Spell It Right ~~Write~~ Dictionary

by Christine Maxwell

Berlitz Publishing
New York Munich Singapore

Spell It ~~Write~~ Right Dictionary

CONTACTING THE EDITORS
Every effort has been made to provide accurate information in this publication, but changes are inevitable. The publisher cannot be responsible for any resulting loss, inconvenience or injury. We would appreciate it if readers would call our attention to any errors or outdated information by contacting Berlitz Publishing, 193 Morris Avenue, Springfield, NJ 07081, USA. email: comments@berlitzbooks.com

Printed in Singapore by Insight Print Services (Pte) Ltd. May 2007
Copy Editor: Jerome Colburn

ACKNOWLEDGEMENTS
I wish to thank Sheryl Olinsky Borg for her unflagging support at Berlitz. Special thanks go to my Spelling Development, Editorial and Database in-house development team and in particular to Bridget Samuels.

American English Spelling Development Team:
Ajay Skreekanth: Electronic Misspelling Program Director
Bridget Samuels: Linguistics, Misspelling rules Consultant Phonology Director

American English Editorial Team:
Bridget Samuels,Veronica Rose Heller, Jackie Roberts, Nancy Dutton

Database Development:
At Publication Services, Inc. I wish to thank Lori Martinsek for her invaluable advice and editorial support and Jerome Colburn for his outstanding editorial work.

Table of Contents

Preface and Introduction v

How to Use This Spelling Dictionary vii

A to Z 1

Commonly Misspelled Words 387

Country, Capital, Citizen, and Language(s) 391

About the Author 396

PREFACE AND INTRODUCTION

More than 80 percent of employers believe that poor grammar and sloppy spelling on the part of their employees spoil otherwise excellent work. For example, a supervisor might not be impressed with an e-mail that reads, "We met with the clyent today." (with "client" misspelled)

A person who has trouble with spelling, however, is often too embarrassed to ask for assistance. This book provides instant self-help for such persons.

Spell It Right is an innovative American-English Spelling Dictionary that goes much farther than any other spelling dictionary in:

- Helping users to find the correct spelling of words even when they don't know the first letters
- Choosing between the correct spellings of words that have similar sounds but very different meanings
- Finding words in the dictionary even when the user is not pronouncing the word correctly
- Enabling the user to find the correct spelling even if he or she starts looking in the wrong part of the alphabet

This dictionary contains a modern vocabulary of over 15,000 headwords, with a further 60,000 word derivatives. The extensive vocabulary includes current terms relating to the Internet and information and communications technology, as well as vocabulary for the workplace.

Who Can Benefit from This Dictionary?

Spell It Right contains many unique features that are particularly helpful for poor spellers, persons with dyslexia and other types of learning difficulties, and students whose first language is not English. Students as young as nine years old and as old as 99 can use this dictionary successfully.

- Common misspellings are printed in **red**, and the corresponding correct spellings are printed alongside the misspelling in **black**. The correct spellings can also be found in their correct alphabetical positions. The user immediately has several opportunities for finding the word being looked for instead of only one.
- If a correctly spelled word, or a misspelling, can be confused with one or more other words, those words are listed to the right of the word or misspelling. A short descriptor, marked with a star *, is placed next to each possibility to suggest the correct meaning.
- Detailed help is also provided for finding the correct spellings of suffixes and compounds. These spelling aids are clearly explained in the Key, which is printed on the inside front cover of this dictionary and at the bottom of each dictionary page.
- There is a special appendix of commonly misspelled words. This appendix also includes stars * and descriptors for many words that can be easily confused with others.

Spell It Right can be a major factor in encouraging reluctant dictionary users of all ages and abilities to become more proficient at using a dictionary independently and to improving their spelling as a consequence.

Christine Maxwell
October 2006
http://www.perfectspelling.com/berlitz

How to Use This Spelling Dictionary

Correct spellings and misspellings are arranged in alphabetical order down the left-hand side of each column. Each misspelling (printed in red) has its correct spelling (printed in **black**) to its right.

First Step

- Think of how the word you want might be spelled (for example, "clyent"), and look in the dictionary at that place in the alphabet (for example, "c").
- Use the two words at the tops of the pages to find the page for your word.
- Look for your spelling in the left-hand side of each column.
- If the spelling you're looking for is printed in **black**, then it's the correct spelling of a word, then proceed to the second and third steps.
- If the word is written in red, then your spelling is wrong. Look across to the right-hand side of the column to find the word correctly spelled in **black**.

clyent client⁺

Extra Spelling Help

If you don't easily find the word you are looking for, your word may begin with a different letter. To help you find the correct first letters of a word, **Information Boxes** are scattered throughout the pages. For example, if you were looking for "cerloin" and didn't find it even as a misspelling, you would find this box nearby:

Unable to find your word under **cer**? Look under **ser**

You would then see where to look next:

serloin sirloin⁺

Second Step

- If the word you have found has a number or a symbol (such as *) after it, look down at the **Key to Spelling Rules** and the **Key to Suffixes and Compounds** at the bottom of the dictionary pages so that you can immediately find out what the number or symbol stands for.
- The stars * are used when there are two or more words that look or sound similar. After a * you will find a brief descriptor, printed in [gray] in brackets, to help you choose the correct spelling to use.
- The numbers give you more help in spelling other forms of the word, such as the present participle of a verb or the plural of a noun.
- A plus sign (⁺) to the right of a word in the right-hand side of the column means that you will find more additional forms of the word (see Third Step on page viii) when you find it in its correct place in the alphabet.
- An @ before a word in the right-hand side of the column means a word that is related to the main word on the left but isn't put together according to the rules in the Keys. An example of this is **say @said**.

Third Step

Sometimes you need to use your word with a suffix (ending) or in a compound word or phrase. Many of these forms are provided alongside the main word in this dictionary. These are printed in gray to the right of the word, introduced with a tilde (~).

strong[1] ~ly ~-arm[1] ~box ~| currency[4]

- When the tilde (~) is immediately in front of the next part, you attach the next part to the main word without a space or hyphen. For example, you would add ***ly*** to ***strong*** to spell ***strongly***; you would add ***box*** to ***strong*** to spell ***strongbox***.
- When there is a hyphen after the tilde (~-), you put a hyphen in between the two parts. For example, you add a hyphen between ***strong*** and ***arm*** to form ***strong-arm***.
- When there is a vertical line and a space after the tilde (~|), you keep the two words separate with a space between them. For example, you keep a space in the phrase ***strong currency***.

Correct Spelling of Suffixes

The "Key to Suffixes and Compounds" gives you the rules for adding suffixes (the letters on the ends of words that make new words.)

The following are examples of these endings and how they are used. In the sample sentences, the example word is in ***boldface italics***.

- **~ing** is used to form the present participle and gerund of a regular verb. You are ***reading*** a sentence that contains a present participle right now. ***Finding*** a gerund in this sentence is easy—just look at the first word.
- **~ed** is used to form the past tense of a regular verb. I ***placed*** a past tense form in this sentence.
- **~er** and **~est** are used to form comparative and superlative adjectives. This dictionary is ***easier*** to use than most dictionaries. It may be the ***easiest*** dictionary of all.
- **~er** is also used to form nouns that mean persons or things that do what a verb means. The ***reader*** can see an example of this form in this sentence.

The numbers marked to the right of the word indicate how to add these endings.

- For words marked with a number **1** or a number **5**, no change is needed when adding these endings: **break**[1] forms **breaking**, **breaker**; **kiss**[5] forms **kissing**, **kissed**.
- Words marked with a number **2** end with an **e** that must be taken off: **seize**[2] forms **seizing**.
- For words marked with a number **3**, the last letter in the word must be doubled before the ending: **dig**[3] forms **digger**, **digging**.

Correct Spelling of Plurals

You can add "**s**" to any noun in this dictionary to make its plural, unless different information is indicated as shown in the following list. So, for example, the plural of ***bed*** can be assumed to be ***beds***.

- For words ending in ***y***, you usually have to take ***y*** off and add ***ies*** to form the plural. Those words are marked with the number **4**: **baby**[4] forms the plural ***babies***.
- If you have to add ***es*** instead of ***s*** to form the plural, the word will have the number **5**: **octopus**[5] forms the plural ***octopuses***.
- Some words ending in ***f*** have plurals in which ***f*** is replaced by ***v***, and ***es*** is added. These words are marked with the number **6**: **calf**[6] has the plural ***calves***.

Words That Can Be Confused with Others

When two words could be confused, as in the following examples, you will find them next to each other, with a star (*) and a simple descriptor next to each to help you pick the right word. People confuse words for several reasons.

- The words sound exactly the same. For example, "The customers at that table over there are asking for their money back."

  their *[possession] there *[place]+

- The words look or sound somewhat similar, but they have totally different meanings. "The *personnel* department keeps files containing *personal* information."

  personal *[private] personnel *[employees]+

Becoming a Successful Dictionary User

As you become used to following the Key to Spelling Rules and the Key to Suffixes and Compounds, you will soon learn the rules and become a better speller as a consequence.

To Marjory Duckworth Malina, my dear mother-in-law,
a woman who loved words,
and who knew how to use them
and write them to great effect.

A

A[1] *[letter] ~-bomb ~-frame ~-OK
ah *[exclamation][+]
aardvark
abacus @abaci
abait abate[2+]
abakis abacus
abandon[1] ~ment
abate[2] ~ment
abattoir
abbot *[monk] about *[to do with]
@abbey
abbreviate[2] @abbreviation
abcent absent[+]
abcentee absentee[+]
abcess abscess[5]
abdamen abdomen
abdicate[2] @abdication
abdomen
abdominal ~ly
abduct[1] ~ion ~or
abel able[2+]
abgect abject *[humiliated][+]
object[1] *[thing, oppose][+]
abide[2]
abie abbey
abil able[2+]
ability[4]
abismal abysmal[+]
abiss abyss[5]
abject *[humiliated] ~ly ~| apology[4]
object[1] *[thing, oppose][+]
able[2] ~-bodied @ably
abnormal ~ly ~| heartbeat ~| return
abnormality[4]
aboard *[on board]
aboart abort[1] *[terminate][+]
abolish[5] ~ment
abolishun abolition
abolition
abominable @abominably
abominate[2] @abomination
aborde aboard *[on board]
Aboriginal @Aborigine
aborshun abortion[+]
abort[1] *[terminate] ~ive
aboard *[on board]
abortion ~ist
abot abbot *[monk][+]
about *[to do with] ~-face ~-turn
abbot *[monk][+]
above ~board ~-the-line costs
abowt about *[to do with][+]
abracadabra
abrasev abrasive[+]
abrasion
abrasive ~ly ~ness
abrawd abroad
abrazion abrasion
abreast
abrest abreast
abreviate abbreviate[2+]
abridge[2]
abroad
abrupt ~ly ~ness
absail abseil[1]
absalushin absolution
absalute absolute[+]
abscent absent[+]
abscess[5]
abscond[1]
abseil[1]
absence
absent ~ly
absentee ~ism

Key to Suffixes and Compounds

These rules are explained on pages vii to ix.

1 Keep the word the same before adding **ed, er, est, ing**
e.g. cool[1] → cooled, cooler, coolest, cooling
2 Take off final **e** before adding **ed, er, est, ing**
e.g. fine[2] → fined, finer, finest, fining
3 Double final consonant before adding **ed, er, est, ing**
e.g. thin[3] → thinned, thinner, thinnest, thinning
4 Change final **y** to **i** before adding **ed, er, es, est, ly, ness**
e.g. tidy[4] → tidied, tidier, tidies, tidiest, tidily, tidiness
Keep final **y** before adding **ing** e.g. tidying
5 Add **es** instead of **s** to the end of the word
e.g. bunch[5] → bunches
6 Change final **f** to **ve** before adding **s**
e.g. calf[6] → calves

absent-minded ~ly ~ness
absurd absurd+
absess abscess[5]
absint absent+
absird absurd+
abskond abscond[1]
absolushun absolution
absolute ~ly ~| priority ~| value ~| zero
absolution
absolutism
absolve[2]
absorb[1] ~able ~ency ~ent
absorption ~| lines
absssess abscess[5]
abstain[1]
abstention
abstinence @abstinent
abstract[1] ~ion
absurd ~ly @absurdity[4]
absyntee absentee+
abucive abusive+
abundance
abundant ~ly
aburn auburn
abuse[2] *[hurt badly]
abuzz *[full of talk]
abusive ~ly ~ness
abuv above+
abuzz *[full of talk]
abuse[2] *[hurt badly]
abyde abide[2]
abysmal ~ly
abyss[5]
acacia
academic ~ally ~ian
academy[4]
acasha acacia
acawn acorn+
accede[2] *[agree] exceed[1] *[be more than]+
accelerate[2] @accelerator
acceleration ~| clause
accent[1] *[speech]
ascent *[incline]
assent[1] *[agree]
accentuate[2]

accept[1] ~ance
acceptable @acceptably
access[5] *[get into] ~ibility[4] ~ible
assess[5] *[examine]+
excess[5] *[too much]+
accession
accessory[4]
accident *[chance event] ~al ~ally ~-prone
occident *[west]+
acclaim[1]
acclimatize[2] @acclimatization
accolade
accommodate[2] @accommodation
accompaniment
accompany[4] @accompanist
accomplice *[crime partner]
accomplish[5] *[complete] ~ment
accord[1] ~ance ~ingly
accordion
accost[1]
account[1] ~ant ~| balance ~| executive
accountable @accountability[4]
accounting ~| insolvency ~| liquidity ~| rules ~| standards
accoustic acoustic
accounts ~| payable ~| receivable
accredit[1] ~ation
accross across+

Unable to find your word under **acc**?
Look under **ac**

accrue[2] @accrual
accrued ~| interest
accumulate[2] @accumulator
accumulation
accuracy[4]
accurate ~ly
accursed
accusative
accusatory
accuse[2] @accusation
accustom[1]

KEY TO SPELLING RULES

Red words are wrong. **Black** words are correct.

~ Add the suffix or word directly to the main word, without a space or hyphen
e.g. ash ~en ~tray → ashen ashtray

~- Add a hyphen to the main word before adding the next word
e.g. blow ~-dry → blow-dry

~| Leave a space between the main word and the next word
e.g. decimal ~| place → decimal place

+ By finding this word in its correct alphabetical order, you can find related words
e.g. abowt about+ → about-face

* Draws attention to words that may be confused

TM Means the word is a trademark

@ Signifies the word is derived from the main word

ace^{2} *[card, expert]
ass^{5} *[animal]
acent — accent^{1} *[speech]
assent^{1} *[agree]
ascent *[incline]
acepsis — asepsis^{+}
acesory — accessory^{4}
acess — assess^{5} *[examine]$^{+}$
access^{5} *[get into]$^{+}$

> Unable to find your word under **ac**?
> Look under **acc**

acetate
acetic *[acid] — ascetic *[austere]$^{+}$
acetone
acetylene
ache^{2} — @achy
acheve — achieve^{2+}
achieve^{2} ~ment — @achievable
Achilles' ~| heel ~| tendon
aching *[hurting] — akin *[similar to]
achord — accord^{1+}
achordian — accordion
acid *[chemical substance] ~ic ~ity^{4}
aside *[on the side]
acid ~| rain ~| test
acident — accident^{+}
acienda — hacienda
Acileys — Achilles'$^{+}$
acknowledge^{2} ~ment
ackredet — accredit^{1+}
acksel — axel *[jump]
axle *[wheel]
axil *[leaf]
ackses — axes *[tools, lines]
axis *[line]
acksess — access^{1} *[get into]$^{+}$
acksiom — axiom^{+}
ackwaint — acquaint^{1+}
ackwilline — aquiline
ackwire — acquire^{2}
ackwit — acquit^{3+}
aclaim — acclaim^{1}
aclimitize — acclimatize^{2+}

acme *[highest achievement]
acne *[skin condition]
acnoledge — acknowledge^{2+}
acolade — accolade
acolite — acolyte
acolyte
acomodate — accommodate^{2+}
acompanie — accompany^{4+}
acompliss — accomplice *[crime partner]
accomplish^{5} *[complete]$^{+}$
acompny — accompany^{4+}
acorn ~| tree
acost — accost^{1}
acount — account^{1+}

> Unable to find your word under **ac**?
> Look under **acc**

acoustic ~ally ~s ~| coupler
acquaint^{1} ~ance
acquiesce^{2}
acquiescence — @acquiescent
acquilene — aquiline
acquire^{2}
Acquired Immune Deficiency Syndrome [AIDS]
acquisishun — acquisition^{+}
acquisition ~| of assets ~| of stock
acquit^{3} — @acquittal
acqusativ — accusative
acqwiess — acquiesce^{2}
acramoney — acrimony^{4}
acre ~age
acrew — accrue^{2+}
acrid
acrilic — acrylic^{+}
acrimonious ~ly
acrimony
acrobat ~ic ~ically ~s
acrofobia — acrophobia
acronym
acrophobia
acropolis

Key to Suffixes and Compounds

These rules are explained on pages vii to ix.

1 Keep the word the same before adding **ed, er, est, ing**
e.g. cool^{1} → cooled, cooler, coolest, cooling
2 Take off final **e** before adding **ed, er, est, ing**
e.g. fine^{2} → fined, finer, finest, fining
3 Double final consonant before adding **ed, er, est, ing**
e.g. thin^{3} → thinned, thinner, thinnest, thinning
4 Change final **y** to **i** before adding **ed, er, es, est, ly, ness**
e.g. tidy^{4} → tidied, tidier, tidies, tidiest, tidily, tidiness
Keep final **y** before adding **ing** e.g. tidying
5 Add **es** instead of **s** to the end of the word
e.g. bunch^{5} → bunches
6 Change final **f** to **ve** before adding **s**
e.g. calf^{6} → calves

across ~-the-board
acrue accrue[2+]
acryd acrid
acrylic ~| acid
acsede accede[2] *[agree]
exceed[1] *[be more than]
acselerate accelerate[2+]
acsenshun ascension
acsent accent[1] *[speech]
ascent *[incline]
assent[1] *[agree]
acsess access[5] *[get into]+
acsessary accessory[4]

> Unable to find your word under **acs**?
> Look under **acc**

acsetic ascetic *[austere]+
acetic *[acid]
acshun action[1+]
acsiom axiom+
act[1] ~| up
acter actor+
actinium
action[1] ~-packed
actionable ~| knowledge
activate[2] @activator
activation
active ~ly ~ness ~| member ~| portfolio strategy[4] ~| server pages
activist
activity[4] @activism
actor @actress
actual ~ly
actuality[4]
actuals
actuary[4]
actyvate activate[2+]
acuity
acumen
acummulate accumulate[2+]
acupuncture @acupuncturist
acurrecy accuracy[4]
acursed accursed
acuse accuse[2+]
acustics acoustics
acustom accustom[1]

> Unable to find your word under **acu**?
> Look under **accu**

acute ~ly ~ness
acwiess acquiesce[2]
acyd acid+
ad *[advertisement]
add[1] *[sum]+
aid[1] *[help]
ad ~| hoc ~| infinitum
adage
adagio
adamant ~ly
Adam's ~| apple
adapt[1] ~able ~ability ~ation
adapter *[person] adaptor *[electric]
adaptive
adaptor *[electric]
adapter *[person]
adaw adore[2+]
adawn adorn[1+]
add[1] *[sum] ~-on
ad *[advertisement]+
addage adage
addament adamant+
addapt adapt[1+]
addaptor adapter *[person]
adaptor *[electric]

> Unable to find your word under **add**?
> Look under **ad**

addendum @addenda
addequate adequate+
adder
addict[1] ~ed ~ion ~ive
addishun addition *[sum]+
addition *[sum] ~al ~ally
edition *[version]
additive
additude attitude
addle[2]
address[5] ~ee ~| book

Key to Spelling Rules

Red words are wrong. **Black** words are correct.

~ Add the suffix or word directly to the main word, without a space or hyphen
e.g. ash ~en ~tray → ashen ashtray

~- Add a hyphen to the main word before adding the next word
e.g. blow ~-dry → blow-dry

~| Leave a space between the main word and the next word
e.g. decimal ~| place → decimal place

+ By finding this word in its correct alphabetical order, you can find related words
e.g. abowt about+ → about-face

* Draws attention to words that may be confused

TM Means the word is a trademark

@ Signifies the word is derived from the main word

ade	aid[1] *[help]
	aide *[helper]
adeckwit	adequate+
adekwate	adequate+
adel	addle[2]
adendum	addendum+
adenoids	
adept ~ly ~ness	
adequate ~ly	@adequacy[4]
ader	adder
adhere[2]	
adherence	@adherent
adhesion	@adhesive
adhoc	ad hoc
adickt	addict[1]+
adict	addict[1]+
adieu *[goodbye]	ado *[fuss]
adige	adage
adinoids	adenoids
adio	audio+
adiquit	adequate+
adishun	addition *[sum]+
adition	edition *[version]
adjacent	
adjar	ajar

Unable to find your word under **adj**?
Look under **aj**

adjective	@adjectival
adjictive	adjective+
adjitate	agitate[2]+
adjourn[1] ~ment	
adjudicate[2]	@adjudicator
adjudication	
adjulation	adulation
adjunct	
adjust[1] ~ment	
adjustable ~-rate mortgage	
adjusted ~| gross income	
ad-lib[3]	
admeral	admiral+
admier	admire[2]+
administer[1]	
administrate[2]	@administrator
administration	
administrative ~ly ~| assistant ~| procedure	
admirable	@admirably
admiral ~ty	
admire[2]	@admiration
admireble	admirable+
admiril	admiral+
admishun	admission
admissible	@admissibility
admission	
admit[3] ~tedly	
admition	admission
admittance	
admonish[5] ~ment	
admyrabul	admirable+
admyral	admiral+
admyre	admire[2]+
admyt	admit[3]+
ado *[fuss]	adieu *[goodbye]
adobe	
adobi	adobe
adolescence	@adolescent
adolesince	adolescence+
Adonis	
adoor	adore[2]+
adoorn	adorn[1]+
adopt[1] ~ion ~ive	
adorable	@adorably
adore[2]	@adoration
adorn[1] ~ment	
adreenil	adrenal+
adrenal ~| gland	
adrenalin	
adress	address[5]+
adrift	
adrinal	adrenal+
adroit ~ly	
adsorb[1] ~able ~ent	
adsorpshin	adsorption
adsorption	
adulation	
adult ~hood	
adulterous ~ly	
adultery	@adulterer

KEY TO SUFFIXES AND COMPOUNDS

These rules are explained on pages vii to ix.

1 Keep the word the same before adding **ed, er, est, ing**
e.g. cool[1] → cooled, cooler, coolest, cooling

2 Take off final **e** before adding **ed, er, est, ing**
e.g. fine[2] → fined, finer, finest, fining

3 Double final consonant before adding **ed, er, est, ing**
e.g. thin[3] → thinned, thinner, thinnest, thinning

4 Change final **y** to **i** before adding **ed, er, es, est, ly, ness**
e.g. tidy[4] → tidied, tidier, tidies, tidiest, tidily, tidiness
Keep final **y** before adding **ing** e.g. tidying

5 Add **es** instead of **s** to the end of the word
e.g. bunch[5] → bunches

6 Change final **f** to **ve** before adding **s**
e.g. calf[6] → calves

advance^{2} ~ment ~| commitment
advanced ~| computational methods
advant advent
advantage ~ous ~ously
advecate advocate^{2}
advencher adventure^{+}
advenchurous adventurous^{+}
advenshur adventure^{+}
advent
adventure ~some
adventurous ~ly ~ness
adverb ~ial
advercity adversity^{4}
adversary^{4}
adverse ~ly ~| effect ~| reaction ~| selection
adversity^{4}
advertise^{2} ~ment
advertising ~| agency ~| campaign
advice *[suggestion]
 advise^{2} *[suggest]$^{+}$
advirse adverse^{+}
advisable @advisability
advise^{2} *[suggest] ~dly
 advice *[suggestion]
advisedly
advisor [also spelled adviser] ~y^{4}
advize advise^{2} *[suggest]
advizidly advisedly
advocacy^{4}
advocate^{2}
advurb adverb^{+}
advursary adversary^{4}
advurse adverse^{+}
advursity adversity^{4}
advurtise advertise^{2+}

> Unable to find your word under **advu**?
> Look under **adve**

advyse advise^{2} *[suggest]
advysedly advisedly
aegis
ael ail *[be ill]
 ale *[beverage]
aeloe aloe *[plant]$^{+}$
aer air^{1} *[gas]$^{+}$
aerate^{2} @aeration
 @aerator
aerial ~ly
aerie *[nest] airy^{4} *[full of air]
aerobatics
aerobic ~ally ~s ~| exercise
aerodrome
aerodynamic ~s
aeronaut ~ical ~ics
aerosol
aerospace
aery aerie *[nest]
 airy^{4} *[full of air]
aesthetic ~ism ~s
afabul affable^{+}
afadavit affidavit
afar *[distant] affair *[business, relationship]
afecshun affection^{+}
afect affect^{1} *[influence]
 effect^{1} *[a result, change]
afectashun affection *[close to love]
 affectation *[pretension]
afectiv affective *[emotional]
 effective *[producing results]$^{+}$
afeeld afield^{+}
affable @affability
 @affably
affair *[business, relationship]
 afar *[distant]
affect^{1} *[influence]
 effect^{1} *[a result, change]
affectation *[pretension]
affection *[close to love] ~ate ~ately
affective *[emotions]
 effective *[producing results]$^{+}$
afferm affirm^{1+}
affermativ affirmative^{+}
afficks affix^{5}
affidavit
affiliate^{2} @affiliation

Key to Spelling Rules

Red words are wrong. **Black** words are correct.

~ Add the suffix or word directly to the main word, without a space or hyphen
e.g. ash ~en ~tray → ashen ashtray

~- Add a hyphen to the main word before adding the next word
e.g. blow ~-dry → blow-dry

~| Leave a space between the main word and the next word
e.g. decimal ~| place → decimal place

+ By finding this word in its correct alphabetical order, you can find related words
e.g. abowt about^{+} → about-face

* Draws attention to words that may be confused

™ Means the word is a trademark

@ Signifies the word is derived from the main word

affinity[4]
affirm[1] ~ation
affirmative ~ly ~| action ~| covenant
affishianado aficionado
affix[5]
afflewance affluence
afflict[1] ~ion
affluence
affluent *[wealthy]
effluent *[liquid waste]
afford[1] ~able ~ability
affrae affray
affray
affrodisiak aphrodisiac
affront[1]
aficionado
afid aphid
afidavit affidavit
afield
afiliate affiliate[2+]
afinity affinity[4]
afire
afirm affirm[1+]
afirmative affirmative[+]
afishenado aficionado
afix affix[5]
aflame
aflict afflict[1+]
afloat
afluence affluence
afluent affluent *[wealthy]
effluent *[liquid waste]
afoot
aford afford[1+]
aforementioned @aforesaid
aforesaid
aforisum aphorism
afrade afraid
afraid
afresh
African ~| American
Afro ~-American
afrodisiac aphrodisiac
afront affront[1]
after ~birth ~care
after ~effect ~-hours ~image ~life ~math ~noon ~-sales ~-school ~shave ~shock ~taste ~thought ~ward

Unable to find your word under **after**? Take off **after** and look again

after-tax ~| profit margin
afyliate affiliate[2+]
again ~st
agane again[+]
agast aghast
age[2] ~less ~| of consent ~| reduction
agectiv adjective[+]
ageing aging
agen again[+]
agency[4] ~| bank ~| basis ~| cost view
agenda
agent
agglomerate[2] @agglomeration
aggrandize[2] ~ment
aggrarian agrarian[+]
aggravate[2] @aggravation
aggreeved aggrieved
aggreived aggrieved
aggregate[2] @aggregation
aggression @aggressor
aggressive ~ly ~ness
aggrieved
aghast
agile @agility
agin again[+]
aging ~| schedule
agint agent
agitate[2] @agitator
agitation
aglomerate agglomerate[2+]
aglow
agnostic ~ism
ago
agonie agony[4]
agonize[2] @agonizingly
agony[4]
agoraphobia

Key to Suffixes and Compounds

These rules are explained on pages vii to ix.

1 Keep the word the same before adding **ed, er, est, ing**
e.g. cool[1] → cooled, cooler, coolest, cooling
2 Take off final **e** before adding **ed, er, est, ing**
e.g. fine[2] → fined, finer, finest, fining
3 Double final consonant before adding **ed, er, est, ing**
e.g. thin[3] → thinned, thinner, thinnest, thinning
4 Change final **y** to **i** before adding **ed, er, es, est, ly, ness**
e.g. tidy[4] → tidied, tidier, tidies, tidiest, tidily, tidiness
Keep final **y** before adding **ing** e.g. tidying
5 Add **es** instead of **s** to the end of the word
e.g. bunch[5] → bunches
6 Change final **f** to **ve** before adding **s**
e.g. calf[6] → calves

agrafobia agoraphobia
agragate aggregate[2+]
agrandise aggrandize[2+]
agrarian ~| reform
agravait aggravate[2+]
agree ~d ~ing ~ment
agreeable @agreeably
agregate aggregate[2+]
agreived aggrieved
agrerien agrarian[+]
agreshun aggression[+]
agresiv aggressive[+]

> Unable to find your word under **agr**?
> Look under **aggr**

agribusiness
agriculcher agriculture
agricultural ~ly ~| revolution
agriculture
agrie agree[+]
agrochemicals
agronomy @agronomist
aground
Agust August
agyle agile[+]
ah *[exclamation] ~ha
A *[letter][+]
ahead
ahoy
aid[1] *[help]
aide ~s *[helpers]
AIDS *[Acquired Immune Deficiency Syndrome]
aifid aphid
aigys aegis
ail[1] *[be ill] ~ment
ale *[beverage]
aim[1] *[hit a target] ~less ~lessly
am *[to be]
aimen amen
ainel anal *[anus]
annul[3] *[not legal][+]
ainshunt ancient[+]

ain't *[is or are not]
ant *[insect][+]
aipex apex[5]
air[1] *[gas] ~bag ~borne ~| brake ~brush[5] ~-condition[1] ~crew ~drop ~fare ~field ~flow ~foil ~| force ~| gun ~lift[1] ~line ~lock ~| mass[5] ~mail ~| miles ~| passage ~plane ~| pocket ~port ~| power ~| sac ~space ~strip ~| raid ~| resistance ~tight ~waves
are *[plural of be]
err[1] *[make a mistake]
heir *[inheritor][+]

> Unable to find your word under **air**?
> Take off **air** and look again

airate aerate[2+]
aircraft ~| carrier
airea area *[surface][+]
aria *[song]
aireal aerial[+]
airey airy[4]
airial aerial[+]
Airian Aryan[+]
airie airy[4]
airobatics aerobatics
airobic aerobic[+]
airodynamics aerodynamic[+]
aironaut aeronaut[+]
airosol aerosol

> Unable to find your word under **ai**?
> Look under **ae**

airy[4]
ais ace[2] *[card, expert]
aisle *[passage] isle *[island]
ait ate *[did eat]
eight *[number][+]
ajacent adjacent
ajar *[open] a jar *[a container]
ajective adjective[+]
ajency agency[4+]
ajenda agenda

Key to Spelling Rules

Red words are wrong. **Black** words are correct.

~ Add the suffix or word directly to the main word, without a space or hyphen
e.g. ash ~en ~tray → ashen ashtray

~- Add a hyphen to the main word before adding the next word
e.g. blow ~-dry → blow-dry

~| Leave a space between the main word and the next word
e.g. decimal ~| place → decimal place

\+ By finding this word in its correct alphabetical order, you can find related words
e.g. abowt about[+] → about-face

★ Draws attention to words that may be confused

TM Means the word is a trademark

@ Signifies the word is derived from the main word

ajent	agent
ajer	azure *[blue]
ajitate	agitate[2+]
ajorne	adjourn[1+]
ajurn	adjourn[1+]
ajust	adjust[1+]
akacia	acacia
akademik	academic[+]
akin *[similar to]	aching *[hurting]
aklame	acclaim[1]
akme	acme *[highest achievement]
aknee	acne *[skin condition]
aknolege	acknowledge[2+]
akordien	accordion
akost	accost[1]
akownt	account[1+]
akrilic	acrylic[+]
akross	across[+]

> Unable to find your word under **ak**?
> Look under **ac**

aksellerate	accelerate[2+]
aksent	accent[1] *[speech]
aksess	access[5] *[get into][+]
aksessary	accessory[4]
aksident	accident[+]
aksium	axiom[+]
akt	act[1+]
aktiv	active[+]
aktor	actor[+]
akuse	accuse[2+]
akwa	aqua[+]
akwarium	aquarium
akwilene	aquiline
akwisishin	acquisition[+]
à la *[according to] ~| carte ~| mode *[food]	Allah *[Moslem God]
Alabama	
alabaster	
alabye	alibi
alacrity	
Alah	Allah *[Moslem God]
alamony	alimony
alarm[1] ~| clock ~ist	
alas	
Alaska	
alay	allay[1] *[calm down] alley *[passage way]
albatross[5]	
albeit	
albem	album
albetross	albatross[5]
albino	
album	
albumen *[egg]	
albumin *[protein]	
albyno	albino
alchemy[4]	@alchemist
alchohol	alcohol[+]
alcohal	alcohol[+]
alcohol ~ic ~ism	
alcove	
alderman	
ale *[beverage]	ail[1] *[be ill][+] all *[every]
alebaster	alabaster
alebye	alibi

> Unable to find your word under **ale**?
> Look under **ali**

aledge	allege[2+]
alegashun	allegation
alein	alien
aleinate	alienate[2+]
alement	ailment
alementary	alimentary *[nutrition][+]
alemony	alimony
alert[1] ~ness	
aleviate	alleviate[2]
alewd	allude[2] *[refer to] elude[2] *[avoid]
alfa	alpha[+]
alfabet	alphabet[+]
algae	
algebra	
algebraic ~| expression	

Key to Suffixes and Compounds

These rules are explained on pages vii to ix.

1 Keep the word the same before adding **ed, er, est, ing**
e.g. cool[1] → cooled, cooler, coolest, cooling
2 Take off final **e** before adding **ed, er, est, ing**
e.g. fine[2] → fined, finer, finest, fining
3 Double final consonant before adding **ed, er, est, ing**
e.g. thin[3] → thinned, thinner, thinnest, thinning
4 Change final **y** to **i** before adding **ed, er, es, est, ly, ness**
e.g. tidy[4] → tidied, tidier, tidies, tidiest, tidily, tidiness
Keep final **y** before adding **ing** e.g. tidying
5 Add **es** instead of **s** to the end of the word
e.g. bunch[5] → bunches
6 Change final **f** to **ve** before adding **s**
e.g. calf[6] → calves

algie	algae
algorithm	
alian	alien
aliance	alliance
alias^{5}	
alibi	
alie	ally^{4} *[friend]
	alley *[passage way]
aliegince	allegiance
alien	
alienait	alienate^{2+}
alienate^{2}	@alienation
alieve	alive
aligater	alligator
aligation	allegation
aligator	alligator
alight^{1}	
align^{1} ~ment	
alike	
alimentary *[nutrition] ~| canal	
	elementary *[simplest]
alimony	
aline	align^{1+}
alirgy	allergy^{4}
alirt	alert^{1+}
alite	alight^{1}
alive	
aliviate	alleviate^{2}
aljebra	algebra
aljee	algae
alkali ~| metal	
alkaline	
alkelye	alkali^{+}
alkemey	alchemy^{4+}
alkohol	alcohol^{+}
alkove	alcove
all *[every] ~-American ~-around ~-in cost ~-in-one ~-inclusive ~| or none ~-purpose ~-star ~| right ~-terrain ~-time	
	awl *[tool]
	ale *[beverage]

> Unable to find your word under **all**?
> take off **all** and look again

Allah *[Moslem God]	
	à la *[according to]$^{+}$
allaie	allay^{1} *[calm down]
	alley *[passage way]
allarm	alarm^{1+}

> Unable to find your word under **all**?
> Look under **al**

allas	alas
allay^{1} *[calm down]	
	alley *[passage way]
allegation	
allegatir	alligator
allege^{2} ~dly	
allegiance	
allegorical ~ly	
allegory^{4}	
allegro	
allergen	
allergic ~| reaction	
allergy^{4}	
allert	alert^{1+}
alleviate^{2}	
allewsion	allusion *[hint]
alley *[passage way]	
	allay^{1} *[calm down]
	ally^{4} *[friend]
alliance	
allied ~| forces	
allienate	alienate^{2+}
alligator	
alligience	allegiance
allirgec	allergic^{+}
alliteration	@alliterative
allive	alive
alliviate	alleviate^{2}
allkali	alkali^{+}
allmighty	almighty
allmost	almost
allocate^{2}	@allocation
alloe	aloe *[plant]$^{+}$
allot^{3} *[give] ~ment	
	a lot *[many]

alloud   allowed *[permitted]
          aloud *[out loud]
allow[1] ~able ~ance
allowed *[permitted]
          aloud *[out loud]
alloy *[metal]   aloe *[plant]+
alltho   although
alltogether   altogether
allude[2] *[refer to]   elude[2] *[avoid]
          illude[2] *[deceive]
allum   alum
allure   @alluring
allurgic   allergic+
allurgie   allergy[4]
allusion *[hint]   elusion *[escape]
          illusion *[false idea]
allusive *[referring to]
          elusive *[hard to find]
alluvial ~| deposit
alluvium
alluzion   allusion *[hint]
          elusion *[escape]
          illusion *[false idea]
allways   always
ally[4] *[friend]   allay[1] *[calm down]
          alley *[passage way]
almanac
almighty
almitee   almighty
almond
almost
alms *[charity]   arms *[limbs, weapons]+
alo   aloe *[plant]+
          alloy *[metal]
aloan   alone
alocate   allocate[2]+
aloe *[plant] ~| vera
          alloy *[metal]
aloft
alokate   allocate[2]+
alone
along ~side
aloof ~ness
aloor   allure+

aloosive   allusive *[suggestive]
          elusive *[hard to find]
a lot *[many]   allot[3] *[give]+
alot   allot[3] *[give]+
          a lot *[many]
aloud *[out loud]   allowed *[permitted]
          aloud *[out loud]
alow   aloe *[plant]+
          allow[1]+
alowed   allowed *[permitted]
          aloud *[out loud]
alown   alone
aloy   alloy *[metal]
          aloe *[plant]+
alp ~ine
alpaca
alpha ~| decay ~| equation ~numeric ~| particle
alphabet ~ical ~ically
alpine ~| retreat
already *[now]   all ready *[prepared]
alright
alrite   alright
also ~-ran
altar *[church] ~piece
alter[1] *[change] ~able ~ation
alter *[other] ~| ego
altercation
alternate[2] ~ly   @alternator
alternate ~| agriculture ~| angles
alternating ~| current
alternative ~ly ~| medicine ~| mortgage instrument
although
althow   although
altimeter
altitude
alto
altogether
altruism
altruist ~ic ~ically
alturnate   alternate[2]+
alturnativ   alternative+

Key to Suffixes and Compounds

These rules are explained on pages vii to ix.

1 Keep the word the same before adding **ed, er, est, ing**
e.g. cool[1] → cooled, cooler, coolest, cooling
2 Take off final **e** before adding **ed, er, est, ing**
e.g. fine[2] → fined, finer, finest, fining
3 Double final consonant before adding **ed, er, est, ing**
e.g. thin[3] → thinned, thinner, thinnest, thinning
4 Change final **y** to **i** before adding **ed, er, es, est, ly, ness**
e.g. tidy[4] → tidied, tidier, tidies, tidiest, tidily, tidiness
Keep final **y** before adding **ing** e.g. tidying
5 Add **es** instead of **s** to the end of the word
e.g. bunch[5] → bunches
6 Change final **f** to **ve** before adding **s**
e.g. calf[6] → calves

Wrong	Correct
alude	allude[2] *[refer to]
	elude[2] *[avoid]
	illude[2] *[deceive]
alumna *[female graduate] ~e [plural]	
alumnus *[male graduate]	
	@alumni [plural]
alure	allure+
alurgy	allergy[4]
alurt	alert[1+]
alushun	allusion *[hint]
	elusion *[escape]
	illusion *[wrong perception]
alusiv	allusive *[suggestive]
	elusive *[hard to find]
always	
aly	ally[4] *[friend]
	alley *[passage way]
alyas	alias[5]
alybi	alibi
alyiance	alliance
alyke	alike
alynement	align[1+]
alyt	alight[1]
alyve	alive
Alzheimer's ~| disease	
am *[to be]	a.m. *[time]
	aim[1] *[hit a target]
amaize	amaze[2+]
amalgam	
amalgamate[2]	@amalgamation
amass[5]	
amateur ~ish ~ism	
amaze[2] ~ment	
Amazon ~ian	
ambassador ~ial	
ambel	amble[2+]
amber	
ambiance	ambience+
ambidekstrous	ambidextrous
ambidextrous	
ambience	@ambient
ambiguity[4]	
ambiguous ~ly ~ness	
ambir	amber
ambishin	ambition
ambishus	ambitious+
ambition	
ambitious ~ly	
ambivalence	@ambivalent
amble[2] ~| along	
ambletory	ambulatory
amboosh	ambush[5]
ambul	amble[2+]
ambulance	
ambulatory	
ambush[5]	
ame	aim[1] *[hit a target]+
	am *[to be]
ameeba	amoeba
ameeno	amino+
ameliorate[2]	@amelioration
amen	
amenable	@amenably
amend[1] ~ment	
amenible	amenable+
amenity[4]	
American ~a ~| dream ~| Stock Exchange	
Americanize[2]	@Americanization
amethyst	
amfetamine	amphetamine
amfibian	amphibian
amfibious	amphibious
amfithiater	amphitheater
amiable	@amiability
	@amiably
amiba	amoeba
amicable	@amicably
amid ~st	
amiebul	amiable+
amikabul	amicable+
amiliorate	ameliorate[2+]
aminabul	amenable+
amino ~| acid	
amiss	
amithist	amethyst
ammalgamate	amalgamate[2+]
ammaze	amaze[2+]
ammo	

KEY TO SPELLING RULES

Red words are wrong. **Black** words are correct.

~ Add the suffix or word directly to the main word, without a space or hyphen
e.g. ash ~en ~tray → ashen ashtray

~- Add a hyphen to the main word before adding the next word
e.g. blow ~-dry → blow-dry

~| Leave a space between the main word and the next word
e.g. decimal ~| place → decimal place

+ By finding this word in its correct alphabetical order, you can find related words
e.g. abowt about+ → about-face

★ Draws attention to words that may be confused

™ Means the word is a trademark

@ Signifies the word is derived from the main word

ammonia
ammunition
ammuse amuse[2+]

Unable to find your word under **amm**? Look under **am**

amnesty[4]
amo ammo
amoeba
amok
amond almond
among ~st
amonia ammonia
amoral ~ity ~ly
amorfus amorphous[+]
amoriss amorous[+]
amorous ~ly
amorphous ~ly ~| computing
amortize[2] @amortization factor
amorus amorous[+]
amount[1]
amownt amount[1]
amp
ampair ampere[+]
ampel ample[+]
ampere @amperage
ampersand
amphetamine
amphibian
amphibious
amphitheater
ampirsand ampersand
ample @amply
amplefy amplify[4]
amplify[4]
ampursand ampersand
amputate[2] @amputation
@amputee
amulet
amung among[+]
amunishin ammunition
amunition ammunition
amuse[2] ~ment
amuze amuse[2+]
amycabul amicable[+]
amyd amid[+]
amyno amino[+]
amyss amiss
amythist amethyst
amyulet amulet
an ~other
anabolic ~| steroid
anachronism
anachronistic ~ally
anacisst anarchist[+]
anaconda
anacronistic anachronistic[+]
anacronisum anachronism
anaemia [also spelled anemia][+]
anagram
anakist anarchist[+]
anakonda anaconda
anakronistic anachronistic[+]
anakronizm anachronism
anal *[anus] annul[3] *[not legal][+]
analgesic
analigie analogy[4]
analist analyst
analisys analysis *[examination, singular][+]
analyses *[examinations, plural]
analize analyze[2]
analog ~| computer ~| signal
analogous ~ly
analogy[4]
analyses *[examinations, plural]
analysis *[examination, singular]
analyst
analytic ~al ~ally
analyze[2]
anarchist ~ic @anarchism
anarchy @anarchic
anarkist anarchist[+]
anarky anarchy[+]
anastehsia anesthesia[+]
anathema
anatomical ~ly
anatomy[4] @anatomist

Key to Suffixes and Compounds

These rules are explained on pages vii to ix.

1 Keep the word the same before adding **ed, er, est, ing**
e.g. cool[1] → cooled, cooler, coolest, cooling
2 Take off final **e** before adding **ed, er, est, ing**
e.g. fine[2] → fined, finer, finest, fining
3 Double final consonant before adding **ed, er, est, ing**
e.g. thin[3] → thinned, thinner, thinnest, thinning
4 Change final **y** to **i** before adding **ed, er, es, est, ly, ness**
e.g. tidy[4] → tidied, tidier, tidies, tidiest, tidily, tidiness
Keep final **y** before adding **ing** e.g. tidying
5 Add **es** instead of **s** to the end of the word
e.g. bunch[5] → bunches
6 Change final **f** to **ve** before adding **s**
e.g. calf[6] → calves

Word	Correct spelling
anceint	ancient+
ancestor	@ancestral
	@ancestry[4]
anchor[1] ~age ~man ~woman	
anchovy[4]	
ancient ~| history	
ancilary	ancillary[4]
ancillary[4]	
ancor	anchor[1]+
and	
andante	
androgenus	androgynous+
androgynous	@androgyny[4]
Andromeda ~| Galaxy	
anealing	annealing
anecdote *[story]	@anecdotal
	antidote *[poison]
aneemia	anemia+
anel	anal *[anus]
	annul[3] *[not legal]+
anemal	animal+
anemia [also spelled anaemia]	
	@anemic
anemone	
anemosity	animosity[4]
anenimity	anonymity
anestetise	anesthetize[2]+
anesthetic	@anesthetist
anesthetize[2]	@anesthesia
anetomical	anatomical+
aneurysm	
aneversary	anniversary[4]
anew	
anex	annex[1]+
aney	any+
angel *[heavenly] ~| dust	
	angle[2] *[geometry]
angelic ~ally	
anger ~| management	
angina	
angir	anger+
angish	anguish+
anglar	angler *[fisherman]
	angular *[pointed]+

Word	Correct spelling
angle[2] *[geometry]	
	angel *[heavenly]+
angler *[fisherman]	
Anglican ~| Church ~ism	
anglicize[2]	
anglir	angler *[fisherman]
Anglo ~phile ~phone ~-Saxon	
anglur	angler *[fisherman]
	angular *[pointed]+
angora	
angrey	angry[4]
angry[4]	
angst	
angstrom	
anguesh	anguish+
anguish ~ed	
angular ~ity	
angulir	angular+
angur	anger+
angwish	anguish+
angyna	angina
anie	any+
anihilate	annihilate[2]+
animal ~| feed ~ism ~istic	
animate[2] ~dly	@animator
animation	
animel	animal+
animia	anemia+
animosity[4]	
aniscede	aniseed
aniseed	
aniversary	anniversary[4]
aniyelate	annihilate[2]+
anjel	angel *[heavenly]+
	angle[2] *[geometry]
anjelic	angelic+
anjina	angina
ankil	ankle+
ankir	anchor[1]+
ankle ~| bone	@anklet
ankor	anchor[1]+
ankshus	anxious+
anksiety	anxiety[4]
annachronysm	anachronism

KEY TO SPELLING RULES

Red words are wrong. **Black** words are correct.

- **~** Add the suffix or word directly to the main word, without a space or hyphen
  e.g. ash ~en ~tray → ashen ashtray
- **~-** Add a hyphen to the main word before adding the next word
  e.g. blow ~-dry → blow-dry
- **~|** Leave a space between the main word and the next word
  e.g. decimal ~| place → decimal place
- **+** By finding this word in its correct alphabetical order, you can find related words
  e.g. abowt about+ → about-face
- ***** Draws attention to words that may be confused
- **TM** Means the word is a trademark
- **@** Signifies the word is derived from the main word

annalisis analysis *[examination, singular]+
analyses *[examinations, plural]
annals
annealing
annex5 ~ation ~es
annihilate2 @annihilation
anniversary4
anno Domini
annoint anoint1+
annonymous anonymous+
annotate2 @annotation
annother another
announce2 ~ment
annoy1 ~ance ~ingly
annoynt anoint1+

Unable to find your word under **ann**?
Look under **an**

annual ~ly ~| meeting ~| report ~| return ~| yield
Annual General Meeting [AGM]
annualized ~| gain
annuity4 ~| due ~| factor ~| in arrears
annul3 *[not legal] ~ment
anal *[anus]
annular
annunciate2 *[announce]
enunciate2 *[speak clearly]
annunciation *[announcement]
enunciation *[clear speaking]
Annunciation *[Christian feast]
anodominie anno Domini
anodyne
anoint1 ~ment
anomalous ~| results
anomaly4
anomelus anomalous+
anonymity4
anonymous ~ly
anoo anew

anorexia ~| nervosa
@anorexic
anotate annotate2+
another
anotomicle anatomical+
anounce announce2+
anownce announce2+
anoy annoy1+
anoynt anoint1+
anser answer1+
ansesstor ancestor+
anshent ancient
ansient ancient
ansillary ancillary4
answer1 ~able ~| print
ant *[insect] ~eater ~hill
ante1 *[pay for]+
ain't *[is or are not]
aunt *[relative]+
antacid
antagonist ~ic ~ically
antagonize2 @antagonism
Antarctic ~| Circle
antartic Antarctic
antasid antacid
antchovy anchovy4
ante1 *[pay for] ~cedent ~cedence
ant *[insect]+
aunt *[relative]+
antebody antibody4
antebyotic antibiotic
antecedent
antechamber
antechrist Antichrist
anteclimax anticlimax+
antecyclone anticyclone+
antediluvian
antedote antidote *[poison]
anecdote *[story]+

Unable to find your word under **ante**?
Look under **anti**

anteek antique *[old]
antic *[prank]

KEY TO SUFFIXES AND COMPOUNDS

These rules are explained on pages vii to ix.

1 Keep the word the same before adding **ed, er, est, ing** e.g. cool1 → cooled, cooler, coolest, cooling
2 Take off final **e** before adding **ed, er, est, ing** e.g. fine2 → fined, finer, finest, fining
3 Double final consonant before adding **ed, er, est, ing** e.g. thin3 → thinned, thinner, thinnest, thinning
4 Change final **y** to **i** before adding **ed, er, es, est, ly, ness** e.g. tidy4 → tidied, tidier, tidies, tidiest, tidily, tidiness
Keep final **y** before adding **ing** e.g. tidying
5 Add **es** instead of **s** to the end of the word e.g. bunch5 → bunches
6 Change final **f** to **ve** before adding **s** e.g. calf6 → calves

antehistamine	antihistamine
ante-inflammatory	anti-inflammatory
antelope	
antenatal	
antenna	@antennae [plural]
anterior	
anteroom	
antesoshall	antisocial^{+}
antesyklone	anticyclone^{+}
anthem	
anther	
anthir	anther
anthology^{4}	
anthracite	
anthrax	
anthresite	anthracite
anthropoid	
anthropologist	
anthropology^{4}	@anthropological
anthum	anthem
anthur	anther
antiaircraft	
antibiotic	
antibody^{4}	
antic *[prank]	antique *[old]
anticedent	antecedent
anticemite	anti-Semite^{+}
anticemitisum	anti-Semitism
anticeptic	antiseptic
Antichrist	
anticipate^{2}	@anticipation

Unable to find your word under **anti**?
Take off **anti** and look again

anticlimax	@anticlimactic
anticlockwise	
anticyclone	@anticyclonic
antidepressant	
antidote *[poison]	anecdote *[story]$^{+}$
antifreeze	
antigen	
antihistamine	
anti-inflammatory	
antilope	antelope
antimatter	
antioxidant	
antipathy^{4}	
anti-personnel	
antipersperant	antiperspirant
antiperspirant	
antipodes	
antiquarian	
antiquary^{4}	
antiquated	
antique *[old]	antic *[prank]
antiquity^{4}	
antiqwaited	antiquated
antiqwarien	antiquarian
antiretroviral	
antirior	anterior
anti-Semite	@anti-Semitic
anti-Semitism	
antiseptic	
antisipait	anticipate^{2+}
antisipate	anticipate^{2+}
antisocial ~ly	
antithesis	@antitheses
antiviral ~| agent	
antler	
antonym	
antybiotic	antibiotic
antybody	antibody^{4}

Unable to find your word under **anty**?
Look under **ante** or **anti**

anual	annual^{+}
anue	anew
anuity	annuity^{4+}
anul	anal *[anus]
	annul^{3} *[not legal]$^{+}$
anular	annular
anunsiate	annunciate^{2} *[announce]
	enunciate^{2} *[speak clearly]

anunsiation	annunciation *[announcement]
	enunciation *[clear speaking]
anurisum	aneurysm
anus	
anuther	another
anvil	
anxiety[4]	
anxious ~ly	
any ~body ~how ~more ~one	
any ~| place ~| time ~thing	
any ~way ~where	

Unable to find your word under **any**? Take off **any** and look again

anyilate	annihilate[2+]
anymal	animal[+]
anymate	animate[2+]
aorta	
Apache ~| Indian	
apal	appall[1]
aparant	apparent[+]
apart	
apartheid	
apartide	apartheid
apartied	apartheid
apartment	
Apatchee	Apache[+]
apathetic	@apathy
apatite *[mineral]	appetite *[desire]
ape[2]	
apeal	appeal[1+]
apear	appear[1+]
apecks	apex[5]
apel	apple[+]
apellate	appellate[+]
apendisitis	appendicitis[+]
apendix	appendix[+]
aperitif	
apertain	appertain[1]
aperture	
apetight	apatite *[mineral]
	appetite *[desire]
apex[5]	
aphid	
aphiliat	affiliate[2+]
aphorism	
aphrodisiac	
apiary[4]	
apiece	
aplaud	applaud[1]
aplawd	applaud[1]
aplie	apply[4+]
aplomb	
aply	apply[4+]
apocalypse	@apocalyptic
apocryphal	
apogee	
apoint	appoint[1+]
apokalipse	apocalypse[+]
apolagise	apologize[2]
apolitical	
apologetic ~ally	
apologize[2]	
apology[4]	@apologist
apoplectic	
apoplexy	
aporshun	apportion[1+]
apostile	apostle
apostle	
apostrofee	apostrophe
apostrophe	
apoynt	appoint[1+]
apoynty	appointee

Unable to find your word under **ap**? Look under **app**

Appalachian	
appall[1]	
appalling ~ly	
apparatus	
apparel	
apparent ~ly	
apparition	
appart	apart

Unable to find your word under **app**? Look under **ap**

Key to Suffixes and Compounds

These rules are explained on pages vii to ix.

1 Keep the word the same before adding **ed, er, est, ing**
e.g. cool[1] → cooled, cooler, coolest, cooling
2 Take off final **e** before adding **ed, er, est, ing**
e.g. fine[2] → fined, finer, finest, fining
3 Double final consonant before adding **ed, er, est, ing**
e.g. thin[3] → thinned, thinner, thinnest, thinning
4 Change final **y** to **i** before adding **ed, er, es, est, ly, ness**
e.g. tidy[4] → tidied, tidier, tidies, tidiest, tidily, tidiness
Keep final **y** before adding **ing** e.g. tidying
5 Add **es** instead of **s** to the end of the word
e.g. bunch[5] → bunches
6 Change final **f** to **ve** before adding **s**
e.g. calf[6] → calves

appartied apartheid
appartment apartment
appeal[1] ~ingly
appear[1] ~ance
appease[2] ~ment
appeel appeal[1+]
appellate ~| court
@appellation
append[1] ~age
appendicitis @appendectomy
appendix @appendices
apperchure aperture
apperitiv aperitif
appertain[1]
appetising ~ly
appetite *[desire] apatite *[mineral]
appetizer
appier appear[1+]
appieree apiary[4]
applaud[1]
applause
apple ~| cart ~| pie ~| sauce
appliance
applicable @applicability
applicant
application ~| form
@applicator
applomb aplomb
apply[4] @application
@appliqué
appocalips apocalypse[+]
appoint[1] ~ee ~ment
appologetick apologetic[+]
appologize apologize[2]
apporshin apportion[1+]
apportion[1] ~ment
apposite *[relevant]
opposite *[contrary]
appossel apostle
appostrofee apostrophe
appraisal ~| ratio ~| rights
appraise[2] *[assess]
apprise[2] *[inform]
appreciable @appreciably
appreciate[2] @appreciation

appreciative ~ly
apprehend[1]
apprehension
apprehensive ~ly ~ness
apprentice ~d ~ship
apprise[2] *[inform]
appraise[2] *[assess]
approach[5] ~able
approbation
appropriate[2] ~ly ~ness
appropriation ~| request
approve[2] @approval
approximate[2] ~ly
@approximation
aprapo apropos
aprayski après-ski
aprechabul appreciable[+]
Aprel April[+]
apren apron[+]
après-ski
apricot ~| jam
April ~| Fool's Day ~| showers
aprise apprise[2] *[inform]
appraise[2] *[assess]
aproach approach[5+]
aprobashun approbation
aproche approach[5+]
apron ~| strings
aproove approve[2+]
apropos
apropriate appropriate[2+]
aprove approve[2+]
aproximate approximate[2+]
apruve approve[2+]
apt ~ly ~ness
aptitude ~| test
apurtain appertain[1]
apyary apiary[4]
aqewus aqueous[+]
aqua ~tic ~lung ~marine ~relle
aquaplane[2]
aquarium
Aquarius
aqueduct
aqueline aquiline

Key to Spelling Rules

Red words are wrong. **Black** words are correct.

~ Add the suffix or word directly to the main word, without a space or hyphen
e.g. ash ~en ~tray → ashen ashtray

~- Add a hyphen to the main word before adding the next word
e.g. blow ~-dry → blow-dry

~| Leave a space between the main word and the next word
e.g. decimal ~| place → decimal place

+ By finding this word in its correct alphabetical order, you can find related words
e.g. abowt about[+] → about-face

* Draws attention to words that may be confused

TM Means the word is a trademark

@ Signifies the word is derived from the main word

aqueous ~| solution	
aquiesense	acquiescence[+]
aquiline	
aqusatory	accusatory
Arab ~ic	
arabesque	
arable ~| farming	
arachnid	
arae	array[1]
araign	arraign[1+]
arain	arraign[1+]
araknid	arachnid
aral	aural *[ear][+]
Aramaic	
arange	arrange[2+]
aray	array[1]
arbeter	arbiter
arbetrage	arbitrage[+]
arbetrary	arbitrary[4]
arbiter	
arbitrage ~ur	
arbitrairie	arbitrary[4]
arbitrait	arbitrate[2+]
arbitraj	arbitrage[+]
arbitrary[4]	
arbitrate[2]	@arbitrator
arbitration	
arboretum	
arbytrate	arbitrate[2+]
arc[1] *[curve, power] ~| light	
	arch[5] *[curved structure][+]
	ark *[boat]
arcade	
arcane	
arch[5] *[curved structure] ~ly ~ness	
	arc[1] *[curve, power][+]
arch *[highest] ~bishop ~diocese ~duke ~-enemy[4]	
archaeology [also spelled archeology]	
	@archaeologist
archaic	
archangel	
archer ~y	
archetype	
Archimedes ~' principle	
archiologey	archaeology[+]
archipelago	
architect ~ure ~ural ~urally	
archive[2]	@archivist
archor	archer[+]
archway	
Arctic ~| Circle ~| sun	
ardent ~ly	
arder	ardor
ardewous	arduous[+]
ardor	
arduous ~ly ~ness	
arduus	arduous[+]
ardvark	aardvark
are *[we are]	air[1] *[gas]
	our *[belonging]
area *[surface] ~| code	
	aria *[song]
areal	aerial[+]
arears	arrears
arebul	arable[+]
areign	arraign[1+]
Aremaic	Aramaic
arena	
aren't *[are not]	aunt *[relative][+]
arest	arrest[1]
argew	argue[2+]
argue[2]	@arguable
	@arguably
argument *[quarrel] ~ative	
	augment[1] *[increase][+]
aria *[song]	area *[surface][+]
arial	aerial[+]
arid *[dry] ~| region	
	aired *[shown]
arie	aerie *[nest]
	airy[4]
	awry
ariel	aerial[+]
Arien	Aryan[+]
arieve	arrive[2+]
arise	@arising
	@arisen
aristocracy[4]	
aristocrat ~ic	

KEY TO SUFFIXES AND COMPOUNDS

These rules are explained on pages vii to ix.

1 Keep the word the same before adding **ed, er, est, ing**
e.g. cool[1] → cooled, cooler, coolest, cooling

2 Take off final **e** before adding **ed, er, est, ing**
e.g. fine[2] → fined, finer, finest, fining

3 Double final consonant before adding **ed, er, est, ing**
e.g. thin[3] → thinned, thinner, thinnest, thinning

4 Change final **y** to **i** before adding **ed, er, es, est, ly, ness**
e.g. tidy[4] → tidied, tidier, tidies, tidiest, tidily, tidiness
Keep final **y** before adding **ing** e.g. tidying

5 Add **es** instead of **s** to the end of the word
e.g. bunch[5] → bunches

6 Change final **f** to **ve** before adding **s**
e.g. calf[6] → calves

arithmetic ~| average ~ian ~| mean ~| progression
arithmia arrhythmia
arive arrive[2+]
arize arise[+]
Arizona
arjewous arduous[+]
ark *[boat] arc[1] *[curve, power][+]
arkaic archaic
arkane arcane
arkangel archangel
Arkansas
arkayick archaic
arketype archetype
arkimides Archimedes[+]
arkiology archaeology[+]
arkipelago archipelago
arkitect architect[+]
arkive archive[2+]
Arktik Arctic[+]
arm[1] ~band ~ful ~pit ~'s length ~twisting
armada
armadillo
Armageddon
armament
armchair
armed ~| forces
armee army[4]
Armenian ~| Apostolic Church
armie army[4]
armistice
armor[1] ~-plated @armory[4]
arms *[limbs, weapons] ~| index
alms *[charity]
army[4]
armystis armistice
arnt aren't *[are not]
aunt *[relative][+]
arobatics aerobatics
arobic aerobic[+]
arodrome aerodrome
arodynamicks aerodynamic[+]
arogance arrogance
arogant arrogant[+]

aroma ~therapy ~tic
aronot aeronaut[+]
arora aurora[+]
arose *[got up] arouse[2] *[stir up][+]
arosol aerosol
around ~| about ~-the-clock
arouse[2] *[stir up] @arousal
arose *[got up]
arow arrow[+]
arowbick aerobic[+]
arownd around[+]
arowse arouse[2] *[stir up][+]
arose *[got up]
aroze arose *[got up]
arouse[2] *[stir up][+]
arpeggio
arraign[1] ~ment
arrain arraign[1+]
arrainge arrange[2+]
arraiy array[1]
arrange[2] ~ment
array[1]
arrears
arrest[1]
arrhythmia
arria aria *[song]
area *[surface][+]
arrible arable[+]
arrid arid *[dry][+]
aired *[shown]
arrise arise[+]
arrithmatic arithmetic[+]

Unable to find your word under **arr**?
Look under **ar**

arrive[2] @arrival
arrogance
arrogant ~ly
arrow ~-head ~root
arse ~hole
arsen arson[+]
arsenal
arsenic
arsin arson[+]

Key to Spelling Rules

Red words are wrong. **Black** words are correct.

~ Add the suffix or word directly to the main word, without a space or hyphen
e.g. ash ~en ~tray → ashen ashtray

~- Add a hyphen to the main word before adding the next word
e.g. blow ~-dry → blow-dry

~| Leave a space between the main word and the next word
e.g. decimal ~| place → decimal place

+ By finding this word in its correct alphabetical order, you can find related words
e.g. abowt about[+] → about-face

★ Draws attention to words that may be confused

™ Means the word is a trademark

@ Signifies the word is derived from the main word

arsinel	arsenal
arsinic	arsenic
arsnal	arsenal
arsnick	arsenic
arson ~ist	
art ~| form ~| gallery ~| theater	
artcher	archer^{+}
artefact	
artefishial	artificial^{+}
arterie	artery^{4}
arteriosclerosis	
artery^{4}	
arteryosklirosis	arteriosclerosis
artesian ~| well	
artful ~ly ~ness	
arthritic	@arthritis
arthropod	
artichoke	
artick	Arctic^{+}
artickel	article^{+}
article ~d	
articles ~| of incorporation	
articulate^{2}	@articulation
artifice	
artificial ~ly ~| intelligence ~| limb	
artifishall	artificial^{+}
artifiss	artifice
artikulate	articulate^{2+}
artillery^{4}	
artirey	artery^{4}
artirisclerosis	arteriosclerosis
artiry	artery^{4}
artisan	
artist *[painter] ~ry	
artiste *[performer]	
artistic *[skillful] ~ally	
	autistic *[condition]$^{+}$
artless ~ly ~ness	
artrey	artery^{4}
artychoke	artichoke
artycle	article^{+}
artyculate	articulate^{2+}
artyfiss	artifice
artysan	artisan

artyst	artist *[painter]$^{+}$
	artiste *[performer]
Aryan ~| race	
aryd	aired *[shown]
	arid *[dry]$^{+}$
arye	awry
arystocrasy	aristocracy^{4}
arystocrat	aristocrat^{+}
as *[comparing, referring]	
	ass^{5} *[animal]
	ace^{2} *[card, expert]
asail	assail^{1+}
ASAP *[as soon as possible]	
asassin	assassin
asassinate	assassinate^{2+}
asault	assault^{1}

> Unable to find your word under **as**?
> Look under **ass**

asbestos ~is	
asc	ask^{1+}
ascance	askance
ascend^{1} ~ancy ~ant	
ascension	
ascent *[incline]	accent^{1} *[speech]
	assent^{1} *[agree]
ascertain^{1} ~able	
ascertane	ascertain^{1+}
ascetic *[austere] ~ally	
	acetic *[acid]
aschore	ashore *[on beach]
ASCII ~| code	
ascorbic ~| acid	
ascorbick	ascorbic^{+}
ascribe^{2}	@ascribable
ase	ace^{2} *[card, expert]
	as *[comparing, referring]
aseatilyne	acetylene
aseksual	asexual^{+}
asembly	assembly^{4+}
asembul	assemble^{2+}

> Unable to find your word under **ase**?
> Look under **ace** or **ass**

Key to Suffixes and Compounds

These rules are explained on pages vii to ix.

1 Keep the word the same before adding **ed, er, est, ing**
e.g. cool^{1} → cooled, cooler, coolest, cooling

2 Take off final **e** before adding **ed, er, est, ing**
e.g. fine^{2} → fined, finer, finest, fining

3 Double final consonant before adding **ed, er, est, ing**
e.g. thin^{3} → thinned, thinner, thinnest, thinning

4 Change final **y** to **i** before adding **ed, er, es, est, ly, ness**
e.g. tidy^{4} → tidied, tidier, tidies, tidiest, tidily, tidiness
Keep final **y** before adding **ing** e.g. tidying

5 Add **es** instead of **s** to the end of the word
e.g. bunch^{5} → bunches

6 Change final **f** to **ve** before adding **s**
e.g. calf^{6} → calves

asend	ascend[1+]
asenshin	ascension
asent	assent[1] *[agree]
	accent[1] *[speech]
	ascent *[incline]
asention	ascension
asepsis	@aseptic
asert	assert[1+]
asertaine	ascertain[1+]
asess	assess[5] *[examine][+]
aset	asset[+]
asetate	acetate
asetic	ascetic *[austere][+]
	acetic *[acid]
asetone	acetone
asetylene	acetylene
asexual ~ly ~| reproduction	
asfixia	asphyxia
asfyxiate	asphyxiate[2+]
ash[5] ~en ~tray	
Ash Wednesday	
ashamed	
ashore *[on beach]	
	assure[2] *[convince]

Unable to find your word under **as**?
Look under **ass**

ashram	
Ashun	Asian[+]
ashurance	assurance
ashur	ashore *[on beach]
	assure[2] *[convince]
ashure	azure *[blue]
ashurence	assurance
Asian	@Asiatic
aside *[on the side]	
	acid *[chemical substance][+]
asiduous	assiduous[+]
asign	assign[1] *[give to]
	asinine *[stupid]
asignee	assignee[+]
asilum	asylum[+]
asimilate	assimilate[2+]
asimptomatic	asymptomatic
asine	assign[1] *[give to][+]
	asinine *[stupid]
asist	assist[1+]
ask[1] ~ing price	
askance	
askanse	askance
askew	
Aski	ASCII[+]
askribe	ascribe[2+]
askue	askew
asleep	
asociate	associate[2+]
asonance	assonance
asorbic	ascorbic[+]
asort	assort[+]
asparagus	
aspartame	
aspect ~| ratio	
aspen *[tree]	aspirin *[medicine]
aspersion	
asphalt	
asphyxia	
asphyxiate[2]	@asphyxiation
aspic	
aspices	auspices
aspidistra	
aspik	aspic
aspin	aspen *[tree]
	aspirin *[medicine]
aspire[2]	@aspirant
	@aspiration
aspiren	aspirin
aspirin *[medicine]	
	aspen *[tree]
aspon	aspen
asprin	aspirin
aspurshun	aspersion
aspydistra	aspidistra
aspyre	aspire[2+]
asque	askew
ass[5] *[animal]	ace[2] *[card, expert]
	as *[comparing, referring]
assail[1] ~able ~ant	
assalt	assault[1]

Key to Spelling Rules

Red words are wrong. **Black** words are correct.

~ Add the suffix or word directly to the main word, without a space or hyphen
e.g. ash ~en ~tray → ashen ashtray

~- Add a hyphen to the main word before adding the next word
e.g. blow ~-dry → blow-dry

~| Leave a space between the main word and the next word
e.g. decimal ~| place → decimal place

+ By finding this word in its correct alphabetical order, you can find related words
e.g. abowt about[+] → about-face

★ Draws attention to words that may be confused

TM Means the word is a trademark

@ Signifies the word is derived from the main word

assap	ASAP+
assassin	
assassinate[2]	@assassination
assault[1]	
assembil	assemble[2+]
assemble[2]	@assemblage
assembly[4] ~| language ~| line	
assend	ascend[1+]
assent[1] *[agree]	accent[1] *[speech]
	ascent *[incline]
assert[1] ~ion ~ive	
assertain	ascertain[1+]
assertane	ascertain[1+]
assess[5] *[examine] ~ment ~or	
	access[5] *[get into]+
asset ~| acquisition ~| activity ratios ~-liability management ~-pricing model ~| substitution problem ~| swap ~| turnover	

> Unable to find your word under **asset**?
> Take off **asset** and look again

asset-based ~| financing	
assetic	acetic *[acid]
	ascetic *[austere]+
assexual	asexual+
assfalt	asphalt
assiduous ~ly	
assidyous	assiduous+
assienda	hacienda
assign[1] *[give to] ~able ~ation ~ment	
	asinine *[stupid]
assignee	@assignor
assimilate[2]	@assimilation
assinine	asinine *[stupid]+
	assign[1] *[give to]
assist[1] ~ance ~ant	
associate[2] ~| degree	
	@association
associative	
assort ~ed ~ment	
assuage[2] ~ment	
assume[2]	@assumable
assumpshin	assumption
assumption	
assurance	
assure[2] *[convince]	
	ashore *[on beach]
assurt	assert[1+]
asswage	assuage[2+]
Astec	Aztec
asteer	austere *[severe]+
aster *[flower]	astir *[waking up]
asterick	asterisk
asterisk	
asterix	asterisk
astern	
asteroid	
asthma ~tic	
astigmatic	@astigmatism
astir *[waking up]	aster *[flower]
astirn	astern
astonish[5] ~ingly ~ment	
astoot	astute+
astound[1] ~ingly	
astownd	astound[1+]
astral	
astray	
astreisk	asterisk
astrel	astral
astreoid	asteroid
astreriss	asterisk
astride	
astringent	
astrisk	asterisk
astrofisicks	astrophysics
astroid	asteroid
astrologer	
astrology	@astrological
astronaut ~ics	
astronomy[4]	
astronot	astronaut+
astrophysics	
Astroturf™	
astryde	astride
astur	aster *[flower]
	astir *[waking up]
asturn	astern
astute ~ly ~ness	

Key to Suffixes and Compounds

These rules are explained on pages vii to ix.

1 Keep the word the same before adding **ed, er, est, ing**
e.g. cool[1] → cooled, cooler, coolest, cooling

2 Take off final **e** before adding **ed, er, est, ing**
e.g. fine[2] → fined, finer, finest, fining

3 Double final consonant before adding **ed, er, est, ing**
e.g. thin[3] → thinned, thinner, thinnest, thinning

4 Change final **y** to **i** before adding **ed, er, es, est, ly, ness**
e.g. tidy[4] → tidied, tidier, tidies, tidiest, tidily, tidiness
Keep final **y** before adding **ing** e.g. tidying

5 Add **es** instead of **s** to the end of the word
e.g. bunch[5] → bunches

6 Change final **f** to **ve** before adding **s**
e.g. calf[6] → calves

astygmatyc	astigmatic[+]
asuage	assuage[2+]
asume	assume[2+]
asumshun	assumption
asunder	
asurance	assurance
asur	ashore *[on beach]
	assure[2] *[convince]
asure	azure *[blue]
aswage	assuage[2+]

> Unable to find your word under **as**?
> Look under **ass**

asyde	acid *[chemical substance][+]
	aside *[on the side]
asylum ~| seeker	
asymmetric ~al ~| information ~| taxes	
	@asymmetry
asymptomatic	
asynine	assign[1] *[give to]
	asinine *[stupid]
at *[a place] ~-risk ~| rest	
	ate *[did eat]
	eight *[number][+]
atach	attach[5+]

> Unable to find your word under **at**?
> Look under **att**

ate *[did eat]	at *[a place]
	eat *[food][+]
	eight *[number][+]
atempt	attempt[1]
atheist ~ic	@atheism
athlete ~'s foot	
athletic ~ism	@athletics
atick	attic
atistic	autistic *[condition][+]
atitude	attitude
Atlantic ~| alliance ~| ocean	
atlas[5]	
ATM *[automatic teller machine]	
atmosfere	atmosphere
atmosphere	

atmospheric ~| pollution ~| pressure	
atoan	atone[2+]
atocrat	autocrat[+]
atoll	
atom ~| bomb	
atomic ~| bomb ~| energy ~| radiation	
atomizer	
atone[2] ~ment	
atonimy	autonomy
atopsy	autopsy[4]
atourney	attorney[+]
atract	attract[1+]
atractiv	attractive[+]
atributible	attributable
atrission	attrition
atrium	
atrochus	atrocious[+]
atrocious ~ly	
atrocitie	atrocity[4]
atrocity[4]	
atrofee	atrophy[4+]
atrophy[4]	@atrophic
atroshice	atrocious[+]
atrosity	atrocity[4]
attach[5] ~able	
attaché ~| case	
attachment	
attack[1] ~| dog	
attain[1] ~able ~ment	
attempt[1]	
attend[1] ~ance ~ant	
attention ~| deficit disorder ~-getter ~getting ~| span	
attentive ~ly ~ness	
attenuate[2]	@attenuation
attest[1] ~ation	
attic	
attire ~d	
attitude	
attorney ~-client privilege ~| general	
attract[1] ~ion	
attractive ~ly ~ness	
attributable	
attribute ~| bias	@attribution
attrition	

Key to Spelling Rules

Red words are wrong. **Black** words are correct.

- **~** Add the suffix or word directly to the main word, without a space or hyphen
  e.g. ash ~en ~tray → ashen ashtray
- **~-** Add a hyphen to the main word before adding the next word
  e.g. blow ~-dry → blow-dry
- **~|** Leave a space between the main word and the next word
  e.g. decimal ~| place → decimal place
- **+** By finding this word in its correct alphabetical order, you can find related words
  e.g. abowt about[+] → about-face
- ***** Draws attention to words that may be confused
- **TM** Means the word is a trademark
- **@** Signifies the word is derived from the main word

attune @attuned
aturney attorney[+]
atypical ~ly
au *[French word] ~| jus ~| pair ~| revoir
oh *[explanation][+]
auburn
auction[1] ~eer ~| markets
audacious ~ly @audacity
audashus audacious[+]
audible @audibly
audience
audio ~| cassette recorder ~| data ~tape ~-visual
audishion audition[1]
audit[1] ~or ~or's report
audition[1]
auditorium
auditory ~| canal ~| nerve
auful awful *[terrible][+]
offal *[meat waste]
auger *[tool] augur[1] *[forecast][+]
aught *[anything] ought *[should do][+]
oat *[grain][+]
augment[1] *[increase] ~ation
argument *[quarrel][+]
augur[1] *[forecast] @augury[4]
auger *[tool]
August
aukshin auction[1+]
auksiliary auxiliary[4]
auksion auction[1+]
aukward awkward[+]
auning awning
aunt *[relative] ~ie
ant *[insect][+]
aren't *[are not]
aura
aural *[ear] ~ly
oral *[mouth][+]
aureole *[halo] oriole *[bird]
auricle *[ear, heart]
oracle *[prophecy]
aurora ~| borealis
auspices
auspicious ~ly ~ness

austere *[severe] ~ly
@austerity
astir *[waking up]
auteur
authentic ~ally ~authenticity
authenticate[2] @authentication
auther author[+]
author ~ship
authoritarian ~ism
authoritative ~ly
authority[4]
authorize[2] @authorization
autistic *[condition]
@autism
artistic *[skillful][+]
auto ~biography[4] ~biographical

Unable to find your word under **auto**?
Take off **auto** and look again

autocrat ~ic ~ically
autograph[1]
automate[2] @automation
automatic ~ally ~| pilot ~| stay
automatism
automaton
automobile @automotive
autonomic ~| computing
autonomous ~ly
autonomy
autopilot
autopsy[4]
autum autumn[+]
autumn ~al
auxiliary[4]
avacado avocado
avail[1]
available @availability
avakado avocado
avalanche
avale avail[1]
avaleble available[+]
avant-garde
avarice @avaricious
avariss avarice[+]

Key to Suffixes and Compounds

These rules are explained on pages vii to ix.

1 Keep the word the same before adding **ed, er, est, ing**
e.g. cool[1] → cooled, cooler, coolest, cooling
2 Take off final **e** before adding **ed, er, est, ing**
e.g. fine[2] → fined, finer, finest, fining
3 Double final consonant before adding **ed, er, est, ing**
e.g. thin[3] → thinned, thinner, thinnest, thinning
4 Change final **y** to **i** before adding **ed, er, es, est, ly, ness**
e.g. tidy[4] → tidied, tidier, tidies, tidiest, tidily, tidiness
Keep final **y** before adding **ing** e.g. tidying
5 Add **es** instead of **s** to the end of the word
e.g. bunch[5] → bunches
6 Change final **f** to **ve** before adding **s**
e.g. calf[6] → calves

avary	aviary⁴
avelanche	avalanche
avencherous	adventurous⁺
avenew	avenue
avenge²	
avenoo	avenue
aventure	adventure⁺
avenue	
average² ~| accounting return ~| life ~| maturity ~| rate of return	
averse	@aversion
avert¹	
aviary⁴	
aviashin	aviation⁺
aviation	@aviator
avid ~ly	
avionics	
avirse	averse⁺
avirt	avert¹
avlanch	avalanche
avocado	
avoid¹ ~able ~ably	
avoyd	avoid¹⁺
avrage	average²⁺
avurse	averse⁺
avurt	avert¹
avyd	avid⁺
await¹	
awake	
awaken¹	
award¹ ~able ~-winning	
aware ~ness	
awash ~| with	
away	
awdience	audience
awdio	audio⁺

Unable to find your word under **aw**?
Look under **au**

awe² *[wonder] ~-inspiring ~some ~struck	
	or *[alternative]⁺
awediense	audience
Awegust	August
awful² *[terrible] ~ly ~ness	
	offal *[meat waste]
awhile	
awile	awhile
awkward ~ly ~ness	
awl *[tool]	all *[every]⁺
	AWOL *[absent]
awlmost	almost
awning	
awoke	
AWOL *[absent]	awl *[tool]
awra	aura
awral	aural *[ear]⁺
	oral *[mouth]
awry	
awspishis	auspicious⁺
awspishus	auspicious⁺
awsteer	austere *[severe]⁺
awt	aught *[anything]
	ought *[should]
awtumn	autumn⁺
ax⁵	
axcession	accession
axel *[jump]	axil *[leaf]
	axle *[wheel]
axes *[tools, lines]	
	axis *[line]
axil *[leaf]	axel *[jump]
	axle *[wheel]
axiom ~atic	
axis *[line]	axes *[tools, lines]
axium	axiom⁺
axle *[wheel]	axel *[jump]
	axil *[leaf]
ayatollah	
ayce	ace² *[card, expert]
	as *[comparing, referring]
ayd	aid¹ *[help]
	aide *[helper]
AYDS	AIDS *[Acquired Immune Deficiency Syndrome]
aye *[yes]	eye *[sight]
	I *[me]
ayerveda	Ayurveda
ayfid	aphid
ayke	ache²⁺

KEY TO SPELLING RULES

Red words are wrong. **Black** words are correct.

~ Add the suffix or word directly to the main word, without a space or hyphen
e.g. ash ~en ~tray → ashen ashtray

~- Add a hyphen to the main word before adding the next word
e.g. blow ~-dry → blow-dry

~| Leave a space between the main word and the next word
e.g. decimal ~| place → decimal place

\+ By finding this word in its correct alphabetical order, you can find related words
e.g. abowt about⁺ → about-face

★ Draws attention to words that may be confused

™ Means the word is a trademark

@ Signifies the word is derived from the main word

aykin — akin *[similar to]
aching *[hurting]
ayle — ail[1] *[be ill]+
ale *[beverage]
aylein — alien
ayleinate — alienate[2+]
aylien — alien
ayling — ailing
aylment — ailment
aym — aim[1] *[hit a target]+
aymen — amen
aynel — anal *[anus]
aypex — apex[5]
ayria — area *[surface]+
aria *[song]

aysexual — asexual+
Aysian — Asian+
aysimtomatic — asymptomatic
ayt — at *[a place]+
ate *[did eat]
eight *[number]

> Unable to find your word under **ay**?
> Take off the **y** and look again

azalea
Aztec
azure *[blue color]
assure[2] *[convince]

B

B *[letter] — be *[exist]+
bee *[insect]
B ~BQ ~-list ~-movie ~-road
~2B [business to business]
~2C [business to consumer]
~2G [business to government]
baa
babble[2] *[chatter] — bauble *[trinket]
babboon — baboon
babe *[baby] — baby[4] *[infant]+
babel — babble[2] *[chatter]
bauble *[trinket]
babisit — baby-sit[3]
babminton — badminton
baboon
babul — babble[2] *[chatter]
bauble *[trinket]
babune — baboon
baby[4] *[infant] ~| boomer ~-sat ~-sit ~-sitting
babe *[baby]
bac — back[1] *[behind, body part]+
bake[2] *[cook]

baccalaureate
bace — base[2] *[bottom]+
bass *[music, fish]+
bacen — bacon+
basin+
Bach *[composer]
batch[1] *[group]+
back[1] *[behind, body part]+
bachaloreate — baccalaureate
bachelor ~hood ~'s degree
bacilika — basilica
bacillus — @bacilli
bacin — bacon+
back[1] *[behind, body part] ~ache ~| bench ~| bone ~breaking ~| burner ~-date[2] ~| door ~door listing ~drop ~end ~fire ~gammon ~ground ~| issue ~lash ~list ~log ~pack ~| pain ~| pay ~pedal[3] ~rest ~scratch ~seat ~space ~stage ~stitch ~stroke ~ward ~wash ~water ~woods

---

Key to Suffixes and Compounds

These rules are explained on pages vii to ix.

1 Keep the word the same before adding **ed, er, est, ing**
e.g. cool[1] → cooled, cooler, coolest, cooling
2 Take off final **e** before adding **ed, er, est, ing**
e.g. fine[2] → fined, finer, finest, fining
3 Double final consonant before adding **ed, er, est, ing**
e.g. thin[3] → thinned, thinner, thinnest, thinning
4 Change final **y** to **i** before adding **ed, er, es, est, ly, ness**
e.g. tidy[4] → tidied, tidier, tidies, tidiest, tidily, tidiness
Keep final **y** before adding **ing** e.g. tidying
5 Add **es** instead of **s** to the end of the word
e.g. bunch[5] → bunches
6 Change final **f** to **ve** before adding **s**
e.g. calf[6] → calves

back[1] ~up [support] ~| up [go backwards, give support]	
	bake[2] *[cook]

> Unable to find your word under **back**?
> Take off **back** and look again

backhand ~ed ~er	
backing *[support]	
	baking *[cooking]+
bacon *[smoked meat] ~| and eggs	
	beacon *[light]
bacteria ~|	@bacterium
	Bactria *[region in Asia]+
bacteriology	@bacteriologist
Bactria *[region in Asia] ~n camel	
	bacteria+
bacyllus	bacillus+
bad *[not good] ~ly ~ness ~| blood ~| debt ~| faith ~mouth[1] ~-tempered	
	bade *[said]
	bayed *[howled]

> Unable to find your word under **bad**?
> Take off **bad** and look again

bade *[said]	bayed *[howled]
badge *[pin]	beige *[color]
badger[1]	
badminton	
badmitton	badminton
bael	bail[1] *[out, pay]
	bale[2] *[bundle]
baffel	baffle[2]
baffle[2]	
bag[3] ~| lady ~pipes	
bager	badger[1]
bagetell	bagatelle
baggage	
bagget	baguette
Baggie™ *[plastic bag]	
	baggy[4] *[loose-fitting]
baggige	baggage
baggy[4] *[loose-fitting]	
	Baggie™ *[plastic bag]
bah	baa
Baha'i	
baib	babe *[baby]
baige	badge *[pin]
	beige *[color]
baik	bake[2] *[cook]
	back[1] *[behind, body part]+
bail[1] *[out, pay]	bale[2] *[bundle]
baileful	baleful+
bailey	
bailiff	
bain	bane *[bore]
bainal	banal+
bair	bare[2] *[naked]+
	bear *[carry, animal]+
baired	bared *[showed]
	bard *[poet]
	barred *[stopped]
bais	base[2] *[bottom]+
	bass *[music]+
	bias[1]+
baisle	basal *[fundamental]+
	basil *[herb]
baiste	baste[2]
bait[1] *[food, torment]	
	bat *[thick stick, animal]+
baited *[trap, teased]	
	bated *[breath]
baithe	bathe[2] *[wash, swim]
	bath[1] *[tub, wash]+
bajer	badger[1]
bak	back[1] *[behind, body part]+
	bake[2] *[cook]
bakaloriate	baccalaureate
bake[2] *[cook]	back[1] *[behind, body part]+
bakery[4]	
baking *[cooking] ~| powder ~| sheet	
	backing *[support]
bakini	bikini
bakon	bacon *[smoked meat]+
bakteria	bacteria+

Key to Spelling Rules

Red words are wrong. **Black** words are correct.

~ Add the suffix or word directly to the main word, without a space or hyphen
e.g. ash ~en ~tray → ashen ashtray

~- Add a hyphen to the main word before adding the next word
e.g. blow ~-dry → blow-dry

~| Leave a space between the main word and the next word
e.g. decimal ~| place → decimal place

+ By finding this word in its correct alphabetical order, you can find related words
e.g. abowt about+ → about-face

★ Draws attention to words that may be confused

™ Means the word is a trademark

@ Signifies the word is derived from the main word

bal — ball[1] *[sport, dance, shout]+
bale[2] *[bundle]
balad — ballad
balalaika
balance[2] ~| of payment ~| of power ~| of trade ~| sheet
balarst — ballast
balay — ballet *[dance]+
balcony[4]
bald *[no hair] ~ing ~ness ~| eagle ~-faced
balled *[shaped into a ball]
bawled *[cried]
bale[2] *[bundle] — bail[1] *[out, pay]
baleful ~ly
balelieka — balalaika
balense — balance[2+]
balerina — ballerina
balet — ballet *[dance]+
ballot[1] *[for voting]+
baligerence — belligerence+
balistic — ballistic+
balittle — belittle[2]

> Unable to find your word under **ba**?
> Look under **be**

balkany — balcony[4]
ball[1] *[sport, dance, shout] ~| bearing ~game ~park ~point
bawl[1] *[cry]
boll *[cotton plant]+
ballad *[song]
ballarina — ballerina
ballast
balled *[shaped into a ball]
bald *[no hair]+
ballad *[song]
bawled *[cried]
ballerina
ballet *[dance] ~| dancer
ballot[1] *[for voting]+
ballistic ~| missile
balloon[1] ~ist
ballot[1] ~| box ~| paper
ballroom ~-dancing
ballsumic — balsamic+

> Unable to find your word under **bal**?
> Look under **ball**

balm ~y
baloon — balloon[1+]
balot — ballet *[dance]+
ballot[1] *[for voting]+
balsa *[tropical tree] ~| wood
balsam *[conifer]
balsamic ~| vinegar
balune — balloon[1+]
bamboo ~| shoot
bamboozle[2]
ban[3] *[stop] — bane *[bore]
banal — @banality[4]
banana ~| skin ~| split
bananza — bonanza
band[1] *[group, stripe]
banned *[not allowed]
band ~stand ~wagon ~width
bandage[2]
Band-Aid™
bandanna
bandige — bandage[2]
bandit ~ry
bandy[4] *[toss about] ~-legged
bane *[bore] — ban[3] *[stop]
baned — band[1] *[group, stripe]+
banned *[not allowed]
banel — banal+
baner — banner+
bang[1] ~-up
bangle
banish[1] ~ment
banister
banjo
bank[1] ~| account ~| card ~| draft ~| holiday ~note ~roll[1]
banking ~| hours
bankrupped — bankrupt[1+]

Key to Suffixes and Compounds

These rules are explained on pages vii to ix.

1 Keep the word the same before adding **ed, er, est, ing** e.g. cool[1] → cooled, cooler, coolest, cooling
2 Take off final **e** before adding **ed, er, est, ing** e.g. fine[2] → fined, finer, finest, fining
3 Double final consonant before adding **ed, er, est, ing** e.g. thin[3] → thinned, thinner, thinnest, thinning
4 Change final **y** to **i** before adding **ed, er, es, est, ly, ness** e.g. tidy[4] → tidied, tidier, tidies, tidiest, tidily, tidiness
Keep final **y** before adding **ing** e.g. tidying
5 Add **es** instead of **s** to the end of the word e.g. bunch[5] → bunches
6 Change final **f** to **ve** before adding **s** e.g. calf[6] → calves

bankrupt[1]	@bankruptcy[4]
bankwet	banquet
bannana	banana+
banned *[not allowed]	
	band[1] *[group, stripe]+
banner ~| headline	
bannish	banish[1+]
bannister	banister
banquet	
bantam ~-weight	
banter[1]	
banysh	banish[1+]
baonnet	bayonet[1]
baptism	@baptist
Baptist ~| General Conference	
baptize[2]	
bar[3] *[stop, line, pub] ~| chart ~| code ~| coding ~| graph ~| hop ~| maid ~man ~| stool ~tender	
	bare[2] *[naked]+

> Unable to find your word under **bar**?
> Take off **bar** and look again

Bar Mitzvah	
baracks	barracks
baracuda	barracuda
barage	barrage
barameter	barometer+
baratone	baritone
barb	
barbarian	@barbarism
barbaric	@barbarous
	@barbarity[4]
barbecue[2]	
barbed ~| wire	
barber ~shop	
barberian	barbarian+
barbican	
Barbie™ ~| doll	
barbiturate	
barc	bark[1]
bard *[poet]	bared *[showed]
	barred *[stopped]
bardge	barge[2+]
bare[2] *[naked] ~ly ~back ~faced ~foot ~headed ~legged	
	bear *[carry, animal]+
bared *[showed]	bard *[poet]
	barred *[stopped]
barekaid	barricade[2]
barel	barrel[3+]
baren	baron *[nobleman]+
	barren *[empty]+
bargain[1] ~| basement	
bargaining ~| chip ~| position	
barge[2] ~-pole	
bargening	bargaining+
bargin	bargain[1+]
baricade	barricade[2]
barier	barrier+
bario	barrio
baritone	
barje	barge[2+]
bark[1]	
barley ~| sugar ~| water	
barmitsva	Bar Mitzvah
barn *[building] ~| dance ~| owl	
	barren *[empty]+
	baron *[nobleman]+
barnacle	
barnical	barnacle
baroke	baroque
barometer	@barometric
baron *[nobleman] ~ial	
	barren *[empty]+
baroque	
barou	bayou
barow	barrow
barracks	
barracuda	
barrage	
barrel[3] ~ful	
barren *[empty] ~ness	
	baron *[nobleman]+
barrette *[hair clip]	
	beret *[hat]
barricade[2]	
barrier ~| reef	
barrio	

Key to Spelling Rules

Red words are wrong. **Black** words are correct.

~ Add the suffix or word directly to the main word, without a space or hyphen
e.g. ash ~en ~tray → ashen ashtray

~- Add a hyphen to the main word before adding the next word
e.g. blow ~-dry → blow-dry

~| Leave a space between the main word and the next word
e.g. decimal ~| place → decimal place

\+ By finding this word in its correct alphabetical order, you can find related words
e.g. abowt about+ → about-face

* Draws attention to words that may be confused

™ Means the word is a trademark

@ Signifies the word is derived from the main word

barrometer	barometer+
barrow	
barter1	
barytone	baritone
bas ~-relief	
	base2 *[bottom]+
	bass *[music, fish]+
basal *[fundamental] ~| metabolism ~| temperature	
	basil *[herb]
	Basel *[city]
basalt	
basc	bask1 *[soak up]
	Basque *[people]
bascet	basket+
baschien	bastion
base2 *[bottom] ~| angle ~ball ~less ~line ~ment	
	bass *[music, fish]+
	bias1+
Basel *[city]	basal *[fundamental]+
	basil *[herb]
basen	basin+
bashful ~ly ~ness	
basic *[simple] ~ally	
BASIC *[program]	
basil *[herb]	basal *[fundamental]+
	Basel *[city]
basilica	
basillus	bacillus+
basin ~ful	
basis	@bases
bask1 *[soak up]	Basque *[people]
basket ~ball ~| case ~ful ~ry ~work	
basle	basal *[fundamental]+
	Basel *[city]
	basil *[herb]
basooka	bazooka
basoon	bassoon+
Basque *[people]	bask1 *[soak up]
bass *[music, fish] ~| clef ~| drum ~| guitar ~| guitarist	
	base2 *[bottom]+
bassilus	bacillus+
bassoon ~ist	
bastard	
bastardize2	
baste2	
bastion	
basturd	bastard
basune	bassoon+
bat3 *[thick stick, animal] ~ty4	
	bait1 *[food, torment]
batallion	battalion
batan	baton *[stick]
	batten1 *[fasten]+
batanical	botanical+
batch1 *[group] ~es ~| processing	
	back1 *[behind, body part]+
batcheler	bachelor+
bate	bat3 *[thick stick, animal]+
	bait1 *[food, torment]
bated *[breath]	baited *[trap, teased]
baten	baton *[stick]
	batten1 *[fasten]+
bater	barter1
	batter1+
batery	battery4+
bath1 *[tub, wash] ~mat ~| oil ~robe ~room	
	bathe2 *[wash, swim]
bathe2 *[wash, swim]	
	bath1 *[tub, wash]+
bathing ~| suit	
batik	
batique	batik
batle	battle2+
baton *[stick]	batten1 *[fasten]+
battalion	
battel	battle2+
batten1 *[fasten] ~| down	
	baton *[stick]
batter1 ~ing ram	
battery4 ~| acid ~| pack	
battin	batten1 *[fasten]+
	baton *[stick]
battle2 ~-axe ~| cry ~dress ~field ~ground ~ments ~-ram ~ship	

KEY TO SUFFIXES AND COMPOUNDS

These rules are explained on pages vii to ix.

1 Keep the word the same before adding **ed, er, est, ing**
e.g. cool1 → cooled, cooler, coolest, cooling

2 Take off final **e** before adding **ed, er, est, ing**
e.g. fine2 → fined, finer, finest, fining

3 Double final consonant before adding **ed, er, est, ing**
e.g. thin3 → thinned, thinner, thinnest, thinning

4 Change final **y** to **i** before adding **ed, er, es, est, ly, ness**
e.g. tidy4 → tidied, tidier, tidies, tidiest, tidily, tidiness
Keep final **y** before adding **ing** e.g. tidying

5 Add **es** instead of **s** to the end of the word
e.g. bunch5 → bunches

6 Change final **f** to **ve** before adding **s**
e.g. calf6 → calves

batton	baton *[stick]
	batten[1] *[fasten]+
batyk	batik
bauble *[trinket]	babble[2] *[chatter]
	bubble[2] *[gas]+
baud *[data] ~| rate	
	bored *[nothing to do]+
baudy	bawdy[4]
baught	bought *[paid for]
	bout *[match, short time]
baujolais	Beaujolais+
baul	ball[1] *[sport, dance, shout]+
	bawl[1] *[cry]
baulk[1]	
bauxite	
bawbl	bauble *[trinket]
	bubble[2] *[gas]+
bawd	baud *[data]+
	bored *[nothing to do]+
bawdy[4]	
bawl[1] *[cry]	ball[1] *[sport, dance, shout]+
bawn	born *[birth]+
bawt	bought *[paid for]
	bout *[match, short time]
bawxite	bauxite
bay[1] ~| leaf ~| window	
bayl	bail[1] *[out, pay]
	bale[2] *[bundle]
bayonet[1]	
bayou	
bayt	bait[1]
baything	bathing+

Unable to find your word under **bay**?
Look under **ba**

bazaar *[sale]	bizarre *[strange]+
bazooka	
be *[I will be] ~ing	
	@been ~| gone
	bee *[insect]+
beach[5] *[shore, sandy] ~es ~| ball ~comber ~combing ~head	
beach	beech[5] *[tree]
	bitch[5] *[female]+
beacon *[light]	bacon *[smoked meat]+
bead[1] *[for a necklace, sweat] ~y	
	bed *[for sleeping]
beaf	beef[1]+
beagle	@beagling
beak *[bird's nose] ~er	
	bike[2] *[bicycle, motorcycle]
beakeeper	beekeeper+
beam[1]	
bean *[vegetable] ~| counter ~curd ~pole ~sprouts ~stalk	
	been *[was]
beanie ~| baby[4]	
beap	beep[1]
bear *[carry, animal] ~able ~ing ~| hug ~| market ~skin	
	bare[2] *[naked]+
	beer *[drink]
	bier *[funeral]
beard *[facial hair] ~ed	
	bared *[showed]
	barred *[stopped]
bearing *[point, carrying]	
	baring *[showing]
beast *[animal, horrible]	
	@beastly[4]
	best *[excellent]+
beastial	bestial+
beat *[hit, win] ~en ~ing	
	beet *[food]+
	bet *[wager]
beata	beta *[test, second, letter]+
beatific ~ation	
beatify[4] *[saint]	beautify[4] *[make beautiful]
beatroot	beetroot
beau *[boyfriend]	bow[1] *[and arrow, bend, tie]+
	bough *[branch]
Beaufort scale	
Beaujolais ~| wine	

Key to Spelling Rules

Red words are wrong. **Black** words are correct.

~ Add the suffix or word directly to the main word, without a space or hyphen
e.g. ash ~en ~tray → ashen ashtray

~- Add a hyphen to the main word before adding the next word
e.g. blow ~-dry → blow-dry

~| Leave a space between the main word and the next word
e.g. decimal ~| place → decimal place

+ By finding this word in its correct alphabetical order, you can find related words
e.g. abowt about+ → about-face

★ Draws attention to words that may be confused

TM Means the word is a trademark

@ Signifies the word is derived from the main word

beautician
beautiful ~ly
beautify[4] *[make beautiful]
beatify[4] *[saint]
beauty[4] *[lovely] ~| parlor ~| queen
booty *[treasure]
beaver[1] ~| away
bebop
becalmed
became
because
beck *[command] ~| and call
beak *[bird's nose]+
beckon[1] *[call] bacon *[smoked meat]+
beacon *[light]
become @becoming
becon beacon *[light]
bacon *[smoked meat]+
beckon[1] *[call]+
becum become+
becuz because
bed[3] *[for sleeping] ~bug ~clothes ~fellow ~| linen ~ridden ~rock ~roll ~room ~side ~sit ~| sore ~spread ~stead ~time
bead[1] *[for a necklace, sweat]+

Unable to find your word under **bed**? Take off **bed** and look again

bedevil[3]
bedlam
Bedouin ~| tribe
bedraggled
bee *[insect] ~hive ~line ~swax
be *[I will be]+
beech[5] *[tree] beach[5] *[shore, sandy]+
bitch[5] *[female]+
beecon beacon *[light]
bacon *[smoked meat]+
beed bead[1]+
beef[1] ~y ~steak ~| up
beegle beagle+
beek beak *[bird's nose]+
beck *[command]+
beekeeper @beekeeping
Beelzebub
beem beam[1]
been *[was] bean *[vegetable]+
beep[1]
beer *[drink] bier *[funeral]
beerd beard *[facial hair]+
bared *[showed]
beest beast *[animal, horrible]+
beet *[food] ~| root
beat *[hit, win]+
beetle *[insect] betel *[nut]
beever beaver[1]+
befall ~en
befit[3]
before ~hand
befrend befriend[1]
befriend[1]
befuddle[2]
beg[3]
began *[past of begin]
begun *[start]
beggar[1]
begile beguile[2]
begin ~ner ~ning
begone
begonia
begrudge[2]
beguile[2]
begun *[start] began *[past of begin]
beguyle beguile[2]
behaf behalf+
behaiv behave[2]
behalf ~| of
behave[2]
behavior ~al ~ism
behead[1]
behed behead[1]
beheld
behest
behind
behold ~en ~er ~ing
beige *[color] badge *[pin]

Key to Suffixes and Compounds

These rules are explained on pages vii to ix.

1 Keep the word the same before adding **ed, er, est, ing**
e.g. cool[1] → cooled, cooler, coolest, cooling
2 Take off final **e** before adding **ed, er, est, ing**
e.g. fine[2] → fined, finer, finest, fining
3 Double final consonant before adding **ed, er, est, ing**
e.g. thin[3] → thinned, thinner, thinnest, thinning
4 Change final **y** to **i** before adding **ed, er, es, est, ly, ness**
e.g. tidy[4] → tidied, tidier, tidies, tidiest, tidily, tidiness
Keep final **y** before adding **ing** e.g. tidying
5 Add **es** instead of **s** to the end of the word
e.g. bunch[5] → bunches
6 Change final **f** to **ve** before adding **s**
e.g. calf[6] → calves

being	
bejeweled	
bek	beak *[bird's nose]+
	beck *[command]
bekause	because
bekome	become+
bekon	beacon *[light]
	beckon[1] *[call]+
bekwest	bequest

> Unable to find your word under **bek**?
> Look under **bec**

bel *[loudness measure]	
	bell *[rings]+
	belle *[beauty]
belabor[1]	
belated ~ly	
belch[5] ~es	
beleaguered	
belei	belie *[wrong idea]+
	belly[4] *[stomach]+
beleif	belief
beleive	believe[2]
belfry[4]	
belie *[wrong idea]	
	belly[4] *[stomach]+
belied	@belying
belief	
believable	@believably
believe[2]	
beligirent	belligerent+
belittle[2]	
bell *[rings] ~boy ~hop ~-ringing	
	bel *[loudness measure]
	belle *[beauty]
bellated	belated+
belle *[beauty]	bel *[loudness measure]
	bell *[rings]+
belligerent ~ly	@belligerence
bellow[1] *[yell]	below *[under]+
bellows *[yells, tool for blowing air]	
	billows *[fills with air, sailing]

belly[4] *[stomach] ~ache ~| button ~| dance[2] ~| flop[3] ~ful ~-up	
	belie *[wrong idea]+
belong[1] ~ings	
beloved	
below *[under] ~-the-line	
	bellow[1] *[yell]
	billow[1] *[fill with air]+
belt[1]	
beltch	belch[5+]
bely	belie *[wrong idea]+
	belly[4] *[stomach]+
bemuse[2]	
bench[5] ~mark[1]	
bend ~able ~ing	
beneath	
benedicshun	benediction
Benedictine ~| monk	
benediction	
beneeth	beneath
benefactor	
beneficial ~ly	
beneficiary[4]	
benefishal	beneficial+
benefisiary	beneficiary[4]
benefit[1] ~| enhancements	
benevolent	@benevolence
benidicshiun	benediction
benign ~ly	
benin	benign+
bent	
bentch	bench+
benzene *[single compound C_6H_6]	
benzine *[petroleum ether mixture]	
bequeath[1]	
bequest	
ber	burr[1]
berate[2]	
berbul	burble[2]
berd	bird+
berden	burden[1+]
bereave[2] ~ment	
bereft	
beret *[hat]	berry[4] *[fruit]
	bury[4] *[cover]

Key to Spelling Rules

Red words are wrong. **Black** words are correct.

~ Add the suffix or word directly to the main word, without a space or hyphen
e.g. ash ~en ~tray → ashen ashtray

~- Add a hyphen to the main word before adding the next word
e.g. blow ~-dry → blow-dry

~| Leave a space between the main word and the next word
e.g. decimal ~| place → decimal place

+ By finding this word in its correct alphabetical order, you can find related words
e.g. abowt about+ → about-face

* Draws attention to words that may be confused

TM Means the word is a trademark

@ Signifies the word is derived from the main word

bereve bereave^{2+}
berger burger
berglar burglar^{+}
bergul burgle^{2} *[steal]
berry^{4} *[fruit] beret *[hat]
bury^{4} *[cover]
berserk
berst burst *[open, in, out]$^{+}$
berth^{1} *[moor, bunk]
birth *[born]$^{+}$
bery beret *[hat]
berry^{4} *[fruit]
bury^{4} *[cover]

Unable to find your word under **ber**?
Look under **bur**

beseech^{5}
beseige besiege^{2}
beserk berserk
beset^{3}
beside ~s
besiege^{2}
besotted
best *[excellent] ~| man ~| practice ~| seller
beast *[animal, horrible]$^{+}$
bestial ~ity
bestow^{1} ~al
bet *[wager] beat *[hit, win]$^{+}$
beta *[test, second, letter] ~| carotene ~-blocker ~| particle ~| ray ~| test
betta *[fish]
better^{1} *[satisfactory]$^{+}$
bettor *[one who bets]
betel *[nut] Beatle *[musician]
beetle *[insect]
betray^{1} ~al
betroth ~ed ~al
betta *[fish] beta *[test, second, letter]$^{+}$
better *[satisfactory]$^{+}$
bettor *[one who bets]
better^{1} *[satisfactory] ~ment
beta *[test, second, letter]$^{+}$
betta *[fish]
bettor *[one who bets]
bettor *[one who bets]
beta *[test, second, letter]$^{+}$
betta *[fish]
better^{1} *[satisfactory]$^{+}$
between
beu beau *[boyfriend]
bow^{1} *[and arrow, bend, tie]
beuge beige *[color]
beuteful beautiful^{+}
beutefy beautify^{4} *[beautiful]
beutician beautician
beutifull beautiful^{+}
beutishun beautician
beuty beauty^{4} *[lovely]$^{+}$
booty *[treasure]
beverage
beware
bewich bewitch^{5}
bewilder^{1} ~ment
bewitch^{5}
bewtane butane^{+}
beyond
bi buy *[shop]$^{+}$
by *[near]$^{+}$
bye *[farewell, sport]$^{+}$
bial bile *[liquid, bitter]$^{+}$
biannual *[twice a year] ~ly
biennial *[every two years]
bias^{5} ~es
Bible ~| belt @biblical
bibliographic ~al
bibliography^{4} @bibliographer
bicarbonate ~| of soda
bicentennial @bicentenary^{4}
biceps
bich bitch^{5} *[female]$^{+}$
beach^{5} *[shore, sandy]$^{+}$
beech^{5} *[tree]
bichimin bitumen
bicker^{1} *[quarrel] biker *[motorcyclist]
bicycle^{2}

KEY TO SUFFIXES AND COMPOUNDS

These rules are explained on pages vii to ix.

1. Keep the word the same before adding **ed, er, est, ing** e.g. cool^{1} → cooled, cooler, coolest, cooling
2. Take off final **e** before adding **ed, er, est, ing** e.g. fine^{2} → fined, finer, finest, fining
3. Double final consonant before adding **ed, er, est, ing** e.g. thin^{3} → thinned, thinner, thinnest, thinning
4. Change final **y** to **i** before adding **ed, er, es, est, ly, ness** e.g. tidy^{4} → tidied, tidier, tidies, tidiest, tidily, tidiness
   Keep final **y** before adding **ing** e.g. tidying
5. Add **es** instead of **s** to the end of the word e.g. bunch^{5} → bunches
6. Change final **f** to **ve** before adding **s** e.g. calf^{6} → calves

bid *[say] ~den ~ding
 bide[2] *[wait]
bide[2] *[wait] bid *[say][+]
bidet
bidevil bedevil[3]
bie by *[near][+]
 buy *[shop][+]
 bye *[farewell, sport][+]
bief beef[1+]
biege beige *[color]
Bielzibub Beelzebub
biennial *[every two years]
 biannual *[twice a year][+]
biep beep[1]
bier *[funeral] beer *[drink][+]
 buyer *[shop]
biet beat *[hit, win][+]
 beet *[food][+]
bietle beetle *[insect]
 betel *[nut]
bifercate bifurcate[2+]
bifocal ~s
bifour before[+]
bifriend befriend[1]
bifurcate[2] @bifurcation
big[3] ~| business ~| deal ~| game ~gie ~head ~hearted ~| leagues ~-mouth ~| name ~| shot ~| top ~| wheel ~wig
Big ~| Apple ~| Bang ~| Brother

> Unable to find your word under **big**?
> Take off **big** and look again

bigamist @bigamous
 @bigamy
bigan began *[past of begin]
bigon begone
bigot ~ed ~ry
bigun begun *[start]
bihalf behalf[+]
bihave behave[2]
bihind behind
bike[2] *[bicycle, motorcycle]
 beak *[bird's nose][+]

> Unable to find your word under **bi**?
> Look under **be**

bikeeni bikini
biker *[motorcyclist]
 bicker[1] *[quarrel]
bikini
bil bill[1] *[invoice][+]
 bile *[liquid, bitter][+]
bilabong billabong
bilateral ~ism ~ly
bilberry[4]
bild billed *[invoiced]
 build *[construct][+]
bildge bilge
bilding building[+]
bile *[liquid, bitter] ~| duct
 bill[1] *[invoice][+]
bilet billet[1]
bilevabul believable[+]
bilge
bilingual ~ism ~ly
bilingwal bilingual[+]
bilion billion[+]
bilittul belittle[2]
bill[1] *[invoice] ~board ~fold
 bile *[liquid, bitter][+]
bill of ~| exchange ~| lading ~| sale
Bill of Rights *[law]

> Unable to find your word under **bill**?
> Take off **bill** and look again

billabong
billbury bilberry[4]
billed *[invoiced] build *[construct][+]
billet[1]
billiards
billion ~aire
billit billet[1]
billow[1] *[fill with air] ~y
 below *[under][+]
billows *[fills with air, sailing]
 bellows *[tool for blowing air]
billy ~| club ~| goat

Key to Spelling Rules

Red words are wrong. **Black** words are correct.

~ Add the suffix or word directly to the main word, without a space or hyphen
e.g. ash ~en ~tray → ashen ashtray

~- Add a hyphen to the main word before adding the next word
e.g. blow ~-dry → blow-dry

~| Leave a space between the main word and the next word
e.g. decimal ~| place → decimal place

+ By finding this word in its correct alphabetical order, you can find related words
e.g. abowt about[+] → about-face

★ Draws attention to words that may be confused

™ Means the word is a trademark

@ Signifies the word is derived from the main word

billyards billiards
biloved beloved
bilow below *[under]+
billow[1] *[fill with air]+
bilt built+
bily billy+
bimbo
bimone bemoan[1]
bimonthly
bimuse bemuse[2]
bin[3] *[box] ~liner
been *[was]
binaculars binoculars
binary ~| number system ~| star
bind ~er ~ing
bindge binge[2]
bineath beneath
binery binary+
binge[2]
bingo
binoculars
binomial ~| system
biocemical biochemical+
biocenser biosensor
biochemical ~ly
biochemist ~ry
biochips
biocomputing
biodegradable
bio-feedback
bio-fuel
biofysics biophysics
biografer biographer
biografy biography[4+]
biographer
biography[4] @biographical
bioinformatics
biokemical biochemical+
biological ~ly ~| activity ~| clock ~| controls ~| research ~| warfare

Unable to find your word under **biological**?
Take off **biological** and look again

biology @biologist

biomass
biomaterials
biomedical ~| computing ~| informatics ~| information
biomedicine
bionic
biopesticide
biophysics
biopsy[4]
biosensor
biosphere
biotechnology
bipartisan
bipass bypass[1]
biped
biplain biplane
biplane
bipolar ~| disorder
biproduct by-product
biqueath bequeath[1]
biquest bequest
birbel burble[2]
birch[5] ~es
bird ~| bath ~-brained ~cage ~| dog ~like ~seed ~| table ~-watching

Unable to find your word under **bird**?
Take off **bird** and look again

birden burden[1+]
birdie
bird's-eye ~| view
birger burger
birgler burglar+
birgul burgle[2] *[steal]
birn burn[1+]
birned burned *[past of burn]
burnt *[that is burned]

Unable to find your word under **bi**?
Look under **bu**

birth *[born] ~day ~| control ~mark ~place ~rate ~right
berth[1] *[moor, bunk]
biscit biscuit

Key to Suffixes and Compounds

These rules are explained on pages vii to ix.

1 Keep the word the same before adding **ed, er, est, ing**
e.g. cool[1] → cooled, cooler, coolest, cooling
2 Take off final **e** before adding **ed, er, est, ing**
e.g. fine[2] → fined, finer, finest, fining
3 Double final consonant before adding **ed, er, est, ing**
e.g. thin[3] → thinned, thinner, thinnest, thinning
4 Change final **y** to **i** before adding **ed, er, es, est, ly, ness**
e.g. tidy[4] → tidied, tidier, tidies, tidiest, tidily, tidiness
Keep final **y** before adding **ing** e.g. tidying
5 Add **es** instead of **s** to the end of the word
e.g. bunch[5] → bunches
6 Change final **f** to **ve** before adding **s**
e.g. calf[6] → calves

bisck bisque
biscuit
biseach beseech[5]
bisecksual bisexual[+]
bisect[1] ~ion ~or
bisectual bisect[1+]
bisexual[+]

Unable to find your word under **bi**?
Look under **by**

biseige besiege[2]
bisekt bisect[1+]
bisen bison
bisentennial bicentennial[+]
biseps biceps
biset beset[3]
bisexual ~ity ~ly
bishop
biside beside[+]
bisk bisque
biskit biscuit
bison
bisoted besotted
bisque
bisquit biscuit
bisson bison
bistander bystander
bistow bestow[1+]
bisycul bicycle[2]
bit *[small piece, past of bite] ~ten
bite *[put teeth into][+]
byte *[data]
bitch[5] *[female] ~es
beach[5] *[shore, sandy][+]
beech[5] *[tree]
bitchumen bitumen
bite[2] *[put teeth into] ~-size ~-sized
byte *[data]
biter *[someone that bites]
bitter *[taste, angry][+]
bitray betray[1+]
bitter *[taste, angry] ~ly ~ness ~| end ~| lemon ~-sweet
bitumen
bitween between
bius bias[5+]
bivouac ~ked ~king
bivuak bivouac[+]
biware beware
biweekly
biwich bewitch[5]
biwilder bewilder[1+]
biword byword
biyond beyond

Unable to find your word under **bi**?
Look under **be**

Bizantine Byzantine
bizarre *[strange] ~ly ~ness
bazaar *[sale]
bizness business[+]
bizy busy[4+]
bla blah[+]
blab[3] ~ber[1] ~bermouth[1]
black[1] *[color] ~| and blue ~| and white ~| ball ~| belt ~berry[4] ~board ~| box ~| currant ~| eye ~head ~| hole ~| ice ~jack ~leg[3] ~list[1] ~| magic ~mail[1] ~| mark ~| market ~out ~smith

Unable to find your word under **black**?
Take off **black** and look again

Black Death *[disease]
blacken[1]
bladder *[sac] blader *[skater]
blade *[cutting part]
blader *[skater] bladder *[sac]
blading
blaggard blackguard
blah ~blah
blahzay blasé *[offhand]
blaze[2] *[fire]
blaid blade *[cutting part]
blaimworthy blameworthy
blair blare[2]
blak black[1+]
blakberry blackberry[4]

Key to Spelling Rules

Red words are wrong. **Black** words are correct.

~ Add the suffix or word directly to the main word, without a space or hyphen
e.g. ash ~en ~tray → ashen ashtray

~- Add a hyphen to the main word before adding the next word
e.g. blow ~-dry → blow-dry

~| Leave a space between the main word and the next word
e.g. decimal ~| place → decimal place

\+ By finding this word in its correct alphabetical order, you can find related words
e.g. abowt about[+] → about-face

* Draws attention to words that may be confused

TM Means the word is a trademark

@ Signifies the word is derived from the main word

blamange	blancmange
blame[2] ~able ~less ~lessly	
blameworthy	
blanch[5] ~es	
blancmange	
bland ~ly ~ness	
blandishments	
blank[1] ~ly ~ness ~| verse	
blanket[1]	
blare[2]	
blarney ~| stone	
blarst	blast[1+]
blarzay	blasé *[offhand]
blasé *[offhand]	blaze[2] *[fire]
blasfeme	blaspheme[2+]
blason	blazon[1]
blaspheme[2]	@blasphemous
blasphemy[4]	
blast[1] ~| furnace ~off	
blatant ~ly	
blatent	blatant[+]
blaze[2] *[fire]	blasé *[offhand]
blazon[1]	
bleach[5] ~es	
bleak[1] ~ly ~ness	
bleary ~-eyed	
bleat[1]	
bleech	bleach[5+]
bleed ~ing	
bleek	bleak[1+]
bleeni	blini *[pancakes]
bleep[1] *[quick sound][+]	
	blip[3] *[short signal]
bleery	bleary[+]
bleet	bleat[1]
blemish[5]	
blend[1]	
bler	blur[3+]
blerb	blurb
blert	blurt[1+]
bless[5]	
blessed ~ness ~| Virgin	
blet	bleat[1]
blew *[wind]	blue *[color][+]
blight[1]	

blimp	
blind[1] ~ly ~ness ~| alley ~| bidding ~| experiment ~| date ~fold[1] ~-man's-buff ~| side[2] ~| spot	

> Unable to find your word under **blind**?
> Take off **blind** and look again

blini *[pancakes]	
blink[1] ~ered ~ers	
bliny	blini *[pancakes]
blip[3] *[short signal]	
	bleep[1] *[quick sound][+]
bliss ~ful ~fully ~fulness	
blister[1]	
blite	blight[1]
blithe ~ly ~ness	
blithering	
blitz[5]	
blizzard	
blo	blow[+]
bloat[1] *[swell up] ~edness	
	blot[3] *[dab]
blob[3]	
bloc *[group]	block[1] *[stop][+]
blocade	blockade[2]
bloch	blotch[5+]
block[1] *[stop] ~age ~buster ~-booking ~| grant ~head ~| vote	
	bloc *[group]

> Unable to find your word under **block**?
> Take off **block** and look again

blockade[2]	
blod	blood[+]
blog[3]	
blond *[light hair-male]	
blonde *[light hair-female]	
blood ~ed ~less ~| bank ~bath ~| cell ~| clot ~-clotting ~count ~curdling ~| donor ~| flow ~| group ~hound ~lust ~| money ~| poisoning ~| pressure ~| profile ~shed ~shot ~stain ~| sugar	

Key to Suffixes and Compounds

These rules are explained on pages vii to ix.

1. Keep the word the same before adding **ed, er, est, ing**
   e.g. cool[1] → cooled, cooler, coolest, cooling
2. Take off final **e** before adding **ed, er, est, ing**
   e.g. fine[2] → fined, finer, finest, fining
3. Double final consonant before adding **ed, er, est, ing**
   e.g. thin[3] → thinned, thinner, thinnest, thinning
4. Change final **y** to **i** before adding **ed, er, es, est, ly, ness**
   e.g. tidy[4] → tidied, tidier, tidies, tidiest, tidily, tidiness
   Keep final **y** before adding **ing** e.g. tidying
5. Add **es** instead of **s** to the end of the word
   e.g. bunch[5] → bunches
6. Change final **f** to **ve** before adding **s**
   e.g. calf[6] → calves

blood ~| test ~thirsty ~| transfusion ~| type ~| vessel

Unable to find your word under **blood**? Take off **blood** and look again

bloody *[covered with blood] ~-minded
Bloody Mary *[drink]
blooper
blossom[1]
blot[3] *[dab] — bloat[1] *[swell up]+
blotch[5] ~es — @blotchy[4]
blote — bloat[1] *[swell up]+
blouse
blow ~er ~ing ~n ~fly ~hole ~out ~pipe ~torch ~-up

Unable to find your word under **blow**? Take off **blow** and look again

blowse — blouse
blubber[1]
blud — blood+
bluddy — bloody *[covered with blood]+
blue *[color] ~bell ~berry[4] ~bird ~| blood ~-blooded ~bonnet ~| cheese ~| chip ~-collar ~grass ~| jeans ~print ~| ribbon ~-rinse
— blew *[wind]

Unable to find your word under **blue**? Take off **blue** and look again

blues ~y
Bluetooth™
bluff[1]
blume — bloom[1+]
blunder[1]
blunt[1] ~ness
bluper — blooper
blur[3] ~ry
blurb
blurt[1] ~| out
blush[5]
bluster[1] ~y

blynd — blind[1+]
blyzzard — blizzard

Unable to find your word under **bly**? Look under **bli**

bo — beau *[boyfriend]
— boo[1] *[surprise]
— bow[1] *[and arrow, bend, tie]+
boa ~| constrictor
boagy — bogey *[golf, threat, wheels]+
boah — boa+
boahmian — bohemian
boan — bone[2+]
boar *[pig] — bore[2] *[drill, no interest]+
board[1] *[get on, panel] ~| meeting ~room
— bored *[nothing to do]+
boarding ~| house ~| pass ~| school
boast[1] ~ful ~fulness ~fully
boat[1] *[water] ~ing ~house ~yard
— bot *[software-related]
bob[3]
bobbal — bauble *[trinket]
— babble[2] *[chatter]
— bubble[2] *[gas]+
bobbin
bobble *[mistake] — bauble *[trinket]
— bubble[2] *[gas]+
bobin — bobbin
boch — botch[1]
bochulism — botulism
bocks — box[5+]
bodice
bodie — body[4+]
bodily ~| harm
bodise — bodice
body[4] ~| bag ~builder ~building ~| cavity ~| clock ~| count ~guard ~| odor ~| shop ~| snatcher ~| suit ~work

Unable to find your word under **body**? Take off **body** and look again

---

Key to Spelling Rules

Red words are wrong. **Black** words are correct.

~ Add the suffix or word directly to the main word, without a space or hyphen
e.g. ash ~en ~tray → ashen ashtray

~- Add a hyphen to the main word before adding the next word
e.g. blow ~-dry → blow-dry

~| Leave a space between the main word and the next word
e.g. decimal ~| place → decimal place

+ By finding this word in its correct alphabetical order, you can find related words
e.g. abowt about+ → about-face

★ Draws attention to words that may be confused

™ Means the word is a trademark

@ Signifies the word is derived from the main word

bofort scale Beaufort scale
bog[3] ~| down
boganvilla bougainvillea
bogel boggle[2]
bogey *[golf, threat, wheels] ~man
boggy[4] *[very wet]
boogie *[dance]+
boggle[2]
boggy[4] *[very wet]
bogey *[golf, threat, wheels]+
bogis bogus
bogus
bohemian
boiant buoyant+
boicott boycott[1]
boil[1] ~| down ~| over
boiled ~| sweet
boiler ~plate ~suit
boisterous ~ly ~ness
bok book[1+]
Bolchevic Bolshevik
bold *[strong] ~ly ~ness ~face
bowled *[ball]
boler bowler+
Boliwood Bollywood *[Indian film industry]
bolk baulk[1]
boll *[cotton plant] ~| weevil
ball[1] *[sport, dance, shout]+
bowl[1] *[food, sport]+
bolled bold *[strong]+
bowled *[sport]
Bollywood *[Indian film industry]
Bolshevik
bolster[1] ~| up
bolt[1] ~-hole
bom bomb[1+]
bomb[1] ~| disposal ~proof ~shell ~| shelter ~sight ~| squad
bombastic ~ally
bon appétit
bon vivant
bon voyage

bona fide @bonafides
bonanza
bond[1] ~age ~holder ~ed
bound[1+]
bone[2] ~| china ~-dry ~head ~| mass ~meal ~| marrow ~| structure
bone appetite bon appétit
bone vivante bon vivant
bone voyage bon voyage
bonfire
bongo ~| drums
bonnafyd bona fide+
bonnanza bonanza
bonus ~| payment ~| track
boo[1] *[surprise] bow[1] *[and arrow, bend, tie]+
boobie booby+
booby ~| prize ~-trap
boofant bouffant+
booger *[mucus] bugger[1]
boogie *[dance] ~| board ~-woogie
bogey *[golf, threat, wheels]+
buggy[4] *[stroller]
boogle bugle[2] *[music]
burgle[2] *[steal]
book[1] ~able ~binder ~case ~| club ~end ~keeping ~let ~mark ~rest ~seller ~shelf ~shop ~worm

Unable to find your word under **book**? Take off **book** and look again

bookay bouquet+
Boolean ~| logic ~| search
boolevard boulevard
Boolian Boolean+
booly bully
boom[1] ~| box ~| town
boomerang
boon ~docks ~doggle ~ies
boorish
boose boos *[sounds of disaprooval]
booze[2] *[drink]+

Key to Suffixes and Compounds

These rules are explained on pages vii to ix.

1 Keep the word the same before adding **ed, er, est, ing**
e.g. cool[1] → cooled, cooler, coolest, cooling
2 Take off final **e** before adding **ed, er, est, ing**
e.g. fine[2] → fined, finer, finest, fining
3 Double final consonant before adding **ed, er, est, ing**
e.g. thin[3] → thinned, thinner, thinnest, thinning
4 Change final **y** to **i** before adding **ed, er, es, est, ly, ness**
e.g. tidy[4] → tidied, tidier, tidies, tidiest, tidily, tidiness
Keep final **y** before adding **ing** e.g. tidying
5 Add **es** instead of **s** to the end of the word
e.g. bunch[5] → bunches
6 Change final **f** to **ve** before adding **s**
e.g. calf[6] → calves

boost[1]
booster ~| seat ~| shot
boot[1] *[shoe] ~| camp ~leg[3] ~strap[3]
bout *[match, short time]
bootee *[shoe] booty *[treasure]
booth *[display, small place]
both *[two things]
booty *[treasure] bootee *[shoe]
booze[2] *[drink] ~-up
boos *[sounds of disaproova]]
borax @boracic
borbul bauble *[trinket]
Bordeaux ~| wine
bordello
border[1] ~line
bording boarding[+]
bordom boredom
bordor border[1+]
bordow Bordeaux[+]
bore[2] *[drill, no interest] ~hole
boar *[pig]
borec boric[+]
bored *[nothing to do] ~| stiff
baud *[data][+]
board[1] *[get on, panel][+]
boreding boarding[+]
boredom
borganvilla bougainvillea
borgwa bourgeois[+]
boric ~| acid
borish boorish
borjwa bourgeois[+]
born *[birth] ~-again
borne *[carried]
borough *[place] borrow[1] *[loan][+]
burrow[1] *[dig, hole]
borrish boorish
borrow[1] *[loan] ~ings
borough *[place]
burrow[1] *[dig, hole]
borte bought *[did buy]
boso bozo
bosom ~y
boson

boss[5] *[in charge] ~y[4]
bows *[bends, ribbons, archery]
bossa nova
bosso nova bossa nova
bost boast[1+]
bot *[software-related]
boat[1] *[water][+]
boot[1] *[shoe][+]
bought *[did buy]
botanical ~| garden
botanist @botany
botch[1]
bote boat[1] *[water][+]
boot[1] *[shoe][+]
bot *[software-related]
both *[two things] booth *[display, small place]
bother[1] ~some
botinist botanist[+]
botique boutique
botle bottle[2+]
botocks Botox™ *[toxin]
buttocks *[bottom]
botom bottom[1+]
Botox™ *[toxin] buttocks *[bottom]
bottanical botanical[+]
bottle[2] ~-feed ~neck ~| opener
bottom[1] ~less ~| line ~| out
botul bottle[2+]
botulism
botum bottom[1+]
bou boo[1] *[surprise]
bow[1] *[and arrow, bend, tie][+]
bouffant ~| hairstyle
bougainvillea
bough *[branch] bow[1] *[and arrow, bend, tie]
bought *[paid for] bout *[match, short time]
bouillon *[soup] ~| cube
bullion *[gold]
boukay bouquet[+]
boulderize bowdlerize[2]
boulevard

KEY TO SPELLING RULES

Red words are wrong. **Black** words are correct.

- ~ Add the suffix or word directly to the main word, without a space or hyphen
  e.g. ash ~en ~tray → ashen ashtray
- ~- Add a hyphen to the main word before adding the next word
  e.g. blow ~-dry → blow-dry
- ~| Leave a space between the main word and the next word
  e.g. decimal ~| place → decimal place
- \+ By finding this word in its correct alphabetical order, you can find related words
  e.g. abowt about[+] → about-face
- ★ Draws attention to words that may be confused
- ™ Means the word is a trademark
- @ Signifies the word is derived from the main word

bounce[2] @bouncy[4]
bound[1] ~less
boundary[4]
bounse bounce[2+]
bounteous ~ly
bountiful ~ly
bounty[4] ~| hunter
bouquay bouquet[+]
bouquet ~| garni
boured board[1] *[get on, panel][+]
bored *[nothing to do][+]
bourgeois ~ie
bourn born *[birth][+]
borne *[carried]
bourzwazee bourgeois[+]
boush bush[+]
bout *[match, short time]
boot[1] *[shoe][+]
bought *[paid for]
boutick boutique
boutique
boutius bounteous[+]
bovine
bow[1] *[and arrow, bend, tie] ~legged
bough *[branch]
beau *[boyfriend]
bowdlerize[2]
bowel *[stomach] ~| movement
bowl[1] *[food, sport][+]
Bowfort Beaufort[+]
Bowjolais Beaujolais[+]
bowl[1] *[food, sport] ~ful
boll *[cotton plant][+]
bowel *[stomach][+]
bowler ~| hat
bowling ~| alley ~| ball
bownd bound[1+]
bownse bounce[2+]
bownty bounty[4+]
bows *[bends, ribbons, archery]
boss[1] *[in charge][+]
bowt bout *[match, short time]
boot[1] *[shoe][+]

Unable to find your word under **bow**?
Look under **bou**

box[5] ~| office ~| spring ~wood
boxer ~| shorts
boxite bauxite
boxsight bauxite
boy *[male] ~friend ~hood
buoy[1] *[float]
Boy Scout *[member]
boyant buoyant[+]
boycott[1]
boyish ~ly ~ness
boyl boil[1+]
boyled boiled[+]
boyler boiler[+]
boystrous boisterous[+]
bozo
bra
brace[2] *[support, teeth]
braise[2] *[food]
brass *[metal][+]
bracelet
bracket[1]
brackish
brade braid[1] *[cloth, hair]
brayed *[donkey]
brag[3]
Brahmin
braid[1] *[cloth, hair]
brayed *[donkey]
braie bray[1]
braik brake[2] *[slow][+]
break *[destroy, end][+]
Braille
brain[1] ~| damage ~-dead ~less ~| cell ~child ~power ~stem ~storm ~-teaser ~| tumor ~wash[1] ~| wave

Unable to find your word under **brain**?
Take off **brain** and look again

brainy[4]

Key to Suffixes and Compounds

These rules are explained on pages vii to ix.

1 Keep the word the same before adding **ed, er, est, ing**
e.g. cool[1] → cooled, cooler, coolest, cooling
2 Take off final **e** before adding **ed, er, est, ing**
e.g. fine[2] → fined, finer, finest, fining
3 Double final consonant before adding **ed, er, est, ing**
e.g. thin[3] → thinned, thinner, thinnest, thinning
4 Change final **y** to **i** before adding **ed, er, es, est, ly, ness**
e.g. tidy[4] → tidied, tidier, tidies, tidiest, tidily, tidiness
Keep final **y** before adding **ing** e.g. tidying
5 Add **es** instead of **s** to the end of the word
e.g. bunch[5] → bunches
6 Change final **f** to **ve** before adding **s**
e.g. calf[6] → calves

Word	Correct spelling / related word
braise[2] *[food]	brace[2] *[support, teeth]
	brass *[metal]+
	braze[2] *[weld]
braiselet	bracelet
braize	braise[2] *[food]
	braze[2] *[weld]
brake[2] *[slow] ~| fluid ~| light ~| pad	
	break *[destroy, end]+.
braket	bracket[1]
brakish	brackish
brale	Braille
brambal	bramble
bramble	
bran *[cereal]	brain[1+]
branch[5] ~| line ~| office	
brand[1] ~| image ~| loyalty ~| name ~-new	
brandie	brandy+
branding ~| iron	
brandish[5] ~es	
brandy ~| butter ~| snap	
brane	brain[1+]
braney	brainy[4]
brase	brace[2] *[support, teeth]
	braise[2] *[food]
	brass *[metal]+
	braze *[weld]
braselet	bracelet
brasen	brazen+
brash ~ly ~ness	
brass *[metal] ~| rubbing	
	brace[2] *[support, teeth]
	braise[2] *[food]
brasseer	brassiere *[undergarment]
	brasserie *[restaurant]
	brazier *[fire pan]
brassiere *[undergarment]	
	brasserie *[restaurant]
	brazier *[fire pan]
brat ~| pack	
brath	broth
braul	brawl[1]
brauny	brawny[4]
braut	brought
bravado	
brave[2]	
bravera	bravura
bravo	
bravura	
brawd	broad+
brawl[1]	
brawny[4]	
brawt	brought
bray[1]	
brayed *[donkey]	braid[1] *[cloth, hair]
brayny	brainy[4]
braze[2] *[weld]	braise[2] *[food]
brazen ~ly ~ness	
brazier *[fire pan]	brassiere *[undergarment]
braziere	brassiere *[undergarment]
	brasserie *[restaurant]
	brazier *[fire pan]
breach[5] *[break]	breech *[back]+
bread *[food] ~ed ~-and-butter ~| basket ~board ~| crumbs ~winner	
	bred *[produced]
	breed *[animals]+

> Unable to find your word under **bread**?
> Take off **bread** and look again

Word	Correct spelling / related word
breadth *[width]	breath *[air]+
break *[destroy, end] ~ing ~even ~line ~down ~neck ~out ~point ~through ~| up	
	brake[2] *[slow]+

> Unable to find your word under **break**?
> Take off **break** and look again

Word	Correct spelling / related word
breakfast[1] ~| television	
breast ~bone ~feed ~plate ~| pocket ~stroke	
	Brest *[city]
breath *[air] ~less ~| test	
	breadth *[width]
	breathe[2] *[in, out]
breathable	
breathalyze[2]	@Breathalyzer™
breathe[2] *[in, out]	
	breath *[air]+

Key to Spelling Rules

Red words are wrong. **Black** words are correct.

- ~ Add the suffix or word directly to the main word, without a space or hyphen
  e.g. ash ~en ~tray → ashen ashtray
- ~- Add a hyphen to the main word before adding the next word
  e.g. blow ~-dry → blow-dry
- ~| Leave a space between the main word and the next word
  e.g. decimal ~| place → decimal place
- + By finding this word in its correct alphabetical order, you can find related words
  e.g. abowt about+ → about-face
- * Draws attention to words that may be confused
- ™ Means the word is a trademark
- @ Signifies the word is derived from the main word

breatheble	breathable
breathilyse	breathalyze[2+]
breathtaking ~ly	
breaze	breeze[2+]
bred *[produced]	bread *[food]+
	breed *[animals]+
bredth	breadth *[width]
breech *[back] ~| birth ~block ~loader	
	breach[5] *[break]
breeches	
breed *[animals] ~ing ground	
	bread *[food]+
breeder ~| reactor	
breef	brief[1+]
breethe	breathe[2] *[in, out]
breeze[2] ~| in ~way	
breezy[4]	
breif	brief[1+]
brekfast	breakfast[1+]
Brest *[city]	breast+
breth	breath *[air]+
	breathe[2] *[in, out]
brethalise	breathalyse[2+]
brethtaking	breathtaking+
brevety	brevity
brevity	
brew[1] *[beer, coffee] ~ed	
	@brewery[4]
brewd	brewed *[beer, coffee]
	brood[1] *[think, family]+
brewnet	brunet+
bribe[2]	@bribery[4]
brick[1] ~layer ~| up ~work	
bridal *[wedding] ~| party ~| suite	
	bridle[2] *[horse]+
bride ~groom ~smaid ~-to-be	
bridge[2] ~head ~| loan	
bridle[2] *[horse] ~| path	
	bridal *[wedding]+
brief[1] ~ly ~s ~case	
brieze	breeze[2+]
brigade	
brigadier ~| general	
brige	bridge[2+]
brigedier	brigadier+

bright ~-eyed	
brighten[1] *[make brighter]	
	Britain *[country]
brigideer	brigadier+
brik	brick[1+]
briket	briquette
brilliant ~ly	@brilliance
brilyant	brilliant+
brim[3] ~ful ~stone	
brine	
bring ~er ~ing	
brink ~manship	
briquette	
brisk[1] ~ly ~ness ~et	
Britain *[country]	brighten[1]
brite	bright+
British ~| Empire ~| Isles	
brittal	brittle+
britten	brighten[1] *[make brighter]
	Britain *[country]
brittle ~ness	
broach[5] *[open]	brooch[5] *[jewelry]
broad ~ly ~band ~bean ~| brush ~cast[1] ~| daylight ~minded ~side ~sheet ~-spectrum	

> Unable to find your word under **broad**?
> Take off **broad** and look again

broaden[1]	
Broadway	
brocade	
brocaid	brocade
broccoli	
broch	broach[5] *[open]
	brooch[5] *[jewelry]
brocher	brochure
brochure	
brockally	broccoli
brod	broad+
brog	brogue
brogue	
broil[1]	
brokade	brocade

Key to Suffixes and Compounds

These rules are explained on pages vii to ix.

1 Keep the word the same before adding **ed, er, est, ing**
e.g. cool[1] → cooled, cooler, coolest, cooling

2 Take off final **e** before adding **ed, er, est, ing**
e.g. fine[2] → fined, finer, finest, fining

3 Double final consonant before adding **ed, er, est, ing**
e.g. thin[3] → thinned, thinner, thinnest, thinning

4 Change final **y** to **i** before adding **ed, er, es, est, ly, ness**
e.g. tidy[4] → tidied, tidier, tidies, tidiest, tidily, tidiness
Keep final **y** before adding **ing** e.g. tidying

5 Add **es** instead of **s** to the end of the word
e.g. bunch[5] → bunches

6 Change final **f** to **ve** before adding **s**
e.g. calf[6] → calves

broke *[did break, no money]	
	brook[1] *[stream]
broken ~-down ~hearted	
broker[1] ~age	
brokn	**broken**+
bromide	
bronchial ~| tube	
bronchitis	
bronco	
bronkial	**bronchial**+
bronkitis	**bronchitis**
bronse	**bronze**[2+]
brontosaurus	
bronze[2] ~| medal ~| metal	
Bronze ~| Age	
brooch[5] *[jewelry]	
	broach[5] *[open]
brood[1] *[think, family]	
	brewed *[beer, coffee]
broody[4]	
brook[1]	
broom ~stick	
broose	**bruise**[2]
broot	**brute**+
brorde	**broad**+
brort	**brought**
broshure	**brochure**
broth	
brothel	
brother ~hood ~-in-law	
brought	
broun	**brown**[1+]
brow ~beat	
brown[1] ~| bag ~| dwarf ~stone	
browse[2]	
browser	
browze	**browse**[2]
broyl	**broil**[1]
bruch	**brooch**[5] *[jewelry]
	brush[5+]
bruck	**brook**[1]
brud	**brewed** *[beer, coffee]
	brood[1] *[think, family]
brue	**brew**[1+]
bruis	**bruise**[2]

bruise[2]	
brume	**broom**+
brunch[5]	
brunet ~te	
brunt	
brush[5] ~es ~-off ~wood ~work	
brusk	**brusque**+
brusque ~ly ~ness	
Brussels ~| sprouts	
brutal ~ity	
brutalize[2]	@**brutalization**
brute ~| force ~| strength	
bruther	**brother**+
brutish ~ly ~ness	
brutle	**brutal**+
brydal	**bridal** *[wedding]+
	bridle[2] *[horse]+
bryde	**bride**+
brydge	**bridge**[2+]
bu	**boo**[1] *[surprise]
	bow[1] *[and arrow, bend, tie]+
bubble[2] *[gas]	@**bubbly**[4]
	bauble *[trinket]
buby	**booby**+
bucher	**butcher**[1+]
buck[1] ~| up	
bucket[1] ~ful	
buckle[2] ~| up	
bucksom	**buxom**+
bud[3]	
Buda	**Buddha**
Buddha	
Buddhism	@**Buddhist**
buddy[4]	
budgerigar	
budget[1] ~ary	
budgie *[budgerigar]	
bufalo	**buffalo**[5+]
buff[1]	
buffalo[5] ~| cowboy	
buffay	**buffet**[1]
buffer[1] ~| state ~| zone	
buffet[1]	
bug[3] ~| out	

Key to Spelling Rules

Red words are wrong. **Black** words are correct.

~ Add the suffix or word directly to the main word, without a space or hyphen
e.g. ash ~en ~tray → ashen ashtray

~- Add a hyphen to the main word before adding the next word
e.g. blow ~-dry → blow-dry

~| Leave a space between the main word and the next word
e.g. decimal ~| place → decimal place

+ By finding this word in its correct alphabetical order, you can find related words
e.g. abowt about+ → about-face

* Draws attention to words that may be confused

™ Means the word is a trademark

@ Signifies the word is derived from the main word

bugel bugle[2] *[music]
burgle[2] *[steal]
buger booger *[mucus]
bugger[1]
buget budget[1+]
bugger[1] booger *[mucus]
buggy[4] *[stroller] bogey *[golf, threat, wheels]+
boogie *[dance]+
bugle[2] *[music] burgle[2] *[steal]
bugy bogey *[golf, threat, wheels]+
buggy[4] *[stroller]
boogie *[dance]+
build *[construct] ~er ~| up
billed *[invoiced]
building ~| site ~| society
buillon bouillon *[soup]+
bullion *[gold]
built ~-in ~| up
buisness business+
bujet budget[1+]
buk book[1+]
buck[1+]
bukle buckle[2+]
bul bull+
bulb ~ous
bulean Boolean+
bulee bully[4]
bulemia bulimia+
bulet bullet+
buletin bulletin+
bulevard boulevard
bulge[2]
bulimia ~| nervosa
@bulimic
bulion bouillon *[soup]+
bullion *[gold]
bulit bullet+
bulitin bulletin+
bulivard boulevard
bulj bulge[2]
bulk ~| buy ~| sales ~| transfer
bull ~dog ~fight ~finch ~frog ~| market ~ring

bulldoze[2] @bulldozer
bullet ~| point ~proof ~| train
bulletin ~| board
bullion *[gold] boullion *[soup]+
bullit bullet+
bull rush *[football]
bulrush[5] *[plant]
bull's eye
bullshit
bully[4]
bulrush[5] *[plant] bull rush *[football]
bulseye bull's eye
bulshit bullshit
bulwark
bulwork bulwark
buly bully[4]
bulymia bulimia+
bum[3] ~| out
bumble[2] ~bee
bumerang boomerang
bumkin bumpkin
bump[1] ~tious ~tiously
bumper ~| sticker ~-to-bumper
bumpkin
bun
bunch[5] ~es
bundle[2] ~| up
bungee ~| jumping
bungel bungle[2]
bungie bungee+
bungle[2]
bunion
bunjie bungee+
bunk ~| bed ~house
bunker[1]
bunny[4] ~| rabbit
Bunsen ~| burner
bunsh bunch[5+]
buoy[1] *[float] boy *[male]+
buoyant @buoyancy
bur burr[1]
burate berate[2]
burau bureau+
buraucracy bureaucracy[4]
buraucrat bureaucrat+

Key to Suffixes and Compounds

These rules are explained on pages vii to ix.

1 Keep the word the same before adding **ed, er, est, ing**
e.g. cool[1] → cooled, cooler, coolest, cooling
2 Take off final **e** before adding **ed, er, est, ing**
e.g. fine[2] → fined, finer, finest, fining
3 Double final consonant before adding **ed, er, est, ing**
e.g. thin[3] → thinned, thinner, thinnest, thinning
4 Change final **y** to **i** before adding **ed, er, es, est, ly, ness**
e.g. tidy[4] → tidied, tidier, tidies, tidiest, tidily, tidiness
Keep final **y** before adding **ing** e.g. tidying
5 Add **es** instead of **s** to the end of the word
e.g. bunch[5] → bunches
6 Change final **f** to **ve** before adding **s**
e.g. calf[6] → calves

burble[2]

burch birch[5+]

burd bird[+]

burden[1] ~some

burdy birdie

bureau *[furniture, agency] ~| de change

bureaucracy[4]

bureaucrat ~ic ~ically

bureave bereave[2+]

bureft bereft

buret *[lab glassware]

beret *[hat]

> Unable to find your word under **bur**?
> Look under **ber**

burgeon ~ing

burger

burgin burgeon[+]

burgindy burgundy *[color]

Burgundy *[wine]

burglar ~| alarm

burglary[4]

burgle[2] *[steal] bugle[2] *[music]

burglery burglary[4]

burgundy *[color]

Burgundy *[wine]

burial ~| ground ~| plot

burido burrito

buriel burial[+]

burito burrito

burlap

burlesque

burley burly[4]

burly[4]

burn[1] ~able ~out

burned *[past of burn]

burnish[1]

burnt *[that is burned]

burned *[past of burn]

burocracy bureaucracy[4]

burocrat bureaucrat[+]

burow burro *[donkey]

burrow[1] *[dig, hole]

bureau[+]

burr[1]

burrito

burro *[donkey] burrow[1] *[dig, hole]

burrow[1] *[dig, hole]

borough *[place]

borrow[1] *[loan][+]

bureau *[furniture, agency][+]

burro *[donkey]

bursitis

burst *[open, in, out] ~ing

bust[1] *[break, sculpture]

bursurk berserk

burth berth[1] *[moor, bunk]

birth *[born][+]

bury[4] *[cover] berry[4] *[fruit]

bus ~| station ~| stop

busel bustle[2]

busem bosom[+]

bush ~ed ~man ~whack[1]

bushle bushel

business[5] ~| card ~| class ~-friendly ~| innovation ~like ~man ~| plan ~| process ~| sector ~| trip ~woman

> Unable to find your word under **business**?
> Take off **business** and look again

business-to ~-business ~-consumer

bussel bustle[2]

bust[1] *[break, sculpture]

burst *[open, in, out][+]

buster *[breaker] booster[+]

bustier *[garment]

bustier *[garment]

bustle[2]

busy[4] ~| bee ~body

but *[however] butt[1] *[end, hit][+]

butane ~| gas

butcher[1] ~y

buten button[1+]

buter butter[1+]

butie beauty[4] *[lovely][+]

booty *[treasure]

butiful beautiful[+]

KEY TO SPELLING RULES

Red words are wrong. **Black** words are correct.

~ Add the suffix or word directly to the main word, without a space or hyphen
e.g. ash ~en ~tray → ashen ashtray

~- Add a hyphen to the main word before adding the next word
e.g. blow ~-dry → blow-dry

~| Leave a space between the main word and the next word
e.g. decimal ~| place → decimal place

+ By finding this word in its correct alphabetical order, you can find related words
e.g. abowt about[+] → about-face

★ Draws attention to words that may be confused

TM Means the word is a trademark

@ Signifies the word is derived from the main word

Unable to find your word under **bu**? Look under **beau**

butique	boutique
butock	buttock
butocks	Botox™ *[toxin]
	buttocks *[bottom]
buton	button[1+]
butt[1] *[end, hit][+]	but *[however]
butter[1] ~y ~fly ~milk ~nut ~scotch	
buttock ~s *[bottom]	
	Botox™ *[toxin]
button[1] ~-down	
buty	beauty[4] *[lovely][+]
	booty *[treasure]
buy *[shop] ~er ~ing ~-out	
	by *[near][+]
	bye *[farewell, sport][+]
buyer *[purchaser]	
	beer *[drink]
	bier *[funeral]
buzz[5] ~es ~word	
buzzard	
by *[near] ~-and-by ~law ~stander	
	buy *[shop][+]
	bye *[farewell, sport][+]
bycarbonate	bicarbonate[+]
byceps	biceps
bycicul	bicycle[2]
bye *[farewell, sport] ~-bye	
	buy *[shop][+]
	by *[near][+]
byer	beer *[drink]
	buyer *[shop]
	bier *[funeral]
bygones	
byngo	bingo
bynoculars	binoculars
byofeedback	biofeedback
bypass[5]	
by-product	
by-sexual	bisexual[+]
bystander	
byte *[data]	bite *[teeth][+]
bytumen	bitumen
byurow	bureau *[furniture, agency][+]
byvouac	bivouac[+]
byword	
Byzantine	
byzarre	bazaar *[sale]
	bizarre *[strange][+]

Unable to find your word under **by**? Look under **bi**

KEY TO SUFFIXES AND COMPOUNDS

These rules are explained on pages vii to ix.

1 Keep the word the same before adding **ed, er, est, ing** e.g. cool[1] → cooled, cooler, coolest, cooling
2 Take off final **e** before adding **ed, er, est, ing** e.g. fine[2] → fined, finer, finest, fining
3 Double final consonant before adding **ed, er, est, ing** e.g. thin[3] → thinned, thinner, thinnest, thinning
4 Change final **y** to **i** before adding **ed, er, es, est, ly, ness** e.g. tidy[4] → tidied, tidier, tidies, tidiest, tidily, tidiness
Keep final **y** before adding **ing** e.g. tidying
5 Add **es** instead of **s** to the end of the word e.g. bunch[5] → bunches
6 Change final **f** to **ve** before adding **s** e.g. calf[6] → calves

C

.com
C *[letter] ~-section
sea *[water]+
see *[eyes]+

> Unable to find your word under **c**?
> Look under **k**

cab ~bie ~driver ~stand
cabal *[conspiracy]
cable² *[rope, wire]+
cabaret
cabbage
cabbaray — cabaret
cabel — cable²+
caberay — cabaret
cabige — cabbage
cabin ~| boy ~| crew ~et ~| cruiser ~| fever
cable² *[rope, wire] ~| car ~| modem ~| stitch ~| television ~| TV
cacao *[seed, tree]
cocoa *[chocolate]
cacaphony — cacophony
Cacasion — Caucasian
cache² *[hide] — catch⁵ *[ball]+
cash¹ *[money]+
cachet *[mark]
cachinial — cochineal
cacing — casing
cackal — cackle²
cackle²
cacktus — cactus+
cacofony — cacophony+
cacophony — @cacophonous
cactus ~| plant — @cacti
cad *[coward]

CAD *[computer-aided design]
cadaver
caddy⁴ *[tea, one who carries]
cadence
cadenza
cadet ~| corps
cadge² *[beg] — cage² *[enclosure]+
cadgole — cajole²+
cadmium
Caesar ~| salad
café *[restaurant] — coffee *[drink]+
cafeteria
caff — calf⁶ *[baby cow]
calve² *[give birth to a calf]
caffe — café *[restaurant]
coffee *[drink]+
caffeine
caftan
cage² *[enclosure]
@cagy⁴
cadge² *[beg]
cagnack — cognac
cagnisent — cognizant+
cagole — cajole²+
cahksus — coccyx
cahoots
cahutes — cahoots
caidence — cadence
caige — cage²+
caik — cake²+
caime — came *[arrived]
Cain *[biblical name]
cane² *[stick]+
can³ *[able, tin]+
cainine — canine *[dog related]
caiotey — coyote

KEY TO SPELLING RULES

Red words are wrong. **Black** words are correct.

~ Add the suffix or word directly to the main word, without a space or hyphen
e.g. ash ~en ~tray → ashen ashtray

~- Add a hyphen to the main word before adding the next word
e.g. blow ~-dry → blow-dry

~| Leave a space between the main word and the next word
e.g. decimal ~| place → decimal place

+ By finding this word in its correct alphabetical order, you can find related words
e.g. abowt about+ → about-face

* Draws attention to words that may be confused

TM Means the word is a trademark

@ Signifies the word is derived from the main word

caiper	caper
cair	care² *[be concerned]⁺
caireful	careful⁺
caireless	careless⁺

> Unable to find your word under **cai**?
> Look under **ca**

cajole² ~ry	
cake² ~| course ~walk	
cakle	cackle²
calamine	
calamity⁴	@calamitous
calcify⁴	@calcification
calcium	
calculate²	@calculable
calculator	
calculation	
calculus	
cale	kale
calemine	calamine
calendar *[time]	calender *[press]
	colander *[draining bowl]
calender *[press]	calendar *[time]
	colander *[draining bowl]
calf⁶ *[baby cow]	calve² *[give birth to a calf]
caliber	
calibrate²	@calibrator
calibration	
calic	colic⁺
calico⁵	
calif	caliph
califlour	cauliflower
caligrapher	calligrapher⁺
caling	calling⁺
calipers	
caliph	
calipso	calypso
calisthenics	
call¹ ~back ~| center ~| for ~| forth ~| girl ~-in ~| off ~| on ~| out ~| up	

> Unable to find your word under **call**?
> Look under **coll**

callamity	calamity⁴⁺
callegen	collagen
callegue	colleague
callendar	calendar *[time]
	calender *[press]
	colander *[draining bowl]
caller ~| ID	
calliedoscope	kaleidoscope⁺
calligrapher	@calligraphy
calling ~| card	
callipers	calipers
callisthenics	
callon	colon *[body part]
	cologne *[perfume]
callony	colony⁴⁺
callous *[unfeeling] ~ly ~ness	
	callus⁵ *[hard skin]
calloused ~| skin	
callow	
callus⁵ *[hard skin]	
	callous *[unfeeling]⁺
calone	cologne *[city, perfume]
	colon *[body part]
calosis	colossus
calow	callow
calquelus	calculus
calqulable	calculable
calqulashun	calculation
calqulate	calculate²⁺
calqulater	calculator
calqulus	calculus

> Unable to find your word under **calqu**?
> Look under **calc**

calsify	calcify⁴⁺
calsium	calcium
calude	collude²⁺
calus	callous *[unfeeling]⁺
	callus⁵ *[hard skin]
Calvary *[hill near Jerusalem]	
	cavalry⁴ *[horse army]
Calvinist ~ic	@Calvinism
calypers	calipers
calyph	caliph

KEY TO SUFFIXES AND COMPOUNDS

These rules are explained on pages vii to ix.

1 Keep the word the same before adding **ed, er, est, ing**
e.g. cool¹ → cooled, cooler, coolest, cooling
2 Take off final **e** before adding **ed, er, est, ing**
e.g. fine² → fined, finer, finest, fining
3 Double final consonant before adding **ed, er, est, ing**
e.g. thin³ → thinned, thinner, thinnest, thinning
4 Change final **y** to **i** before adding **ed, er, es, est, ly, ness**
e.g. tidy⁴ → tidied, tidier, tidies, tidiest, tidily, tidiness
Keep final **y** before adding **ing** e.g. tidying
5 Add **es** instead of **s** to the end of the word
e.g. bunch⁵ → bunches
6 Change final **f** to **ve** before adding **s**
e.g. calf⁶ → calves

calypso	
cam *[wheel] ~shaft	
	came *[arrived]
camaflage	camouflage[2]
camamele	chamomile
camaphlage	camouflage[2]
camaraderie	
camcorder	
came *[arrived]	cam *[wheel][+]
camel ~| hair ~| train	
camelion	chameleon
Camelot	
Camembert	
camemorate	commemorate[2+]
cameo	
camera ~| bag ~| equipment ~| shy	
camfer	camphor
	chamfer *[notch]
camfor	camphor
camiflage	camouflage[2]
camikazi	kamikaze
Camilot	Camelot
camimiel	camomile
camio	cameo
camisole	
cammando	commando[+]
camoflage	camouflage[2]
camomile	
Camonber	Camembert
camouflage[2]	
camp[1] ~fire ~ground ~site	
campaign[1]	
campain	campaign[1]
campfer	camphor
camphor	
campus[5]	
camputation	computation
camra	camera[+]
camraderee	camaraderie
camul	camel[+]
camune	commune[2]
camunicate	communicate[2+]
can[3] *[able, tin] ~-do ~not	
	cane[2] *[stick][+]
canabiss	cannabis
canal	
canapé *[food]	canopy[4] *[covering]
canary[4] *[bird]	cannery[4] *[factory]
canasta *[card game]	
	canister *[box]
cancan	
cancel[3] ~lation	
cancer *[illness] ~ous	
	canker *[sore]
Cancer *[zodiac]	
canch	conch
cancil	cancel[3+]
candee	candy[4+]
candel	candle[+]
candelabra	
cander	candor
candey	candy[4+]
candicy	candidacy[4]
candid *[frank] ~ly ~ness	
	candied *[sugared]
candidacy[4]	
candidait	candidate[+]
candidasy	candidacy[4]
candidate	@candidature
candied *[sugared]	
	candid *[frank][+]
candle ~light ~lit ~stick	
candone	condone[2]
candor	
candy[4] ~| bar ~| cane	
cane[2] *[stick] ~| sugar	
	can[3] *[able, tin][+]
canery	cannery[4] *[factory]
canew	canoe[+]
cangaroo	kangaroo[+]
canibal	cannibal[+]
canibis	cannabis
canine *[dog related]	
	cannon[1] *[gun][+]
	canon *[writings][+]
canion	canyon
canister *[box]	canasta *[card game]
canker *[sore]	cancer *[illness][+]
cannabis	
cannal	canal

Key to Spelling Rules

Red words are wrong. **Black** words are correct.

~ Add the suffix or word directly to the main word, without a space or hyphen
e.g. ash ~en ~tray → ashen ashtray

~- Add a hyphen to the main word before adding the next word
e.g. blow ~-dry → blow-dry

~| Leave a space between the main word and the next word
e.g. decimal ~| place → decimal place

\+ By finding this word in its correct alphabetical order, you can find related words
e.g. abowt about[+] → about-face

★ Draws attention to words that may be confused

TM Means the word is a trademark

@ Signifies the word is derived from the main word

cannen cannon[1] *[gun]+
canon *[writings]+
cannery[4] *[factory]
canary[4] *[bird]
cannibal ~ism ~istic
cannibalize[2]
cannible cannibal+
cannister canister *[box]
canasta *[card game]
cannon[1] *[gun] ~ball ~| fodder
canine *[dog related]
canon *[writings]+
canny[4]
canoe ~d ~ing ~ist
canon *[writings] ~ical
canine *[dog related]
cannon[1] *[gun]+
canonize[2] @canonization
canoo canoe+
canopay canapé *[food]
canopy[4] *[covering]
canopy[4] *[covering]
canapé *[food]
canquer canker *[sore]
conquer[1] *[defeat]+
cansel cancel[3+]
canser cancer *[illness]+
Cancer *[zodiac]
cant *[slant, hypocrisy]
can't *[cannot]
cantada cantata
cantaloupe
cantankerous ~ly ~ness
cantata
canteen
canter[1] *[horse] cantor *[religious singer]
cantilever[1]
cantor *[religious singer]
canter[1] *[horse]
cantsumay consommé
canue canoe+
canvas[5] *[cloth]
canvass[5] *[ask for votes] ~es
cany canny[4]
canyon

caos chaos+
cap[3] *[hat, covering]
cape *[cloak, land]
capability[4]
capable @capably
capacious ~ness
capacitor
capacity[4]
capashus capacious+
capasiter capacitor
capasity capacity[4]
caparison *[horse decoration]
comparison
capaytious capacious+
capchen caption[1]
capcher capture[2] *[catch]
cape *[cloak, land]
cap[3] *[hat, covering]
capechino cappuccino
caper
capichulate capitulate[2+]
capillary[4]
capital *[city, wealth] ~| asset ~| city ~| gain ~| letter ~| punishment
capitol *[building]
capitalist ~ic @capitalism
capitalize[2] @capitalization
capitle capital *[city, wealth]+
capitulate[2] @capitulation
capor caper
cappuccino
caprice
capricious ~ly ~ness
Capricorn
caprise caprice
caprishus capricious+
capshure capture[2] *[catch]
capsil capsule[2]
capsize[2]
capsule[2]
captain[1] ~cy
capter captor *[person who captures]
captin captain[1+]
caption[1]

Key to Suffixes and Compounds

These rules are explained on pages vii to ix.

1 Keep the word the same before adding **ed, er, est, ing**
e.g. cool[1] → cooled, cooler, coolest, cooling
2 Take off final **e** before adding **ed, er, est, ing**
e.g. fine[2] → fined, finer, finest, fining
3 Double final consonant before adding **ed, er, est, ing**
e.g. thin[3] → thinned, thinner, thinnest, thinning
4 Change final **y** to **i** before adding **ed, er, es, est, ly, ness**
e.g. tidy[4] → tidied, tidier, tidies, tidiest, tidily, tidiness
Keep final **y** before adding **ing** e.g. tidying
5 Add **es** instead of **s** to the end of the word
e.g. bunch[5] → bunches
6 Change final **f** to **ve** before adding **s**
e.g. calf[6] → calves

captivate[2]
captive ~| market
@captivity
captology
captor *[person who captures]
capture[2] *[catch]
capucheeno cappuccino
car *[vehicle] ~| bomb ~jack[1] ~| pool[1] ~port ~| sharing
care[2] *[be concerned]+
caracter character+
caracteristic characteristic+
carafe
caramel ~ize[2]
carat *[weight of gem]
caret *[mark]
carrot *[food]
karat *[purity of gold]
carati karate *[fighting]
caravan ~ning ~| site
caraway ~| seed
carbaretta carburetor
carben carbon+
carbenize carbonize[2]
carbin carbon+
carbinize carbonize[2]
carbohydrate
carbolic ~| acid
carbon ~ated ~| copy ~| dating ~| dioxide ~| monoxide ~| paper
carbonize[2]
carbord cardboard
carburetor
carcass[5]
carcinogen ~| ic
carcinoma
card[1] ~board ~holder ~| sharp ~| table
cardboard
cardiac ~| arrest
cardigan
cardinal ~| number
cardiogram
cardiology @cardiologist
cardiovascular ~| disease

care[2] *[be concerned] ~free ~worn
car *[vehicle]+
careckteristik characteristic+
careen[1]
career *[job] ~| ladder ~| path
carrier *[carries]+
careful ~ly ~ness
careless ~ly ~ness
caress[1]
caret *[mark] carat *[weight of gem]
carrot *[vegetable]
karat *[purity of gold]
caretaker
carette carat *[weight of gem]
caret *[mark]
carrot *[vegetable]
karat *[purity of gold]
carey carry[4]+
cargo[5] ~| carrier
Carian *[ancient people]
carrion *[dead animal]
caribou
caribu caribou
caricature
carie carry[4]+
caries *[tooth decay]
carier career *[job]
carrier *[carries]+
carisma charisma
carivan caravan+
carless careless+
carmel caramel+
carnal ~ly ~| knowledge
carnashion carnation
carnation
carnij carnage
carnil carnal+
carnival
carnivore @carnivorous
carol[3] *[song] ~-singing
carrel *[study desk]
carossell carousel
carot carat *[weight of gem]
caret *[mark]

Key to Spelling Rules

Red words are wrong. **Black** words are correct.

~ Add the suffix or word directly to the main word, without a space or hyphen
e.g. ash ~en ~tray → ashen ashtray

~- Add a hyphen to the main word before adding the next word
e.g. blow ~-dry → blow-dry

~| Leave a space between the main word and the next word
e.g. decimal ~| place → decimal place

+ By finding this word in its correct alphabetical order, you can find related words
e.g. abowt about+ → about-face

* Draws attention to words that may be confused

TM Means the word is a trademark

@ Signifies the word is derived from the main word

carot	carrot *[vegetable]
	karat *[purity of gold]
carotene *[carrots]	
	keratin *[protein]
carotid ~| artery	
carotte	carat *[weight of gem]
	carrot *[vegetable]
	karate *[fighting]
carouse[2]	
carousel	
carowse	carouse[2]
carp *[complain, fish]	
carpal *[wrist] ~| tunnel syndrome	
	carpel *[flower part]
carpel *[flower part]	
	carpal *[wrist]+
carpenter	@carpentry
carpet[1] ~bagger ~| bomb[1]	
carraway	caraway+
carrel *[study desk]	
	carol[3] *[song]+
carrie	carry[4]+
carrier *[carries] ~| bag ~| pigeon	
	career *[job]
carrige	carriage+
carrine	careen[1]
carrion *[dead animal]	
carrot *[vegetable]	
	carat *[weight of gem]
	caret *[mark]
	karat *[purity of gold]
carrotid	carotid+
carrousel [also spelled carousel]	
carry[4] ~-on ~out ~| over	
carsanoma	carcinoma
carsinigin	carcinogen+
cart[1] *[transport] ~horse	
	kart *[go-kart]
cart ~load ~wheel	
carte blanche	
cartel	
carten	carton *[box]
	cartoon *[comic strip]+
cartilage	
cartography	@cartographer

carton *[box]	
cartoon *[comic strip] ~ist	
cartouche	
cartridge ~| paper	
cartune	cartoon *[comic strip]+
carumba	caramba
caruze	carouse[2]
carve[2] *[cut]	calve[2] *[give birth to a calf]
carving ~| fork ~| knife[6]	
caryon	carrion *[dead animal]
Casanova	
casarole	casserole[2]
cascade[2]	
case[2] ~| history ~load ~| study[4]	
casel	castle[2]
caserole	casserole[2]
caset	cassette+
cash[1] *[money] ~| cow ~| flow ~| reserve	
	cache[2] *[hide]
	catch[5] *[ball]+
cashay	cachet *[mark]
cashelty	casualty[4]
cashew ~| nut	
cashier	
cashmere ~| sweater	
cashoo	cashew+
cashulty	casualty[4]
casing	
casino	
cask *[container]	casque *[helmet]
casket	
casm	chasm
casock	cassock *[robe]
casque *[helmet]	cask *[container]
cassel	castle[2]
casserole[2]	
casset	cassette+
cassette ~| deck ~| player ~| recorder	
cassle	castle[2]
cassock *[robe]	Cossack *[in Ukraine]
Cassonova	Casanova
cassrole	casserole[2]

Key to Suffixes and Compounds

These rules are explained on pages vii to ix.

1 Keep the word the same before adding **ed, er, est, ing**
e.g. cool[1] → cooled, cooler, coolest, cooling

2 Take off final **e** before adding **ed, er, est, ing**
e.g. fine[2] → fined, finer, finest, fining

3 Double final consonant before adding **ed, er, est, ing**
e.g. thin[3] → thinned, thinner, thinnest, thinning

4 Change final **y** to **i** before adding **ed, er, es, est, ly, ness**
e.g. tidy[4] → tidied, tidier, tidies, tidiest, tidily, tidiness
Keep final **y** before adding **ing** e.g. tidying

5 Add **es** instead of **s** to the end of the word
e.g. bunch[5] → bunches

6 Change final **f** to **ve** before adding **s**
e.g. calf[6] → calves

cast *[select, throw] ~er ~ing ~| iron ~off *[clothing] ~| off *[depart]
caste *[social class]
castanets
castaway
caste *[social class]
cast *[select, throw]+
caster *[thrower, wheel]
castor *[oil, sugar]+
castigate[2] @castigator
castigation
castinets castanets
castle[2]
castor *[oil, sugar] ~| bean ~| oil ~| sugar
caster *[thrower, wheel]
castrate[2] @castration
casual *[informal] ~ly ~ness
causal *[cause and effect]
casualty[4]
cat ~call ~| litter ~nip ~walk
CAT scan
cataclysm ~ic
catacomb
catagoric categoric+
catagorize categorize[2]
catagory category[4]
cataleptic
catalog[3] ~| search
catalytic ~| converter
catalyze[2] @catalyst
catamaran
catapult[1]
catar catarrh
cataract
catarrh
catastrofee catastrophe
catastrofic catastrophic+
catastrophe
catastrophic ~ally
catatonic
catch[5] *[ball] ~ing ~all ~word
cache[2] *[hide]
ketch[5] *[boat]

catechism
cateclysum cataclysm+
catee catty[4]
categoric ~al ~ally
categorize[2]
category[4]
catekism catechism
catekome catacomb
catel cattle+
cateleptic cataleptic
catelize catalyze[2+]
catelog catalog[1+]
catemaran catamaran
catepolt catapult[1]
cater[1]
caterakt cataract
caterpillar
catetonic catatonic
catharsis
cathartic
cathedral
catheter
cathode
catholic *[varied]
Catholic *[religion] ~ism
caticlism cataclysm+
catimaran catamaran
catipiller caterpillar
catitonic catatonic
catnap[3]
catscan CAT scan
catsup [also spelled ketchup]
cattapiller caterpillar
cattle ~| grid ~| prod
catty[4]
Caucasian
caucious cautious+
caucus[5]
cauff cough[1] *[throat irritation]+
caught *[past of catch]
cot *[bed]
court[1] *[law]+
caul *[covering] call[1+]
cowl *[hood]
cauldron

Key to Spelling Rules

Red words are wrong. **Black** words are correct.

~ Add the suffix or word directly to the main word, without a space or hyphen
e.g. ash ~en ~tray → ashen ashtray

~- Add a hyphen to the main word before adding the next word
e.g. blow ~-dry → blow-dry

~| Leave a space between the main word and the next word
e.g. decimal ~| place → decimal place

+ By finding this word in its correct alphabetical order, you can find related words
e.g. abowt about+ → about-face

★ Draws attention to words that may be confused

TM Means the word is a trademark

@ Signifies the word is derived from the main word

cauliflower
caulk[1] *[seal] — **cock**[1] *[chicken]+
causal *[cause and effect] — **casual** *[informal]+
cause[2] ~| of action ~| célèbre ~way
caushin — **caution**[1+]
caushus — **cautious**+
caustic ~ally
cauterize[2] — @**cauterization**
caution[1] ~ary
cautious ~ly ~ness
cavalcade
cavalier *[noble, offhand]
cavalry[4] *[horse army] — **Calvary** *[hill near Jerusalem]
cave[2] ~man ~woman
caveat
cavelry — **cavalry**[4] *[horse army]; **Calvary** *[hill near Jerusalem]
cavern ~ous
caviar
caviat — **caveat**
cavilcade — **cavalcade**
caviler *[complainer] — **cavalier** *[noble, offhand]
cavilier — **cavalier** *[noble, offhand]; **caviler** *[complainer]
cavity[4]
cavort[1]
cavurn — **cavern**+
caw[1] *[crow] — **core** *[center]; **corps** *[army, ballet]
Cawcasian — **Caucasian**
cawcus — **caucus**[5]
cawk — **caulk**[1] *[seal]; **cork**[1] *[stopper]+
cawldren — **cauldron**
cawling — **calling**+
cawnsintrate — **concentrate**[2]
cawpulense — **corpulence**+
cawstic — **caustic**+
cawterize — **cauterize**[2+]
cawz — **cause**[2+]; **coarse**[2] *[rough]+; **course**[2] *[order, path]+

> Unable to find your word under **caw**?
> Look under **cau**

cayenne ~| pepper
cayge — **cadge**[2] *[beg]; **cage**[2] *[enclosure]+
caym — **came** *[arrived]
caynine — **canine** *[dog related]
cazmeer — **cashmere**+
cazym — **chasm**
CB *[Citizen's Band] ~| radio
CD *[recording, investment] ~| burner ~| player ~-ROM
cea — **seedy**[4] *[poor condition]; **C** *[letter]+; **sea** *[water]+; **see** *[eyes]+
cease[2] *[stop] ~fire ~less ~lessly — **seize**[2] *[grab hold]
cecsation — **cessation** *[halt]; **session** *[period]
cecsepit — **cesspit**+
cecure — **secure**[2+]
cedar *[tree] — **Seder** *[Jewish meal]; **seeder** *[plants seeds]
cedate — **sedate**[2+]
cede[2] *[give up] — **seed**[1] *[plant, number]+
cedenza — **cadenza** *[music]; **credenza** *[table]
ceder — **cedar** *[tree]; **Seder** *[Jewish meal]
cedilla
cee — **sea** *[water]+; **see** *[eyes]+
ceeje — **siege**+
ceeling — **ceiling** *[roof]; **sealing** *[fastening]
Cee-Tee-scan — **CT scan**
ceiling *[roof] — **sealing** *[fastening]

cel *[transparent sheet]
  cell *[prison, unit]
  sell *[goods]+
celary — celery[4] *[vegetable]
  salary[4] *[pay]+
Celcius — Celsius
celebrate[2] *[occasion]
  @celebration
  celibate *[unmarried]+
celebrity[4] *[fame]
celenium — selenium
celerity[4] *[speed]
celery[4] *[vegetable]
  salary[4] *[pay]+
celestial ~| body ~| object
celibate *[unmarried]
  @celibacy
  celebrate[2] *[occasion]+
celifane — cellophane
cell *[prison, unit] ~| biology ~| division ~| function ~| phone
  cel *[transparent sheet]
  sell *[goods]
cellar *[space underground]
  seller *[sales person]
cellfone — cell phone
cello — @cellist
cellofane — cellophane
cellophane
Cellsius — Celsius
cellular ~| computing ~| level ~| phone
cellule — @celluloid
cellulite
cellulose
celphone — cell phone
celry — celery[4] *[vegetable]
  salary[4] *[pay]+
Celsius
Celtic ~| cross ~| fringe
celular — cellular+
celule — cellule+
celulite — cellulite
celulose — cellulose
cemen — seaman *[sailor]
  semen *[sperm]
cement[1] ~| mixer
cemetery[4] *[graveyard]
  symmetry[4] *[similar]
cemicle — chemical+
cemitary — cemetery[4] *[graveyard]
  symmetry[4] *[similar]
cenataf — cenotaph
cene — scene *[theater]+
  seen *[eyes]
cenile — senile+
cenior — senior+
cenotaph
censer *[incense holder]
  censor[1] *[restrict]+
  censure *[disapprove of]
  sensor *[detector]
censis — census
censor[1] *[restrict] ~ship
  censer *[incense holder]
  censure *[disapprove of]
  sensor *[detector]
censual — sensual *[dominated by senses]+
censuous — sensuous *[appealing to senses]+
censure[2] *[disapprove of]
  censer *[incense holder]
  censor[1] *[restrict]+
  sensor *[detector]
census *[count of population]
  senses *[sight, hearing, touch]
censuus — sensuous *[appealing to senses]+
  census *[count of population]
cent *[money] — scent *[perfume]
  sent *[away]
centapide — centipede
centar — center[2]+
  centaur
centaur
centenarian
centenary[4] — @centennial
center

Key to Spelling Rules

Red words are wrong. **Black** words are correct.

~ Add the suffix or word directly to the main word, without a space or hyphen
e.g. ash ~en ~tray → ashen ashtray

~- Add a hyphen to the main word before adding the next word
e.g. blow ~-dry → blow-dry

~| Leave a space between the main word and the next word
e.g. decimal ~| place → decimal place

+ By finding this word in its correct alphabetical order, you can find related words
e.g. abowt about+ → about-face

* Draws attention to words that may be confused

TM Means the word is a trademark

@ Signifies the word is derived from the main word

center^2 ~fold ~| forward ~piece ~| stage
centigrade
centiliter
centimeter
centipede
centir — center^{2+}
central ~ity ~ly ~| heating ~| nervous system ~| processing unit

> Unable to find your word under **central**? Take off **central** and look again

centralize^2 — @centralization
centrifugal ~| force
centrifuge
centrist
centrul — central$^+$
centry — century
sentry^{4+}
centryst — centrist
cents *[money] — scents *[perfumes]
sense^2 *[become aware]
centual — sensual *[dominated by senses]$^+$
centuous — sensuous *[appealing to senses]$^+$
centuple^2
centurion
century^4
CEO *[Chief Executive Officer]
ceptic — septic *[infected]
ceramic
ceratine — carotene *[carrots]
keratin *[protein]
cerca — circa
cercuit — circuit^{1+}
cercul — circle^2
cercus — circus^5
cerd — curd *[from milk]
cerdul — curdle^2
cereal *[grain] — serial *[one after another]$^+$
cerebellum
cerebral ~| palsy ~| trauma
cerebrum
ceremonial ~ly
ceremonious ~ly
ceremony^4
cerf — serf *[slave]$^+$
surf^1 *[sea]$^+$
cerfew — curfew
cerial — cereal *[grain]
serial *[one after another]$^+$
cerialize — serialize^{2+}
ceribral — cerebral$^+$
ceriel — cereal *[grain]
serial *[one after another]$^+$
ceries — series
cerif — serif$^+$
cerikature — caricature
cerimony — ceremony^4
cerkit — circuit^{1+}
cerl — curl^{1+}
cerlue — curlew
cername — surname
cernel — colonel *[officer]
kernel *[seed]
cerse — curse^2 *[bad spell]
cersor — cursor *[computer]
cersory — cursory^4
certail — curtail^{1+}
certain *[sure] ~ly
curtain *[screen]$^+$
certainty^4
certale — curtail^{1+}
certen — certain *[sure]$^+$
curtain *[screen]$^+$
certifiable — @certifiably
certificate ~| of deposit ~| of origin
certified ~| check
certify^4 — @certification
certinty — certainty^4
certitude
certsy — curtsy^4 *[bow]
cervashus — curvaceous$^+$
cerve — curve^{2+}
cervical ~| cancer ~| smear
cervix

Key to Suffixes and Compounds

These rules are explained on pages vii to ix.

1 Keep the word the same before adding **ed, er, est, ing** e.g. cool^1 → cooled, cooler, coolest, cooling
2 Take off final **e** before adding **ed, er, est, ing** e.g. fine^2 → fined, finer, finest, fining
3 Double final consonant before adding **ed, er, est, ing** e.g. thin^3 → thinned, thinner, thinnest, thinning
4 Change final **y** to **i** before adding **ed, er, es, est, ly, ness** e.g. tidy^4 → tidied, tidier, tidies, tidiest, tidily, tidiness
Keep final **y** before adding **ing** e.g. tidying
5 Add **es** instead of **s** to the end of the word e.g. bunch^5 → bunches
6 Change final **f** to **ve** before adding **s** e.g. calf^6 → calves

Unable to find your word under **cer**? Look under **cir**, **cur**, **ser**, **sir**, or **sur**

cesar Caesar+
Cesarean ~| birth ~| operation ~| section
cessation *[halt]
cession *[yielding]
session *[period]+
cesspit @cesspool
cetarr catarrh
cew cue[2] *[sign]
queue *[line]
ceyabata ciabatta
ceymotheripy chemotherapy

Unable to find your word under **ce**? Look under **se**

chachay cachet *[mark]
chador *[clothing] chatter[1] *[talk]+
chafe[2] *[rub]
chaff *[grain husks]
chagrin ~ed
chaif chafe[2] *[rub]
chaff *[grain husks]
chaim chime[2]
chaimber chamber+
chaimberlin chamberlain
chain[1] ~| gang ~| letter ~-link ~| mail ~| reaction ~-smoke[2] ~| store
chainge change[2+]
chainging changing+
chair[1] ~man ~person ~woman
chairish cherish[1]
chaised chased *[pursued]
chaste *[pure]
chaiste chased *[pursued]
chaste *[pure]
chalay chalet
chalesteral cholesterol+
chalet
chalice
chalinge challenge[2+]
chalis chalice
chalk[1] *[white substance] ~y ~board
choke[2] *[stop breathing]+
challenge[2] ~| match
chamber ~| music ~| pot
Chamber ~| of Commerce
chameleon
chamfer *[notch]
chamize chemise[2] *[blouse]
chamois *[animal, cloth]
chamomile
champ[1] ~| at the bit
champagne *[wine]
campaign[1]
champain champagne *[wine]
campaign[1]
champion[1] ~ship
Chanaka Chanukah+
chance[2] @chancy
chancellor
chandelier *[light holder]
chandler *[ship's]
chane chain[1+]
chanel channel[3]
change[2] ~able ~ling ~over
changing ~| room
chanj change[2+]
channel[3]
chanse chance[2+]
chanseller chancellor
chant[1]
Chanukah [also spelled Hanukkah]
chaos ~| theory @chaotic
chaparone chaperon[1]
chapel
chaperon[1]
chaplain @chaplaincy[4]
chaple chapel
chaplin chaplain+
chappati
chapped ~| lips
chaps
ChapStick™
chapt chapped+
chapter
chapul chapel

Key to Spelling Rules

Red words are wrong. **Black** words are correct.

~ Add the suffix or word directly to the main word, without a space or hyphen
e.g. ash ~en ~tray → ashen ashtray

~- Add a hyphen to the main word before adding the next word
e.g. blow ~-dry → blow-dry

~| Leave a space between the main word and the next word
e.g. decimal ~| place → decimal place

\+ By finding this word in its correct alphabetical order, you can find related words
e.g. abowt about+ → about-face

★ Draws attention to words that may be confused

™ Means the word is a trademark

@ Signifies the word is derived from the main word

character ~| actor ~| assassination
characteristic ~ally
characterize[2] @characterization
charade
charcoal
chard *[beet] charred *[burned]
chaired *[a meeting]
shard *[fragment]
chare chair[1+]
chared chard *[beet]
charred *[burned]
chaired *[a meeting]
charge[2] ~able ~| account ~| card
chariot ~eer
charisma
charitable @charitably
charity[4] ~| shop
charivari [also spelled shivaree]
charj charge[2+]
charlatan *[fraud]
Charleston *[dance, city]
charm[1] ~| offensive
charred *[burned]
chard *[beet]
chaired *[a meeting]
shard *[fragment]
chart[1] ~er flight
charute cheroot
charysma charisma
chase[2]
chased *[pursued]
chaste *[pure]
chasen chasten[1]
chasie chassis
chasm
chassis
chaste *[pure] chased *[pursued]
chasten[1]
chastise[2] ~ment
chastity ~| belt
chastize chastise[2+]
chasym chasm
chat[3] ~| room ~| show
chateau ~x *[plural]
chatow chateau[+]

chatter[1] *[talk] ~box
chador *[clothing]
chatty[4]
chauffeur[1] *[driver] ~-driven
shofar *[horn]
chauk chalk[1] *[white substance][+]
chauvinism
chauvinist ~ic ~ically
chaw chore *[job]
cheap[1] *[inexpensive] ~ly ~ness ~| shot ~| skate
cheep[1] *[bird]
chip[3] *[piece][+]
sheep *[animals]
ship[3] *[boat][+]
cheapen[1]
cheary cheery[4]
cheat[1]
check[1] *[control, money] ~| box ~book ~-in ~list ~mate[2] ~out ~point ~| up
Czech *[citizen]
Cheddar ~| cheese
cheef chief *[leader][+]
chef *[cook][+]
cheek[1] *[face, rudeness] ~bone
chic *[elegant]
chick *[bird][+]
cheeky[4]
cheep[1] *[bird] cheap[1] *[inexpensive][+]
chip[3] *[piece][+]
sheep *[animals]
ship[3] *[boat][+]
cheepin cheapen[1]
cheer[1] ~less ~| leader ~y[4]
cheerful ~ly ~ness
cheese ~board ~burger ~cake
@cheesy[4]
cheet cheat[1]
cheetah
cheewawa Chihuahua
cheezy cheesy[4]
chef *[cook] ~| d'oeuvre
chief *[leader][+]

KEY TO SUFFIXES AND COMPOUNDS

These rules are explained on pages vii to ix.

1 Keep the word the same before adding **ed, er, est, ing**
e.g. cool[1] → cooled, cooler, coolest, cooling
2 Take off final **e** before adding **ed, er, est, ing**
e.g. fine[2] → fined, finer, finest, fining
3 Double final consonant before adding **ed, er, est, ing**
e.g. thin[3] → thinned, thinner, thinnest, thinning
4 Change final **y** to **i** before adding **ed, er, es, est, ly, ness**
e.g. tidy[4] → tidied, tidier, tidies, tidiest, tidily, tidiness
Keep final **y** before adding **ing** e.g. tidying
5 Add **es** instead of **s** to the end of the word
e.g. bunch[5] → bunches
6 Change final **f** to **ve** before adding **s**
e.g. calf[6] → calves

cheita cheetah
cheite Shiite *[branch of Islam]
shit *[feces]+
chello cello+
chemeez chemise[2] *[blouse]
chemical ~ly ~| agent ~| engineer ~| engineering ~| warfare ~| weapons

> Unable to find your word under **chemical**?
> Take off **chemical** and look again

chemise[2] *[blouse]
chemist ~ry
chemotherapy
cheos chaos+
cherch church[5+]
cherchyard churchyard
cherey cheery[4]
cherish[1]
cherlish churlish+
chern churn[1]
cheroot
cherp chirp[1+]
cherry[4] ~| bomb
cherry-pick[1]
cherub ~ic
chess *[board game] ~board ~men ~| piece
chest *[body, box] ~nut ~| of drawers
chew[1] ~ing gum ~y
chews *[grinds food]
choose *[pick]+
Chianti
chic *[elegant] cheek[1] *[face, rudeness]+
chick *[bird]+
sheikh *[Arab chief]
chicanery
Chicano
chi-chi
chick *[bird] ~adee ~pea
chic *[elegant]
cheek[1] *[face, rudeness]+
Chickano Chicano
chicken[1] ~-and-egg ~feed ~hearted ~pox

chickery chicory
chicle *[gum]
chicory
chide[2]
chief *[leader] ~ly ~tain
chef *[cook]+
Chief ~| Executive Officer ~| Justice ~| Financial Officer ~| Operating Officer
chier cheer[1+]
chierful cheerful+
chiese cheese+
chietah cheetah

> Unable to find your word under **chi**?
> Look under **che**

chiffon
Chihuahua
chiite Shiite *[branch of Islam]
shit *[feces]+
chikin chicken[1+]
child ~| abuse ~bearing ~birth ~| care ~hood ~less ~like ~minder ~proof ~ren ~ish ~'s play

> Unable to find your word under **child**?
> Take off **child** and look again

chile *[pepper] ~| powder
Chile *[country]
chili[5] *[food] ~| con carne
chilly *[cold]
chill[1] ~| out
chilli[5] [also spelled chile, chili]
chilly *[cold] chili[5] *[food]+
Chile *[country]
chime[2]
chimera
chimney ~| stack ~| sweep
chimp ~anzee
chin ~-up
china ~| clay
Chinatown
chinchilla
Chinese ~| lantern ~| puzzle

KEY TO SPELLING RULES

Red words are wrong. **Black** words are correct.

~ Add the suffix or word directly to the main word, without a space or hyphen
e.g. ash ~en ~tray → ashen ashtray

~- Add a hyphen to the main word before adding the next word
e.g. blow ~-dry → blow-dry

~| Leave a space between the main word and the next word
e.g. decimal ~| place → decimal place

\+ By finding this word in its correct alphabetical order, you can find related words
e.g. abowt about+ → about-face

★ Draws attention to words that may be confused

™ Means the word is a trademark

@ Signifies the word is derived from the main word

chink
chintilla chinchilla
chintz ~y
chip[3] *[piece] ~board ~| off the old block
cheap[1] *[inexpensive]
cheep[1] *[bird]
ship[3] *[boat]+
sheep *[animals]
chipmunk
chirad charade
chirch church[5]+
chirn churn[1]
chiropractor @chiropractic
chirp[1] @chirpy[4]
chisel[3]
chit *[ticket, girl] ~chat[3]
shit[3] *[feces]
chivalry @chivalrous
chives
chivlery chivalry+
chiwawa chihuahua
chizle chisel[3]
chloride
chlorinate[2]
chlorine
chloroform[1]
chlorophyll
chloroplast
choak choke[2] *[stop breathing]+
chock *[holds in place] ~ful
chalk[1] *[white substance]+
choke[2] *[stop breathing]+
chuck[1] *[throw]
shock[1] *[blow]+
chocolate ~| bar ~-box ~| cake ~-chip cookie
chofer chauffeur[1] *[driver]+
shofar *[horn]
choice
choir *[singers] ~boy ~girl ~master
coir *[coconut fiber]
quire *[paper]
choise choice
choke[2] *[stop breathing] ~| chain

choler *[rage] collar[1] *[seize, neckband]
cholera *[disease]
cholesterol ~-free
choose *[pick] @choosing
chews *[grinds food]
choot chute *[slide]
shoot *[weapon, goal]+
chop[3] ~stick ~-suey
choppie choppy[4]+
chopping ~| board ~| block
choppy[4] ~| sea
choral *[singing] coral *[colored stone]+
chorale *[hymn] corral[3] *[animals]
chord *[music] cord *[rope]+
chore *[job] shore *[sea, prop up]+
sure[2] *[certain]+
choreographer @choreography
chortel chortle[2]
chortle[2]
chorus[5] *[singing]
chose *[past of choose] ~n
choose *[pick]+
chovinist chauvinist+
chow *[food] ~der ~| mein
ciao *[greeting]
choys choice
chramatic chromatic
chrank crank[1]+
shrank
chreshendo crescendo
Christ @Christendom
christal crystal+
christen[1]
Christian ~ity
Christmas ~| card ~| carol ~| cookie ~| Day ~| Eve ~time ~| tree

> Unable to find your word under **Christmas**? Take off **Christmas** and look again

chriteria criteria+
chromate @chromatography
chromatic
chrome
chromium

KEY TO SUFFIXES AND COMPOUNDS

These rules are explained on pages vii to ix.

1 Keep the word the same before adding **ed, er, est, ing**
e.g. cool[1] → cooled, cooler, coolest, cooling
2 Take off final **e** before adding **ed, er, est, ing**
e.g. fine[2] → fined, finer, finest, fining
3 Double final consonant before adding **ed, er, est, ing**
e.g. thin[3] → thinned, thinner, thinnest, thinning
4 Change final **y** to **i** before adding **ed, er, es, est, ly, ness**
e.g. tidy[4] → tidied, tidier, tidies, tidiest, tidily, tidiness
Keep final **y** before adding **ing** e.g. tidying
5 Add **es** instead of **s** to the end of the word
e.g. bunch[5] → bunches
6 Change final **f** to **ve** before adding **s**
e.g. calf[6] → calves

chromosome	
chronic ~ally ~| disease ~| fatigue	
chronicle^{2}	
chronograph	
chronological ~ly	
chronology^{4}	
chronometer	
chroshay	crochet^{1}
chrysalis^{5}	
chrysanthemum	
chrystaline	crystalline
chrystallize	crystallize^{2+}
chubby^{4}	
chuck^{1} *[throw]	shuck *[corn]
chuckle^{2}	
chue	chew^{1+}
chug^{3}	
chukka	
chukle	chuckle^{2}
chum ~my	
chunck	chunk^{+}
chunk	@chunky^{4}
church^{5} ~goer ~yard	
Church ~| of England ~| of Scotland	
churlish ~ly	
churn^{1}	
churp	chirp^{1+}
chuse	choose *[pick]$^{+}$
	shoes *[footwear]
chush	shush^{1}
chute *[slide]	shoot *[weapon, goal]$^{+}$

> Unable to find your word under **ch**?
> Look under **sh**

chutney	
chutzpah	
chuw	chew^{1+}
chyde	chide^{2}
chyli	chili^{5} *[food]$^{+}$
	chilly^{4} *[cold]
chyme *[partly digested food]	
	chime^{2}
chyna	china^{+}
Chynatown	Chinatown
Chynese	Chinese^{+}
chyntz	chintz^{+}
chyves	chives
cianide	cyanide

> Unable to find your word under **chy**?
> Look under **chi**

ciantee	Chianti
ciao *[greeting]	chow *[food]$^{+}$
ciatic	sciatic^{+}
ciatica	sciatica^{+}
cibernetics	cybernetics
cicada	
ciclamate	cyclamate
ciclamen	cyclamen
cicle	chicle *[gum]
	cycle^{2} *[turning]
	sickle *[blade]
ciclick	cyclic^{+}
ciclist	cyclist
ciclone	cyclone
Ciclops	Cyclops
ciclotron	cyclotron
cider	
cience	science^{+}
cientific	scientific^{+}
cifer	cipher *[code]
cifi	sci-fi *[science fiction]
cigar	
cigarette ~| butt ~| holder ~| lighter ~| paper ~| smoke	
cignet	cygnet *[swan]
	signet *[ring]
cilindrical	cylindrical^{+}
cilium *[hairlike]	@cilia
	psyllium *[seed]
cimbal	cymbal *[music]
	symbol *[sign]$^{+}$
cimera	chimera
cimian	simian
cinamin	cinnamon
cinary	canary^{4} *[bird]
cinch^{5} *[binding]	
cinder ~block	

Key to Spelling Rules

Red words are wrong. **Black** words are correct.

~ Add the suffix or word directly to the main word, without a space or hyphen
e.g. ash ~en ~tray → ashen ashtray

~- Add a hyphen to the main word before adding the next word
e.g. blow ~-dry → blow-dry

~| Leave a space between the main word and the next word
e.g. decimal ~| place → decimal place

\+ By finding this word in its correct alphabetical order, you can find related words
e.g. abowt about^{+} → about-face

★ Draws attention to words that may be confused

™ Means the word is a trademark

@ Signifies the word is derived from the main word

Cinderella
cine ~| camera ~| film
cinema ~tic ~tically
cinematographer @cinematography
cinfront confront[1+]
cinic cynic[+]
cinical cynical[+]
cinima cinema[+]
cinnamon
cinosure cynosure
cinsentrick concentric
cinsern concern[1]

> Unable to find your word under **cin**?
> Look under **con**

cintch cinch[5] *[binding]
cintillating scintillating
cinus sinus[5]
ciny cine[+]
cipher *[code] siphon[1] *[tube, take away]
cipress cypress
circa
circadian ~| rhythm
circimsize circumcise[2+]
circis circus[5]
circle[2]
circuit[1] ~| board ~| breaker ~| judge ~| switch ~| training
circuitous ~ly
circuitry
circular
circulate[2] @circulation
circumcise[2] @circumcision
circumference
circumflex
circumlocution
circumnavigate[2]
circumscribe[2]
circumscription
circumspect ~ly ~ion ~ive
circumstance
circumstantial ~ly ~| evidence
circumvent[1] ~ion

circus[5]
cirf serf *[slave][+]
surf[1] *[sea][+]
Cirillic Cyrillic
cirka circa
cirkadian circadian[+]
cirkit circuit[1+]
cirogenics cryogenics
ciropracter chiropractor[+]
cirosis cirrhosis
cirrhosis
cirrocumulus
cirrostratus
cirrus
cisors scissors
cissie sissy[4]
cissors scissors
cist cyst[+]
cistern
citadel
citation
citazen citizen[+]
cite[2] *[quote] sight *[seeing][+]
site *[place]

> Unable to find your word under **ci**?
> Look under **cy** or **s**

citee city[4+]
citidel citadel
citizen ~ship
citizen's arrest
Citizen's Band [CB radio]
citric ~| acid
citrus ~| fruit
city[4] ~| hall ~| slicker
ciube cube[+]
ciukumber cucumber
civic ~-minded ~s
civies civvies
civik civic[+]
civil ~| defense ~| disobedience ~| engineer ~| engineering ~| law ~| liberties ~| rights ~| service ~| war

---

KEY TO SUFFIXES AND COMPOUNDS

These rules are explained on pages vii to ix.

1 Keep the word the same before adding **ed, er, est, ing**
e.g. cool[1] → cooled, cooler, coolest, cooling
2 Take off final **e** before adding **ed, er, est, ing**
e.g. fine[2] → fined, finer, finest, fining
3 Double final consonant before adding **ed, er, est, ing**
e.g. thin[3] → thinned, thinner, thinnest, thinning
4 Change final **y** to **i** before adding **ed, er, es, est, ly, ness**
e.g. tidy[4] → tidied, tidier, tidies, tidiest, tidily, tidiness
Keep final **y** before adding **ing** e.g. tidying
5 Add **es** instead of **s** to the end of the word
e.g. bunch[5] → bunches
6 Change final **f** to **ve** before adding **s**
e.g. calf[6] → calves

> Unable to find your word under **civil**?
> Take off **civil** and look again

civilian
civility^{4}
civilization
civilize^{2} — @civilization
civilyan — civilian
clacissisum — classicism *[classics]$^{+}$
— classism *[prejudice]
clad *[clothed]
clade *[genetic tree]
claim^{1} *[ownership] ~ant ~| check ~| ticket
— clam^{3} *[sea creature]$^{+}$
clairion — clarion^{+}
clairity — clarity
clairvoyant — @clairvoyance
clabbered *[curdled]
— clapboard *[wood]
clam^{3} *[sea creature] ~bake ~| up
— claim^{1} *[ownership]$^{+}$
clamber^{1} ~| down ~| up
clame — claim^{1} *[ownership]$^{+}$
— clam^{3} *[sea creature]$^{+}$
clammer — clamor^{+}
clammy^{4}
clamor — @clamorous
clamp^{1} ~down
clan ~nish
clanc — clank^{1}
clandestine ~ly
clang^{1} ~or
clank^{1}
clap^{3} — @clapper board
clapboard *[wood]
— clabbered *[curdled]
claret
clarety — clarity
clarevoyant — clairvoyant^{+}
clarify^{4} — @clarification
clarinet ~ist
clarion ~| call
clarity
clash^{5}
clasic — classic^{+}
clasified — classified^{+}
class^{5} ~| action suit ~| consciousness ~mate ~room ~work

> Unable to find your word under **class**?
> Take off **class** and look again

classic ~al ~ally
classicism *[classics]
— @classicist
— classism *[prejudice]
classified ~| ad ~| directory
classify^{4} — @classification
classism *[prejudice]
— classicism *[classics]$^{+}$
clastraphobia — claustrophobia^{+}
clatter^{1}
clause *[sentence]
— claws *[animal]
claustrophobia — @claustrophobic
clavekord — clavichord
clavical — clavicle
clavichord
clavicle
claw^{1}
claws *[animal] — clause *[sentence]
clawstraphobia — claustrophobia^{+}
clawted — clotted^{+}
clay ~| pigeon shooting
claym — claim^{1} *[ownership]$^{+}$
clean^{1} ~able ~liness ~ly ~-cut ~-living ~-shaven
cleanse^{2}
clear^{1} ~ance ~ly ~| blue ~-headed ~-sighted
clearing ~| bank ~house
cleavage
cleave^{2} *[slice in two]
cleaver *[knife] — clever *[intelligent]$^{+}$
cleek — clique *[group]$^{+}$
cleen — clean^{1+}
cleer — clear^{1+}
cleering — clearing^{+}
cleeshay — cliché

Key to Spelling Rules

Red words are wrong. **Black** words are correct.

~ Add the suffix or word directly to the main word, without a space or hyphen
e.g. ash ~en ~tray → ashen ashtray

~- Add a hyphen to the main word before adding the next word
e.g. blow ~-dry → blow-dry

~| Leave a space between the main word and the next word
e.g. decimal ~| place → decimal place

\+ By finding this word in its correct alphabetical order, you can find related words
e.g. abowt about^{+} → about-face

★ Draws attention to words that may be confused

™ Means the word is a trademark

@ Signifies the word is derived from the main word

cleevage	cleavage
cleeve	cleave[2] *[slice in two]
clef *[music symbol]	
	cleft *[split in two]+
	cliff+
cleft *[split in two] ~| palate	
	clef *[music symbol]
	cliff+
clemency	@clement
clench[1]	
clenze	cleanse[2]
cleph	clef *[music symbol]
	cleft *[split in two]+
clephed	cleft *[split in two]+
	clef *[music symbol]
clergy[4] ~man ~woman	
cleric ~al	
clerk[1]	
cleve	cleave[2] *[slice in two]
	clever[1] *[intelligent]+
clever[1] *[intelligent] ~ly ~ness	
	cleaver *[knife]
clew	clue[2]+
cliant	client+
cliché	
click[1] *[snap] ~able ~rate	
	clique *[group]+
clicks ~-and-mortar	
client ~-server	
clientele	
cliff ~hanger	
clik	click[1] *[snap]+
	clique *[group]+
climactic ~ally	
climate ~| change	
climax[5] ~es	
climb[1] *[up, down] ~down	
	clime *[climate]
climbing ~| frame ~| wall	
clime *[climate]	climb[1] *[up, down]+
climing	climbing+
clinch[5] ~es	
clinck	clink[1]
clinex	Kleenex™
cling ~ing	

clinic ~al ~ally ~ian	
clink[1]	
cliontell	clientele
clip[3] ~| art ~-clop ~-on	
clique *[group]	@cliquish
	click[1] *[snap]+
clirk	clerk[1]
clitoris	
cloak[1] ~-and-dagger	
cloan	clone
clobber[1]	
cloche	
clock[1] ~| in ~wise ~work	
clockwatch[5]	
clod *[lump of earth]	
	clawed *[attacked]
	clot[3] *[blood]
clog[3]	
cloister ~ed	
cloke	cloak[1]+
clone	
clorafill	chlorophyll
cloraform	chloroform[1]
cloreen	chlorine
cloride	chloride
clorinate	chlorinate[2]
clorine	chlorine
clorofill	chlorophyll
cloroform	chloroform[1]
cloryde	chloride

> Unable to find your word under **clo**?
> Look under **chlo**

close[2] ~ly ~ness ~| call ~-fitting ~-knit ~-out ~| quarters ~-run ~| shave ~-up

> Unable to find your word under **close**?
> Take off **close** and look again

closed ~-circuit TV ~| shop	
closet[1]	
closhe	cloche
closure *[closing]	cloture *[stop debate]
clot[3] *[blood]	clod *[lump of earth]

Key to Suffixes and Compounds

These rules are explained on pages vii to ix.

1 Keep the word the same before adding **ed, er, est, ing**
e.g. cool[1] → cooled, cooler, coolest, cooling

2 Take off final **e** before adding **ed, er, est, ing**
e.g. fine[2] → fined, finer, finest, fining

3 Double final consonant before adding **ed, er, est, ing**
e.g. thin[3] → thinned, thinner, thinnest, thinning

4 Change final **y** to **i** before adding **ed, er, es, est, ly, ness**
e.g. tidy[4] → tidied, tidier, tidies, tidiest, tidily, tidiness
Keep final **y** before adding **ing** e.g. tidying

5 Add **es** instead of **s** to the end of the word
e.g. bunch[5] → bunches

6 Change final **f** to **ve** before adding **s**
e.g. calf[6] → calves

cloth *[piece of fabric]
clothe[2] *[put clothes on]
clothes *[wear] ~| horse ~| line ~| peg
close[2+]
clothing
clotted ~| blood ~| cream
cloture *[stop debate]
closure *[closing]
cloud[1] ~burst @cloudy[4]
cloun clown[1+]
clout[1]
clove @clover leaf[5]
clowd cloud[1+]
clown[1] ~ish
clowt clout[1]
cloyster cloister[+]
clozed closed[+]
clozher closure
club[3] ~| foot ~house ~| sandwich ~| soda
cluch clutch[1+]
cluck[1]
clue[2] ~less
clump[1] ~y
clumsy[4]
clung
clunk[1] @clunky[4]
clurgy clergy[4+]
clurk clerk[1]
cluster[1] ~| bomb
clutch[5] ~es
clutter[1]
clyent client[+]
clyme climb[1] *[up, down][+]
clime *[climate]
clynic clinic[+]
coach[5] ~ful ~load
coafficiant coefficient
coagulate[2] @coagulant
coak coke[2] *[drug, coal]
Coke™ *[cola]
coaksial coaxial[+]
coal *[carbon] ~field ~mine ~| scuttle
cool[1] *[cold][+]
coalesce[2]
coalescence @coalescent
coalition
coarse[2] *[rough] ~ly ~ness
course[2] *[order, path][+]
coarsen[1]
coast[1] *[land] ~al ~line
cost[1] *[amount][+]
Coast Guard
coat[1] *[covering] ~| hanger ~| of arms ~stand ~-tails
court[1] *[law][+]
coax[5] *[persuade]
Cokes *[colas]
co-axeal coaxial[+]
coaxial ~| cable
cobalt ~| blue
cobble[2] *[put together] ~stone
COBOL *[computer language]
cobolt cobalt[+]
cobra
cobweb
coca *[cocaine plant]
cocoa *[chocolate]
Coca-Cola™ *[drink]
cocaine
cocanut coconut
cocao cacao *[seed, tree]
coca *[cocaine plant]
cocoa *[chocolate]
cocayne cocaine
coccoon cocoon
coccyx
coch coach[1+]
cochineal
cock[1] *[chicken] @cocky[4]
caulk[1] *[seal]
coke[2] *[drug, coal]
Coke™ *[cola]
cook[1] *[food][+]
cock ~-and-bull story ~-a-doodle-do ~amamie ~chafer ~crow ~erel ~eyed ~-up ~pit ~roach ~tail

Unable to find your word under **cock**?
Take off **cock** and look again

Key to Spelling Rules

Red words are wrong. **Black** words are correct.

~ Add the suffix or word directly to the main word, without a space or hyphen
e.g. ash ~en ~tray → ashen ashtray

~- Add a hyphen to the main word before adding the next word
e.g. blow ~-dry → blow-dry

~| Leave a space between the main word and the next word
e.g. decimal ~| place → decimal place

\+ By finding this word in its correct alphabetical order, you can find related words
e.g. abowt about[+] → about-face

* Draws attention to words that may be confused

™ Means the word is a trademark

@ Signifies the word is derived from the main word

<table>
<tr><td>Cockasian</td><td>Caucasian</td></tr>
<tr><td>cockatoo</td><td></td></tr>
<tr><td>cocker ~| spaniel</td><td></td></tr>
<tr><td>cocket</td><td>coquette[+]</td></tr>
<tr><td>cockfight ~ing</td><td></td></tr>
<tr><td>cockle ~| shell</td><td></td></tr>
<tr><td>cockoon</td><td>cocoon</td></tr>
<tr><td>cocks *[birds]</td><td>cooks *[makes food]</td></tr>
<tr><td></td><td>cox[5] *[rowing][+]</td></tr>
<tr><td>cocksis</td><td>coccyx</td></tr>
<tr><td>cocktail ~| lounge ~| dress ~| party</td><td></td></tr>
<tr><td>cocky[4] *[arrogant]</td><td></td></tr>
<tr><td></td><td>cookie *[biscuit]</td></tr>
<tr><td>coco *[coconut]</td><td>coca *[cocaine plant]</td></tr>
<tr><td></td><td>cacao *[seed, tree]</td></tr>
<tr><td></td><td>cocoa *[chocolate]</td></tr>
<tr><td>Coco Cola</td><td>Coca-Cola™ *[drink]</td></tr>
<tr><td>cocoa *[chocolate]</td><td></td></tr>
<tr><td></td><td>coca *[cocaine plant]</td></tr>
<tr><td></td><td>cacao *[seed, tree]</td></tr>
<tr><td>coconut</td><td></td></tr>
<tr><td>cocoon</td><td></td></tr>
<tr><td>cocsyx</td><td>coccyx</td></tr>
<tr><td>cod *[fish] ~ling ~| liver oil</td><td></td></tr>
<tr><td>coda *[music]</td><td>code[2] *[information][+]</td></tr>
<tr><td>coddle[2]</td><td></td></tr>
<tr><td>code[2] *[information] ~breaking ~| name ~| red</td><td></td></tr>
<tr><td></td><td>coda *[music]</td></tr>
<tr><td>codeine</td><td></td></tr>
<tr><td>codex *[book]</td><td>@codices</td></tr>
<tr><td>codgitate</td><td>cogitate[2]</td></tr>
<tr><td>codicil</td><td></td></tr>
<tr><td>codify[4]</td><td></td></tr>
<tr><td>codine</td><td>codeine</td></tr>
<tr><td>codisil</td><td>codicil</td></tr>
<tr><td>coed ~ucation ~ucational</td><td></td></tr>
<tr><td>coefficient</td><td></td></tr>
<tr><td>coegsist</td><td>coexist[1+]</td></tr>
<tr><td>coenside</td><td>coincide[2]</td></tr>
<tr><td>coequal ~ly ~ity</td><td></td></tr>
<tr><td>coerce[2]</td><td>@coercible</td></tr>
<tr><td>coercion</td><td>@coercive</td></tr>
<tr><td>coexist[1] ~ence ~ent</td><td></td></tr>
<tr><td>coff</td><td>cough[1] *[throat irritation][+]</td></tr>
<tr><td>coffed</td><td>coiffed *[hairdo]</td></tr>
<tr><td></td><td>coughed *[throat noise]</td></tr>
<tr><td>coffee *[drink] ~| break ~| machine ~| shop ~| table</td><td></td></tr>
<tr><td></td><td>café *[restaurant]</td></tr>
<tr><td>coffer *[treasure chest]</td><td></td></tr>
<tr><td>coffin *[funeral casket]</td><td></td></tr>
<tr><td>coffur</td><td>coffer *[treasure chest]</td></tr>
<tr><td></td><td>coiffure *[hair][+]</td></tr>
<tr><td>cog ~wheel</td><td></td></tr>
<tr><td>cogent ~ly</td><td>@cogency</td></tr>
<tr><td>cogitate[2]</td><td></td></tr>
<tr><td>cognac</td><td></td></tr>
<tr><td>cognishin</td><td>cognition</td></tr>
<tr><td>cognition</td><td></td></tr>
<tr><td>cognitive ~ly</td><td></td></tr>
<tr><td>cognizant</td><td>@cognizance</td></tr>
<tr><td>cohabit[1] ~ation</td><td></td></tr>
<tr><td>coheezion</td><td>cohesion</td></tr>
<tr><td>coherence</td><td></td></tr>
<tr><td>coherent ~ly</td><td></td></tr>
<tr><td>cohesion</td><td></td></tr>
<tr><td>cohesive ~ly ~ness</td><td></td></tr>
<tr><td>cohort</td><td></td></tr>
<tr><td>coie</td><td>coy *[shy][+]</td></tr>
<tr><td>coiffed</td><td></td></tr>
<tr><td>coiffure *[hair]</td><td>@coiffed</td></tr>
<tr><td>coil[1]</td><td></td></tr>
<tr><td>coilessence</td><td>coalescence[+]</td></tr>
<tr><td>coin[1] ~age</td><td></td></tr>
<tr><td>coincide[2]</td><td></td></tr>
<tr><td>coincidence</td><td></td></tr>
<tr><td>coincident ~ally</td><td></td></tr>
<tr><td>coinsurance</td><td></td></tr>
<tr><td>coir *[coconut fiber]</td><td></td></tr>
<tr><td></td><td>choir *[singers][+]</td></tr>
<tr><td></td><td>quire *[paper]</td></tr>
<tr><td>coitus</td><td></td></tr>
<tr><td>cojency</td><td>cogency</td></tr>
<tr><td>cojent</td><td>cogent[+]</td></tr>
<tr><td>cojitate</td><td>cogitate[2]</td></tr>
</table>

Unable to find your word **coj**?
Look under **cog**

Key to Suffixes and Compounds

These rules are explained on pages vii to ix.

1 Keep the word the same before adding **ed, er, est, ing**
e.g. cool[1] → cooled, cooler, coolest, cooling

2 Take off final **e** before adding **ed, er, est, ing**
e.g. fine[2] → fined, finer, finest, fining

3 Double final consonant before adding **ed, er, est, ing**
e.g. thin[3] → thinned, thinner, thinnest, thinning

4 Change final **y** to **i** before adding **ed, er, es, est, ly, ness**
e.g. tidy[4] → tidied, tidier, tidies, tidiest, tidily, tidiness
Keep final **y** before adding **ing** e.g. tidying

5 Add **es** instead of **s** to the end of the word
e.g. bunch[5] → bunches

6 Change final **f** to **ve** before adding **s**
e.g. calf[6] → calves

Wrong	Correct
cokaine	cocaine
cokatoo	cockatoo
cokchafer	cockchafer
coke^{2} *[drug, coal]	
	Coke™ *[cola]
	cook^{1} *[food]
Coke™ *[cola]	coke^{2} *[drug, coal]
Cokes *[beverages]	
	coax^{1} *[persuade]$^{+}$
cokette	coquette^{+}
cok-eyed	cock-eyed
cokinut	coconut
cokker	cocker^{+}
coko	coca *[cocaine plant]
	cocoa *[chocolate]
cokrel	cockerel
col *[mountain ridge]	
	coal *[carbon]$^{+}$
	cool^{1} *[cold]$^{+}$
cola *[drink]	collar^{1} *[seize, neckband]
colaberait	collaborate^{2+}
colage	collage *[picture]
	college *[university]$^{+}$
colagen	collagen
colander *[draining bowl]	
	calendar *[time]
	calender^{1} *[press]
colaps	collapse^{2}
colate	collate^{2}
colatteral	collateral^{+}
cold *[freeze] ~ly ~ness ~| blood ~-blooded ~-call ~| cream ~| cuts ~| front ~-hearted ~| shoulder ~| snap ~| sore ~| spell ~| storage ~| sweat ~| turkey ~| war	
	could *[can]$^{+}$

> Unable to find your word under **cold**?
> Take off **cold** and look again

Wrong	Correct
coldren	cauldron
coldslaw	coleslaw
cole	coal^{+}
colectiv	collective^{+}
coleeg	colleague
colege	college *[university]$^{+}$
	collage *[picture]
colen	colon *[body part]
	cologne *[perfume]
coler	choler *[rage]
	collar^{1} *[seize, neckband]
colera	cholera *[disease]
	choler *[rage]
colerbone	collarbone
colerful	colorful^{+}
coleslaw	
colesteral	cholesterol^{+}
colic ~ky	
colide	collide^{2}
coligin	collagen

> Unable to find your word under **col**?
> Look under **coll**

Wrong	Correct
colitis	
collaborate^{2}	@collaborator
collaboration	
collaborative ~ly	
collage *[picture]	college *[university]$^{+}$
collagen	
collapse^{2}	
collar^{1} *[seize, neckband]	
	choler *[rage]
collara	cholera *[disease]
collarbone	
collard *[vegetable] ~| greens	
collasil	colossal^{+}
collate^{2}	
collateral ~| damage	
collateralize^{2}	
colleague	
collecshin	collection^{+}
collect^{1} ~able ~or	
collection ~| agency^{4}	
collective ~ly ~| bargaining	
collectivism	
college *[university] ~| degree ~| dorm	
	collage *[picture]
coller	collar^{1} *[seize, neckband]
collerfull	colorful^{+}

collide[2]
collidge — college *[university]+ collage *[picture]
collie
colliflower — cauliflower
colligrapher — calligrapher+
collirbown — collarbone
collision ~| course ~| damage waiver
collitis — colitis
collocate[2] — @collocation
collonaide — colonnade
colloneal — colonial+
colloquial ~ism ~ly
colloquy[4]
collor — color[1+]
collude[2] — @collusion
collum — column+
collumbien — columbine
collun — colon *[body part] cologne *[perfume]

> Unable to find your word under **coll**?
> Look under **col**

colly — collie
colocate — collocate[2+]
colocuial — colloquial+
cologne *[perfume] colon *[body part]
colokait — collocate[2+]
colon *[body part] cologne *[perfume]
colonel *[officer] kernel *[seed] coronal *[vertical plane, circlet]
colonial ~ism ~ist
colonie — colony[4+]
coloniel — colonial+
colonize[2] — @colonization
colonnade
colony[4] — @colonist
colonyse — colonize[2+]
colood — collude[2+]
coloquee — colloquy[4]
coloquiel — colloquial+

color[1] ~less ~-blind ~| change ~| correction ~fast ~| scheme ~| supplement ~| temperature ~| wheel

> Unable to find your word under **color**?
> Take off **color** and look again

colorful ~ly ~ness
colossal ~ly
colossus
colt ~ish
colude — collude[2+]
columbine
column ~ist
colyc — colic+
colyer — collier
colyery — colliery[4]
colytis — colitis
com — comb[1] *[for hair]+ come *[arrive]+
coma *[unconscious] comma *[punctuation]
comand — command[1] *[be in charge]+ commend[1] *[praise]+
comando — commando+
comb[1] *[for hair] ~| out ~| through come *[arrive]+
combat[1] ~ant ~ive ~| fatigue
combine[2] — @combination
combo
combustion — @combustible
come *[arrive] ~back ~down ~uppance @coming comb[1] *[for hair]+
come on *[hurry up] come-on *[invitation] common *[ordinary]+
comedian — @comedienne
comedy[4]
comemorate — commemorate[2+]
comence — commence[2+]
comend — commend[1] *[praise]+ command[1] *[be in charge]+

KEY TO SUFFIXES AND COMPOUNDS

These rules are explained on pages vii to ix.

1 Keep the word the same before adding **ed, er, est, ing**
e.g. cool[1] → cooled, cooler, coolest, cooling
2 Take off final **e** before adding **ed, er, est, ing**
e.g. fine[2] → fined, finer, finest, fining
3 Double final consonant before adding **ed, er, est, ing**
e.g. thin[3] → thinned, thinner, thinnest, thinning
4 Change final **y** to **i** before adding **ed, er, es, est, ly, ness**
e.g. tidy[4] → tidied, tidier, tidies, tidiest, tidily, tidiness
Keep final **y** before adding **ing** e.g. tidying
5 Add **es** instead of **s** to the end of the word
e.g. bunch[5] → bunches
6 Change final **f** to **ve** before adding **s**
e.g. calf[6] → calves

comenplace commonplace
comensurate commensurate
coment comment[1+]
comerse commerce[+]
comershal commercial[+]
comet *[in the sky]
commit[3] *[to do][+]
comfort[1] ~able ~ably
comfortable @comfortably
comic ~al ~ally ~| strip
comidian comedian[+]
comidy comedy[4]
comity *[friendly behavior]
comission commission[1+]
comit comet *[in the sky]
commit[3] *[to do][+]
comitee comity *[friendly behavior]
committee
comity *[friendly behavior]
comizerate commiserate[2+]
comma *[punctuation]
coma *[unconscious]
command[1] *[be in charge] ~ant ~ment
commend[1] *[praise][+]
commandeer[1] *[take over]
commander *[one who is in charge]
~-in-chief
commando ~| raid
commemorate[2] @commemoration
commen common[+]
come on *[hurry up]
commence[2] ~ment
commend[1] *[praise] ~ation
command[1] *[be in charge][+]
commendable @commendably
commensurate
comment[1] ~ator
commentary[4]
commerce ~| server
commercial ~ism ~ly ~| bank
~| presence
commercialize[2] @commercialization
commet comet *[in the sky]
commit[3] *[to do][+]
commic comic[+]
commiserate[2] @commiseration
commission[1] ~| basis ~ed officer
commit[3] *[to do] ~ment ~tal
comet *[in the sky]
committee
commity comity *[friendly behavior]
committee
commode
commodity[4]
common ~ly ~ness ~| cold
~| denominator ~| factor ~| ground
~| law ~| knowledge ~place
~| sense ~wealth

Unable to find your word under **common**?
Take off **common** and look again

commotion
communal ~ly
commune[2]
communicable
communicashuns
communications[+]
communicate[2] @communication
communications ~| satellite
communicative ~ly
communicible communicable
communion
communiqué
communism @communist
community[4] ~| college ~| service
commute[2]
comodity commodity[4]
comon common[+]
comoshun commotion

Unable to find your word under **com**?
Look under **comm**

comp ~| time
compact ~| disc player
@CD-ROM
compair compare[2]
companion ~able ~ship

Key to Spelling Rules

Red words are wrong. **Black** words are correct.

~ Add the suffix or word directly to the main word, without a space or hyphen
e.g. ash ~en ~tray → ashen ashtray

~- Add a hyphen to the main word before adding the next word
e.g. blow ~-dry → blow-dry

~| Leave a space between the main word and the next word
e.g. decimal ~| place → decimal place

+ By finding this word in its correct alphabetical order, you can find related words
e.g. abowt about[+] → about-face

* Draws attention to words that may be confused

TM Means the word is a trademark

@ Signifies the word is derived from the main word

company⁴ ~| car ~| law
comparable @comparably
comparative ~ly
compare²
comparison caparison *[horse decoration]
compartment
compartmentalize²
compashun compassion⁺
compass⁵
compassion ~ate ~ately
compatible @compatibility
compatriot
compeet compete² *[struggle]
compel³
compendium
compensate² @compensation
compete² *[struggle]
complete² *[finish]⁺
competence @competent
@competently
competishun competition
competition
competitive ~ly ~ness ~| advantage ~| intelligence
competitor
compile² @compilation
compitince competence⁺
compitishun competition
complacency
complacent ~ly
complain¹ ~t
complaisansie complacency
complamint complement¹ *[go well with]
compliment¹ *[praise]⁺
complane complain¹⁺
complasensy complacency
complasent complacent⁺
complecks complex⁺
complekshun complexion
complement¹ *[go well with]
compliment¹ *[praise]⁺
complementary ~| angle
compleshin completion

complete² *[finish] ~ly ~ness
@completion
compete² *[struggle]
complex @complexity⁴
complexion
compliance @compliant
complicate² @complication
complicity
complie comply⁴
compliment¹ *[praise] ~ary
complement¹ *[go well with]
complisitie complicity
comply⁴
component
comportment
compose² *[make up]
comprise² *[include]
composishun composition
composite @compositor
composition
compost
composure
compote
compound¹ ~| fracture ~| interest
comprable comparable⁺
comprehend¹ @comprehensible
comprehension
comprehensive ~ly ~| policy
compress⁵ ~ible ~ion ~or
comprihenshun comprehension
comprise² *[include]
compose² *[make up]
compromise²
compulsion @compulsive
compulsory⁴
compunction
computation
computational ~| assistance ~| genomics ~| modeling ~| pharmacology ~| power ~| research ~| scientists ~| system ~| technologies ~| therapeutics

KEY TO SUFFIXES AND COMPOUNDS

These rules are explained on pages vii to ix.

1 Keep the word the same before adding **ed, er, est, ing**
e.g. cool¹ → cooled, cooler, coolest, cooling
2 Take off final **e** before adding **ed, er, est, ing**
e.g. fine² → fined, finer, finest, fining
3 Double final consonant before adding **ed, er, est, ing**
e.g. thin³ → thinned, thinner, thinnest, thinning
4 Change final **y** to **i** before adding **ed, er, es, est, ly, ness**
e.g. tidy⁴ → tidied, tidier, tidies, tidiest, tidily, tidiness
Keep final **y** before adding **ing** e.g. tidying
5 Add **es** instead of **s** to the end of the word
e.g. bunch⁵ → bunches
6 Change final **f** to **ve** before adding **s**
e.g. calf⁶ → calves

> Unable to find your word under **computational**?
> Take off **computational** and look again

compute[2] @computation
computer ~-aided design ~| game ~| graphics ~| hardware ~-literate ~| program ~| science ~| screen ~| software

> Unable to find your word under **computer**?
> Take off **computer** and look again

computerize[2]
computing ~| systems
comrade ~ship ~ry
comunal communal+
comune commune[2]
comunicate communicate[2]+
comunicative communicative+
comunikay communiqué
comunity community[4]+
comunizm communism+
comute commute[2]

> Unable to find your word under **com**?
> Look under **comm**

con[3] *[against, trick] ~| artist ~| man
cone[2] *[pointed object]
conasewer connoisseur
conatation connotation
concave
conceal[1] ~ment
concecion concession+
concede[2]
conceit ~ed ~edly ~edness
conceivable @conceivably
conceive[2]
concensus consensus
concent consent[1]+
concentrate[2]
concentration ~| camp
concentric
concepshun conception
concept ~ual ~ually
conception
conceptualize[2]
concequense consequence
concequenshal consequential+
concequent consequent+
concern[1]
concert ~ed ~| hall
concertina[1]
concerto
concerve conserve[2]+
concervation conservation
concession ~ary
concete conceit+
conch
conchairtoe concerto
concider consider[1]+
concienshious conscientious+
concilashin conciliation+
conciliation @conciliatory
concine consign[1]+
concious conscious *[awake]+
concise ~ly ~ness
concist consist[1]+
conclave
conclewd conclude[2]+
conclewsiv conclusive+
conclude[2] @conclusion
conclusive ~ly
concoct[1] ~ion
concomitant
concord ~ance ~ant
concourse
concrete ~ly ~ness
concubine
concur[3] *[agree] ~rence
conquer[1] *[defeat]+
concurrent ~ly
concussed
concussion
concust concussed
concyst consist[1]+
condamint condiment
condawit conduit
condemm condemn[1]+
condemn[1] ~ation

Key to Spelling Rules

Red words are wrong. **Black** words are correct.

~ Add the suffix or word directly to the main word, without a space or hyphen
e.g. ash ~en ~tray → ashen ashtray

~- Add a hyphen to the main word before adding the next word
e.g. blow ~-dry → blow-dry

~| Leave a space between the main word and the next word
e.g. decimal ~| place → decimal place

+ By finding this word in its correct alphabetical order, you can find related words
e.g. abowt about+ → about-face

* Draws attention to words that may be confused

TM Means the word is a trademark

@ Signifies the word is derived from the main word

condense^{2} @condensation
condescend^{1} @condescension
condiment
condisend — condescend^{1+}
condishin — condition^{1+}
condition^{1} ~al ~ally
condolences
condominium
condone^{2}
conducive
conduct^{1} ~ion ~or
conductive @conductivity
conduit
condwit — conduit
cone^{2} *[pointed object]
con^{3} *[against, trick]$^{+}$
conect — connect^{1+}
conerbashun — conurbation
confab
confeckshin — confection^{+}
confection ~er ~ery
confeddy — confetti
confederacy^{4}
confederate^{2} @confederation
confer^{3} *[give, discuss]
conifer *[tree]$^{+}$
conference^{2} ~| call
conferm — confirm^{1+}
confess^{5} ~or
confession ~al
confetti
conffer — confer^{3} *[give, discuss]
conifer *[tree]$^{+}$
confidant *[trusted male]
confident *[self-assured]$^{+}$
confidante *[trusted female]
confide^{2}
confidence ~| trick ~| trickster
confident *[self-assured] ~ly
confidant *[trusted male]
confidential ~ity ~ly
confidinse — confidence^{+}
configure^{2} @configuration
confine^{2} ~ment

confir — confer^{3} *[give, discuss]
conifer *[tree]$^{+}$
confirm^{1} ~ation ~ative
confiscate^{2} @confiscation
conflagration
conflict^{1}
confond — confound^{1}
conform^{1} ~ation
conformist @conformity
confound^{1}
confourm — conform^{1+}
confourmist — conformist^{+}
confownd — confound^{1}
confront^{1} ~ation ~ational
Confucius @Confucianism
confur — confer^{3} *[give, discuss]
conifer *[tree]$^{+}$
confuse^{2} @confusion
Confushis — Confucius^{+}
confyde — confide^{2}
congar — conger *[eel]
conjure^{2} *[imagine]$^{+}$
congeal^{1}
congecture — conjecture^{2+}
congegate — conjugate^{2+}
congenial ~ity ~ly
congenital ~ly
conger *[eel] — conjure^{2} *[imagine]$^{+}$
congestion
congestive ~| heart failure
congir — conger *[eel]
conjure^{2} *[imagine]$^{+}$
conglomerate^{2} @conglomeration
congrats
congratulate^{2} @congratulations
congratulatory
congregate^{2} @congregation
congress ~ional
congrigate — congregate^{2+}
congriss — congress^{+}
congruence @congruent
congugal — conjugal
congur — conger *[eel]
conjure^{2} *[imagine]$^{+}$
conical

Key to Suffixes and Compounds

These rules are explained on pages vii to ix.

1 Keep the word the same before adding **ed, er, est, ing** e.g. cool^{1} → cooled, cooler, coolest, cooling
2 Take off final **e** before adding **ed, er, est, ing** e.g. fine^{2} → fined, finer, finest, fining
3 Double final consonant before adding **ed, er, est, ing** e.g. thin^{3} → thinned, thinner, thinnest, thinning
4 Change final **y** to **i** before adding **ed, er, es, est, ly, ness** e.g. tidy^{4} → tidied, tidier, tidies, tidiest, tidily, tidiness
Keep final **y** before adding **ing** e.g. tidying
5 Add **es** instead of **s** to the end of the word e.g. bunch^{5} → bunches
6 Change final **f** to **ve** before adding **s** e.g. calf^{6} → calves

conifer *[tree] ~ous	
	confer[3] *[give, discuss]
coniffer	conifer *[tree]+
	confer[3] *[give, discuss]
conive	connive[2+]
conjagil	conjugal
conjecture[2]	@conjectural
conjir	conger *[eel]
	conjure[2] *[imagine]+
conjugal	
conjugate[2]	@conjugation
conjunction	
conjunctivitis	
conjure[2] *[imagine] ~| up	
	conger *[eel]
conkamitant	concomitant
conkeestidore	conquistador
conker	canker *[sore]
	concur[3] *[agree]+
	conquer[1] *[defeat]+
conkorce	concourse
conkreet	concrete+
conkur	concur[3] *[agree]+
	conquer[1] *[defeat]+
conkwest	conquest
connect[1] ~ion	
connective ~| tissue	
connectivity	
conniseur	connoisseur
connive[2]	@connivance
connoisseur	
connotation	
connote[2]	

> Unable to find your word under **conn**?
> Look under **con**

conossir	connoisseur
conote	connote[2]
conqubine	concubine
conquer[1] *[defeat] ~or	
	concur[3] *[agree]+
conquest	
conquistador	
consacrate	consecrate[2+]
conscience ~-stricken	
conscientious ~ly ~ness ~| objector	
conscious *[awake] ~ly ~ness	
	conscience+
conscript[1] ~ion	
conseal	conceal[1+]
conseat	conceit+
consecrate[2]	@consecration
consecutive ~ly	
conseed	concede[2]
conseel	conceal[1+]
conseenshus	conscientious+
conseevable	conceivable+
conseit	conceit+
conseivabul	conceivable+
conseive	conceive[2]
consensus	
consent[1] ~ual	
consentrashun	concentration+
consentrate	concentrate[2]
consentric	concentric
consept	concept+
conseptualize	conceptualize[2]
consequence	
consequent ~ly	
consequential ~ly	
consequitiv	consecutive+
consern	concern[1]
consert	concert+
consertina	concertina[1]
conservancy	
conservative ~ly ~ness	
conservatoire	
conservatory[4]	
conserve[2]	@conservation
conseshon	concession+
consessin	concession+
conshence	conscious *[awake]+
	conscience+
consherto	concerto
conshienshus	conscientious+
conshince	conscious *[awake]+
conshuns	conscience+
conshus	conscious *[awake]+
consicrait	consecrate[2+]

Key to Spelling Rules

Red words are wrong. **Black** words are correct.

- ~ Add the suffix or word directly to the main word, without a space or hyphen
  e.g. ash ~en ~tray → ashen ashtray
- ~- Add a hyphen to the main word before adding the next word
  e.g. blow ~-dry → blow-dry
- ~| Leave a space between the main word and the next word
  e.g. decimal ~| place → decimal place
- \+ By finding this word in its correct alphabetical order, you can find related words
  e.g. abowt about+ → about-face
- ★ Draws attention to words that may be confused
- TM Means the word is a trademark
- @ Signifies the word is derived from the main word

consider[1] ~able ~ably ~ately
considerate @consideration
consievable conceivable⁺
consign[1] ~ment
consikwense consequence
consiliashun conciliation⁺
consillation conciliation⁺
consimmait consummate[2+]
consine consign[1+]
cosine⁺
consintrait concentrate[2]
consintrashin concentration⁺
consiquent consequent⁺
consirn concern[1]
consirt concert⁺
consirv conserve[2+]
consirvatorie conservatory[4]
consirvency conservancy
consise concise⁺
consist[1] ~ency[4] ~| of
conskript conscript[1+]
consolable
console[2] *[comfort, controls]
@consolation
consul *[official]⁺
consoleble consolable
consolidate[2] @consolidation
consommé
consonant
consoom consume[2+]
consordium consortium⁺
consort[1]
consortium @consortia
consoul console[2] *[comfort, controls]⁺
consul *[official]⁺
consperesy conspiracy[4]
conspicuous ~ly ~ness
conspiracy[4]
conspirator ~ial ~ially
conspire[2]
conspyre conspire[2]
conssession concession⁺

Unable to find your word under **cons**? Look under **conc**

constant ~ly @constancy
constellation
constepait constipate[2+]
consternation
constetoot constitute[2]
constichuent constituent
constint constant⁺
constipate[2] @constipation
constituency[4] @constituent
constitute[2]
constitution ~al ~ally
constomme consommé
constrain[1] ~t
constrew construe[2]
constrict[1] ~ion
construcshun construction⁺
construct[1]
construction ~| line ~| paper
constructive ~ly
construe[2]
consturnasion consternation
consul *[official] ~ar ~ate
console[2] *[comfort, controls]⁺
consult[1] *[ask advice] ~ant ~ation
consultancy[4]
consumate consummate[2+]
consume[2] @consumable
consumer ~| credit ~ism ~| durables ~| goods ~| price index
consummate[2] ~ly
consumpshun consumption
consumption
consurvancy conservancy
consurvativ conservative⁺
consurvatory conservatory[4]
consurvatwa conservatoire
consurve conserve[2+]
contact[1] ~| lens
contagion
contagious ~ly ~ness
contain[1] ~ment

KEY TO SUFFIXES AND COMPOUNDS

These rules are explained on pages vii to ix.

1 Keep the word the same before adding **ed, er, est, ing**
e.g. cool[1] → cooled, cooler, coolest, cooling
2 Take off final **e** before adding **ed, er, est, ing**
e.g. fine[2] → fined, finer, finest, fining
3 Double final consonant before adding **ed, er, est, ing**
e.g. thin[3] → thinned, thinner, thinnest, thinning
4 Change final **y** to **i** before adding **ed, er, es, est, ly, ness**
e.g. tidy[4] → tidied, tidier, tidies, tidiest, tidily, tidiness
Keep final **y** before adding **ing** e.g. tidying
5 Add **es** instead of **s** to the end of the word
e.g. bunch[5] → bunches
6 Change final **f** to **ve** before adding **s**
e.g. calf[6] → calves

contajion contagion
contajis contagious[+]
contaminate[2] @contamination
contane contain[1+]
contch conch
contemplate[2] @contemplation
contemplative ~ly
contemporaneous ~ly ~ness
contemporary[4]
contempt ~ible
contemptuous ~ly
contenant continent *[land mass]
contend[1]
contenshun contention[+]
content[1] ~ment ~| management ~| value
contention @contentious
contermperenius contemporaneous[+]
contest[1] *[competition] ~ant
context *[information]
contigewis contiguous[+]
contiguous ~ly
continence *[self-control]
continents *[land masses]
continent *[land mass]
continental ~| drift ~| shelf
contingency[4] @contingent
continins continence *[self-control]
continual ~ly
continuance @continuation
continue[2] @continuity
continuous ~ly ~ness
continuum
continyew continue[2+]
contoosian contusion
contorshin contortion[+]
contort[1]
contortion ~ist
contour
contourt contort[1]
contraband
contraception @contraceptive
contract[1] ~ion
contractual ~ly
contradict[1] ~ion ~ory
contralto
contraption
contrary[4]
contrasepshin contraception[+]
contrast[1]
contratom contretemps
contravene[2] @contravention
contreband contraband
contrecepshun contraception[+]
contredict contradict[1+]
contrery contrary[4]
contretemps
contreveen contravene[2+]
contriband contraband
contribute[2] @contributor
contribution @contributory
contrified countrified
contriseption contraception[+]
contrite ~ly ~ness @contrition
contrive[2] @contrivance
contriveen contravene[2+]
control[3] ~lable ~| group ~| room ~| tower
controlled ~| experiment ~| substance ~| trial
controlling ~| variables
controversial ~ly
controversy[4]
controvurshal controversial[+]
contry contrary[4]
country[4] *[nation][+]
contryte contrite[+]
contumplait contemplate[2+]
contur contour
contusion
conurbation
convalesce[2]
convalescence @convalescent
convalluted convoluted
convay convey[1+]
convayance conveyance[+]
convecshun convection[+]

KEY TO SPELLING RULES

Red words are wrong. **Black** words are correct.

~ Add the suffix or word directly to the main word, without a space or hyphen
e.g. ash ~en ~tray → ashen ashtray

~- Add a hyphen to the main word before adding the next word
e.g. blow ~-dry → blow-dry

~| Leave a space between the main word and the next word
e.g. decimal ~| place → decimal place

+ By finding this word in its correct alphabetical order, you can find related words
e.g. abowt about[+] → about-face

* Draws attention to words that may be confused

TM Means the word is a trademark

@ Signifies the word is derived from the main word

convection	@convector
conveks	convex
conveless	convalesce[2]
convelessence	convalescence[+]
convene[2]	
convenience ~| store	
convenient ~ly	
convenshin	convention[+]
convent	
convention ~al ~ly	
converce	converse[2+]
converge[2]	
convergent	
conversation ~al ~alist	
converse[2] ~ly	@conversant
conversion	
convert[1] ~ible	
conveveal	convivial[+]
convex	
convey[1] ~or belt	
conveyance	@conveyancing
conveyor ~| belt	
convict[1] ~ion	
convince[2]	@convincingly
convine	convene[2]
convinience	convenience[+]
convinient	convenient[+]
convinse	convince[2+]
convirsashin	conversation[+]
convivial ~ity ~ly	
convoie	convoy[1]
convoke[2]	@convocation
convoluted	@convolution *[fold]
convoy[1]	
convulse[2]	@convulsion
convurge	converge[2]
convursashun	conversation[+]
convurse	converse[2+]
convurshun	conversion
convurt	convert[1+]
conyak	cognac
coo[1] *[sound]	cue[2] *[sign]
	coup[1] *[stroke][+]
	queue[2] *[line][+]

cook[1] *[food] ~book ~ware ~out	
	cock[1] *[chicken][+]
	kook *[eccentric]
cookery ~| book	
cookie *[biscuit]	cocky[4] *[arrogant]
cool[1] *[calm, cold] ~ant ~ly ~ness ~-headed	
	cull[1] *[remove]
	cowl
coop[1] *[enclosure] ~| up	
	coup[1] *[stroke][+]
	coupe *[car][+]
co-op *[co-operative]	
	co-opt[1] *[take over]
co-operate[2]	@co-operation
co-operative ~ly ~ness	
co-opt[1] *[take over]	
	co-op *[co-operative]

> Unable to find your word under **co-**?
> Take off **co-** and look again

co-ordinashun	coordination
coordinate[2] ~| pair ~| point	
coordination	
cop *[police officer] ~-out	
	cope[2] *[manage]
copayment	
cope[2] *[manage]	cop *[police officer][+]
Copernican ~| system	
copie	copy[4+]
copilot[1]	
copious ~ly	
copiright	copyright *[ownership]
	copywrite[2] *[write copy][+]
copius	copious[+]
copper ~plate	
copulate[2]	
Copurnican	Copernican[+]
copy[4] ~book ~cat ~| editor	
co-pylot	copilot[1]
copyright *[ownership]	
copywrite[2] *[write copy]	
	@copywriter

Key to Suffixes and Compounds

These rules are explained on pages vii to ix.

1 Keep the word the same before adding **ed, er, est, ing**
e.g. cool[1] → cooled, cooler, coolest, cooling

2 Take off final **e** before adding **ed, er, est, ing**
e.g. fine[2] → fined, finer, finest, fining

3 Double final consonant before adding **ed, er, est, ing**
e.g. thin[3] → thinned, thinner, thinnest, thinning

4 Change final **y** to **i** before adding **ed, er, es, est, ly, ness**
e.g. tidy[4] → tidied, tidier, tidies, tidiest, tidily, tidiness
Keep final **y** before adding **ing** e.g. tidying

5 Add **es** instead of **s** to the end of the word
e.g. bunch[5] → bunches

6 Change final **f** to **ve** before adding **s**
e.g. calf[6] → calves

coque coke[2] *[coal, drug]
Coke™ *[cola]
cock *[chicken]+
coquette @coquettish
@coquetry
coragaited corrugated+
corage courage+
coral *[colored stone] ~| reef
choral *[singing]
chorale *[hymn]
corral[3] *[animals]
coralait correlate[2]+
corallary corollary
Coran Koran *[holy book]
Corcasian Caucasian
cord *[rope] ~age ~less
chord *[music]
cordan cordon[1]+
cordaroy corduroy
corde cord *[rope]+
chord *[music]
cordeal cordial+
corden cordon[1]+
cordial ~ity ~ly
cordite
cordon[1] ~| bleu ~| off
corduroy
core *[center] caw[1] *[crow]
corps *[army, ballet]
coreckt correct[1]+
coredial cordial+
corel choral *[singing]
coral *[colored stone]+
corelate correlate[2]+
corespond correspond[1]
co-respondent *[divorce]
correspondent *[reporter, writer]
corevet corvette
coriagrafer choreographer+
corida corrida *[bullfight]
corridor *[passage]
coridor corridor *[passage]
corrida *[bullfight]
corillate correlate[2]+

corinette cornet *[horn]
coronet *[crown]
Corinthian
coriographer choreographer+
corispond correspond[1]
corister chorister
corjial cordial+
cork[1] *[stopper] ~screw
caulk[1] *[seal]
cormorant
corn ~flakes ~-on-the-cob ~y
cornflower *[flower]
corn flour *[cooking]
cornea
corner[1] *[point] ~stone
corona *[sun]
coroner *[investigator]
cornet *[horn]
cornia cornea
cornice
cornucopia
coroborate corroborate[2]
corode corrode[2]
corollary
corona *[sun] corner[1] *[point]+
coroner *[investigator]
coronal *[vertical plane, circlet]
kernel *[seed]
coronary[4] ~| heart disease
coronashin coronation
coronation
coronel colonel *[officer]
coronal *[vertical plane, circlet]
kernel *[seed]
coroner *[investigator]
corner[1] *[point]+
corona *[sun]
coronet *[crown]
coroshun corrosion+

Unable to find your word under **cor**?
Look under **corr**

corperel corporal+

Key to Spelling Rules

Red words are wrong. **Black** words are correct.

~ Add the suffix or word directly to the main word, without a space or hyphen
e.g. ash ~en ~tray → ashen ashtray

~- Add a hyphen to the main word before adding the next word
e.g. blow ~-dry → blow-dry

~| Leave a space between the main word and the next word
e.g. decimal ~| place → decimal place

+ By finding this word in its correct alphabetical order, you can find related words
e.g. abowt about+ → about-face

* Draws attention to words that may be confused

™ Means the word is a trademark

@ Signifies the word is derived from the main word

corpis corpus
corpiulance corpulence+
corporal ~| punishment ~| seargent
corporashin corporation
corporate ~| culture ~| image ~| ladder
corporation ~| headquarters
corpral corporal+
corprate corporate+
corps *[army, ballet]
core *[center]
corpse *[body]
corpse *[body] corps *[army, ballet]
corpsel corpuscle
corpulence @corpulent
corpus
corpuscle
corral3 *[animals] choral *[singing]
chorale *[hymn]
coral *[colored stone]+
correct1 ~ion ~ive
correlate2 @correlation
correspond1
correspondent *[reporter, writer]
co-respondent *[divorce]
correspondence ~| course
corresponding ~| angle
corrida *[bullfight]
corridor *[passage]
corrigible
corroad corrode2
corroborate2
corroborative ~ly
corrode2
corrosion @corrosive
corrugated ~| iron
corrupt1 ~ly ~ness
corruptible
cors cause2 *[reason]+
caws *[crow]
coarse2 *[rough]+
chorus5 *[singing]
corsage
corsen coarsen1
corset ~ed

cort caught *[past of catch]
court1 *[law]+
cortège
corteks cortex
cortesan courtesan *[prostitute]
cortisone *[drug]
cortesy courtesy4
cortex
cortier courtier
cortisone *[drug]
cortizan courtesan *[prostitute]
cortisone *[drug]
cortmarshall court-martial3
corugated corrugated+
corupt corrupt1+
coruptibul corruptible
corvette
Cosack Cossack
coset cosset1
cosie cozy4
cosignatory4
cosine ~| function
cosmetic ~| surgery
cosmetologist
cosmetology *[beauty]
cosmology *[universe]+
cosmic ~ally ~| ray
cosmography
cosmology *[universe]
cosmetology *[beauty]+
cosmonaut
cosmopolitan ~ism
cosmos
cosponsor3
Cossack *[in Ukraine]
cassock *[robe]
cosset1
cost1 *[amount] ~ly ~-benefit analysis ~| cutting
coast *[land]+
costar3
cost-effective ~ly ~ness
costic caustic+
costlie costly4
costly4

Key to Suffixes and Compounds

These rules are explained on pages vii to ix.

1 Keep the word the same before adding **ed, er, est, ing**
e.g. cool1 → cooled, cooler, coolest, cooling
2 Take off final **e** before adding **ed, er, est, ing**
e.g. fine2 → fined, finer, finest, fining
3 Double final consonant before adding **ed, er, est, ing**
e.g. thin3 → thinned, thinner, thinnest, thinning
4 Change final **y** to **i** before adding **ed, er, es, est, ly, ness**
e.g. tidy4 → tidied, tidier, tidies, tidiest, tidily, tidiness
Keep final **y** before adding **ing** e.g. tidying
5 Add **es** instead of **s** to the end of the word
e.g. bunch5 → bunches
6 Change final **f** to **ve** before adding **s**
e.g. calf6 → calves

cost-of-living ~| adjustment ~| index
costume ~| jewelry
cot *[bed] — caught *[past of catch] / coat[1] *[covering]+ / court[1] *[law]+
cotangent
cotchineal — cochineal
coterize — cauterize[2+]
cotin — cotton+
cotion — caution[1+]
coton — cotton+
cotorize — cauterize[2+]
cottage ~| cheese ~| industry[4]
cotton ~-picking ~| reel ~wood ~| wool
couch[5] ~es ~| potato
cougar
cough[1] *[throat irritation] ~| drop ~| syrup
— cuff[1] *[fold, blow]+
coul — cool[1] *[calm, cold]+ / cowl *[hood] / cull[1] *[remove]
could *[can] — couldn't *[could not] / cold[1] *[freeze]+
council *[assembly] ~man ~woman
— consul *[official]+ / counsel[3] *[give advice]
counsel[3] *[give advice]
— consul *[official]+ / council *[assembly]+
counselor *[adviser]
counsilor *[council member]
count[1] ~less ~ess
countenance
counter[1] ~act[1] ~attack[1] ~balance ~charge ~claim ~clockwise ~culture ~espionage ~feit[1] ~foil[1] ~mand[1] ~mine[2] ~offer[1] ~pane[2] ~part ~point ~productive ~sign ~sue[2] ~weigh ~weight

> Unable to find your word under **counter**?
> Take off **counter** and look again

counterfeit[1]
countrified
country[4] *[nation] ~| and western ~| dancing ~| house ~| music ~side
— county[4] *[an area within a state]
county[4] *[an area within a state]
— country[4] *[nation]+
coup[1] *[stroke] ~| d'état
— coo[1] *[sound] / coop *[enclosure]+ / coupe *[car] / cup[3] *[container]+
coupe *[car] — coop *[enclosure]+ / coup[1] *[stroke]+
couple[2] ~t — @coupling
coupling
coupon
courage ~ous ~ously ~ousness
courd — cord *[rope]+ / chord *[music]
courduroy — corduroy
courier
courk — cork[1] *[stopper]+
courpulince — corpulence+
course[2] *[order, path]
— coarse[2] *[rough]+
course ~| book ~work
courset — corset+
court[1] *[law] ~ly ~house ~-martial[3] ~| order ~ship ~yard
— caught *[past of catch] / coat[1] *[covering]+
courtayzh — cortège
courteous ~ly ~ness
courtesan *[prostitute]
courtesy[4]
courtier
cousin
cove
covenant
cover[1] *[hide] ~age ~| letter ~-up
covert *[hidden]
cow ~boy ~girl ~slip
coward *[runaway] ~ice ~ly[4]
— cowered *[cringed]
cowch — couch[5+]

Key to Spelling Rules

Red words are wrong. **Black** words are correct.

- ~ Add the suffix or word directly to the main word, without a space or hyphen
  e.g. ash ~en ~tray → ashen ashtray
- ~- Add a hyphen to the main word before adding the next word
  e.g. blow ~-dry → blow-dry
- ~| Leave a space between the main word and the next word
  e.g. decimal ~| place → decimal place
- + By finding this word in its correct alphabetical order, you can find related words
  e.g. abowt about+ → about-face
- ★ Draws attention to words that may be confused
- ™ Means the word is a trademark
- @ Signifies the word is derived from the main word

cower[1]	
cowered *[cringed]	
	coward *[runaway]+
cowl *[hood]	caul *[covering]
	cool[1] *[calm, cold]+
	cull[1] *[remove]
cowla	cola *[drink]
	collar[1] *[seize, neckband]
cowld	cold[1+]
	could *[can]+
cownsel	counsel[3] *[give advice]
	council *[assembly]+
cownseller	counselor *[adviser]
cownsellor	councilor *[council member]
cownt	count[1+]
cowntinince	continence
	countenance

Unable to find your word under **cow**?
Look under **cou**

coworker	
cowur	cower[1]
cox[5] *[rowing] ~swain	
	coax[5] *[encourage]
	cocks *[birds]
	Cokes *[drinks]
coy *[shy] ~ly ~ness	
	koi *[fish]
coyn	coin[1+]
coyote	
coytus	coitus
cozmanot	cosmonaut
cozmetic	cosmetic+
cozmic	cosmic+
cozmografee	cosmography
cozmology	cosmology *[universe]+
cozmopolitan	cosmopolitan+
cozmos	cosmos

Unable to find your word under **coz**?
Look under **cos**

cozy[4]	
cra	craw+
crab ~| apple ~meat	
crack[1] ~| cocaine ~down ~er ~erjack ~| shot ~up	
crackle[2]	
cradle[2]	
craft ~y[4]	
crafts ~man ~manship ~woman	
crag ~gy	
craifish	crayfish
crain	crane[2]
crainium	cranium
craink	crank[1+]
craion	crayon
craip	crepe *[wrinkled fabric]+
	crêpe *[pancake]
	creep *[move slowly]+
craiv	crave[2+]
craize	craze[2+]
craizee	crazy[4]

Unable to find your word under **crai**?
Look under **cra**

crak	crack[1+]
craknel	cracknel
cram[3]	
cramp[1] ~on	
cranberry[4]	
crane[2]	
cranium	
crank[1] ~case ~shaft ~y[4]	
cranny[4]	
crap[3] *[feces, rubbish]	
crape	crepe *[wrinkled fabric]+
cras	crass+
crash[5] *[accident] ~| barrier ~| helmet ~-land[1]	
	crush[5] *[press hard]+
crass ~ly ~ness	
crassant	croissant
crate[2] *[box]	@crater
	create[2] *[make]+
	krait *[snake]
craul	crawl[1] *[creep along]
cravat	

KEY TO SUFFIXES AND COMPOUNDS

These rules are explained on pages vii to ix.

1 Keep the word the same before adding **ed, er, est, ing**
e.g. cool[1] → cooled, cooler, coolest, cooling

2 Take off final **e** before adding **ed, er, est, ing**
e.g. fine[2] → fined, finer, finest, fining

3 Double final consonant before adding **ed, er, est, ing**
e.g. thin[3] → thinned, thinner, thinnest, thinning

4 Change final **y** to **i** before adding **ed, er, es, est, ly, ness**
e.g. tidy[4] → tidied, tidier, tidies, tidiest, tidily, tidiness
Keep final **y** before adding **ing** e.g. tidying

5 Add **es** instead of **s** to the end of the word
e.g. bunch[5] → bunches

6 Change final **f** to **ve** before adding **s**
e.g. calf[6] → calves

<table>
<tr><td>crave[2]</td><td>@cravings</td></tr>
<tr><td>cravit</td><td>cravat</td></tr>
<tr><td>craw ~fish</td><td></td></tr>
<tr><td>crawl[1] *[creep along]</td><td></td></tr>
<tr><td></td><td>Creole *[language]</td></tr>
<tr><td>crayfish</td><td></td></tr>
<tr><td>crayon</td><td></td></tr>
<tr><td>craze[2]</td><td></td></tr>
<tr><td>crazy[4]</td><td></td></tr>
<tr><td>creacher</td><td>creature[+]</td></tr>
<tr><td>cread</td><td>creed *[beliefs][+]</td></tr>
<tr><td>creak[1] *[noise] ~y[4]</td><td></td></tr>
<tr><td></td><td>creek *[stream]</td></tr>
<tr><td></td><td>crick[1] *[muscle cramp]</td></tr>
<tr><td>cream[1] *[top of milk] ~| cheese ~puff ~| soda ~| tea</td><td></td></tr>
<tr><td></td><td>crème *[sweet cream][+]</td></tr>
<tr><td>creamatorium</td><td>crematorium</td></tr>
<tr><td>creamy[4]</td><td></td></tr>
<tr><td>creap</td><td>creep *[move slowly][+]</td></tr>
<tr><td>crease[2]</td><td>creased *[wrinkled]</td></tr>
<tr><td></td><td>crest[1] *[top, shield][+]</td></tr>
<tr><td>create[2] *[make]</td><td>@creator</td></tr>
<tr><td></td><td>crate[2] *[box][+]</td></tr>
<tr><td>creation ~ism</td><td></td></tr>
<tr><td>creative ~ly ~ness ~| accounting ~| writing</td><td></td></tr>
<tr><td>creativity[4]</td><td></td></tr>
<tr><td>creature ~| comforts</td><td></td></tr>
<tr><td>crèche</td><td></td></tr>
<tr><td>crecher</td><td>creature[+]</td></tr>
<tr><td>credence</td><td></td></tr>
<tr><td>credentials</td><td></td></tr>
<tr><td>credenza *[table]</td><td>cadenza *[music]</td></tr>
<tr><td>credible</td><td>@credibility</td></tr>
<tr><td>credit[1] ~or ~able ~| card ~| line ~| limit ~| memo ~| rating ~| terms</td><td></td></tr>
<tr><td>creditworthy</td><td>@creditworthiness</td></tr>
<tr><td>credo</td><td></td></tr>
<tr><td>credulity[2]</td><td>@credulous</td></tr>
<tr><td>creed *[beliefs] ~al</td><td></td></tr>
<tr><td></td><td>cried *[past of cry]</td></tr>
<tr><td>creedance</td><td>credence</td></tr>
</table>

<table>
<tr><td>creek *[stream]</td><td>creak[1] *[noise][+]</td></tr>
<tr><td></td><td>crick[1] *[muscle cramp]</td></tr>
<tr><td>creem</td><td>cream[1] *[top of milk][+]</td></tr>
<tr><td>creemate</td><td>cremate[2+]</td></tr>
<tr><td>creep *[move slowly] ~er ~ing ~y[4]</td><td></td></tr>
<tr><td></td><td>crepe *[wrinkled fabric][+]</td></tr>
<tr><td>creese</td><td>crease[2+]</td></tr>
<tr><td>creetcher</td><td>creature[+]</td></tr>
<tr><td>crejulity</td><td>credulity[+]</td></tr>
<tr><td>cremate[2]</td><td>@cremation</td></tr>
<tr><td>crematorium</td><td></td></tr>
<tr><td>crème *[sweet cream] ~| brûlée ~| fraiche</td><td></td></tr>
<tr><td></td><td>cream[1] *[top of milk][+]</td></tr>
<tr><td>cremetoriam</td><td>crematorium</td></tr>
<tr><td>crenelated</td><td>crenellated</td></tr>
<tr><td>crenellated</td><td></td></tr>
<tr><td>Creole *[language]</td><td></td></tr>
<tr><td></td><td>crawl[1] *[creep along]</td></tr>
<tr><td>crepe *[wrinkled fabric] ~| paper</td><td></td></tr>
<tr><td></td><td>creep *[move slowly][+]</td></tr>
<tr><td>crêpe *[pancake]</td><td></td></tr>
<tr><td>crept *[crawled]</td><td>crypt *[underground room][+]</td></tr>
<tr><td>crescendo</td><td></td></tr>
<tr><td>crescent ~| moon</td><td></td></tr>
<tr><td>creshendo</td><td>crescendo</td></tr>
<tr><td>cressent</td><td>crescent[+]</td></tr>
<tr><td>crest[1] *[top, shield] ~fallen</td><td></td></tr>
<tr><td></td><td>creased *[wrinkled]</td></tr>
<tr><td>Creutzfeldt-Jakob disease *[CJD]</td><td></td></tr>
<tr><td>crevasse *[large crack in ice]</td><td></td></tr>
<tr><td></td><td>crevice *[small crack]</td></tr>
<tr><td>crevat</td><td>cravat</td></tr>
<tr><td>crevice *[small crack]</td><td></td></tr>
<tr><td></td><td>crevasse *[large crack in ice]</td></tr>
<tr><td>crew[1] ~| cut ~| neck</td><td></td></tr>
<tr><td>crewdity</td><td>crudity *[coarseness]</td></tr>
<tr><td></td><td>crudités *[food]</td></tr>
<tr><td>crewel *[yarn]</td><td>cruel[3] *[hurtful][+]</td></tr>
<tr><td>crewit</td><td>cruet</td></tr>
<tr><td>crews *[teams]</td><td>cruise[2] *[trip][+]</td></tr>
<tr><td>criashun</td><td>creation[+]</td></tr>
<tr><td>criate</td><td>create[2+]</td></tr>
<tr><td>criativ</td><td>creative[+]</td></tr>
<tr><td>criativity</td><td>creativity[4]</td></tr>
</table>

crib[3] ~| death	
cribbage	
crick[1] *[muscle cramp]	
	creak[1] *[noise][+]
	creek *[stream]
cricket ~| captain	
cried *[past of cry]	
	creed *[beliefs][+]
crie	cry[4+]
crik	creak[1] *[noise][+]
	creek *[stream]
	crick[1] *[muscle cramp]
crikit	cricket[+]
crimate	cremate[2+]
crime ~| and punishment ~| wave	
criminal ~ly	
criminalize[2]	@criminality
criminologist	@criminology
crimp[1]	
crimson	
crinaline	crinoline
crindge	cringe[2]
cringe[2]	
crinkle[2]	@crinkly
crinoline	
criogenics	cryogenics
criole	creole
cripple[2]	
cript	crypt *[underground room][+]
criptogram	cryptogram
criptograph	cryptograph[+]
cripul	cripple[2]
crisanthimum	chrysanthemum
crisis ~| management	
	@crises
crisp[1]	@crispy[4]
crisscross[5]	
crissen	christen[1]
Crist	Christ[+]
cristal	crystal[+]
cristaline	crystalline
cristalize	crystallize[2+]
cristallografee	crystallography
cristel	crystal[+]
cristeleen	crystalline

> Unable to find your word under **cri**?
> Look under **cry**

Cristian	Christian[+]
Cristmas	Christmas[+]
criteek	critique *[criticism]
	critic *[evaluator]
criteria	@criterion
critic *[evaluator]	critique *[criticism]
critical ~ly ~| point	
criticism	
criticize[2]	
critique *[criticism]	
	critic *[evaluator]
croak[1]	
croch	crotch[+]
crochet[1]	
crock ~ery	
crocodile	
crocus[5]	
croissant	
Croitsfeld-Jacob disease	
	Creutzfeldt-Jakob disease
crokay	croquet *[game]
croke	croak[1]
crokodile	crocodile
crokus	crocus[5]
cromasome	chromosome
cromate	chromate[+]
cromatic	chromatic
crome	chrome
cronic	chronic[+]
crony[4] ~ism	
crood	crud *[dirt]
	crude *[rough][+]
crook[1]	
crooks *[criminals]	
	crux *[central point]
crooked ~edly ~edness	
croon[1]	
croopyay	croupier
crop[3] ~| circle ~| rotation	

Key to Suffixes and Compounds

These rules are explained on pages vii to ix.

1 Keep the word the same before adding **ed, er, est, ing**
e.g. cool[1] → cooled, cooler, coolest, cooling

2 Take off final **e** before adding **ed, er, est, ing**
e.g. fine[2] → fined, finer, finest, fining

3 Double final consonant before adding **ed, er, est, ing**
e.g. thin[3] → thinned, thinner, thinnest, thinning

4 Change final **y** to **i** before adding **ed, er, es, est, ly, ness**
e.g. tidy[4] → tidied, tidier, tidies, tidiest, tidily, tidiness
Keep final **y** before adding **ing** e.g. tidying

5 Add **es** instead of **s** to the end of the word
e.g. bunch[5] → bunches

6 Change final **f** to **ve** before adding **s**
e.g. calf[6] → calves

croquet *[game]
croquette *[food]
croshay — crochet[1]
cross[1] ~ly ~beam ~bow ~bred ~breed ~bones ~-check[1] ~| collateralization ~-country ~-cultural ~current ~cut ~cutting ~-dressing ~-eyed ~-examine[2] ~-examination ~-fertilize[2] ~| fire ~hatch ~-legged ~over ~patch ~-purposes ~-question[1] ~-reference[2] ~road ~| section ~walk ~wind ~word

Unable to find your word under **cross**? Take off **cross** and look again

crotch ~ety[4]
crouch[5]
croud — crowed *[cock]; crowd[1] *[people]
croupier
crow[1] ~bar
crowch — crouch[5]
crowd[1] *[people]
crowed *[cock]
crowkay — croquet *[game]
crowket — croquette *[food]
crown[1] ~| jewels
cruch — crutch[5]
crucial ~ly
crucible
crucifix ~ion
crucify[4]
crucks — crux[5] *[central point]
crud *[dirt]
crude *[rough] ~ly ~ness
crudity *[coarseness]
— crudités *[food]
crue — crew[1+]
cruel[3] *[hurtful] ~ly ~ty
— crewel *[yarn]
cruet
cruise[2] *[trip] ~| control ~| liner ~| missile
— crews *[teams]
cruk — crook[1]
cruks — crooks *[criminals]; crux[5] *[central point]
crule — crewel *[yarn]; cruel[3] *[hurtful]+
crumb
crumble[2] *[break up]
— crumple[2] *[crease]
crummy[4]
crumple[2] *[crease]
— crumble[2] *[break up]
crunch[1] — @crunchy[4]
crune — croon[1]
cruntch — crunch[1+]
crupiay — croupier
crusade[2]
crush[1] *[press hard] ~| barrier
— crash[1] *[accident]+
crushal — crucial+
crusibel — crucible
crusifix — crucifix+
crusify — crucify[4]
crust — @crusty[4]
crustacean
crustashun — crustacean
crutch[5]
cruw — crew[1+]
cruwel — crewel *[yarn]; cruel[3] *[hurtful]+
crux[5] *[central point]
— crooks *[criminals]
cruze — cruise[2] *[trip]+; crews *[teams]
cry[4] ~baby
crymp — crimp[1]
crynolyne — crinoline
cryogenics
crypt *[underground room] ~ic ~ography
— crept *[crawled]
crysalis — chrysalis[5]
crysanthemum — chrysanthemum
crysilis — chrysalis[5]

Key to Spelling Rules

Red words are wrong. **Black** words are correct.

~ Add the suffix or word directly to the main word, without a space or hyphen
e.g. ash ~en ~tray → ashen ashtray

~- Add a hyphen to the main word before adding the next word
e.g. blow ~-dry → blow-dry

~| Leave a space between the main word and the next word
e.g. decimal ~| place → decimal place

\+ By finding this word in its correct alphabetical order, you can find related words
e.g. abowt about+ → about-face

★ Draws attention to words that may be confused

TM Means the word is a trademark

@ Signifies the word is derived from the main word

crysis	crisis+
crystal ~| ball ~| clear	
crystalline	
crystallize2	@crystallization
crystallography	
cryteria	criteria+
crytic	critic *[evaluator]
	critique *[criticism]
cryticysum	criticism
cryticyze	criticize2
CT scan	
cu	coo1 *[sound]
	coup1 *[stroke]+
	cue2 *[sign]
	queue2 *[line]
cub	
Cub Scout	
cube ~d ~| number ~| root	
cubical *[cube-shaped]	
cubicle *[small room]	
cubism	@cubist
cuckold1	
cuckoo ~| clock	
cucoo	cuckoo+
cucumber	
cud *[cow-related]	
	queued *[waited in line]
cuddle2	@cuddly4
cudgel3	
cudjel	cudgel3
cue *[sign]	coo1 *[sound]
	queue2 *[line]
cuelinery	culinary
cuenayiform	cuneiform
cueue	cue2 *[sign]
	queue2 *[line]
cuff1 *[fold, blow] ~link	
	cough1 *[throat irritation]+
cuger	cougar
cuier	choir *[singers]+
	coir *[coconut fiber]
	quire *[paper]
cuisine	
cuk	cook1 *[food]+
cul	cull1 *[remove]
culcher	culture2+
cul-de-sac	
culdisack	cul-de-sac
cule	cool1 *[calm, cold]+
	cull1 *[remove]
culinary	
cull1 *[remove]	cool1 *[calm, cold]+
culminate2	@culmination
culpable	@culpability
culprit	
cult	
cultivate2	@cultivator
cultivation	
cultural ~ly ~| barrier ~| norms ~| value	
culture2 ~| shock	
culvert	
cum	come *[arrive]+
	comb1 *[for hair]+
cum laude	
cumbersome ~ly ~ness	
cumemorate	commemorate2+
cumfurt	comfort1+
cumlawday	cum laude
cummand	command1 *[be in charge]+
cumpany	company4+
cumparison	comparison
cumpeditor	competitor
cumpell	compel3
cumpete	compete2 *[struggle]
cumpile	compile2+
cumplete	complete2 *[finish]+

Unable to find your word under **cum**?
Look under **com**

cumulative	
cumulus	
cunclude	conclude2+
cuncubine	concubine
cuneiform	
cunfine	confine2+
cunning ~ly	
cunsern	concern1

KEY TO SUFFIXES AND COMPOUNDS

These rules are explained on pages vii to ix.

1 Keep the word the same before adding **ed, er, est, ing**
e.g. cool1 → cooled, cooler, coolest, cooling
2 Take off final **e** before adding **ed, er, est, ing**
e.g. fine2 → fined, finer, finest, fining
3 Double final consonant before adding **ed, er, est, ing**
e.g. thin3 → thinned, thinner, thinnest, thinning
4 Change final **y** to **i** before adding **ed, er, es, est, ly, ness**
e.g. tidy4 → tidied, tidier, tidies, tidiest, tidily, tidiness
Keep final **y** before adding **ing** e.g. tidying
5 Add **es** instead of **s** to the end of the word
e.g. bunch5 → bunches
6 Change final **f** to **ve** before adding **s**
e.g. calf6 → calves

cunsult	consult[1] *[ask advice]+
cuntree	country[4] *[nation]+
cuntrified	countrified
cuoperate	co-operate[2+]
cup[3] *[container] ~cake ~ful	
	coop[1] *[enclosure]+
cupboard	
Cupid	
cuple	couple[2+]
cupola	
cupon	coupon
cupple	couple[2+]
cuppling	coupling
cuppola	cupola
curable	
curate[2]	@curator
curb[1] *[stop] ~stone	
curd *[from milk]	Kurd *[person]
curdle[2]	
cure[2] ~-all	@curative
curensy	currency[4]
curent	currant *[fruit]
	current *[flow]+
curey	curry[4+]
curfew	
curiculum	curriculum+
curier	courier
curige	courage+
curio	
curiosity[4]	
curious ~ly ~ness	
curl[1] ~y[4] ~ew	
curlew	
currage	courage+
currageous	courageous+
currant *[fruit]	current *[flow]+
currency[4]	
current *[flow] ~ly ~| account ~| affairs ~| assets ~| liabilities	
	currant *[fruit]
curriculum ~| vitae	
	@curricula
currier	courier
curry[4] ~| powder	
curse[2] *[bad spell]	
curser	cursor *[computer]
cursery	cursory[4]
cursive	
cursor *[computer]	
	curse[2] *[bad spell]
cursory[4]	
curt ~ly ~ness	
curtail[1] ~ment	
curtain *[screen] ~| call ~| rail	
	certain *[sure]+
curtesy	courtesy[4]
	curtsy[4] *[bow]
curtsy[4] *[bow]	courtesy[4]
curvaceous ~ness	
curvashuss	curvaceous+
curve[2]	@curvature
cury	curry[4+]
cus	cuss[1]
cushion[1]	
cusin	cousin
cusp	
cuss[5]	
custard	
custidy	custody+
custody	@custodial
	@custodian
custom ~er ~-made	
customary[4]	
customer ~| base ~| service	
cut[3] *[with a knife] ~back ~-and-dried ~-and-paste ~off ~-rate ~throat ~| through ~up	
	cute[2] *[sweet]+

> Unable to find your word under **cut**?
> Take off **cut** and look again

cute[2] *[sweet] ~ly ~ness	
	cut[3] *[with a knife]+
cuticle	
cutlass[5]	
cutlery	
cutlet	
cutlus	cutlass[5]
cutting ~| edge	

Key to Spelling Rules

Red words are wrong. **Black** words are correct.

~ Add the suffix or word directly to the main word, without a space or hyphen
e.g. ash ~en ~tray → ashen ashtray

~- Add a hyphen to the main word before adding the next word
e.g. blow ~-dry → blow-dry

~| Leave a space between the main word and the next word
e.g. decimal ~| place → decimal place

\+ By finding this word in its correct alphabetical order, you can find related words
e.g. abowt about+ → about-face

* Draws attention to words that may be confused

TM Means the word is a trademark

@ Signifies the word is derived from the main word

cuvenant	covenant
cuver	cover[1+]
cuwd	could *[can]+
cuzin	cousin

Unable to find your word under **cu**?
Look under **co** or **cou**

CV *[curriculum vitae]	
cworum	quorum
cyanide	
cybernetics	
cyberspace	
cyclamate	
cyclamen	
cycle[2] *[turning]	sickle *[blade]
cyclemait	cyclamate
cyclic ~al	
cyclist	
cyclone	
Cyclops	
cyclotron	
cyder	cider
cyenn	cayenne+
cyfer	cipher *[code]
	siphon[1] *[tube, take away]
cygnet *[swan]	signet *[ring]
cyklatron	cyclotron
cylinder	
cylindrical ~ly	
cymbal *[music]	symbol *[sign]+
cymbolic	symbolic+
cymbolical	symbolical+
cymbolise	symbolize[2+]
cynch	cinch[5]
cynder	cinder+
Cynderella	Cinderella
cyne	sign[1+]
cynema	cinema+
cynic ~ism	
cynical ~ly	
cynonim	synonym+
cynosure	
cynus	sinus[5]
cypher	cipher *[code]
	siphon[1] *[tube, take away]
cypress	
cyrcle	circle[2]
cyrculer	circular
Cyrillic	
cyringe	syringe
cyris	cirrus
cyrosis	cirrhosis
cyrup	syrup+
cyst ~itis	
cystem	system+
cyte	cite[2] *[quote]
	sight *[seeing]+
	site *[place]

Unable to find your word under **cy**?
Look under **ci**, **si**, or **sy**

czar [also spelled tsar] ~ina	
Czech *[citizen]	check[1] *[book, control]+

Key to Suffixes and Compounds

These rules are explained on pages vii to ix.

1. Keep the word the same before adding **ed, er, est, ing**
   e.g. cool[1] → cooled, cooler, coolest, cooling
2. Take off final **e** before adding **ed, er, est, ing**
   e.g. fine[2] → fined, finer, finest, fining
3. Double final consonant before adding **ed, er, est, ing**
   e.g. thin[3] → thinned, thinner, thinnest, thinning
4. Change final **y** to **i** before adding **ed, er, es, est, ly, ness**
   e.g. tidy[4] → tidied, tidier, tidies, tidiest, tidily, tidiness
   Keep final **y** before adding **ing** e.g. tidying
5. Add **es** instead of **s** to the end of the word
   e.g. bunch[5] → bunches
6. Change final **f** to **ve** before adding **s**
   e.g. calf[6] → calves

D

D ~-day
dabble[2] ~| in
dabel dabble[2]+
dachshund
dackery daiquiri
dacore décor
Dacron™
dad
dael dale *[valley]
daily[4] *[every day]
daffodil
daft
dagger
daily[4] *[every day]
dally[4] *[wait around]
daim dame *[lady]
damn[1] *[curse]+
dain Dane *[Denmark, dog]
deign[1] *[bother]
dainty[4]
daiquiri
dair dare[2]+
dairy[4] *[milk] ~| farm
diary[4] *[journal]
daisy[4] ~| chain
Dakron Dacron™
dalfin dolphin+
dally[4] *[wait around]
daily[4] *[every day]
Dalmatian
dalya dahlia
dam[3] *[water] dame *[lady]
damn[1] *[curse]+
damage[2] ~| control
dame *[lady] dam[3] *[water]
damn[1] *[curse]+
damige damage[2]+
damize demise
damn[1] *[curse] ~ation
dam[3] *[water]
damp[1] ~en[1] ~ness
dampen[1]
damson
dance[2] ~| craze ~| floor ~| music
dandelion
dandruff
dandy[4]
Dane *[Denmark, dog]
deign[1] *[bother]
danety dainty[4]
danger ~ous ~ously
dangle[2]
danjer danger+
dank
danse dance[2]+
dapal dapple[2]
dapper
dapple[2]
dare[2] ~devil
darey dairy[4] *[milk]+
diary[4] *[journal]
dark[1] ~ly ~ness ~| horse ~| room
Dark Ages
darken[1]
darling
darn[1]
dart[1] ~board
dash[1] ~board
dashhund dachshund
dastardly ~| deed
data ~| acquisition ~| analysis
~| architecture ~bank ~base
~| capture ~| cleaning ~| entry
~| exploration ~| extraction ~| file

Key to Spelling Rules

Red words are wrong. **Black** words are correct.

~ Add the suffix or word directly to the main word, without a space or hyphen
e.g. ash ~en ~tray → ashen ashtray

~- Add a hyphen to the main word before adding the next word
e.g. blow ~-dry → blow-dry

~| Leave a space between the main word and the next word
e.g. decimal ~| place → decimal place

+ By finding this word in its correct alphabetical order, you can find related words
e.g. abowt about+ → about-face

★ Draws attention to words that may be confused

™ Means the word is a trademark

@ Signifies the word is derived from the main word

data ~| integration ~| mapping ~| mining ~| munging ~| preservation ~| processing ~| record ~| set ~| source ~| stream ~| storage ~| structure ~| visualization ~| warehouse ~| warehousing

> Unable to find your word under **data**?
> Take off **data** and look again

date² ~| line ~| of birth ~| rape ~-stamp¹
daub¹
daudel — dawdle²
daughter ~-in-law
daun — dawn¹⁺
daunt¹ ~ingly ~less
dauter — daughter⁺
dawb — daub¹
dawdle²
dawn¹ ~| chorus ~| patrol ~| raid
dawnt — daunt¹⁺
dawter — daughter⁺
day ~break ~| care ~dream ~light ~| nursery ~| player ~| rates ~| release ~time ~trader ~-to-day ~| trip

> Unable to find your word under **day**?
> Take off **day** and look again

daybue — début
daycor — décor
dayfacto — de facto

> Unable to find your word under **day**?
> Look under **de**

Day-Glo
dayly — daily⁴ *[every day]
 dally⁴ *[wait around]
days *[dates] — daze² *[stun]
dayt — date²⁺
daze² *[stun] — days *[dates]
dazzle²

de facto
dead *[not alive] ~ly⁴ ~bolt ~| duck ~| end ~head ~| heat ~line ~| loss ~weight ~wood
 deed *[action]⁺

> Unable to find your word under **dead**?
> Take off **dead** and look again

deaden¹
deaf *[not hearing] ~ness ~-and-dumb ~-mute
 deft *[clever]⁺
deafen¹ *[harm hearing] ~ingly
 define² *[explain]⁺
deal *[trade] ~ing ~er ~ership
 dele *[proofreader's mark]
dealt
dean *[college] ~'s list
 den *[shelter]
dear *[loved] ~est ~ly
 deer *[animal]⁺
dearth *[not enough]
death *[being dead] ~ly ~bed ~| benefit ~blow ~| penalty ~| rate ~| sentence ~| toll ~| trap ~| warrant ~| wish

> Unable to find your word under **death**?
> Take off **death** and look again

débâcle
debait — debate²⁺
debar³
debase²
debate² — @debatable
debauched — @debauchery
debilitate²
debit¹ *[accounting transaction] ~| balance ~| card ~| column
 debt *[amount owed]⁺
debonair ~ly
debree — debris
debrief¹
debris

Key to Suffixes and Compounds

These rules are explained on pages vii to ix.

1 Keep the word the same before adding **ed, er, est, ing** e.g. cool¹ → cooled, cooler, coolest, cooling
2 Take off final **e** before adding **ed, er, est, ing** e.g. fine² → fined, finer, finest, fining
3 Double final consonant before adding **ed, er, est, ing** e.g. thin³ → thinned, thinner, thinnest, thinning
4 Change final **y** to **i** before adding **ed, er, es, est, ly, ness** e.g. tidy⁴ → tidied, tidier, tidies, tidiest, tidily, tidiness
Keep final **y** before adding **ing** e.g. tidying
5 Add **es** instead of **s** to the end of the word e.g. bunch⁵ → bunches
6 Change final **f** to **ve** before adding **s** e.g. calf⁶ → calves

debt *[amount owed] ~or ~| collection
debunk[1]
début
debutant *[man]
debutante *[woman]
decade *[10 years]
    decayed *[rotted]
decadent *[morally declining]
    @decadence
    decedent *[dead person]
decaffeinated
decamp[1]
decant[1]
decapitate[2]   @decapitation
decathlon
decay[1]
decayed *[rotted]   decade[1] *[10 years]
deceased *[dead]
    diseased *[ill]
decedent *[dead person]
    decadent *[morally declining][+]
deceeve   deceive[2]
deceit ~ful ~fully ~fulness
deceive[2]
December
decency
decend   descend[1+]
decent *[good] ~ly
    descent *[down]
    dissent[1] *[argue]
decentralize[2]   @decentralization
decepshin   deception
deception
deceptive ~ly ~ness
decete   deceit[+]
decibel
decide[2] ~dly
deciduous ~| tree
decifir   decipher[1+]
decimal ~| fraction ~| number ~| place ~| point
decimalize[2]
decimate[2]   @decimation
decimil   decimal[+]

decint   decent *[good][+]
    descent *[down]
    dissent[1] *[argue]
decipher[1] ~able
decision ~| making ~| maker ~| support system
decisive ~ly ~ness
deck[1] ~| chair ~hand ~| of cards
deckade   decade[1] *[10 years]
deckadent   decadent *[morally declining][+]
declaration   @declaratory
declare[2]   @declared value
declassify[4]
declension
decline[2]
decode[2]
décolleté   @décolletage
decompose[2]   @decomposition
decompress[5] ~ion ~or
decongestant
deconstruct[1]
decontaminate[2]   @decontamination
décor
decorate[2]   @decoration
    @decorator
decorative ~ly
decorum
decoy[1]
decrativ   decorative[+]
decrease[2]   @decreasingly
decree *[order] ~d ~ing
    decry[4] *[condemn]
    degree *[amount, study]
decrepit ~ude
decrie   decree *[order][+]
    degree *[amount, study]
decriminalize[2]   @decriminalization
decry[4] *[condemn]
    decree *[order][+]
    degree *[amount, study]
decryption
decsend   descend[1+]
ded   dead *[not alive][+]
    deed *[action][+]

Key to Spelling Rules

Red words are wrong. **Black** words are correct.

~ Add the suffix or word directly to the main word, without a space or hyphen
e.g. ash ~en ~tray → ashen ashtray

~- Add a hyphen to the main word before adding the next word
e.g. blow ~-dry → blow-dry

~| Leave a space between the main word and the next word
e.g. decimal ~| place → decimal place

+ By finding this word in its correct alphabetical order, you can find related words
e.g. abowt about[+] → about-face

* Draws attention to words that may be confused

TM Means the word is a trademark

@ Signifies the word is derived from the main word

dedacated — dedicated[+]
deden — deaden[1]
dedicate[2] — @dedication
dedicated ~| line
dedin — deaden[1]
deduce[2]
deduct[1] ~ible ~ion
deecint — decent *[good][+]
descent *[down]
dissent[1] *[argue]
deed *[action] ~| of transfer ~| poll
dead *[not alive][+]
Deeday — D-Day
deefalt — default[1]
deeitie — deity[4]
deel — deal *[trade][+]
deeler — dealer[+]
deem[1]
deen — dean *[college][+]
deep[1] ~ly ~| freeze ~-frozen ~-fry[4] ~-rooted ~-seated ~-set
deepart — depart[1+]
deepen[1]
deer *[animal] ~skin
dear *[loved][+]
de-escalate[2]
deetach — detach[1+]
deetor — detour *[go around]
deeva — diva
deevalue — devalue[2]
deevius — devious[+]
deezel — diesel
def — deaf *[not hearing][+]
deface[2] *[damage] ~ment
dephase[2] *[waves]
defalt — default[1]
defamation — @defamatory
defase — deface[2] *[damage][+]
dephase[2] *[waves]
defasit — deficit[+]
default[1]
defeat[1] ~ism ~ist
defecate[2] — @defecation
defect[1] ~ion ~ive
defend[1] ~able ~ant

defens — defense[+]
defense ~less ~| counsel ~| mechanism
defensible
defensive ~ly ~ness
defer[3] *[put off] — differ[1] *[disagree]
deference *[submission]
deferenshial — deferential *[submitting][+]
differential *[difference][+]
deferential *[submitting] ~ly
defermashun — defamation[+]
deferred ~| creditor ~| payment
deffen — deafen[1] *[harm hearing][+]
defiance — @defiant
@defiantly
defianse — defiance[+]
deficiency[4]
deficient
deficit ~| financing ~| spending
defie — defy[4] *[oppose]
deify[4] *[worship]
defien — define[2] *[explain][+]
defile[2]
defin — deafen[1] *[harm hearing][+]
define[2] *[explain][+]
define[2] *[explain] — @definable
deafen[1] *[harm hearing][+]
definishun — definition
definite ~ly
definition
definitive ~ly
defir — defer[3] *[put off]
differ[1] *[disagree]
defishensy — deficiency[4]
defisit — deficit[+]
deflate[2] — @deflation
deflationary[4]
deflect[1] ~ion ~or
deforest[1] ~ation
deform[1] ~ation
deformity[4]
defraud[1]
defray[1] ~able ~| costs
defrost[1]

KEY TO SUFFIXES AND COMPOUNDS

These rules are explained on pages vii to ix.

1 Keep the word the same before adding **ed, er, est, ing**
e.g. cool[1] → cooled, cooler, coolest, cooling
2 Take off final **e** before adding **ed, er, est, ing**
e.g. fine[2] → fined, finer, finest, fining
3 Double final consonant before adding **ed, er, est, ing**
e.g. thin[3] → thinned, thinner, thinnest, thinning
4 Change final **y** to **i** before adding **ed, er, es, est, ly, ness**
e.g. tidy[4] → tidied, tidier, tidies, tidiest, tidily, tidiness
Keep final **y** before adding **ing** e.g. tidying
5 Add **es** instead of **s** to the end of the word
e.g. bunch[5] → bunches
6 Change final **f** to **ve** before adding **s**
e.g. calf[6] → calves

deft *[clever] ~ly ~ness	
	deaf *[not hearing]
defunct	
defunkt	defunct
defuse[2] *[calm]	@defusion
	diffuse[2] *[spread][+]
defy[4] *[oppose]	deify[4] *[worship]
degeneracy	
degenerasie	degeneracy
degenerate[2]	@degeneration
degrade[2]	@degradation
degree *[amount, study]	
	decree *[order][+]
dehumanize[2]	@dehumanization
dehydrate[2]	@dehydration
de-ice[2]	
deify[4] *[worship]	defy[4] *[oppose]
deign[1] *[bother]	Dane *[Denmark, dog]
deism	@deist
deity[4]	
déjà vu	
deject[1] ~ion	
dek	deck[1+]
dekorate	decorate[2+]
dekorativ	decorative[+]
dekorum	decorum

Unable to find your word under **dek**?
Look under **dec**

dekstroze	dextrose *[sugar]
dekstrus	dexterous *[skillful][+]
delay[1]	
dele *[proofreader's mark]	
	deal *[trade][+]
delectable	
deleete	delete[2+]
delegate[2]	@delegation
delete[2]	@deletion
deliberate[2] ~ly	@deliberation
delicacy[4]	
delicate ~ly ~ness	
delicatessen	
delicious ~ly ~ness	
delight[1] ~ful ~fully	

delikatessen	delicatessen
delinquent	@delinquency[4]
delirious ~ly	
delirium	
delishus	delicious[+]
deliver[1] ~ance	
delivery[4] ~| date ~| order ~| time	
dell	
delouse[2]	
delta	
delude[2]	@delusion
	@delusional
deluge[2]	
delusory	
deluxe	
delve[2] ~| into	
demagogue ~ry	
demand[1] ~-pull inflation	
demarcate[2]	@demarcation
demean[1] ~or	
demensha	dementia
demented	@dementor
dementia	
demer	demur[3] *[refuse]
	demure *[shy][+]
demesne *[property]	
	domain *[realm][+]
demicrat	Democrat[+]
demilitarize[2]	@demilitarization
demise	
demo	
demobilize[2]	@demobilization
democracy[4]	
Democrat ~ic Party	
democratic ~ally	
democratize[2]	@democratization
demographic ~s	@demography
demolish[1]	
demolition	
demon ~ic	
demonstrable	@demonstrably
demonstrate[2]	@demonstrator
demonstration ~| model	
demonstrative ~ly	
demoralize[2]	

KEY TO SPELLING RULES

Red words are wrong. **Black** words are correct.

~ Add the suffix or word directly to the main word, without a space or hyphen
e.g. ash ~en ~tray → ashen ashtray

~- Add a hyphen to the main word before adding the next word
e.g. blow ~-dry → blow-dry

~| Leave a space between the main word and the next word
e.g. decimal ~| place → decimal place

+ By finding this word in its correct alphabetical order, you can find related words
e.g. abowt about[+] → about-face

* Draws attention to words that may be confused

TM Means the word is a trademark

@ Signifies the word is derived from the main word

demote² @demotion
demur³ *[refuse]
demure *[shy] ~ly
demygod demigod
demystify⁴
den *[shelter] dean *[college]+
dence dense² *[thick]+
dencher denture
dencity density⁴
dene dean *[college]+
den *[shelter]
denegrait denigrate²+
denial
deniel denial
denigrate² @denigration
denim
denizen
denomination ~al
denominator
denounce² @denunciation
denownce denounce²
denowns denounce²
dense² *[thick] ~ly
dents *[bangs]
density⁴
dent¹
dental ~| hygiene
dentin
dentist ~ry
denture
denude²
denum denim
denumaw denouement
deny⁴
denyal denial
denygreat denigrate²+
deodorant
deodorize²
depart¹ ~ure
department ~al ~ally ~| store
departmentalize²
depend¹ ~able
dependence *[trust]
dependency⁴ *[need]
dependent *[needy] ~| variable
depersonalize²
depewty deputy⁴+
dephase² *[waves]
deface² *[damage]+
depict¹ ~ion
depilate² @depilation
deplete² @depletion
deploma diploma

Unable to find your word under **de**?
Look under **di**

deplore² @deplorable
@deplorably
deploy¹ ~ment
depopulate² @depopulation
deport¹ ~ation ~ee ~ment
depose²
deposit¹ ~| account ~ory⁴ ~| slip
deposition
depot
depraved² @depravity
deprecate² *[disapprove]
depreciate² *[value]
@depreciation rate
depress⁵ ~ant ~ive
depression *[sadness, mental illness]
Depression *[economic disaster, 1929–1941]
depressurize²
deprishiate deprecate² *[disapprove]
depreciate² *[value]+
deprive² @deprivation
depth ~| charge ~| of field
depthirea diphtheria
deputation
deputie deputy⁴+
deputize²
deputy⁴ ~| director ~| manager
derail¹ ~leur *[bicycle gears] ~ment
derange² ~ment
derby⁴
deregulate² @deregulation
derelict ~ion

Key to Suffixes and Compounds

These rules are explained on pages vii to ix.

1 Keep the word the same before adding **ed, er, est, ing**
e.g. cool¹ → cooled, cooler, coolest, cooling
2 Take off final **e** before adding **ed, er, est, ing**
e.g. fine² → fined, finer, finest, fining
3 Double final consonant before adding **ed, er, est, ing**
e.g. thin³ → thinned, thinner, thinnest, thinning
4 Change final **y** to **i** before adding **ed, er, es, est, ly, ness**
e.g. tidy⁴ → tidied, tidier, tidies, tidiest, tidily, tidiness
Keep final **y** before adding **ing** e.g. tidying
5 Add **es** instead of **s** to the end of the word
e.g. bunch⁵ → bunches
6 Change final **f** to **ve** before adding **s**
e.g. calf⁶ → calves

deride[2] *[make fun of]	
	@derisive
	@derisory
	dried *[made dry]
derision	
derivative	
derive[2]	@derivation
derizion	derision
dermatitis	
dermatology	@dermatologist
derogatory	
derrick	
derride	deride[2] *[make fun of]+
derrive	derive[2+]
dert	dirt+
derth	dearth *[not enough]
derty	dirty[4]
dervish	
desalinate[2]	@desalination
descend[1] ~ant	
descent *[down]	decent *[good]+
	dissent[1] *[argue]
descrete	discreet *[careful]+
	discrete *[separate]
describe[2]	@describable
description	@descriptive
descurage	discourage[2+]
desdain	disdain[1+]
desecrate[2]	@desecration
deseedent	decedent
deseet	deceit+
deseeve	deceive[2]
desegregate[2]	@desegregation
desend	descend[1+]
desensitize[2]	
desent	decent *[good]+
	descent *[down]
	dissent[1] *[argue]
desentralize	decentralize[2+]
deseption	deception
desert[1] *[leave, sand] ~ion	
	dessert *[food]
deserve[2] ~dly	
deseve	deceive[2]
desibell	decibel
desiccate[2]	
desiduous	deciduous+
desied	decide[2+]
design[1] ~| defect ~| fault	
designate[2]	@designation
desimait	decimate[2+]
desimal	decimal+
desimalize	decimalize[2]
desimilize	decimalize[2]

Unable to find your word under **des**?
Look under **dec**

desirable	@desirability
desire[2]	@desirous
desist[1]	
desk ~| job	
desktop ~| computer ~| grid ~| publishing	
desolate	@desolation
despair[1] ~ingly	
despare	despair[1+]
desperado[5]	
desperate *[need] ~ly	
	disparate *[distinct]+
desperation	
desperse	disperse[2] *[scatter]+
despicable	@despicably
despiet	despite
despirashin	desperation
despiration	desperation
despirse	disperse[2] *[scatter]+
	disburse[2] *[pay out]+
despise[2]	
despite	
despondent	
despot ~ic ~ically ~ism	
despute	dispute[2]
dessend	descend[1+]
dessert *[food]	desert[1] *[leave, sand]+
dessicate	desiccate[2]
destichute	destitute+
destiny[4]	@destined
destitute	@destitution
destroy[1]	

Key to Spelling Rules

Red words are wrong. **Black** words are correct.

~ Add the suffix or word directly to the main word, without a space or hyphen
e.g. ash ~en ~tray → ashen ashtray

~- Add a hyphen to the main word before adding the next word
e.g. blow ~-dry → blow-dry

~| Leave a space between the main word and the next word
e.g. decimal ~| place → decimal place

\+ By finding this word in its correct alphabetical order, you can find related words
e.g. abowt about+ → about-face

* Draws attention to words that may be confused

TM Means the word is a trademark

@ Signifies the word is derived from the main word

destruction	@destructible
destructive ~ly	
desurve	deserve[2+]
det	debt *[amount owed]+
detach[5] ~ment	
detail[1]	
detain ~ee	
detect[1] ~able ~ion ~or	
detective ~| agency	
détente	
detention ~| center	
deter[3] *[stop] ~rence	
	detour *[go around]
deterant	deterrent
detergent	
deteriorate[2]	@deterioration
determinant	
determination	
determine[2]	@determinism
determinent	determinant
deterrent	
detest[1] ~able	
deth	death *[being dead]+
	dearth *[not enough]
dethrone[2]	
detonate[2]	@detonation
	@detonator
detour *[go around]	
	deter[3] *[stop]+
detriment ~al	
dette	debt *[amount owed]+
deturjent	detergent
deturmin	determine[2+]
deuce[2] *[card, carburetor]	
	douche[2] *[hygiene]
	juice[2] *[drink]+
deuration	duration
deva	diva
devaluate[2]	
devalue[2]	
devastate[2]	@devastation
develop[1] ~ment	
deviance	@deviant
deviate[2]	@deviation
device *[thing]	devise[2] *[invent]

devide	divide[2]
devil ~ry ~'s advocate	
devilish ~ly	
devious ~ly ~ness	
devise[2] *[invent]	device *[thing]
devolution	
devorse	divorce[2] *[end of marriage]+
devoshin	devotion+
devote[2] ~dly	@devotee
devotion ~al	
devour[1]	
devout ~ly	
devulge	divulge[2+]

> Unable to find your word under **de**?
> Look under **di**

devyce	device *[thing]
	devise[2] *[invent]
dew *[drops]	do *[get done]+
	due *[owing, expected]+
	Jew *[person of Jewish ethnicity]+
dewel	dual *[two]+
	duel[3] *[fight]
dewet	duet
dewn	dune *[sand hill]

> Unable to find your word under **dew**?
> Look under **du**

dexterity	
dexterous *[skillful] ~ly	
	dextrose *[sugar]
dextrin	
dextrose *[sugar]	dexterous *[skillful]+
dezign	design[1]
diabetes	@diabetic
diabolic ~al ~ally	
diafanus	diaphanous
diafram	diaphragm
diagnose[2]	
diagnosis	@diagnoses
diagnostic ~ally ~ian ~s	
diagonal ~ly	

Key to Suffixes and Compounds

These rules are explained on pages vii to ix.

1 Keep the word the same before adding **ed, er, est, ing**
e.g. cool[1] → cooled, cooler, coolest, cooling

2 Take off final **e** before adding **ed, er, est, ing**
e.g. fine[2] → fined, finer, finest, fining

3 Double final consonant before adding **ed, er, est, ing**
e.g. thin[3] → thinned, thinner, thinnest, thinning

4 Change final **y** to **i** before adding **ed, er, es, est, ly, ness**
e.g. tidy[4] → tidied, tidier, tidies, tidiest, tidily, tidiness
Keep final **y** before adding **ing** e.g. tidying

5 Add **es** instead of **s** to the end of the word
e.g. bunch[5] → bunches

6 Change final **f** to **ve** before adding **s**
e.g. calf[6] → calves

diagram ~matic ~matically
dial[1] ~| direct
dialect
dialing ~| code ~| tone
dialog
dial-up ~| connection
dialysis
diameter
diametrically ~| opposed
diamond ~| jubilee ~| ring
diaphanous
diaphragm
diar — dire *[bad][+] / dear *[loved][+] / deer *[animal][+]
diarrhea
diary[4] *[journal] — dairy[4] *[milk][+]
diatribe
dibate — debate[2+]
dibree — debris
dice[2] *[for playing]
— dies *[stop living]
diceive — deceive[2]
dicent — decent *[good][+] / descent *[down] / dissent[1] *[argue]
dicerne — discern[1+]
dichotomy[4]
diciduous — deciduous[+]
dicipel — disciple
dicipline — discipline[2+]
dickshin — diction
dickshinery — dictionary[4]
dicktaiter — dictator[+]
dicktate — dictate[2+]
dicktem — dictum
dicree — decree *[order][+]
dicshun — diction
dicshunry — dictionary[4]
dictaphone
dictate[2] — @dictation
dictator ~ial ~ship
diction
dictionary[4]
dictum

did *[past of do] — died *[past of die] / dyed *[changed color]
didactic ~ally
diddle[2]
didgeridoo
didn't [did not]
diduct — deduct[1+]
die *[death, dice] ~| away ~| down ~-hard ~| off ~| out
— dye *[change color][+]
— @dying
died *[past of die] — did *[past of do] / dyed *[changed color]
dieing — dyeing *[to change color] / dying *[about to die]
diek — dyke
dielate — dilate[2+]
dielect — dialect
dienamic — dynamic[+]
dier — dire *[bad][+] / dear *[loved][+] / deer *[animal][+]
diernal — diurnal[+]
diesel
diet[1] ~ary ~ician
dietary ~| fiber
dietetic ~s
diety — deity[4]
difacto — de facto

> Unable to find your word under **di**?
> Look under **de**

difamatry — defamatory
difase — deface[2] *[damage][+] / dephase[2] *[waves]
diference — difference *[unlike]
diferentiate — differentiate[2+]
difewse — defuse[2] *[calm][+] / diffuse[2] *[spread][+]
differ[1] *[disagree] — defer[3] *[put off]
difference *[unlike]
— deference *[submission]
different ~ly

differential *[difference] ~| tariffs
  deferential *[submitting]$^{+}$
differentiate^{2} — **@differentiation**
difficult — **@difficulty**^{4}
diffidence — **@diffident**
diffurenshal — **deferential** *[submitting]$^{+}$
  differential *[difference]$^{+}$
diffurenshiate — **differentiate**$^{2+}$
diffuse^{2} *[spread] — **@diffusion**
  defuse^{2} *[calm]$^{+}$
difine — **define**^{2} *[explain]$^{+}$
difishincie — **deficiency**^{4}
difrens — **difference** *[unlike]
difunct — **defunct**
difurunce — **difference** *[unlike]
difuse — **defuse**^{2} *[calm]$^{+}$
  diffuse^{2} *[spread]$^{+}$
dify — **defy**^{4} *[oppose]
  deify^{4} *[worship]
dig^{3} ~| in ~| out ~| up
  @dug
digenerasy — **degeneracy**
digenerate — **degenerate**$^{2+}$
digerati
digest^{1} ~ible ~ion ~ive
digestien — **digestion**
digit ~alis ~ally
digital ~| camera ~| cash ~| certificate ~| computer ~| data ~| library^{4} ~| object ~| signature ~| stream ~| wallet

> Unable to find your word under **digital**?
> Take off **digital** and look again

digitization
dignify^{4}
dignitary^{4} *[important person]
dignity^{4} *[importance]
digrade — **degrade**$^{2+}$

> Unable to find your word under **di**?
> Look under **de**

digree — **degree** *[amount, study]
digress^{5} ~ion

diing — **dyeing** *[to change color]
  dying *[about to die]
dijeradoo — **didgeridoo**
dijeratti — **digerati**

> Unable to find your word under **dij**?
> Look under **dig**

dike *[canal, dam]
  dyke *[lesbian]
dilait — **dilate**$^{2+}$
dilapidated — **@dilapidation**
dilate^{2} — **@dilation**
dilay — **delay**^{1}
dilect — **dialect**
dileete — **delete**$^{2+}$
dilemma
dilete — **delete**$^{2+}$
dilettante
dilewd — **delude**$^{2+}$
dilewte — **dilute**$^{2+}$
dilicious — **delicious**$^{+}$
diligence — **@diligent**
  @diligently
diling — **dialing**$^{+}$
dilinquent — **delinquent**$^{+}$
dilishus — **delicious**$^{+}$
dilude — **delude**$^{2+}$
dilute^{2} — **@dilution**
dim^{3} *[not bright] ~ly ~ness ~| sum ~-wit
  dime *[money]
dimand — **demand**$^{1+}$
dime *[money] — **dim**^{3} *[not bright]$^{+}$
dimensha — **dementia**
dimension
dimentid — **demented**$^{+}$
dimentor — **dementor**
diminish^{1} ~ing returns
diminution
diminutive
dimise — **demise**
dimmer *[light]
dimple^{2}

Key to Suffixes and Compounds

These rules are explained on pages vii to ix.

1 Keep the word the same before adding **ed, er, est, ing**
e.g. cool^{1} → cooled, cooler, coolest, cooling
2 Take off final **e** before adding **ed, er, est, ing**
e.g. fine^{2} → fined, finer, finest, fining
3 Double final consonant before adding **ed, er, est, ing**
e.g. thin^{3} → thinned, thinner, thinnest, thinning
4 Change final **y** to **i** before adding **ed, er, es, est, ly, ness**
e.g. tidy^{4} → tidied, tidier, tidies, tidiest, tidily, tidiness
Keep final **y** before adding **ing** e.g. tidying
5 Add **es** instead of **s** to the end of the word
e.g. bunch^{5} → bunches
6 Change final **f** to **ve** before adding **s**
e.g. calf^{6} → calves

dimur demur^{3} *[refuse]
demure *[shy]$^{+}$
dimmer *[light]
dinamic dynamic^{+}
dinamoe dynamo
dinasty dynasty^{4+}
dine^{2} *[eat] din *[noise]
dyne *[unit of force]
diner *[one who dines]
dinner *[meal]$^{+}$
dinesore dinosaur
ding ~-dong
dinghy^{4} *[boat] dingy^{4} *[shabby]
dingo^{5}
dingy^{4} *[shabby] dinghy^{4} *[boat]
dinial denial
dining ~| car ~| room ~| table
dinner *[meal] ~| jacket ~| table ~time
diner *[one who dines]
dinnir dinner *[meal]$^{+}$
dinosaur
diocese @diocesan
diode
diodorant deodorant
diosees diocese^{+}
dioxide
dioxin
dip^{3} ~stick
dipart depart^{1+}
diparture departure
diphtheria
diphthong
dipict depict^{1+}
diplete deplete^{2+}
diploema diploma
diploie deploy^{1+}
diploma
diplomacy^{4}
diplomat ~ic ~ically
diplor deplore^{2+}
diplore deplore^{2+}
diploy deploy^{1+}
dipozit deposit^{1+}
dipraved depraved^{+}
dipreshiate depreciate^{2} *[value]$^{+}$

diptheria diphtheria
dipthong diphthong
dirby derby^{4}
dire *[bad] ~| need
dear *[loved]$^{+}$
deer *[animal]$^{+}$
direct^{1} ~ly ~| advertising ~| broadcast ~| connection ~| debit ~| deposit ~| mail ~| marketing ~| proportion

> Unable to find your word under **direct**?
> Take off **direct** and look again

direction @directive
director ~ate ~ship
directory^{4} ~| assistance
dirijun derision
dirmatitis dermatitis
dirt ~-cheap ~| road ~| track
dirth dearth *[not enough]
dirty^{4}
dirvish dervish

> Unable to find your word under **dir**?
> Look under **der**

disabil disable^{2+}
disability^{4} ~| insurance ~| retirement
disable^{2} ~ment
disabuse^{2}
disadvantage
disaffected @disaffection
disagree ~able ~d ~ably ~ment
disallow^{1}
disapere disappear^{1+}
disaplin discipline^{2+}
disappear^{1} ~ance
disappoint^{1} ~ment
disapproval
disapprove^{2} *[bad]
disprove^{2} *[false]
disarm^{1} ~ament
disassemble^{2} *[take apart]
dissemble^{2} *[conceal]$^{+}$
disassociate^{2} @disassociation

Key to Spelling Rules

Red words are wrong. **Black** words are correct.

- **~** Add the suffix or word directly to the main word, without a space or hyphen
  e.g. ash ~en ~tray → ashen ashtray
- **~-** Add a hyphen to the main word before adding the next word
  e.g. blow ~-dry → blow-dry
- **~|** Leave a space between the main word and the next word
  e.g. decimal ~| place → decimal place
- **+** By finding this word in its correct alphabetical order, you can find related words
  e.g. abowt about^{+} → about-face
- **★** Draws attention to words that may be confused
- **™** Means the word is a trademark
- **@** Signifies the word is derived from the main word

disaster @disastrous
@disastrously
disavow[1] ~al
disband[1] ~ment
disbar[3]
disbelief
disbelieve[2]
disburse[2] *[pay out]
@disbursal
disperse[2] *[scatter]+
disc *[compact, music] ~| jockey
disk *[magnetic, spine]+
discard[1]
discend descend[1+]
discendent descendant
discern[1] ~ible ~ment
discharge[2]
disciple
discipline[2] @disciplinary
disclaim[1] ~er
disclose[2] @disclosure
disco[5] ~| dance[2] ~theque
discolor[1] @discoloration
discomfort
disconcerted @disconcerting
disconnect[1]
disconsolate ~ly
discontent ~ed
discontinue[2]
discord
discoteck discotheque
discount[1] ~| card ~| price ~| rate ~| store
discourage[2] ~ment
discourse[2]
discourteous ~ly ~ness
discourtesy[4]
discover[1] @discovery[4]
discredit[1] ~able
discreet *[careful] ~ly
discrete *[separate]
discrepancy[4]
discrete *[separate]
discreet *[careful]+
discretion ~ary

discribe describe[2+]
discriminate[2] @discrimination
discripshun description+
discumfort discomfort
discurige discourage[2+]
discursion @discursive
discurtesy discourtesy[4]
discus[5] *[sport]
discuss[5] *[debate] ~es ~ion
disdain[1] ~ful ~fully
disease
diseased *[ill] deceased *[dead]
disect dissect[1+]
disembark[1] ~ation
disembody[4] @disembodiment
disembowel[3]
disenchanted @disenchantment
disendent descendant
disenfranchise[2] ~ment
disengage[2] ~ment
disenshun dissension
disent decent *[good]+
descent *[down]
dissent[1] *[argue]
disentangle[2] ~ment
disepshun deception
diseptiv deceptive+
disert desert[1] *[leave, sand]+
dessert *[food]
disertashin dissertation
disertation dissertation
diserve deserve[2+]
diseve deceive[2]
disfavor[1]
disfigure[2] ~ment
disgorge[2]
disgrace[2] ~ful ~fully
disgruntled
disguise[2]
disgust[1]
dish[5] ~cloth ~pan ~washer ~water
disharmony
dishearten[1]
disheveled
dishonest ~ly @dishonesty

Key to Suffixes and Compounds

These rules are explained on pages vii to ix.

1 Keep the word the same before adding **ed, er, est, ing**
e.g. cool[1] → cooled, cooler, coolest, cooling
2 Take off final **e** before adding **ed, er, est, ing**
e.g. fine[2] → fined, finer, finest, fining
3 Double final consonant before adding **ed, er, est, ing**
e.g. thin[3] → thinned, thinner, thinnest, thinning
4 Change final **y** to **i** before adding **ed, er, es, est, ly, ness**
e.g. tidy[4] → tidied, tidier, tidies, tidiest, tidily, tidiness
Keep final **y** before adding **ing** e.g. tidying
5 Add **es** instead of **s** to the end of the word
e.g. bunch[5] → bunches
6 Change final **f** to **ve** before adding **s**
e.g. calf[6] → calves

dishonor[1] ~able ~ably
diside decide[2+]
disiduus deciduous+
disign design[1+]

Unable to find your word under **di**?
Look under **de**

disillusion[1] ~ment
disincentive
disinclined
disine design[1+]
disinfect[1] ~ant
disinflation
disingenuous ~ly ~ness
disinherit[1] ~ance
disintegrate[2] @disintegration
disinter[3] ~ment
disinterest ~ed
disinvestment
disiphir decipher[1+]
disirabul desirable+
disire desire[2+]
disirve deserve[2+]
disist desist[1]
disjointed
disk *[magnetic, spine] ~| drive
disc *[compact, music]+
diskerage discourage[2+]
diskette
diskomfort discomfort
diskreet discreet *[careful]+
discrete *[separate]
dislexsia dyslexia+
dislike[2]
dislocate[2] @dislocation
dislodge[2]
disloyal ~ty[4]
dismal ~ly
dismantle[2]
dismay[1]
dismember[1] ~ment
dismiss[5] ~al
dismount[1]
Disney ~land

disobedience @disobedient
disobey[1]
disorder[1] ~ly
disorganize[2] @disorganization
disorient[2] @disorientation
disown[1]
dispair despair[1+]
disparage[2] ~ment
disparate *[distinct] ~ly
desperate *[need]+
dispare despair[1+]
disparity[4]
dispassionate ~ly
dispatch[5] ~es
dispear despair[1+]
dispel[3]
dispensary[4]
dispense[2] @dispensation
disperse[2] *[scatter]
@dispersal
disburse[2] *[pay out]+
dispiese despise[2]
dispikabul despicable+
dispirited @dispiriting
dispise despise[2]
dispite despite
displace[2] ~ment
display[1] ~| ad ~| advertising ~| case
displease[2] @displeasure
dispondunt despondent
dispose[2] @disposable
@disposal
disposition
dispossess[5] ~ion
disproportion ~ate ~ately
disprove[2] *[false] disapprove[2] *[bad]
dispurse disburse[2] *[pay out]+
disperse[2] *[scatter]+
dispute[2]
disqualify[4] @disqualification
disque disk *[magnetic, spine]+
disc *[compact, music]+
disquiet[1]
disregard[1]
disrepair

Key to Spelling Rules

Red words are wrong. **Black** words are correct.

~ Add the suffix or word directly to the main word, without a space or hyphen
e.g. ash ~en ~tray → ashen ashtray

~- Add a hyphen to the main word before adding the next word
e.g. blow ~-dry → blow-dry

~| Leave a space between the main word and the next word
e.g. decimal ~| place → decimal place

+ By finding this word in its correct alphabetical order, you can find related words
e.g. abowt about+ → about-face

★ Draws attention to words that may be confused

™ Means the word is a trademark

@ Signifies the word is derived from the main word

disreputable @disreputably
disrepute
disrespect ~ful ~fully
disrobe[2]
disrupt[1] ~ion
disruptive ~ly ~ness
dissability disability[4+]
dissapear disappear[1+]
dissapoint disappoint[1+]
dissatisfy[4] @dissatisfaction
disscurrage discourage[2+]
dissect[1] @dissection
dissemble[2] *[conceal]
@dissemblance
disassemble[2] *[take apart]
disseminate[2] @dissemination
dissendent descend[1+]
dissenshin dissension
dissension
dissent[1] *[argue] decent *[good]+
descent *[down]
dissern discern[1+]
dissert desert[1] *[leave, sand]+
dessert *[food]
dissertation
disservice
dissident @dissidence
dissimilar ~ity
dissipate[2] @dissipation
dissiplin discipline[2+]
dissolute ~ly @dissolution
dissolve[2]
dissonance @dissonant
dissproov disapprove[2] *[bad]
disprove[2] *[false]
dissuade[2] @dissuasion
@dissuasive
dissypul disciple
distal *[further outward]
distill *[purify]+
distance ~| time graph
distant ~ly
distaste ~ful ~fully
distemper ~ed

distend[1]
distill *[purify] ~ation
distal *[further outward]
distillery[4]
distinct ~ion
distinctive ~ly ~ness
distinguish[1] ~able
distort[1] ~ion
distract[1] ~edly ~ion
distrafy dystrophy
distraught
distress[5] ~ingly
distribushun distribution+
distribute[2] @distributor
distributed ~| computing environment ~| database ~| expenses ~| object computing

> Unable to find your word under **distributed**? Take off **distributed** and look again

distribution ~| chain ~| channel ~| cost ~| network
district ~| attorney ~| court
District of Colombia
distrofee dystrophy
distrot distraught
distroy destroy[1]
distruction destruction+
distrust[1] ~ful
disturb[1] ~ance
disunited @disunity
disurtashun dissertation
disused
diswade dissuade[2+]
disypher decipher[1+]
ditach detach[1+]
ditain detain+
ditch[5]
ditect detect[1+]
dither[1]
ditto
ditty[4]
ditur deter[3] *[stop]+
detour *[go around]

Key to Suffixes and Compounds

These rules are explained on pages vii to ix.

1 Keep the word the same before adding **ed, er, est, ing**
e.g. cool[1] → cooled, cooler, coolest, cooling
2 Take off final **e** before adding **ed, er, est, ing**
e.g. fine[2] → fined, finer, finest, fining
3 Double final consonant before adding **ed, er, est, ing**
e.g. thin[3] → thinned, thinner, thinnest, thinning
4 Change final **y** to **i** before adding **ed, er, es, est, ly, ness**
e.g. tidy[4] → tidied, tidier, tidies, tidiest, tidily, tidiness
Keep final **y** before adding **ing** e.g. tidying
5 Add **es** instead of **s** to the end of the word
e.g. bunch[5] → bunches
6 Change final **f** to **ve** before adding **s**
e.g. calf[6] → calves

diuretic

diurnal ~ly

diva

divalue devalue[2]

divan

dive[2] ~-bomb ~-bomber

divelop develop[1+]

diverge[2]

divergence @divergent

divers *[into water]

diverse *[very different] ~ly

diversify[4] @diversification

diversion ~ary

diversity[4]

divert[1]

divest[1] ~iture

divians deviance+

diviate deviate[2+]

divice device *[thing]

divide[2]

dividend ~| cover ~| warrant ~| yield

dividing ~| line

divine[2] ~ly @divination

diving ~| board ~| bell

divinity[4]

divious devious+

divirge diverge[2]

divisible

division

divisive ~ly ~ness

diviss device *[thing]
devise[2] *[invent]

> Unable to find your word under **di**?
> Look under **de**

divorce[2] *[end of marriage] divorcé *[male]

divulge[2] @divulgence

divurge diverge[2]

divurgence divergence+

divurs divers *[into water]
diverse *[very different]+

divurt divert[1]

dizease disease

dizzy[4]

DJ [disk jockey]

DNA ~| profiling ~| testing

do *[get done, musical note] ~able ~ing
doe *[deer]
doer *[gets things done]
d'oh *[silly]
dough *[bread]+
dour *[gloomy]

Doberman ~| pinscher

dock[1] ~lands ~side ~yard

docket[1]

docking ~| station

dockit docket[1]

dockter doctor[1+]

docterin doctrine+

doctor[1] ~al ~ate ~'s certificate
@Dr. [title]

doctrine @doctrinaire

docudrama

document[1] ~ation ~| type

documentary[4] ~| evidence ~| proof

doddering @dodderer
@doddery

dodge[2] dodgy[4] *[problematic]
doge *[ruler of Venice]
doggy[4] *[dog]+

dodo

doe *[deer] do *[get done]+
d'oh *[silly]
dough *[bread]+

doer *[gets things done]
door *[entrance]+

does *[acts, female deer / rabbits]
dose[2] *[of medicine]+

doesn't [does not]

doff[1]

dog[3] ~| paddle ~trot ~watch

doge *[ruler of Venice]
dodge[2+]
doggy[4] *[dog]+
dogie *[calf]

doggy[4] *[dog] ~| paddle[2]
dodgy[4] *[problematic]
doge *[ruler of Venice]
dogie *[calf]

Key to Spelling Rules

Red words are wrong. **Black** words are correct.

~ Add the suffix or word directly to the main word, without a space or hyphen
e.g. ash ~en ~tray → ashen ashtray

~- Add a hyphen to the main word before adding the next word
e.g. blow ~-dry → blow-dry

~| Leave a space between the main word and the next word
e.g. decimal ~| place → decimal place

\+ By finding this word in its correct alphabetical order, you can find related words
e.g. abowt about+ → about-face

★ Draws attention to words that may be confused

™ Means the word is a trademark

@ Signifies the word is derived from the main word

dogie *[calf] dodgy[4] *[problematic]
doge *[ruler of Venice]
doggy[4] *[dog][+]
dogma ~tic ~tically ~tism
d'oh *[silly] do *[get done, musical note][+]
doe *[deer]
dough *[bread][+]
doj dodge[2+]
doge *[ruler of Venice]
dok dock[1+]
doket docket[1]
doksend dachshund
dokter doctor[1+]
doktrine doctrine[+]
doldrums
dole[2] *[provide] ~ful
doll *[toy][+]
dolfin dolphin[+]
doll *[toy] ~'s house
@dolly[4]
dull[1] *[tedious, not bright][+]
dollar ~| bill ~| diplomacy ~| sign
dollop
dolomite
dolphin ~arium
dolya dahlia
domain *[realm] ~| name
demesne *[property]
Domain Name System [DNS]
dome *[shape] ~ed
doom[1] *[destruction]
domestic ~ally ~ity ~| arts ~| market ~| production ~| rights ~| sales ~| science ~| syndication ~| trade ~| violence

> Unable to find your word under **domestic**?
> Take off **domestic** and look again

domesticate[2]
domicile ~d
dominance @dominant
dominate[2] @domination
domineer[1]
dominion
domino[5] ~| effect
dominyin dominion
don[3] *[put on] done *[finished]
dun *[color]
dune *[sand][+]
donate[2] @donation
done *[finished] don[3] *[put on]
dun *[color]
dune *[sand][+]
donkey ~| derby ~work
donor
doobius dubious[+]
dooche douche[2]
doodle[2]
doom[1] *[destruction]
dome *[shape][+]
doon dune *[sand][+]
door *[entrance] ~bell ~knob ~knocker ~step ~-to-door ~way
doer *[gets things done]
dope[2] @dopey
Doppler ~| effect ~| radar
dormant
dormitory[4]
dormitrey dormitory[4]
dormouse @dormice
dorsal
DOS *[program] doss *[cheap sleeping place]
dose[2] *[of medicine]
@dosage
doze[2] *[sleep][+]
dossier
dot[3] ~.com ~ty[4]
double[2] ~| agent ~| back ~-barrelled ~| bass ~-blind ~-breasted ~-check ~| chin ~-click[1] ~-cross[1] ~-cursed ~-dip[3] ~-decker ~-edged ~| glazing ~-jointed ~-park[1] ~| quick ~| standard ~take ~| talk ~think ~| time

> Unable to find your word under **double**?
> Take off **double** and look again

Key to Suffixes and Compounds

These rules are explained on pages vii to ix.

1 Keep the word the same before adding **ed, er, est, ing**
e.g. cool[1] → cooled, cooler, coolest, cooling
2 Take off final **e** before adding **ed, er, est, ing**
e.g. fine[2] → fined, finer, finest, fining
3 Double final consonant before adding **ed, er, est, ing**
e.g. thin[3] → thinned, thinner, thinnest, thinning
4 Change final **y** to **i** before adding **ed, er, es, est, ly, ness**
e.g. tidy[4] → tidied, tidier, tidies, tidiest, tidily, tidiness
Keep final **y** before adding **ing** e.g. tidying
5 Add **es** instead of **s** to the end of the word
e.g. bunch[5] → bunches
6 Change final **f** to **ve** before adding **s**
e.g. calf[6] → calves

doubly
doubt[1] ~ful ~fully ~less ~lessly
douche[2] *[hygiene]
deuce[2] *[card, carburetor]
dough *[bread] ~y ~nut
do *[get done, musical note]+
doe *[deer]
d'oh *[silly]
dour *[gloomy] — doer *[gets things done]
dourey — dowry[4]
douse[2] *[drench] — dowse[2] *[search]
dove ~cote[2] ~tail[1]
Dow ~| Jones Average
dowager
dowdy[4]
down[1] ~beat ~cast ~fall ~grade ~-hearted ~hill ~| payment ~play[1] ~pour ~size[2] ~stairs ~stream ~time ~-to-earth ~trend ~trodden ~turn ~wards ~wind

> Unable to find your word under **down**?
> Take off **down** and look again

Down syndrome
dowry[4]
dowse[2] *[search] — douse[2] *[drench]
doze[2] *[sleep] — @dozy[4]
dose[2] *[of medicine]+
dozen
drab ~ly ~ness
draft[1]
draftsman ~ship
drafty
drag[3]
dragin — dragon+
dragon *[monster] ~fly
dragoon[1] *[soldier]
drain[1] *[liquid] ~age ~pipe
drake
dral — drawl[1] *[speech]
dram
drama ~tist
dramatic ~ally

dramatize[2] — @dramatization
dran — drain[1] *[liquid]
drawn *[stretched]+
drank *[had drunk]
drunk *[be drunk]+
drape[2]
drapery[4]
drastic ~ally
drau — draw+
draul — drawl[1]
draun — drawn+
draw *[pull, sketch] ~back ~bridge ~-up
drawer *[furniture] ~s *[underwear]
drawing ~| paper ~| pin ~| room
drawl[1] *[speech] — droll *[humorous]
drawn *[stretched] ~-out
dray *[cart] — drey *[nest]
dread[1] ~ful ~fully ~locks ~nought
dream[1] — @dreamt
@dreamy[4]
dreary[4]
dred — dread[1+]
dredge[2] ~| up
dreem — dream[1+]
dregs
dreidel [also spelled dreidl]
dreive — drive[2+]
drej — dredge[2+]
dreme — dream[1+]
drench[5]
dresaj — dressage
dress[5] *[clothing] ~es ~maker ~| rehearsal ~| shirt ~y[4]
duress *[hardship]
dressage
dressing ~-down ~| gown ~| room
dressy[4]
drew
drewl — drool[1]
drey *[nest] — dray *[cart]
dribble[2]
dribs and drabs
dride — deride[2] *[make fun of]+
dried *[made dry]
drie — dry[4+]

Key to Spelling Rules

Red words are wrong. **Black** words are correct.

~ Add the suffix or word directly to the main word, without a space or hyphen
e.g. ash ~en ~tray → ashen ashtray

~- Add a hyphen to the main word before adding the next word
e.g. blow ~-dry → blow-dry

~| Leave a space between the main word and the next word
e.g. decimal ~| place → decimal place

\+ By finding this word in its correct alphabetical order, you can find related words
e.g. abowt about+ → about-face

★ Draws attention to words that may be confused

™ Means the word is a trademark

@ Signifies the word is derived from the main word

dried *[made dry] deride[2] *[make fun of]+
drier *[less wet] dryer *[machine]
drift[1] ~| net ~wood
drill[1] ~| down ~| sergeant ~| team
drily
drink ~able
drinking ~| water
drip[3] ~-dry ~-feed ~-feeding
drive[2] ~-by ~-in @driven
drivel
driver ~'s education ~'s seat ~| discount
drizzle[2]
droa droit+
droit ~| du seigneur ~| moral
droll *[humorous] drawl[1] *[speech]
dromedary[4]
dromidery dromedary[4]
drone[2]
drool[1]
droop[1] *[hang down]
drop[3] *[let fall]+
drop[3] *[let fall] ~| back ~| by ~-down menu ~| in ~-kick[1] ~let ~-off ~| out *[withdraw] ~out *[one who drops out] ~| shot ~| zone

> Unable to find your word under **drop**?
> Take off **drop** and look again

drore draw *[pull, sketch]+
drawer *[furniture]+
drorl drawl[1] *[speech]
drorn drawn+
drought
droup drop[3] *[let fall]+
droop[1] *[hang down]
drowse[2] @drowsy[4]
drowt drought
drubbing
drudge[2] *[boring work] ~ry
drug[3] *[substance, put to sleep]+
drue drew

drug[3] *[substance, put to sleep] ~| addict ~| delivery ~store
drudge[2] *[boring work]+

> Unable to find your word under **drug**?
> Take off **drug** and look again

Druid
drule drool[1]
drum[3] ~stick ~| major
drummedary dromedary[4]
drunk *[be drunk] ~ard ~| driving ~en ~enly ~enness
drank *[had drunk]
drupe droop[1] *[hang down]
drop[3] *[let fall]+
dry[4] ~ness ~-clean ~| run
dryde deride[2] *[make fun of]+
dried *[made dry]
dryer *[machine] drier *[less wet]
dryve drive[2+]
du dew *[drops]
do *[get done]+
due *[owed]+
dual *[two] ~ism ~ity
duel[3] *[fight]
jewel *[gem]+
dub[3]
dubble double[2+]
dubious ~ly ~ness
duche douche[2]
duchy[4] @duchess[5]
duck[1] *[bird, avoid contact] ~ling
duke *[royalty]
duct *[tube] ~ile ~| tape
ducked *[bent down]
dud *[not working]
dude *[a man]
due *[owed] ~| process
dew *[drops]
do *[get done]+
Jew *[person of Jewish ethnicity]+
duel[3] *[fight] dual *[two]+
jewel *[gem]

KEY TO SUFFIXES AND COMPOUNDS

These rules are explained on pages vii to ix.

1 Keep the word the same before adding **ed, er, est, ing**
e.g. cool[1] → cooled, cooler, coolest, cooling
2 Take off final **e** before adding **ed, er, est, ing**
e.g. fine[2] → fined, finer, finest, fining
3 Double final consonant before adding **ed, er, est, ing**
e.g. thin[3] → thinned, thinner, thinnest, thinning
4 Change final **y** to **i** before adding **ed, er, es, est, ly, ness**
e.g. tidy[4] → tidied, tidier, tidies, tidiest, tidily, tidiness
Keep final **y** before adding **ing** e.g. tidying
5 Add **es** instead of **s** to the end of the word
e.g. bunch[5] → bunches
6 Change final **f** to **ve** before adding **s**
e.g. calf[6] → calves

dues *[entry cost] does *[gets done]+
Jews *[Jewish people]+
duet
duffel ~| bag
dug ~out
dukbox jukebox
duke *[royalty] duck[1] *[bird, avoid contact]+
dukt ducked *[bent down]
duct *[tube]+
dulcet
dull[1] *[tedious, not bright] ~ish
doll *[toy]+
duel[3] *[fight]
jewel *[gem]+
dully *[not bright] duly *[due]
July *[month]
dulset dulcet
duly *[due] dully *[not bright]
July *[month]
dum dumb[1]+
dumb[1] ~ly ~ness ~bell ~| down ~found ~struck ~waiter
dummy[4]
dump[1] ~ster ~y
dumpling
dun *[color] done *[finished]
dune *[sand hill]
dunce
dune *[sand hill] ~| buggy[4]
dun *[color]
done *[finished]
dung
dungarees
dungeon
dunse dunce
duodenal
dupe[2]
duplex
duplicate[2] @duplication
duplicity @duplicitous
durable @durability
durashin duration
duration
duresce duress *[hardship]
dress[1] *[clothing]+
duribil durable+
duride deride[2] *[make fun of]+
durishun derision

Unable to find your word under **dur**?
Look under **der** or **dir**

durmatology dermatology+
durth dearth *[not enough]
dusc dusk+
dusk ~y[4]
dust[1] ~| bowl ~| bunny ~| devil ~| jacket ~pan
dust ~| storm ~-up ~y[4]
dutiful ~ly
duty[4] ~-bound ~-free ~-paid
duv dove+
duvay duvet
duvet
duwel dual *[two]+
duel[3] *[fight]
duz does *[gets done]+
dues *[entry cost]
Jews *[Jewish people]
duzen dozen
DVD ~| player
dwarf[1] ~| star
dwell[1] *[live in] @dwelt
duel[3] *[fight]
dwharf dwarf[1]+
dwindle[2]
dworf dwarf[1]+
dyaretic diuretic
dyaria diarrhea
dyatary dietary+
dyatetic dietetic+
dye *[change color] ~ing
die *[death, dice]+
dyed *[changed color]
died *[past of die]
dyeing *[changing color]
dying *[passing away]
dyening dining+

Key to Spelling Rules

Red words are wrong. **Black** words are correct.

~ Add the suffix or word directly to the main word, without a space or hyphen
e.g. ash ~en ~tray → ashen ashtray

~- Add a hyphen to the main word before adding the next word
e.g. blow ~-dry → blow-dry

~| Leave a space between the main word and the next word
e.g. decimal ~| place → decimal place

+ By finding this word in its correct alphabetical order, you can find related words
e.g. abowt about+ → about-face

* Draws attention to words that may be confused

TM Means the word is a trademark

@ Signifies the word is derived from the main word

dyernal diurnal+
dying *[about to die]
dyjerati digerati
dyke *[lesbian] dike *[canal, dam]
dylait dilate[2+]
dylate dilate[2+]
dylute dilute[2+]
dynamic ~ally @dynamism
dynamite[2]
dynamo
dynasty[4] @dynastic
dyne *[unit of force]
din *[noise]
dine[2] *[eat]
dyner diner *[one who dines]
dinner *[meal]+
dyning dining+
dynosaur dinosaur
dyre dire *[bad]+
dear *[loved]+
deer *[animal]+

dysability disability[4+]
dysabul disable[2+]
dysagrie disagree+
dysentery
dysfunction ~al
dysifer decipher[1+]
dysintrie dysentery
dysk disk *[magnetic, spine]+
disc *[compact, music]+

Unable to find your word under **dys**?
Look under **dis**

dyslexia @dyslexic
dystrophy
dyurnil diurnal+

Unable to find your word under **dy**?
Look under **di**

E

e ~-book ~-business ~-cash ~-commerce ~-mail ~-tailing
each *[per piece] ~| other
etch[5] *[draw]
itch[5] *[scratch]+
eager ~ly ~ness ~| beaver
eagle ~-eyed @eaglet
eal eel
ear *[body part] ~ache ~drum ~lobe ~phone ~plug ~ring ~shot ~wig
ere *[before]

Unable to find your word under **ear**?
Take off **ear** and look again

eara era *[a time]

early[4] ~| bird ~| distribution ~| redemption ~| withdrawal
earmark[1]
earn[1] *[receive payment] ~-out ~-up
urn *[vase]
earnest ~ly ~ness
earnings
earth ~ly ~y ~bound ~ling ~-shaking ~-shattering ~worm
earthen ~ware
earthquake
eary eerie *[scary]+
Erie *[lake]+
ease[2] ~ment ~| of use
easel
east ~erly ~ern ~ward

Key to Suffixes and Compounds

These rules are explained on pages vii to ix.

1 Keep the word the same before adding **ed, er, est, ing**
e.g. cool[1] → cooled, cooler, coolest, cooling
2 Take off final **e** before adding **ed, er, est, ing**
e.g. fine[2] → fined, finer, finest, fining
3 Double final consonant before adding **ed, er, est, ing**
e.g. thin[3] → thinned, thinner, thinnest, thinning
4 Change final **y** to **i** before adding **ed, er, es, est, ly, ness**
e.g. tidy[4] → tidied, tidier, tidies, tidiest, tidily, tidiness
Keep final **y** before adding **ing** e.g. tidying
5 Add **es** instead of **s** to the end of the word
e.g. bunch[5] → bunches
6 Change final **f** to **ve** before adding **s**
e.g. calf[6] → calves

Easter *[Christian feast] ~| Bunny ~| egg ~| Sunday
ester *[chemical]
eastern ~er
Eastern ~| Hemisphere ~| Standard Time
easy[4] ~-care ~| chair ~-going ~| terms
eat *[food] ~able ~en ~ing
ate *[did eat food]
eating ~| disorder
eau ~| de cologne ~| de toilette
au *[French word]+
owe[2] *[be in debt]+
eave *[overhang] eve *[night before]
eaves ~drop[3] eves *[evening]
eays ease[2+]
ebany ebony+
ebb[1]
ebony @ebonite
eboolyent ebullient+
ebullient @ebullience
eccentric ~ally ~ity
ecclesiastic ~al ~ally
ecconamise economize[2+]
ecconomic economic+

> Unable to find your word under **ecc**?
> Look under **ec**

ECG [electrocardiogram]
ech each *[every]+
etch[1] *[draw]
echelon
echo[5] ~es
ecksact exact[1+]
ecksagerate exaggerate[2+]
ecksamine examine[2]
ecksampul example
eckscite excite[2] *[very happy]+

> Unable to find your word under **ecks**?
> Look under **ex**

eclair
eclectic
eclesiastic ecclesiastic+
eclipse[2] *[of the sun]
@ecliptic
ellipse *[mathematical curve]+
eco ~climate ~-friendly ~system
E. coli
ecological ~ly
ecology @ecologist
economic ~al ~ally ~s ~| climate ~| cycle ~| development ~| exposure ~| growth ~| indicator ~| model ~| outlook ~| planning ~| policy ~| risk system ~| surplus ~| union

> Unable to find your word under **economic**?
> Take off **economic** and look again

economize[2] @economist
economy[4] ~| class ~| of scale
ecosystem
ecoterrorism @ecoterrorist
ecotourism @ecotourist
ecsama eczema
ecsentric eccentric+
ecstasy *[great happiness]
ecstasy™ *[drug]
ecstatic ~ally
ectopic ~| pregnancy
ectoplasm
ecumenical
eczema
edable edible+
edafiss edifice
edafy edify[4+]
edatoreal editorial+
eddy[4]
edebul edible+
edema
edge[2] ~| numbers ~ways
edgy[4]
edi eddy[4]
edible @edibility
edict
edifice
edifie edify[4+]

Key to Spelling Rules

Red words are wrong. **Black** words are correct.

~ Add the suffix or word directly to the main word, without a space or hyphen
e.g. ash ~en ~tray → ashen ashtray

~- Add a hyphen to the main word before adding the next word
e.g. blow ~-dry → blow-dry

~| Leave a space between the main word and the next word
e.g. decimal ~| place → decimal place

+ By finding this word in its correct alphabetical order, you can find related words
e.g. abowt about+ → about-face

★ Draws attention to words that may be confused

™ Means the word is a trademark

@ Signifies the word is derived from the main word

edifiss edifice
edify[4] @edification
edima edema
edit[1]
edition *[version] addition *[sum]+
editor ~ial
editorialize[2]
edj edge[2+]
educashin education+
educate[2] @educator
education ~al ~ally ~ist
edukayt educate[2+]
edy eddy[4]
edyt edit[1]
edytor editor+
eech each *[every]+
etch[5] *[draw]
eedict edict
eefishent efficient *[gets things done]+
eegar eager+
eek *[exclamation]
eke[2] *[earn with difficulty]+
eekanomic economic[1+]

Unable to find your word under **eek**?
Look under **ec**

eekoleye E. coli
eel
eeleet elite+
eer ear *[body part]+
ere *[before]
err[1] *[make a mistake]+
eerie *[scary] ~ly ~ness
Erie *[lake]+
eermark earmark[1]
eet eat[1] *[food]+
ate *[did eat]
eether ether *[air, liquid]+
eev eve
eeves eaves+

Unable to find your word under **ee**?
Look under **ea**

efacasy efficacy
eface efface[2+]
efajy effigy[4]
efarvess effervesce[2]
efect effect[1] *[a result, change]+
affect[1] *[feeling, emotion]+
efeet effete
efemeral ephemeral+
efeminate effeminate+
efert effort+

Unable to find your word under **ef**?
Look under **eff**

efface[2] ~ment
effagey effigy[4]
effect[1] *[a result, change] ~ive ~ively
affect[1] *[feeling, emotion]+
effective *[producing results]
~| communication ~| date
~| interest rate ~| spread
affective *[relating to feelings or emotions]+

Unable to find your word under **effective**?
Take off **effective** and look again

effeminate ~ly @effeminacy
effervesce[2]
effervescence @effervescent
effete
efficacious ~ly ~ness
efficacy
efficiency[4]
efficient *[gets things done] ~ly
~| diversification
officiant *[officiates]
effigy[4]
effikashus efficacious+
effluent *[liquid waste]
@effluence
affluent *[wealthy]
effort ~less ~lessly
effrontery[4]

Key to Suffixes and Compounds

These rules are explained on pages vii to ix.

1 Keep the word the same before adding **ed, er, est, ing**
e.g. cool[1] → cooled, cooler, coolest, cooling
2 Take off final **e** before adding **ed, er, est, ing**
e.g. fine[2] → fined, finer, finest, fining
3 Double final consonant before adding **ed, er, est, ing**
e.g. thin[3] → thinned, thinner, thinnest, thinning
4 Change final **y** to **i** before adding **ed, er, es, est, ly, ness**
e.g. tidy[4] → tidied, tidier, tidies, tidiest, tidily, tidiness
Keep final **y** before adding **ing** e.g. tidying
5 Add **es** instead of **s** to the end of the word
e.g. bunch[5] → bunches
6 Change final **f** to **ve** before adding **s**
e.g. calf[6] → calves

effusive ~ly	
efishent	efficient *[gets things done]+
efluent	effluent *[liquid waste]+
	affluent *[wealthy]
efort	effort+
eg	e.g. *[for example]
	egg1+
e.g. *[for example]	
egalitarian ~ism	
ege	edge2+
egect	eject1+
egel	eagle+
eger	eager+
egg1 ~cup ~head ~nog ~| on ~plant ~| roll ~shell ~| timer ~| white ~| yolk	

Unable to find your word under **egg**?
Take off **egg** and look again

eggzima	eczema
egiptology	Egyptology+
egnore	ignore2+
ego ~ism ~tism ~| trip	
egocentric ~ity	
egoist ~ic ~ical ~ically	
egomania ~c	
egosentric	egocentric+
egret	
egsact	exact1+
egsam	exam+
egsema	eczema

Unable to find your word under **egs**?
Look under **ex**

egul	eagle+
egy	edgy4
Egyptology	@Egyptologist
eiderdown	
Eiffel *[Tower]	eyeful *[amount, in your eye]
eight *[number] ~| ball ~een ~eenth	
	ate *[food]
eighty4	@eightieth
eirie	eerie *[scary]+
	Erie *[lake]+
either *[or]	ether *[air, liquid]+
ejaculate2	@ejaculation
eject1 ~ion ~or	
eji	edgy4
ejis	aegis
ejucayt	educate2+
ekcentrik	eccentric+
eke2 *[earn with difficulty] ~| out	
	eek *[exclamation]
eklektik	eclectic
eklipse	eclipse2 *[of the sun]+
eko	echo5+
ekology	ecology+

Unable to find your word under **ek**?
Look under **ec**

eksact	exact1+
eksampul	example
eksetra	et cetera *[and other similar things]
eksorsize	exorcise2 *[remove evil]
	exercise2 *[physical activity]

Unable to find your word under **eks**?
Look under **ex**

ekwalize	equalize2
ekwity	equity4+

Unable to find your word under **ekw**?
Look under **equ**

ekzema	eczema
elaborate2 ~ly	@elaboration
elacution	elocution+
elajy	elegy4 *[poem]+
elament	element+
elamenterey	elementary *[basic]+
	alimentary *[nutrition]+
elapse2 *[pass] ~d time	
	ellipse *[mathematical curve]

KEY TO SPELLING RULES

Red words are wrong. **Black** words are correct.

~ Add the suffix or word directly to the main word, without a space or hyphen
e.g. ash ~en ~tray → ashen ashtray

~- Add a hyphen to the main word before adding the next word
e.g. blow ~-dry → blow-dry

~| Leave a space between the main word and the next word
e.g. decimal ~| place → decimal place

+ By finding this word in its correct alphabetical order, you can find related words
e.g. abowt about+ → about-face

★ Draws attention to words that may be confused

TM Means the word is a trademark

@ Signifies the word is derived from the main word

elaquense	eloquence+
elastic ~ity	
elated	@elation
elavate	elevate[2+]
elayted	elated+
elbow[1] ~| grease ~| room	
elc	elk
elder ~ly	@eldest
ele	eel
elecshin	election+
elect[1] ~ive ~or ~orate	
election ~eering	
Electoral ~| College	
electric ~al ~ally ~| chair ~| eye ~| generator	
electricity	@electrician
electrify[4]	@electrification
electrocardiogram	
electrocute[2]	@electrocution
electrode	
electrolysis	
electrolyte	@electrolytic
electromagnet ~ic ~ism	
electromotive	
electron	
electronic ~ally ~| banking ~| daily capture ~| data interchange ~| funds transfer ~| mail ~| publishing ~| signature	

> Unable to find your word under **electronic**?
> Take off **electronic** and look again

electroplate[2]	
electroscope	
eleet	elite+
elefant	elephant+
elegance	@elegant
eleganse	elegance+
elegy[4] *[poem]	@elegiac
	eulogy *[funeral oration]
elekshin	election+
elekt	elect[1+]
elektrik	electric+
elektrisity	electricity+
elektronik	electronic+

> Unable to find your word under **elek**?
> Look under **elec**

element ~al	
elementary *[basic] ~| particle ~| school	
	alimentary *[nutrition]+
elephant ~ine	
elevate[2]	@elevator
elevation	
eleven	@eleventh hour
elf[6] ~in ~ish	
elicit[1] *[get]	illicit *[illegal]+
elicution	elocution+
eligans	elegance+
eligible	@eligibility
eliksir	elixir
elikwense	eloquence+
eliminate[2]	@eliminator
elimination	
elips	eclipse[2] *[of the sun]+
	ellipse *[mathematical curve]+
eliptic	elliptic+
elisit	elicit[1] *[get]
	illicit *[illegal]+
elite	@elitism
	@elitist
eliterashun	alliteration+
elixir	
elk	
ellipse *[mathematical curve]	
	@ellipsis
	eclipse[2] *[of the sun]+
elliptic ~al ~ally	
ellisit	elicit[1] *[get]
	illicit *[illegal]+
ellizhun	elision
elm ~| tree	
eloap	elope[2+]
elocution ~ist	
elokwence	eloquence+
elongate[2]	@elongation
elope[2] ~ment	

Key to Suffixes and Compounds

These rules are explained on pages vii to ix.

1 Keep the word the same before adding **ed, er, est, ing**
e.g. cool[1] → cooled, cooler, coolest, cooling

2 Take off final **e** before adding **ed, er, est, ing**
e.g. fine[2] → fined, finer, finest, fining

3 Double final consonant before adding **ed, er, est, ing**
e.g. thin[3] → thinned, thinner, thinnest, thinning

4 Change final **y** to **i** before adding **ed, er, es, est, ly, ness**
e.g. tidy[4] → tidied, tidier, tidies, tidiest, tidily, tidiness
Keep final **y** before adding **ing** e.g. tidying

5 Add **es** instead of **s** to the end of the word
e.g. bunch[5] → bunches

6 Change final **f** to **ve** before adding **s**
e.g. calf[6] → calves

eloquence	@eloquent
eloqushun	elocution^{+}
else ~where	
elucidate^{2}	@elucidation
elude^{2} *[avoid]	allude^{2} *[refer to]
	illude *[deceive]
elumentarey	elementary *[basic]$^{+}$
	alimentary *[nutrition]$^{+}$
elushun	illusion *[false idea]
	elusion *[escape]
	allusion *[hint]
elusidate	elucidate^{2+}
elusion *[escape]	illusion *[false idea]
	allusion *[hint]
elusive *[hard to find]	
	illusive *[deceptive]
emaciated	@emaciation
emagrant	emigrant *[exits]
	immigrant *[arrives]
emagrasion	emigration *[exit]
	immigration *[arrival]
emagreat	emigrate^{2} *[exit]
	immigrate^{2} *[arrive]
emale	e-mail
emanate^{2}	
emancipate^{2}	@emancipation
emanent	eminent *[repected]$^{+}$
	immanent *[everywhere]
emansapate	emancipate^{2+}
emasculate^{2}	@emasculation
emasiate	emaciate^{2+}
emayl	e-mail
embalm^{1}	
embankment	
embarass	embarrass^{5+}
embargo^{5} ~es	
embark^{1} ~ation card	
embarm	embalm^{1}
embarrass^{5} ~ment	
embassy^{4}	
embattle^{2}	
embed^{3}	
embellish^{5} ~ment	
ember	
embew	imbue^{2}

embezzle^{2} ~ment	
embitter^{1} ~ment	
emblazon^{1}	
emblem ~atic ~atically	
embody^{4}	@embodiment
embolden	
embolism	
emboss^{1}	
embrace^{2}	
embrio	embryo^{+}
embriology	embryology^{+}
embroider^{1} ~y	
embroil^{1} ~ment	
embroyder	embroider^{1+}
embryo ~nic	
embryology	@embryologist
emeer	emir
emegracion	emigration *[exit]
	immigration *[arrival]
emegrant	emigrant *[exits]
	immigrant *[arrives]
emegrate	emigrate^{2} *[exit]
	immigrate^{2} *[arrive]
emenate	emanate^{2}
emenent	eminent *[respected]$^{+}$
	immanent *[everywhere]
	imminent *[soon]$^{+}$
emerald ~| green	
emerge^{2}	
emergence	@emergent
emergency^{4} ~| fund ~| room ~| services	
emerjency	emergency^{4+}
emery ~| board	
emetic	
emfasis	emphasis^{+}
emfasize	emphasize^{2}
emfatic	emphatic^{+}
emfyseema	emphysema
emigrant *[exits]	immigrant *[arrives]
emigrate^{2} *[exit]	immigrate^{2} *[arrive]
emigration *[exit]	immigration *[arrival]
eminate	emanate^{2}
eminent *[respected] ~ly	
	@eminence

KEY TO SPELLING RULES

Red words are wrong. **Black** words are correct.

- ~ Add the suffix or word directly to the main word, without a space or hyphen
  e.g. ash ~en ~tray → ashen ashtray
- ~- Add a hyphen to the main word before adding the next word
  e.g. blow ~-dry → blow-dry
- ~| Leave a space between the main word and the next word
  e.g. decimal ~| place → decimal place
- \+ By finding this word in its correct alphabetical order, you can find related words
  e.g. abowt about^{+} → about-face
- ★ Draws attention to words that may be confused
- ™ Means the word is a trademark
- @ Signifies the word is derived from the main word

eminent imminent *[soon]+
immanent *[everywhere]
emir
emisary emissary[4]
emishun emission
emissary[4]
emission
emit[3]
emity enmity[4]
emmense immense+
Emmy[4] ~| award
emoshun emotion+
emoticon
emotion ~al ~ally
emotive
emp imp+
empact impact[1]
empair impair[1+]
empartial impartial+
empathic *[having the same feeling]
@empathy
emphatic *[forceful]+
empeach impeach[5+]
empending impending
emperor @empress
emphasis @emphases
emphasize[2]
emphatic *[forceful] ~ally
empathic *[having the same feeling]+
emphysema
empinge impinge[2]
empire *[lands] ~-building
umpire *[game]
empirical ~ly
empiricism @empiricist
empish impish+
emplicit implicit+
emplore implore[2]
employ[1] ~able ~ee ~er
employee ~| contribution ~-owned ~| stock ownership
employment ~| agency[4]
emporium @emporia
empose impose[2+]
emposter impostor *[swindler]+
imposture *[deception]
empower[1] ~ment
emprer emperor+
empresario impresario
empress *[royalty]
impress[5] *[cause admiration]+
empression impression+
emprint imprint[1]
emprudence imprudence
emprudent imprudent+
empty[4] ~-handed ~-headed ~| nest
empulsave impulsive+

Unable to find your word under **em**?
Look under **im**

empuror emperor+
empyre empire *[lands]+
emrald emerald+
emrie emery+
emtee empty[4+]
emulate[2] @emulation
emulshun emulsion
emulsify[4] @emulsification
emulsion
emurge emerge[2]
emy Emmy[4+]
en route
enabel enable[2] *[to make able]+
enable[2] *[to make able] ~ment
unable *[not able]
enabling ~| technology
enact[1] ~able ~ment
enaction inaction
enactive inactive
enamel[3]
enamored
enane inane+
encamp[1] ~ment
encapsulate[2] @encapsulation
encase[2] ~ment
encefalitis encephalitis
encephalitis

Key to Suffixes and Compounds

These rules are explained on pages vii to ix.

1 Keep the word the same before adding **ed, er, est, ing**
e.g. cool[1] → cooled, cooler, coolest, cooling
2 Take off final **e** before adding **ed, er, est, ing**
e.g. fine[2] → fined, finer, finest, fining
3 Double final consonant before adding **ed, er, est, ing**
e.g. thin[3] → thinned, thinner, thinnest, thinning
4 Change final **y** to **i** before adding **ed, er, es, est, ly, ness**
e.g. tidy[4] → tidied, tidier, tidies, tidiest, tidily, tidiness
Keep final **y** before adding **ing** e.g. tidying
5 Add **es** instead of **s** to the end of the word
e.g. bunch[5] → bunches
6 Change final **f** to **ve** before adding **s**
e.g. calf[6] → calves

encercle	encircle[2+]
enchant[1] ~ment ~ress	
enciclopeedia	encyclopedia[+]
encircle[2] ~ment	
enclave	
encline	incline[2+]
enclose[2]	@enclosure
enclude	include[2+]
enclusive	inclusive[+]
encoar	encore
encode[2]	
encompass[5]	
encore	
encounter[1]	
encourage[2] ~ment	
encownter	encounter[1]
encripsion	encryption
encroach[5] ~ment	
encrust[1]	
encryption	
encumber[1]	
encumpass	encompass[5]
encur	incur[3+]
encurige	encourage[2+]
encyclopedia	@encyclopedic
encyst *[enclose] ~ment	
	insist[1] *[be firm][+]
end[1] ~less ~lessly ~| product ~| user	
endanger[1] ~ed species	
endaws	endorse[2+]
endear[1] ~ment	
endeavor[1]	
endeer	endear[1+]
endent	indent[1+]
endever	endeavor[1]
endive	
endorse[2] ~ment	
endow[1] ~ment	
endure[2] *[survive]	
	@endurable
	@endurance
	injure[2] *[harm][+]
enema	
enemy[4]	
energetic ~ally	
energize[2]	
energy[4] ~| transfer	
enerjetic	energetic[+]
enerjy	energy[4+]
enervate[2] *[weaken]	
	@enervation
	innervate[2] *[supply with nerves]
enfold[1]	
enforce[2] ~ment	
enforceable	@enforceability
enform	inform[1+]
enforse	enforce[2+]
enfranchise[2] ~ment	
engage[2] ~ment ring	
engayg	engage[2+]
engender[1]	
engine ~| driver	
engineer[1]	
English ~| Channel ~| language ~man ~| muffin ~woman	
engraiv	engrave[2]
engrave[2]	
engrayned	ingrained
engross[5]	
engulf[1]	
enhance[2] ~ment	
enie	any[+]
enigma ~tic	
enjender	engender[1]
enjine	engine[+]
enjineer	engineer[1]
enjoiabul	enjoyable[+]
enjoin[1] *[prevent]	@injunction
enjoy[1] *[get pleasure] ~ment	
enjoyable	@enjoyably
enjure	endure[2] *[survive][+]
	injure[2] *[harm][+]
enkamp	encamp[1+]
enkounter	encounter[1]
enkourage	encourage[2+]

Unable to find your word under **enk**?
Look under **enc**

Key to Spelling Rules

Red words are wrong. **Black** words are correct.

~ Add the suffix or word directly to the main word, without a space or hyphen
e.g. ash ~en ~tray → ashen ashtray

~- Add a hyphen to the main word before adding the next word
e.g. blow ~-dry → blow-dry

~| Leave a space between the main word and the next word
e.g. decimal ~| place → decimal place

\+ By finding this word in its correct alphabetical order, you can find related words
e.g. abowt about[+] → about-face

★ Draws attention to words that may be confused

TM Means the word is a trademark

@ Signifies the word is derived from the main word

enkwire	enquire *[ask about]
	inquire[2] *[ask about]
enlarge[2] ~ment	
enlighten[1] ~ment	
enlist[1]	
enliten	enlighten[1+]
enliven[1]	
enlyst	enlist[1]
enlyten	enlighten[1+]
enmie	enemy[4]
enmity[4]	
ennema	enema
ennoble[2] ~ment	
ennui	
ennumerate	enumerate[2+]

Unable to find your word under **enn**?
Look under **en**

enormity[4]	
enormous ~ly	
enough	
enquire *[ask about]	
	@enquiry
	inquire[2] *[ask about]
enrage[2]	
enrapture[2]	
enrich[5] ~ment	
enroll[1] ~ment	
enrych	enrich[5+]
ensconce[2]	
ensemble	
ensen	ensign
ensew	ensue[2] *[follow]
enshrine[2]	
enshure	ensure[2] *[make sure]
	insure *[money]
ensign	
ensiklopedia	encyclopedia+
ensime	enzyme
ensine	ensign
ensircul	encircle[2+]
enskonce	ensconce[2]
enslave[2] ~ment	
ensnare[2]	
ensue[2] *[follow]	
ensure[2] *[make sure]	
	insure *[money]
ensyclopeedia	encyclopedia+
entail[1]	
entamologist	entomologist
entamology	entomology *[study of insects]+
entangle[2] ~ment	
enter[1] *[go into]	inter[3] *[bury]+
enteritis	
enterprise ~| resource planning ~| value	
	@enterprising
entertain[1] ~ment	
enterytis	enteritis
enthooze	enthuse[2]
enthooziasm	enthusiasm+
enthooziastic	enthusiastic+
enthrall[1]	
enthrone[2] ~ment	
enthuse[2]	
enthusiasm	@enthusiast
enthusiastic ~ally	
entice[2] ~ment	
entimologist	entomologist
entimology	entomology *[study of insects]+
	etymology *[study of words]+
entire ~ly ~ty	
entise	entice[2+]
entitee	entity[4]
entitle[2] ~ment	
entity[4]	
entomb[1] ~ment	
entomologist	
entomology *[study of insects]	
	@entomological
	etymology *[study of words]
entoom	entomb[1+]
entrails	
entrance[2] ~| fee ~ment	
entrant	
entrap[3] ~ment	

Key to Suffixes and Compounds

These rules are explained on pages vii to ix.

1 Keep the word the same before adding **ed, er, est, ing**
e.g. cool[1] → cooled, cooler, coolest, cooling
2 Take off final **e** before adding **ed, er, est, ing**
e.g. fine[2] → fined, finer, finest, fining
3 Double final consonant before adding **ed, er, est, ing**
e.g. thin[3] → thinned, thinner, thinnest, thinning
4 Change final **y** to **i** before adding **ed, er, es, est, ly, ness**
e.g. tidy[4] → tidied, tidier, tidies, tidiest, tidily, tidiness
Keep final **y** before adding **ing** e.g. tidying
5 Add **es** instead of **s** to the end of the word
e.g. bunch[5] → bunches
6 Change final **f** to **ve** before adding **s**
e.g. calf[6] → calves

entrapranoor entrepreneur[+]
entray entrée *[meal]
entry[4] *[going into]
entreat[1] ~ingly
entreaty[4]
entrée *[meal] entry[4] *[going into]
entreet entreat[1+]
entreety entreaty[4]
entrench[5] ~ment
entrense entrance[2+]
entrent entrant
entrepreneur ~ial
entrust[1]
entry[4] *[going into] ~-level
entrée *[meal]
entume entomb[1+]
entur enter[1] *[go into]
inter[3] *[bury][+]
enturitus enteritis
enturprise enterprise[+]
enturtain entertain[1+]
entwine[2]
entyce entice[2+]
entyre entire[+]
entytal entitle[2+]
enuff enough
enumerable *[can be counted]
innumerable *[cannot be counted]
enumerate[2] @enumeration
enunciate[2] *[speak clearly]
enunciation *[clear speaking]
annunciation *[announcement]
enurjetic energetic[+]
enurjise energize[2]
enurvate enervate[2] *[weaken][+]
innervate[2] *[supply with nerves]
envee envy[4+]
envelop[1] *[surround]
envelope *[paper]
envent invent[1+]
enventive inventory[4+]
envie envy[4] *[begrudge][+]

envious ~ly ~ness
environment ~alist
environmental ~ly ~| conditions ~| fund ~| protection
envisage[2]
envisige envisage[2]
envlope envelop[1] *[surround]
envolve involve[2+]
envoi *[end of poem]
envoy *[ambassador]
envy[4] *[begrudge]
@enviable
envyronment environment[+]
enwee ennui
eny any[+]
enygma enigma[+]
enzyme
eon
epaucksy epoxy[4+]
epaulet
ephemeral ~ly
epic ~ally
epicenter
epicure @epicurean
epidemic
epidemiology
epidermis @epidermal
epidural
Epifany Epiphany *[Christian celebration]
epiglottis
epigraf epigraph[+]
epigram ~matic ~matically
epigraph ~ic
epik epic[+]
epikure epicure[+]
epilepsy @epileptic
epilogue
epiphany *[revelation]
Epiphany *[Christian celebration]
episcopacy
Episcopal ~ian ~| Church
episentre epicenter
episewd episode
episkopacy episcopacy

Key to Spelling Rules

Red words are wrong. **Black** words are correct.

~ Add the suffix or word directly to the main word, without a space or hyphen
e.g. ash ~en ~tray → ashen ashtray

~- Add a hyphen to the main word before adding the next word
e.g. blow ~-dry → blow-dry

~| Leave a space between the main word and the next word
e.g. decimal ~| place → decimal place

\+ By finding this word in its correct alphabetical order, you can find related words
e.g. abowt about[+] → about-face

* Draws attention to words that may be confused

TM Means the word is a trademark

@ Signifies the word is derived from the main word

episkopal Episcopal+
episode
episodic ~ally
epissel epistle+
epistle @epistolary
epitaph *[inscription at grave]
epithet *[descriptive phrase]
epitome
epitomize[2]
epoch ~al ~-making
epoksy epoxy[4]+
epolet epaulet
epoxy[4] ~| resin
epydemyc epidemic
epydermys epidermis+

> Unable to find your word under **epy**?
> Look under **epi**

eqewstrian equestrian
equable *[steady]
 @equably
 equitable *[fair]+
equadistant equidistant
equait equate[2]+
equal[3] ~ly ~| opportunity[4] ~| sign
equalataral equilateral
equalibrium equilibrium+
equality[4]
equalize[2] @equalizer
equanimity
equanocks equinox
equate[2] @equation
equator ~ial
equayt equate[2]+
equerry[4]
equestrian
equible equable *[steady]+
 equitable *[fair]+
equidistant
equilateral
equilibrium ~| price
equilize equalize[2]+
equine
equinimity equanimity

equinox
equip[3] ~ment
equitable *[fair] @equitably
 equable *[steady]+
equity[4] ~| cap ~| capital ~| claim ~| floor ~| fund ~| kicker ~| market ~| options ~| swap ~| holder ~| method

> Unable to find your word under **equity**?
> Take off **equity** and look again

equivacate equivocate[2]+
equivalent ~| annual benefit ~| annual cost ~| bond yield ~| loan
 @equivalence
equivocal ~ly
equivocate[2] @equivocation
er ere *[before]
 heir *[inheritance]+
era *[a time] ere *[before]
 error *[mistake]+
erace erase[2]+
eradicate[2] @eradication
 @eradicator
erand errand *[brief trip]
erant errant *[straying]
erar era *[a time]
 error *[mistake]+
erase[2] @eraser
eratic erotic *[sexual]+
 erratic *[uneven movement]+
eratum erratum+
erb herb+
erbaycious herbaceous+
erbicide herbicide
ere *[before] air *[breathe]
 ear *[body part]+
 err[1] *[make a mistake]+
 heir *[inheritor]+
erect[1] ~ion
erend errand *[brief trip]
 errant *[straying]
erer error *[mistake]+

Key to Suffixes and Compounds

These rules are explained on pages vii to ix.

1 Keep the word the same before adding **ed, er, est, ing**
e.g. cool[1] → cooled, cooler, coolest, cooling
2 Take off final **e** before adding **ed, er, est, ing**
e.g. fine[2] → fined, finer, finest, fining
3 Double final consonant before adding **ed, er, est, ing**
e.g. thin[3] → thinned, thinner, thinnest, thinning
4 Change final **y** to **i** before adding **ed, er, es, est, ly, ness**
e.g. tidy[4] → tidied, tidier, tidies, tidiest, tidily, tidiness
Keep final **y** before adding **ing** e.g. tidying
5 Add **es** instead of **s** to the end of the word
e.g. bunch[5] → bunches
6 Change final **f** to **ve** before adding **s**
e.g. calf[6] → calves

ergonomics
Erie *[lake] ~| Canal
eerie *[scary]
erk irk[1+]
erl earl *[noble][+]
URL *[uniform resource locator]
erly early[4+]
ermine
ern earn[1] *[receive payment][+]
urn *[vase]
ernest earnest[+]
ernings earnings[+]
erobic aerobic[+]
erode[2]
erodynamic aerodynamic[+]
eronaut aeronaut[+]

Unable to find your word under **ero**?
Look under **aero**

eroneous erroneous[+]
eror error *[mistake][+]
erosion
erotic *[sexual] ~a ~ally ~ism
erratic *[uneven movement][+]
err[1] *[make a mistake] ~ant
air[1] *[gas]
ear *[body part][+]
heir *[inheritor][+]
errand *[brief trip]
errant *[straying]
erratic *[uneven movement] ~ally
erotic *[sexual][+]
erratum @errata
erroneous ~ly
error *[mistake] ~| message
era *[a time]
errupt erupt[1+]
erstwhile
erth earth[+]
erthen earthen[+]
erthquake earthquake

erudite ~ly @erudition
erupt[1] ~ion
ervre oeuvre[+]
esanse essence
esay essay[1+]
escalate[2] @escalator
escalation
escalator ~| clause
escapade
escape[2] ~| artist ~| clause
escapism @escapist
@escapee
escargot
escarpment
eschaton *[end of the world]
@eschatology
eschew[1] *[do without]
issue[2] *[come out][+]
eschuary estuary[4]
eschue eschew[1]
Escimo Eskimo
escort[1]
escrow ~| receipt
esens essence
esenshul essential[+]
eshalon echelon
eskalate escalate[2+]
eskapisum escapism[+]
Eskimo
eskwire esquire
esophagus
esoteric ~ally
especial ~ly
espionage
espouse[2] @espousal
espresso
espyonnage espionage
essay[1] ~ist
essence
essential ~ly
establish[5] ~ment
estate ~| planning ~| tax
estchuary estuary[4]
esteem[1]
ester *[chemical] Easter *[Christian feast][+]

Key to Spelling Rules

Red words are wrong. **Black** words are correct.

~ Add the suffix or word directly to the main word, without a space or hyphen
e.g. ash ~en ~tray → ashen ashtray

~- Add a hyphen to the main word before adding the next word
e.g. blow ~-dry → blow-dry

~| Leave a space between the main word and the next word
e.g. decimal ~| place → decimal place

+ By finding this word in its correct alphabetical order, you can find related words
e.g. abowt about[+] → about-face

* Draws attention to words that may be confused

TM Means the word is a trademark

@ Signifies the word is derived from the main word

estern eastern+
esthetic
estimable
estimate[2] @estimation
estime esteem[1]
estimebul estimable
estranged @estrangement
estrogen
estuary[4]
estymate estimate[2+]
estyooary estuary[4]
esy easy[4+]
et cetera *[and other similar things]
etakit etiquette
etamology entomology *[study of insects]+
etymology *[study of words]+
etch[5] *[draw] each *[every]+
eternal ~ly
eternity[4]
ether *[air, liquid] ~eal
either *[or]
Esther *[woman's name]
Ethernet
ethic ~al ~ally ~s
ethnic ~ity ~| cleansing
ethnology @ethnological
ethos
ethur either *[or]
ether *[air, liquid]+
Ethurnet Ethernet
etiket etiquette
etimology etymology *[study of words]+
etiquette
etsetra et cetera *[and other similar things]+
eturnity eternity[4]
etymology *[study of words]
@etymologist
entomology *[study of insects]+
eucalaylee ukulele
eucalyptus

Eucharist
Euclid
eue ewe *[sheep]
you *[person]
yew *[tree]
eufemistic euphemistic+
eufemisum euphemism
euforia euphoria+
eugenics
eukalyptus eucalyptus
eukulele ukulele
eulogize[2] @eulogist
eulogy *[funeral oration]
elegy[4] *[poem]+
eunanimous unanimous
eunique unique *[one and only]+
eunison unison
eunuch *[castrated male]
unique *[one and only]+
UNIX *[operating system]
euphemism
euphemistic ~ally
euphoria @euphoric
eurythmy @eurythmics
euro ~| currency ~dollar
European ~| Exchange Rate ~| Monetary System ~| Union
eustachian ~| tube
euthanasia
eutopia utopia+

Unable to find your word under **eu**?
Look under **u**

evacuate[2] @evacuation
@evacuee
evade[2]
evaluate[2] @evaluation
evalution evaluation
evolution+
evalutionery evolutionary+
evangelic ~al ~ally
evangelist @evangelical
evangelize[2] @evangelism
evaporate[2] @evaporation

KEY TO SUFFIXES AND COMPOUNDS

These rules are explained on pages vii to ix.

1 Keep the word the same before adding **ed, er, est, ing**
e.g. cool[1] → cooled, cooler, coolest, cooling
2 Take off final **e** before adding **ed, er, est, ing**
e.g. fine[2] → fined, finer, finest, fining
3 Double final consonant before adding **ed, er, est, ing**
e.g. thin[3] → thinned, thinner, thinnest, thinning
4 Change final **y** to **i** before adding **ed, er, es, est, ly, ness**
e.g. tidy[4] → tidied, tidier, tidies, tidiest, tidily, tidiness
Keep final **y** before adding **ing** e.g. tidying
5 Add **es** instead of **s** to the end of the word
e.g. bunch[5] → bunches
6 Change final **f** to **ve** before adding **s**
e.g. calf[6] → calves

evasion
evasive ~ly ~ness
eve
even[1] ~ly ~ness ~song ~tide
evenchual eventual+
even-handed ~ly ~ness
evening ~| classes ~| dress
event ~ful ~-driven ~| risk ~| study
eventual ~ly
eventuality[4]
ever ~green ~lasting ~more
every ~body ~day ~one ~thing ~where
eves *[evenings] eaves+
evict[1] ~ion
evidence @evidential
evident ~ly
evikt evict[1+]
evil ~ly ~-minded
evilution evolution+
evilutionery evolutionary+
evning evening+
evocative ~ly
evoke[2] @evocation
evolution ~ist
evolutionary ~| computation ~| process
evolve[2]
evon even[1+]
evry every+
evur ever+
evury every+
evydent evident+
evyl evil+
ewe *[sheep] you *[person]
yew *[tree]
ewes *[sheep] use[2] *[utilize]
us *[group of two or more]
exacerbate[2] @exacerbation
exact[1] ~ly ~ness
exaggerate[2] @exaggeration
exale exhale[2+]
exalt[1] ~ation
exam ~ination
examine[2]
example

exasperate[2] @exasperation
exaut exhort[1+]
excavate[2] @excavator
excavation
exceed[1] *[be more than] ~ingly
accede[2] *[agree]
excel[3]
excellence @excellent
@excellently
excellent ~ly
excepshun exception+
except[1] *[other than] ~ance
accept[1] *[take]+
exception ~al ~ally
excerpt *[extract] exert[1] *[effort]+
excershun exertion *[effort]
excursion *[visit]
excess ~| baggage ~| profits ~| returns ~ive ~ively ~| accumulation ~| reserves ~| ratio ~| margin

Unable to find your word under **excess**? Take off **excess** and look again

excetra et cetera *[and other similar things]
exchange[2] ~able ~| controls ~| fund ~| rate ~| student ~| value
excise[2] *[tax] ~| duty[4] ~| officer[4]
exercise[2] *[physical activity]
exorcise[2] *[remove evil]+
excitable @excitability
excite[2] *[very happy] ~ment
exit[1] *[leave, way out]+
excited *[very happy] ~ly
exited *[left, went out]
exclaim[1]
exclamation @exclamatory
exclude[2] @exclusion
exclusive ~ly @exclusivity
excommunicate[2] @excommunication
excrement
excruciating ~ly

KEY TO SPELLING RULES

Red words are wrong. **Black** words are correct.

~ Add the suffix or word directly to the main word, without a space or hyphen
e.g. ash ~en ~tray → ashen ashtray

~- Add a hyphen to the main word before adding the next word
e.g. blow ~-dry → blow-dry

~| Leave a space between the main word and the next word
e.g. decimal ~| place → decimal place

+ By finding this word in its correct alphabetical order, you can find related words
e.g. abowt about+ → about-face

* Draws attention to words that may be confused

TM Means the word is a trademark

@ Signifies the word is derived from the main word

excursion
excuse[2] @excusable
excytabel excitable+
execute[2] @executor
execution ~er
executive ~| officer ~| order ~| secretary[4]
exellent excellent
exema eczema
exemplary
exemplify[4]
exempt[1] ~ion
exercise[2] *[physical activity]
excise[2] *[tax]+
exorcise[2] *[remove evil]
exert[1] *[effort] ~ion
excerpt *[extract]
exertion *[effort] excursion *[visit]
exetra et cetera *[and other similar things]
exhale[2] @exhalation
exhaust[1] ~ible ~ion ~ive ~| pipe
exhibit[1] ~or
exhibition ~| hall ~ism ~ist
exhilarate[2] @exhilaration
exhort[1] ~ation
exhume[2]
exibishun exhibition+
exibit exhibit[1]+
exigence
exile[2]
exilerate exhilarate[2]+
exima eczema
exist[1] ~ence ~ent
exit[1] *[leave, way out] ~| poll ~| visa
excite[2] *[very happy]+
exklude exclude[2]+
exklusiv exclusive+
exkuse excuse[2]+

> Unable to find your word under **exk**?
> Look under **exc**

exmas Xmas
exonerate[2] @exoneration
exooberance exuberance+
exood exude[2]
exorbitance @exorbitant
exorcise[2] *[remove evil]
exercise[2] *[physical activity]
exorcist @exorcism
exort exhort[1]+
exotic ~a ~ally ~ism
expand[1]
expanse *[wide area]
@expansion
expense *[cost]+
expansive ~ly ~ness
exparation expiration+
expatriate[2] @expatriation
expect[1] ~ancy ~ation
expectant *[waiting] ~ly
expectorant *[coughing up]
@expectorate
expedience @expedient
@expediency
expedishun expedition+
expedishus expeditious+
expedite[2]
expedition ~| outfitter
expeditionary ~| force
expeditious ~ly
expel[3]
expend[1] ~iture
expendable @expendability
expense *[cost] ~| account
@expensive
expanse *[wide area]+
expergate expurgate[2]
experience[2]
experiment[1] ~ation
experimental ~ly
expert ~ise ~ly ~ness
expirament experiment[1]+
expiration ~| cycle ~| date ~| review
expire[2]
expiriance experience[2]
explain[1] ~able
explanation @explanatory

Key to Suffixes and Compounds

These rules are explained on pages vii to ix.

1 Keep the word the same before adding **ed, er, est, ing**
e.g. cool[1] → cooled, cooler, coolest, cooling
2 Take off final **e** before adding **ed, er, est, ing**
e.g. fine[2] → fined, finer, finest, fining
3 Double final consonant before adding **ed, er, est, ing**
e.g. thin[3] → thinned, thinner, thinnest, thinning
4 Change final **y** to **i** before adding **ed, er, es, est, ly, ness**
e.g. tidy[4] → tidied, tidier, tidies, tidiest, tidily, tidiness
Keep final **y** before adding **ing** e.g. tidying
5 Add **es** instead of **s** to the end of the word
e.g. bunch[5] → bunches
6 Change final **f** to **ve** before adding **s**
e.g. calf[6] → calves

explane explain[1+]
expletive
explicable
explicit ~ly
explisit explicit[+]
expload explode[2]
exploar explore[2]
explode[2]
exploit[1] ~ation
exploration @exploratory
explore[2]
explosion @explosive
exployt exploit[1+]
expo
exponent
export[1] ~ation ~| deal ~| department ~| duty ~| earnings ~| license ~| market ~| permit ~| trade

> Unable to find your word under **export**?
> Take off **export** and look again

exporting ~| company[4] ~| country[4]
expose[2] *[make known] @exposure
exposé *[scandalous disclosure]
express[5] ~ible ~ly ~| delivery[4] ~| letter
expression ~less
expressionism @expressionist
expressive ~ly
expresso espresso
expropriate[2] @expropriation
expulshin expulsion
expulsion
expunge[2]
expurgate[2]
expurt expert[+]
exquisite ~ly ~ness
exray X-ray[1]
exseed exceed[1+]
exsellense excellence[+]
exsept except[1] *[other than][+]
exsert excerpt *[extract]
exert[1] *[effort][+]
ex-service
exsess excess[+]
exsite excite[2] *[very happy][+]

> Unable to find your word under **exs**?
> Look under **exc**

extemporaneous ~ly
extemporize[2]
extend[1]
extended ~| credit[4] ~| family[4]
extensible ~| markup language ~| stylesheet
extension ~| number
extensive ~ly
extent
extenuating ~| circumstances
exterior
exterminate[2] @exterminator
extermination
external ~ly ~| account ~| audit ~| auditor ~| financing ~| market ~| partner

> Unable to find your word under **external**?
> Take off **external** and look again

externalize[2]
extinct ~ion
extinguish[1]
extirior exterior
extol[3]
extorsion extortion[+]
extort[1]
extortion ~ist
extra ~| charges ~curricular ~net ~marital relations ~sensory perception ~terrestrial ~| time

> Unable to find your word under **extra**?
> Take off **extra** and look again

extract[1] ~ion
extradite[2] @extradition
extramural
extraneous ~ly ~ness
extraordinary @extraordinarily

KEY TO SPELLING RULES

Red words are wrong. **Black** words are correct.

~ Add the suffix or word directly to the main word, without a space or hyphen
e.g. ash ~en ~tray → ashen ashtray

~- Add a hyphen to the main word before adding the next word
e.g. blow ~-dry → blow-dry

~| Leave a space between the main word and the next word
e.g. decimal ~| place → decimal place

+ By finding this word in its correct alphabetical order, you can find related words
e.g. abowt about[+] → about-face

* Draws attention to words that may be confused

TM Means the word is a trademark

@ Signifies the word is derived from the main word

extrapolate[2] @extrapolation
extravagance
extravagant ~ly
extravaganza
extravert extrovert+
extream extreme+
extredite extradite2+
extreme ~ly @extremist
extremity[4]
extricate[2] @extrication
extrikate extricate2+
extrordinary extraordinary+
extrovert ~ed
exturminate exterminate2+
exturnal external+
exuberance @exuberant
exude[2]
exult[1] ~ant ~ation
exume exhume[2]
exurcise exercise[2] *[physical activity]
exorcise[2] *[remove evil]
exurt exert[1] *[effort]+
eyce ice2+
eydict edict
eye[2] *[sight] ~ball[1] ~| brow ~| contact ~lash ~| level ~lid ~| liner ~-opener ~piece ~sight ~sore ~| teeth ~| tooth ~wash ~witness
aye *[yes]
I *[me]

Unable to find your word under **eye**?
Take off **eye** and look again

eyed *[watched] I'd *[I had, would]
ID *[identification]
id *[psyche]
eyederdown eiderdown
eyeds ides *[Roman calendar]+
eyeful *[amount, in your eye]
Eiffel *[Tower]
eyelet *[hole] islet *[island]
eyemax IMAX+
eye-o-you IOU [I owe you]
eye-tee IT *[Information Technology]+
eyether either *[or]
ether *[air, liquid]+
eylit eyelet *[hole]
islet *[island]
eyris iris *[part of the eye]
Irish *[from Ireland]
eyt eight *[number]+
eytem item+

Unable to find your word under **ey**?
Look under **i**

eytey eighty4+
eyther ether *[air, liquid]+
either *[or]
ezy easy4+

KEY TO SUFFIXES AND COMPOUNDS

These rules are explained on pages vii to ix.

1 Keep the word the same before adding **ed, er, est, ing**
e.g. cool[1] → cooled, cooler, coolest, cooling
2 Take off final **e** before adding **ed, er, est, ing**
e.g. fine[2] → fined, finer, finest, fining
3 Double final consonant before adding **ed, er, est, ing**
e.g. thin[3] → thinned, thinner, thinnest, thinning
4 Change final **y** to **i** before adding **ed, er, es, est, ly, ness**
e.g. tidy[4] → tidied, tidier, tidies, tidiest, tidily, tidiness
Keep final **y** before adding **ing** e.g. tidying
5 Add **es** instead of **s** to the end of the word
e.g. bunch[5] → bunches
6 Change final **f** to **ve** before adding **s**
e.g. calf[6] → calves

F

fable ~d
fabric
fabricate[2]
fabrication
fabulous ~ly ~ness
facade
face[2] *[head] ~less ~| card ~cloth ~-lift ~| mask ~-off ~| pack ~| paint ~-saving ~-to-face ~| value
faze[2] *[bother]
phase[2] *[stage]

Unable to find your word under **face**?
Take off **face** and look again

faces *[more than one face]
feces *[excrement]+
facet *[surface] ~ed
faucet *[for water]
facetious *[joking] ~ly ~ness
fachen — fashion[1+]
fachisum — fascism+
fachuous — fatuous+
facial *[face]
facile *[easy]
facilitate[2] — @facilitation
facility[4]
facinate — fascinate[2+]
facism — fascism+
facitious — facetious *[joking]+
factitious *[artificial]
facshun — faction *[political group]
facsimile ~| transmission
fact *[event] ~-finding ~oid ~otum ~ual ~ually
faked *[pretended]

Unable to find your word under **fact**?
Take off **fact** and look again

facter — factor+
factery — factory[4+]
faction *[political group]
fraction *[small part]+
factitious *[artificial]
fictitious *[imaginary]+
factor ~ial
factory[4] ~| floor ~| gate ~| outlet ~| ship
facts *[realities] — fax[5] *[send a fax]+
faculty[4]
fad *[fashion] ~dish
fade[2] *[go away]
faheeta — fajita
Fahrenheit
faid — fade[2] *[go away]
faik — fake[2+]
fail[1] *[not succeed] ~ure ~-safe
fall *[tumble, decline]+
fain *[willingly] — fane *[holy place]
feign[1] *[deceive]
faint[1] *[weak] ~ly ~ness
feint *[deceptive move]
fair *[just, event] ~| dealing ~| game ~ground ~-haired ~-minded ~| play ~| price ~| test ~| trade ~| use ~way ~-weather
fare[2] *[bus, food, manage]+

Unable to find your word under **fair**?
Take off **fair** and look again

Key to Spelling Rules

Red words are wrong. **Black** words are correct.

~ Add the suffix or word directly to the main word, without a space or hyphen
e.g. ash ~en ~tray → ashen ashtray

~- Add a hyphen to the main word before adding the next word
e.g. blow ~-dry → blow-dry

~| Leave a space between the main word and the next word
e.g. decimal ~| place → decimal place

+ By finding this word in its correct alphabetical order, you can find related words
e.g. abowt about+ → about-face

★ Draws attention to words that may be confused

TM Means the word is a trademark

@ Signifies the word is derived from the main word

fairy[4] *[imaginary creature] ~| cake ~| godmother ~land ~| lights ~| story[4] ~tale
ferry[4] *[boat]+

Unable to find your word under **fairy**? Take off **fairy** and look again

fait accompli
faite — fate *[destiny]
fete *[festival]
faith ~ful ~fully ~fulness
fajita
fake[2] ~| out ~ry
faked *[pretended]
fact *[event]+
faker *[pretender]
fakir *[holy man]
fakt — fact *[event]+
faked *[pretended]
fakts — fax[5] *[send a fax]+
facts *[realities]

Unable to find your word under **fak**? Look under **fac**

falafel
falanx — phalanx[5]
falasy — fallacy[4+]
falcify — falsify[4+]
falcon ~er ~ry
fale — fail[1][not succeed]+
fall *[tumble, decline]+
falesy — fallacy[4+]
falken — falcon+
fall *[tumble, decline] ~en ~back ~| behind ~| due ~| guy ~| through ~out *[nuclear explosion] ~| out *[break with someone]
fail[1] *[not succeed]+

Unable to find your word under **fall**? Take off **fall** and look again

fallacy[4] — @fallacious
fallible — @fallibility
fallic — phallic+
fallopian ~| tube
fallow ~| field
falls *[down] — false *[untrue]+
falo — fallow+
false *[untrue] ~ly ~| alarm ~| bottom ~-hearted ~hood ~| pretense ~| teeth
falsify[4] — @falsification
falsity[4]
falter[1]
falufel — falafel
fame ~d
familial *[about one's family]
familiar *[well known] ~ity
familiarize[2] — @familiarization
family[4] ~| name ~| planning ~| practice ~| tree ~| values
famine
famished
famous ~ly
fan[3] ~| belt ~| club ~fare ~| mail ~zine
fanatic ~al ~ally ~ism
fanciful ~ly
fancy[4] ~| dress ~| face ~-free
fane *[holy place] — fain *[willingly]
feign[1] *[deceive]
fang
fanny ~| pack
fansiful — fanciful+
fansy — fancy[4+]
fantacize — fantasize[2]
fantasha — fantasia
fantasia
fantasize[2]
fantastic ~ally
fantasy[4]
fantisize — fantasize[2]
fantisy — fantasy[4]
fantom — phantom
faquir — fakir *[holy man]
faker *[pretender]
far *[distant] ~away ~-fetched ~-flung ~| gone ~-off ~-out ~-reaching

KEY TO SUFFIXES AND COMPOUNDS

These rules are explained on pages vii to ix.

1 Keep the word the same before adding **ed, er, est, ing**
e.g. cool[1] → cooled, cooler, coolest, cooling
2 Take off final **e** before adding **ed, er, est, ing**
e.g. fine[2] → fined, finer, finest, fining
3 Double final consonant before adding **ed, er, est, ing**
e.g. thin[3] → thinned, thinner, thinnest, thinning
4 Change final **y** to **i** before adding **ed, er, es, est, ly, ness**
e.g. tidy[4] → tidied, tidier, tidies, tidiest, tidily, tidiness
Keep final **y** before adding **ing** e.g. tidying
5 Add **es** instead of **s** to the end of the word
e.g. bunch[5] → bunches
6 Change final **f** to **ve** before adding **s**
e.g. calf[6] → calves

far ~sighted
fare[2] *[bus, food, manage]+
fair *[just, event]+

Unable to find your word under **far**?
Take off **far** and look again

faraoh pharaoh
farce @farcical
@farcically
fare[2] *[bus, food, manage] ~well
fair *[just, event]+
far *[distant]+
Farenheight Fahrenheit
faringeal pharyngeal+
Farisee Pharisee
farm[1] ~| hand ~house ~land ~yard
farmacist pharmacist
farmacy pharmacy[4]

Unable to find your word under **far**?
Look under **phar**

farrier *[blacksmith]
farse farce+
farst fast[1+]
fart[1]
farther *[distant] father[1] *[dad]+
farthing *[old English coin]
fary fairy[4] *[imaginary creature]+
ferry[4] *[boat]+
farynx pharynx
fasade facade
fascia *[layer]
fascinate[2] @fascination
fascism @fascist
fase face[2] *[head]+
faze[2] *[bother]
phase[2] *[stage]
faseeshus facetious *[joking]+
fasen fasten[1]
faset facet *[surface]+
faucet *[for water]

fashall facial *[face]
facile *[easy]
fashion[1] ~able ~ably ~| house ~| show
fashisum fascism+
fasile facial *[face]
facile *[easy]
fasilitate facilitate[2+]
fasility facility[4]
fassen fasten[1]
fasset facet *[surface]+
fassinate fascinate[2+]
fast[1] ~-acting ~| food ~-forward ~| lane ~-talking ~| track

Unable to find your word under **fast**?
Take off **fast** and look again

fasten[1]
fastidious ~ly ~ness
fat[3] *[big] ~ness ~| cat ~-free ~head
fate *[destiny]+
fête[2] *[festival]
fatal *[deadly] ~ly
fetal *[before birth]+
fatalist ~ic ~ically
@fatalism
fatality[4]
fate *[destiny] ~ful ~fully
feta *[cheese]
fête[2] *[festival]
fateakomplee fait accompli
fated *[destined] feted *[honored]
fetid *[decaying]
fateeg fatigue[2+]
faten fatten[1+]
father[1] *[dad] ~ly ~hood
farther *[distant]
father-in-law
Father's Day
fathom[1] ~less
fatie fatty[4+]
fatigue[2] ~s
fatten[1] ~| up
fatty[4] ~| acids
fatuous ~ly

Key to Spelling Rules

Red words are wrong. **Black** words are correct.

~ Add the suffix or word directly to the main word, without a space or hyphen
e.g. ash ~en ~tray → ashen ashtray

~- Add a hyphen to the main word before adding the next word
e.g. blow ~-dry → blow-dry

~| Leave a space between the main word and the next word
e.g. decimal ~| place → decimal place

+ By finding this word in its correct alphabetical order, you can find related words
e.g. abowt about+ → about-face

★ Draws attention to words that may be confused

™ Means the word is a trademark

@ Signifies the word is derived from the main word

fatwah [also spelled fatwa]	
faucet *[for water]	
	facet *[surface]+
fault[1] ~y ~-finding ~less	
faun *[in myths]	fawn[1] *[color, deer, flatter]
fauna *[animals]	
faux pas	
favor[1] ~able ~ably	
favorite	@favoritism
fawlt	fault[1+]
fawn[1] *[color, deer, flatter]	
	faun *[in myths]
fawna	fauna *[animals]
fax[5] *[send a fax] ~es ~| machine	
	facts *[realities]
faximilee	facsimile+
fay *[fairy]	fey *[strange]
fayr	fair *[just, event]+
	fare[2] *[bus, food, manage]+
faysha	fascia *[layer]
fayta	feta *[cheese]
fayth	faith+
faythless	faithless+
faze[2] *[bother]	phase[2] *[stage]
fead	feed *[give food]+
feading	feeding+
feal	feel+
feald	field[1+]
fear[1] *[afraid] ~some	
	fire[2] *[burning]+
fearful ~ly ~ness	
fearless ~ness	
feasant	pheasant *[bird]
feasible	@feasibility
feast[1]	
feat *[action]	feet *[more than one foot]
	fête[2] *[festival]
feather ~ed ~y ~weight	
feature[2] ~| film	
featus	fetus[5]
February	
Febuary	February

feces *[excrement]	
	@fecal
	faces *[more than one face]
fech	fetch[5]
feckless	
fed *[given food]	feed *[give food]+
Fed *[Federal Reserve System]	
federal ~ly	
Federal Reserve ~| System	
federalist	@federalism
fedral	federal+
fee	
feeble[2] ~-minded	
feecher	feature[2+]
feed *[give food] ~er ~back	
	fed *[given food]
feeding ~| bottle ~| frenzy ~| ground	
feefdom	fiefdom
feel ~er ~ing	
feeld	field[1+]
feer	fear[1+]
feerse	fierce+
feest	feast[1]
feet *[more than one foot]	
	feat *[action]
	fête[2] *[festival]
feeture	feature[2+]

Unable to find your word under **fee**?
Look under **fie** or **fea**

feid	feed *[give food]+
feign[1] *[deceive]	fain *[willingly]
	fane *[holy place]
feil	feel+
feild	field[1+]
feint *[deceptive move]	
	faint[1] *[weak]+
feir	fear[1+]
feirce	fierce+
feirful	fearful+
fekless	feckless
fekund	fecund+
feline	

Key to Suffixes and Compounds

These rules are explained on pages vii to ix.

1 Keep the word the same before adding **ed, er, est, ing**
e.g. cool[1] → cooled, cooler, coolest, cooling
2 Take off final **e** before adding **ed, er, est, ing**
e.g. fine[2] → fined, finer, finest, fining
3 Double final consonant before adding **ed, er, est, ing**
e.g. thin[3] → thinned, thinner, thinnest, thinning
4 Change final **y** to **i** before adding **ed, er, es, est, ly, ness**
e.g. tidy[4] → tidied, tidier, tidies, tidiest, tidily, tidiness
Keep final **y** before adding **ing** e.g. tidying
5 Add **es** instead of **s** to the end of the word
e.g. bunch[5] → bunches
6 Change final **f** to **ve** before adding **s**
e.g. calf[6] → calves

fell
fellow ~ship
felon @felony[4]
felow fellow+
felt ~-tip
female ~| impersonator
femer femur
feminine @femininity
feminist @feminism
feminize[2]
femme ~| fatale
femur
fen ~land
fence[2]
fend[1] *[ward off] fiend *[monster]+
feng ~| shui
fenix phoenix
fennel *[spice] ~| seed
phenyl *[chemical group]+
feral *[wild] ~| animal
ferrule *[metal sleeve]
ferule *[corporal punishment]
ferlong furlong
ferm firm[1]
ferment[1] *[yeast] ~ation
firmament *[sky]
foment[1] *[trouble]+
fern
fernace furnace *[fireplace]
fernish furnish[5] *[add furniture]+
ferniture furniture
fero pharaoh
ferocious ~ly ~ness
ferocity
feroshus ferocious+
ferret[1] ~| around ~| out
Ferris wheel
ferrous *[iron]
ferrule *[metal sleeve]
feral *[wild]+
ferule *[corporal punishment]

ferry[4] *[boat] ~man
fairy[4] *[imaginary creature]+
ferst first *[number one]+
ferther further[1] *[distant]+
father[1] *[dad]+
ferthest furthest
fertile *[life-giving]
fertility ~| drug
fertilize[2] @fertilization
fertive furtive+
ferule *[corporal punishment]
feral *[wild]+
ferrule *[metal sleeve]
fervent ~ly
ferver fervor
fervid ~ly ~ness
fervor
fes fez
fester[1]
festival
festive ~ly ~ness
festivity[4]
festoon[1]
festun festoon[1]
fet accomply fait accompli
feta *[cheese]
fetal *[before birth] ~| monitor
fatal *[deadly]+
fetch[1]
fête[2] *[festival] fate *[destiny]+
feat *[action]
feet *[more than one foot]
feta *[cheese]
feted *[honored] fated *[destined]
fetid *[decaying]
fetel fetal *[before birth]+
fettle[2] *[condition]
feter fetter[1+]
fether feather+
fetid *[decaying] fated *[destined]
feted *[honored]
fetish[5] ~ism ~ist
fetlock
fetoochinee fettuccine

KEY TO SPELLING RULES

Red words are wrong. **Black** words are correct.

~ Add the suffix or word directly to the main word, without a space or hyphen
e.g. ash ~en ~tray → ashen ashtray

~- Add a hyphen to the main word before adding the next word
e.g. blow ~-dry → blow-dry

~| Leave a space between the main word and the next word
e.g. decimal ~| place → decimal place

+ By finding this word in its correct alphabetical order, you can find related words
e.g. abowt about+ → about-face

★ Draws attention to words that may be confused

™ Means the word is a trademark

@ Signifies the word is derived from the main word

fetter[1] ~s
fettle[2] *[condition]
fettuccine
fetus[5]
feud[1] *[quarrel]
feudal *[in Middle Ages] ~ism ~ist ~istic
futile *[useless][+]
fever ~ed ~| pitch
feverish ~ly ~ness
few *[not many] ~| and far between
phew *[exclamation]
fewgitive fugitive
fewl fool[1] *[deceive, stupid person][+]
fuel *[to burn][+]
fewm fume[2]
fewrius furious[+]
fewse fuse[2] *[electrical][+]
fewsha fuchsia
fewzyun fusion

> Unable to find your word under **few**?
> Look under **fu**

fez
fial file[2] *[document, tool, line][+]
fiancé *[man] finance[2] *[put up money][+]
fiancée *[woman]
fiansay fiancé *[man]
fiancée *[woman]
fiasco
fib[3]
fiber ~board ~fill ~glass ~| optics
fibrillation
fibroid ~s
fibrosis
fibrous
fibula ~r
fibur fiber[+]
fices feces *[excrement][+]
fichery fishery[4]
fickle ~ness
ficks fix[5+]
fickst fixed[+]
fiction *[story] ~al
friction *[rubbing]
fictishus fictitious *[imaginary][+]
fictitious *[imaginary] ~ly
fiddle[2] ~sticks @fiddly[4]
fidel fiddle[2+]
fidelity
fidget[1] ~y
fieble feeble[2+]
fied feed *[give food][+]
fiel feel[+]
file[2] *[document, tool, line][+]
field[1] ~| day ~| glasses ~| marshal ~mouse ~| trip ~work ~| sports ~| test ~| trial

> Unable to find your word under **field**?
> Take off **field** and look again

fiend *[monster] ~ish ~ishly ~ishness
friend[+]
fier fear[1+]
fire[2] *[flame][+]
fierce ~ly ~ness
fierse fierce[+]
fiery[4] *[flames, passionate]
furry[4] *[hairy]
fiest feast[1]
fiesta
fifteen ~th
fifth ~| column
Fifth Amendment
fifty[4] ~-fifty @fiftieth
fig ~| tree
figer figure[2+]
figerativ figurative[+]
figet fidget[1+]
fight *[argue] ~| back ~ing
fit[3] *[right size]
figment
figurative ~ly
figure[2] ~| drawing ~head ~| skating
fijit fidget[1+]
fiksed fixed[+]
fikshun fiction *[story][+]

Key to Suffixes and Compounds

These rules are explained on pages vii to ix.

1 Keep the word the same before adding **ed, er, est, ing**
e.g. cool[1] → cooled, cooler, coolest, cooling
2 Take off final **e** before adding **ed, er, est, ing**
e.g. fine[2] → fined, finer, finest, fining
3 Double final consonant before adding **ed, er, est, ing**
e.g. thin[3] → thinned, thinner, thinnest, thinning
4 Change final **y** to **i** before adding **ed, er, es, est, ly, ness**
e.g. tidy[4] → tidied, tidier, tidies, tidiest, tidily, tidiness
Keep final **y** before adding **ing** e.g. tidying
5 Add **es** instead of **s** to the end of the word
e.g. bunch[5] → bunches
6 Change final **f** to **ve** before adding **s**
e.g. calf[6] → calves

filabuster **filibuster**[1]
filagree **filigree**
filament
filander **philander**[1]+

> Unable to find your word under **fi**?
> Look under **phi**

filanthropy **philanthropy**+
filay **filet** *[steak]+
fillet *[meat or fish]
filly[4]
filch[5]
file[2] *[document, tool, line] ~| clerk ~| server ~| type ~| transfer protocol [FTP]

> Unable to find your word under **file**?
> Take off **file** and look again

filement **filament**
filet *[steak] ~| mignon
fillet *[meat or fish]
filial
filibuster[1]
filigree
filine **feline**
filing *[scraping] ~| cabinet ~| requirement
filling *[making full]+
fill[1] *[make full] ~-in
file[2] *[document, tool, line]+
fillet *[meat or fish]
filet *[steak]+
filling *[making full] ~| station
fillip *[sudden motion]
Philip *[man's name]
fill-up *[fuel]
filly[4]
film[1] ~| clip ~| festival ~maker ~making ~| star ~strip ~| stock
filmy[4]
filo ~| dough ~| pastry

> Unable to find your word under **filo**?
> Look under **philo**

filter[1] *[sieve] **philter** *[love potion]
filth **@filthy**[4]
filtration
fimale **female**+
fimur **femur**
fin *[fish] **fine**[2] *[money paid, quality]+
Finn *[from Finland]
final *[last] ~| cut ~| Four ~ist ~ly
finale *[last event]
finality
finalize[2]
finance[2] *[put up money] ~| charge
@financier
fiancé *[man]
financial ~ly ~| asset ~| accounting ~| crisis ~| institution ~| position ~| resources ~| risk ~| statement ~| settlement ~| year

> Unable to find your word under **financial**?
> Take off **financial** and look again

finch[5]
find *[discover] ~er ~ing ~| out
fined *[charged a fine]
finned *[having fins]
fine[2] *[money paid, quality] ~ly ~| art ~-drawn ~| print ~| spun
fin *[fish]
Finn *[from Finland]
fined *[charged a fine]
fineness *[high quality]
finesse *[skill]
finery
finesse *[skill] **fineness** *[high quality]
fine-tooth ~| comb
finger[1] ~| bowl ~nail ~print
finish[5] ~ed goods
finite
fink *[tattler] **think**+
Finn *[from Finland]
fin *[fish]
fine[2] *[money paid, quality]+

Key to Spelling Rules

Red words are wrong. **Black** words are correct.

~ Add the suffix or word directly to the main word, without a space or hyphen
e.g. ash ~en ~tray → ashen ashtray

~- Add a hyphen to the main word before adding the next word
e.g. blow ~-dry → blow-dry

~| Leave a space between the main word and the next word
e.g. decimal ~| place → decimal place

\+ By finding this word in its correct alphabetical order, you can find related words
e.g. abowt about+ → about-face

★ Draws attention to words that may be confused

™ Means the word is a trademark

@ Signifies the word is derived from the main word

finned *[having fins]
find *[discover]+
fined *[charged a fine]
finsh — finch[5]
finish[1]
fiord
fir *[tree] — fur[3] *[coat]+
fire[2] *[burning] ~| alarm ~arm ~ball ~bomb[1] ~brand[1] ~break[1] ~| brigade ~cracker ~| department ~| drill ~-eater ~| engine ~| escape ~| extinguisher ~fighter ~fly ~| hydrant ~man ~place ~power ~proof ~-resistant ~| sale ~| station ~trap ~wall ~work
fear[1] *[afraid]+
fiery[4] *[flames, passionate]

> Unable to find your word under **fire**?
> Take off **fire** and look again

firing ~| line ~| squad
firm[1]
firmament *[sky]
firment — ferment[1] *[yeast]+
foment[1] *[trouble]+
firn — fern
firnace — furnace *[fireplace]
firry — fiery[4] *[flames, passionate]
furry[4] *[hairy]
first *[number one] ~ly ~| aid ~-class ~-rate ~| run
fist *[part of the arm]
fits *[attacks]
First ~| Lady ~| World War

> Unable to find your word under **first**?
> Take off **first** and look again

firther — father *[relative]+
further[1] *[distant]+
firtile — fertile *[life-giving]
firtilise — fertilize[2+]
firtiv — furtive+
firvor — fervor

> Unable to find your word under **fir**?
> Look under **fer** or **fur**

firy — fiery[4] *[flames, passionate]
fisabul — feasible+
fiscal *[money] ~ly ~| policy ~| year
physical *[matter and energy]+
fish[5] ~| cake ~| farming ~| sticks
fisher *[catching fish]
fissure *[crack]
fishery[4]
fishun — fission *[splitting apart]
fishure — fissure *[crack]
fishy[4]
fisical — fiscal *[money]+
physical *[matter and energy]+
fision — fission *[splitting apart]
fusion *[putting together]
fiskle — fiscal *[money]+
physical *[matter and energy]+
fission *[splitting apart]
fissure *[crack] — fisher *[catching fish]
fist *[part of the arm]
first *[number one]
fits *[attacks]
fit[3] *[right size] — fight *[argue]+
five ~-and-dime ~-and-ten
fix[5] ~es
fixate[2] — @fixation
fixative
fixed ~| assets ~| income ~| salary
fixitive — fixative
fixture
fizhen — fission *[splitting apart]
fizher — fissure *[crack]
fizz[5] — @fizzle[2]
fjord
flabbergasted
flabby[4]

Key to Suffixes and Compounds

These rules are explained on pages vii to ix.

1 Keep the word the same before adding **ed, er, est, ing**
e.g. cool[1] → cooled, cooler, coolest, cooling
2 Take off final **e** before adding **ed, er, est, ing**
e.g. fine[2] → fined, finer, finest, fining
3 Double final consonant before adding **ed, er, est, ing**
e.g. thin[3] → thinned, thinner, thinnest, thinning
4 Change final **y** to **i** before adding **ed, er, es, est, ly, ness**
e.g. tidy[4] → tidied, tidier, tidies, tidiest, tidily, tidiness
Keep final **y** before adding **ing** e.g. tidying
5 Add **es** instead of **s** to the end of the word
e.g. bunch[5] → bunches
6 Change final **f** to **ve** before adding **s**
e.g. calf[6] → calves

flaccid ~ly
flag[3] ~| day ~| of convenience ~pole ~ship ~stone
flagrant
flair *[instinct] flare[2] *[light, widen]
flajelate flagellate[2+]
flak *[antiaircraft] ~| jacket
flake[2] *[snow] @flaky[4]
flamboyance @flamboyant
flame[2]
flamenco *[dance]
flamingo *[bird]
flammable @flammability
flan
flanal flannel[3]
flange
flank[1]
flannel[3]
flap[3] ~jack
flare[2] *[light, widen]
flair *[instinct]
flasc flask
flash[5] ~back ~bulb ~| card ~| flood ~light ~| point
flashy[4]
flask
flat ~ly ~bed ~-cap ~-chested ~-footed ~iron ~lands ~| rate ~| spin ~worm

> Unable to find your word under **flat**?
> Take off **flat** and look again

flatly *[plainly] philately[4] *[stamp collecting]+
flatten[1]
flatter[1] ~y
flaunt[1] *[display] flounce[2] *[move dramatically]
flout[1] *[defy]
flautist
flaver flavor[1]
flavor[1]
flaw *[blemish] ~ed
floor[1] *[ground]+

flawnt flaunt[1] *[display]
flawtist flautist
flea *[insect] ~bag ~bite ~-bitten ~pit
flee *[run away]+
flebitis phlebitis *[blood vessel disease]
fleck ~ed
flecks *[spots] flex[5] *[muscles]+
flecksibul flexible+
fledgling
flee *[run away] ~ing
flea *[insect]+
fleece[2] *[sheep's wool]
fleas *[insects]+
fleet *[boats]
fleeting ~ly
fleksibel flexible+
flem phlegm+
flerdelee fleur-de-lis
flert flirt[1+]
flesh[5] ~y ~-colored ~| out ~| wound
fleur-de-lis
flew *[flight] flu *[disease]
flue *[metal tube]
flex[5] *[muscles] ~es ~| time
flecks *[spots]
flexible @flexibility
flick[1]
flicker[1]
flie flea *[insect]+
flee *[run away]+
fly *[insect, travel]+
fliece fleece[2] *[sheep's wool]
flies *[plural of fly]
fleece[2] *[sheep's wool]
fliet fleet *[boats]
flight *[flying]+
flight *[flying] ~less ~| attendant ~| deck ~| information ~| lieutenant ~| path ~| recorder ~| simulator ~| test

> Unable to find your word under **flight**?
> Take off **flight** and look again

KEY TO SPELLING RULES

Red words are wrong. **Black** words are correct.

~ Add the suffix or word directly to the main word, without a space or hyphen
e.g. ash ~en ~tray → ashen ashtray

~- Add a hyphen to the main word before adding the next word
e.g. blow ~-dry → blow-dry

~| Leave a space between the main word and the next word
e.g. decimal ~| place → decimal place

+ By finding this word in its correct alphabetical order, you can find related words
e.g. abowt about+ → about-face

★ Draws attention to words that may be confused

TM Means the word is a trademark

@ Signifies the word is derived from the main word

flighty[4]
fliing fling *[throw]+
flying *[airborne]+
flimsy[4]
flinch[5] ~es
fling *[throw] ~ing
flint ~y ~| glass ~lock
flip[3] ~chart ~-flop ~side
flippant ~ly
flirt[1] *[invite romance] ~ation ~atious ~y
flit *[move quickly]
flisse fleece[2] *[sheep's wool]
flit[3] *[move quickly]
flight *[flying]+
flity flighty[4]
float[1] @flotation
flock[1]
flocks *[sheep] flux *[flow]
phlox *[flower]
floe *[ice] flow[1] *[river]+
flog[3]
flood[1] *[overflow] ~gate ~light ~lit ~| plain
fluid *[capable of flowing]+
floor[1] *[ground] ~board ~| lamp ~| plan ~| sample ~| show
flaw *[blemish]+
flour[1] *[food]+
floordali fleur-de-lis
floot flute+
floozy[4]
flop[3] ~house
floppy[4] ~| disk ~| diskette ~| hat
flora
floral
flore floor[1] *[ground]+
florid *[flowery] fluoride *[chemical]
florist
flornt flaunt[1] *[display]
flortist flautist
floss[5]
flote float[1+]
flotilla
flotsam

flounce[1] *[move dramatically]
flaunt *[display]
flout[1] *[defy]
flounder[1]
flour[1] *[food] ~y ~| mill
floor[1] *[ground]+
flower[1] *[plant]+
flourescent fluorescent
flourish[1]
flout[1] *[defy] flaunt[1] *[display]
flounce[2] *[move dramatically]
flow[1] *[river] ~chart ~| diagram
floe *[ice]
follow[1] *[go after]+
flower[1] *[plant] ~| bed ~| pot ~| power
flour[1] *[food]+
flown
flownder flounder[1]

Unable to find your word under **flow**?
Look under **flou**

flox flocks *[sheep]
flux *[flow]
phlox *[flower]
flu *[disease] flew *[flight]
flue *[metal tube]
fluch flush[5]
flucks flocks *[sheep]
flux *[flow]
phlox *[flower]
fluctuate[2] @fluctuation
flud flood[1] *[overflow]+
fluid *[capable of flowing]+
flue *[metal tube] flew *[flight]
flu *[disease]
fluent ~ly @fluency
fluff[1] ~y[4]
fluid ~| mechanics ~| ounce
fluke[2]
fluks flocks *[sheep]
flux *[flow]
phlox *[flower]
fluktuate fluctuate[2+]

Key to Suffixes and Compounds

These rules are explained on pages vii to ix.

1 Keep the word the same before adding **ed, er, est, ing**
e.g. cool[1] → cooled, cooler, coolest, cooling
2 Take off final **e** before adding **ed, er, est, ing**
e.g. fine[2] → fined, finer, finest, fining
3 Double final consonant before adding **ed, er, est, ing**
e.g. thin[3] → thinned, thinner, thinnest, thinning
4 Change final **y** to **i** before adding **ed, er, es, est, ly, ness**
e.g. tidy[4] → tidied, tidier, tidies, tidiest, tidily, tidiness
Keep final **y** before adding **ing** e.g. tidying
5 Add **es** instead of **s** to the end of the word
e.g. bunch[5] → bunches
6 Change final **f** to **ve** before adding **s**
e.g. calf[6] → calves

flummox ~ed
flung
flunk[1] ~y[4]
fluorescent ~| light
fluoride *[chemical]
@fluorine
florid *[flowery]
fluorocarbon
fluride — fluoride *[chemical]
flurish — flourish[1]
flurocarbon — fluorocarbon
flurry[4]
flurt — flirt[1] *[invite romance]+
flit *[move quickly]
flush[5]
fluster[1]
flute ~d
flutter[1]
fluvial
flux *[flow] — flocks *[sheep]
phlox *[flower]
fluzy — floozy[4]
fly *[insect, travel] ~ing ~-by ~-by-night ~catcher ~-fishing ~leaf ~over ~paper ~swatter ~weight ~wheel
@flies
@flew
flee *[run away]+
flea *[insect]+

Unable to find your word under **fly**?
Take off **fly** and look again

flyck — flick[1]
flying *[airborne] ~| buttress ~| circus ~| fish ~| saucer ~| start ~| visit

Unable to find your word under **flying**?
Take off **flying** and look again

foal[1] — foaled *[horse's birth]
fold[1] *[bend something]
foam[1] ~| rubber — @foamy[4]
fobia — phobia+
focal ~| length ~| point
focsle — forecastle *[on ship]
foxhole *[on battlefield]
focus[5] ~es ~| group
@foci
fod — food *[eat]+
fodder
foe
foenix — phoenix
foepa — faux pas
fog[3] ~| up — @foggy[4]
foible
foie gras
foier — foyer
foil[1]
foist[1]
fokal — focal+
foke — folk+
fokelore — folklore
foks — folks *[people]
fox *[animal]+
foksul — forecastle *[on ship]
foxhole *[on battlefield]
fokus — focus[5]+
fold[1] *[bend something]
foaled *[horse's birth]
foldaway ~| bed
fole — foal[1]+
foleeo — folio
foliage
folic ~| acid
folicul — follicle
folij — foliage
folio
folk ~lore ~| music ~| song
folken — falcon+
foll — fall *[down]+
follicle
follow[1] *[go after] ~-through ~| up
flow[1] *[river]+
folly[4]
folsify — falsify[4]+
folt — fault[1]+
folter — falter[1]
fome — foam[1]+

Key to Spelling Rules

Red words are wrong. **Black** words are correct.

~ Add the suffix or word directly to the main word, without a space or hyphen
e.g. ash ~en ~tray → ashen ashtray

~- Add a hyphen to the main word before adding the next word
e.g. blow ~-dry → blow-dry

~| Leave a space between the main word and the next word
e.g. decimal ~| place → decimal place

+ By finding this word in its correct alphabetical order, you can find related words
e.g. abowt about+ → about-face

* Draws attention to words that may be confused

TM Means the word is a trademark

@ Signifies the word is derived from the main word

foment[1] *[trouble] ~ation
    ferment[1] *[yeast]+
fond[1]
fondle[2]
fondue
fone   **phone**[2+]
fonology   **phonology**+
font
fony   **phony**[4+]

> Unable to find your word under **fon**?
> Look under **phon**

food *[eat] ~| additive ~| allergen ~| allergy[4] ~| bank ~borne ~| chain ~| irradiation ~| poisoning ~| preservatives ~| processor ~| processing ~| product ~| web
    feud[1] *[quarrel]

> Unable to find your word under **food**?
> Take off **food** and look again

fool[1]   **fuel** *[to burn]+
foolhardy[4]
foolish ~ly ~ness
fool's ~| gold ~| paradise
foolscap
foonreal   **funeral** *[ceremony]
    funereal *[gloomy]
foot[1] ~| and mouth disease ~ball ~fall ~hills ~hold ~lights ~loose ~note ~print ~rest ~sore ~step ~stool ~wear ~work

> Unable to find your word under **foot**?
> Take off **foot** and look again

footage
football ~er ~ing
fopaw   **faux pas**
for *[used by]   **fore** *[front]+
    four *[number]+
forage[2] *[for food]
    forge[2] *[metal]
forbade

forbear *[not do] ~ance ~ing
    forebear *[ancestor]
forbid[3]   **@forbade**
force[2] ~| majeure ~| meter ~| of nature
forced ~| labor ~| landing
forceful ~ly ~ness
forceps
forchen   **fortune**+
forchenet   **fortunate**+
forcible   **@forcibly**
ford[1] ~able
fore *[front] ~arm ~cast ~court ~fathers ~finger ~front ~ground ~hand ~head ~knowledge ~leg ~lock ~man ~most ~play ~runner ~shorten ~sight[1] ~skin ~warn[1]
    for *[used by]
    four *[number]+
forebear *[ancestor]
    forbear *[not do]+
foreboding ~ly
forecastle *[on ship]
    foxhole *[on battlefield]
foreclose[2]   **@foreclosure**
foregave   **forgave**
forego *[precede] ~ing
    forgo *[do without]
foregone *[predetermined] ~| conclusion
    forgone *[done without]
foregot   **forgot**+
foreign ~er ~| body ~| currency ~| distribution ~| exchange ~| market ~| rights ~| service

> Unable to find your word under **foreign**?
> Take off **foreign** and look again

foren   **foreign**+
foresaw
foresee ~able ~ing ~n
foreshadow[1]
forest[1] ~ation ~ry
forestall[1]
foretell ~ing   **@foretold**
forever ~more

KEY TO SUFFIXES AND COMPOUNDS

These rules are explained on pages vii to ix.

1 Keep the word the same before adding **ed, er, est, ing**
e.g. cool[1] → cooled, cooler, coolest, cooling
2 Take off final **e** before adding **ed, er, est, ing**
e.g. fine[2] → fined, finer, finest, fining
3 Double final consonant before adding **ed, er, est, ing**
e.g. thin[3] → thinned, thinner, thinnest, thinning
4 Change final **y** to **i** before adding **ed, er, es, est, ly, ness**
e.g. tidy[4] → tidied, tidier, tidies, tidiest, tidily, tidiness
Keep final **y** before adding **ing** e.g. tidying
5 Add **es** instead of **s** to the end of the word
e.g. bunch[5] → bunches
6 Change final **f** to **ve** before adding **s**
e.g. calf[6] → calves

foreword *[in book]
forward[1] *[advance]+

> Unable to find your word under **fore**?
> Look under **for** or **four**

forfeit[1] ~ure
forgave
forge[2] *[metal] forage[2] *[for food]
forgery[4]
forget[3] ~-me-not
forgetful ~ness
forgivable
forgive ~n ~ness
@forgiving
forgo *[do without] ~ing
forego *[precede]+
forgone *[done without]
foregone *[predetermined]+
forgot ~ten
forhand forehand
forige forage[2] *[for food]
forist forest[1+]
forj forage[2] *[for food]
forge[2] *[metal]
forjery forgery[4]
fork[1] ~lift ~ed lightening
forlorn
forlt fault[1+]
form[1] *[shape] ~ation
forum *[public speaking]+
from *[preposition]
formal @formality[4]
formaldehyde
formalize[2] @formalization
formally *[officially]
formerly *[before]
formashun formation+
format[3]
formation @formative
forment ferment[1] *[yeast]+
firmament *[sky]
foment[1] *[trouble]+
former
formerly *[before] formally *[officially]
formidable @formidably
formula ~e ~s
formulate[2] @formulation
forn faun *[in myths]
fawn[1] *[color, deer, flatter]
forna fauna *[animals]
fornicate[2] @fornication
for-profit
forrest forest[1+]
forsake ~n @forsaking
forse force[2+]
forsed forced+
forseful forceful+
forseps forceps
forsithia forsythia
forsook
forswear ~ing
forswore @forsworn
forsythia
fort *[castle] ~ress
fought *[battle]
thought *[think]
Fort Knox *[place]
fortay forte *[strong point]
forte *[strong point]
fought *[battle]
forty[4] *[number]+
forteen fourteen+
forth *[forward] ~coming
fourth *[number]+

> Unable to find your word under **fo**?
> Look under **fou**

forth ~right ~with
fortieth
fortify[4] @fortification
fortissimo
fortitude
fortuitous ~ly ~ness
fortunate ~ly
fortune ~-hunter ~-teller

KEY TO SPELLING RULES

Red words are wrong. **Black** words are correct.

~ Add the suffix or word directly to the main word, without a space or hyphen
e.g. ash ~en ~tray → ashen ashtray

~- Add a hyphen to the main word before adding the next word
e.g. blow ~-dry → blow-dry

~| Leave a space between the main word and the next word
e.g. decimal ~| place → decimal place

\+ By finding this word in its correct alphabetical order, you can find related words
e.g. abowt about+ → about-face

★ Draws attention to words that may be confused

TM Means the word is a trademark

@ Signifies the word is derived from the main word

forty[4] *[number] ~| winks
@fortieth
forte *[strong point]
fortyfie fortify[4+]
forum *[public speaking]
@fora
forward[1] *[advance] ~| pass ~| slash
foreword *[in book]
fosfate phosphate

> Unable to find your word under **fo**?
> Look under **pho**

fossil ~| fuel
fossilize[2] @fossilization
foster[1] ~-child ~-father ~-mother
foto photo[+]

> Unable to find your word under **foto**?
> Look under **photo**

fought *[battle] fort *[castle][+]
thought *[think]
foul[1] *[dirty] ~ly ~ness ~-mouthed
fowl *[bird]
found[1] ~ation ~ling
founding ~| father
foundry[4]
fountain ~head ~| pen
four *[number] ~-by-four ~fold
~-leaf clover ~-letter-word
~-poster ~-stroke ~score ~some
~square ~| star
for *[used by]
fore *[front][+]

> Unable to find your word under **four**?
> Look under **for,** or take off **four** and look again

fourbid forbid[3+]
fource force[2+]
fourhand forehand
fourm form[1] *[shape][+]
forum *[public speaking][+]

fourt fought *[battle]
fort *[castle][+]
fourth *[number][+]
thought *[think]
fourteen ~th
fourth *[number] ~| dimension ~| estate
forth *[forward][+]
Fourth of July *[holiday]
fourtnight fortnight[+]
fow foe
fowl *[bird] foul[1] *[dirty][+]
fowpas faux pas
fox[5] *[animal] ~glove ~| hunting
~| terrier
folks *[people]
foxhole *[on battlefield]
forecastle *[on ship]
foxtrot[3]
foybul foible
foyer
foyl foil[1]
foyst foist[1]
foyyay foyer
fracas
fractal
fraction *[small part] ~al
faction *[political group]
fractious ~ly
fracture[2]
frael frail[1+]
fragile @fragility
fragment[1] ~ary ~ation
fragrance @fragrant
fragrense fragrance[+]
frail[1] @frailty[4]
fraim frame[2+]
frait freight *[goods][+]
frajile fragile[+]
fraksher fracture[2]
frakshun fraction *[small part][+]
frakshus fractious[+]
frale frail[1+]
frame[2] ~| of mind ~| of reference ~work
franc *[money] frank[1] *[blunt][+]
franchise[2] ~e ~| system

Key to Suffixes and Compounds

These rules are explained on pages vii to ix.

1 Keep the word the same before adding **ed, er, est, ing**
e.g. cool[1] → cooled, cooler, coolest, cooling
2 Take off final **e** before adding **ed, er, est, ing**
e.g. fine[2] → fined, finer, finest, fining
3 Double final consonant before adding **ed, er, est, ing**
e.g. thin[3] → thinned, thinner, thinnest, thinning
4 Change final **y** to **i** before adding **ed, er, es, est, ly, ness**
e.g. tidy[4] → tidied, tidier, tidies, tidiest, tidily, tidiness
Keep final **y** before adding **ing** e.g. tidying
5 Add **es** instead of **s** to the end of the word
e.g. bunch[5] → bunches
6 Change final **f** to **ve** before adding **s**
e.g. calf[6] → calves

Francophile
Francophone
frank[1] *[blunt] ~ly ~ness ~furter ~incense
| franc *[money]
frantic ~ally
frap[3] *[bind tightly]
frappé *[milk shake]
frase | frays *[fights, wears out] phrase[2] *[words]+
fraternal ~ly
fraternity[4]
fraternize[2] | @fraternization
fraud ~ster
fraudulence | @fraudulent
fraught
frawd | fraud+
frawdulence | fraudulence+
frawt | fraught
fray[1]
frayl | frail[1+]
frays *[fights, wears out] | phrase[2] *[words]+
frazzle[2] *[upset] | phrasal *[short phrase]+
frea | free+
freak[1] ~ish ~ishly
freckle ~d
free ~ing ~ly ~r ~st ~| agent ~bie ~| enterprise ~| fall ~-floating ~lance[2] ~| love ~| market ~| radical ~-range ~| speech ~style ~thinker ~| throw ~| trade ~wheel ~| will

> Unable to find your word under **free**?
> Take off **free** and look again

freed *[set free] | fried *[cooked]
freedom ~| fighter ~| of speech
freehold ~er ~ing
Freemason ~ry
frees *[releases] | freeze *[cold]+ frieze *[pattern]
freesia
freeze *[cold] | @freezing frees *[releases] frieze *[pattern]
freeze ~-dried ~-frame
freezha | freesia
freight *[goods] ~er ~| car ~| train
| fret[3] *[worry]+ fright *[fear]
freind | friend+
frekwency | frequency[4]
frekwent | frequent[1+]
French ~| bread ~| dressing ~| fry[4] ~| horn ~| kiss ~man

> Unable to find your word under **French**?
> Take off **French** and look again

frend | friend+
frenetic
frenzy | @frenzied
frequency[4]
frequent[1] ~ly
fresco[5]
fresh[1] ~ly ~ness ~-faced ~man ~water
freshen[1]
fresko | fresco[5]
fret[3] *[worry] ~ful ~fully
| freight *[goods]+
fret ~| saw
Freudian ~| slip
frew | threw *[ball] through *[go through]
frey | fray[1]
friar *[religious] | fryer *[food]
friction *[rubbing] | fiction *[story]+
Friday
fridge
frie | free+ fry[4]
fried *[cooked] | freed *[set free] friend+
friedom | freedom+
friend ~ship
friendly[4] ~| fire ~| takeover

KEY TO SPELLING RULES

Red words are wrong. **Black** words are correct.

~ Add the suffix or word directly to the main word, without a space or hyphen
e.g. ash ~en ~tray → ashen ashtray
~- Add a hyphen to the main word before adding the next word
e.g. blow ~-dry → blow-dry
~| Leave a space between the main word and the next word
e.g. decimal ~| place → decimal place
+ By finding this word in its correct alphabetical order, you can find related words
e.g. abowt about+ → about-face
* Draws attention to words that may be confused
TM Means the word is a trademark
@ Signifies the word is derived from the main word

frieze *[pattern] freeze *[cold]+
frigate ~| bird
fright *[fear] freight *[goods]+
frighten[1]
frightful ~ly ~ness
frigid ~ity
frik freak[1+]
frill[1] ~y
fringe[2] ~| benefit
frippery[4]
Frisbee™
frisk[1] ~y[4]
fritefull frightful+
friten frighten[1]
fritter[1]
frivolous ~ly @frivolity[4]
frizbee Frisbee™
frizz[5] @frizzy[4]
frog ~man
Froidian Freudian+
frolic @frolicked
@frolicking
from *[preposition]
form[1] *[shape]+
frond
frong throng[1]
front[1] ~age ~al ~ally ~| burner
~| crawl ~-loader ~| line ~| man
~| office ~-page ~-row ~-runner
~-wheel drive

> Unable to find your word under **front**?
> Take off **front** and look again

frontier ~sman ~swoman
frooishun fruition
froot fruit[1+]
frord fraud+
frordulence fraudulence+
frosh *[first-year student]
frost[1] ~bite ~bitten
frosty[4]
frot fraught
froth[1] @frothy[4]
frown[1]

Froydian Freudian+
froze ~n
fructose
frugal ~ity ~ly
fruit[1] ~| cake ~| cocktail ~| fly ~| salad
@fruity[4]

> Unable to find your word under **fruit**?
> Take off **fruit** and look again

fruitful ~ly ~ness
fruition
fruitless ~ly ~ness
fruity[4]
frump @frumpy[4]
frunt front[1+]
fruntier frontier+
frustrate[2] @frustration
frut fruit[1+]
fry[4]
fryction friction *[rubbing]
fryer *[food] friar *[religious]
frying pan
frynge fringe[2+]
fryt fright *[fear]
fryzz frizz[5+]

> Unable to find your word under **fry**?
> Look under **fri**

fucher future
fuchsia
fuchure future
fuddy-duddy[4]
fude feud[1] *[quarrel]
fudge[2]
fue few *[not many]+
phew *[exclamation]
fuel *[to burn] ~| cell ~-injection
fool[1] *[deceive, stupid person]+
fuge fudge[2]
fugue
fugitive
fugue

KEY TO SUFFIXES AND COMPOUNDS

These rules are explained on pages vii to ix.

1 Keep the word the same before adding **ed, er, est, ing**
e.g. cool[1] → cooled, cooler, coolest, cooling
2 Take off final **e** before adding **ed, er, est, ing**
e.g. fine[2] → fined, finer, finest, fining
3 Double final consonant before adding **ed, er, est, ing**
e.g. thin[3] → thinned, thinner, thinnest, thinning
4 Change final **y** to **i** before adding **ed, er, es, est, ly, ness**
e.g. tidy[4] → tidied, tidier, tidies, tidiest, tidily, tidiness
Keep final **y** before adding **ing** e.g. tidying
5 Add **es** instead of **s** to the end of the word
e.g. bunch[5] → bunches
6 Change final **f** to **ve** before adding **s**
e.g. calf[6] → calves

Fuhrer *[also spelled Fuehrer]
furor *[rage]
ful fool[1] *[deceive, stupid person]+
full[1] *[complete]+
fulcrum
fule fool[1] *[deceive, stupid person]+
fuel *[to burn]+
fulfill ~ment
full[1] *[complete] ~ness ~back ~| blast ~-blooded ~-blown ~-face ~-fledged ~-length ~-on ~-page ~-scale ~-size ~-time
fool[1] *[deceive, stupid person]+

Unable to find your word under **full**?
Take off **full** and look again

fully ~| grown
fulsome ~ly ~ness
fumble[2]
fume[2]
fumigate[2] @fumigator
fun
function[1]
functional ~ly ~| component ~| genomics
fund[1]
fundamental ~ist ~ly
fundraise[2]
funel funnel[3]
funeral *[ceremony]
funereal *[gloomy]
fungible
fungus @fungi @fungicide
funjable fungible
funk
funkshun function[1]
funkshunal functional+
funky[4]
funnel[3]

funny[4] ~| bone ~| business
fur[3] *[coat] ~| up
fir *[tree]
furious ~ly ~ness
furlong
furmament firmament *[sky]
furment ferment[1] *[yeast]+
foment[1] *[trouble]+
furn fern
furnace *[fireplace]
furnish[1] *[add furniture] ~ings
furniture
furor *[rage] Fuhrer *[Hitler]
furoshus ferocious+
furrier
furrow[1]
furry[4] *[hairy] fury[4] *[anger]
furst first *[number one]+
further[1] *[distant] @furthest
father[1] *[dad]+
further ~ance ~more ~most
furtile fertile *[life-giving]
futile *[useless]
furtilise fertilize[2]+
furtility fertility+
furtive ~ly ~ness
furvent fervent+
furver fervor
furvour fervor

Unable to find your word under **fur**?
Look under **fer** or **fir**

fury[4] *[anger] furry[4] *[hairy]
fuse[2] *[electrical] ~| box
fuss[5] *[worry]+
fuselage
fushia fuchsia
fusillade
fusion *[putting together]
fuss[5] *[worry] ~budget
@fussy[4]
fuzz[5] *[fluffy material]

Key to Spelling Rules

Red words are wrong. **Black** words are correct.

~ Add the suffix or word directly to the main word, without a space or hyphen
e.g. ash ~en ~tray → ashen ashtray

~- Add a hyphen to the main word before adding the next word
e.g. blow ~-dry → blow-dry

~| Leave a space between the main word and the next word
e.g. decimal ~| place → decimal place

+ By finding this word in its correct alphabetical order, you can find related words
e.g. abowt about+ → about-face

* Draws attention to words that may be confused

TM Means the word is a trademark

@ Signifies the word is derived from the main word

fusty[4]
fut — foot+
futball — football+
futile *[useless] — @futility
future
futurist ~ic ~ically
futyle — futile *[useless]+
feudal *[in Middle Ages]+
fuzz[5] *[fluffy material]
fuss[5] *[worry]+
fuzzy[4] ~| logic
fwagra — foie gras
fyoocher — future
fyoorer — Fuhrer *[Hitler]
furor *[rage]
fyoory — fury[4] *[anger]
furry[4] *[hairy]
fyootle — futile *[useless]+
feudal *[in Middle Ages]+
fyooze — fuse[2] *[electrical]+
fyord — fjord
fyshun — fission

> Unable to find your word under **fy**?
> Look under **fi**

fysical — physical+
fysician — physician
fysics — physics+
fysiotherapist — physiotherapist+
fyt — fight *[argue]+
fit[3] *[right size]
fyx — fix[5]+

G

G ~| clef ~-string ~-suit
gabble[2] *[talk]
gable *[on roof]
gad[3] ~| about
gadget ~ry
Gael *[Scot, Irish] — gale *[wind]+
Gail *[woman's name]
gaff *[spear, sail]
gaffe *[mistake]
gaffer *[old man]
gag[3]
gage — gauge[2]
gaggle ~| of geese
Gaia ~| hypothesis
gaiety
Gail *[woman's name]
Gael *[Scot, Irish]
gale *[wind]+
gall[1] *[nerve]+
gaily
gain[1] ~ful ~fully
gainsay ~ing — @gainsaid
gaip — gape[2] *[open]
gait *[walk] — gate[2] *[barrier]+
gaje — gauge[2]
gajet — gadget+
gak — gawk[1]+
gala
galactic
galant — gallant+
galaxy[4]
gale *[wind] ~-force
Gael *[Scot, Irish]
Gail *[woman's name]
gall[1] *[nerve]+
galeksy — galaxy[4]
galent — gallant+
galery — gallery[4]
galivant — gallivant[1]

Key to Suffixes and Compounds

These rules are explained on pages vii to ix.

1 Keep the word the same before adding **ed, er, est, ing**
e.g. cool[1] → cooled, cooler, coolest, cooling
2 Take off final **e** before adding **ed, er, est, ing**
e.g. fine[2] → fined, finer, finest, fining
3 Double final consonant before adding **ed, er, est, ing**
e.g. thin[3] → thinned, thinner, thinnest, thinning
4 Change final **y** to **i** before adding **ed, er, es, est, ly, ness**
e.g. tidy[4] → tidied, tidier, tidies, tidiest, tidily, tidiness
Keep final **y** before adding **ing** e.g. tidying
5 Add **es** instead of **s** to the end of the word
e.g. bunch[5] → bunches
6 Change final **f** to **ve** before adding **s**
e.g. calf[6] → calves

gall[1] *[nerve] ~bladder
Gael *[Scot, Irish]
Gail *[woman's name]
gale *[wind]+
gallant ~ry
gallen gallon
gallery[4]
galley
gallon
gallop[1] *[horse] Gallup *[poll]
Gallup *[poll] gallop[1] *[horse]
galon gallon
galop gallop[1] *[horse]
Gallup *[poll]
galore
galosh *[boot]
galvanize[2]
galy gaily
galley
gambit *[trick] gamut *[range]
gamble[2] *[games]
gambol[3] *[frolic]
game ~| bird ~keeper ~| plan ~| point ~| over ~| reserve ~| warden
gamesmanship
gamet gamut
gaming
gamut *[range] gambit *[trick]
gander
gane gain[1+]
ganesay gainsay+
gang[1] ~land ~plank ~way
gangling
gangrene @gangrenous
gangster ~ism ~| rap
gannet
gap *[opening, space] ~-toothed
gape[2] *[open]
garage
garantey guarantee *[goods]+
guaranty *[debt]+
garb
garbage
garble[2]
gard guard[1+]

garden[1] ~| center ~| party ~| shed
gardenia
gardian guardian+
gargal gargle[2] *[throat]
gargoyle *[figure]
gargantuan
gargle[2] *[throat]
gargoyle *[figure]
garish
garland[1]
garlic ~ky
garment
garner[1]
garnet
garnish[5] ~es
garrison
garrulous ~ly ~ness
garter ~| snake
gas[5] ~es ~| chamber ~| fire ~| mask ~ohol ~| oven ~| pressure ~| ring ~| station ~| tank

Unable to find your word under **gas**?
Take off **gas** and look again

gascet gasket
gase gaze[2]
gaseleen gasoline
gaselle gazelle
gasette gazette
gash[5] ~es
gasket
gasohol
gasoline
gasp[1]
gaspacho gazpacho
gastly ghastly[4]
gastric ~ulcer @gastritis
gastrointestinal
gastronomy @gastronomic
gassaleen gasoline
gate[2] *[barrier] ~house ~keeper ~way
gait *[walk]
gate-crash[5] ~er ~es
gather[1]

KEY TO SPELLING RULES

Red words are wrong. **Black** words are correct.

~ Add the suffix or word directly to the main word, without a space or hyphen
e.g. ash ~en ~tray → ashen ashtray

~- Add a hyphen to the main word before adding the next word
e.g. blow ~-dry → blow-dry

~| Leave a space between the main word and the next word
e.g. decimal ~| place → decimal place

+ By finding this word in its correct alphabetical order, you can find related words
e.g. abowt about+ → about-face

* Draws attention to words that may be confused

TM Means the word is a trademark

@ Signifies the word is derived from the main word

Gatorade™
gauche *[rude] gosh *[surprise]
gouache *[painting]
gaudy[4]
gauge[2]
gaunt
gauntlet
gauze *[cloth] gorse *[bush]
gave
gavel
gaw gore[2+]
gawk[1] ~y
gay ~| rights
Gaya Gaia[+]
gayety gaiety
gayla gala
gayly gaily
gayn gain[1+]
gaysha geisha
gayt gate[2] *[barrier][+]
gait *[walk]
gayter gaiter[+]
gaze[2]
gazebo
gazelle
gazette
gazpacho
gear[1] *[equipment] ~shift ~stick
gecko
gee ~| whiz
geek ~y
geese
geezer *[old person]
geyser *[fountain]
Geiger ~| counter
geisha
geko gecko
Gekyll Jekyll[+]
gel[3] *[soft substance]
jell[1] *[become firm]
gelatin @gelatinous
geld[1]
gelignite
gelly jelly[4+]
gem

Gemini
gemmy jimmy[4]
gender ~-bender ~-specific ~| studies
gene *[DNA, cell] ~| bank ~| pool ~| recognition ~| sequencing ~| therapy
jeans *[trousers]

Unable to find your word under **gene**? Take off **gene** and look again

genealogy @genealogist
general ~ly ~| anesthetic ~| election ~| knowledge ~| officer ~| practitioner ~| public ~| staff ~| store ~| strike

Unable to find your word under **general**? Take off **general** and look again

generality[4]
generalize[2] @generalization
generate[2] @generator
generative *[productive] ~| grammar
genitive *[possessive][+]
generation ~al ~| X
generic *[unbranded] ~ally
genetic *[DNA][+]
generosity[4]
generous ~ly ~ness
genes *[DNA, cells]
jeans *[trousers]
genetic *[DNA] ~ally ~| abnormality[4] ~| algorithm ~| code ~| engineering ~| enhancement ~| modification ~| programming
generic *[unbranded][+]

Unable to find your word under **genetic**? Take off **genetic** and look again

genetically ~| modified
genial ~ity
genie

KEY TO SUFFIXES AND COMPOUNDS

These rules are explained on pages vii to ix.

1 Keep the word the same before adding **ed, er, est, ing**
e.g. cool[1] → cooled, cooler, coolest, cooling
2 Take off final **e** before adding **ed, er, est, ing**
e.g. fine[2] → fined, finer, finest, fining
3 Double final consonant before adding **ed, er, est, ing**
e.g. thin[3] → thinned, thinner, thinnest, thinning
4 Change final **y** to **i** before adding **ed, er, es, est, ly, ness**
e.g. tidy[4] → tidied, tidier, tidies, tidiest, tidily, tidiness
Keep final **y** before adding **ing** e.g. tidying
5 Add **es** instead of **s** to the end of the word
e.g. bunch[5] → bunches
6 Change final **f** to **ve** before adding **s**
e.g. calf[6] → calves

genital *[reproductive] ~ia ~s
gentile *[not Jewish]
gentle *[kind, soft touch]+
genitive *[possessive] ~| case
generative *[productive]+
genius[5]
genocide @genocidal
genome
genomic ~| computing
genotype
genral general+
genralize generalize[2]+
genre ~-bending
genteel *[social class]
@gentility
gentile *[not Jewish]
genital *[reproductive]+
gentle *[kind, soft touch]
gentle[2] *[kind, soft touch] ~ness
~man's agreement
genital *[reproductive]+
gentile *[not Jewish]
@gently
gentrify[4] @gentrification
gentry
genuine ~ly ~ness
genus @genera
geocentric
geodesic ~| dome
geofysical geophysical
geofysics geophysics+
geographic ~al ~ally
geography @geographer
geological ~ly
geology @geologist
geometric ~al ~ally
geometry
geophysical
geophysics @geophysicist
geospatial ~| data
geranium
gerbil
gerd gird[1]
gerdul girdle[2]
gergle gurgle[2]
geriatric ~s
gerila gorilla *[ape]
guerrilla *[war]
gerk jerk[1]+
gerkin gherkin
gerl girl+
germ ~| warfare
German *[people] ~ic ~| measles
~| shepherd
germane *[relevant] ~ly ~ness
germicide
germinate[2] @germination
gerontology @gerontologist
gerrymander[1]
gerth girth

Unable to find your word under **ge**?
Look under **gi**

gerund ~ive
geshtapo Gestapo
gess guess[5]+
gest guessed *[estimated]
guest *[visitor]+
jest[1] *[joke]
gestalt
Gestapo
gestate[2] @gestation
gesticulate[2] @gesticulation
gesture[2]
Gesuit Jesuit
get ~ting ~-together ~-up-and-go
getsam jetsam *[cargo overboard]
gettison jettison[1] *[throw away]
getto ghetto+
Gew dew *[drops]
Jew *[person of Jewish ethnicity]+
gewel jewel[3] *[gem]+
joule *[unit]
gewelry jewelry *[gems]
gewish Jewish+

Unable to find your word under **ge**?
Look under **je**

Key to Spelling Rules

Red words are wrong. **Black** words are correct.

~ Add the suffix or word directly to the main word, without a space or hyphen
e.g. ash ~en ~tray → ashen ashtray

~- Add a hyphen to the main word before adding the next word
e.g. blow ~-dry → blow-dry

~| Leave a space between the main word and the next word
e.g. decimal ~| place → decimal place

\+ By finding this word in its correct alphabetical order, you can find related words
e.g. abowt about+ → about-face

★ Draws attention to words that may be confused

™ Means the word is a trademark

@ Signifies the word is derived from the main word

<table>
<tr><td>geyser *[fountain]</td><td>geezer *[old person]</td></tr>
<tr><td>gezel</td><td>gazelle</td></tr>
<tr><td>gezet</td><td>gazette</td></tr>
<tr><td>gezibo</td><td>gazebo</td></tr>
<tr><td colspan="2">ghastly[4]</td></tr>
<tr><td colspan="2">gherkin</td></tr>
<tr><td colspan="2">ghetto ~| blaster</td></tr>
<tr><td colspan="2">ghost[1] ~ly ~| town ~| train ~| word</td></tr>
<tr><td colspan="2">ghostwrite[2]</td></tr>
<tr><td>ghoul</td><td>ghoulish *[morbid]</td></tr>
<tr><td></td><td>goulash *[dish]</td></tr>
<tr><td colspan="2">giant ~ess ~| panda</td></tr>
<tr><td>gib *[metal plate]</td><td>gibe[1] *[to taunt]</td></tr>
<tr><td></td><td>jib *[part of a crane]</td></tr>
<tr><td colspan="2">gibber[1] ~ish</td></tr>
<tr><td colspan="2">gibbon</td></tr>
<tr><td>gibe[2] *[to taunt]</td><td>gib *[metal plate]</td></tr>
<tr><td></td><td>jib *[part of a crane]</td></tr>
<tr><td colspan="2">giblets</td></tr>
<tr><td>gidanse</td><td>guidance+</td></tr>
<tr><td colspan="2">giddy[4]</td></tr>
<tr><td>gide</td><td>guide[2]+</td></tr>
<tr><td>giek</td><td>geek+</td></tr>
<tr><td>gier</td><td>gear[1] *[equipment]+</td></tr>
<tr><td></td><td>jeer[1] *[ridicule]</td></tr>
<tr><td>giese</td><td>geese</td></tr>
<tr><td colspan="2">gift[1] ~| certificate ~| shop ~-wrap[3]</td></tr>
<tr><td colspan="2">gig *[public performance]</td></tr>
<tr><td></td><td>jig[3] *[dance]+</td></tr>
<tr><td colspan="2">gigabyte</td></tr>
<tr><td colspan="2">gigantic ~ally</td></tr>
<tr><td>giggle[2] *[laugh]</td><td>jiggle[2] *[move]</td></tr>
<tr><td colspan="2">gigolo</td></tr>
<tr><td>gihad</td><td>jihad</td></tr>
<tr><td>gild[1] *[gold cover]</td><td>guild *[association]</td></tr>
<tr><td>gile</td><td>guile+</td></tr>
<tr><td>gill *[fish]</td><td>guile+</td></tr>
<tr><td>gilotine</td><td>guillotine[2]</td></tr>
<tr><td colspan="2">gilt *[gold leaf] ~-edged</td></tr>
<tr><td></td><td>guilt *[shame]</td></tr>
<tr><td>giltey</td><td>guilty[4]</td></tr>
<tr><td colspan="2">gimlet</td></tr>
<tr><td colspan="2">gimmick ~ry ~y</td></tr>
<tr><td colspan="2">gin ~| and tonic ~| rummy</td></tr>
<tr><td>ginea</td><td>guinea+</td></tr>
<tr><td>gineal</td><td>genial+</td></tr>
<tr><td>ginecological</td><td>gynecological</td></tr>
<tr><td>ginecology</td><td>gynecology+</td></tr>
<tr><td colspan="2">ginger ~ly ~| ale ~| beer ~bread</td></tr>
<tr><td colspan="2">gingivitis</td></tr>
<tr><td>gingle</td><td>jingle[2]</td></tr>
<tr><td>gingoism</td><td>jingoism+</td></tr>
<tr><td>ginie</td><td>genie</td></tr>
<tr><td>ginks</td><td>jinks *[high]</td></tr>
<tr><td></td><td>jinx[5] *[spell]+</td></tr>
<tr><td>ginny</td><td>guinea+</td></tr>
<tr><td colspan="2">ginseng</td></tr>
<tr><td>ginx</td><td>jinx[5] *[spell]+</td></tr>
<tr><td></td><td>jinks *[high]</td></tr>
<tr><td colspan="2">giraffe</td></tr>
<tr><td>girdal</td><td>girdle[2]</td></tr>
<tr><td colspan="2">gird[1]</td></tr>
<tr><td colspan="2">girder</td></tr>
<tr><td colspan="2">girdle[2]</td></tr>
<tr><td>girgle</td><td>gurgle[2]</td></tr>
<tr><td colspan="2">girl ~ie ~ish ~friend</td></tr>
<tr><td colspan="2">Girl ~| Scout</td></tr>
<tr><td>giro</td><td>gyro+</td></tr>
<tr><td colspan="2">girth</td></tr>
<tr><td>gise</td><td>guise *[pretense]</td></tr>
<tr><td colspan="2">gist *[rough translation]</td></tr>
<tr><td></td><td>jest[1] *[joke]</td></tr>
<tr><td>gitar</td><td>guitar+</td></tr>
<tr><td colspan="2">give ~n ~-and-take ~| -away</td></tr>
<tr><td></td><td>@giving</td></tr>
<tr><td>giy</td><td>guy</td></tr>
<tr><td>gize</td><td>guise *[pretence]</td></tr>
<tr><td></td><td>guys *[people]</td></tr>
<tr><td colspan="2">gizmo</td></tr>
<tr><td colspan="2">gizzard</td></tr>
<tr><td>glacé *[cherry]</td><td>glacier *[ice]</td></tr>
<tr><td>glacial</td><td>@glaciation</td></tr>
<tr><td>glacier *[ice]</td><td>glazier *[glass repairer]</td></tr>
<tr><td colspan="2">glad[3] *[happy] ~ly</td></tr>
<tr><td></td><td>glade *[forest clearing]</td></tr>
<tr><td colspan="2">gladden[1]</td></tr>
<tr><td colspan="2">glade *[forest clearing]</td></tr>
<tr><td></td><td>glad[3] *[happy]+</td></tr>
<tr><td colspan="2">gladiator</td></tr>
<tr><td>glaishall</td><td>glacial+</td></tr>
</table>

Key to Suffixes and Compounds

These rules are explained on pages vii to ix.

1 Keep the word the same before adding **ed, er, est, ing**
e.g. cool[1] → cooled, cooler, coolest, cooling

2 Take off final **e** before adding **ed, er, est, ing**
e.g. fine[2] → fined, finer, finest, fining

3 Double final consonant before adding **ed, er, est, ing**
e.g. thin[3] → thinned, thinner, thinnest, thinning

4 Change final **y** to **i** before adding **ed, er, es, est, ly, ness**
e.g. tidy[4] → tidied, tidier, tidies, tidiest, tidily, tidiness
Keep final **y** before adding **ing** e.g. tidying

5 Add **es** instead of **s** to the end of the word
e.g. bunch[5] → bunches

6 Change final **f** to **ve** before adding **s**
e.g. calf[6] → calves

glaisher	glacier *[ice]
	glazier *[glass]
glamorize[2]	@glamorization
glamorous ~ly ~ness	
glance[2]	
gland ~ular fever	
glanse	glance[2]
glare[2]	
glashal	glacial+
glasher	glacier *[ice]
	glazier *[glass repairer]
glasnost	
glass[5] ~es ~-blower ~| ceiling ~ware	
glassy *[like glass]	
	glacé *[cherry]
glaucoma	
glaycial	glacial+
glaysure	glacier *[ice]
	glazier *[glass repairer]
glaze[2]	
glazier *[glass repairer]	
	glacier *[ice]
glaznost	glasnost
gleam[1] *[shine]	
glean[1] *[gather]	
glee ~ful ~fully	
glib ~ly ~ness	
glicerine	glycerin
glicojen	glycogen
glide[2]	
glimmer[1]	
glimpse[2]	
glint[1]	
glisserall	glycerol
glisserin	glycerin
glisten[1]	
glitch	
glits	glitz+
glitter[1] ~ati	
glitz	@glitzy[4]
gloat[1]	
glob *[drop of something]	
	globe *[world]+
global ~ly ~| village ~| warming	
globalize[2]	@globalization

globe *[world] ~trotter ~trotting	
	glob *[drop of something]
globule	@globular
glocoma	glaucoma
gloocose	glucose
gloom	@gloomy[4]
glootemate	glutamate
glootin	gluten *[substance]+
	glutton *[person]+
glorify[4]	@glorification
glorious ~ly ~ness	
glory[4]	
gloss[5] ~es	@glossy[4]
glossary[4]	
glote	gloat[1]
glottis	
glove ~| compartment	
glow[1] ~-worm	
glowcoma	glaucoma
glower[1]	
glucose	
glue[2] ~y ~-sniffing	
glukose	glucose
glum[3] ~ly ~ness	
glut[3] *[excess]	
glutamate	
gluten *[substance]	
	@glutinous
glutton *[person] ~ous ~y	
glycerin	
glycerol	
glycogen	
glymse	glimpse[2]
gnarled	
gnash[5]• ~es	
gnat	
gnaw[1] *[bite]	nor *[neither]
gneiss *[rock]	nice[2] *[pleasant]+
gnew	gnu *[animal]
	knew *[had knowledge]
	new *[not old]+
	nu *[Greek letter]
gnome *[dwarf]	@gnomish
	nom+

KEY TO SPELLING RULES

Red words are wrong. **Black** words are correct.

~ Add the suffix or word directly to the main word, without a space or hyphen
e.g. ash ~en ~tray → ashen ashtray

~- Add a hyphen to the main word before adding the next word
e.g. blow ~-dry → blow-dry

~| Leave a space between the main word and the next word
e.g. decimal ~| place → decimal place

\+ By finding this word in its correct alphabetical order, you can find related words
e.g. abowt about+ → about-face

★ Draws attention to words that may be confused

TM Means the word is a trademark

@ Signifies the word is derived from the main word

gnu *[animal] knew *[had knowledge]
new *[not old]+
nu *[Greek letter]
go[5] ~er ~ing ~-ahead ~-between ~-kart
goad[1]
goal ~less ~ie ~keeper ~| kick ~| line ~post
goat *[animal] ~ee ~herd ~skin
gout *[illness]
gobble[2] ~degook
goblet
goblin
god *[being, spirit] ~ly ~dess ~-awful ~child ~daughter ~father ~-forsaken ~head ~like ~mother ~send ~son
goad[1] *[incite]
good *[favorable]+
God *[Supreme Being] ~| forbid ~-given ~| knows ~speed

Unable to find your word under **god**?
Take off **god** and look again

gofer gopher
goggle[2] ~-eyed
goiter
gold ~-digger ~finch ~fish ~| leaf ~| medal ~| medalist ~| mine ~| rush ~smith ~| standard

Unable to find your word under **gold**?
Take off **gold** and look again

golden ~| age ~| eagle ~| handshake ~| jubilee ~| oldie ~| parachute ~| retriever ~rod ~| rule

Unable to find your word under **golden**?
Take off **golden** and look again

gole goal+
golf *[game] gulf *[bay]
gonads
gonarea gonorrhea
gondola @gondolier
gone ~r
gong
gonorrhea
gontlet gauntlet
goober *[peanut]
goobernatorial gubernatorial
good *[favorable] ~ness ~| afternoon ~bye ~| day ~| evening ~-for-nothing ~| humored ~-looking ~| morning ~-natured ~| night ~will

Unable to find your word under **good**?
Take off **good** and look again

Good Friday *[religious day]
goody[4] ~-bag ~-goody
goof ~y
Google™ *[web search]
googol *[very large number] ~| plex
gool ghoul+
goolish ghoulish *[death]
goulash *[dish]
goolog Gulag
goolush goulash *[dish]
ghoulish *[death]
goop
goose ~bumps
gopher
gord gourd *[fruit]
gored *[bull]
Gordian knot
gordy gaudy[4]
gore[2] @gory[4]
gored *[bull] gourd *[fruit]
gorge[2]
gorgeous ~ly ~ness
Gorgonzola
gorilla *[ape] guerrilla *[war]
gorjes gorgeous+
gork gawk[1]+
gormay gourmet+
gornt gaunt
gorse *[bush] gauze *[cloth]

Key to Suffixes and Compounds

These rules are explained on pages vii to ix.

1 Keep the word the same before adding **ed, er, est, ing**
e.g. cool[1] → cooled, cooler, coolest, cooling
2 Take off final **e** before adding **ed, er, est, ing**
e.g. fine[2] → fined, finer, finest, fining
3 Double final consonant before adding **ed, er, est, ing**
e.g. thin[3] → thinned, thinner, thinnest, thinning
4 Change final **y** to **i** before adding **ed, er, es, est, ly, ness**
e.g. tidy[4] → tidied, tidier, tidies, tidiest, tidily, tidiness
Keep final **y** before adding **ing** e.g. tidying
5 Add **es** instead of **s** to the end of the word
e.g. bunch[5] → bunches
6 Change final **f** to **ve** before adding **s**
e.g. calf[6] → calves

gosh *[surprise] gauche *[rude]
gouache *[painting]
gosip gossip[1+]
gosling
gospel ~| choir ~| music ~| singer ~| truth
gossamer
gossip[1] ~y ~| column ~| hound ~| rag
gost ghost[1+]
gostwrite ghostwrite[2]
gosumer gossamer
got *[past of get] goat[+]
Gothic
gouache *[painting]
gauche *[rude]
gosh *[surprise]
Gouda
gouge[2]
goul ghoul[+]
goal[+]
goulash *[dish] ghoulish *[death]
gourd *[fruit] gored *[bull]
gourmand
gourmet ~| cook
gout *[illness] goat *[animal][+]
govern[1] ~able ~ance
governatorial gubernatorial
governess
government ~al ~| bonds ~-controlled ~-regulated ~-sponsored
governor
gowge gouge[2]
gown
gowsh gauche *[rude]
gosh *[surprise]
gouache *[painting]
gowt goat *[animal][+]
gout *[illness]
goz gauze *[cloth]
gorse *[bush]
grab[3] ~-bag
grace[2] ~ful ~fully ~ness ~| period
gracious ~ly ~ness
grade[2] @gradation
gradient

gradual ~ly
graduate[2] @graduation
graf graph
grafficle graphical[+]
graffiti *[writing on wall]
grafite graffiti *[writing on wall]
graphite *[pencil lead]
grafitti graffiti *[writing on wall]
graft[1] *[plant, bribe]
graph *[drawing]
graid grade[2+]
grail
grain ~y
grait grate[2] *[fire, cheese]
great[1] *[big][+]
graiteful grateful[+]
gramafone gramophone
grammar *[language] ~ian
grandma *[grandmother]
grammatical ~ly
Grammy[4]
gramophone
granade grenade[+]
granary[4]
grand ~child ~children ~dad ~daughter ~eur ~father ~| jury ~| mal ~mother ~parent ~| piano ~| slam ~son ~stand

> Unable to find your word under **grand**? Take off **grand** and look again

grandiose @grandiosity
grandma *[grandmother]
grammar *[language][+]
granet granite
grange
granite
grannery granary[4]
granny[4] ~| square
grant[1] ~-making
granular ~ity
granulate[2] @granulation
granule
granyul granule

Key to Spelling Rules

Red words are wrong. **Black** words are correct.

- ~ Add the suffix or word directly to the main word, without a space or hyphen
  e.g. ash ~en ~tray → ashen ashtray
- ~- Add a hyphen to the main word before adding the next word
  e.g. blow ~-dry → blow-dry
- ~| Leave a space between the main word and the next word
  e.g. decimal ~| place → decimal place
- \+ By finding this word in its correct alphabetical order, you can find related words
  e.g. abowt about[+] → about-face
- ★ Draws attention to words that may be confused
- ™ Means the word is a trademark
- @ Signifies the word is derived from the main word

granyular granular+
granulate granulate2+
grape ~fruit ~seed ~shot ~vine
graph *[drawing] graft1 *[plant, bribe]
graphic ~ally ~| data ~| novel
graphical ~| user interface [GUI]
graphite *[pencil lead]
graffiti *[writing on wall]
graphology
grapple2
grase grace2+
graze2
grashus gracious+
grasp1
grass5 ~hopper ~land ~roots ~| snake
grate2 *[fire, cheese]
great1 *[big]+
grateful ~ly ~ness
grater *[cheese] greater *[bigger]+
gratest greatest+
gratify4 @gratification
gratis
gratitude
gratuitous ~ly ~ness
gratuity4
grave2 ~ly ~digger ~yard
gravel3 ~ly
gravitate2 @gravitation
gravitational ~| attraction
gravity
gravy ~| boat ~| train
gray1 ~| area
grayhound greyhound
grayl grail
grayling
grayn grain+
graze2
grease2 *[thick oil] ~paint ~proof
Greece *[country]+
greasy4
great1 *[big] ~ly ~ness
grate2 *[fire, cheese]
greater *[bigger] ~| than
grater *[cheese]

Greece *[country]
@Greek
grease2 *[thick oil]+
greed @greedy4
greef grief+
green ~ery ~ness ~back ~| card ~-eyed ~horn ~house effect
Greenwich ~| Mean Time
greese grease2 *[thick oil]+
Greece *[country]+
greesy greasy4
greet1 ~ings
greev grieve2+
greevious grievous+
gregarious ~ly ~ness
Gregorian ~| calendar ~| chant
greif grief+
greive grieve2+
gremlin
grenade @grenadier
Grenitch Greenwich+
grew
grewl gruel *[oatmeal]+
growl1 *[low sound]
grewsome gruesome+
greyhound
greyling grayling
grid ~| computing ~| technology
griddle2
gridiron
gried greed+
grief ~-stricken
grien green+
griet greet1+
grieve2 @grievance
grievous ~ly ~ness
griffin
grill1 ~| room
grim3 *[harsh] ~ly ~ness
grime *[dirt]+
grimace2
grime *[dirt] @grimy4
grim3 *[harsh]+
grimiss grimace2
grin3

Key to Suffixes and Compounds

These rules are explained on pages vii to ix.

1 Keep the word the same before adding **ed, er, est, ing**
e.g. cool1 → cooled, cooler, coolest, cooling
2 Take off final **e** before adding **ed, er, est, ing**
e.g. fine2 → fined, finer, finest, fining
3 Double final consonant before adding **ed, er, est, ing**
e.g. thin3 → thinned, thinner, thinnest, thinning
4 Change final **y** to **i** before adding **ed, er, es, est, ly, ness**
e.g. tidy4 → tidied, tidier, tidies, tidiest, tidily, tidiness
Keep final **y** before adding **ing** e.g. tidying
5 Add **es** instead of **s** to the end of the word
e.g. bunch5 → bunches
6 Change final **f** to **ve** before adding **s**
e.g. calf6 → calves

grind[1] ~stone
gringo[5]
grip[3] *[hold]
gripe[2] *[pain, complain]
grippe[2] *[disease]
grisel — gristle *[on meat]+
grizzle[2] *[gray, complain]
grisly[4] *[horrid] — gristly *[meat]
grizzly[4] *[bear]
grist
gristle *[on meat] — @gristly
grizzle[2] *[gray, complain]
grit[3] — @grits
@gritty[4]
grizzle[2] *[gray, complain]
gristle *[on meat]+
grizzly[4] ~| bear
grisly[4] *[horrid]
gristly *[meat]
groan[1] *[moan] — grown *[bigger]+
groap — grope[2]
groce — gross[5+]
grocer *[shop] — grosser *[fatter]
grocery[4] ~| store
groggy[4]
groin
grone — groan[1] *[moan]
grown *[bigger]+
groom[1]
groop — grope[2] *[touch]
group[1+]
groove[2] *[indent] — grove *[trees]
groovy[4]
grope[2] *[touch]
groser — grocer *[shop]
grosser *[fatter]
gross[5] *[disgusting, big] ~ly ~| domestic product ~| margin ~| profit ~| receipts
grows *[develop]

> Unable to find your word under **gross**?
> Take off **gross** and look again

grotesque ~ly
grotto[5]

grouch ~y
groul — growl[1] *[low sound]
gruel *[oatmeal]+
ground[1] ~less ~breaking ~| floor ~hog ~| rule ~swell ~work

> Unable to find your word under **ground**?
> Take off **ground** and look again

Groundhog ~| Day
groundskeeper
group[1] ~| practice ~| therapy ~ware
grouper *[fish]
groupie *[fan]
grouse[2]
grove *[trees] — groove[2] *[indent]
grovel[3]
grow ~er ~ing
growl[1] *[low sound]
gruel *[oatmeal]+
grown *[bigger] ~-up
groan[1] *[moan]
grownd — ground[1+]
growse — grouse[2]
growth ~| factor ~| fund ~| hormone ~| industry ~| rate

> Unable to find your word under **growth**?
> Take off **growth** and look again

grub[3] — @grubby[4]
grudge — @grudging
@grudgingly
grue — grew
gruel *[oatmeal] ~ling
growl[1] *[low sound]
gruesome ~ly ~ness
gruff[1] ~ly ~ness
gruge — grudge+
grumble[2]
grumpy[4]
grunge — @grungy[4]
grunt[1]
grupe — group[1+]
gryd — grid+
gryddle — griddle[2]

Key to Spelling Rules

Red words are wrong. **Black** words are correct.

- ~ Add the suffix or word directly to the main word, without a space or hyphen
  e.g. ash ~en ~tray → ashen ashtray
- ~- Add a hyphen to the main word before adding the next word
  e.g. blow ~-dry → blow-dry
- ~| Leave a space between the main word and the next word
  e.g. decimal ~| place → decimal place
- \+ By finding this word in its correct alphabetical order, you can find related words
  e.g. abowt about+ → about-face
- ★ Draws attention to words that may be confused
- ™ Means the word is a trademark
- @ Signifies the word is derived from the main word

gryt grit[3+]

> Unable to find your word under **gry**?
> Look under **gri**

guacamole
guache gauche *[rude]
gouache *[painting]
guano
guarantee *[goods] ~d ~ing
guaranty *[debt] @guarantor
guard[1] ~sman ~room
guardian ~| angel ~ship
guava
gubernatorial ~| race
gud god *[being, spirit]+
good *[favorable]+
gudbye goodbye
guerrilla *[war] gorilla *[ape]
guess[5] *[estimate] ~timate ~work
guest *[visitor]+
guessed *[estimated]
guest *[visitor] ~| house ~| room ~| worker
GUI [Graphical User Interface]
guidance ~| system
guide[2] ~book ~| dog ~line ~post
guided ~| missile
guild *[association]
gild[1] *[gold cover]
guile ~less
guillotine[2]
guilt *[shame] gilt *[gold leaf]+
guilty[4]
guinea ~| fowl ~| pig
guise *[pretense] guys *[people]
guitar ~ist ~| player
guizer geezer *[old person]
geyser *[fountain]
gulable gullible+
Gulag
gulash galosh *[boot]
goulash *[dish]
ghoulish *[death]
gulf *[bay] golf *[game]
Gulf Stream
gull
gullet
gullible @gullibility
gully[4]
gulp[1]
gum[3] ~drop ~shoe ~| tree
gumption
gun[3] ~boat ~dog ~fight ~man ~point ~powder ~running ~ship ~shot ~slinger

> Unable to find your word under **gun**?
> Take off **gun** and look again

gunnell gunwale
gunner ~y
gunwale
guppy
gurbil gerbil
gurd gird[1]
gurdul girdle[2]
gurgle[2]
gurkin gherkin *[food]
jerkin *[jacket]
gurl girl+
gurth girth
guseberry gooseberry[4]
gush[5] ~er ~es
gusse goose+
gust[1] @gusto
gut[3] ~| feeling
gutter ~ing ~| press ~snipe
guttural ~ly
guvern govern[1+]
guverner governor
guvernment government+
guy
guynecological gynecological
guynecology gynecology+
guys *[people] guise *[pretence]
guyser geyser
guzzle[2]
gwacamole guacamole
gwano guano

Key to Suffixes and Compounds

These rules are explained on pages vii to ix.

1 Keep the word the same before adding **ed, er, est, ing**
e.g. cool[1] → cooled, cooler, coolest, cooling
2 Take off final **e** before adding **ed, er, est, ing**
e.g. fine[2] → fined, finer, finest, fining
3 Double final consonant before adding **ed, er, est, ing**
e.g. thin[3] → thinned, thinner, thinnest, thinning
4 Change final **y** to **i** before adding **ed, er, es, est, ly, ness**
e.g. tidy[4] → tidied, tidier, tidies, tidiest, tidily, tidiness
Keep final **y** before adding **ing** e.g. tidying
5 Add **es** instead of **s** to the end of the word
e.g. bunch[5] → bunches
6 Change final **f** to **ve** before adding **s**
e.g. calf[6] → calves

gwashe — gauche *[rude]
gouache *[painting]
gwava — guava
gya — Gaia+
gybe — gibe[2] *[to taunt]
jib *[part of a crane]
gyddy — giddy[4]
gyft — gift[1+]
gyg — gig *[public performance]
gyggle — giggle[2] *[laugh]
gyle — guile+
gylt — gilt *[gold leaf]+
guilt *[shame]
gym ~khana ~nasium

gymnast ~ic ~ics
gynecological
gynecology @gynecologist
gypsum
gypsy[4]
gyrate[2] @gyration
gyro ~compass ~scope
gyzer — geezer *[old person]
geyser *[fountain]
gyzmo — gizmo

Unable to find your word under **gy**?
Look under **gi**

H

habeas corpus
habit ~able ~-forming
habitat ~ion
habitual ~ly
habitué
hacienda
hack[1] *[chop] ~saw
hackle *[feathers] heckle[2] *[pester]
hackney ~ed
had ~n't *[had not]
haddock
Hadj [also spelled Hajj]
haduck — haddock
hagad — Haggadah *[Jewish text]+
haggard *[worn]
hage — Hajj
hagel — haggle[2]
Haggadah *[Jewish text]
@Haggadoth
@haggadist
haggard *[worn]
haggle[2]

hail[1] *[ice, salute] ~stone
hale *[hearty]
hair *[on head] ~brush ~cut ~do ~dresser ~dressing ~line ~net ~pin ~-raising ~| salon ~-splitting ~style
hare *[animal]+
heir *[inherit]+

Unable to find your word under **hair**?
Take off **hair** and look again

hairloom — heirloom
hairy[4] *[with hair] harry[4] *[pursue]
Hajj [also spelled Hadj]
hak — hack[1] *[chop]+
hawk[1] *[bird, clear throat]+
hale *[hearty] hail[1] *[ice, salute]+
half[6] ~-baked ~-day ~-hearted ~| hour ~-life ~-light ~-price ~term ~time *[game] ~-time *[job] ~way ~-wit ~| year ~-yearly

KEY TO SPELLING RULES

Red words are wrong. **Black** words are correct.

~ Add the suffix or word directly to the main word, without a space or hyphen
e.g. ash ~en ~tray → ashen ashtray

~- Add a hyphen to the main word before adding the next word
e.g. blow ~-dry → blow-dry

~| Leave a space between the main word and the next word
e.g. decimal ~| place → decimal place

\+ By finding this word in its correct alphabetical order, you can find related words
e.g. abowt about+ → about-face

★ Draws attention to words that may be confused

TM Means the word is a trademark

@ Signifies the word is derived from the main word

Unable to find your word under **half**?
Take off **half** and look again

halibut
halijen — halogen
hall *[room] ~mark ~way
— haul[1] *[pull]
Hall ~| of Fame
hallelujah
Halloween [also spelled Hallowe'en]
hallucinate[2] — @hallucination
hallucinogen
halo[5] *[disk of light]
— hello *[greeting]
halogen
halt[1] ~ingly
halusinate — hallucinate[2+]
halusinogen — hallucinogen
halve[2] *[cut in half]
— have *[possess]+
ham[3] ~burger ~-fisted ~string ~| up
hammer[1]
hammock
hamper[1]
hamster
hamuck — hammock
hanch — haunch[5] *[thigh]
hand[1] ~ful ~| luggage ~made ~| over ~shake

Unable to find your word under **hand**?
Take off **hand** and look again

handal — Handel *[composer]
— handle[2] *[hold]+
handcuff[1]
Handel *[composer]
— handle[2] *[hold]+
handicap[3]
handicraft — @handiwork
handkerchief
handle[2] *[hold] ~bar
— Handel *[composer]
handling ~| charge
hands ~-on ~-free

handsome *[good-looking] ~ly ~ness
— hansom *[carriage]+
handwriting — @handwritten
handy[4]
Hanekka — Hanukkah+
hang[1] ~man ~over ~-up
hangar *[plane]
hanger *[clothes]
hanker[1] ~| after
hankerchif — handkerchief
hankuff — handcuff[1]
hanky ~-panky
Hannaka — Hanukkah+
hansom *[carriage] ~| cab
— handsome+
hant — haunt[1+]
Hanukkah [also spelled Chanukah]
haphazard ~ly ~ness
hapless ~ly ~ness
happen[1]
happy[4] ~-go-lucky
hara-kiri
harang — harangue[2]
harangue[2]
harass[5] ~ment
harbinger
harbor[1]
hard ~est ~ly ~ness ~ball ~-bitten ~-boiled ~| disk ~-hearted ~ship ~-wired ~-working

Unable to find your word under **hard**?
Take off **hard** and look again

harden[1]
hardware ~| application ~| engineer ~| neutral
hardy[4]
hare *[animal] ~bell ~-brained ~-lip
— hair *[on head]+
harem
hark[1] ~| back
harlot
harm[1] ~ful ~fully
harmenize — harmonize[2+]
harmless ~ly ~ness

Key to Suffixes and Compounds

These rules are explained on pages vii to ix.

1 Keep the word the same before adding **ed, er, est, ing**
e.g. cool[1] → cooled, cooler, coolest, cooling
2 Take off final **e** before adding **ed, er, est, ing**
e.g. fine[2] → fined, finer, finest, fining
3 Double final consonant before adding **ed, er, est, ing**
e.g. thin[3] → thinned, thinner, thinnest, thinning
4 Change final **y** to **i** before adding **ed, er, es, est, ly, ness**
e.g. tidy[4] → tidied, tidier, tidies, tidiest, tidily, tidiness
Keep final **y** before adding **ing** e.g. tidying
5 Add **es** instead of **s** to the end of the word
e.g. bunch[5] → bunches
6 Change final **f** to **ve** before adding **s**
e.g. calf[6] → calves

harmonic ~a ~ally
harmonious ~ly
harmonize[2] @harmonization
harmony[4]
harness[5] ~es
harp[1] ~ist ~| on
harpoon[1]
harpsichord
harrass harass[5+]
harried
harrow[1]
harry[4] *[pursue] hairy[4] *[with hair]
harry-carry hara-kiri
harsh[1] ~ly ~ness
hart *[male deer] heart *[part of body]+
harten hearten[1]
hartless heartless+
harty hearty[4]
harvest[1]
has ~-been ~n't [has not]
hasal hassle[2] *[annoy]
hazel *[bush]+
hash[5]
hashish
hassienda hacienda
hassle[2] *[annoy] hazel *[bush]+
hassock
haste *[great speed]
@hasten[1]
hasty[4] *[done in a hurry]
hastle hassle[2] *[annoy]
hazel *[bush]+
hasty[4] *[done in a hurry]
haste *[great speed]+
hat *[head clothing] ~pin
hate[2] *[dislike]
hot[3] *[burning]+
hatch[5] ~es ~way
hatchery[4]
hatchet ~| job ~| man
hate[2] *[dislike] hat *[head clothing]+
hateful ~ly ~ness
hathorn hawthorn
hatred
haughty[4]

haul[1] *[pull] hall *[room]+
haunch[5] *[thigh] hunch *[bend, guess]
haunt[1] ~ed house
haute *[fancy] ~| couture ~| cuisine
oat *[grain]+
have *[possess] @had
@has
@having
halve[2] *[cut in half]
haven
havoc
hawk[1] *[bird, clear throat] ~-eyed ~ish
hock[1] *[pawn, ankle]+
hawkey hockey
hawl hall *[room]+
haul[1] *[pull]
hawnch haunch[1] *[thigh]
hawnt haunt[1+]
hawse hoarse *[voice]+
horse *[animal]+

Unable to find your word under **ha**?
Look under **ho**

hawser
hawtey haughty[4]
hawthorn
hay *[grass] ~| fever ~lage ~| stack ~| wire
hey *[greeting]
hayl hail[1] *[ice, salute]+
hale *[hearty]
haylo halo[5] *[disk of light]
haynus heinous+
hazard[1] ~ous
haze @hazy[4]
hazel *[bush] ~-eyed ~nut
hassle[2]
he ~'d *[he would]
heed[1] *[take notice of]+
hid *[past of hide]
head[1] *[body, lead] ~ache ~board ~| count ~dress ~first ~gear ~hunter ~lamp ~land ~master ~mistress ~| office ~-over-heels

head ~phones ~quarters ~rest ~room ~set ~stone ~strong ~s-up ~| teacher ~waiter ~way ~| wind

heed[1] *[take notice of]+
hid *[past of hide]

> Unable to find your word under **head**?
> Take off **head** and look again

headhunt[1]
heads *[body, leads] ~-up
heeds[1] *[takes notice]+
heads ~| or tails
heal[1] *[cure] — heel *[foot]
he'll *[he will]
hill *[mound, slope]+
healed *[cured] — held *[past of hold]
health ~ful ~| care ~| center ~| claim ~| club ~| food ~| hazard ~| insurance

> Unable to find your word under **health**?
> Take off **health** and look again

healthy[4]
heap[1] *[pile] — hip *[body part, in fashion]+
hear *[sound] ~ing ~say
her *[female]+
here *[place]+
heard *[sound] — herd[1] *[animals]
Hurd *[servers]
hearing *[sound] ~-impaired
hearken[1] ~| after
hearsay *[word of mouth]
hearse *[funeral vehicle]
heart *[part of body] ~| attack ~beat ~break ~breaking ~broken ~burn ~| disease ~felt ~land ~-rending ~sick ~strings ~throb ~-to-heart ~warming
hart *[male deer]
hearth *[fireplace]
hurt *[injure]+

> Unable to find your word under **heart**?
> Take off **heart** and look again

hearten[1]
hearth *[fireplace]
heart *[part of body]+
heath *[scrubland]
heartless ~ly ~ness
hearty[4]
heat[1] ~edly ~proof ~| lightning ~stroke ~| wave
heath *[scrubland]
hearth *[fireplace]
heathen
heather
heave[2] *[lift] ~-ho
heavy[4] *[weight]+
hive[2] *[bee]
heaven ~ly ~ward
heavy[4] *[weight] ~-duty ~| goods ~-handed ~| industry
heave[2] *[lift]+
Hebrew ~| language
heckle[2] *[pester] — hackle *[feathers]
hectare *[land area]
hector *[harangue]
hectic ~ally
hector *[harangue]
hectare *[land area]
hed — heed[1] *[take notice of]+
he'd *[he had]
head[1] *[body, lead]+
he'd *[he had] — heed[1] *[take notice of]+
hid *[past of hide]
hide *[conceal]+
hedge[2] ~| clipper ~hog ~row
hedonist ~ic — @hedonism
heds — heads *[body, leads]+
heeds *[takes notice of]
heed[1] *[take notice of] ~ful ~less
he'd *[he had]
head[1] *[body, lead]+

Key to Suffixes and Compounds

These rules are explained on pages vii to ix.

1 Keep the word the same before adding **ed, er, est, ing**
e.g. cool[1] → cooled, cooler, coolest, cooling
2 Take off final **e** before adding **ed, er, est, ing**
e.g. fine[2] → fined, finer, finest, fining
3 Double final consonant before adding **ed, er, est, ing**
e.g. thin[3] → thinned, thinner, thinnest, thinning
4 Change final **y** to **i** before adding **ed, er, es, est, ly, ness**
e.g. tidy[4] → tidied, tidier, tidies, tidiest, tidily, tidiness
Keep final **y** before adding **ing** e.g. tidying
5 Add **es** instead of **s** to the end of the word
e.g. bunch[5] → bunches
6 Change final **f** to **ve** before adding **s**
e.g. calf[6] → calves

heel *[foot]	heal[1] *[cure]
	he'll *[he will]
	hill *[mound, slope]+
heer	hear *[sound]+
	here *[place]+
heering	hearing+
heeve	heave[2] *[lift]+
heffer	heifer
hefty[4]	
heifer	
height *[vertical measurement]	
	hit *[strike]+
heighten[1]	
Heimlich ~| maneuver	
heinous ~ly ~ness	
heir *[inherit] ~ess ~| apparent ~loom	
	hair *[on head]+
heiritable	heritable+
heiritage	heritage
heist *[robbery]	highest *[tallest]+
	hoist[1] *[raise]
heksagon	hexagon+
heksahedron	hexahedron
held *[past of hold]	
	healed *[cured]
helicopter	@helipad
	@heliport
helium	
helix[5]	
he'll *[he will]	
hell *[punishment] ~-bent ~fire ~hole	
hellish ~ly ~ness	
hello *[greeting]	halo[5] *[disk of light]
helm *[steers ship]	
helmet *[on head]	
help[1]	
helpful ~ly ~ness	
helpless ~ly ~ness	
helth	health+

Unable to find your word under **he**?
Look under **hea**

hem[3] ~line ~-stitch	
hemaroids	hemorrhoids
hematology	
hematoma	
hemerage	hemorrhage[2]
hemisphere	
hemlock	
hemofilia	hemophilia+
hemoglobin	
hemophilia ~c	
hemoroids	hemorrhoids
hemorrhage[2]	
hemorrhoids	
hemorrige	hemorrhage[2]
hemp	
hen ~house ~pecked	
hena	henna
hence ~forth ~forward	
henchman	@henchmen
henna	
hense	hence+
hepatitis	
her *[female] ~self	
	hear *[sound]+
	here *[place]+
herald[1] ~ry	
herb ~al ~alist ~| garden	
herbaceous ~| border	
herbicide	
herbivore	@herbivorous
herd[1] *[animals]	heard *[sound]
	Hurd *[servers]
herdul	hurdle[2] *[obstacle]
	hurtle[2] *[move rapidly]
here *[place] ~abouts ~after ~by ~in ~with	
	hear *[listen]+
hereditary *[handed down]	
heredity *[handing down]	
heresy[4]	
heretic ~al	
heritable ~| disease	
heritage *[handed down]	
	hermitage *[hermit's home]
	Hermitage *[Russian museum]

Key to Spelling Rules

Red words are wrong. **Black** words are correct.

~ Add the suffix or word directly to the main word, without a space or hyphen
e.g. ash ~en ~tray → ashen ashtray

~- Add a hyphen to the main word before adding the next word
e.g. blow ~-dry → blow-dry

~| Leave a space between the main word and the next word
e.g. decimal ~| place → decimal place

\+ By finding this word in its correct alphabetical order, you can find related words
e.g. abowt about+ → about-face

★ Draws attention to words that may be confused

™ Means the word is a trademark

@ Signifies the word is derived from the main word

heritige	**heritage**
herl	**hurl**[1]
hermaphrodite	
hermetic ~ally	
hermit	
hermitage *[hermit's home]	
	heritage *[handed down]
Hermitage *[Russian museum]	
hernia	
hero[5] ~ic ~ically ~-worship	
heroin *[drug]	
heroine *[female hero]	
heroism	
heron	
herpes	
herring	
herry	**hairy**[4] *[with hair]
	harry[4] *[pursue]
hers *[possessive pronoun]	
herse	**hearse** *[funeral vehicle]
hert	**hurt** *[injure]+
	hut *[shed]
hertul	**hurtle**[2]
hertz *[frequency measure]	
	hurts *[pain]
hesitant ~ly	**@hesitancy**
hesitate[2]	**@hesitation**
heterogeneous	
heterosexual	
hether	**heather**
hetrogenious	**heterogeneous**
hetrosexual	**heterosexual**
heven	**heaven**+
hevie	**heavy**[4] *[weight]+
hew[1] *[cut] ~n	
	hue *[tint, fuss]
	who *[what, which]
hewj	**huge** *[large]+
hewmor	**humor**[1]
hexagon ~al	
hey *[greeting]	**hay** *[grass]+
hi *[greeting] ~-fi	
	high *[tall]+
hiacinth	**hyacinth**
hiatus	

hibernate[2]	**@hibernation**
hibrid	**hybrid**
Hibrue	**Hebrew**+
hiccup[3]	
hich	**hitch**[5+]
hichhike	**hitch-hike**[2]
hickup	**hiccup**[3]
hid *[past of hide]	**he'd** *[he had]
	hide *[conceal]+
hidden ~| asset ~| reserves	
hide *[conceal] ~-and-seek ~-out	
	hid *[past of hide]
hideous ~ly ~ness	
hiding ~| place	
hidious	**hideous**+
hidra	**hydra**+
hidrangea	**hydrangea**
hidrant	**hydrant**
hidrolic	**hydraulic**+
hie	**hi** *[greeting]+
	high *[tall]+
hieght	**height** *[vertical measurement]
hieghten	**heighten**[1]
hiena	**hyena**
hienous	**heinous**+
hier	**hear** *[sound]+
	higher *[further up]+
	hire[2] *[employ]+
hierarchical ~ly	
hierarchy[4]	
hieroglyph ~ic ~ics	
hiest	**highest** *[tallest]+
	heist *[robbery]
hieve	**heave**[2] *[lift]+
	hive[2] *[for bees]
hiewey	**highway**+
hifen	**hyphen**
hifenate	**hyphenate**[2]
higene	**hygiene**+
higenist	**hygienist**
high *[tall] ~ly ~ness ~-bandwidth ~brow ~| court ~| chair ~-class ~| command ~| finance ~flyer ~-handed ~-level ~light	

Key to Suffixes and Compounds

These rules are explained on pages vii to ix.

1 Keep the word the same before adding **ed, er, est, ing**
e.g. cool[1] → cooled, cooler, coolest, cooling

2 Take off final **e** before adding **ed, er, est, ing**
e.g. fine[2] → fined, finer, finest, fining

3 Double final consonant before adding **ed, er, est, ing**
e.g. thin[3] → thinned, thinner, thinnest, thinning

4 Change final **y** to **i** before adding **ed, er, es, est, ly, ness**
e.g. tidy[4] → tidied, tidier, tidies, tidiest, tidily, tidiness
Keep final **y** before adding **ing** e.g. tidying

5 Add **es** instead of **s** to the end of the word
e.g. bunch[5] → bunches

6 Change final **f** to **ve** before adding **s**
e.g. calf[6] → calves

high ~-performance computing ~-pitched ~-priced ~-profile ~| quality ~-ranking ~-rent ~-rise ~| roller ~| school ~-speed ~-spirited ~| tech ~-yield
hi *[greeting]+

> Unable to find your word under **high**?
> Take off **high** and look again

higher *[further up] ~| education ~-up
hire[2] *[employ]+
highest *[tallest] ~| common factor
heist *[robbery]
highlight[1]
highly ~| motivated ~| qualified ~| paid
highman hymen
highway ~man
higiene hygiene+
hijack[1]
hike[2]
hil hill *[mound, slope]+
heal[1] *[cure]
heel *[foot]
he'll *[he will]
hilarious ~ly ~ness
hilium helium
hilix helix[5]
hill *[mound, slope] ~ly[4] ~billy[4] ~side
heal *[cure]
heel[1] *[foot]
he'll *[he will]
him *[male] ~self
hymn *[song]+
himelick Heimlich+
himen hymen *[membrane]
hind ~quarters ~sight
hinder[1]
Hindoo Hindu+
hindrance
Hindu ~ism
hinge[2]
hint[1]
hinterland

hip *[body part, in fashion] ~| hop
@hippie
heap[1] *[pile]
hype[2] *[publicity]
hipacrit hypocrite
hipacritical hypocritical *[false]+
hipe hip *[body part, in fashion]
hype[2] *[publicity]
hipertext hypertext
hipnosis hypnosis
hipnotize hypnotize[2]
hipocrasy hypocrisy[4]
hipotanuse hypotenuse
hipothasis hypothesis+
hippie
hippocracy hypocrisy[4]
Hippocratic ~| oath
hippodrome
hippopotamus
hir hear *[sound]+
here *[place]+
her *[female]+
hire[2] *[employ]+
hirdel hurdle[2] *[obstacle]
hurtle[2] *[move rapidly]
hire[2] *[employ] ~| purchase
hear *[sound]+
here *[place]+
higher *[further up]+
hirl hurl[1]
his *[possessive of 'he']
he's *[he is]
hiss[5] *[sound]+
Hispanic
hiss[5] *[sound] ~es
his *[possessive of 'he']
histerectemy hysterectomy[4]
histeria hysteria+
histerical hysterical+

> Unable to find your word under **hi**?
> Look under **hy**

historian

KEY TO SPELLING RULES

Red words are wrong. **Black** words are correct.

~ Add the suffix or word directly to the main word, without a space or hyphen
e.g. ash ~en ~tray → ashen ashtray

~- Add a hyphen to the main word before adding the next word
e.g. blow ~-dry → blow-dry

~| Leave a space between the main word and the next word
e.g. decimal ~| place → decimal place

+ By finding this word in its correct alphabetical order, you can find related words
e.g. abowt about+ → about-face

* Draws attention to words that may be confused

TM Means the word is a trademark

@ Signifies the word is derived from the main word

historic ~al ~ally
historik historic⁺
history[4]
histrionic ~ally ~s
hit *[strike] ~-and-run ~| list ~ter ~ting ~-and-miss
height *[vertical measurement]
hitch[5] ~es ~-hike[2]
hiten heighten[1]
HIV *[disease]
hive[2] *[for bees] heave[2] *[lift]⁺

Unable to find your word under **hi**?
Look under **he**

hiway highway⁺
ho *[shout] hoe[2] *[digging tool]
who *[question]⁺
hoaks hoax[5+]
hoan hone[2+]
hoar *[gray] ~frost
whore[2] *[prostitute]⁺
hoard[1] *[collect] horde *[swarm]
hoarse *[voice] ~ly ~ness
horse *[animal]⁺
hoax[5] ~es
hob ~goblin ~nailed
hobble[2]
hobby[4] ~-horse
hobnob[3]
hock[1] *[pawn, ankle] ~shop
hawk[1] *[bird, clear throat]⁺
hockey *[game]
hodgepodge
hoe[2] *[digging tool]
ho *[shout]
hog[3] ~shead ~wash
hoist[1] *[raise] heist *[robbery]
hok hock[1] *[pawn, ankle]⁺
hook[1+]
hokes hoax[5+]
hokey *[sentimental]
hockey *[game]

holacawst holocaust *[blood sacrifice]
hold ~er ~| fast ~| on ~| out ~| over ~-up
holding ~| company[4]
hole[2] *[cavity] ~| up
whole *[complete]⁺
holy *[sacred]
holegram hologram
holey *[holes] holy *[sacred]
wholly *[fully]
holiday[1] *[vacation]
Holy Day *[religious day]
holistic
Holiwood Hollywood
hollandaise ~| sauce
hollocost holocaust *[blood sacrifice]
hollow[1]
holly *[tree] ~berry ~hock
holy *[sacred]
wholly *[fully]
Hollywood
holocaust *[blood sacrifice]
Holocaust *[slaughter of Jews]
hologram
holster[1]
holy[4] *[sacred] holly *[tree]
wholly *[fully]
Holy ~| Bible ~| Ghost ~| Grail ~| Land ~| See ~| Spirit ~| Trinity
Holy Day *[religious day]
holiday[1] *[vacation]
homage
home[2] *[dwelling, seek] ~boy ~coming ~| consumption ~| ground ~grown ~| made ~| market ~| movie ~owner ~| shopping ~| page ~| plate

Unable to find your word under **home**?
Take off **home** and look again

homeless ~ness
homely[4] *[comfortable]
homily[4] *[sermon]

Key to Suffixes and Compounds

These rules are explained on pages vii to ix.

1 Keep the word the same before adding **ed, er, est, ing**
e.g. cool[1] → cooled, cooler, coolest, cooling
2 Take off final **e** before adding **ed, er, est, ing**
e.g. fine[2] → fined, finer, finest, fining
3 Double final consonant before adding **ed, er, est, ing**
e.g. thin[3] → thinned, thinner, thinnest, thinning
4 Change final **y** to **i** before adding **ed, er, es, est, ly, ness**
e.g. tidy[4] → tidied, tidier, tidies, tidiest, tidily, tidiness
Keep final **y** before adding **ing** e.g. tidying
5 Add **es** instead of **s** to the end of the word
e.g. bunch[5] → bunches
6 Change final **f** to **ve** before adding **s**
e.g. calf[6] → calves

homeopath ~ic ~y
homesick ~ness
homicide @homicidal
homige homage
homily[4] *[sermon]
homely[4] *[comfortable]
homing ~| instinct ~| pigeon
homiopath homeopath+
homiside homicide+
homo sapiens
homofobia homophobia+
homogeneous @homogeneity
homograph
homojenous homogeneous+
homonym
homophobia @homophobic
homosexual ~ity
hone[2] *[sharpen] honey *[bees]+
honer honor[1]+
honest ~ly ~y
honey *[bees] ~bunch ~comb ~suckle
honeymoon[1]
honk[1]
honor[1] ~able ~ably
honorarium
honorific
hont haunt[1]+
hood[1] *[head cover, gangster]
who'd *[who had, who would]
hoodlum
hoodwink[1]
hoof[6] *[animal foot]
huff[1] *[pant]+
hook[1] ~-up ~worm
hoolahoop hula hoop™
hooligan ~ism
hoop[1] *[circle] whoop[1] *[shout]+
hoopla
hoot[1] *[loud cry, owl]
hot *[burning]+
hop[3] *[jump] ~scotch
hope[2] *[wish] ~ful ~fully
hopeless ~ly ~ness
horde *[swarm] hoard[1] *[collect]
horer horror+
horible horrible+

Unable to find your word under **hor**?
Look under **horr**

horizon
horizontal ~lly ~| integration
hormone
horn[1] ~beam ~pipe ~-rimmed
hornet
horny[4]
horoscope
horrer horror+
horrible @horribly
horrid ~ness
horrific ~ally
horrify[4]
horror ~| film ~| story ~| struck
hors-d'oeuvre ~s
horse *[animal] ~back ~| box ~| riding ~shoe ~| chestnut ~-drawn ~fly[4] ~hair ~meat ~play ~power ~'s ass ~-trading ~whip[3]
hoarse *[voice]+
whores *[prostitutes]

Unable to find your word under **horse**?
Take off **horse** and look again

horticultural ~ist
horticulture @horticultural
hose[2] *[water] hoes *[digs]
horse *[animal]+
who's *[who is, who has]
whose *[possessive]
hosiery
hospitable @hospitably
hospital ~ity
hospitalize[2] @hospitalization
hospitle hospital+
host[1] ~ess
hostage
hostel *[lodging]
hostile *[enemy] ~| takeover
@hostility[4]

hot[3] *[burning] ~ly ~bed ~-blooded ~| chocolate ~| dog ~foot ~headed ~house ~| key ~line ~| pants ~| plate ~| potato ~| rod ~| seat ~shot ~-tempered
hoot[1] *[loud cry, owl]

> Unable to find your word under **hot**?
> Take off **hot** and look again

hotel ~ier
hound[1]
hour *[time] ~ly ~glass
our *[possessive]+
hours *[time] ours *[possessive]+
house[2] ~ful ~| arrest ~boat ~breaking ~cleaning ~hold ~| lights ~plant ~-sit ~-trained ~wife[6] ~work ~warming
House ~| of Representatives

> Unable to find your word under **house**?
> Take off **house** and look again

hovel
hover[1] ~craft
how *[question] ~ever
who *[what, which]

> Unable to find your word under **ho**?
> Look under **who**

howitzer
howl[1]
hownd hound[1]
howse house[2+]
howswife housewife[6]
howswork housework

> Unable to find your word under **how**?
> Look under **hou**

hoyst hoist[1]
hu hew[1] *[cut]+
hue *[tint, fuss]
who *[what, which]

hub ~bub ~cap
Hubble ~'s constant ~'s law ~| Space Telescope
huch hutch[5]
hud hood[1] *[head cover, gangster]+
who'd *[who had, who would]
huddle[2]
hudwink hoodwink[1]
hue *[tint, fuss] hew[1] *[cut]+
who *[what, which]+
huff[1] *[pant] ~y[4]
hoof[6] *[animal foot]
hug[3] *[embrace]
huge *[large] ~ly
hula ~| dance ~| hoop™
hulk ~ing
hull[1] *[shell] who'll *[who will]
hum[3] ~bug ~drum ~ming bird
human *[person] ~ly ~| body ~| condition ~| computer interface ~| genome ~kind ~| rights
humane *[kindly]+
Human Resources [HR]

> Unable to find your word under **human**?
> Take off **human** and look again

humane *[kindly] ~ly
human *[person]+
humanist ~ic ~ism
humanitarian ~ism
humanity[4]
humanize[2]
humble[2] ~ness @humbly
humbug
humdrum
humer humor[1]
humerus *[bone] humorous *[funny]
humid ~ity
humidify[4]
humiliate[2] @humiliation
humility
humming ~bird

Key to Suffixes and Compounds

These rules are explained on pages vii to ix.

1 Keep the word the same before adding **ed, er, est, ing**
e.g. cool[1] → cooled, cooler, coolest, cooling
2 Take off final **e** before adding **ed, er, est, ing**
e.g. fine[2] → fined, finer, finest, fining
3 Double final consonant before adding **ed, er, est, ing**
e.g. thin[3] → thinned, thinner, thinnest, thinning
4 Change final **y** to **i** before adding **ed, er, es, est, ly, ness**
e.g. tidy[4] → tidied, tidier, tidies, tidiest, tidily, tidiness
Keep final **y** before adding **ing** e.g. tidying
5 Add **es** instead of **s** to the end of the word
e.g. bunch[5] → bunches
6 Change final **f** to **ve** before adding **s**
e.g. calf[6] → calves

hummus *[food]	humus *[soil]
humor[1]	
humorist	
humorous *[funny]	
	humerus *[bone]
hump[1] ~back	
humus *[soil]	hummus *[food]
hunch[5] *[bend, guess] ~back	
	haunch[5] *[thigh]
hundred ~th ~fold ~weight	
hung ~over	
hunger[1] ~| pang ~| strike	
hungry[4]	
hunk	
hunny	honey+
hunnymoon	honeymoon[1]
hunt[1] ~-and-peck ~sman	
hunta	junta
hunter ~-gatherer	
hupe	hoop[1] *[circle]+
	whoop[1] *[shout]+
hurb	herb+
hurbaceous	herbaceous+
hurbiside	herbicide
hurbivor	herbivore+
Hurd *[servers]	heard *[sound]
	herd[1] *[animals]
hurdle[2] *[obstacle]	
	hurtle[2] *[move rapidly]
hurikane	hurricane
hurl[1]	
hurmafrodyte	hermaphrodite
hurmetic	hermetic+
hurmit	hermit
hurnia	hernia
hurpes	herpes
hurray	
hurricane	
hurry[4] ~| up	
hurse	hearse *[funeral vehicle]
	hers *[possessive pronoun]
hurt *[injure] ~ful ~ing	
	hut *[shed]

hurtle[2] *[move rapidly]	
	hurdle[2] *[obstacle]
hurtz	hertz *[frequency measure]

> Unable to find your word under **hur**?
> Look under **her**

husband[1] ~ry	
hush[5] ~-hush ~| money	
husk[1]	@husky[4]
hussel	hustle[2]
hustle[2]	
hut *[shed]	hurt *[injure]+
hutch[5]	
hy	hi *[greeting]+
	high *[tall]+
hyacinth	
hyatus	hiatus
hybernate	hibernate[2]+
hybrid	
hyd	hid *[past of hide]
	hide *[conceal]+
hyddeus	hideous+
hyde	hide *[conceal]+
	hid *[past of hide]
hydra	
hydrangea	
hydrant	
hydraulic ~ally	@hydraulics
hydro ~electric ~foil ~therapy	
hydrocarbon	
hydrochloric ~| acid	
hydrocortisone	
hydrogen ~| bomb	
hydrokloric	hydrochloric+
hydrokside	hydroxide
hydrolic	hydraulic+
hydrolysis	
hydrometer	
hydropath	
hydrophobia	
hydroplane	
hydrostatic	
hydrotherapy	

hydroxide

hye	hi *[greeting]+
	high *[tall]+

hyena

hyer	higher *[further up]+
	hire² *[employ]+
hyerarcky	hierarchy⁴
hyest	highest *[tallest]+
	heist *[robbery]
hyfen	hyphen
hyfenate	hyphenate²
hygiene	@hygienist
hygienic ~ally	
hyjack	hijack¹
hyjene	hygiene+
hyjenic	hygienic+
hyke	hike²
hylarious	hilarious+
hymen *[membrane]	
hymlick	Heimlich+
hymn *[song] ~al	
	him *[male]+
	hymen *[membrane]
hynder	hinder¹
Hyndoo	Hindu+
hyndrance	hindrance
Hyndu	Hindu+
hynge	hinge²
hynt	hint¹
hype² *[publicity]	heap¹ *[pile]
	hip *[body part, in fashion]

hyper ~active ~activity ~inflation ~link ~| media ~sensitive ~tension ~ventilate²

> Unable to find your word under **hyper**?
> Take off **hyper** and look again

hyperbole
hyperbolic ~al ~ally
hypercritical
hypertext
hyphen
hyphenate²
hypnosis
hypnotic ~ally

hypnotist	@hypnotism

hypnotize²
hypoallergenic
hypochondria ~c
hypocrisy⁴
hypocrite

hypocritical *[false] ~ly	
	hypercritical
hypodermic ~| needle	
hypotenuse	
hypothermia	
hypothesis	@hypotheses
hypothesize²	
hypothetical ~ly	
hypothetikal	hypothetical+
hyppodrome	hippodrome
hyppopotamus	hippopotamus
hyppy	hippie
hyre	higher *[further up]+
	hire² *[employ]+
hyrogliph	hieroglyph+
Hyspanic	Hispanic
hyst	heist *[robbery]
hysterectomy⁴	
hysteria	@hysterics
hysterical ~ly	
hystorick	historic+
hyt	height *[vertical measurement]
	hit *[strike]+
hytch	hitch⁵+
hytch-hyke	hitch-hike²

> Unable to find your word under **hy**?
> Look under **hi**

hyu	hue *[tint, fuss]
	who *[what or which]
hyuman	human *[person]+
hyway	highway+

KEY TO SUFFIXES AND COMPOUNDS

These rules are explained on pages vii to ix.

1 Keep the word the same before adding **ed, er, est, ing** e.g. cool¹ → cooled, cooler, coolest, cooling
2 Take off final **e** before adding **ed, er, est, ing** e.g. fine² → fined, finer, finest, fining
3 Double final consonant before adding **ed, er, est, ing** e.g. thin³ → thinned, thinner, thinnest, thinning
4 Change final **y** to **i** before adding **ed, er, es, est, ly, ness** e.g. tidy⁴ → tidied, tidier, tidies, tidiest, tidily, tidiness
Keep final **y** before adding **ing** e.g. tidying
5 Add **es** instead of **s** to the end of the word e.g. bunch⁵ → bunches
6 Change final **f** to **ve** before adding **s** e.g. calf⁶ → calves

I

I *[me, letter of the alphabet]
aye *[yes]
eye *[see]+
I ~| see *[seeing with your eyes]
icy4 *[freezing]
iambic ~| pentameter

Unable to find your word under **i**?
Look under **e**

ibuprofen
ice2 *[frozen water] ~| age ~berg ~-cold ~| cream ~| hockey ~| pack ~| pick ~| rink ~-skate2
icy4 *[freezing]

Unable to find your word under **ice**?
Take off **ice** and look again

ich — each *[per piece]
itch5 *[scratch]+
icicle
icing ~| sugar
iclair — eclair
iclispe — eclipse2+
icon ~oclast ~oclastic
icy4 *[freezing] — I see *[seeing with your eyes]
icycle — icicle
id *[psyche] — I'd *[I had, would]
it *[pronoun]+
ID *[identification]
I'd *[I had, would] — eyed *[watched]
id *[psyche]
ID *[identification]
ideal ~ism ~ly
idealize2

idealogical — ideological+
idealogy — ideology4
ideel — ideal+
ideelise — idealize2
ideer — idea
idel — idle2 *[lazy]+
idol *[worship]
idyll *[poem]+
idendify — identify4+
identical ~ly
identify4 — @identification
identity4 ~| card
ideoligy — ideology4
ideological ~ly
ideology4
ideom — idiom+
ideosyncrasy — idiosyncrasy4+
ideot — idiot+
iderdown — eiderdown
ides *[Roman calendar] ~| of March
ideum — idiom+
idill — idyll *[poem]+
idiocy
idiological — ideological+
idiology — ideology4
idiom ~atic ~atically
idiosey — idiocy4
idiosyncrasy — @idiosyncratic
idiot ~ic ~| savant
idium — idiom+
idle2 *[lazy] ~ness
idyll *[poem]+
idol *[worship] — idyll *[poem]+
idolatry — @idolatrous
idolize2
idollatry — idolatry+

Key to Spelling Rules

Red words are wrong. **Black** words are correct.

~ Add the suffix or word directly to the main word, without a space or hyphen
e.g. ash ~en ~tray → ashen ashtray

~- Add a hyphen to the main word before adding the next word
e.g. blow ~-dry → blow-dry

~| Leave a space between the main word and the next word
e.g. decimal ~| place → decimal place

+ By finding this word in its correct alphabetical order, you can find related words
e.g. abowt about+ → about-face

* Draws attention to words that may be confused

TM Means the word is a trademark

@ Signifies the word is derived from the main word

idyll *[poem] ~ic ~ically	
	idle[2] *[lazy][+]
	idol *[worship]
idyot	idiot[+]
i.e. *[that is]	aye *[yes]
	eye *[see][+]
	I *[me]
ieght	eight *[number][+]
ieghth	eighth[+]
ieghty	eighty[4+]
ier	ire
iern	iron[1+]
iery	eery[4] *[strange]
	Erie *[lake]
iether	either *[or]
	ether *[air, liquid][+]
if ~fy ~| ever ~| only	
Iffel	eyeful *[amount, in your eye]
	Eiffel [Tower]
igalitarian	egalitarian[+]
Igiptology	Egyptology[+]
igkneeous	igneous[+]
igknowble	ignoble
igknowminious	ignominious[+]
igloo	
igneminy	ignominy
igneous ~| rock	
igneramus	ignoramus
ignerence	ignorance
ignite[2]	@ignition
ignius	igneous[+]
ignoble	
ignominious ~ly ~ness	
ignominy	
ignor	ignore[2]
ignoramus	
ignorance	
ignorant ~ly	
ignore[2]	
ignorent	ignorant[+]
ignour	ignore[2]
ignyte	ignite[2+]
igo	ego[+]
igocentric	egocentric[+]
igotist	egotist[+]
iguana	
ihmahm	imam
ijaculate	ejaculate[2+]
ijambic	iambic[+]
iject	eject[1+]
ikon	icon[+]
il	aisle *[passage]
	ill *[sick][+]
	I'll *[I will, I shall][+]
	isle *[island]
iland	island[+]
ilapse	elapse[2+]
ilastic	elastic[+]
ilate	elate[2+]
ile	aisle *[passage]
	isle *[island]
I'le	I'll *[I will, I shall]
	aisle *[passage]
ileagle	illegal[+]
ilegible	illegible[+]
ilegitimate	illegitimate[+]
ilett	eyelet *[hole]
	islet *[island]
ilicit	elicit[1] *[get]
	illicit *[illegal]
iligitimate	illegitimate[+]
iliminate	eliminate[2+]
ilind	island[+]
ilistrate	illustrate[2+]
ill ~ness ~-advised ~-bred ~-conceived ~-considered ~-defined ~-equipped ~-fated ~| feeling ~-founded ~| health ~-prepared	

> Unable to find your word under **ill**?
> Take off **ill** and look again

I'll *[I will, I shall]	aisle *[passage]
	isle *[island]
illegal ~ly	@illegality[4]
illegible	@illegibility
illegitimacy	
illegitimate ~ly	

Key to Suffixes and Compounds

These rules are explained on pages vii to ix.

1. Keep the word the same before adding **ed, er, est, ing**
   e.g. cool[1] → cooled, cooler, coolest, cooling
2. Take off final **e** before adding **ed, er, est, ing**
   e.g. fine[2] → fined, finer, finest, fining
3. Double final consonant before adding **ed, er, est, ing**
   e.g. thin[3] → thinned, thinner, thinnest, thinning
4. Change final **y** to **i** before adding **ed, er, es, est, ly, ness**
   e.g. tidy[4] → tidied, tidier, tidies, tidiest, tidily, tidiness
   Keep final **y** before adding **ing** e.g. tidying
5. Add **es** instead of **s** to the end of the word
   e.g. bunch[5] → bunches
6. Change final **f** to **ve** before adding **s**
   e.g. calf[6] → calves

illicit *[illegal] ~ness	
	elicit^{1} *[get]
illistrate	illustrate^{2+}
illiteracy	@illiterate
illogical	
illuminate^{2}	@illumination
illusion *[wrong perception]	
	allusion *[reference]
	elusion *[escape]
illusive *[deceptive]	
	allusive *[suggestive]$^{+}$
	elusive *[evasive]$^{+}$
illusory	
illustrate^{2}	@illustrator
illustration	
illustrative	
illustrious ~ly ~ness	
ilness	illness
ilongate	elongate^{2+}
ilope	elope^{2+}
ilushun	allusion *[reference]
	illusion *[false idea]
ilusive	illusive *[deceptive]

Unable to find your word under **il**?
Look under **ill**

I'm [I am]	
imaciate	emaciate^{2+}
Imacks	IMAX™
imaculate	immaculate^{+}
image^{2}	@imaginable ~| map
imaginary ~| number	
imaginative ~ly	
imagine^{2}	@imagination
imaks	IMAX™$^{+}$
imam	
imanent	immanent *[everywhere]
	imminent *[soon]$^{+}$
	eminent *[respected]$^{+}$
imansipate	emancipate^{2+}
imaqulate	immaculate^{+}
imarm	imam
IMAX™ ~| film	
imbalance	

imbecile	
imbed^{3}	
imbew	imbue^{2}
imbibe^{2}	
imbicile	imbecile
imbue^{2}	
imbybe	imbibe^{2}
imediate	immediate^{+}
imens	immense^{+}
imesurable	immeasurable^{+}
imidiate	immediate^{+}
imige	image^{2+}
imigrant	emigrant *[exits]
	immigrant *[arrives]
imij	image^{2+}
iminent	imminent *[soon]$^{+}$
	eminent *[respected]$^{+}$
imit	emit^{3}
imitate^{2}	@imitation
imiterial	immaterial
immachure	immature^{+}
immaculate ~ly ~ness	
immam	imam
immanent *[everywhere]	
	imminent *[soon]$^{+}$
	eminent *[respected]$^{+}$
immaterial	
immature	@immaturity
immeasurable	@immeasurably
immediacy	
immediate ~ly	
immemorial	
immense ~ly	@immensity
immerse^{2}	@immersion
immigrant *[arrives]	
	emigrant *[exits]
immigrate^{2} *[arrive]	
	emigrate^{2} *[exit]
immigration *[arrival]	
	emigration *[exit]
imminent *[soon] ~ly	
	eminent *[respected]$^{+}$
	immanent *[everywhere]

Key to Spelling Rules

Red words are wrong. **Black** words are correct.

~ Add the suffix or word directly to the main word, without a space or hyphen
e.g. ash ~en ~tray → ashen ashtray

~- Add a hyphen to the main word before adding the next word
e.g. blow ~-dry → blow-dry

~| Leave a space between the main word and the next word
e.g. decimal ~| place → decimal place

+ By finding this word in its correct alphabetical order, you can find related words
e.g. abowt about^{+} → about-face

* Draws attention to words that may be confused

™ Means the word is a trademark

@ Signifies the word is derived from the main word

Unable to find your word under **imm**? Look under **em**

immitate	imitate²⁺
immobile	@immobility
immobilize²	@immobilization
immoderate ~ly	
immoral *[wicked] ~ity ~ly	
immortal *[doesn't die]	
immortalize²	@immortality
immosion	emotion⁺
immovable	
immpecable	impeccable⁺
immune	@immunity
immune ~| response ~| system	
immunize²	@immunization
immunoglobulin	
immunology	
immunotherapy	
immurse	immerse²⁺
immutable	
imobil	immobile⁺

Unable to find your word under **im**? Look under **imm**

imorul	immoral⁺
imotiv	emotive
imp ~ish ~ishly ~ishness	
impact¹	
impair¹ ~ment	
impakt	impact¹
impalpable	@impalpably
imparshal	impartial⁺
impart¹	
impartial ~ity ~ly	
impashent	impatient⁺
impasiont	impatient⁺
impasiv	impassive⁺
impassable	
impasse	
impassioned	
impassive ~ly ~ness	
impassivity	
impasture	imposture *[deception] impostor *[swindler]
impatience	
impatient ~ly	
impatus	impetus *[encouragement]
impeach⁵ *[accuse] ~able ~ment	
impearial	imperial *[empire]⁺ imperil³ *[put in danger]
impearialist	imperialist⁺
impeccable	@impeccably
impechuosity	impetuosity
impechuous	impetuous *[done quickly]⁺
impeckable	impeccable⁺
impecunious ~ness	
impede²	
impediment ~a	
impeech	impeach⁵⁺
impeed	impede²
impeeriel	imperial *[empire]⁺
impekunious	impecunious⁺
impel³	
impending	
impenetrable	
impenge	impinge²
impenitence	
impequnious	impecunious⁺
imperal	imperil³ *[put in danger] imperial *[empire]⁺
imperative ~ly ~ness	
imperceptible	@imperceptibly
imperfect ~ion	
imperial *[empire] ~ism ~ly	imperil³ *[put in danger]
imperialist ~ic	
imperil³ *[put in danger]	imperial *[empire]⁺
imperious ~ly ~ness	
imperitive	imperative⁺
impermeable	
imperseptable	imperceptible⁺
impersonal ~ly	
impersonate²	@impersonator
impertinence	@impertinent
impervious ~ly ~ness	
impetuosity	

Key to Suffixes and Compounds

These rules are explained on pages vii to ix.

1 Keep the word the same before adding **ed, er, est, ing** e.g. cool¹ → cooled, cooler, coolest, cooling
2 Take off final **e** before adding **ed, er, est, ing** e.g. fine² → fined, finer, finest, fining
3 Double final consonant before adding **ed, er, est, ing** e.g. thin³ → thinned, thinner, thinnest, thinning
4 Change final **y** to **i** before adding **ed, er, es, est, ly, ness** e.g. tidy⁴ → tidied, tidier, tidies, tidiest, tidily, tidiness
Keep final **y** before adding **ing** e.g. tidying
5 Add **es** instead of **s** to the end of the word e.g. bunch⁵ → bunches
6 Change final **f** to **ve** before adding **s** e.g. calf⁶ → calves

impetuous *[done quickly] ~ly	
impetus[5] *[encouragement]	
impeure	impure+
impeurity	impurity[4]
impewdance	impudence
impewdent	impudent+
impewn	impugn[1]
impewnity	impunity
impich	impeach[5] *[accuse]+
	impish *[mischievous]+
impily	imply[4+]
impinge[2]	
impious ~ly	
impirialist	imperialist+
impirious	imperious+
impish *[mischievous] ~ness	
impitent	impotent *[weak]
impius	impious+
implacable	@implacably
implacate	implicate[2+]
implament	implement[1+]
implant[1] ~ation	
implausible	
implawsable	implausible
implecate	implicate[2+]
implement[1] ~ation	
implemint	implement[1+]
implicate[2]	@implication
implicit ~ly ~ness	
implie	imply[4+]
impliment	implement[1+]
implisit	implicit+
implore[2]	
implorsibul	implausible
implour	implore[2]
imply[4]	@implication
impolite ~ly ~ness	
impolitic	
imponderable	
imporchune	importune[2+]
import[1] ~able ~ation ~| duty[4] ~-export ~| license ~| quota ~| restrictions ~| surcharge ~| tax	

Unable to find your word under **import**? Take off **import** and look again

importance *[value]	
	impotence *[weakness]+
important *[valuable] ~ly	
	impotent *[weak]
importune[2]	@importunity
imposcher	impostor *[swindler]
	imposture *[deception]
impose[2]	@imposition
imposibility	impossibility[4]
imposible	impossible+
impossibility[4]	
impossible	@impossibly
impostor *[swindler]	
imposture *[deception]	
impotence *[weakness]	
	@impotent
	importance *[value]
	impudence *[boldness]
impotent *[weak]	important *[valuable]+
	impudent *[bold]+
impound[1]	
impourt	import[1+]
impourtance	importance *[value]
impourtant	important *[valuable]+
impourtants	importance *[value]
impouse	impose[2+]
impoverish[5] ~ment	
impoverished	
impownd	impound[1]
impracise	imprecise+
impracticable	
impractical ~ly	
impracticality[4]	
impravise	improvise[2+]
imprecation *[curse]	
imprecion	impression+
imprecionism	impressionism+
imprecise ~ly	
impregnable	
impregnate[2]	
impreprietie	impropriety[4]
impresario	

Key to Spelling Rules

Red words are wrong. **Black** words are correct.

~ Add the suffix or word directly to the main word, without a space or hyphen
e.g. ash ~en ~tray → ashen ashtray

~- Add a hyphen to the main word before adding the next word
e.g. blow ~-dry → blow-dry

~| Leave a space between the main word and the next word
e.g. decimal ~| place → decimal place

\+ By finding this word in its correct alphabetical order, you can find related words
e.g. abowt about+ → about-face

★ Draws attention to words that may be confused

TM Means the word is a trademark

@ Signifies the word is derived from the main word

impreshionism impressionism+
impresise imprecise+
impresiv impressive+
impress[5] *[cause admiration]
empress *[royalty]
impression ~able
impressionism @impressionist
impressive ~ly ~ness
imprint[1]
imprison[1] ~ment
improbable @improbability
impromptu
improper ~ly
impropriety[4]
impropur improper+
improve[2] ~ment
improvident ~ly
improvise[2] @improvisation
imprudence *[rashness]
impudence *[boldness]
imprudent *[unwise] ~ly
impudent *[bold]
impruve improve[2+]
impruvise improvise[2+]
imprynt imprint[1]
impudant impudent+
impudence *[boldness]
imprudence *[rashness]
impudent *[bold] ~ly
impotent *[weak]
imprudent *[unwise]+
impugn[1]
impulsave impulsive+
impulse ~| buyer
impulsian impulsion
impulsion
impulsive ~ly
impune impugn[1]
impunity
impure @impurity
impurfect imperfect+
impursonal impersonal+
impursonate impersonate[2+]
impurtinence impertinence+
impurvious impervious+

impyur impure+
imulsify emulsify[4+]
imulsion emulsion
imune immune+
imunise immunize[2+]
imunology immunology
imuteable immutable
imytate imitate[2+]
imyune immune+
in *[go in] ~| absentia ~-box ~-fighting ~-group ~-house ~-line skates ~| loco parentis ~| situ
inn *[hotel]+

> Unable to find your word under **in**?
> Take off **in** and look again

inability[4]
inaccessible @inaccessibility
inaccuracy[4]
inaccurate ~ly
inacsessible inaccessible+
inaction
inactive @inactivity
inacuracy inaccuracy[4]
inacurate inaccurate+
inadequacy[4]
inadequate ~ly
inadmissible @inadmissibility
inadvertent ~ly ~ness
inaksessible inaccessible+
inakshun inaction
inaksuracy inaccuracy[4]
inaktion inaction
inaktive inactive
inaktivity inactivity
inalienable
inane ~ly ~ness
inanimate
inanity[4]
inapplicable
inappropriate ~ly ~ness
inarticulate
inaskapable inescapable+
inasmuch ~| as

KEY TO SUFFIXES AND COMPOUNDS

These rules are explained on pages vii to ix.

1 Keep the word the same before adding **ed, er, est, ing** e.g. cool[1] → cooled, cooler, coolest, cooling
2 Take off final **e** before adding **ed, er, est, ing** e.g. fine[2] → fined, finer, finest, fining
3 Double final consonant before adding **ed, er, est, ing** e.g. thin[3] → thinned, thinner, thinnest, thinning
4 Change final **y** to **i** before adding **ed, er, es, est, ly, ness** e.g. tidy[4] → tidied, tidier, tidies, tidiest, tidily, tidiness
Keep final **y** before adding **ing** e.g. tidying
5 Add **es** instead of **s** to the end of the word e.g. bunch[5] → bunches
6 Change final **f** to **ve** before adding **s** e.g. calf[6] → calves

inate	innate^{+}
inatension	inattention^{+}
inattention	@inattentive
inaudible	@inaudibility
inaugerate	inaugurate^{2+}
inaugural	
inaugurate^{2}	@inauguration
inauspicious ~ly	
inavate	innervate^{2} *[supply with nerves]
	innovate^{2} *[invent]$^{+}$
	enervate^{2} *[weaken]$^{+}$
inawdibel	inaudible^{+}
inawganic	inorganic^{+}
inawgural	inaugural
inbed	imbed^{3}
in-between	
inborn	
inbourn	inborn
inbred	@inbreeding
inc. *[incorporated]	
	ink^{1} *[writing]$^{+}$
incalculable	
incandescent	
incantation	
incapable	
incapacitate^{2}	
incapacity	
incapasatate	incapacitate^{2}
incapible	incapable
incarcerate^{2}	@incarceration
incarnate^{2}	@incarnation
incarserate	incarcerate^{2+}
incect	incest *[sex with near relative]
	insect *[bug]$^{+}$
inceminate	inseminate^{2+}
incendiary^{4}	
incense^{2}	
incensible	insensible
incensitiv	insensitive^{+}
incensitivity	insensitivity^{4}
incentive ~| bonus ~| payment	
inceprable	inseparable
incepshun	inception

inception	
incequre	insecure^{+}
incerection	insurrection
incersion	incursion
incert	insert^{1} *[put in]$^{+}$
incertitude	
incesant	incessant^{+}
inceschuous	incestuous^{+}
incessant ~ly	
incest *[sex with near relative]	
	insect *[bug]$^{+}$
incestuous ~ly ~ness	
incet	incest *[sex with near relative]
	inset^{3} *[smaller part inside larger]
inch^{5} ~es	
inchoir	inquire^{2+}
inchuitive	intuitive^{+}
incide	inside *[internal]$^{+}$
incidence *[how often]	
	incidents *[events]
incident *[event] ~al ~ally	
incidents *[events]	
	incidence *[how often]
incider	insider^{+}
incidint	incident^{+}
inciduous	insidious *[sneaky]$^{+}$
incight	incite^{2} *[stir up]$^{+}$
	insight *[understanding]
incignificint	insignificant^{+}
incillin	insulin *[hormone]
incincere	insincere^{+}
incinerate^{2} *[burn]	
	@incinerator
	insinuate^{2} *[imply]
incipid	insipid *[bland]$^{+}$
	incipit *[beginning]
incipit *[beginning]	
incipient	
incision	
incisive ~ly ~ness	
incisor	
incist	insist^{1+}

incite[2] *[stir up] ~ment	
	insight *[understanding]
incizion	incision
inclement	
incline[2] ~d	@inclination
incling	inkling
include[2]	@inclusion
inclusive ~ly ~ness	
incognito	
incoherence	@incoherent
incombencie	incumbency[4+]
income ~| statement ~| tax	
incoming ~| call ~| mail	
incommunicado	
incomparable	@incomparably
incompetence	
incompetent ~ly ~ness	
incomplete ~ness	
incomprehensible	
incomunicado	incommunicado
inconceivable	@inconceivably
inconcistency	inconsistency[4]
inconcistent	inconsistent[+]
inconclusive ~ly ~ness	
incongrewity	incongruity[4]
incongrewus	incongruous[+]
incongruity[4]	
incongruous ~ness	
inconpspickuous	inconspicuous[+]
inconseivable	inconceivable[+]
inconsiderable	
inconsiderate ~ness	
inconsistency[4]	
inconsistent ~ly	
inconsolable	
inconspicuous ~ly	
inconstancy	@inconstant
incontestable	
incontinence	@incontinent
incontrovertible	@incontrovertibly
inconvenience[2]	@inconvenient
incorporate[2]	@incorporation
incorrect ~ly ~ness	
incorruptible	
incrament	increment[+]

increase[2]	
incredeulity	incredulity[+]
incredible	@incredibly
incredulity	@incredulous
increese	increase[2]
increment ~al cost	
incriminate[2]	@incrimination
incubashun	incubation
incubate[2]	@incubator
incubation	
inculcate[2]	
incum	income[+]
incumbency[4]	@incumbent
incuming	incoming[+]
incumparable	incomparable[+]
incumplete	incomplete[+]
incur[3] ~| debt	
incurable	@incurably
incurible	incurable[+]
incurr	incur[3+]
incursion	
incygnia	insignia
incynerate	incinerate[2] *[burn][+]
incypient	incipient
incysive	incisive[+]
incysor	incisor
incyst	insist[1+]
incyte	incite[2] *[stir up][+]
	insight *[understanding]

Unable to find your word under **inc**?
Look under **ins**

indacate	indicate[2+]
indacator	indicator
indalinse	indolence[+]
indamnify	indemnify[4+]
indastinct	indistinct
indastinguishable	indistinguishable
indavidjual	individual[+]
indavisabul	indivisible *[cannot be divided]
indebted ~ness	
indecency[4]	

Key to Suffixes and Compounds

These rules are explained on pages vii to ix.

1 Keep the word the same before adding **ed, er, est, ing**
e.g. cool[1] → cooled, cooler, coolest, cooling

2 Take off final **e** before adding **ed, er, est, ing**
e.g. fine[2] → fined, finer, finest, fining

3 Double final consonant before adding **ed, er, est, ing**
e.g. thin[3] → thinned, thinner, thinnest, thinning

4 Change final **y** to **i** before adding **ed, er, es, est, ly, ness**
e.g. tidy[4] → tidied, tidier, tidies, tidiest, tidily, tidiness
Keep final **y** before adding **ing** e.g. tidying

5 Add **es** instead of **s** to the end of the word
e.g. bunch[5] → bunches

6 Change final **f** to **ve** before adding **s**
e.g. calf[6] → calves

indecent ~ly ~| assault
indecision
indecisive ~ly ~ness
indecks index[5+]
indeed
indeesent indecent+
indefatigable
indefensible
indefinite ~ly ~| article
indeginus indigenous
indekorum indecorum
indeks index[5+]
indelable indelible+
indelible @indelibly
indelicacy[4]
indelicate ~ly
indellable indelible+
indemnify[4] @indemnification
indemnity[4]
indent[1] ~ure
independence
independent ~ly ~| company[4]
indescribable @indescribably
indesent indecent+
indesiferable indecipherable
indesisive indecisive+
indeskribable indescribable+
indestructible
indeterminate ~ly
indetted indebted+
indewbitable indubitable+
indewse induce[2+]
index[5] ~ation ~es ~| card ~| finger ~-linked ~| corn ~| ink ~| summer
@indices
Indian
indicate[2] @indication
indicative
indicator
indiciferable indecipherable
indicision indecision
indicisive indecisive+
indict[1] ~ment
Indien Indian+
indifensable indefensible
indifference @indifferent
indifrens indifference+
indigenous *[native]
indigent *[poor] @indigence
indignant *[offended]+
indigenus indigenous *[native]
indigestible
indigestion @indigestive
indight indict[1+]
indiginus indigenous
indignant *[offended]
@indignation
indigent *[poor]+
indignity[4]
indigo
indihct indict[1+]
indijenous indigenous *[native]
indijent indigent *[poor]+
indijestible indigestible
indijestion indigestion+
indike indict[1+]
indipendent independent+
indirect ~ly ~| object ~| taxation
indiscreet *[careless]
indiscrete *[joined]
indiscretion
indiscribable indescribable+
indiscriminate
indiskreshin indiscretion
indispensable @indispensably
indisposed
indisputable @indisputably
indistinct
indistinguishable
indistructable indestructible
indistry industry[4]
inditerminat indeterminate+
individual ~ity ~ly
individualism @indvidualist
indivisible *[cannot be divided]
invisible *[cannot be seen]+
indoctrinate[2] @indoctrination
indolence @indolent
indomitable @indomitably

Key to Spelling Rules

Red words are wrong. **Black** words are correct.

~ Add the suffix or word directly to the main word, without a space or hyphen
e.g. ash ~en ~tray → ashen ashtray

~- Add a hyphen to the main word before adding the next word
e.g. blow ~-dry → blow-dry

~| Leave a space between the main word and the next word
e.g. decimal ~| place → decimal place

+ By finding this word in its correct alphabetical order, you can find related words
e.g. abowt about+ → about-face

★ Draws attention to words that may be confused

TM Means the word is a trademark

@ Signifies the word is derived from the main word

indoor ~s
indoos induce[2+]
indubitable @indubitably
induce[2] ~ment
inducshin induction[+]
induction ~| course
indugo indigo
indulge[2] @indulgence
@indulgent
indulinse indolence[+]
indurect indirect[+]
induse induce[2+]
industreal industrial[+]
industrial ~ism ~ist ~ly ~| accident
~| design ~| capacity ~| dispute
~| espionage ~| estate ~| expansion
~-grade ~| process ~| relations
~| tribunal

Unable to find your word under **industrial**? Take off **industrial** and look again

industrialize[2] @industrialization
industrialized ~| nation
industrious ~ly ~ness
industry[4]
induvidual individual[+]
indycatyve indicative
indyrect indirect[+]
indyspensabul indispensable[+]
indyte indict[1+]
indyvidual individual[+]
inebriated
ineckspensive inexpensive[+]
inedible
ineffective ~ly ~ness
ineffectual ~ly
inefficiency[4]
inefficient ~ly
inefishint inefficient[+]
inekwality inequality[4]
inekwity inequity[4] *[unfairness]
iniquity[4] *[badness]
inelegance @inelegant
ineligible @ineligibility

inept *[foolish] ~ly
ineptichude ineptitude
ineptitude
inequality[4]
inequity[4] *[unfairness]
iniquity[4] *[badness]
iner inner[+]
inersha inertia
inert ~ly ~| gas
inertia
inescapable @inescapably
inessential
inestimable
inevitable @inevitably
@inevitability
inexact ~itude
inexaustible inexhaustible
inexcusable
inexhaustible
inexorable @inexorably
inexpensive ~ly
inexperience ~d
inexplicable @inexplicably
inexpressible
inexqusabul inexcusable
inextinguishable
inextricable
infachuated infatuated[+]
infadel infidel
infadelity infidelity[4]
infallible @infallibility
infamie infamy
infamous ~ly
infamus infamous[+]
infamy
infancy *[babyhood]
infanite infinite[+]
infansy infancy
infant ~icide ~ile
infantry[4] *[soldiers]
infarction *[death of tissue]
infraction *[wrongdoing]
infatuated @infatuation
infect[1] *[cause disease] ~ion
inflect[1] *[modify][+]

Key to Suffixes and Compounds

These rules are explained on pages vii to ix.

1 Keep the word the same before adding **ed, er, est, ing**
e.g. cool[1] → cooled, cooler, coolest, cooling
2 Take off final **e** before adding **ed, er, est, ing**
e.g. fine[2] → fined, finer, finest, fining
3 Double final consonant before adding **ed, er, est, ing**
e.g. thin[3] → thinned, thinner, thinnest, thinning
4 Change final **y** to **i** before adding **ed, er, es, est, ly, ness**
e.g. tidy[4] → tidied, tidier, tidies, tidiest, tidily, tidiness
Keep final **y** before adding **ing** e.g. tidying
5 Add **es** instead of **s** to the end of the word
e.g. bunch[5] → bunches
6 Change final **f** to **ve** before adding **s**
e.g. calf[6] → calves

infectious ~ly ~ness ~| disease	
infekshis	infectious+
infent	infant+
infentry	infantry[4] *[soldiers]
infer[3] ~ence	
inferior ~ity	
inferm	infirm+
infermary	infirmary[4]
infermity	infirmity[4]
infernal ~ly	
inferno	
infertile	@infertility
infest[1] ~ation	
infidel	
infidelity[4]	
infiding	infighting
infighting	
infiltrate[2]	@infiltration
infimous	infamous+
infinidy	infinity[4]
infinite ~ly	
infinitesimal ~ly	
infinitive	
infinity[4]	
infint	infant+
infintrie	infantry[4] *[soldiers]
infir	infer[3]+
infirior	inferior+
infirm	@infirmary[4]
infirmary[4]	
infirmation	information+
infirmity[4]	
infirnel	infernal+
infirno	inferno
infirtile	infertile+
infiting	infighting
inflait	inflate[2]+
inflame[2]	@inflammable
inflammatory	
inflashun	inflation+
inflate[2]	@inflatable
inflation ~ary ~-proof	
inflaym	inflame[2]+
inflayshin	inflation+
inflayt	inflate[2]+

inflect[1] *[modify] ~ion	
	infect[1] *[cause disease]+
	inflict[1] *[cause to suffer]+
infleksible	inflexible+
inflekt	inflect[1] *[modify]+
inflewnce	influence[2]
inflewnza	influenza
inflexible	@inflexibility
inflict[1] *[cause to suffer] ~ion	
	inflect[1] *[modify]+
in-fliet	in-flight+
in-flight ~| entertainment	
inflooence	influence[2]
inflooenza	influenza
inflow	
influcks	influx
influence[2]	
influenshil	influential+
influential ~ly	
influenza	
influks	influx
influx	
inform[1] ~atics ~ative	
informal ~ity ~ly	
informant	
informashin	information+
information ~| asset ~| base ~| management ~| overload ~| repository ~| superhighway ~| technology	

> Unable to find your word under **information**? Take off **information** and look again

informint	informant
infourm	inform[1]+
infourmal	informal+
infourmation	information+
infraction *[wrongdoing]	
	infarction *[death of tissue]
infrared ~| astronomy ~| telescope	
infrastructure	
infrequency	
infrequent ~ly	

KEY TO SPELLING RULES

Red words are wrong. **Black** words are correct.

~ Add the suffix or word directly to the main word, without a space or hyphen
e.g. ash ~en ~tray → ashen ashtray

~- Add a hyphen to the main word before adding the next word
e.g. blow ~-dry → blow-dry

~| Leave a space between the main word and the next word
e.g. decimal ~| place → decimal place

\+ By finding this word in its correct alphabetical order, you can find related words
e.g. abowt about+ → about-face

★ Draws attention to words that may be confused

TM Means the word is a trademark

@ Signifies the word is derived from the main word

infrered	infrared[+]
infrestructure	infrastructure
infringe[2] ~ment	
infrured	infrared[+]
infrustructure	infrastructure
infudel	infidel
infumy	infamy
infuncy	infancy *[babyhood]
infunitesimul	infinitesimal[+]
infunt	infant[+]
infuntry	infantry[4] *[soldiers]
infur	infer[3+]
infuriate[2]	
infurm	infirm[+]
infurmashin	information[+]
infurmidy	infirmity[4]
infurno	inferno
infurnul	infernal[+]
infurtile	infertile[+]
infuryate	infuriate[2]
infuse[2]	@infusion
infydel	infidel
infyltrate	infiltrate[2+]
infynite	infinite[+]
infynitesymal	infinitesimal[+]
infynity	infinity[4]
infynityve	infinitive
infyuriate	infuriate[2]
infyuse	infuse[2+]
ingenious *[clever] ~ly ~ness	
	ingenuous *[trusting][+]
ingenuity	
ingenuous *[trusting] ~ly ~ness	
	ingenious *[clever][+]
ingest ~ion	
inget	ingot
inginuity	ingenuity
inglorious ~ly	
ingot	
ingraditude	ingratitude
ingrained	
ingrashiate	ingratiate[2]
ingratiate[2]	
ingratitude	
ingredient	

ingroan	ingrown[+]
ingrone	ingrown[+]
ingrow ~ing	
ingrown ~| toenail	
inhabit[1] ~ant	
inhail	inhale[2+]
inhairint	inherent[+]
inhairit	inherit[1+]
inhale[2]	@inhalation
inharit	inherit[1+]
inhayl	inhale[2+]
inherent ~ly	
inherit[1] ~ance ~or	
inhewmane	inhumane *[cruel]
inhibid	inhibit[1+]
inhibit[1] ~ion ~or	
inhospitable	
inhuman *[not human] ~ity ~ly	
inhumane *[cruel]	
inhybit	inhibit[1+]
inhyooman	inhuman *[not human][+]
	inhumane *[cruel]
inibriated	inebriated
inikwitey	iniquity[4] *[badness]
	inequity[4] *[unfairness]
inikwitous	iniquitous
inimical	
inimitable	
ining	inning
iniquitous	
iniquity[4] *[badness]	
	inequity[4] *[unfairness]
inirt	inert[+]
inirtia	inertia
inishiate	initiate[2+]
inishil	initial[3+]
inishulize	initialize[2+]
inishyative	initiative
initial[3] ~ly ~| capital	
initialize[2]	@initialization
initiate[2]	@initiation
initiative	
inject[1] ~ion ~or	
injenious	ingenious *[clever][+]
	ingenuous *[trusting][+]

Key to Suffixes and Compounds

These rules are explained on pages vii to ix.

1 Keep the word the same before adding **ed, er, est, ing**
e.g. cool[1] → cooled, cooler, coolest, cooling

2 Take off final **e** before adding **ed, er, est, ing**
e.g. fine[2] → fined, finer, finest, fining

3 Double final consonant before adding **ed, er, est, ing**
e.g. thin[3] → thinned, thinner, thinnest, thinning

4 Change final **y** to **i** before adding **ed, er, es, est, ly, ness**
e.g. tidy[4] → tidied, tidier, tidies, tidiest, tidily, tidiness
Keep final **y** before adding **ing** e.g. tidying

5 Add **es** instead of **s** to the end of the word
e.g. bunch[5] → bunches

6 Change final **f** to **ve** before adding **s**
e.g. calf[6] → calves

injenuity	ingenuity
injer	injure[2+]
injery	injury[4]
injest	ingest[+]
injir	injure[2+]
injunction	
injunkshin	injunction
injure[2] *[harm]	@injurious
	endure[2] *[survive][+]
injury[4]	
injustice	
injustis	injustice
ink[1] *[writing] ~| in ~-jet	
	inc. *[incorporated]
inkalkulable	incalculable
inklement	inclement
inkling	
inklude	include[2+]
inklusive	inclusive[+]
inkompetant	incompetent[+]
inkorect	incorrect[+]
inkrease	increase[2]
inkredible	incredible[+]
inkur	incur[3+]
inkwest	inquest
inkwire	inquire[+]
inkwisitive	inquisitive[+]
inlah	in-law
inland	
in-law	
inlay	@inlaid
inled	inlet
inlet	
inley	inlay[+]
inlund	inland
inmate	
inmemorial	immemorial
inmost	
inn *[hotel] ~keeper	
	in *[go in][+]
innability	inability[4]
innaccurate	inaccurate[+]
innacurate	inaccurate[+]
innapproriate	inappropriate[+]
innate ~ly ~ness	
innegrate	integrate[2+]
inner ~| city ~most	
innercourse	intercourse

> Unable to find your word under **inner**?
> Look under **inter**

innert	inert[+]
innervate[2] *[supply with nerves]	
	enervate[2] *[weaken][+]
	innovate[2] *[invent][+]
innigrate	integrate[2+]
inning	
innmost	inmost
innocence	
innocent ~ly	
innoculate	inoculate[2+]
innocuous ~ly	
innofencive	inoffensive[+]
innopurtune	inopportune[+]
innordinit	inordinate[+]
innorganik	inorganic[+]
innosent	innocent[+]
innovate[2] *[invent]	
	@innovation
innovative ~ly	
innquest	inquest
innstil	instill[1] *[give by example][+]
	install[1] *[put in][+]
innuendo	
innumerable *[cannot be counted]	
	enumerable *[can be counted]
innumeracy	
innundate	inundate[2+]
innure	inure[2]
inocence	innocence
inoculate[2]	@inoculation
inocuous	innocuous[+]
inoffensive ~ly ~ness	
inokulate	inoculate[2+]
inoperative	
inopportune ~ly	
inordinate ~ly	
inorganic ~| chemistry ~| compound	

KEY TO SPELLING RULES

Red words are wrong. **Black** words are correct.

~ Add the suffix or word directly to the main word, without a space or hyphen
e.g. ash ~en ~tray → ashen ashtray

~- Add a hyphen to the main word before adding the next word
e.g. blow ~-dry → blow-dry

~| Leave a space between the main word and the next word
e.g. decimal ~| place → decimal place

+ By finding this word in its correct alphabetical order, you can find related words
e.g. abowt about[+] → about-face

★ Draws attention to words that may be confused

TM Means the word is a trademark

@ Signifies the word is derived from the main word

inorgural	inaugural
inormity	enormity[4]
inormous	enormous[+]
inorspishus	inauspicious[+]
inourdinate	inordinate[+]
inovate	innovate[2+]
inpediment	impediment[+]

Unable to find your word under **in**? Look under **im**

inprision	imprison[1+]
inpursonate	impersonate[2+]

Unable to find your word under **inp**? Look under **imp**

input[3]	
inqubate	incubate[2+]
inquest	
inquire	@inquiry
inquisitive ~ly ~ness	
inquisitor	
inroads	
insabordination	insubordination
insalen	insolent *[disrespectful][+]
	insulin *[hormone]
insane ~ly	
insanitary	unsanitary *[dirty]
	insanity[4] *[mental illness]
insanity[4] *[mental illness]	
insatiable	@insatiably
insayshable	insatiable[+]
inscrewtable	inscrutable
inscribe[2]	
inscription	
inscrutable	
insect *[bug] ~icide	
	incest *[sex with near relative]
insecure ~ly	
insecurity[4]	
insedent	incident[+]
insedents	incidents *[events]
	incidence *[how often]
insekt	insect *[animal][+]
insekure	insecure[+]
inseminate[2]	@insemination
insendiary	incendiary[4]
insensative	insensitive[+]
insense	incense[2]
insensible	
insensitive ~ly	
insensitivity[4]	
insentive	incentive[+]
inseparable	
inserginse	insurgence *[revolt][+]
insermountable	insurmountable
inserrection	insurrection
insert[1] *[put in] ~ion	
	inset[3] *[smaller part inside larger]
insertitude	incertitude
insessant	incessant[+]
insest	incest *[sex with near relative]
	insist[1] *[be firm][+]

Unable to find your word under **ins**? Look under **inc**

inset[3] *[smaller part inside larger]	
	incest *[sex with near relative]
	insect *[bug]
	insert *[put in][+]
inseyed	inside *[internal][+]
inshaw	inshore *[coast]
insher	ensure[2] *[make sure]
	insure[2] *[money]
	inshore *[coast]
insherince	insurance[+]
inshore *[coast]	ensure[2] *[make sure]
	insure[2] *[money]
insibordinate	insubordinate[+]
insicure	insecure[+]
inside *[internal] ~| out	
	insight *[understanding]
insidence	incidence *[how often]
	incidents *[events]
insident	incident *[event][+]

Key to Suffixes and Compounds

These rules are explained on pages vii to ix.

1 Keep the word the same before adding **ed, er, est, ing** e.g. cool[1] → cooled, cooler, coolest, cooling
2 Take off final **e** before adding **ed, er, est, ing** e.g. fine[2] → fined, finer, finest, fining
3 Double final consonant before adding **ed, er, est, ing** e.g. thin[3] → thinned, thinner, thinnest, thinning
4 Change final **y** to **i** before adding **ed, er, es, est, ly, ness** e.g. tidy[4] → tidied, tidier, tidies, tidiest, tidily, tidiness
Keep final **y** before adding **ing** e.g. tidying
5 Add **es** instead of **s** to the end of the word e.g. bunch[5] → bunches
6 Change final **f** to **ve** before adding **s** e.g. calf[6] → calves

insider ~| dealing ~| trading	
insidious *[sneaky] ~ly ~ness	
insidur	insider^{+}
insied	inside *[internal]$^{+}$
insiet	insight *[understanding]
insifishint	insufficient^{+}
insight *[understanding]	
	incite^{2} *[stir up]$^{+}$
insignia	
insignificance	
insignificant ~ly	
insilate	insulate^{2+}
insilense	insolence
insilent	insolent *[disrespectful]$^{+}$
insilin	insulin *[hormone]
insilur	insular^{+}
insincere ~ly	@insincerity
insinerate	incinerate^{2} *[burn]$^{+}$
	insinuate^{2} *[imply]
insinsear	insincere^{+}
insinuashin	insinuation
insinuate^{2} *[imply]	
	incinerate^{2} *[burn]$^{+}$
insinuation	
insipid *[bland] ~ly ~ness	
insipient	incipient
insirt	insert^{1} *[put in]$^{+}$
insishun	incision
insisive	incisive^{+}
insisor	incisor
insist^{1} *[be firm] ~ence ~ent ~ently	
	encyst *[enclose]$^{+}$
insite	incite^{2} *[stir up]$^{+}$
	inside *[internal]$^{+}$
	insight *[understanding]
insizer	incisor
inskribe	inscribe^{2}
insofar	
insolence	
insolent *[disrespectful] ~ly	
insoluble	@insolubility
insolvency	@insolvent
insomnia ~c	
insowfar	insofar
inspect^{1} ~ion ~or	

inspectorate	
inspire^{2}	@inspiration
instability	
instagashin	instigation
instagate	instigate^{2+}
install^{1} *[put in] ~ation ~ment	
	instill^{1} *[give by example]$^{+}$
instance^{2} *[example]	
	instants *[moments]
instantaneous ~ly	
instants *[moments]	
	instance^{2} *[example]
instatushinalize	institutionalize^{2}
instatute	institute^{2}
instatution	institution^{+}
instawl	install^{1} *[put in]$^{+}$
instead	
instense	instance^{2} *[example]
	instants *[moments]
instep	
instichute	institute^{2}
instigate^{2}	@instigator
instigation	
instill^{1} *[give by example] ~ation	
	install^{1} *[put in]$^{+}$
instince	instants *[moments]
	instance^{2} *[example]
instinct *[sense] ~ive ~ively	
	instant *[very fast]$^{+}$
instintaneous	instantaneous^{+}
institushin	institution^{+}
institute^{2}	
institution ~al	
institutionalize^{2}	
instrament	instrument^{+}
instramental	instrumental^{+}
instruct^{1} ~ion ~or	
instructive ~ly	
instrument ~ation	
instrumental ~ist ~ity	
instubility	instability
instunt	instant^{+}
instynct	instinct *[sense]$^{+}$
insubordinate ~ly	
insubordination	

insufferable @insufferably
insufficiency[4]
insufficient ~ly ~| funds
insufrable insufferable+
insular ~ity
insulashun insulation
insulate[2] @insulator
insulation
insulin *[hormone]
insullen insolent *[disrespectful]+
insulin *[hormone]
insult[1]
insuncere insincere+
insurance ~| broker ~| contract ~| company[4] ~| coverage ~| policy[4] ~| premium ~| rate

Unable to find your word under **insurance**? Take off **insurance** and try again

insure[2] *[money] ensure[2] *[make sure]
inshore *[coast]
insurgence *[revolt]
@insurgent
@insurgency
insurgents *[those who are rebelling]
insurmountable
insurrection
insurt insert[1] *[put in]+
insygnia insignia
insyncere insincere+
intact
intake
intangible ~| asset
intch inch[5+]
inteerior interior
integer
integrait integrate[2+]
integral ~ly
integrate[2] @integration
integrated ~| circuit ~| network
integrity
intejer integer
inteligent intelligent+
intellect
intellectual ~| property
intellectual ~ize[2] ~ly
intelligence
intelligent ~ly ~sia
intelligible
intemperance
intemperate ~ly
intempranse intemperance
intempurate intemperate+
intence intense *[strong feeling]+
intend[1] *[plan to do]
intent *[purpose]
intense *[strong feeling] ~ly
intents *[purposes]
intenshin intention+
intensify[4] @intensification
intensity[4]
intensive ~ly ~ness ~| care
intent *[purpose] intense *[strong feeling]+
intention ~al ~ally
inter[3] *[bury] enter[1] *[go into]
interact[1] ~ion
interactive ~| computing ~| video
interagayshin interrogation
interbred @interbreeding
intercede[2]
intercellular *[between cells]
intracellular *[within one cell]+
intercept[1] ~ion ~or
intercession *[pleading for another]
intersession *[time between semesters]
interchange[2] ~able
intercom
interconnect[1] ~ion
intercontinental
intercourse
interdenominational
interdependence
interdict[1] ~ion
interdisciplinary
interest[1] ~| bearing ~| charges ~| free ~| rate
interface

Key to Suffixes and Compounds

These rules are explained on pages vii to ix.

1 Keep the word the same before adding **ed, er, est, ing**
e.g. cool[1] → cooled, cooler, coolest, cooling
2 Take off final **e** before adding **ed, er, est, ing**
e.g. fine[2] → fined, finer, finest, fining
3 Double final consonant before adding **ed, er, est, ing**
e.g. thin[3] → thinned, thinner, thinnest, thinning
4 Change final **y** to **i** before adding **ed, er, es, est, ly, ness**
e.g. tidy[4] → tidied, tidier, tidies, tidiest, tidily, tidiness
Keep final **y** before adding **ing** e.g. tidying
5 Add **es** instead of **s** to the end of the word
e.g. bunch[5] → bunches
6 Change final **f** to **ve** before adding **s**
e.g. calf[6] → calves

Word	Correct / related
interfere[2] ~nce	
interferon	
interim ~| dividend ~| payment ~| report	
interior	
interist	interest[1+]
interject[1] ~ion	
interkom	intercom
interkours	intercourse
interleave[2]	
interlock[1]	
interlocutor	
interloper	
interlude	
intermarry[4]	
intermediary[4]	
intermediate	
interment *[burial]	
	internment *[prison]
interminable	@interminably
intermingle[2]	
intermission	
intermittent	
intermix[5]	
intermology *[study of insects]+	
intern[1] *[imprison, learner] ~ship	
	in turn *[next]
internal ~ly ~| audit ~| report	
Internal Revenue Service [IRS]	
internashinal	international+
international ~ly ~| call ~| law ~| trade	
internaut	
internecine	
internegative *[negative film made from a negative]	
internesine	internecine
Internet *[global network]+	
	intranet *[internal network]
Internet ~| relay chat ~| service provider	
internment *[prison]	
	interment *[burial]
internought	internaut
internul	internal+
interogait	interrogate[2+]
interoperability ~| standards	
interpid	intrepid+
interplanetary	
interplay[1]	
Interpol *[international police]	
interpolate[2] *[insert between numbers]	
interpret[1] ~ation ~ive	
interrelate[2]	
interrogate[2]	
interrogation	
interrupt[1] ~ion	
intersect[1] ~ion	
intersede	intercede[2]
intersept	intercept[1+]
intersession *[time between semesters]	
	intercession *[pleading for another]
intersperse[2]	
interstate *[highway]	
	intestate *[without a will]
intertwine[2]	
interum	interim+
interval	
intervene[2]	@intervention
interview[1]	
intervue	interview[1]
interweave	@interweaving
interwove ~n	
intestate *[without a will]	
	interstate *[highway]
intestine	@intestinal
intiger	integer
intigral	integral+
intigrate	integrate[2+]
intigrated	integrated+
intimacy	
intimait	intimate[2+]
intimasey	intimacy
intimate[2] ~ly	
intimidate[2]	@intimidation
intimit	intimate[2+]
intir	inter[3] *[bury]+
	enter[1] *[go into]
intiract	interact[1+]
intirier	interior
intirn	intern[1]

KEY TO SPELLING RULES

Red words are wrong. **Black** words are correct.

~ Add the suffix or word directly to the main word, without a space or hyphen
e.g. ash ~en ~tray → ashen ashtray

~- Add a hyphen to the main word before adding the next word
e.g. blow ~-dry → blow-dry

~| Leave a space between the main word and the next word
e.g. decimal ~| place → decimal place

+ By finding this word in its correct alphabetical order, you can find related words
e.g. abowt about+ → about-face

★ Draws attention to words that may be confused

TM Means the word is a trademark

@ Signifies the word is derived from the main word

Intirnet	Internet *[global network]+
	Intranet *[internal network]
into	
intocksicant	intoxicant
intocksicate	intoxicate[2+]
intoen	intone[2]
intolerable	@intolerably
intolerance	@intolerant
intonashin	intonation
intonation	
intone[2]	
intoo	into
intooishun	intuition
intooitive	intuitive+
intoxicant	
intoxicate[2]	@intoxication
intracellular *[within one cell] ~| location	
	intercellular *[between cells]
intractable	
intraduction	introduction+
intraduse	introduce[2]
intramuscular	
Intranet *[internal network]	
	Internet *[global network]+
intransative	intransitive+
intransigence	@intransigent
intransitive ~| verb	
intraseluler	intracellular+
intravenous ~ly	
intravurt	introvert+
intreeg	intrigue[2]
intrepid ~ly ~ness	
intreplanetary	interplanetary
intrepol	Interpol *[international police]
intrewd	intrude[2]
intrewshun	intrusion+
intricacy[4]	
intricate ~ly	
intrigue[2]	
intrikasey	intricacy[4]
intrikit	intricate+
intrim	interim+
intrinsic ~ally	
intrist	interest[1+]
introduce[2]	
introduction	@introductory
introod	intrude[2]
introoshun	intrusion+
introspection	@introspective
introvert ~ed	
intrude[2]	
Intrunet	Intranet *[internal network]
	Internet *[global network]+
intrushun	intrusion+
intrusion	@intrusive
intrynsyc	intrinsic+
intuition	
intuitive ~ly	
intur	inter[3] *[bury]+
	enter[1] *[go into]
inturest	interest[1+]
inturfase	interface[2]
inturfeir	interfere[2+]
inturlude	interlude
inturment	interment *[burial]
	internment *[prison]
inturmerry	intermarry[4]
inturmishin	intermission
in turn *[next]	intern[1] *[imprison, learner]+
inturnashinul	international+
Inturnet	Internet *[global network]+
	intranet *[internal network]
inturpret	interpret[1+]
intursect	intersect[1+]
intursept	intercept[1+]
inturupt	interrupt[1+]
intwo	into
intymate	intimate[2+]
intymidate	intimidate[2+]
inuendo	innuendo
inumerable	innumerable *[cannot be counted]
	enumerable *[can be counted]
inumeracy	innumeracy
inundate[2]	@inundation
inure[2]	

KEY TO SUFFIXES AND COMPOUNDS

These rules are explained on pages vii to ix.

1 Keep the word the same before adding **ed, er, est, ing**
e.g. cool[1] → cooled, cooler, coolest, cooling

2 Take off final **e** before adding **ed, er, est, ing**
e.g. fine[2] → fined, finer, finest, fining

3 Double final consonant before adding **ed, er, est, ing**
e.g. thin[3] → thinned, thinner, thinnest, thinning

4 Change final **y** to **i** before adding **ed, er, es, est, ly, ness**
e.g. tidy[4] → tidied, tidier, tidies, tidiest, tidily, tidiness
Keep final **y** before adding **ing** e.g. tidying

5 Add **es** instead of **s** to the end of the word
e.g. bunch[5] → bunches

6 Change final **f** to **ve** before adding **s**
e.g. calf[6] → calves

inursha	inertia
inurt	inert+
inurtia	inertia
invade[2]	
invagel	inveigle[2] *[deceive]
invalid ~ity	
invalidate[2]	
invaluable	
invariable	@invariably
invaryible	invariable+
invasion	
invasive	
invay	inveigh[1] *[complain]
invayd	invade[2]
invaysive	invasive
invective	
inveigh[1] *[complain]	
inveigle[2] *[deceive]	
invektive	invective
invent[1] ~ion ~or	
inventive ~ness	
inventory[4] ~| control	
inverse	
invert[1]	@inversion
invertebrate	
invest[1] ~ment ~or	
investichur	investiture
investigate[2]	@investigation
investigator	
investiture	
inveterate	
in-vetro	in vitro+
invey	inveigh[1] *[complain]
invialit	inviolate
invidious ~ly ~ness	
inviet	invite[2+]
invigerate	invigorate[2]
invight	invite[2+]
invigorate[2]	
invincible	
inviolate	
invirse	inverse
invirt	invert[1+]
invirtibrate	invertebrate
invisibility	
invisible *[cannot be seen] ~| assets ~| earnings	
	indivisible *[cannot be divided]
invite[2]	@invitation
in vitro ~| fertilization	
invoak	invoke[2]
invoice[2] ~| number	
invoke[2]	
involuntary	@involuntarily
involve[2] ~ment	
invoyce	invoice[2+]
invulnerable	@invunerability
invurse	inverse
invurt	invert[1+]
invurtebrate	invertebrate
invydious	invidious+
inward ~ly ~ness ~s	
inwerd	inward+
inymical	inimical
inymitable	inimitable
inyour	inure[2]
inyuendo	innuendo
ioda	iota
iodine	
iodize[2]	
ion ~ic ~ize[2]	
ionosfere	ionosphere
ionosphere	
iota	
ipoch	epoch+
iquidistant	equidistant
iradiate	irradiate[2+]
iradicate	eradicate[2+]
irait	irate+
irascible	@irascibility
irase	erase[2+]

Unable to find your word under **i**?
Look under **e**

irashinal	irrational+
irate ~ly ~ness	
irational	irrational+
irayt	irate+

Key to Spelling Rules

Red words are wrong. **Black** words are correct.

~ Add the suffix or word directly to the main word, without a space or hyphen
e.g. ash ~en ~tray → ashen ashtray

~- Add a hyphen to the main word before adding the next word
e.g. blow ~-dry → blow-dry

~| Leave a space between the main word and the next word
e.g. decimal ~| place → decimal place

+ By finding this word in its correct alphabetical order, you can find related words
e.g. abowt about+ → about-face

* Draws attention to words that may be confused

TM Means the word is a trademark

@ Signifies the word is derived from the main word

ire	
ireconcilable	irreconcilable
irefutible	irrefutable⁺
iregular	irregular⁺
irelevant	irrelevant⁺
ireparable	irreparable
iresistible	irresistible⁺
iresponsable	irresponsible⁺
irevocable	irrevocable

> Unable to find your word under **ire**?
> Look under **irre**

iridium	
irigait	irrigate[2+]
iris	
Irish ~| coffee ~| stew	
iritable	irritable⁺
irk[1] ~some	
irly	early[4+]
irmine	ermine
irn	earn[1] *[money]
	urn *[vase]
irnest	earnest⁺
irning	ironing⁺
iron[1] ~| age ~clad ~| curtain ~| lung ~| out ~sides ~wood ~work	

> Unable to find your word under **iron**?
> Take off **iron** and look again

ironic ~al ~ally	
ironing ~| board	
irony[4]	
irradiate[2]	@irradiation
irrashunal	irrational⁺
irrate	irate⁺
irrational ~ly ~| number	
irreconcilable	
irredeemable	
irrefutable	@irrefutably
irregular ~ly	
irregularity[4]	
irrelevancy[4]	
irrelevant ~ly	@irrelevance
irremovable	
irreparable	
irreplaceable	
irrepressible	@irrepressibly
irreproachable	
irresistible	@irresistibly
irrespective	
irresponsibility	
irresponsible	@irresponsibly
irretrievable	
irreverence	
irreverent ~ly	
irreversible	
irrevocable	
irridium	iridium
irrigate[2]	@irrigation
irritable	@irritably
	@irritability
irritant	
irritate[2]	@irritation
irth	earth⁺
irthen	earthen⁺
irydium	iridium
irys	iris
isabar	isobar
isametriks	isometrics⁺
isasuleze	isosceles⁺
isatherm	isotherm
isatope	isotope
iscing	icing⁺
ise	ice[2+]
ishoo	issue[2] *[come out]⁺
	eschew[1] *[do without]
isibar	isobar
isicle	icicle
isilashin	isolation⁺
isilate	isolate[2]
ising	icing⁺
isint	isn't *[is not]
isite	eyesight
Islam ~ic ~ist	
island ~er	
isle *[island]	aisle *[passage]
	I'll *[I shall, I will]
islet *[island]	eyelet *[hole]
ismus	isthmus

Key to Suffixes and Compounds

These rules are explained on pages vii to ix.

1 Keep the word the same before adding **ed, er, est, ing**
e.g. cool[1] → cooled, cooler, coolest, cooling
2 Take off final **e** before adding **ed, er, est, ing**
e.g. fine[2] → fined, finer, finest, fining
3 Double final consonant before adding **ed, er, est, ing**
e.g. thin[3] → thinned, thinner, thinnest, thinning
4 Change final **y** to **i** before adding **ed, er, es, est, ly, ness**
e.g. tidy[4] → tidied, tidier, tidies, tidiest, tidily, tidiness
Keep final **y** before adding **ing** e.g. tidying
5 Add **es** instead of **s** to the end of the word
e.g. bunch[5] → bunches
6 Change final **f** to **ve** before adding **s**
e.g. calf[6] → calves

isn't *[is not]
isobar
isolate[2]
isolation ~ism ~ist
isometrics @isometrically
isosceles ~| triangle
isosiles isosceles+
isotherm
isotope
issicle icicle
issing icing+
issue[2] *[come out] ~| instructions
eschew[1] *[do without]
issy icy[4] *[freezing]
ice[2] *[frozen water]+
isthmus
isue issue[2] *[come out]+
it *[pronoun] ~self
id *[psyche]
I'd *[I would]+
IT *[Information Technology]+
italicize[2]
italics
itch[5] *[scratch] ~y[4]
each *[per piece]
item
itemize[2]
itemized ~| account ~| deductions ~| invoice
iterbium ytterbium
iternal eternal+
iternity eternity[4]
ither either *[or]
ether *[air, liquid]+
ithos ethos

> Unable to find your word under **i**?
> Look under **e**

itinerant
itinerary[4]

it'll *[it will]
itrium yttrium
its *[possessive] it's *[it is, it has]
it's *[it is, it has] its *[possessive]
itum item
itumize itemize[2]
itumized itemized+
iturnity eternity[4]
itynerant itinerant
itz its *[possessive]
it's *[it is, it has]
IV *[intravenous] I've *[I have]
ivacuate evacuate[2+]
ivade evade[2+]
ivaluate evaluate[2+]
ivangelic evangelic+
ivaporate evaporate[2+]
I've *[I have] ivy[4] *[leaf]
IV *[intravenous]
iverie ivory *[tusk]+
ivie ivy *[green plant]
IV *[intravenous]
ivoke evoke[2]
ivolve evolve[2]
ivory[4] *[tusk] ~| tower
ivy[4] *[green plant] ~| league
IV *[intravenous]
iyambic iambic+
iye I *[me]
aye *[yes]
eye *[see]+
iyer ire
iylet islet *[island]
iyota iota
Iyrish Irish+
iyrnie irony[4]
iyrning ironing+
Izlam Islam+
izzint isn't *[is not]

Key to Spelling Rules

Red words are wrong. **Black** words are correct.

~ Add the suffix or word directly to the main word, without a space or hyphen
e.g. ash ~en ~tray → ashen ashtray

~- Add a hyphen to the main word before adding the next word
e.g. blow ~-dry → blow-dry

~| Leave a space between the main word and the next word
e.g. decimal ~| place → decimal place

+ By finding this word in its correct alphabetical order, you can find related words
e.g. abowt about+ → about-face

* Draws attention to words that may be confused

™ Means the word is a trademark

@ Signifies the word is derived from the main word

J

jab[3]

> Unable to find your word under **J**?
> Look under **G**

jabber[1]
jack[1] ~ass ~boot ~hammer ~-in-the-box ~knife ~| o' lantern ~pot ~| rabbit ~| of all trades
jackal *[animal]   Jekyll *[good side]+
jacket
Jacuzzi™
jade ~d
jagged ~ly ~ness
jaguar
jaid   jade+
jail[1] ~bait ~bird ~break
jak   jack[1+]
jaket   jacket
jakoozee   Jacuzzi™
jakul   jackal
jale   jail[1+]
jalopy[4]
jam[3] *[food, squeeze]
jamb *[side post]
jamboree
Jane Doe
jangel   jangle[2]
jangle[2]
janitor
January
jar[3]
jargon
jasmine
jasper
jaundice ~d
jaundise   jaundice+
jaunt ~y[4]
java *[coffee]
Java™ *[language] ~Beans ~Script
javelin
jaw ~bone
jawndiss   jaundice+
jawnt   jaunt+
Jaycees
jayd   jade+
jaywalk[1]
jazz[5] ~man ~| music ~| musician ~| up ~y[4]
jealous ~ly ~y
jeans *[trousers]   genes *[DNA, cells]
Jeckal   jackal *[animal]
   Jekyll *[good side]+
jeehad   jihad
Jeep™
jeer[1] *[ridicule]
Jehovah ~'s Witness
Jekyll ~| and Hyde
   jackal *[animal]
jell[1] *[become firm]
   gel[3] *[soft substance]
Jell-O™
jelly[4] ~| bean ~fish
jelus   jealous+
jenital   genital+
jeopardize[2]   @jeopardy
jepardize   jeopardize[2+]
jepodize   jeopardize[2+]
jeranium   geranium
jeriatric   geriatric+
jerk[1] ~water   @jerky[4]
jernal   journal+
jerney   journey[1+]
jersey

Key to Suffixes and Compounds

These rules are explained on pages vii to ix.

1 Keep the word the same before adding **ed, er, est, ing**
e.g. cool[1] → cooled, cooler, coolest, cooling
2 Take off final **e** before adding **ed, er, est, ing**
e.g. fine[2] → fined, finer, finest, fining
3 Double final consonant before adding **ed, er, est, ing**
e.g. thin[3] → thinned, thinner, thinnest, thinning
4 Change final **y** to **i** before adding **ed, er, es, est, ly, ness**
e.g. tidy[4] → tidied, tidier, tidies, tidiest, tidily, tidiness
Keep final **y** before adding **ing** e.g. tidying
5 Add **es** instead of **s** to the end of the word
e.g. bunch[5] → bunches
6 Change final **f** to **ve** before adding **s**
e.g. calf[6] → calves

jescher gesture[2]
jest[1] *[joke]+ gist *[rough translation]
jestate gestate[2+]
jesticulate gesticulate[2+]

Unable to find your word under **je**?
Look under **ge**

Jesuit
Jesus ~| Christ
jet[3] ~-black ~| engine ~| lag ~-lagged ~-propelled ~| set ~| stream

Unable to find your word under **jet**?
Take off **jet** and look again

jetsam *[cargo overboard]
jettison[1] *[throw away]
jetty[4]
Jew *[person of Jewish ethnicity]
due *[owed]+
jewel *[gem] ~ed ~lry
joule *[energy]
Jewish ~| faith ~ness
jewn June
Jewry *[Jews] jury[4] *[court]+
Jews *[Jewish people]
dues *[entry cost]
deuce *[card, car]
juice[2] *[drink]+
jewt jute *[cloth]

Unable to find your word under **jew**?
Look under **ju**

jib *[part of a crane]
jibe
jiblets giblets
jig[3] ~saw *[puzzle]
gig *[public performance]
jigger[1]
jiggle[2]
jihad
jilt[1]
jimmy[4]
jingle[2]
jingoism @jingoistic
jinks *[high]
jinx[5] *[spell] ~es
jipsum gypsum
jist gist *[rough translation]+
jest[1] *[joke]

Unable to find your word under **ji**?
Look under **gi** or **gy**

jitter[1] ~s @jittery
jive[2]
job[3] ~less ~| application ~| action ~| center ~| description ~| lot ~| satisfaction ~| security ~| specification ~| title

Unable to find your word under **job**?
Take off **job** and look again

jockey[1]
jockstrap
jockulir jocular+
jocular ~ly ~ity
jodhpurs
Joe ~| public
jog[3]
John ~| Doe ~| Hancock
Johnny ~-come-lately
joi joy+
join[1] ~| up
joint[1] ~ly ~| account ~| management ~| ownership ~| signatory ~| venture
Joint Chiefs of Staff
joist[1]
joistick joystick
joke[2] @jokingly
jokuler jocular+
jolly[4]
jolt[1]
jondis jaundice+
jonkwil jonquil
jonkwill jonquil
jont jaunt+

Key to Spelling Rules

Red words are wrong. **Black** words are correct.

~ Add the suffix or word directly to the main word, without a space or hyphen
e.g. ash ~en ~tray → ashen ashtray

~- Add a hyphen to the main word before adding the next word
e.g. blow ~-dry → blow-dry

~| Leave a space between the main word and the next word
e.g. decimal ~| place → decimal place

+ By finding this word in its correct alphabetical order, you can find related words
e.g. abowt about+ → about-face

* Draws attention to words that may be confused

TM Means the word is a trademark

@ Signifies the word is derived from the main word

joo	due *[owed]+
	Jew *[person of Jewish ethnicity]
joos	dues *[owed]+
	Jews *[Jewish people]+
jooish	Jewish+
jool	jewel *[gem]+
	joule *[energy]
Joon	June
joos	Jews *[Jewish people]
	juice[2] *[drink]+
	dues *[entry cost]
joote	jute *[cloth]
josel	jostle[2]
josh[5]	
jostle[2]	
jot[3] ~tings	
joule *[energy]	jewel *[gem]+
journal ~ese ~ism ~ist ~istic	
journey[1] ~man	
joust[1] *[medieval combat]	
	just *[fair]+
jovial ~ly ~ity	
jowl	
jowst	joust[1] *[medieval combat]
joy ~ful ~fully ~ride ~rider ~-riding	
joyn	join[1+]

> Unable to find your word under **joy**?
> Look under **joi**

joyous ~ly ~ness	
joystick	
joyus	joyous+
jubalee	jubilee+
jubilant ~ly	@jubilance
jubilee	@jubilation
juce	deuce *[card, car]
	juice[2] *[drink]+
	Jews *[Jewish people]
jucuzi	Jacuzzi™
Judaism	
Judas	
judge[2] *[official] ~ment ~mental	
	jug[3] *[pot]
Judgment Day	

judicial ~ly ~| process	
judiciary[4]	
judicious ~ly ~ness	
judo	
Judyism	Judaism
juel	duel[1] *[fight]
	jewel *[gem]+
	joule *[unit]
jug[3] *[pot]	
juge	judge[2] *[official]+
juggernaut	
juggle[2]	
juggler *[throws]	
jugular *[neck]	
juice[2] *[drink]	@juicy[4] ~| bar
	deuce *[card, car]
	Jews *[Jewish people]
Juish	Jewish+
jujitsu	
jukebox	
jukstapose	juxtapose[2+]
jule	duel[1] *[fight]
	jewel *[gem]+
	joule *[unit]
July *[month]	dully *[not bright]
	duly *[due]
jumble[2]	
jumbo ~| jet ~| meal	
jump[1] ~| rope ~| seat ~-start ~suit ~y[4]	
jumper ~| cable	
jumping ~| bean ~-off place	
junaper	juniper+
junction ~| box	
juncture	
June	
juneur	junior+
jungle	
junior ~| college ~| high school ~| league ~| executive ~| partner	
juniper ~| berry ~| bush	
junk[1] ~| bond ~| food ~| mail ~yard	
junket	
junkie	
junksher	juncture

Key to Suffixes and Compounds

These rules are explained on pages vii to ix.

1 Keep the word the same before adding **ed, er, est, ing**
e.g. cool[1] → cooled, cooler, coolest, cooling

2 Take off final **e** before adding **ed, er, est, ing**
e.g. fine[2] → fined, finer, finest, fining

3 Double final consonant before adding **ed, er, est, ing**
e.g. thin[3] → thinned, thinner, thinnest, thinning

4 Change final **y** to **i** before adding **ed, er, es, est, ly, ness**
e.g. tidy[4] → tidied, tidier, tidies, tidiest, tidily, tidiness
Keep final **y** before adding **ing** e.g. tidying

5 Add **es** instead of **s** to the end of the word
e.g. bunch[5] → bunches

6 Change final **f** to **ve** before adding **s**
e.g. calf[6] → calves

junkshin	junction+
junta *[ruling group]	
	hunter *[horse, one who hunts]
Jupiter	
jurer	juror
jurisdiction	
jurisprudence	@jurisprudent
jurist	
jurnal	journal+
jurny	journey[1+]
juror	
jursey	jersey
jury[4] *[court] ~| box ~| duty ~-rigged	
	Jewry *[Jews]
juse	dues *[entry cost]
	Jews *[Jewish people]
	juice[2] *[drink]+
jussdis	justice+
just *[fair] ~ly ~ness ~| deserts	
	joust[1] *[medieval combat]
justafiabel	justifiable+
justice ~| of the peace	
justifiable	@justifiably
justify[4]	@justification
justiss	justice+
jut[3] *[stick out]	
jute *[fiber]	
juvanal	juvenile+
juvenile ~| delinquent ~| delinquency ~| diabetes	
juwel	duel[3] *[fight]
	jewel *[gem]+
	joule *[energy]
juxtapose[2]	@juxtaposition
juze	dues *[entry cost]
	Jews *[Jewish people]
	juice[2] *[drink]+
jym	gym+
jynks	jinks *[high]
	jinx[5] *[spell]+

kab	cab+

> Unable to find your word under **K**?
> Look under **C**

kabbige	cabbage
kache	cache[2] *[hide]
kael	kale
kafé	café *[restaurant]
	coffee *[drink]
kage	cage[2] *[enclosure]+
	cadge[2] *[beg]+
kail	kale
kaki	khaki
kalculate	calculate[2+]
kalculater	calculator
kalculus	calculus
kale	
kaleidoscope	@kaleidoscopic
kalender	calendar *[time]
	calender *[press]
kalidoscope	kaleidoscope+
kama	comma *[punctuation]
	karma *[consequences]
kame	came
kamikaze	
kamono	kimono
kamp	camp[1+]
kan	can[3] *[able, tin]+
kangaroo ~| court	
kanji	
kanoo	canoe+

KEY TO SPELLING RULES

Red words are wrong. **Black** words are correct.

~ Add the suffix or word directly to the main word, without a space or hyphen
e.g. ash ~en ~tray → ashen ashtray

~- Add a hyphen to the main word before adding the next word
e.g. blow ~-dry → blow-dry

~| Leave a space between the main word and the next word
e.g. decimal ~| place → decimal place

\+ By finding this word in its correct alphabetical order, you can find related words
e.g. abowt about+ → about-face

★ Draws attention to words that may be confused

TM Means the word is a trademark

@ Signifies the word is derived from the main word

kaos	chaos+
kapchur	capture2
karaoke	
karaseen	kerosene
karat *[purity of gold]	
	carat *[weight of gem]
	caret *[mark]
	carrot *[vegetable]
karate *[fighting]	
kareer	career *[job]
	carrier *[carrying]+
karioke	karaoke
karma *[consequences]	
karnival	carnival
kasett	cassette+
kaution	caution1+
kave	cave2+
kavity	cavity4
kayak ~ing	
kayolin	kaolin
keal	keel1+
kean	keen1+
Keanti	Chianti+
keap	keep+
kebab	
kech	ketch5 *[boat]
	catch5 *[ball]+
	kitsch *[tasteless]
	quiche *[food]+
kechup	ketchup+
kee	key1 *[lock, computer, important]
	quay *[by the sea]
keel1 ~| over	
keelow	kilo+
keen1 ~ly ~ness ~| competition	
keenote	keynote+
keep ~er ~ing ~| fit ~sake ~| up	
keersh	kirsch
keesh	quiche *[food]+
keetch	kitsch *[tasteless]
keewee	kiwi+
keeyosk	kiosk
keg	
kelidoscope	kaleidoscope+
kelp	
kelvin	
kennel	
kept	
kerabeener	karabiner
keraseen	kerosene
keratey	karate *[fighting]
keratin *[protein]	carotene *[carrots]
kereyoke	karaoke
kernel *[seed] ~| technology	
	colonel *[officer]
kerosene	
kestrel	
ketal	kettle+
ketch5 *[boat]	catch5 *[ball]+
ketchup [also spelled catsup]	
kettle ~drum	
key1 *[lock, computer, important] ~board ~boarding ~hole ~| industry4 ~pad ~punch ~| ring ~stroke ~| up ~word	
	quay *[by the sea]+

> Unable to find your word under **key**?
> Take off **key** and look again

keynote ~| address ~| speech ~| speaker	
khaki	
kibab	kebab
kibbutz *[collective farm]	
	@kibbutzim
kibitz *[make comments]	
kibosh	
kic	kick1+
kiche	quiche *[food]+
	kitsch *[tasteless]
kichen	kitchen+
kick1 ~back ~boxing ~off ~stand ~-start	
kid3 ~| gloves ~stuff	
kiddie *[child] ~| tax	
	kitty4 *[cat, money]+
kidknee	kidney+
kidnap3	
kidney ~| bean ~| damage ~| failure	

Key to Suffixes and Compounds

These rules are explained on pages vii to ix.

1 Keep the word the same before adding **ed, er, est, ing**
e.g. cool1 → cooled, cooler, coolest, cooling
2 Take off final **e** before adding **ed, er, est, ing**
e.g. fine2 → fined, finer, finest, fining
3 Double final consonant before adding **ed, er, est, ing**
e.g. thin3 → thinned, thinner, thinnest, thinning
4 Change final **y** to **i** before adding **ed, er, es, est, ly, ness**
e.g. tidy4 → tidied, tidier, tidies, tidiest, tidily, tidiness
Keep final **y** before adding **ing** e.g. tidying
5 Add **es** instead of **s** to the end of the word
e.g. bunch5 → bunches
6 Change final **f** to **ve** before adding **s**
e.g. calf6 → calves

kiel	keel[1+]
kien	keen[1+]
kight	kite *[flying toy]
kik	kick[1+]
kill[1] *[cause to die] ~joy ~| off	
	kiln *[oven]
killer ~| application ~| bee ~| instinct ~| whale	
kiln *[oven]	kill[1] *[cause to die]+
kilo ~byte ~cycle ~gram ~hertz ~meter ~watt	
kilt	
kilter	
kimono	
kin ~sfolk ~ship ~sman ~swoman	
kinasthetic	kinesthetic+
kinck	kink+
kind ~ly ~ness ~-hearted	
kindal	kindle[2]
kindergarten	
kindle[2]	
kindred ~| spirit	
kindrid	kindred+
kinesthetic ~ally	
kinetic ~| art ~| energy	
king ~dom ~fisher ~ly ~pin ~-size ~-sized	
kink ~y[4]	
kiosk	
kirb	curb[1] *[stop]+
kirsch	
kiss[5] ~es ~| of death ~| of life ~off	
kit[3] *[equipment] ~bag	
	kite *[flying toy]
kitchen ~ette ~ware	
kite *[flying toy]	kit[3] *[equipment]+
kith ~| and kin	
kitsch *[tasteless]	
kitten	
kitty[4] *[cat, money] ~-corner ~| litter	
	kiddie *[child]+
kiwi ~| fruit	
Kleenex™	
kleeshay	cliché
kleptomania	@kleptomaniac
klerk	clerk[1]
klorafill	chlorophyll+
Klu Klux Klan	Ku Klux Klan
klue	clue[2+]
kluts	klutz+
klutz ~y	
knack	
knapsack	
knave *[bad person, Jack in cards]	
	nave *[church]
knead[1] *[dough]	kneed *[touched with knee]
	need[1] *[must have]+
knee ~ing ~| brace ~cap ~-deep ~-high ~-jerk ~-length	
kneed *[touched with knee]	
	knead *[dough]
	need[1] *[must have]+
kneel *[on knees] ~ing ~| down	
knell *[sound of a bell]	
knelt ~| down	
knew *[had knowledge]	
	new *[not old]
	gnu *[animal]
	nu *[Greek letter]
knick-knack	
knife[6] ~-edge	
knight *[rank] ~hood	
	knit[3] *[with needles]
	night *[dark]+
knit[3] *[with needles]	
	nit *[insect]
	night *[dark]+
knite	knight *[rank]+
	knit[3] *[with needles]
	night *[dark]+
knob[3] *[door handle] ~bly	
	nob *[cribbage]
knock[1] *[strike] ~back ~-kneed ~| off ~-on ~out	
	nock *[notch]
knoll	
knot[3] *[tie] ~ty	
	not *[negation]

Key to Spelling Rules

Red words are wrong. **Black** words are correct.

~ Add the suffix or word directly to the main word, without a space or hyphen
e.g. ash ~en ~tray → ashen ashtray

~- Add a hyphen to the main word before adding the next word
e.g. blow ~-dry → blow-dry

~| Leave a space between the main word and the next word
e.g. decimal ~| place → decimal place

+ By finding this word in its correct alphabetical order, you can find related words
e.g. abowt about+ → about-face

★ Draws attention to words that may be confused

™ Means the word is a trademark

@ Signifies the word is derived from the main word

knot[3] *[tie] note[2] *[short message, remark]
know *[information] ~ing ~ingly ~-all ~-how
no *[negative response]+
now *[at present]+
knowledge ~able ~| acquisition ~| asset ~| base ~| creation ~| exchange ~| infrastructure ~| initiative ~| integration ~| management ~| object ~| preservation ~| processes ~| product ~| production ~| representation ~| synthesis

> Unable to find your word under **knowledge**? Take off **knowledge** and look again

known *[had knowlede] ~| about
knows *[has knowledge]
nose *[on face]
knuckle[2] ~head ~| down ~duster

> Unable to find your word under **kn**? Look under **n**

koala ~| bear
kobalt cobalt+
kock cock *[chicken]+
cook[1] *[food]+
Kodak™
kokacola Coca Cola™
kollekshun collection+
komikauzy kamikaze
kompete compete[2] *[struggle]+
komplete complete[2] [finish]+
konjy kanji
kontest contest[1] *[competition]
context *[information]
know know *[knowledge]+
now *[immediately]
Koo Klucks Klan Ku Klux Klan
koodows kudos
kook *[eccentric] cock *[chicken]+
cook[1] *[food]+
kookaburra
kool cool[1] *[calm, cold]+
cull[1] *[remove]
cowl *[robe]
kop cop *[police officer]+
cope[2] *[manage]
Koran *[also spelled Qur'an]
korden cordon[1]+
kore core *[center]
corps *[army, ballet]
korespondens correspondence+
koridor corridor *[passage]
corrida *[bullfight]
kornflower cornflower *[flower]
corn flour *[cooking]
koroshun corrosion+
korps core *[center]
corps *[army, ballet]
corpse *[body]
kort caught *[past of catch]
cot *[bed]
court *[law]
kosher
Kouran Koran *[holy book]
kowala koala+
kowtow[1]
krait *[snake] crate[2] *[box]+
krate crate[2] *[box]+
create[2] *[make]+
krait *[snake]
krave crave[2]+
krawfish crayfish
kraze craze[2]+
kreese crease[2] *[wrinkle]+
Kremlin
krest crest *[top, shield]
creased *[wrinkled]
krew crew[1]+
krews crews *[teams]
cruise[2] *[trip]+
krick creak *[noise]
creek *[stream]
crick[1] *[muscle cramp]
krill
krime crime+
kripton krypton

Key to Suffixes and Compounds

These rules are explained on pages vii to ix.

1 Keep the word the same before adding **ed, er, est, ing** e.g. cool[1] → cooled, cooler, coolest, cooling
2 Take off final **e** before adding **ed, er, est, ing** e.g. fine[2] → fined, finer, finest, fining
3 Double final consonant before adding **ed, er, est, ing** e.g. thin[3] → thinned, thinner, thinnest, thinning
4 Change final **y** to **i** before adding **ed, er, es, est, ly, ness** e.g. tidy[4] → tidied, tidier, tidies, tidiest, tidily, tidiness
Keep final **y** before adding **ing** e.g. tidying
5 Add **es** instead of **s** to the end of the word e.g. bunch[5] → bunches
6 Change final **f** to **ve** before adding **s** e.g. calf[6] → calves

Krishna
krypton
Ku Klux Klan
kudos
kukaburra kookaburra
kumlawday cum laude+
kumquat
kung fu
kurb curb *[stop]+
kurnel kernel *[seed]
colonel *[officer]
kwack quack[1]
Kwanzaa *[African American holiday]
kweezeen cuisine
kwerty QWERTY+
kwestshun question[1]+
kwick quick+
kwiet quiet[1] *[calm]+
quite *[completely]
kwier choir *[singers]
queer[1] *[strange]+
quire *[paper]
kworum quorum *[enough members]
Koran *[holy book]

Unable to find your word under **kw**?
Look under **qu**

kydnap kidnap[3]
kydnee kidney+
kyln kiln
kylo kilo+
kylt kilt

L

lab ~| test
labatory laboratory[4] *[science workplace]
lavatory[4] *[washroom]
labeedo libido+
label
laber labor[1]+
labirinth labyrinth
lable label
labor[1] ~| costs ~| dispute ~| force ~-intensive ~| pains ~-saving ~| union
Labor Day
laboratory[4] *[science workplace]
lavatory[4] *[washroom]
laborious ~ly ~ness
Labrador ~| dog ~| retriever
labratory laboratory[4] *[science workplace]
labyrinth
lacadaysickle lackadaisical+
lace[2] @lacy[4]
lase[2] *[emit laser light]
lach latch[1]+
lacitude lassitude
lack[1] *[not have] ~luster
lake *[water]+
lackadaisical ~ly
lacker lacquer[1]
lacks *[does not possess]
lakes *[bodies of water]
lax *[careless]+
lacksativ laxative
laconic ~ally
lacquer[1]
lacrosse
lactate[2] @lactation
lactic ~| acid
lactose ~| intolerance ~| intolerant
lad *[boy] lade[2] *[load]
laid *[past of lay]+

Key to Spelling Rules

Red words are wrong. **Black** words are correct.

~ Add the suffix or word directly to the main word, without a space or hyphen
e.g. ash ~en ~tray → ashen ashtray

~- Add a hyphen to the main word before adding the next word
e.g. blow ~-dry → blow-dry

~| Leave a space between the main word and the next word
e.g. decimal ~| place → decimal place

+ By finding this word in its correct alphabetical order, you can find related words
e.g. abowt about+ → about-face

★ Draws attention to words that may be confused

TM Means the word is a trademark

@ Signifies the word is derived from the main word

ladder[1] *[for climbing]
later *[afterwards]
latter *[last]+
lade[2] *[load] laid *[past of lay]+
lad *[boy]
laden
ladies' ~| man ~| room ~| wear
ladle[2]
lady[4] *[woman] ~bug ~-killer ~like
laity *[not clergy]
laff laugh[1]+
lafter laughter
lag[3] ~| behind
lager *[beer] larger *[bigger]
lagging
lagoon
lagubrius lugubrious+
lagune lagoon
laid *[past of lay] ~-back
lad *[boy]
lade[2] *[load]
laik lake *[water]+
lack[1] *[not have]+
laim lame[2] *[limp, weak]+
lain *[down] lane *[path]
lair *[den] layer[1] *[thickness]
laissez-faire
laity *[not clergy] lady[4] *[woman]+
lak lack[1] *[not have]+
lake *[water]+
lakadaisical lackadaisical+
lake *[water] ~front ~side
lack[1] *[not have]+
lakonik laconic+
lakrosse lacrosse
laks lacks *[does not possess]
lax *[careless]+
laktik lactic+
laktose lactose+
lam[3] *[flight] lamb[1] *[sheep]+
lame[2] *[limp, weak]+
lama *[Tibetan monk]
llama *[animal]
lamanate laminate[2+]
lamay lamé *[gold cloth]

Lamaze [childbirth] ~| class
lamb[1] *[sheep] ~skin
lam[3] *[flight]
lambaste[2]
lambent ~ly
lame[2] *[limp, weak] ~ly ~ness ~| duck
lamb[1] *[sheep]+
lam[3] *[flight]
lamé *[gold cloth]
lament[1] ~able ~ation
@lamentably
laminate[2] @laminator
lamozz Lamaze *[childbirth]+
lamp ~light ~post ~shade
lampoon[1] ~ist
lanalin lanolin
lance[2] ~-corporal
land[1] ~fall ~fill ~form ~holding ~lady ~locked ~lord ~mark ~mine ~owner ~slide ~ward

> Unable to find your word under **land**?
> Take off **land** and look again

landing ~| field ~| gear ~| place ~| strip
landscape[2] ~| gardener ~| gardening
lane *[path] lain *[down]
langer languor+
langeree lingerie *[underwear]
language ~-independent ~| laboratory
languid ~ly
languish[5]
languor ~ous ~ously ~ousness
langwid languid+
langwij language+
langwish languish[5]
lanjeree lingerie *[underwear]
lanky[4]
lanolin
lanse lance[2+]
lansit lancet
lantern
lanyard
lap[3] ~-dance[2] ~| dog ~top

Key to Suffixes and Compounds

These rules are explained on pages vii to ix.

1 Keep the word the same before adding **ed, er, est, ing**
e.g. cool[1] → cooled, cooler, coolest, cooling
2 Take off final **e** before adding **ed, er, est, ing**
e.g. fine[2] → fined, finer, finest, fining
3 Double final consonant before adding **ed, er, est, ing**
e.g. thin[3] → thinned, thinner, thinnest, thinning
4 Change final **y** to **i** before adding **ed, er, es, est, ly, ness**
e.g. tidy[4] → tidied, tidier, tidies, tidiest, tidily, tidiness
Keep final **y** before adding **ing** e.g. tidying
5 Add **es** instead of **s** to the end of the word
e.g. bunch[5] → bunches
6 Change final **f** to **ve** before adding **s**
e.g. calf[6] → calves

laparoscope *[instrument]
laparoscopy[4] *[small-incision surgery]
laparotomy[4] *[open abdominal surgery]
lapel
lapis lazuli
lapse[2]
larceny[4] @larcenist
larch[5]
lard
lare lair *[den]
layer[1] *[thickness]
larf laugh[1+]
large ~ly
larger *[bigger] lager *[beer]
largesse *[generosity]
largest *[biggest]
largur lager *[beer]
larger *[bigger]
larinjitis laryngitis
larinx larynx[+]
larj large[+]
larjess largesse *[generosity]
largest *[biggest]
lark[1] ~| about
larmay lamé *[gold cloth]
larseny larceny[4+]
larva *[insect] @larvae [plural]
lava *[volcano]
laryngitis
larynx @larynges
@laryngeal
lasagna [also spelled lasagne]
lascivious ~ly ~ness
lase[2] *[emit laser light]
lace[2+]
laze[2] *[not work][+]
laser ~| disk ~| gun ~| printer
laserate lacerate[2+]
lash[1] @lashings
laso lasso[5+]
lass ~ie
lassay fair laissez-faire
lassitude
lassivius lascivious[+]
lasso[5] ~es

last[1] ~ly ~-ditch ~| gasp ~-minute ~| name ~| quarter ~| post ~| rites ~| straw
Last Supper

> Unable to find your word under **last**?
> Take off **last** and look again

lasue lasso[5+]
latarel lateral[+]
latatood latitude
latay latté
latch[5] ~key child
late[2] *[not early] ~ly ~comer
latté *[drink]
latency
latent ~| heat
later *[afterwards] ladder[1] *[for climbing]
latter *[last][+]
lateral ~| thinking
latex
lath *[wooden strip]
lathe *[machine]
lather[1]
Latin ~| America ~| Mass
Latino @Latina
latiss lattice[+]
latitude
latrine
latté *[drink] late[2] *[not early][+]
latter *[last] ~-day ~ly
ladder[1] *[for climbing]
later *[afterwards]
lattice ~d ~| window ~work
laud[1] *[praise] lord[1] *[noble][+]
laudable @laudably
@laudatory
laugh[1] ~able ~ingstock
laughter
launch[5] ~es ~| pad
launching ~| costs ~| date
launder[1]
laundromat
laundry[4] ~| basket ~| list
launjeray lingerie *[underwear]

KEY TO SPELLING RULES

Red words are wrong. **Black** words are correct.

~ Add the suffix or word directly to the main word, without a space or hyphen
e.g. ash ~en ~tray → ashen ashtray

~- Add a hyphen to the main word before adding the next word
e.g. blow ~-dry → blow-dry

~| Leave a space between the main word and the next word
e.g. decimal ~| place → decimal place

+ By finding this word in its correct alphabetical order, you can find related words
e.g. abowt about[+] → about-face

★ Draws attention to words that may be confused

™ Means the word is a trademark

@ Signifies the word is derived from the main word

laureate
laurel[3]
lava *[volcano] larva *[insect]+
lavander lavender+
lavatory[4] *[washroom]
laboratory[4] *[science workplace]
lavender ~| oil
lavish[5] ~es ~ly ~ness
law *[rule] ~-abiding ~breaker
lore *[learning]
law ~| court ~| enforcement ~suit
lawful ~ly ~ness
lawless ~ness
lawn ~| mower ~| tennis
lawyer

Unable to find your word under **law**?
Look under **lau**

lax *[careless] ~ity ~ness
lacks *[does not possess]
laxative
lay *[put down] ~about ~away ~man
lei *[Hawaiian garland]
lay ~out ~person
laydle ladle[2]
layer[1] *[thickness]
lair *[den]
layety laity *[not clergy]
laysay fair laissez-faire
laytecks latex
layth lathe *[machine]
lath *[wooden strip]
laze[2] *[not work] ~| around
lace[2]+
lase[2] *[emit laser light]
lazer laser+
lazonya lasagna+
lazy[4] ~bones
lea *[open ground]
lee *[shelter]+
leach[5] *[drain away] ~es
leech[5] *[worm]
lead *[guide, result] ~ing ~| time
lead *[substance] ~ed ~en ~| balloon ~-free
led *[past of lead]
leader ~ship
leading ~| article ~| edge ~| lady ~| man
leaf[1] *[turn pages] ~| through
lief *[gladly]
leaf[6] *[trees] ~y
leaflet[1]
league ~| tables
leak[1] *[hole] @leaky[4]
leek *[vegetable]
leakage
lean[1] *[bend, no excess] ~| cuisine ~-to
line[2] *[narrow mark]+
leant *[past of lean]
lent *[past of lend]
leap[1] ~frog ~| year
leapt
learn[1]
learning ~| curve ~| disability ~| style
lease[2] *[rent] ~| back ~| equipment ~hold ~holder
less *[smaller]
leased *[rented] ~| equipment
least *[smallest]+
leash[5] ~es
leason liaison+
least *[smallest] ~| common denominator
leased *[rented]+
leather ~ed ~| goods ~neck ~y
leave[2] *[go away from] ~| of absence
@left
leavened ~| bread
leayzon liaison+
leccher lecher+
lecture[2]+
lecher ~ous ~y
lecithin
lectern
lecture[2] ~ship ~| theater
lecturn lectern
led *[past of lead] lead *[substance]+
ledge

Key to Suffixes and Compounds

These rules are explained on pages vii to ix.

1. Keep the word the same before adding **ed, er, est, ing**
   e.g. cool[1] → cooled, cooler, coolest, cooling
2. Take off final **e** before adding **ed, er, est, ing**
   e.g. fine[2] → fined, finer, finest, fining
3. Double final consonant before adding **ed, er, est, ing**
   e.g. thin[3] → thinned, thinner, thinnest, thinning
4. Change final **y** to **i** before adding **ed, er, es, est, ly, ness**
   e.g. tidy[4] → tidied, tidier, tidies, tidiest, tidily, tidiness
   Keep final **y** before adding **ing** e.g. tidying
5. Add **es** instead of **s** to the end of the word
   e.g. bunch[5] → bunches
6. Change final **f** to **ve** before adding **s**
   e.g. calf[6] → calves

ledger *[account book] ~| entry	
	leger *[off staff in music]+
leding	leading+
lee *[shelter] ~ward ~way	
	lea *[open ground]
leeayzon	liaison+
Leebra	Libra
leece	lease[2+]
leech[5] *[worm]	leach[5] *[drain away]+
leechee	lychee *[fruit]
leed	lead *[substance]+
	led *[past of lead]
leeding	leading+
leef	leaf[6] *[trees]+
	lief *[gladly]
leeflet	leaflet[1]
leeg	league+
leek *[vegetable]	leak[1] *[hole]+
leekige	leakage
leemer	lemur
leen	lean[1] *[bend, no excess]+
leep	leap[1+]
leer[1]	@leery[4]
leesay	lycée *[French school]
leeshun	lesion *[injury]
	legion *[large number, military unit]+
leest	least+
leeter	liter *[measurement]
leethal	lethal+
leev	leave[2] *[go away from]+
	leaf[1] *[turn pages]+
	leaf[6] *[trees]+
	lief *[gladly]
leezhure	leisure+
left ~| over ~overs ~-wing ~| field ~-footer ~-handed ~ist	
leftenant	lieutenant+
leg[3] ~| iron ~room ~-up ~work	
legacy[4] ~| application ~| data ~| system	
legal ~ly ~| action ~| adviser ~| aid ~| costs ~| department ~| expenses ~| holiday ~| proceedings ~| status ~| system ~| tender	

Unable to find your word under **legal**? Take off **legal** and look again

legalize[2]	@legalization
legend ~ary	
leger *[off staff in music] ~| line	
	ledger *[account book]+
leggo	Lego™ *[blocks]
	let go *[release]
legible	@legibility
	@legibly
legion *[large number, military unit]	
	@legionary[4]
	lesion *[injury]
legionnaire	@Legionnaires' disease
legislate[2]	@legislator
legislation	
legislature	
legisy	legacy[4+]
legitimacy	
legitimate ~ly	
legle	legal+
Lego™ *[blocks]	let go *[release]
legume	@leguminous
lei *[Hawaiian garland]	
	lay *[put down]+
leisure ~ly ~| center	
lej	ledge
lejion	legion *[large number, military unit]+
leksicograffer	lexicographer+
lemming	
lemon ~ade ~| curd ~grass	
lemur	
lend ~er ~ing	@lent
lene	lean[1] *[bend, no excess]+
length ~wise	
lengthen[1]	
lengthy[4]	
leniency	
lenient ~ly	
lens[5]	
lent *[past of lend]	
	leant *[past of lean]
Lent *[before Easter]	

Key to Spelling Rules

Red words are wrong. **Black** words are correct.

~ Add the suffix or word directly to the main word, without a space or hyphen
e.g. ash ~en ~tray → ashen ashtray

~- Add a hyphen to the main word before adding the next word
e.g. blow ~-dry → blow-dry

~| Leave a space between the main word and the next word
e.g. decimal ~| place → decimal place

+ By finding this word in its correct alphabetical order, you can find related words
e.g. abowt about+ → about-face

* Draws attention to words that may be confused

™ Means the word is a trademark

@ Signifies the word is derived from the main word

lentil
lenz lens[5]
leopard
leotard
leper ~| colony
lepperd leopard
leprechaun
leprosy @leprous
lept leapt
lerch lurch[5+]
lerk lurk[1]
lern learn[1]
lesbian ~ism
lesher leisure+
lesion *[injury] legion *[large number, military unit]+
  lessen[1] *[make less]
  lesson *[learn]
less *[smaller] lease[2] *[rent]+
lessathin lecithin
lessee *[tenant]
lessen[1] *[make less]
  lesson *[learn]
lesser *[smaller, less important]
  lessor *[landlord]
lesson *[learn] lessen[1] *[make less]
lessor *[landlord] lesser *[smaller, less important]
lest *[so that not] leased *[rented]+
  least *[smallest]+
let ~| go @letting
letcher lecher+
  lecture[2+]
leter letter[1] *[writing]+
  liter *[measurement]
lethal ~ly ~| injection
lethargic ~ally @lethargy
lethargy
lether leather[1+]
letiss lettuce
letreen latrine
letter[1] *[writing] ~box ~| bomb ~head ~| of credit ~-perfect ~| writing
  liter *[measurement]
  litter *[rubbish]+

lettuce
leukemia
leukocyte
Levant
levee *[wall] levy[4] *[require to pay]
level[3] ~-crossing ~-headed ~-pegging
levened leavened+
lever[1] ~age
leveraged ~| buy-out
leviathan
levies *[charges]
Levis™ *[jeans]
levitate[2] @levitation
levity
levvay levee *[wall]
levy[4] *[require to pay]
  levee *[wall]
lewd ~ly ~ness
lexicographer @lexicography
lexicon
lexis *[lexicon]
LexisNexis™ *[law search engine]
Lexus™ *[car]
lezbien lesbian+
liability[4]
liable *[likely, responsible]
  libel[1] *[lies]
liaise[2]
liaison ~| officer
liar *[tells lies] lyre *[musical]+
liase liaise[2]
liason liaison+
liatard leotard
libary library[4+]
libeedo libido+
libel[1] *[lies] liable *[likely, responsible]
libelous ~ly
liberal ~ly ~ism ~| arts ~| studies
liberalize[2] @liberalization
liberate[2] @liberator
liberation
libertine
liberty[4]
libido @libidinous

Key to Suffixes and Compounds

These rules are explained on pages vii to ix.

1 Keep the word the same before adding **ed, er, est, ing**
e.g. cool[1] → cooled, cooler, coolest, cooling
2 Take off final **e** before adding **ed, er, est, ing**
e.g. fine[2] → fined, finer, finest, fining
3 Double final consonant before adding **ed, er, est, ing**
e.g. thin[3] → thinned, thinner, thinnest, thinning
4 Change final **y** to **i** before adding **ed, er, es, est, ly, ness**
e.g. tidy[4] → tidied, tidier, tidies, tidiest, tidily, tidiness
Keep final **y** before adding **ing** e.g. tidying
5 Add **es** instead of **s** to the end of the word
e.g. bunch[5] → bunches
6 Change final **f** to **ve** before adding **s**
e.g. calf[6] → calves

lible — liable *[likely, responsible]
libel[1] *[lies]
Libra
libral — liberal+
libralize — liberalize[2+]
librarian ~ship
library[4] ~| science
libretto — @librettist
librury — library[4+]
lice *[nits] — lycée *[French school]
license[2] *[a permit] ~| plate
licensee *[someone with permit]
licensing ~| hours ~| laws
licentiate
licentious ~ly ~ness
lichen *[plant] — liken *[compare]
lichi — lychee *[fruit]
lycée *[French school]
lick[1] *[with tongue]
like[2] *[same]+
licker *[one who licks]
liqueur *[sweet alcohol]
liquor *[alcohol, liquid]
lickety-split
licorice
licra — Lycra™
lid *[top] ~ded
lied *[told an untruth]
lide — lied *[told an untruth]
lie *[down, untruth]
@lying
lye *[liquid]
lie ~| detector
liebraree — library[4+]
lied *[told an untruth]
lid *[top]
lief *[gladly] — leaf[1] *[turn pages]+
leaf[6] *[trees]+
life[6] *[being, living]+
liege
liek — leak[1] *[hole]+
leek *[vegetable]
like[2] *[same]+
lien *[legal hold] — lean[1] *[bend, no excess]+
line[2] *[narrow mark]+

lier — leer[1+]
liar *[tells lies]
lyre *[musical]+
lieu *[place] ~| of
loo *[washroom]
lieutenant ~| governor
life[6] *[being, living] ~less ~-and-death ~boat ~blood ~buoy ~| cycle ~| force ~guard ~| insurance ~| jacket ~like ~line ~long ~| preserver ~| raft ~| saver ~| sciences ~-size ~-sized ~span ~| story ~style ~| support ~-threatening ~| vest
live[2] *[be alive]+

> Unable to find your word under **life**?
> Take off **life** and look again

lift[1] ~-off
ligal — legal+
ligament
ligature
light[1] *[shining, not heavy] ~| bulb ~| filter ~-fingered ~-footed ~-headed ~hearted ~house ~| intensity ~| industry[4] ~ness ~| meter ~s-out ~weight ~-year
lit *[past of light]

> Unable to find your word under **light**?
> Take off **light** and look again

lighten[1]
lightening *[making lighter]
lightning[1] *[flash]
lighter *[flame, weight]
liter *[measurement]
lightning *[flash] ~| conductor ~| rod ~| strike
lightening *[making lighter]
ligicher — ligature
ligue — league+
liing — lying+

Key to Spelling Rules

Red words are wrong. **Black** words are correct.

~ Add the suffix or word directly to the main word, without a space or hyphen
e.g. ash ~en ~tray → ashen ashtray

~- Add a hyphen to the main word before adding the next word
e.g. blow ~-dry → blow-dry

~| Leave a space between the main word and the next word
e.g. decimal ~| place → decimal place

\+ By finding this word in its correct alphabetical order, you can find related words
e.g. abowt about+ → about-face

★ Draws attention to words that may be confused

™ Means the word is a trademark

@ Signifies the word is derived from the main word

like[2] *[same] ~able ~ness ~-minded ~wise
lick[1] *[with tongue]
likely @likelihood
liken *[compare] lichen *[plant]
likerish licorice
likwid liquid+
lilac
lilt[1]
lily[4] ~| pad ~-white
lim limb *[arm, leg]+
lime *[fruit, chemical]+
limb *[arm, leg] ~ed ~less
lime *[fruit, chemical]+
limber[1] ~| up
limbo[1]
lime *[fruit, chemical] ~light ~stone ~| tree
limb *[arm, leg]+
Lime disease Lyme disease
limerick
limezeen limousine+
limf lymph *[fluid]+
limit[1] ~ation ~free ~less
limited ~| liability company [LLC] ~| market ~| partnership
limousine ~| service
limp[1] *[not firm] ~ly ~ness
lymph *[fluid]+
limrick limerick
linage *[number of lines]
lineage *[ancestry]
linch lynch[5+]
linchpin
line[2] *[narrow mark] ~| editor ~| graph ~| manager ~| management ~| of credit ~| of fire ~| printer ~sman ~| up *[to order] ~up *[criminal]
lean[1] *[bend, no excess]+
lien *[legal hold]

> Unable to find your word under **line**?
> Take off **line** and look again

lineage *[ancestry]
linage *[number of lines]

lineament *[features]
liniment *[ointment]
linear ~| accelerator ~| algebra
linen ~| basket ~| cupboard
linger[1] *[stay behind] ~ing
lingerie *[underwear]
lingo[5]
linguist ~ic ~ics
liniment *[ointment]
lineament *[features]
lining
link[1] ~age ~-up
links *[joins] lynx[5] *[animal]
lino ~cut
linoleum
linseed ~-oil
lint
Linux™
linx links *[joins]
lynx[5] *[animal]
lion *[cat] ~ess ~-hearted ~ize
loin *[body part]+
lip ~| gloss ~-read ~| service ~stick
lipid ~| profile
liquefy[4] @liquefaction
liqueur *[sweet alcohol]
liquor *[alcohol, liquid]
licker *[one who licks]
liquid ~| asset ~ity crisis
liquidate[2] @liquidator
liquidation
liquor *[alcohol, liquid]
liqueur *[sweet alcohol]
licker *[one who licks]
lirch lurch[5+]
lire liar *[tells lies]
lyre *[musical]+
liric lyric+
liricist lyricist+
lirk lurk[1]
lise lease[2+]
lice *[nits]
lycée *[French school]
lisence license[2+]
lisenshus licentious+

Key to Suffixes and Compounds

These rules are explained on pages vii to ix.

1 Keep the word the same before adding **ed, er, est, ing**
e.g. cool[1] → cooled, cooler, coolest, cooling
2 Take off final **e** before adding **ed, er, est, ing**
e.g. fine[2] → fined, finer, finest, fining
3 Double final consonant before adding **ed, er, est, ing**
e.g. thin[3] → thinned, thinner, thinnest, thinning
4 Change final **y** to **i** before adding **ed, er, es, est, ly, ness**
e.g. tidy[4] → tidied, tidier, tidies, tidiest, tidily, tidiness
Keep final **y** before adding **ing** e.g. tidying
5 Add **es** instead of **s** to the end of the word
e.g. bunch[5] → bunches
6 Change final **f** to **ve** before adding **s**
e.g. calf[6] → calves

lisp[1]
lissen listen[1]
lissening listening+
lissome
list[1] ~| price ~| processing
listen[1]
listening ~| device ~| post
listeria *[germ] wisteria *[vine]
listless ~ly ~ness
lit *[past of light] light[1] *[shining, not heavy]+
litany[4]
litel little[2+]
liten lighten[1]
liter *[measurement]
lighter *[flame, weight]
litter *[rubbish]+
literacy
literal ~ly
literary
literate
literature
litergy liturgy[4+]
lithe ~ly ~some
lithium ~| battery
lithograph @lithography
litigant
litigate[2] @litigant
@litigator
litigation
litigious ~ly ~ness
litmus ~| paper ~| test
litning lightening *[making lighter]
lightning *[flash]+
litter[1] *[rubbish] ~bug
lighter *[flame, weight]
liter *[measurement]
letter[1] *[writing]+
little[2] ~| finger ~| toe
Little League
littrasy literacy
liturgy[4] @liturgical
live[2] *[be alive] ~-action ~-in
life[6] *[being, living]+

live ~stock ~| wire
livelihood
lively[4]
liven[1] ~| up
liver ~ish ~| function ~| sausage ~| spot ~wort ~wurst
livery[4] ~| stable
livid
living ~| death ~| fossil ~| hell ~| quarters ~| room ~| wage ~| will
lizard
llama *[animal] lama *[Tibetan monk]
loab lobe *[ear]
load[1] *[weight] ~ing dock ~stone
lode *[mineral]+
loaf[1] *[lazy] ~| around
loaf[6] *[bread]
loam *[rich soil] loom[1] *[large, weaving]
loan[1] *[lend] ~| capital ~| shark
lone *[alone]+
loath *[reluctant] ~some ~| to
loathe[2] *[hate]
lob[3] *[throw] lobe *[ear]
lobby[4] ~ist
lobe *[ear] lob[3] *[throw]
lobotomy[4]
lobster ~man ~| pot
local ~| authority[4] ~| distributor ~| anesthesia ~| anesthetic ~| variable
Local ~| Area Network [LAN]

> Unable to find your word under **local**?
> Take off **local** and look again

locality[4]
localize[2] @localization
locate[2] @locator
location
loch *[lake] ~| Ness Monster
lock[1] *[door]+
lock[1] *[door] ~jaw ~out ~smith ~step ~up
loch *[lake]+
locker *[closed space] ~| room

Key to Spelling Rules

Red words are wrong. **Black** words are correct.

~ Add the suffix or word directly to the main word, without a space or hyphen
e.g. ash ~en ~tray → ashen ashtray

~- Add a hyphen to the main word before adding the next word
e.g. blow ~-dry → blow-dry

~| Leave a space between the main word and the next word
e.g. decimal ~| place → decimal place

\+ By finding this word in its correct alphabetical order, you can find related words
e.g. abowt about+ → about-face

★ Draws attention to words that may be confused

TM Means the word is a trademark

@ Signifies the word is derived from the main word

locket
locomotion @locomotive
locus *[path] @loci
locust *[tree, insect]
lod laud[1] *[praise]
lord[1] *[noble]+
lodable laudable+
lode *[mineral] ~star ~stone
load[1] *[weight]+
lodge[2] *[living space] ~ment
loge *[seating section]
loft[1] @lofty[4]
lofull lawful+
log[3] ~book ~| cabin ~jam ~| off ~| on ~| out
loganberry[4]
logarithm ~ic
loge *[seating section]
lodge[2] *[living space]+
loggerheads
logic ~al ~ally ~ian
logistics
logo *[sign]
LOGO™ *[computer language]
loin *[body part] ~cloth ~s
lion *[cat]+
loiter[1]
lojic logic+
lok loch *[lake]+
lock[1] *[door]+
lokal local+
lokalise localize[2+]
lokality locality[4]
lokate locate[2+]
lokomoshun locomotion+
lokus locus *[path]+
lokust locust *[tree, insect]
loless lawless+
loll[1]
lollipop
lon lawn+
lonch launch[1+]
lonching launching+
londer launder[1]
londermat laundromat
londry laundry[4+]
lone *[alone] ~r ~some ~| wolf
loan[1] *[lend]+
lonely[4] ~| hearts
long[1] ~-distance ~| division ~hand ~| haul ~| johns ~| jump ~-lasting ~-life ~-lived ~-lost ~-standing ~-suffering ~-term ~-wave ~-winded

> Unable to find your word under **long**?
> Take off **long** and look again

longevity
longing ~ly
longitude
longitudinal ~ly
lonjeray lingerie *[underwear]
lonjevity longevity
loo *[washroom] lieu *[place]+
lood lewd+
loofah
look[1] *[see] ~alike ~-in ~ism ~out *[keeping watch] ~| out *[pay attention, protect oneself]
luck *[chance]+
lookeemia leukemia
looker *[one who looks]
locker *[enclosed space]+
lucre *[money]
loom[1] *[large, weaving]
loam *[rich soil]
loominessens luminescence+

> Unable to find your word under **loom**?
> Look under **lum**

loonatic lunatic+
loony[4]
loop[1] *[circle] ~hole
loupe *[magnifier]
loopis lupus
loopy[4]
loose[2] *[not tight] ~ly ~ness ~-leaf
lose *[not win]+
louse *[insect]+
loosen[1] ~| up

Key to Suffixes and Compounds

These rules are explained on pages vii to ix.

1 Keep the word the same before adding **ed, er, est, ing** e.g. cool[1] → cooled, cooler, coolest, cooling
2 Take off final **e** before adding **ed, er, est, ing** e.g. fine[2] → fined, finer, finest, fining
3 Double final consonant before adding **ed, er, est, ing** e.g. thin[3] → thinned, thinner, thinnest, thinning
4 Change final **y** to **i** before adding **ed, er, es, est, ly, ness** e.g. tidy[4] → tidied, tidier, tidies, tidiest, tidily, tidiness Keep final **y** before adding **ing** e.g. tidying
5 Add **es** instead of **s** to the end of the word e.g. bunch[5] → bunches
6 Change final **f** to **ve** before adding **s** e.g. calf[6] → calves

loot[1] *[stolen goods]
lute *[musical]
lootenent lieutenant+
lootheran Lutheran
lop[3] *[cut] ~sided
lope[2] *[run]
loquacious ~ly ~ness
lord[1] *[noble] ~ly ~ship
laud[1] *[praise]
Lord ~| God ~'s Prayer
lordable laudable+
lore *[learning] law *[rule]+
loriet laureate
lorrel laurel[3]
lose *[not win] @loser
@losing
loose[2] *[not tight]+
louse *[insect]+
loshun lotion
loss *[thing lost] ~| adjuster ~-making
lost *[past of lose] ~-and-found ~| property
lot *[amount] loot[1] *[stolen goods]
loth loath *[reluctant]+
loathe[2] *[hate]
lotion
lotis lotus
lottay latté
lottery[4]
lotto
lotus
loud[1] ~ly ~ness ~mouth ~speaker
lounge[2] ~| suit
loupe *[magnifier] loop[1] *[circle]+
louse[2] *[insect] ~| up
loose[2] *[not tight]+
lose *[not win]+
lousy[4]
lout ~ish
love[2] ~| affair ~bird ~| child ~| letter ~| life ~making ~sick ~| seat ~| song

Unable to find your word under **love**?
Take off **love** and look again

lovely[4] @lovable
low[1] ~brow ~-budget ~-calorie ~-cut ~down ~er ~-fat ~-flying ~-grade ~-key ~lands ~life ~-lying ~-paid ~-pressure ~| profile ~-risk ~-spirited ~-tech ~| tide

Unable to find your word under **low**?
Take off **low** and look again

lowd loud[1]+
lower[1] ~case ~-class
lowest ~| common denominator
lowly[4]
lownge lounge[2]+
lowngeray lingerie *[underwear]
lowse louse[2] *[insect]+
lowzy lousy[4]
loyal ~ism ~ist ~ly
loyalty[4]
loyer lawyer
loyn loin *[body part]+
loyter loiter[1]
lozenge
LSD *[illegal drug]
lu loo *[washroom]
lieu+
lubricant
lubricate[2] @lubricator
lubrication
lucid ~ity ~ly ~ness
Lucifer
luck *[chance] @lucky[4]
look[1] *[see]+
lucksuriant luxuriant+
lucosite leukocyte *[white blood cell]
lucrative ~ly
lucre *[money] looker *[one who looks]
ludicrous ~ly
lufa loofah
lug[3] *[carry] ~| around ~| nut
luge *[sled]
luggage ~| rack
lugubrious ~ly ~ness

Key to Spelling Rules

Red words are wrong. **Black** words are correct.

~ Add the suffix or word directly to the main word, without a space or hyphen
e.g. ash ~en ~tray → ashen ashtray

~- Add a hyphen to the main word before adding the next word
e.g. blow ~-dry → blow-dry

~| Leave a space between the main word and the next word
e.g. decimal ~| place → decimal place

+ By finding this word in its correct alphabetical order, you can find related words
e.g. abowt about+ → about-face

★ Draws attention to words that may be confused

TM Means the word is a trademark

@ Signifies the word is derived from the main word

lukasite	leukocyte *[white blood cell]
lukemia	leukemia
luker	looker *[one who looks]
	lucre *[money]
lukewarm	
lukrative	lucrative[+]
lull[1]	
lullaby[4]	
lumbago	
lumbar *[back] ~| puncture ~| vertebra	
lumber[1] *[wood, move] ~jack ~yard	
lume	loom[1] *[large, weaving]
luminary[4]	
luminescence	@luminescent
luminous	@luminosity
lump[1] ~y[4] ~| sum	
lunacy[4]	
lunar ~| calendar ~| module ~| month	
lunasy	lunacy[4]
lunatic ~| fringe	
lunch[5] ~| counter ~es ~| hour ~| meat ~time	
luncheon	
luner	lunar[+]
luney	loony[4]
lung *[breathing] ~| disease ~fish	
lunge[2] *[move]	
lunisy	lunacy[4]
lunj	lunge[2] *[move]
lunshun	luncheon
luntch	lunch[5+]
lupus	
lurch[5] ~es ~| forward	
lure[2]	
lurid ~ly	
lurk[1]	
lurn	learn[1]
lurning	learning[+]
lurtch	lurch[5+]
luscious ~ly ~ness	
luse	loose[2] *[not tight][+]
	lose *[not win][+]
	louse *[insect][+]
lush[5] ~ly ~ness	

lushus	luscious[+]
lusid	lucid[+]
Lusifer	Lucifer
lusse	loose[2] *[not tight][+]
lussen	loosen[1+]
lust[1] ~ful ~fully	
luster	@lustrous
lusty[4]	
lute *[musical]	loot[1] *[stolen goods]
Lutheran	
luv	love[2+]
luvly	lovely[4+]
luxuriant ~ly	@luxuriance
luxuriate[2]	
luxurious ~ly ~ness	
luxury[4]	
ly	lie *[down, untruth][+]
	lye *[liquid]
lyaise	liaise[2]
lybel	liable *[likely, responsible]
	libel[3] *[lies]
lyberal	liberal[+]
lybrary	library[4+]
lyce	lice *[nits]
lycée *[French school]	
	lice *[nits]
lychee *[fruit]	
lychen	lichen *[plant]
	liken *[compare]
lyckoriss	licorice
Lycra™	
lye *[liquid]	lie *[down, untruth][+]
lyer	liar *[tells lies]
	lyre *[musical][+]
lying ~-in-state	
lyme	lime[+]
Lyme disease	
lymf	lymph *[fluid][+]
lymp	limp[1] *[not firm][+]
lymph *[fluid] ~atic ~| node ~| vessel	
	limp[1] *[not firm][+]
lymphocyte	
lymphoma	
lynch[5] ~| mob	
lynt	lint

KEY TO SUFFIXES AND COMPOUNDS

These rules are explained on pages vii to ix.

1 Keep the word the same before adding **ed, er, est, ing**
e.g. cool[1] → cooled, cooler, coolest, cooling
2 Take off final **e** before adding **ed, er, est, ing**
e.g. fine[2] → fined, finer, finest, fining
3 Double final consonant before adding **ed, er, est, ing**
e.g. thin[3] → thinned, thinner, thinnest, thinning
4 Change final **y** to **i** before adding **ed, er, es, est, ly, ness**
e.g. tidy[4] → tidied, tidier, tidies, tidiest, tidily, tidiness
Keep final **y** before adding **ing** e.g. tidying
5 Add **es** instead of **s** to the end of the word
e.g. bunch[5] → bunches
6 Change final **f** to **ve** before adding **s**
e.g. calf[6] → calves

lyntchpin linchpin
lynx[5] *[animal] links *[joins]
lyon lion *[cat]+
lyp lip+
lyre *[musical] ~bird
liar *[tells lies]

lyric ~al @lyrics
lyricist @lyricism
lysp lisp[1]

Unable to find your word under **ly**? Look under **li**

M

ma
ma'am *[polite address]
maim[1] *[hurt]
macabre
macadamia ~| nut
macaque *[monkey]
macaroni *[pasta]
macaroon *[cookie]
macaw *[bird]
mace *[spice, stick]
maize *[corn]
maze *[labyrinth]
macerate[2] *[soak]
@maceration
Mach *[unit of speed]
make *[create]+
mock[1] *[ridicule]+
machete
Machiavellian
machinations
machine[2] ~| gun ~-made ~-readable ~| tool ~-translation ~| vision
machinery
machinist
macho @machismo
machure mature[2+]
mackerel
mackeroni macaroni *[pasta]
mackeroon macaroon *[cookie]
mackramay macramé
macock macaque *[monkey]
macramé

macro ~biotic ~cosm ~-economics
macroscopic
mad[3] *[crazy] ~ly ~ness ~cap ~house
made *[built]+
maid *[girl, servant]+
madden[1]
made *[built] ~-to-order
mad[3] *[crazy]+
maid *[girl, servant]+
maden madden[1]
maiden+
Madonna
madrigal
maelstrom
maer mayor *[official]+
maestro
mafia @mafioso
magazine ~| insert
magenta
magestic majestic+
magesty majesty[4]
maggot
magic ~al ~ally
magician
magisterial ~ly
magistrate
magit maggot
magma
magnam magnum+
magnanimity @magnanimous
magnate *[person]
magnet *[attracts iron]+

Key to Spelling Rules

Red words are wrong. **Black** words are correct.

~ Add the suffix or word directly to the main word, without a space or hyphen
e.g. ash ~en ~tray → ashen ashtray

~- Add a hyphen to the main word before adding the next word
e.g. blow ~-dry → blow-dry

~| Leave a space between the main word and the next word
e.g. decimal ~| place → decimal place

\+ By finding this word in its correct alphabetical order, you can find related words
e.g. abowt about+ → about-face

★ Draws attention to words that may be confused

™ Means the word is a trademark

@ Signifies the word is derived from the main word

magnesia @magnesium
magnet *[attracts iron] ~ism
magnate *[person]
magnetic ~| tape ~| track
magnetize[2] @magnetization
magnificence
magnificent ~ly
magnify[4] @magnification
magnifying ~| glass
magnitude
magnizha magnesia+
magnolia
magnum ~| opus
magority majority[4+]
magpie
mahagony mahogany
maharaja *[prince]
@maharani
maharishi *[religious teacher]
mah-jongg
mahm ma'am *[polite address]
maim[1] *[hurt]
mom *[mother]+
mahogany
maid *[girl, servant] ~enly ~| of honor
made *[built]+
maiden ~| name
mail[1] *[post] ~bag ~box ~ing list ~| man ~-order
male *[man]+
mailstrum maelstrom
maim[1] *[hurt] ma'am *[polite address]
main *[most important] ~ly ~frame ~land ~line ~stay ~stream
mane *[hair]
Main Street
maintain[1]
maintenance
mais mace *[spice, stick]
maize *[corn]
maze *[labyrinth]
mait mate[2] *[partner]
maitre d'
maize *[corn] mace *[spice, stick]
maze *[labyrinth]

Unable to find your word under **mai**?
Look under **ma** or **may**

majenta magenta
majestic ~ally
majesty[4]
majic magic+

Unable to find your word under **maj**?
Look under **mag**

majong mah-jongg
major[1] ~ette ~| shareholder ~| shareholding
majority[4] ~| shareholder
mak Mach *[unit of speed]
make *[create]+
makaroni macaroni *[pasta]
makaroon macaroon *[cookie]
makaw macaw *[bird]
make *[create] ~-believe ~shift ~up
@maker
@making
Mach *[unit of speed]
Makiavellian Machiavellian
makob macabre
makok macaque *[monkey]
makramay macramé

Unable to find your word under **mak**?
Look under **mac**

maksi maxi+

Unable to find your word under **maks**?
Look under **max**

malachite
maladicksion malediction
maladjusted @maladjustment
malady[4]
malafacter malefactor
malaise
malajusted maladjusted+
malakite malachite
malapropism

KEY TO SUFFIXES AND COMPOUNDS

These rules are explained on pages vii to ix.

1 Keep the word the same before adding **ed, er, est, ing**
e.g. cool[1] → cooled, cooler, coolest, cooling
2 Take off final **e** before adding **ed, er, est, ing**
e.g. fine[2] → fined, finer, finest, fining
3 Double final consonant before adding **ed, er, est, ing**
e.g. thin[3] → thinned, thinner, thinnest, thinning
4 Change final **y** to **i** before adding **ed, er, es, est, ly, ness**
e.g. tidy[4] → tidied, tidier, tidies, tidiest, tidily, tidiness
Keep final **y** before adding **ing** e.g. tidying
5 Add **es** instead of **s** to the end of the word
e.g. bunch[5] → bunches
6 Change final **f** to **ve** before adding **s**
e.g. calf[6] → calves

malard mallard+
malaria
malathion
malaze malaise
male *[man] ~-dominated
mail[1] *[post]+
malediction
malefactor
malerd mallard+
malestrom maelstrom
malevolence @malevolent
malform[1] ~ation
malfunction[1]
maliable malleable+
malice
malicious ~ly ~ness
malign[1]
malignancy[4]
malignant ~| tumor
maline malign[1]
malishus malicious+
maliss malice
mall *[shops] maul[1] *[hurt]
mallard ~| duck
malleable @malleability
mallerd mallard+

> Unable to find your word under **mall**?
> Look under **mal**

malnutrition
malodorous
Malpighian layer
malpractice
malt ~ed ~| ball ~| extract ~| liquor ~| shake ~| whisky
maltreat[1] ~ment
mam ma'am *[polite address]
mom *[mother]+
mame ma'am *[polite address]
maim[1] *[hurt]
mammal *[animal that produces milk] ~ian
mammary[4] *[producing milk] ~| gland
memory[4] *[remembering]+
mammon *[greed]
mammoth *[large animal]
man[3] *[male] ~ly ~-eater ~fully ~hole ~hood ~hunt ~kind ~-of-war ~power
mane *[hair]

> Unable to find your word under **man**?
> Take off **man** and look again

manacle[2] *[handcuff]
monocle[2] *[eyeglass]
manafest manifest[1+]
manage[2] *[cope] ~able
ménage *[household]+
management ~| course ~| information system ~| style ~| team ~| training

> Unable to find your word under **management**?
> Take off **management** and look again

manager ~ial
managing ~| director ~| partner
mandabel mandible
mandait mandate[2]
mandarin
mandatary *[receives mandate]
mandatory *[compulsory]
mandate[2]
mandatory *[compulsory]
mandatary *[receives mandate]
mandible
mandolin *[music]
mandoline *[kitchen tool]
mane *[hair] main *[most important]+
manequin mannequin *[model]
maner manner *[method]+
manor *[estate]
manetane maintain[1]
maneuver[1] ~able
manewer manure *[excrement]
manganese
manger

Key to Spelling Rules

Red words are wrong. **Black** words are correct.

- ~ Add the suffix or word directly to the main word, without a space or hyphen e.g. ash ~en ~tray → ashen ashtray
- ~- Add a hyphen to the main word before adding the next word e.g. blow ~-dry → blow-dry
- ~| Leave a space between the main word and the next word e.g. decimal ~| place → decimal place
- \+ By finding this word in its correct alphabetical order, you can find related words e.g. abowt about+ → about-face
- ★ Draws attention to words that may be confused
- TM Means the word is a trademark
- @ Signifies the word is derived from the main word

mangle[2]
mango[5]
mangrove
manhandle[2]
mania
maniac *[mad person] ~al
 manic *[mad]+
 manioc *[root]
manic *[mad] ~| depressive
manickle manacle[2]
manicure[2] @manicurist
manifest[1] ~ly ~ation
manifesto
manifold[1]
manige manage[2] *[cope]+
manijing managing+
manijment management+
manikin [Also spelled mannequin]
manila ~| envelope
manioc *[root] manic *[mad]+
 maniac *[mad person]+
manipulate[2] @manipulator
manipulation @manipulative
maniqure manicure[2]+
manjer manger
Manks Manx
manna *[food] manner *[method]+
 manor *[estate]
mannequin *[Also spelled manikin]
manner *[method] ~ed ~ism
 manna *[food]
 manor *[estate]
manners
mannifest manifest[1]+
manoover maneuver[1]+
manoor manure *[excrement]
manor *[estate] manna *[food]
 manner *[method]+
manshun mansion
mansion
manslaughter
manslotter manslaughter
mantel *[fireplace] ~piece
 mantle[2] *[cloak]
mantle[2] *[cloak] mantel *[fireplace]+

manual ~ly ~| work ~| worker
manufacture[2]
manufacturing ~| capacity ~| costs ~| overhead
manupilation manipulation+
manure *[excrement]
 manor *[estate]
manuscript
manuver maneuver[1]+
Manx
many
manyac maniac *[mad person]+
 manic *[mad]+
 manioc *[root]
manyfest manifest[1]+
Maoism
Maori
map[3] *[directions]
 mop[3] *[clean]
maple ~| leaf ~| sugar ~| syrup
mar[3] *[spoil] mare *[horse]
 mayor *[official]+
maraschino ~| cherry
marathon
maraud[1]
marawana marijuana
marble[2]
march[5] *[walk] ~es ~-past
March *[month]
Mardi Gras
mare *[horse] mayor *[official]+
mareen Marine+
mareshino maraschino+
margarine
margarita
margin ~al ~ally
marige marriage+
marigold
marijuana
marina *[harbor] marine *[soldier, sea]
marinate[2]
marine *[soldier, sea]
 marina *[harbor]
Marine ~| Corps
marionette

Key to Suffixes and Compounds

These rules are explained on pages vii to ix.

1. Keep the word the same before adding **ed, er, est, ing**
 e.g. cool[1] → cooled, cooler, coolest, cooling
2. Take off final **e** before adding **ed, er, est, ing**
 e.g. fine[2] → fined, finer, finest, fining
3. Double final consonant before adding **ed, er, est, ing**
 e.g. thin[3] → thinned, thinner, thinnest, thinning
4. Change final **y** to **i** before adding **ed, er, es, est, ly, ness**
 e.g. tidy[4] → tidied, tidier, tidies, tidiest, tidily, tidiness
 Keep final **y** before adding **ing** e.g. tidying
5. Add **es** instead of **s** to the end of the word
 e.g. bunch[5] → bunches
6. Change final **f** to **ve** before adding **s**
 e.g. calf[6] → calves

marital *[marriage]
martial *[war]+
maritime ~| law ~| trade
marjarin margarine
marjin margin+
marjoram
mark[1] ~edly ~sman ~smanship ~-to-market
markee marquee *[tent]
marquis *[nobleman]
market[1] ~| economy[4] ~| penetration ~place ~| research ~share ~| value
marketing ~| agreement ~| concept ~| department ~| division ~| manager ~| mix ~| strategy[4] ~| technique
markey marquee *[tent]
marquis *[nobleman]
markit market[1+]
markiting marketing+
Marksism Marxism+
markup ~| language
marlin *[fish] merlin *[bird, magician]
marmalade
marod maraud[1]
maroon[1]
marquee *[tent]
marquis *[nobleman]
marriage ~| certificate ~| license
marriage ~able ~| broker
marriwahna marijuana
marrow ~bone
marry[4] *[matrimony]
@married
merry[4] *[happy]+
Mary *[woman's name]
Mars *[planet] @Martian
mares *[horses]
marsewpial marsupial
marsh ~mallow @marshy
marshal *[arrange]
martial *[war]+
Marshan Martian
marsipan marzipan
marsupial
marteeny martini
marten *[animal] martin *[bird]
marter martyr[1+]
marterise martyrize[2]
martial *[war] ~| arts ~| law
marshal *[arrange]
marital *[marriage]
Martian
martin *[bird] marten *[animal]
martini
marty graw Mardi Gras
martyr[1] ~dom
martyrize[2]
marune maroon[1]
marvel[3]
marvellous ~ly
Marxism @Marxist
Mary *[woman's name]
marry[4] *[matrimony]+
merry[4] *[happy]+
maryjuana marijuana

Unable to find your word under **mary**?
Look under **mari**

marzipan
masage massage[2] *[body]
masaker massacre[2] *[slaughter]
mascara *[eye makeup]
massacre[2] *[slaughter]
mascot
masculine @masculinity
mase mace *[spice, stick]
maize *[corn]
maze *[labyrinth]
maser *[microwave laser]
maserre masseur+
mash[5]
mashettee machete

Unable to find your word under **mash**?
Look under **mach**

masiv massive+
mask[1] *[cover] masque *[entertainment]

maskara mascara *[eye make-up]
massacre[2] *[slaughter]
maskerade masquerade[2]
masking tape
maskot mascot
maskuline masculine[+]
masochism
masochist ~ic ~ically
mason ~ry
masonic
masoor masseur[+]
masoos masseuse
masque *[entertainment]
mask[1] *[cover]
masquerade[2]
masqulin masculine[+]
mass[5] *[amount] ~es ~| market ~| media ~-produced ~| production
Mass *[religious service]

> Unable to find your word under **mass**?
> Take off **mass** and look again

massacre[2] *[slaughter]
mascara *[eye makeup]
massage[2] *[body]
message *[information][+]
massectomee mastectomy
massed *[large group]
mast *[of a ship]
masseur *[male]
masseuse *[female]
Massia Messiah[+]
massive ~ly
mast *[of a ship] massed *[large group]
mastacate masticate[2] *[chew][+]
mastectomy
master[1] ~ly ~| key ~piece ~| plan
Master ~| of Arts ~| of Science
Master of Ceremonies [MC]
masterbate masturbate[2+]
mastercate masticate[2] *[chew]
masterful ~ly
mastermind[1]
Master's ~| Degree [M.A.]

masticate[2] *[chew]
@mastication
mastiff
masturbate[2] @masturbation
masure masseur[+]
measure[2+]
mat[3] *[rug] mate[2] *[partner]
matte *[dull]
matador
match[5] ~es ~box ~less ~maker ~| point ~stick ~wood
mate[2] *[partner] mat[3] *[rug]
matte *[dull]
matedor matador
matenence maintenance
mater dee maitre d'
material ~ly
materialist ~ic @materialism
materialize[2] @materialization
maternal ~ly
maternity ~| leave ~| ward
mateyay métier *[specialty]
math ~ematical ~ematics
mathematician
maticulate matriculate[2+]
maticulous meticulous[+]
matinée
matiriel material[+]
matirielize materialize[2+]
matriarch ~al ~y
matriculate[2] @matriculation
matrimony @matrimonial
matris mattress[5] *[bed]
matrix *[mathematics]
@matrices
matron ~ly ~| of honor
matte *[dull] mat[3] *[rug]
mate[2] *[partner]
matter[1]
matting
mattress[5] *[bed] matrix *[mathematics][+]
mature[2] ~ly ~| economy[4]
@maturity
maturnal maternal[+]
maturnity maternity[+]

Key to Suffixes and Compounds

These rules are explained on pages vii to ix.

1 Keep the word the same before adding **ed, er, est, ing**
e.g. cool[1] → cooled, cooler, coolest, cooling
2 Take off final **e** before adding **ed, er, est, ing**
e.g. fine[2] → fined, finer, finest, fining
3 Double final consonant before adding **ed, er, est, ing**
e.g. thin[3] → thinned, thinner, thinnest, thinning
4 Change final **y** to **i** before adding **ed, er, es, est, ly, ness**
e.g. tidy[4] → tidied, tidier, tidies, tidiest, tidily, tidiness
Keep final **y** before adding **ing** e.g. tidying
5 Add **es** instead of **s** to the end of the word
e.g. bunch[5] → bunches
6 Change final **f** to **ve** before adding **s**
e.g. calf[6] → calves

matzo *[bread] mezzo *[middle range]+
maul[1] *[hurt] mall *[shops]
mausoleum
mauve
maverick
mawkish ~ness
mawl mall *[shops]
maul[1] *[hurt]
mawrayz mores
mawv mauve
maxi ~| pad
maxim
maximal ~ly
maximize[2]
maximum
may *[perhaps] ~be
May *[month] @mayfly[4]
May Day *[1st of May]
mayday *[call for help]
mayanaze mayonnaise
mayce mace *[spice, stick]
mayde made *[built]+
maid *[girl, servant]+
mayday *[call for help]
Mayflower *[Pilgrims' ship]
mayhem
maylay mêlée
maym maim[1] *[hurt]
ma'am *[polite address]
mayonnaise
mayor *[official] ~al
mare *[horse]
mays mace *[spice, stick]
maize *[corn]
maze *[labyrinth]
mayt mate[2] *[partner]
matte *[dull]
maytyay métier *[specialty]
mazalium mausoleum
maze *[labyrinth] maize *[corn]
me *[pronoun] my *[pronoun]+
mi *[musical note]
meadow
meager ~ly
meak meek *[mild]+

meal ~call ~time
mealy ~-mouthed
mean *[middle, harsh] ~er ~est ~ie ~ly ~ness
mien *[appearance]
meander[1]
meaning ~ful ~fully ~less
means ~-tested
meant
meantime @meanwhile
measles
measurable @measurably
measure[2] ~ment
meat *[flesh] ~y ~ball ~loaf
meet *[come together]+
mete[2] *[out]
meatier *[more meaty]
meteor *[rock]
mecanic mechanic+
mecanize mechanize[2]+
Mecca
mechanic ~al ~ally
mechanism
mechanize[2] @mechanization
mecka Mecca
medal *[award] ~ist
meddle[2] *[interfere]+
mettle *[spirit]
Medal ~| of Honor
medallion
medaly medley
meddle[2] *[interfere] ~some
medal *[award]+
meddler *[interferes]
medlar *[fruit]
medeval medieval
media ~| coverage ~| hype
median *[central] Midian *[country in Bible]
mediate[2] @mediation
@mediator
medic
medical ~ly ~| insurance ~| practitioner ~| school ~| examiner ~| expense
medicate[2] @medication

Key to Spelling Rules

Red words are wrong. **Black** words are correct.

~ Add the suffix or word directly to the main word, without a space or hyphen
e.g. ash ~en ~tray → ashen ashtray

~- Add a hyphen to the main word before adding the next word
e.g. blow ~-dry → blow-dry

~| Leave a space between the main word and the next word
e.g. decimal ~| place → decimal place

+ By finding this word in its correct alphabetical order, you can find related words
e.g. abowt about+ → about-face

★ Draws attention to words that may be confused

TM Means the word is a trademark

@ Signifies the word is derived from the main word

medicine @medicinal
medieval
mediocre @mediocrity[4]
meditate[2] @meditation
Mediterranean
medium ~-sized ~-term ~| wave
medlar *[fruit] meddler *[interferes]
medle medal *[award]+
mettle *[spirit]
medley
medow meadow
medulla ~| oblongata
meeger meager+
meek *[mild] ~ly ~ness
mike *[microphone]
meel meal+
meen mean *[middle, harsh]+
mien *[appearance]
meentime meantime+
meer mere *[only]+
mare *[horse]
meet *[come together] ~ing place
meat *[flesh]+
mete[2] *[out]
meetier meatier *[more meaty]
meteor *[rock]
meezels measles
meezonsenn mise-en-scène
mega ~hertz ~phone ~star ~ton ~bit ~bucks ~byte ~cycle ~dose
megafone megaphone
megalith ~ic
megalomania @megalomaniac
megrane migraine
Meka Mecca
mekanic mechanic+
mekanistic mechanistic
mekanize mechanize[2]+
mekka Mecca
melancholic
melancholy @melancholia
melanoma
melay mêlée
meld[1]
mêlée

melen melon
melledy melody[4]
mellifluous
mellody melody[4]
mellow[1]
melo mellow[1]
melodic
melodrama @melodramatic
melody[4]
melon
melstrom maelstrom
melt[1] ~down
melting ~| pot
memary memory[4] *[remembering]+
mammary[4] *[producing milk]+
member ~ship
membrane
memento[5]
memmorial Memorial+
memmory memory[4] *[remembering]+
mammary[4] *[producing milk]+
memo
memoir
memorabilia
memorable @memorably
memorandum
memorial
Memorial ~| Day
memorize[2]
memory[4] *[remembering] ~-mapped
mammary[4] *[producing milk]+
memrabilia memorabilia
men *[males] ~swear
mean *[middle, harsh]
menace[2]
ménage *[household] ~| à trois
menagerie
menajery menagerie
menapoz menopause
@menopausal

Key to Suffixes and Compounds

These rules are explained on pages vii to ix.

1. Keep the word the same before adding **ed, er, est, ing**
   e.g. cool[1] → cooled, cooler, coolest, cooling
2. Take off final **e** before adding **ed, er, est, ing**
   e.g. fine[2] → fined, finer, finest, fining
3. Double final consonant before adding **ed, er, est, ing**
   e.g. thin[3] → thinned, thinner, thinnest, thinning
4. Change final **y** to **i** before adding **ed, er, es, est, ly, ness**
   e.g. tidy[4] → tidied, tidier, tidies, tidiest, tidily, tidiness
   Keep final **y** before adding **ing** e.g. tidying
5. Add **es** instead of **s** to the end of the word
   e.g. bunch[5] → bunches
6. Change final **f** to **ve** before adding **s**
   e.g. calf[6] → calves

menastic monastic+
menchen mention[1]
mend[1]
menial ~ly
meningitis
meniss menace[2]
menjitis meningitis
menopause @menopausal
menshun mention[1]
menstrual ~| period
menstruate[2] @menstruation
mental ~ly ~| arithmetic ~| illness ~| retardation
mentality[4]
menthol
mention[1]
mentor[1]
menu
meny many
meow[1] [also spelled miaow]
mer mare *[horse]
mere *[only]+
myrrh *[perfume]
merang meringue
mercantile @mercantilism
mercenary[4]
merchandise[2]
merchandising ~| rights
merchant ~| bank ~| marine
merciful ~ly
merciless ~ly ~ness
mercury *[metal] @mercurial
@mercuric
Mercury *[planet]
mercy[4] *[kindness]
merder murder[1]+
merdle myrtle
mere *[only] ~ly ~st
mare *[horse]
myrrh *[perfume]
merge[2] @merger
mergers ~| and acquisitions [M&A]
meridian
meridional
meringue
merit[1]
merj merge[2]+
merjers mergers+
merkanteel mercantile+
merkury mercury *[metal]+
merlin *[bird, magician]
marlin *[fish]
mermaid @merman
mermer murmur[1]
merriment
merry[4] *[happy] ~-go-round ~-making
marry[4] *[matrimony]+
Mary *[woman's name]
Mersey *[English river]
mercy[4] *[kindness]
mersiless merciless+
mersinary mercenary[4]
mersy mercy[4] *[kindness]
Mersey *[English river]
mertel myrtle
merth mirth
mesels measles
mesh[5] ~| interface
meshurabul measurable+
meshure measure[2]+
mesia messiah+
mesige massage[2] *[body]
message *[information]+
mesmerize[2]
mess[5] @messy[4]
message *[information] ~| board
massage[2] *[body]
messenger
messiah @messianic
metabolic @metabolism
metabolize[2]
metacarpal *[bone in hand]
metadata
metafor metaphor+
metafysicul metaphysical+
metal *[material] ~| fatigue ~work
medal *[award]+
mettle *[spirit]
metallic
metallurgist

Key to Spelling Rules

Red words are wrong. **Black** words are correct.

~ Add the suffix or word directly to the main word, without a space or hyphen
e.g. ash ~en ~tray → ashen ashtray

~- Add a hyphen to the main word before adding the next word
e.g. blow ~-dry → blow-dry

~| Leave a space between the main word and the next word
e.g. decimal ~| place → decimal place

+ By finding this word in its correct alphabetical order, you can find related words
e.g. abowt about+ → about-face

★ Draws attention to words that may be confused

TM Means the word is a trademark

@ Signifies the word is derived from the main word

metallurgy	@metallurgical
metamorphose^{2}	@metamorphosis
metaphor ~ic ~ical ~ically	
metaphysical ~ly	@metaphysics
metastasis	
metatarsal *[bone in foot]	
mete^{2} *[out]	meat *[flesh]$^{+}$
	meet *[come together]$^{+}$
meteor *[rock]	meatier *[more meaty]
meteorite	
meteorology	@meteorological
meter *[machine, measure]	
	mete^{2} *[out]
	miter *[hat, joint]$^{+}$
methadone	
methane	
method ~ical ~ically	
Methodist	@Methodism
methodology^{4}	
meticulous ~ly	
métier *[specialty]	
metior	meteor *[rock]
metric ~ation	
metronome	
metropolis	@metropolitan
metsaneen	mezzanine
metso	mezzo *[middle range]$^{+}$
	matzo *[bread]
mettle *[spirit]	medal *[award]$^{+}$
	metal *[material]$^{+}$
metyay	métier *[specialty]
	meteor *[rock]
mew^{1}	
mewchual	mutual^{+}
mewl^{1} *[cry]	mule *[donkey]
mews *[cat, stable]	
	muse^{2} *[think, inspiration]

> Unable to find your word under **mew**?
> Look under **mu**

meximatosis	myxomatosis
mezaneen	mezzanine
mezels	measles
mezher	measure^{2+}
mezzanine	
mezzo ~-soprano	
mi *[musical note]	me *[pronoun]
	my *[pronoun]$^{+}$
miander	meander^{1}
miaow [also spelled meow]	
mica	
mice	
micro ~biology ~biologist ~cosm ~economic ~electronics ~fiche ~film ~management ~organism ~phone ~scope ~scopic ~wave	

> Unable to find your word under **micro**?
> Take off **micro** and look again

microbe	@microbial
micron	
mid ~day ~night ~point ~-range ~riff ~shipman ~summer	
middle ~| age ~-aged ~brow ~man ~| school ~ware ~weight	
Middle ~| Ages ~| East	
midevil	medieval
Mideast	
midget	
midia	media^{+}
Midian *[country in Bible]	
	median *[central]
midiate	mediate^{2+}
midium	medium^{+}
midivil	medieval
midst *[middle]	mist *[fog]
	missed *[did not get]
Midwest	
midwife^{6}	@midwifery
mien *[appearance]	
	mean *[middle, harsh]$^{+}$
	mine^{2} *[belonging to me, tunnel, explosive]$^{+}$
miget	midget
might *[strength, may] ~y^{4}	
	mite *[small child, parasite]
	mitt *[glove]$^{+}$

KEY TO SUFFIXES AND COMPOUNDS

These rules are explained on pages vii to ix.

1 Keep the word the same before adding **ed, er, est, ing**
e.g. cool^{1} → cooled, cooler, coolest, cooling
2 Take off final **e** before adding **ed, er, est, ing**
e.g. fine^{2} → fined, finer, finest, fining
3 Double final consonant before adding **ed, er, est, ing**
e.g. thin^{3} → thinned, thinner, thinnest, thinning
4 Change final **y** to **i** before adding **ed, er, es, est, ly, ness**
e.g. tidy^{4} → tidied, tidier, tidies, tidiest, tidily, tidiness
Keep final **y** before adding **ing** e.g. tidying
5 Add **es** instead of **s** to the end of the word
e.g. bunch^{5} → bunches
6 Change final **f** to **ve** before adding **s**
e.g. calf^{6} → calves

migraine
migrant
migrate[2] @migration
migratory
migrent migrant
mijit midget
mika mica
mike *[microphone]
meek *[mild]+
mikro micro+

> Unable to find your word under **mik**?
> Look under **mic**

milapeed millipede
mild[1] ~ly ~ness
mildew
mile ~age ~stone
milenium millennium+
milisha militia
militancy @militant
military[4] ~| service
@militarism
militate[2]
militia
milk[1] ~y[4] ~| float ~| run ~shake
~| tooth
Milky Way
mill[1] ~pond ~stone
millennium @millennia
millet ~| seed
milligram @milliliter
millimeter
milliner @millinery
million ~aire ~airess
millipede
millivolt @milliwatt
mime[2] *[silent acting] ~sis ~tic
MIME *[file type]
mimic @mimicked
@mimicking
mimicry
mimosa
minacher miniature+
minacherization miniaturization

minaret
mince[2] ~meat ~| pie
mind[1] *[awareness] ~ful ~-bending
~-blowing ~-boggling ~| reader ~set
mined *[excavated, planted explosives]
mindless ~ly ~ness
mine[2] *[belonging to me, tunnel, explosive] ~sweeper
mien *[appearance]
mined *[excavated, planted explosives]
mind[1] *[awareness]+
miner *[works in mine]
minor *[lesser]+
mynah *[bird]
mineral
mineralogy @mineralogist
minestrone
mingle[2]
mini ~| series ~skirt
minial menial+
miniature @miniaturist
miniaturization
minimal @minimalize[2]
minimize[2]
minimum ~| wage
minion
miniret minaret
miniscule minuscule
minister[1] ~ial
ministration
ministronee minestrone
ministry[4]
mink ~| fur
minks *[animals] minx[5]
minnow
minor *[lesser] ~| league ~| offense
~| scale
miner *[works in mine]
mynah *[bird]
minority[4]
minoxidil
minse mince[2+]
minstrel
mint[1] ~| sauce

Key to Spelling Rules

Red words are wrong. **Black** words are correct.

~ Add the suffix or word directly to the main word, without a space or hyphen
e.g. ash ~en ~tray → ashen ashtray

~- Add a hyphen to the main word before adding the next word
e.g. blow ~-dry → blow-dry

~| Leave a space between the main word and the next word
e.g. decimal ~| place → decimal place

\+ By finding this word in its correct alphabetical order, you can find related words
e.g. abowt about+ → about-face

★ Draws attention to words that may be confused

™ Means the word is a trademark

@ Signifies the word is derived from the main word

minuet *[dance] ~| and trio
minute *[small, time]+
minus ~| sign
minuscule
minute[2] *[small, time] ~ly ~ness
minuet *[dance]+
minutiae
minx[5]
minyon minion
minyooet minuet *[dance]+
miopia myopia+
miracle @miraculous
mirage
mirang meringue
mirder murder[1+]
mire[2]
mirge merge[2+]
miriad myriad
mirk murk+
mirmade mermaid+
mirmer murmur[1]
mirror[1] ~| image
mirth
mirtle myrtle
mis miss[1] *[fail to hit, loss]+
Miss *[title]
Ms. [title]
misadventure
misajeny misogyny+
misanthrope @misanthropic
misanthropist @misanthropy
misapply[4]
misapprehension
misappropriate[2] @misappropriation
misbehave[2] @misbehavior
miscalculate[2] @miscalculation
miscarry[4] @miscarriage
miscast
miscellany[4] @miscellaneous
mischance
mischief @mischievous
misconceive[2]
misconception
misconduct
misconstrue[2]
misdeed
misdemeanor

Unable to find your word under **mis**?
Take off **mis** and look again

mise mice
mise-en-scène
miser @miserly[4]
miserable @miserably
misery[4]
misfire[2]
misfit
misfortune
misgide misguide[2+]
misgivings
misgovern[1] ~ment
misguide[2] @misguidance
mishandle[2]
mishap
mishapen misshapen[1]
mishun mission+
misil missile *[weapon]
missal *[prayer book]
misinform[1] ~ation
mising missing+
misinterpret[1] ~ation
misiv missive
misjudge[2] @misjudgment
miskondukt misconduct

Unable to find your word under **misk**?
Look under **misc**

miskwote misquote[2]
mislay ~ing @mislaid
misle missal *[prayer book]
missile *[weapon]
misletoe mistletoe
mislead *[deceive] ~ing
misled *[past of mislead]
mismatch ~ed
misnomer
misogyny @misogynist
mispel misspell+
mispend misspend+

Key to Suffixes and Compounds

These rules are explained on pages vii to ix.

1 Keep the word the same before adding **ed, er, est, ing**
e.g. cool[1] → cooled, cooler, coolest, cooling
2 Take off final **e** before adding **ed, er, est, ing**
e.g. fine[2] → fined, finer, finest, fining
3 Double final consonant before adding **ed, er, est, ing**
e.g. thin[3] → thinned, thinner, thinnest, thinning
4 Change final **y** to **i** before adding **ed, er, es, est, ly, ness**
e.g. tidy[4] → tidied, tidier, tidies, tidiest, tidily, tidiness
Keep final **y** before adding **ing** e.g. tidying
5 Add **es** instead of **s** to the end of the word
e.g. bunch[5] → bunches
6 Change final **f** to **ve** before adding **s**
e.g. calf[6] → calves

misplace[2] ~ment	
misprint[1]	
mispronounce[2]	
mispronunciation	
misquote[2]	
misread ~ing	
misrepresent[1] ~ation	
misrule[2]	
miss[5] *[fail to hit, loss] ~es	
Miss	Ms. *[title] Mrs. *[title]
missal *[prayer book]	
	missile *[weapon]
missed *[did not get]	
	midst *[middle]
	mist *[fog]
missel ~| thrush	
misseltoe	mistletoe
missellany	miscellany[4+]
misshapen[1]	
missile *[weapon]	
	missal *[prayer book]
missing ~| in action ~| link ~| person	
mission	@missionary[4]
missive	
missletoe	mistletoe
misspell ~ing	@misspelt
misspend ~ing	@misspent
misstake	mistake[+]
misstate[2] ~ment	
misstook	mistook
misstriss	mistress[5]
missty	misty[4]
missyoor	monsieur
mist *[fog] ~y[4]	
	midst *[middle]
	missed *[did not get]
mistakable	
mistake ~n ~nly	
	@mistaking
mistate	misstate[2+]
misteek	mystique *[mystery]
	mystic *[spiritual][+]
Mister *[abbreviated Mr.]	
misterius	mysterious[+]
mistic	mystic *[spiritual][+]
	mystique *[mystery]
mistify	mystify[4+]
mistime[2]	
mistique	mystic *[spiritual][+]
	mystique *[mystery]
mistletoe	
mistook	
mistress[5]	
mistrial	
mistrust[1] ~ful	
mistry	mystery[4]
misunderstand ~ing	
misunderstood	
misure	monsieur
misuse[2]	
mite *[small child, parasite]•	
	might *[strength, may]
miter *[hat, joint] ~| box	
	meter *[machine, measure]
mith	myth *[legend][+]
mithane	methane
mitigate[2]	@mitigation
mitior	meteor *[rock]
mitiorology	meteorology[+]
mitt *[glove] ~en	
mity	mighty[4]
mix[5] ~ture	
mixamatosis	myxomatosis
mixed ~| bag ~| blessing ~| doubles ~| economy ~| grill ~| metaphor	
mizer	miser[+]
mizery	misery[4]
mizrabul	miserable[+]
mnemonic *[memory]	
	pneumonic *[lungs][+]
moad	mode *[manner][+]
	mowed *[grass]
moal	mole *[animal, mark, chemical amount][+]
moan[1] *[complain]	
	mown *[grass]
moat *[ditch] ~ed	
	mote *[small speck]

Key to Spelling Rules

Red words are wrong. **Black** words are correct.

~ Add the suffix or word directly to the main word, without a space or hyphen
e.g. ash ~en ~tray → ashen ashtray

~- Add a hyphen to the main word before adding the next word
e.g. blow ~-dry → blow-dry

~| Leave a space between the main word and the next word
e.g. decimal ~| place → decimal place

+ By finding this word in its correct alphabetical order, you can find related words
e.g. abowt about[+] → about-face

* Draws attention to words that may be confused

TM Means the word is a trademark

@ Signifies the word is derived from the main word

mob[3]	
mobile ~| home ~| phone	
mobility	
mobilize[2]	@mobilization
moccasin	
mocha	
mock[1] *[ridicule] ~ery	
	Mach *[unit of speed]
mocka	mocha
mockasin	moccasin
modal *[verb, music] ~| dialog	
	model *[example]
moddle	model *[example]
	mottle *[speckled]
	muddle[2] *[mix up]+
mode *[manner]	@modish
	mowed *[grass]
model *[example]	modal *[verb, music]+
	mottle *[speckled]
modem	
moderate[2]	@moderator
moderation	
modern ~ism ~ity	
modernize[2]	@modernization
modest ~y	
modgeler	modular+
modicum	
modify[4]	@modification
modis	modus+
modular ~ity	
modulate[2]	
modulation	
module	
modum	modem
modurn	modern+
modurnize	modernize[2]+
modus ~| operandi ~| vivendi	
modyuler	modular+
modyool	module
modyoolate	modulate[2]
	modulator
moed	mode *[manner]+
	mowed *[grass]
mohair	
moisin	moisten[1]

moist[1] ~ness ~ure	
moisten[1]	
mojuler	modular+
moka	mocha
mokasin	moccasin
mokok	macaque *[monkey]
molar *[tooth, chemical concentration]	
molasses	
mold[1] *[shape, fungus] ~board plow ~er ~ing	
mole *[animal, mark, chemical amount] ~| fraction ~| rat	
molecular ~| biology ~| computing ~| medicine ~| modeling	
molecule	
moler	molar *[tooth, chemical concentration]
molest[1] ~ation	
mollify[4]	
mollusk	
molt[1] *[shed skin, feathers]	
molten *[liquid]	
mom *[mother] ~-and-pop store	
	mum *[quiet, mother, chrysanthemum]+
moment	
momentary[4]	
momentous	
momentum	
mommy[4] *[mother]	
	mummy *[dead]+
monarch ~ic ~ical	
monarchy[4]	@monarchist
monastery[4]	
monastic ~ism	
Monday	
mone	moan[1] *[complain]
	mown *[grass]
monetary	@monetarism
money ~bags ~ed ~-changer ~| laundering ~lender ~-making ~| market ~| order	
	@monies

Key to Suffixes and Compounds

These rules are explained on pages vii to ix.

1 Keep the word the same before adding **ed, er, est, ing**
e.g. cool[1] → cooled, cooler, coolest, cooling

2 Take off final **e** before adding **ed, er, est, ing**
e.g. fine[2] → fined, finer, finest, fining

3 Double final consonant before adding **ed, er, est, ing**
e.g. thin[3] → thinned, thinner, thinnest, thinning

4 Change final **y** to **i** before adding **ed, er, es, est, ly, ness**
e.g. tidy[4] → tidied, tidier, tidies, tidiest, tidily, tidiness
Keep final **y** before adding **ing** e.g. tidying

5 Add **es** instead of **s** to the end of the word
e.g. bunch[5] → bunches

6 Change final **f** to **ve** before adding **s**
e.g. calf[6] → calves

Unable to find your word under **money**? Take off **money** and look again

money's worth
mongoose
mongrel
Monica *[woman's name]
moniker *[name]
monickle — monocle[2] *[eyeglass]
monie — money+
moniker *[name] — Monica *[woman's name]
monitor[1]
monitoring ~| system
monk ~ish ~fish
monkey ~| business
monochrome — @monochromatic
monocle[2] *[eyeglass]
manacle[2] *[handcuff]
monogamous
monogamy — @monogamist
monogram — @monograph
monokrome — monochrome+
monokside — monoxide
monolingual
monolith ~ic
monologue
monoplane
monopolization
monopolize[2] — @monopolist
monopoly[4]
monorail
monosodium ~| glutamate
monosyllable — @monosyllabic
monotone
monotonous — @monotony
monoxide
monoxidyl — minoxidil
monsieur
monsoon
monster — @monstrous
monstrosity[4]
monsune — monsoon
month ~ly statement
montin — mountain+
monument ~al ~ally

moo[1] *[cow]
mood *[emotional state]
mooed *[cow]
mud *[dirt]+
moody[4]
mooed *[cow]
moon[1] ~beam ~light ~lit ~scape ~shine ~stone
moor[1] *[ground, boat]
more *[greater quantity]+
Moore's ~| law
moose *[deer] — mouse *[computer, rodent]+
mousse *[pudding]
moot[1] *[open to debate] ~| point
mute[2] *[silent]+
moovee — movie+
mop[3] *[clean] — map[3] *[directions]
mope[2] *[do nothing]
moped *[bike]
mopped *[cleaned]
morabund — moribund
moral *[good] ~ly ~| majority
morel *[mushroom]
mortal *[will die]+
morale *[confidence]
morality[4] *[right and wrong] ~| play
moralize[2]
morass
moratorium
morays *[eels] — mores *[beliefs]
morbid ~ity
morchuary — mortuary[4]+
more *[greater quantity] ~over
moor[1] *[ground, boat]
morel *[mushroom]
moral *[good]+
mores *[beliefs] — morays *[eels]
moretorium — moratorium
morf — morph[1]
morfeem — morpheme *[language]
morfine — morphine *[drug]
morg — morgue
morgige — mortgage[2]+
morgue

Key to Spelling Rules

Red words are wrong. **Black** words are correct.

~ Add the suffix or word directly to the main word, without a space or hyphen
e.g. ash ~en ~tray → ashen ashtray

~- Add a hyphen to the main word before adding the next word
e.g. blow ~-dry → blow-dry

~| Leave a space between the main word and the next word
e.g. decimal ~| place → decimal place

\+ By finding this word in its correct alphabetical order, you can find related words
e.g. abowt about+ → about-face

★ Draws attention to words that may be confused

™ Means the word is a trademark

@ Signifies the word is derived from the main word

moribund
morn *[morning] mourn[1] *[grieve]
mornful mournful+
morning
moron ~ic
morose ~ly
morph[1]
morpheme *[language]
morphine *[drug]
Morse ~| code
morsel
mortal *[will die] ~ity ~ly
moral *[good]+
mortar[1] ~| board
mortgage[2] ~| payment
mortify[4] @mortification
mortuary[4] @mortician
mosaic
mosey[1] *[move] ~| along
moshun motion[1]+
mosk mosque
moskito mosquito[5]+
Moslem [Also spelled Muslim]
mosque
mosquito[5] ~| net
moss[5] ~y
most ~ly
mote *[small speck]
moat *[ditch]+
moteef motif *[pattern]
motive *[cause]
moth ~eaten
mother[1] ~ly ~board ~hood ~-in-law ~less ~| tongue
Mother ~| Earth ~| Nature ~'s Day
motif *[pattern] motive *[cause]
motion[1] ~less
motivate[2] @motivator
motivation ~al
motive *[cause] motif *[pattern]
motley ~| crew
motor[1] ~bike ~boat ~cade ~cycle ~| home ~| vehicle
motorist
motorize[2]

Motown
motto[5]
mound[1]
mount[1] ~ain ~ainous
mountain ~eer
Mountie
mourn[1] *[grieve] morn *[morning]
mournful ~ly
mouse *[computer, rodent] ~trap
mousse *[pudding]
moussaka
mousse *[pudding]
moose *[deer]
mouse *[computer, rodent]+
mousy
mouth[1] ~ful ~piece ~-to-mouth ~wash
movable ~| feast
move[2] *[motion] ~ment
movie *[film] ~| star ~| theater
mow ~er ~ing
mowed *[grass] mode *[manner]+
Mowism Maoism
mown *[grass] moan[1] *[complain]
mownd mound[1]
Mowri Maori
mowse mouse *[computer, rodent]+
mousse *[pudding]

> Unable to find your word under **mow**? Look under **mou**

mowtown Motown
moyst moist[1]+
moysten moisten[1]
MRI [magnetic resonance imaging]
MS-DOS [program]
MSG [monosodium glutamate]
much ~-heralded
muchual mutual+
muck[1] ~-raking ~y[4]
mucosa
mucous *[relating to mucus] ~| membrane
mucus *[moist substance]

Key to Suffixes and Compounds

These rules are explained on pages vii to ix.

1 Keep the word the same before adding **ed, er, est, ing** e.g. cool[1] → cooled, cooler, coolest, cooling
2 Take off final **e** before adding **ed, er, est, ing** e.g. fine[2] → fined, finer, finest, fining
3 Double final consonant before adding **ed, er, est, ing** e.g. thin[3] → thinned, thinner, thinnest, thinning
4 Change final **y** to **i** before adding **ed, er, es, est, ly, ness** e.g. tidy[4] → tidied, tidier, tidies, tidiest, tidily, tidiness
Keep final **y** before adding **ing** e.g. tidying
5 Add **es** instead of **s** to the end of the word e.g. bunch[5] → bunches
6 Change final **f** to **ve** before adding **s** e.g. calf[6] → calves

mud3 *[dirt] ~bath ~| pie
mood *[emotional state]+
muddle2 *[mix up] ~-headed
mue mew1
moo1 *[cow]+
muel mewl1 *[cry]
mule *[donkey]
mufel muffle2
muff
muffin
muffle2
mufti *[Islamic jurist, casual dress]
mug3 ~shot ~gy4
mukus mucous *[relating to mucus]+
mula mullah
mulberry4
mulch5
mule *[donkey] mewl1 *[cry]
mullah
multch mulch5
multicolored
multicultural ~ism
multifarious
multilateral ~ly
multilingual
multimedia ~| player ~| presentation
multi-millionaire
multinational

Unable to find your word under **multi**? Take off **multi** and look again

multiple ~-choice ~| sclerosis
multiplex5
multiplicity
multiply4 @multiplication
multiracial
multi-tasking
multitude @multitudinous
multi-user
mum *[quiet, mother, chrysanthemum] ~'s the word
mom *[mother]+
mumble2
mumbo-jumbo
mummify4 @mummification
mummy4 *[dead] ~| bag
mommy4 *[mother]
mumps
munch5
munches *[eats]
munchies *[desire to eat]
mundane
Mundy Monday
mune moon1+
munetry monetary+
muney money+
munging ~| technique
mungrel mongrel
municipal
municipality4
munificence @munificent
munitions
munk monk+
munkey monkey+
munny money+
munsh munch5
mural
murang meringue
murcantile mercantile+
murcenary mercenary4
murchandise merchandise2
murchant merchant+
murcury mercury *[metal]+
murcy mercy4 *[kindness]
Mersey *[English river]
murder1 ~er ~ess ~ous
murge merge2+
murk @murky4
murmaid mermaid+
murmur1
murr myrrh *[perfume]
mere *[only]+
mursee mercy4 *[kindness]
Mersey *[English river]
mursiful merciful+
murtel myrtle
musarka moussaka
muscatel

Key to Spelling Rules

Red words are wrong. **Black** words are correct.

~ Add the suffix or word directly to the main word, without a space or hyphen
e.g. ash ~en ~tray → ashen ashtray

~- Add a hyphen to the main word before adding the next word
e.g. blow ~-dry → blow-dry

~| Leave a space between the main word and the next word
e.g. decimal ~| place → decimal place

+ By finding this word in its correct alphabetical order, you can find related words
e.g. abowt about+ → about-face

* Draws attention to words that may be confused

TM Means the word is a trademark

@ Signifies the word is derived from the main word

muscle^2 *[in body]
 mussel *[shellfish]
muscular @muscularity
muse^2 *[think, inspiration]
 mews *[cat, stable]
museum ~| piece
mush @mushy^4
mushroom^1
music ~al ~ally ~| video
musician ~ship
musik music+
musishan musician+
musium museum+
musk ~rat ~y
musket ~eer ~ry
Muslim *[Also spelled Moslem]
muslin *[cloth]
musse moose *[deer]
 mousse *[pudding]
mussel *[shellfish]
 muscle^2 *[in body]
must ~n't [must not]
mustache
mustang
mustard *[spice] ~| gas
 muster^1 *[assemble]
mustash
muster^1 *[assemble]
mustle muscle^2 *[in body]+
 mussel *[shellfish]
musturd mustard *[spice]+
 muster^1 *[assemble]
musty^4
mutant
mutar mutter^1
mutate^2 @mutation
mutchual mutual+
mute^2 *[silent] ~ly
 moot^1 *[open to debate]+
muten mutton
mutilate^2 @mutilation
mutineer @mutinous
mutiny^4

mutter^1
mutton
mutual ~ly ~| advantage ~| fund
muvabul movable+
muve move^2 *[motion]+
muvy movie *[film]+
muze muse^2 *[think, inspiration]
 mews *[cat, stable]
muzzle^2
muzzy^4
my *[pronoun] ~| own ~self
 me *[pronoun]
 mi *[musical note]
myaow meow^1
myld mild^{1+}
mylion million+
myll mill^{1+}
myllennium millennium+
mynah *[bird] miner *[works in mine]
 minor *[lesser]+
mynaret minaret
mynx minx^5
myoot mute^2 *[silent]+
 moot^1 *[open to debate]+
myopia @myopic
myracle miracle+
myrage mirage
myriad
myrrh *[perfume] mare *[horse]
 mere *[only]+
myrror mirror^{1+}
myrtle
myss miss^5 *[fail to hit, loss]+
 Miss *[title]
 Ms. *[title]
myst midst *[middle]
 missed *[did not get]
 mist *[fog]
mystake mistake+
mysterious ~ly ~ness
mystery^4
mystic *[spiritual] ~al ~ism
 mystique *[mystery]
mystify^4 @mystification

KEY TO SUFFIXES AND COMPOUNDS

These rules are explained on pages vii to ix.

1 Keep the word the same before adding **ed, er, est, ing**
e.g. cool^1 → cooled, cooler, coolest, cooling
2 Take off final **e** before adding **ed, er, est, ing**
e.g. fine^2 → fined, finer, finest, fining
3 Double final consonant before adding **ed, er, est, ing**
e.g. thin^3 → thinned, thinner, thinnest, thinning
4 Change final **y** to **i** before adding **ed, er, es, est, ly, ness**
e.g. tidy^4 → tidied, tidier, tidies, tidiest, tidily, tidiness
Keep final **y** before adding **ing** e.g. tidying
5 Add **es** instead of **s** to the end of the word
e.g. bunch^5 → bunches
6 Change final **f** to **ve** before adding **s**
e.g. calf^6 → calves

mystique *[mystery]
mystic *[spiritual]+
mystro maestro
myt might *[strength, may]
mite *[small child, parasite]
mitt *[glove]+
myth *[legend] ~ical
mythology4 @mythological
mytre meter *[machine, measure]
miter *[hat, joint]+

Unable to find your word under **my**? Look under **mi**

myxomatosis

N

nab
nacher nature+
nacheral natural+
nacheralize naturalize2+
nacherist naturist+
nachos
nack knack
nafarius nefarious+
naftha naphtha+
nag3
nail1 ~-biter ~-biting ~| clipper ~| file ~| polish
naim name2+
naip nape *[back of neck]
nairow narrow1+
naïve *[trusting] ~ly ~ty
nave *[church]
knave *[Jack card]
navy4 *[sea army]
naked ~ness ~| eye
nale nail1+
name2 ~ly ~less ~| brand ~-drop3 ~plate ~sake
namonic mnemonic *[memory]
pneumonic *[lungs]+
nanny
nanoscale ~| object
nanoscience
nanosecond
nanostructure
nanotechnology

Unable to find your word under **nano**? Take off **nano** and look again

nap3 *[sleep] nape *[back of neck]
napalm
nape *[back of neck]
nap3 *[sleep]
naphtha ~lene
napkin ~| ring
napsack knapsack
naptha naphtha+
narait narrate2+
narashen narration+
narc *[police] nark *[informer]
narcissist ~ic @narcissism
narcolepsy
narcotic @narcosis
nark *[informer] narc *[police]
narkotic narcotic+
naro narrow1+
narrate2 @narrator
narration @narrative
narrow1 ~ly ~ness ~band ~boat ~-gauge ~-minded
narsasist narcissist+
nasal ~ly
nascent
NASDAQ

Key to Spelling Rules

Red words are wrong. **Black** words are correct.

~ Add the suffix or word directly to the main word, without a space or hyphen
e.g. ash ~en ~tray → ashen ashtray

~- Add a hyphen to the main word before adding the next word
e.g. blow ~-dry → blow-dry

~| Leave a space between the main word and the next word
e.g. decimal ~| place → decimal place

+ By finding this word in its correct alphabetical order, you can find related words
e.g. abowt about+ → about-face

★ Draws attention to words that may be confused

TM Means the word is a trademark

@ Signifies the word is derived from the main word

nashenal	national+
nashenalist	nationalist+
nashenality	nationality[4]
nashenalize	nationalize[2]+
nasty[4]	
natal	
natchos	nachos
nation ~-state ~wide	
national ~| anthem ~| costume ~| debt ~| park ~| security ~| service	

> Unable to find your word under **national**? Take off **national** and look again

nationalist ~ic	@nationalism
nationality[4]	
nationalize[2]	@nationalization
native ~| speaker	
	@nativist
Nativity	
natural ~ly ~| gas ~ist ~| history ~| selection	
naturalize[2]	@naturalization
nature ~| reserve ~| trail	
naturist	@naturism
naught	
naughty[4]	
nausea	nauseous *[causing nausea]
nauseate[2] ~d *[suffering from nausea]	
nautical ~| mile	
naval *[navy]	navel *[stomach]+
nave *[church]	naïve *[trusting]+
	knave *[Jack card]
navegait	navigate[2]+
navegashun	navigation
navegible	navigable+
navel *[stomach] ~| orange	
	naval *[navy]
navigable	@navigability
navigate[2]	@navigator
navigation	
navy[4] ~| blue	
nawjool	nodule
nawt	naught
nawty	naughty[4]
nay *[negative] ~sayer	
	neigh[1] *[horse's sound]
nayber	neighbor+
nayeev	naïve *[trusting]+
	nave *[church]
	knave *[Jack card]
nayshen	nation+
naytev	native+
nazdack	NASDAQ
nazel	nasal+
Nazi	
nea	nay *[negative]+
	knee *[body part]+
nead	knead[1] *[dough]
	kneed *[struck]
	need[1] *[must have]+
Neanderthal	
Neapolitan	
near[1] ~by ~ly ~ness ~-sighted	
neat *[orderly] ~ly ~ness	
	net[3] *[mesh, web]+
nebula ~r	@nebulous
necessary	@necessarily
necessitate[2]	
necessity[4]	
neck ~lace ~line ~tie	
necksis	nexus
necropolis	
necrosis	@necrotic
nectar	@nectarine
neece	niece *[relative]
	Nice *[city in France]
need[1] *[must have] ~ful	
	knead[1] *[dough]
	kneed *[struck]
needle[2] ~craft ~point ~work	
needless ~ly ~ness	
needy[4]	
neel	kneel *[on knees]+
	knell *[sound of a bell]
neer	near[1]+
neese	niece *[relative]
	Nice *[city in France]+

neet — **neat** *[orderly]+
net[3] *[mesh, web]+
neether — **neither**
nefarious ~ly ~ness
nefyoo — **nephew**
negate[2] — @negation
negative ~| cash flow ~| growth ~ly
@negativity
neglazhay — **negligee**
neglect[1] ~ful
negligee
negligence — @negligent
negligible
negotiable
negotiate[2] — @negotiator
negotiation
neigh[1] *[horse's sound]
nay *[negative]+
neighbor ~ing ~ly
neighborhood ~| watch
neither *[not one or the other]
nether *[lower]
nekropalis — **necropolis**
nekter — **nectar**+
nell — **knell** *[sound of a bell]
kneel *[on knees]+
nelt — **knelt**+
nemesis
nemonic — **mnemonic** *[memory]
pneumonic *[lungs]+
Neolithic
neon ~| light
Nepal *[country] ~i
nipple *[protrusion]+
nephew
nepotism — @nepotist
Neptune
nerve ~| center ~| gas ~-wracking
nervis — **nervous**+
nervous ~ly ~ness ~| breakdown ~| system
nervy
nesesary — **necessary**+
nesesitate — **necessitate**[2]
nesesity — **necessity**[4]

nest[1] ~ling
net[3] *[mesh, after subtractions] ~| assets ~| loss ~| margin ~| price ~| profit ~| sales ~speak ~| weight ~| worth ~work ~| yield
neat *[orderly]+

> Unable to find your word under **net**?
> Take off **net** and look again

nether *[lower] — **neither** *[not one or the other]
netiquette
netivity — **Nativity**
netizen
nettle[2] ~| rash
network ~| multiple
neural ~| net ~| network
neuralgia
neurological — @neurology
neurologist
neuron
neurosis — @neuroses
neurotic ~ally
neuter[1]
neutral ~ity
neutralize[2] — @neutralization
neutron ~| activation analysis ~| bomb ~| star
never ~-ending ~more ~theless
new *[not old] ~ly ~ness ~| age ~born ~comer ~| idea ~| product development
knew *[had knowledge]
gnu *[animal]
nu *[Greek letter]
New ~| Year's Day ~| Year's Eve

> Unable to find your word under **new**?
> Take off **new** and look again

newbie *[beginner]
newbile — **nubile**
newclear — **nuclear**+
newd — **nude**+
newkewlar — **nuclear**+

Key to Spelling Rules

Red words are wrong. **Black** words are correct.

~ Add the suffix or word directly to the main word, without a space or hyphen
e.g. ash ~en ~tray → ashen ashtray

~- Add a hyphen to the main word before adding the next word
e.g. blow ~-dry → blow-dry

~| Leave a space between the main word and the next word
e.g. decimal ~| place → decimal place

+ By finding this word in its correct alphabetical order, you can find related words
e.g. abowt about+ → about-face

★ Draws attention to words that may be confused

TM Means the word is a trademark

@ Signifies the word is derived from the main word

newmrasy numeracy

> Unable to find your word under **new**?
> Look under **nu**

news ~desk ~| flash ~group ~letter ~paper ~print ~reader ~room ~stand

> Unable to find your word under **news**?
> Take off **news** and look again

newt
newtron neutron+
next ~-door ~-of-kin
nexus
ni nigh
niacin
nialithic Neolithic
nianderthal Neanderthal
nibble[2]
nice[2] *[pleasant] ~ly ~ness ~ty[4]
gneiss *[rock]
Nice *[city in France]
niece *[relative]
niche ~| market
nick[1] *[cut, steal]
nickateen nicotine+
nickel
nicknack knick-knack
nickname ~d
nicotine ~| gum ~| patch
nid need[1] *[must have]+
knead[1] *[dough]
kneed *[struck]
nidle needle[2+]
niece *[relative] Nice *[city in France]
gneiss *[rock]
nife knife[6+]
nifty[4]
nigal niggle[2+]
niggle[2] @niggly
nigh
night *[dark] knight *[rank]+

> Unable to find your word under **n**?
> Look under **kn**

night ~club ~fall ~gown ~life ~| light ~shade ~| shift ~shirt ~time ~| watchman

> Unable to find your word under **night**?
> Take off **night** and look again

nightingale
nightmare @nightmarish
Nike™
nilon nylon+
nimbis nimbus+
nimble ~ness @nimbly
nimbus @nimbi
nimf nymph+
nincompoop
nine @ninth
nineteen ~th
ninety[4] @ninetieth
nini ninny[4]
ninja
ninkumpoop nincompoop
ninny[4]
ninteen nineteen+
ninty ninety[4+]
nion neon+
niopolitan Neapolitan
nip[3] ~-and-tuck @nippy[4]
nipal nipple *[protrusion]+
Nepal *[country]+
nipple *[protrusion] ~| ring
nise nice[2] *[pleasant]+
niece *[relative]
gneiss *[rock]
nit *[insect] knight *[rank]+
knit[3] *[with needles]
night *[dark]+
nitch niche+
nite knight *[rank]+
knit[3] *[with needles]
night *[dark]
nit *[insect]
nitemare nightmare+

Key to Suffixes and Compounds

These rules are explained on pages vii to ix.

1 Keep the word the same before adding **ed, er, est, ing**
e.g. cool[1] → cooled, cooler, coolest, cooling
2 Take off final **e** before adding **ed, er, est, ing**
e.g. fine[2] → fined, finer, finest, fining
3 Double final consonant before adding **ed, er, est, ing**
e.g. thin[3] → thinned, thinner, thinnest, thinning
4 Change final **y** to **i** before adding **ed, er, es, est, ly, ness**
e.g. tidy[4] → tidied, tidier, tidies, tidiest, tidily, tidiness
Keep final **y** before adding **ing** e.g. tidying
5 Add **es** instead of **s** to the end of the word
e.g. bunch[5] → bunches
6 Change final **f** to **ve** before adding **s**
e.g. calf[6] → calves

nitengail nightingale
nitrate
nitric ~| acid
nitrogen
nitroglycerine
nitrous ~| oxide
nitwit
no *[negative response] ~-brainer ~body ~-claims bonus ~-fly zone ~-go area ~| man's land ~| one ~-show ~| way ~where
know *[information]

Unable to find your word under **no**?
Take off **no** and look again

noad node *[lump, in computing]
nob *[cribbage] knob[3] *[door handle]+
Nobel *[prize] noble *[class, worthy]
nobility[4]
noble *[class, worthy]
Nobel *[prize]
nod[3] *[bow head] ~| off
node *[lump, in computing]
nodule
nock *[notch] knock[1] *[strike]+
noise ~less ~lessly
@noisy
nolledge knowledge+
nom *[name] ~| de guerre ~| de plume
gnome *[dwarf]+
nomad ~ic
nominal ~ly
nominate[2] @nomination
non *[prefix] ~-profit ~-negotiable
none *[not any]
nun *[religious]+
nonconformist @nonconformism
nonconformity
nondescript
none *[not any] nun *[religious]+
nonentity[4]
nonkunformity nonconformity
non-negotiable
nonplussed
nonprofit ~-profit-making
nonreturnable
nonsense @nonsensical
non-starter
nonvolatile

Unable to find your word under **non**?
Take off **non** and look again

noo knew *[had knowledge]
new *[not old]+
gnu *[animal]
nu *[Greek letter]
nooby newbie *[beginner]
noobyle nubile
noodist nudist+
nookyular nuclear+
noomatick pneumatic+
noomizmatick numismatic *[coin collecting]
noomonia pneumonia
noomerater numerator
noomerus numerous+
noon *[midday] ~day
no one *[not any person]
nun *[religious]+
noosinse nuisance

Unable to find your word under **noo**?
Look under **nu**

noot newt
nooter neuter[1]
nootron neutron+
nooze news+
nor *[neither] gnaw[1] *[bite]
norm
normal ~cy
normalize[2] @normalization
north ~-east ~ern ~-west ~| wind
nose *[on face] knows *[has knowledge]
nosedive[2]
nosey nosy[4]
noshen notion+
nostril
nosy[4]

not *[negation]	knot[3] *[tie][+]
	note[2] *[short message, remark][+]
notable	@notably
notarize[2]	@notary
note[2] *[short message, remark] ~book ~card ~pad ~paper ~worthy	
	knot *[tie]
	not *[negation]

Unable to find your word under **note**? Take off **note** and look again

noterize	notarize[2]
nothing ~ness	
notible	notable[+]
notical	nautical[+]
notice[2] ~able ~| board	
notion ~al	
notiss	notice[2+]
notorious ~ly	
notsee	Nazi
nougat	
nought	knot *[tie]
	not *[negation]
noun *[part of speech] ~| phrase	
	known *[had knowledge][+]
nourish[5] ~ment	
nova	@novae
novel ~ist ~la	
novelty[4]	
November	
novice *[beginner]	
novitiate *[state of being a novice]	
novle	novel[+]
now *[at present] ~adays	
	know *[information][+]
nowbell	Nobel *[prize]
	noble *[class, worthy]
nowmad	nomad[+]
nown	known *[had knowledge]
	noun *[part of speech][+]
noyze	noise[+]
noze	knows *[has knowledge]
	nose *[on face]
nozedive	nosedive[2]
nozia	nausea[+]
noziate	nauseate[2]
nu *[Greek letter]	knew *[had knowledge]
	new *[not old][+]
	gnu *[animal]
nuance	
nubile	
nuckel	knuckle[2+]
nuclear ~| energy ~| family ~| fission ~| medicine ~| physics ~| power	
nucleus	@nucleii
nucular	nuclear[+]
nude	@nudity
nudge[2]	
nudist	@nudism
nugget	
nugit	nougat
nuisance	
nuj	nudge[2]
null ~| and void	
nullify[4]	
num	numb[1+]
	nom[+]
numb[1] ~ly ~ness	
number[1] *[quantity] ~| crunching ~| line ~s racket ~| theory	
number *[more numb, anesthetic]	
numbskull	
numeracy	
numerator	
numerical	
numerous ~ly	
numismatic *[coin collecting]	
numskull	numbskull
nun *[religious] ~nery	
	none *[not any]
	noon *[midday][+]
nupchuals	nuptials
nuptials	
nuralja	neuralgia
nurcher	nurture[2]
nurish	nourish[5+]
nurolagist	neurologist

KEY TO SUFFIXES AND COMPOUNDS

These rules are explained on pages vii to ix.

1. Keep the word the same before adding **ed, er, est, ing** e.g. cool[1] → cooled, cooler, coolest, cooling
2. Take off final **e** before adding **ed, er, est, ing** e.g. fine[2] → fined, finer, finest, fining
3. Double final consonant before adding **ed, er, est, ing** e.g. thin[3] → thinned, thinner, thinnest, thinning
4. Change final **y** to **i** before adding **ed, er, es, est, ly, ness** e.g. tidy[4] → tidied, tidier, tidies, tidiest, tidily, tidiness Keep final **y** before adding **ing** e.g. tidying
5. Add **es** instead of **s** to the end of the word e.g. bunch[5] → bunches
6. Change final **f** to **ve** before adding **s** e.g. calf[6] → calves

nuron	neuron
nurosis	neurosis+
nurotic	neurotic+
nurrish	nourish5+
nurse2 ~| practitioner	
nursery4	
nursing ~| home	
nurture2	
nut ~ty4 ~cracker ~meg ~shell	
nutral	neutral+
nutrient	
nutrition ~ist	
nutritious	
nutron	neutron+

Unable to find your word under **nu**?
Look under **neu**

nuze	news+
nyasin	niacin
nye	nigh
nykie	Nike™
nylon ~| stockings	
nymph ~omaniac	
nytrait	nitrate
nytrick	nitric+
nytrogliserin	nitroglycerine

Unable to find your word under **ny**?
Look under **ni**

O

O [letter of the alphabet]	
	au *[French word]+
	oh *[exclamation]
	owe2 *[be in debt]
O.K. [okay]	
oad	ode *[poem]
	owed *[money]
oaf *[stupid person] ~ish ~ishness	
	off *[away from]+
oak ~en	
oan	own1 *[belonging]+
oapn	open1+
oar *[boat]	awe2 *[wonder]+
	or *[alternative]
	ore *[mineral]
oasis	@oases
oat *[grain] ~| bran ~cake ~meal	
	haute *[fancy]+
oath *[swear]	
obay	obey1
obdurate ~ly	@obduracy
obedient ~ly	@obedience
obeece	obese+
obeediyent	obedient+
obese	@obesity
obey1	
obgect	object1 *[thing, oppose]+
	abject *[humiliated]+
obichuary	obituary4
obidyant	obedient+
obise	obese+
obituary4	
objaydar	objet d'art
object1 *[thing, oppose] ~-oriented ~| program	
	abject *[humiliated]+
objection ~able	
objective ~ly	@objectivity
	@objectivism
objekt	object1+
objet d'art	
objurate	obdurate+
oblagacion	obligation
obleek	oblique+

Key to Spelling Rules

Red words are wrong. **Black** words are correct.

~ Add the suffix or word directly to the main word, without a space or hyphen
e.g. ash ~en ~tray → ashen ashtray

~- Add a hyphen to the main word before adding the next word
e.g. blow ~-dry → blow-dry

~| Leave a space between the main word and the next word
e.g. decimal ~| place → decimal place

+ By finding this word in its correct alphabetical order, you can find related words
e.g. abowt about+ → about-face

★ Draws attention to words that may be confused

™ Means the word is a trademark

@ Signifies the word is derived from the main word

oblick	oblique[+]
obligation	
oblige[2]	@obligatory
oblique ~ly ~ness	
obliterate[2]	@obliteration
oblivious *[unaware] ~ly	
	@oblivion
	obvious *[clearly seen][+]
oblong	
oblyge	oblige[2+]
oblyterate	obliterate[2+]
oblyvius	oblivious *[unaware][+]
obnoxious ~ly	
oboe	@oboist
obow	oboe[+]
obsaleet	obsolete
obsalesense	obsolescence[+]
obscene ~ly	@obscenity[4]
obscure[2] ~ly	@obscurity[4]
obseen	obscene[+]
obsequious *[subservient] ~ly ~ness	
obsequy[4] *[funeral service]	
observant	
observatory[4]	
observe[2]	@observation
obsessed	
obsidian	
obskure	obscure[2+]
obsolescence	@obsolescent
obsolete	
obsqure	obscure[2+]
obstacle ~| course	
obstetric ~ian ~s	
obstickle	obstacle[+]
obstinacy	
obstinait	obstinate[+]
obstinasey	obstinacy
obstinate ~ly	
obstreperous	
obstruct[1] ~ion ~ive	
obsturkul	obstacle[+]
obstynate	obstinate[+]
obsurvatory	observatory[4]
obsurve	observe[2+]
obtain[1] ~able	

obtrusive	
obtuse ~ly ~ness ~| angle	
obverse	
obvious *[clearly seen] ~ly ~ness	
	oblivious *[unaware][+]
obzhaydar	objet d'art
ocashun	occasion[+]
occasion ~al ~ally	
occhre *[color]	ocher *[color]
	occur[3] *[happen][+]
	okra *[vegetable]
occident *[west] ~al	
	accident *[chance event][+]
occular	ocular[+]
occult	
occupant	@occupancy rate
occupation ~al therapy	
occupy[4]	
occur[3] *[happen]	@occurrence
	ochre *[color]
	okra *[vegetable]
ocean ~| current ~| ridge ~side	
oceanography	
ocelot	
ocher *[color]	occur[3] *[happen][+]
	okra *[vegetable]
ocksajen	occasion[+]
ockur	occur[3] *[happen][+]
	ocher *[color]
	okra *[vegetable]
o'clock	
ocsident	occident *[west][+]
octagon ~al	
octain	octane[+]
octajenerian	octogenarian
octane ~| rating	
octave	
octet ~| rule	
octive	octave
October	
octogenarian	
octopus[5]	
ocular	@oculist
ocupant	occupant[+]

Key to Suffixes and Compounds

These rules are explained on pages vii to ix.

1 Keep the word the same before adding **ed, er, est, ing**
e.g. cool[1] → cooled, cooler, coolest, cooling

2 Take off final **e** before adding **ed, er, est, ing**
e.g. fine[2] → fined, finer, finest, fining

3 Double final consonant before adding **ed, er, est, ing**
e.g. thin[3] → thinned, thinner, thinnest, thinning

4 Change final **y** to **i** before adding **ed, er, es, est, ly, ness**
e.g. tidy[4] → tidied, tidier, tidies, tidiest, tidily, tidiness
Keep final **y** before adding **ing** e.g. tidying

5 Add **es** instead of **s** to the end of the word
e.g. bunch[5] → bunches

6 Change final **f** to **ve** before adding **s**
e.g. calf[6] → calves

ocur occur[3] *[happen]+
ocher[3] *[color]
okra *[vegetable]

Unable to find your word under **oc**?
Look under **occ**

OD[1] *[overdose]
odd *[not even] ~ly ~ball ~| job ~ment ~| number
ode *[poem]
owed *[money]
oddessee odyssey
oddit audit[1+]
oddity[4]
oddometre odometer
odds ~-on ~| and ends
ode *[poem] odd *[not even]
owed *[money]
OD[1] *[overdose]
Oder *[European river]
odor+
odeum *[theater] odium *[contempt]
odious *[hateful] ~ly ~ness
odorous *[scented]+
odissee odyssey
odit audit[1+]
odity oddity[4]
odium *[contempt]
odeum *[theater]
odius odious *[hateful]+
odometer
odor ~-free ~less
Oder *[European river]
odorous *[scented] ~ly ~ness
odious *[hateful]+
ods odds+
odyssey
odyum odium *[contempt]
odeum *[theater]
oeuvre ~| d'art
of *[belonging to] ~| course
oaf *[stupid person]+
off *[away from]+

ofal awful *[terrible]
offal *[meat waste]
ofen often
ofence offense
ofend offend[1]
ofer offer[1]
off *[away from] ~beat ~| balance ~-color ~| center ~-chance ~-duty ~line ~-limits ~load ~-peak ~-ramp ~-road ~-season ~shoot ~shore ~side ~-site ~spring ~stage ~-the-cuff ~-the-rack ~-the-record ~-the-wall ~-white ~-year
of *[belonging to]+
oaf *[stupid person]+

Unable to find your word under **off**?
Take off **off** and look again

offal *[meat waste]
awful *[terrible]+
offen often
offend[1]
offense
offensive ~ly ~ness
offer[1]
offhand ~ed ~edness
office ~| equipment ~| furniture ~holder ~| hours ~| space ~| worker
officer
official ~ly ~| receiver ~| return
officiant *[officiates]
efficient *[gets things done]+
officiate[2]
officious ~ly ~ness
offset[3]
offten often

Unable to find your word under **off**?
Look under **of**

ofice office+
ofiser officer
ofishall official+
ofset offset[3]

Key to Spelling Rules

Red words are wrong. **Black** words are correct.

~ Add the suffix or word directly to the main word, without a space or hyphen
e.g. ash ~en ~tray → ashen ashtray

~- Add a hyphen to the main word before adding the next word
e.g. blow ~-dry → blow-dry

~| Leave a space between the main word and the next word
e.g. decimal ~| place → decimal place

+ By finding this word in its correct alphabetical order, you can find related words
e.g. abowt about+ → about-face

★ Draws attention to words that may be confused

TM Means the word is a trademark

@ Signifies the word is derived from the main word

often
ofthalmologist ophthalmologist+
ogle[2]
ogre ~ss
oh *[exclamation] au *[French word]+
ohm *[measurement]
ow *[pain]
owe[2] *[be in debt]
ohe ow *[pain]
owe[2] *[be in debt]
ohm *[measurement] ~ic
oh *[exclamation]
om *[Hindu sacred word]
Ohm's ~| law
oil[1] ~y[4] ~can ~cloth ~field ~| paint ~| painting ~seed ~| skin ~| spill ~| well

Unable to find your word under **oil**? Take off **oil** and look again

ointment
oister oyster+
okashun occasion+
okcupation occupation+
okcupy occupy[4]
okcur occur[3] *[happen]+
ochre *[color]
oker ochre *[color]
occur[3] *[happen]+
okra *[vegetable]
o'klock o'clock
okra *[vegetable] ochre *[color]
occur[3] *[happen]+
oksygen oxygen+
Oktober October
okult occult

Unable to find your word under **ok**? Look under **occ**

old ~| age ~-fashioned ~| guard ~| maid ~| school ~-timer
Old ~| Glory ~| Testament ~| World
oleander
olegarky oligarchy[4]
olev olive+
olfactory
oligarchy[4]
olive ~| branch ~| green ~| oil
olyander oleander
Olympic ~| Games ~s
@Olympian
olyve olive+
om *[Hindu sacred word]
ohm *[measurement]+
Oman *[country] omen *[sign]
omayga omega
ombudsman
omega
omelet
omen *[sign] Oman *[country]
omenous ominous+
omiga omega
ominous ~ly ~ness
omishun omission
omission
omit[3]
omlet omelet
omminus ominous+
ommit omit[3]
omnipotence @omnipotent
omniscient @omniscience
omnivore
omnivorous ~ly ~ness
omnysient omniscient+
omnyvorous omnivorous+
omyshun omission
on *[surface of] ~-air ~coming ~going ~line ~rush ~side ~shore ~-screen ~set ~slaught ~stage
one *[single]+
own[1] *[belonging]+

Unable to find your word under **on**? Take off **on** and look again

onamotapia onomatopoeia+
once *[one time] ~-over
wants *[needs, desires]
oncology @oncologist

KEY TO SUFFIXES AND COMPOUNDS

These rules are explained on pages vii to ix.

1 Keep the word the same before adding **ed, er, est, ing**
e.g. cool[1] → cooled, cooler, coolest, cooling
2 Take off final **e** before adding **ed, er, est, ing**
e.g. fine[2] → fined, finer, finest, fining
3 Double final consonant before adding **ed, er, est, ing**
e.g. thin[3] → thinned, thinner, thinnest, thinning
4 Change final **y** to **i** before adding **ed, er, es, est, ly, ness**
e.g. tidy[4] → tidied, tidier, tidies, tidiest, tidily, tidiness
Keep final **y** before adding **ing** e.g. tidying
5 Add **es** instead of **s** to the end of the word
e.g. bunch[5] → bunches
6 Change final **f** to **ve** before adding **s**
e.g. calf[6] → calves

oncor encore

one *[single] ~| another ~-armed bandit ~-horse ~-night stand ~| off ~self ~-sided ~-to-one ~-track mind ~-upmanship ~-up ~-way

on *[surface of]
own[1] *[belonging]+
wan *[pale]
won *[victory]

Unable to find your word under **one**?
Take off **one** and look again

oner owner+
honor[1]+

onerous

ones *[individuals]
once *[one time]+

onion *[vegetable]
union *[uniting]

onis onus

onix onyx

onkolegy oncology+

online ~| system

onlooker

only

onlyne online+

onomatopoeia @onomatopoeic @onomatopoetic

onous onus

onroot en route

onse once *[one time]+

onset

onto

ontology

onus

onwards

onwee ennui

onyun onion *[vegetable]
union *[uniting]

onyx

ooze[2]

opacity

opake opaque+

opal ~ine

opan open[1]+

opaque ~ly

opassity opacity

op-ed ~| page

open[1] ~ly ~ness ~er ~| air ~-and-shut ~-ended ~| house ~-market ~| minded ~-plan ~| season ~| society

Unable to find your word under **open**?
Take off **open** and look again

opening ~| balance ~| bid ~| hours ~| price

opera ~tic ~tically

operashun operation+

operate[2] @operable @operative

operating ~| budget ~| costs ~| expense ~| room ~| system ~| theater

operation ~al

operator *[handles something]

operetta *[opera]

ophthalmic

ophthalmologist @ophthalmology

opiam opium

opiate

opinion ~ated ~| poll

opis opus

opium

opiyet opiate

oponent opponent

oportunity opportunity[4]

oposit opposite *[contrary]+

opossum

opous opus

opoze oppose[2]+

Unable to find your word under **op**?
Look under **opp**

oppera opera+

opperate operate[2]+

opponent

opportune ~ly ~ness

Key to Spelling Rules

Red words are wrong. **Black** words are correct.

~ Add the suffix or word directly to the main word, without a space or hyphen
e.g. ash ~en ~tray → ashen ashtray

~- Add a hyphen to the main word before adding the next word
e.g. blow ~-dry → blow-dry

~| Leave a space between the main word and the next word
e.g. decimal ~| place → decimal place

+ By finding this word in its correct alphabetical order, you can find related words
e.g. abowt about+ → about-face

* Draws attention to words that may be confused

TM Means the word is a trademark

@ Signifies the word is derived from the main word

opportunism
opportunist ~ic ~ically
opportunity[4]
oppose[2] @opposition
opposite *[contrary] ~| angles
apposite *[appropriate]
opposum opossum
opposyte opposite *[contrary]+
oppress[1] ~ion ~ive
opra opera+
opress oppress[5+]
opretta operetta *[opera]
opshun option+
opt[1] ~| out
optamist optimist+
opthalmic ophthalmic
optic ~s ~| nerve
optical ~ly ~| disc ~| fiber ~| illusion
optician
optickle optical+
optimist ~ic ~ically
@optimism
optimize[2] @optimization
optimum
option ~al ~ally
optishun optician
optometrist
optyc optic+
opulence @opulent
opurate operate[2+]
opuration operation+
opus
opyate opiate
opyoolense opulence+
or *[alternative] ~| else
awe[2] *[wonder]+
oar *[boat]
ore *[mineral]
oracle *[prophecy]
auricle *[ear, heart]
oral *[mouth] ~ly ~| contraceptive ~| fixation
aural *[ear]+
orange ~| juice
orangutan
oration
orator
oratorio *[music]
oratory[4] *[speech, prayer place]
orb[1]
orbit[1] ~al
orchard
orchestra ~l
orchestrate[2] @orchestration
orchid
ordain[1]
ordeal
order[1] *[command] ~ly[4] ~| book ~| fulfillment ~| number ~| of reactivity ~| processing
ordure *[filth]

> Unable to find your word under **order**?
> Take off **order** and look again

orderve hors-d'oeuvre
ordinal ~| number
ordinance *[regulation]
ordnance *[artillery]
ordinary @ordinarily
ordination
ordnance *[artillery]
ordinance *[regulation]
ordnary ordinary+
ordnense ordinance *[regulation]
ordnance *[artillery]
ordure *[filth] order[1] *[command]+
ore *[mineral] awe[2] *[wonder]+
oar *[boat]
or *[alternative]
oregano
orel oral *[mouth]+
aural *[ear]+
orfan orphan[1+]
organ ~ist ~-grinder
organic ~ally ~| chemistry ~| farming ~| industry
organism
organizational ~| methods
organize[2] @organization

KEY TO SUFFIXES AND COMPOUNDS

These rules are explained on pages vii to ix.

1 Keep the word the same before adding **ed, er, est, ing**
e.g. cool[1] → cooled, cooler, coolest, cooling
2 Take off final **e** before adding **ed, er, est, ing**
e.g. fine[2] → fined, finer, finest, fining
3 Double final consonant before adding **ed, er, est, ing**
e.g. thin[3] → thinned, thinner, thinnest, thinning
4 Change final **y** to **i** before adding **ed, er, es, est, ly, ness**
e.g. tidy[4] → tidied, tidier, tidies, tidiest, tidily, tidiness
Keep final **y** before adding **ing** e.g. tidying
5 Add **es** instead of **s** to the end of the word
e.g. bunch[5] → bunches
6 Change final **f** to **ve** before adding **s**
e.g. calf[6] → calves

orgasm ~ic	
orginizashunal	organizational[+]
orginize	organize[2+]
orgy[4]	@orgiastic
oriant	orient[1+]
orickle	auricle *[ear, heart]
	oracle *[prophecy]
oriel	oriole *[bird]
	aureole *[halo]
orient[1] ~eering ~al ~ally ~ation	
orifice	
origin	
original ~ity ~ly	
originate[2]	@origination
	@originator
orijin	origin
oriole *[bird]	aureole *[halo]
Orion ~'s belt	
orkestra	orchestra[+]
orkestrate	orchestrate[2+]
orkid	orchid
orl	all *[every][+]
	awl *[tool]
	oil[1+]
ormanent	ornament[1+]
ornait	ornate[+]
ornament[1] ~al ~ation	
ornate ~ly	
ornithology	@ornithological
orphan[1] ~age	
orrangatang	orangutan
ort	aught *[anything]
	ought *[should do]
	oat *[grain]
orthodontist	@orthodontics
orthodox	@orthodoxy[4]
Orthodox ~| Church ~| Judaism	
orthography	
orthopedic ~s	@orthopedist
oryan	Orion[+]
Oscar	
oscillate[2]	@oscillation
	@oscillator
oscilloscope	
osefy	ossify[4]

oselot	ocelot
oshun	ocean[+]
osilate	oscillate[2+]
osiliscope	oscilloscope
osmosis	
osofogus	esophagus
osprey	
ossalot	ocelot
ossifer	officer
ossify[4]	
ostensible	@ostensibly
ostentatious ~ly	@ostentation
osteoarthritis	
osteopath ~y	
osteoporosis	
ostio-arthritis	osteoarthritis
ostiopath	osteopath[+]
ostracize[2]	@ostracism
ostrich[5]	
ostrisize	ostracize[2+]
ote	oat *[grain][+]
	oath *[swear]
	ought *[should do][+]
	haute *[fancy][+]
oter	otter *[mammal]
	other *[alternative][+]
othe	oath *[swear]
	other *[alternative][+]
other *[alternative] ~| half ~wise	
	otter *[mammal]
	author[1+]
otherize	authorize[2+]
otter *[mammal]	other *[alternative][+]
ottoman	
ouch	
ought *[should do] ~| to	
	oat *[grain][+]
oul	owl[+]
ounce *[weight, fluid]	
our *[belonging] ~selves	
	are *[we are]
	hour *[time][+]
ourangatang	orangutan
ours *[possessive]	
	hours *[time]

Key to Spelling Rules

Red words are wrong. **Black** words are correct.

- ~ Add the suffix or word directly to the main word, without a space or hyphen
  e.g. ash ~en ~tray → ashen ashtray
- ~- Add a hyphen to the main word before adding the next word
  e.g. blow ~-dry → blow-dry
- ~| Leave a space between the main word and the next word
  e.g. decimal ~| place → decimal place
- + By finding this word in its correct alphabetical order, you can find related words
  e.g. abowt·about[+] → about-face
- ★ Draws attention to words that may be confused
- ™ Means the word is a trademark
- @ Signifies the word is derived from the main word

oust[1]

out[1] ~back ~bid ~break ~board ~bound[1] ~burst[1] ~cast[1] ~class[5] ~come ~crop ~cry ~dated ~distance ~doors ~house ~field ~fit ~going ~law ~let ~line[2] ~look ~-maneuver[1] ~moded ~number[1] ~-of-court settlement ~| of date ~| of pocket ~| of stock ~put ~perform[1] ~patient ~pouring ~rank[1] ~reach[5] ~right ~run[3] ~set[1] ~sider ~skirts ~spend[1] ~standing ~stretched ~wear ~weigh[1] ~wit[3]

> Unable to find your word under **out**?
> Take off **out** and look again

outdo ~ing — @**outdoes** @**outdone**

outer ~most ~| space ~wear

outpatient ~| clinic ~| procedure

outplace ~ment

outrage[2] ~ous ~ously

outside ~| lane

outsource[2]

outspoken

outstanding ~ly ~| debts ~| orders

outward ~-bound ~ly

oval

ovarian

ovary[4]

ovashun — **ovation**

ovation

ovel — **oval**

ovem — **ovum**+

oven ~proof ~ware

over *[above] ~abundance[2] ~achieve[2] ~all ~awed ~board ~book[1] ~capacity ~charge[2] ~coat ~come[2] ~do ~doing ~done ~draft ~draw ~drawn ~due ~fish ~extended ~head ~hear ~heat ~joyed ~lap ~lay ~look ~night ~qualified ~payment ~production ~ride ~seas ~shadow[1] ~sight[1] ~spend[1] ~stay[1] ~stock[1] ~throw[1] ~throwing ~thrown ~-the-counter ~time ~tone ~turn[1] ~view[1] ~winter[1] ~work[1] ~wrought

> Unable to find your word under **over**?
> Take off **over** and look again

overall *[general] ~| losses ~| majority — **overhaul** *[rebuild]

overalls *[clothing]

overdose[2] — @**overdosage**

overestimate[2]

overhaul *[rebuild] — **overall** *[general]+

overpopulate — @**overpopulation**

oversee ~n ~ing

oversell ~ing — @**oversold**

overt

overtake ~n — @**overtaking**

overture

overwait — **overweight**

overwhelm[1] ~ingly

overy — **ovary**[4]

oviduct

oviry — **ovary**[4]

ovulate[2] — @**ovulation**

ovule

ovum — @**ova**

ovursee — **oversee**+

ovurt — **overt**

> Unable to find your word under **ovu**?
> Look under **ove**

ow *[pain] — **au** *[French word]+ **oh** *[exclamation] **owe**[2] *[be in debt]

owaysis — **oasis**+

owch — **ouch**

owe[2] *[be in debt] — **au** *[French word]+ **oh** *[exclamation] **ow** *[pain]

owed *[money] — **ode** *[poem]

owl ~ish

Key to Suffixes and Compounds

These rules are explained on pages vii to ix.

1. Keep the word the same before adding **ed, er, est, ing**
   e.g. cool[1] → cooled, cooler, coolest, cooling
2. Take off final **e** before adding **ed, er, est, ing**
   e.g. fine[2] → fined, finer, finest, fining
3. Double final consonant before adding **ed, er, est, ing**
   e.g. thin[3] → thinned, thinner, thinnest, thinning
4. Change final **y** to **i** before adding **ed, er, es, est, ly, ness**
   e.g. tidy[4] → tidied, tidier, tidies, tidiest, tidily, tidiness
   Keep final **y** before adding **ing** e.g. tidying
5. Add **es** instead of **s** to the end of the word
   e.g. bunch[5] → bunches
6. Change final **f** to **ve** before adding **s**
   e.g. calf[6] → calves

own[1] *[belonging] ~| up
on *[surface of]+
one *[single]+
ownce ounce
owner ~ship ~-operator
ownley only
ownse ounce *[weight, fluid]
owst oust[1]
owt out[1+]

Unable to find your word under **ow**? Look under **ou**

ox ~en ~tail
oxadacion oxidation+
oxadyze oxidize[2]
oxajen oxygen+
oxidation ~| number
oxide
oxidize[2]
oxigen oxygen+
oximoron oxymoron
oxyde oxide
oxygen ~| mask ~| tent
oxygenate[2] @oxygenation
oxymoron
oyel oil[1+]
oyly oily[4]
oyntment ointment
oyster ~-bed ~-catcher
ozone ~-depletion ~| layer

P

P *[letter of the alphabet]
pea *[vegetable]+
pee[1] *[urine]
pa *[dad] par *[even]+
PA *[personal assistant]
pace[2] ~maker ~setter
paced *[walked] paste[2] *[food, glue]+
pachyderm
pacific *[peaceful]
Pacific *[Ocean] ~| Rim
specific *[particular]
pacifism @pacifist
pacify[4] @pacification
pack[1] ~horse ~| ice ~rat
package[2] ~| deal
packed *[case] ~| up
pact *[agreement]
packet
packiderm pachyderm
packing ~| case ~| charges ~| list
pact *[agreement] packed *[case]+
pad[3] *[cushion] paid *[given money]
paddle[2] ~| wheel
paddock
paddy[4] *[pond] ~wagon
patty[4] *[round food shape]
padlock[1]
padre
paella
pagan ~ism
page[2] ~| view @pager
pageant ~ry
paginate[2] @pagination
pagoda
paid *[given money]
pad[3] *[cushion]
pail *[bucket] pale[2] *[lose color]+
pain[1] *[suffering] ~less ~-free
pan[3] *[utensil, criticize]+
pane *[glass]
painful ~ly
painkiller
painstaking

Key to Spelling Rules

Red words are wrong. **Black** words are correct.

~ Add the suffix or word directly to the main word, without a space or hyphen
e.g. ash ~en ~tray → ashen ashtray

~- Add a hyphen to the main word before adding the next word
e.g. blow ~-dry → blow-dry

~| Leave a space between the main word and the next word
e.g. decimal ~| place → decimal place

\+ By finding this word in its correct alphabetical order, you can find related words
e.g. abowt about+ → about-face

★ Draws attention to words that may be confused

TM Means the word is a trademark

@ Signifies the word is derived from the main word

paint[1] ~brush
pair[1] *[two] — par *[even]+
pare[2] *[trim]
pear *[fruit]+
pairable *[can be matched]
parable *[example]
paj — page[2]+
pajamas
pajent — pageant+
pakage — package[2]+
paket — packet
pakt — pact *[agreement]
packed *[case]+
pal *[friend] ~ly
pail *[bucket]
pale[2] *[lose color]+
pall *[covering, weaken]+
pawl *[ratchet]
Paul *[name]
palace *[building] — @palatial
police[2] *[law and order]+
palamino — palomino
palatable
palate *[mouth] — pallet *[stack]
palette *[artist's]+
pale[2] *[lose color] ~face ~ness
pail *[bucket]
pal *[friend]+
paleontology
palette *[artist's] ~| knife
palate *[mouth]
pallet *[stack]
palindrome
palisade
paliss — palace *[building]+
police[2] *[law and order]+
pall *[covering, weaken] ~bearer
pal *[friend]+
Paul *[name]
pawl *[ratchet]
pallet *[stack] — palate *[mouth]
palette *[artist's]+
palliative
pallid
pallitabul — palatable

pallor *[lack of color]
paler *[light in color]
palm[1] ~ist ~istry
Palm ~| Sunday
palomino
palpable — @palpably
palpitate[2] — @palpitation
paltry[4]
palundrome — palindrome
palus — palace *[building]+
palusade — palisade
palyative — palliative
pamento — pimento
pamflet — pamphlet[1]+
pamp — pomp *[ceremony]+
pampas *[plains] ~| grass
pompous *[self-important]+
pamper[1]
pamphlet[1] ~eer
pampis — pampas *[plains]+
pampur — pamper[1]
pampus — pampas *[plains]+
pan[3] *[cooking, criticize] ~cake
pain[1] *[suffering]+
pane *[glass]
Pan ~| African ~| American ~| European
panacea
panache
Panama ~| hat
panamime — pantomime[2]
panasia — panacea
pancreas — @pancreatic
pand — panned *[criticized, camera, gold]
pond *[water]
panda *[animal] — pander[1] *[indulge]
ponder[1] *[think]+
pandemonium
pander[1] *[indulge]
panda *[animal]
ponder[1] *[think]
pandimonium — pandemonium

Key to Suffixes and Compounds

These rules are explained on pages vii to ix.

1 Keep the word the same before adding **ed, er, est, ing**
e.g. cool[1] → cooled, cooler, coolest, cooling
2 Take off final **e** before adding **ed, er, est, ing**
e.g. fine[2] → fined, finer, finest, fining
3 Double final consonant before adding **ed, er, est, ing**
e.g. thin[3] → thinned, thinner, thinnest, thinning
4 Change final **y** to **i** before adding **ed, er, es, est, ly, ness**
e.g. tidy[4] → tidied, tidier, tidies, tidiest, tidily, tidiness
Keep final **y** before adding **ing** e.g. tidying
5 Add **es** instead of **s** to the end of the word
e.g. bunch[5] → bunches
6 Change final **f** to **ve** before adding **s**
e.g. calf[6] → calves

panduh panda *[animal]
pander[1] *[indulge]
ponder[1] *[think]+
pandumonium pandemonium
pane *[glass] pan[3] *[utensil, criticize]+
pain[1] *[suffering]+
pane-killer painkiller
panel[1] ~ist ~| discussion
panestaking painstaking
panic ~| attack ~| selling ~-stricken
panicked @panicking
panil panel[1]+
paniply panoply[4]
panirama panorama+
pankrias pancreas+
panned *[criticized, camera, gold]
pond *[water]
pawned *[sold]
pannel panel[1]+
pannik panic+

> Unable to find your word under **pann**?
> Look under **pan**

panoply[4]
panorama @panoramic
pant[1] *[breathe loudly]
paint[1]+
pantamime pantomime[2]
panther
pantomime[2]
panty[4] ~hose
panul panel[1]+
panuma Panama+
panuply panoply[4]
panurama panorama+
Pap ~| smear ~| test
papacy[4] @papal
@papist
paparazzi
papasy papacy[4]+
papaya
paper[1] ~back ~chase ~| clip ~knife ~| profit ~weight ~work
pepper[1]+
paper-mashay papier-mâché
papicy papacy[4]+
papier-mâché
papiratsi paparazzi
papirus papyrus
paprika
papyrus
par *[even] ~| excellence
pair[1] *[two]
pear *[fruit]+
parable *[example]
parabola *[curve] @parabolic
parachute[2] @parachutist
parade[2]
paradigm ~| shift
paradise
paradox ~ical ~ically
paraffin
parafinalia paraphernalia
paragon
paragraph
parakeet
parallel[1] @parallelogram
paralysis @paralytic
paralyze[2]
parameter *[function input]
perimeter *[distance around]
paramilitary
paramount
paranoia @paranoiac
@paranoid
paranormal
parapet
paraphernalia
paraphrase[2]
paraplegic
parashoot parachute[2]+
parasite
parasitic ~al ~ally
parasol
paratrooper

> Unable to find your word under **para**?
> Look under **peri**

Key to Spelling Rules

Red words are wrong. **Black** words are correct.

- ~ Add the suffix or word directly to the main word, without a space or hyphen
  e.g. ash ~en ~tray → ashen ashtray
- ~- Add a hyphen to the main word before adding the next word
  e.g. blow ~-dry → blow-dry
- ~| Leave a space between the main word and the next word
  e.g. decimal ~| place → decimal place
- \+ By finding this word in its correct alphabetical order, you can find related words
  e.g. abowt about+ → about-face
- ★ Draws attention to words that may be confused
- ™ Means the word is a trademark
- @ Signifies the word is derived from the main word

parboil[1]	
parce	parse[2]
parcel[3]	
parcen	parson *[religious]
	person *[being]+
parch[5] ~ment	
parck	park[1+]
parckay	parquet *[floor]
pardicle	particle+

> Unable to find your word under **pard**?
> Look under **part**

pardon[1] ~able	
pare[2] *[trim]	pair[1] *[two]
	pear *[fruit]+
parebul	parable *[example]
	pairable *[can be matched]
parent ~age ~al ~ing ~| company[4]	
parenthesis	@parentheses
pariah	
parible	parable *[example]
	pairable *[can be matched]
paridy	parity[4] *[being even]
	parody[4] *[imitation]
paridyme	paradigm+
parilell	parallel[1+]
parinoya	paranoia+
parint	parent+
Parisian *[person from Paris]	
Parisienne *[woman from Paris]	
parisit	parasite
parit	parrot[1]
parity[4] *[being even]	
	parody[4] *[imitation]
park[1] ~| and ride ~| keeper ~land ~| ranger	
parka	
parking ~| lot ~| meter ~| ticket	
Parkinson's ~| disease	
parlament	parliament+
parlay *[leverage]	parley[1] *[negotiate]
parlement	parliament+
parley[1] *[negotiate]	
	parlay *[leverage]
parliament ~arian ~ary	
parlument	parliament+
parm	palm[1+]
parmesan ~| cheese	
parochial ~ism	
parocksisum	paroxysm
parody[4] *[imitation]	
	parity[4] *[being even]
parokial	parochial+
parole[2] *[release]	payroll *[pay]
paroxysm	
parquet *[floor]	
parr	par *[even]+
	pair[1] *[two]
	pear *[fruit]+
parrch	parch[5+]
parrot[1]	
parry[4]	
parsamoniyis	parsimonious+
parscher	pasture
parse[2]	
parsel	parcel[3]
parsen	parson *[religious]
	person *[being]+
parshialitee	partiality[4]
parsimonious	@parsimony
parsley	
parsnip	
parson *[religious]	
	person *[being]+
parsul	parcel[3]
part[1] ~ly ~| of speech ~-time	
partake ~n	@partaking
partasippul	participle
partee	party[4] *[celebration]+
partial ~ly ~| loss ~| payment	
partiality[4]	
participant	
participate[2]	@participation
	@participatory
participative	
participle	
particle ~| physics	

Key to Suffixes and Compounds

These rules are explained on pages vii to ix.

1 Keep the word the same before adding **ed, er, est, ing**
e.g. cool[1] → cooled, cooler, coolest, cooling

2 Take off final **e** before adding **ed, er, est, ing**
e.g. fine[2] → fined, finer, finest, fining

3 Double final consonant before adding **ed, er, est, ing**
e.g. thin[3] → thinned, thinner, thinnest, thinning

4 Change final **y** to **i** before adding **ed, er, es, est, ly, ness**
e.g. tidy[4] → tidied, tidier, tidies, tidiest, tidily, tidiness
Keep final **y** before adding **ing** e.g. tidying

5 Add **es** instead of **s** to the end of the word
e.g. bunch[5] → bunches

6 Change final **f** to **ve** before adding **s**
e.g. calf[6] → calves

particular ~ity ~ly
particularize[2]
partikle particle+
partisan ~ship
partishun partition[1]
partisippul participle
partissipait participate[2+]
partition[1] *[division]
perdition *[damnation]
partizin partisan+
partner[1] ~ship
partook *[did partake]
partridge
partukle particle+
party[4] *[celebration] ~| animal ~| line ~pooper
partysan partisan+
parudime paradigm+
parunt parent+
parut parrot[1]
pasay passé *[no longer relevant]
pascherize pasteurize[2+]
paschir pasture
pase pace[2+]
paser passer+
pash posh[1] *[smart]
pasha
pashent patient *[calm, person treated]+
pashin passion+
pashuh pasha
pashun passion+
pasible passable *[can pass, be passed]+
passible *[can suffer]
possible *[can be done]+
pasific pacific *[peaceful]
Pacific *[Ocean]
specific *[particular]+
pasinjer passenger
pasishin position
pasity paucity

pasover Passover *[Jewish celebration]
pass over *[go over]
pass[5] ~book ~| key ~| over ~port ~word
passable *[can pass, be passed]
@passably
passible *[can suffer]
possible *[can be done]+
passage ~way
passé *[no longer relevant]
passed *[did pass]
past *[time, beyond]+
passenger
passer ~-by
passible *[can suffer]
passable *[can pass, be passed]+
possible *[can be done]+
passify pacify[4+]
passij passage+
passion ~ate ~ately ~fruit
passive ~ly ~ness
Passover *[Jewish celebration]
pass over *[go over]
passta pasta *[noodles]
passtel pastel *[color]
passunjer passenger
past *[time, beyond] ~| master
passed *[did pass]
pasta *[noodles] pastor+
pastashio pistachio
pastcher pasture
paste[2] *[food, glue] ~board ~-up
paced *[walked]
past *[time, beyond]+
pasta *[noodles]
pasteche pastiche
pasteesh pastiche
pastel *[color] pastille *[air freshener, lozenge]
paster *[one who pastes]
pasta *[noodles]
pastor *[shepherd]+
pasteurize[2] @pasteurization

KEY TO SPELLING RULES

Red words are wrong. **Black** words are correct.

~ Add the suffix or word directly to the main word, without a space or hyphen
e.g. ash ~en ~tray → ashen ashtray

~- Add a hyphen to the main word before adding the next word
e.g. blow ~-dry → blow-dry

~| Leave a space between the main word and the next word
e.g. decimal ~| place → decimal place

+ By finding this word in its correct alphabetical order, you can find related words
e.g. abowt about+ → about-face

★ Draws attention to words that may be confused

TM Means the word is a trademark

@ Signifies the word is derived from the main word

pastiche
pastille *[air freshener, lozenge]
    pastel *[color]
pastime
pastor *[shepherd] ~al
    pasture *[grazing]
    paster *[one who pastes]
pastrami
pastry[4] *[baked goods]
    pasty *[meat pie, pastelike]
pasture *[grazing]
    pastor *[shepherd][+]
pasturize   pasteurize[2+]
pasty[4] *[meat pie, pastelike]
    pastry[4] *[baked goods]
pasuble   passable *[can pass, be passed][+]
    passible *[can suffer]
pasufism   pacifism[+]
pat[3] *[tap]
patay   pâté *[food]
    party[4] *[celebration][+]
patch[5] ~work   @patchy[4]
pâté *[food]   party[4] *[celebration][+]
pateena   patina
pateet   petite
patella
patent[1] *[opening, invention] ~able ~ly ~| leather ~| pending
patential   potential[+]
pater   patter[1]
paternal ~ism ~ly
paternalist ~ic
paternity
patey   party[4] *[celebration][+]
    pâté *[food]
path ~finder ~way
pathetic ~ally ~| fallacy
pathological ~ly
pathology   @pathologist
pathos
patience *[calmness]
    patients *[persons treated]

patient *[calm, person treated] ~ly
    patent[1] *[opening, invention][+]
patina
patint   patent[1] *[opening, invention][+]
    patient *[calm, person treated][+]
patio ~| door
patishin   petition[1]
pâtisserie
patramony   patrimony[4]
patreeit   patriot[+]
patriarch ~al
patricide
patrimony[4]
patrin   patron[+]
patriot ~ism
patriotic ~ally
patriside   patricide
patrol[3] *[guard rounds]
    petrol *[fuel][+]
patron ~ess ~| saint
patronage
patronize[2]
patrumony   patrimony[4]
patrun   patron[+]
patter[1]
pattern[1]
patty[4] *[round food shape]
    paddy[4] *[pond][+]
patuitary   pituitary[+]
patunt   patent[1+]
paturn   pattern[1]
paturnal   paternal[+]
paucity
Paul *[name]   pall *[covering, weaken][+]
    pawl *[ratchet]
paunch ~y
paund   pawned *[sold]
    pond *[water]
    pound[1] *[weight, money][+]
pauper
pause[2] *[stop]   paws *[feet]
pave[2] ~ment

KEY TO SUFFIXES AND COMPOUNDS

These rules are explained on pages vii to ix.

1 Keep the word the same before adding **ed, er, est, ing**
e.g. cool[1] → cooled, cooler, coolest, cooling
2 Take off final **e** before adding **ed, er, est, ing**
e.g. fine[2] → fined, finer, finest, fining
3 Double final consonant before adding **ed, er, est, ing**
e.g. thin[3] → thinned, thinner, thinnest, thinning
4 Change final **y** to **i** before adding **ed, er, es, est, ly, ness**
e.g. tidy[4] → tidied, tidier, tidies, tidiest, tidily, tidiness
Keep final **y** before adding **ing** e.g. tidying
5 Add **es** instead of **s** to the end of the word
e.g. bunch[5] → bunches
6 Change final **f** to **ve** before adding **s**
e.g. calf[6] → calves

pavilion
paw[1] *[foot] — poor[1] *[needy]+
pore[2] *[skin, over]
pour[1] *[a drink]
pawch — porch[5]
pawkupine — porcupine
pawl *[ratchet] — pall *[covering, weaken]+
Paul *[name]
pawn[1] *[deposit, chess] ~broker ~shop
porn *[sex]
pawnch — paunch+
pawpur — pauper
paws *[feet] — pause[2] *[stop]
pawshun — portion[1]
pawsity — paucity
pay[1] ~able ~ee ~er ~ing ~back ~check ~day ~| dirt ~ment ~off ~load ~| phone
@paid

> Unable to find your word under **pay**?
> Take off **pay** and look again

payd — paid *[given money]
payge — page[2]+
paygun — pagan+
payl — pale[2] *[lose color]+
pail *[bucket]
payn — pain[1] *[suffering]+
payncreas — pancreas+
paynt — paint[1]+
payper — paper[1]+
payroll *[pay] — parole[2] *[release]
payshunt — patient *[calm, person treated]+
payso — peso
payst — paste[2] *[food, glue]+
paced *[walked]
paystry — pastry[4] *[baked goods]
paytriark — patriarch+
paytriot — patriot+
payv — pave[2]+
PC *[personal computer, politically correct]
pea *[vegetable] ~brain ~shooter
pee[1] *[urine]
peace *[calm] ~ably ~-loving ~-offering ~| officer ~| pipe ~time
peas *[vegetables]
pees *[urinates]
Peace Corps
peaceful ~ly ~ness
peacekeeping — @peacekeeper
peach[5] ~y[4]
peacock — @peahen
peak *[top] ~| output ~| period
peek[1] *[look]+
Peke *[dog]
pick[1] *[select, tool]+
pique *[anger]
peal[1] *[bells] — peel[1] *[skin]
peanut ~| brittle ~| butter ~| oil
pear *[fruit] ~-shaped ~| tree
par *[even]+
pare[2] *[trim]
peer[1] *[look, noble, equal]+
pier *[structure]
pearish — perish[5]+
pearitonitys — peritonitis
pearl *[gem] ~y
Perl *[computer language]
purl[1] *[knitting]
pearse — pierce[2] *[make a hole]
peary — parry[4]
peasant *[rustic] ~ry
pheasant *[bird]
pleasant *[enjoyable]+
pease — piece[2] *[part]+
peasfle — peaceful+
peaskiping — peacekeeping+
peat *[substance] ~| bog
pit[3] *[hole, fight]+
peaved — peeved
pebble — @pebbly
pecan
peccadillo
pechalins — petulance
peck[1] *[bite, measure] ~ish
pick[1] *[select, tool]+

pecking ~| order
pecks *[bites, measure]
pecs *[muscles]
pectin
pectoral
peculiar ~ly
peculiarity[4]
pedafile pedophile+
pedagogic ~al @pedagogy
pedagree pedigree+
pedakur pedicure+
pedal[1] *[on a bike, foot lever]
peddle[2] *[sell]
petal *[flower]
pedaler *[cyclist] peddler *[seller]
pedant ~ic
peddle[2] *[sell] pedal[1] *[on a bike, foot lever]
piddle[2] *[trifle, urinate]
peddler *[seller] pedaler *[cyclist]
peddy petty+
pedestal
pedestrian ~| crossing ~| zone
pediatric ~ian ~s
pedicoat petticoat
pedicure @pedicurist
pedigojy pedagogic+
pedigree ~d
pedint pedant+
pedistil pedestal
pedle pedal[1] *[on a bike, foot lever]
peddle[2] *[sell]
petal *[flower]
pedofile pedophile+
pedometer
pedophile @pedophilia
pedugojy pedagogic+
pedunt pedant+
pee[1] *[urine] pea *[vegetable]+
peece peace *[calm]+
piece[2] *[part]+
peas *[vegetables]
peech peach[5]+

peek[1] *[look] ~aboo
peak *[top]+
Peke *[dog]
pick[1] *[select, tool]+
pique *[anger]
peekant piquant+
peel[1] *[skin] peal[1] *[bells]
peenal penal+
peenalize penalize[2]
peenis penis
peenut peanut+
peep[1] *[look] ~hole ~| show ~ing Tom
pipe[2] *[tube]+
peeple people[2]
peer[1] *[look, noble, equal] ~less
pier *[structure]
peerage
peeriodd period+
peerse pierce[2] *[make a hole]
pees *[urinates] peace *[harmony]+
peas *[vegetables]
piece[2] *[part]+
Pees Core Peace Corps
peesee PC *[personal computer, politically correct]
peesful peaceful+
peest piste *[skiing]
pissed *[angry, drunk]
peeta pita+
peetsa pizza+
peeved
peevish ~ly ~ness
peeza pizza+
peg[3] ~board ~-leg
pegorativ pejorative
pehr pair[1] *[two]
pear *[fruit]+
peice peace *[calm]+
piece[2] *[part]+
pejorative
pek peak *[top]+
peck[1] *[bite, measure]+
peek[1] *[look]+
Peke *[dog]
pique *[anger]

Key to Suffixes and Compounds

These rules are explained on pages vii to ix.

1 Keep the word the same before adding **ed, er, est, ing**
e.g. cool[1] → cooled, cooler, coolest, cooling
2 Take off final **e** before adding **ed, er, est, ing**
e.g. fine[2] → fined, finer, finest, fining
3 Double final consonant before adding **ed, er, est, ing**
e.g. thin[3] → thinned, thinner, thinnest, thinning
4 Change final **y** to **i** before adding **ed, er, es, est, ly, ness**
e.g. tidy[4] → tidied, tidier, tidies, tidiest, tidily, tidiness
Keep final **y** before adding **ing** e.g. tidying
5 Add **es** instead of **s** to the end of the word
e.g. bunch[5] → bunches
6 Change final **f** to **ve** before adding **s**
e.g. calf[6] → calves

pekadilo peccadillo
pekan pecan
Peke *[dog] peak *[top]+
peek[1] *[look]
pique *[anger]
Peking *[Beijing, China] ~| duck
peaking *[highest]
pecking *[biting]
peeking *[looking]
Pekingese *[dog]
pektin pectin
Pele *[soccer player, volcano goddess]
peal[1] *[bells]
peel[1] *[skin]
pelican
pellet
pell-mell
pelt[1]
pelukin pelican
pelut pellet
pelvis @pelvic exam
pen[3] *[writing, enclosure] ~| name ~| pal
penal *[of punishment] ~| code
penile *[of penis]
penalize[2]
penalty[4]
penance *[repentant action]
pennants *[flags]
penitence *[repentant attitude]
penchant
pencil[3] ~case
pendant
pending
pendulum
penetrable
penetrate[2] @penetration
penguin
penicillin
penile *[of penis] penal *[of punishment]+
penilty penalty[4]
penins penance *[repentant action]
penis
pennants *[flags]

peninsula
penis
penisillin penicillin
penitence *[repentant attitude]
penance *[repentant action]
penitent ~ly
penitentiary[4]
penitrate penetrate[2+]
penitribil penetrable
penitunse penitence *[repentant attitude]
penitunt penitent+
penjulum pendulum
pennants *[flags] penance *[repentant action]
pennife penknife[6]
penniless ~ness
penninsula peninsula
penny[4] ~-pincher ~-pinching
penshant penchant
penshun pension[1+]
pensil pencil[3+]
pension[1] ~able ~| fund ~| scheme
pensive ~ly ~ness
pent ~-up
pentacost Pentecost+
pentagon *[shape] ~al
Pentagon *[U.S. Military Headquarters]
pentameter
pentathlon
Pentecost ~al
penthouse
penticost Pentecost+
pentigon pentagon *[shape]+
Pentagon *[U.S. Military Headquarters]
pentous penthouse
penucilin penicillin
penulize penalize[2]
penultimate
penulty penalty[4]
penunse pennants *[flags]
penance *[repentant action]

Key to Spelling Rules

Red words are wrong. **Black** words are correct.

~ Add the suffix or word directly to the main word, without a space or hyphen
e.g. ash ~en ~tray → ashen ashtray

~- Add a hyphen to the main word before adding the next word
e.g. blow ~-dry → blow-dry

~| Leave a space between the main word and the next word
e.g. decimal ~| place → decimal place

+ By finding this word in its correct alphabetical order, you can find related words
e.g. abowt about+ → about-face

★ Draws attention to words that may be confused

™ Means the word is a trademark

@ Signifies the word is derived from the main word

penusilun **penicillin**
penutrate **penetrate**[2+]
peny **penny**[4+]
peony[4] *[flower]
people[2]
pep ~| talk
pepe **peep**[1] *[look][+]
pepironi **pepperoni**
pepper[1] ~y ~corn ~mint
paper[1+]
pepperoni
pepsin
peptic ~| ulcer
peptide
pepur **pepper**[1+]
paper[1+]
per *[rate] ~| annum ~| capita ~cent ~| day ~| diem ~| hour ~| person
purr[1] *[cat]
pair *[two][+]
peer[1] *[look, noble, equal][+]
pier *[structure]

> Unable to find your word under **per**?
> Take off **per** and look again

peralisis **paralysis**[+]
perameter **parameter** *[function input]
perimeter *[distance around]
peraskope **periscope**
perceive[2]
percentage ~| discount ~| increase ~| point
percentile
perceptible **@perceptibly**
perception **@perceptual**
perceptive ~ly ~ness
percession **precession** *[wobbling][+]
procession *[march][+]
perch[5]
perchance
perchis **purchase**[2+]
perchising **purchasing**[+]
percieve **perceive**[2]
percist **persist**[1+]
percolate[2] **@percolator**
percussion **@percussive**
perdah **purdah**
perdikshun **prediction**
perdition *[damnation]
partition[1] *[division]
pere **peer**[1] *[look, noble, equal][+]
pier *[structure]
peremptory
perennial ~ly
perenthesis **parenthesis**[+]
perfect[1] *[flawless]
@perfectionist
prefect *[official][+]
perforate[2] **@perforation**
perform[1] ~ance
perfume[2] **@perfumery**[4]
perfunctory[4]
perfur **prefer**[3+]
pergatory **purgatory**
perge **purge**[2]
pergress **progress**[1+]
pergressive **progressive**[+]
perhaps
peria **pariah**
perifery **periphery**[+]
peril ~ous ~ously
perimeter *[distance around]
parameter *[function input]
period ~ic
peripatetic
periphery **@peripheral**
periscope
perish[5] ~able goods
peritonitis

> Unable to find your word under **per**?
> Look under **par**

perj **purge**[2]

Key to Suffixes and Compounds

These rules are explained on pages vii to ix.

1 Keep the word the same before adding **ed, er, est, ing**
e.g. cool[1] → cooled, cooler, coolest, cooling
2 Take off final **e** before adding **ed, er, est, ing**
e.g. fine[2] → fined, finer, finest, fining
3 Double final consonant before adding **ed, er, est, ing**
e.g. thin[3] → thinned, thinner, thinnest, thinning
4 Change final **y** to **i** before adding **ed, er, es, est, ly, ness**
e.g. tidy[4] → tidied, tidier, tidies, tidiest, tidily, tidiness
Keep final **y** before adding **ing** e.g. tidying
5 Add **es** instead of **s** to the end of the word
e.g. bunch[5] → bunches
6 Change final **f** to **ve** before adding **s**
e.g. calf[6] → calves

perjure[2] @perjury
perk[1] ~y[4]
perkolate percolate[2+]
Perl *[computer language]
pearl *[gem]+
purl[1] *[knitting]
perloin purloin[1]
perm[1] ~afrost
permanence @permanency
permanent ~ly
permanganate
permeable
permeate[2]
permission @permissible
permissive ~ness
permit[3]
permutation
pernicious ~ly ~ness
pernunseeayshun
pronunciation
perockside peroxide
peroggative prerogative
perooz peruse[2+]
peroxide
perpell propel[3+]
perpendicular
perpetchual perpetual+
perpetrate[2] @perpetrator
perpetual ~ly ~| motion
perpetuate[2]
perpetuity[4]
perpisful purposeful+
perpitrate perpetrate[2+]
perple purple
perplex[5] ~ingly @perplexity[4]
perport purport[1]
perpose purpose[2] *[intent]+
porpoise[2] *[animal]
propose[2] *[suggest]+
perposfle purposeful+
perposs purpose[2] *[intent]+
porpoise[2] *[animal]
perpulshun propulsion+
perr per *[rate]+
purr[1] *[cat]

perrfekt perfect[1] *[flawless]+
perrogativ prerogative
perscribe prescribe[2] *[write an order]
proscribe[2] *[forbid]
perscripshun prescription *[order]+
proscription *[ban]
perse purse[2]
persecute[2] *[harass]
@persecutor
prosecute[2] *[in court]+
persecution
perseev perceive[2]
persevere[2] @perseverance
Persian ~| rug
persicute persecute[2] *[harass]+
persicution persecution
persimmon
persinal personal *[private]+
persinality personality[4]
persinilize personalize[2+]
persist[1] ~ent ~ently
persistence @persistency
perskribe prescribe[2] *[write an order]
proscribe[2] *[forbid]
person *[being] ~able ~age
parson *[religious]
persona ~| non grata
personal *[private] ~ly ~| allowance ~| assistant ~| computer ~| organizer ~| property
personnel *[employees]+
personality[4]
personalize[2] @personalization
personify[4] @personification
personnel *[employees] ~| department
personal *[private]+
persoot pursuit
perspective
perspicacious @perspicacity
perspier perspire[2+]
perspikashis perspicacious+
perspire[2] @perspiration
persuade[2] @persuadable

Key to Spelling Rules

Red words are wrong. **Black** words are correct.

~ Add the suffix or word directly to the main word, without a space or hyphen
e.g. ash ~en ~tray → ashen ashtray

~- Add a hyphen to the main word before adding the next word
e.g. blow ~-dry → blow-dry

~| Leave a space between the main word and the next word
e.g. decimal ~| place → decimal place

+ By finding this word in its correct alphabetical order, you can find related words
e.g. abowt about+ → about-face

* Draws attention to words that may be confused

TM Means the word is a trademark

@ Signifies the word is derived from the main word

persuant	pursuant
persuasion	
persuasive ~ly ~ness	
persue	pursue[2+]
persunel	personal *[private][+]
	personnel *[employees][+]
perswayd	persuade[2+]
pert ~ly ~ness	
pertain[1]	
pertanins	pertinence[+]
pertend	pretend[1] *[make believe]
	portend[1] *[foretell]
perterb	perturb[1]
pertikuler	particular[+]
pertinence	@pertinent
perturb[1]	
peruse[2]	@perusal
pervade[2]	@pervasive
perverse ~ly ~ness	
perversion	@perversive
pervert[1]	
pervey	purvey[1+]
pervious	
perypatetik	peripatetic
pesant	peasant *[rustic][+]
pesimism	pessimism
pesmist	pessimist[+]
peso	
pessamism	pessimism
pessamist	pessimist[+]
pessel	pestle
pessimism	
pessimist ~ic ~ically	
pesso	peso
pesster	pester[1]
pest *[annoying] ~icide	
	piste *[skiing]
	pissed *[angry, drunk]
pester[1]	
pesticide	
pestilence	@pestilent
pestir	pester[1]
pestiside	pesticide
pestle	
pestur	pester[1]
pet[3] ~| name	
petal *[flower]	peddle[2] *[sell]
	pedal[1] *[on a bike, foot lever]
peter[1] ~| out	
petil	petal *[flower]
petite	
petition[1]	
petrafy	petrify[4]
petrel *[bird]	petrol *[fuel][+]
petrify[4]	
petrol *[fuel] ~eum	
	petrel *[bird]
	patrol[3] *[guard rounds]
petrology	@petrologist
petrufy	petrify[4]
petteet	petite
petticoat	
petty ~| cash ~| expenses ~| officer	
petul	petal *[flower]
petulance	
petulant ~ly	
petunia	
petur	peter[1+]
pety	petty[+]
peuny	peony[4] *[flower]
	puny[4] *[small]
peved	peeved
pew *[church seating]	
pewder	pewter
pewny	puny[4] *[small]
pewpa	pupa *[of insect][+]
pewse	puce *[color]
pewter	
pex	pecs *[muscles]
	pecks *[bites, measure]
pey	pay[1+]
peye	pie *[food][+]
	pi *[number]
pezant	peasant *[rustic][+]
phalanx[5]	
phalatily	philately *[stamp collecting][+]
phallus[5]	@phallic

Key to Suffixes and Compounds

These rules are explained on pages vii to ix.

1 Keep the word the same before adding **ed, er, est, ing**
e.g. cool[1] → cooled, cooler, coolest, cooling

2 Take off final **e** before adding **ed, er, est, ing**
e.g. fine[2] → fined, finer, finest, fining

3 Double final consonant before adding **ed, er, est, ing**
e.g. thin[3] → thinned, thinner, thinnest, thinning

4 Change final **y** to **i** before adding **ed, er, es, est, ly, ness**
e.g. tidy[4] → tidied, tidier, tidies, tidiest, tidily, tidiness
Keep final **y** before adding **ing** e.g. tidying

5 Add **es** instead of **s** to the end of the word
e.g. bunch[5] → bunches

6 Change final **f** to **ve** before adding **s**
e.g. calf[6] → calves

phanetik phonetic+
fanatic+
phanominon phenomenon+
phantasm ~agoric ~agorical
phantom
pharaoh
pharingeal pharyngeal+
pharinks pharynx
Pharisee
pharmaceutical
pharmacology^4
pharmacy^4 @pharmacist
pharoah pharaoh
pharynx
phase^2 *[a stage] ~| in ~| out
faze^2 *[worry]
pheasant *[bird] peasant *[rustic]
pheenix phoenix^5
phenol
phenomenal ~ly
phenomenon @phenomena
phenyl *[chemical group] ~alanine ~ephrine
fennel *[spice]+
phew *[exclamation]
few *[not many]+

> Unable to find your word under **ph**?
> Look under **F**

phezant pheasant *[bird]
philaligy philology+
philander^1 ~er
philanthropic ~ally
philanthropy @philanthropist
philately^4 *[stamp collecting]
@philatelist
flatly *[plainly]
phile file^2 *[document, tool, line]+
philharmonic
Philip *[man's name]
fillip *[sudden motion]
fill-up *[fuel]
philistine
philology @philologist
philosifize philosophize^2
philosiphur philosopher+
philosiphy philosophy
philosopher ~'s stone
philosophical ~ly
philosophize^2
philosophy
philter *[love potion]
filter^1 *[sieve]
phizikly physically
phizix physics+

> Unable to find your word under **phi**?
> Look under **phy**

phlebitis *[blood vessel disease]
phlegm @phlegmatic
phlem phlegm+
phlox *[flower] flocks *[of birds, sheep]
phoan phone^{2+}
phobia @phobic
phoenix^5
phone^2 ~| call ~| card ~| line ~| number
phoneme @phonemic
phonetic ~ally ~s
phoney phony^{4+}
phonic ~s
phonograph
phonology @phonological
phony^4 @phoniness
phosfate phosphate
phosforis phosphorus
phosphate
phosphorescent
phosphorus
photigraph photograph
photo ~-finish ~genic ~journalism ~| opportunity ~| shoot ~tropism ~| voltaic

> Unable to find your word under **photo**?
> Take off **photo** and look again

photocopy^4 @photocopiable
@photocopier

KEY TO SPELLING RULES

Red words are wrong. **Black** words are correct.

~ Add the suffix or word directly to the main word, without a space or hyphen
e.g. ash ~en ~tray → ashen ashtray

~- Add a hyphen to the main word before adding the next word
e.g. blow ~-dry → blow-dry

~| Leave a space between the main word and the next word
e.g. decimal ~| place → decimal place

+ By finding this word in its correct alphabetical order, you can find related words
e.g. abowt about+ → about-face

* Draws attention to words that may be confused

TM Means the word is a trademark

@ Signifies the word is derived from the main word

photoelectric ~| cell
photofit
photograph
photographer @photography
photographic ~| memory
photokopy photocopy^{4+}
photon
photosensitive
photosynthesis
phrasal *[short phrase] ~| verb
frazzle^{2} *[upset]
phrase^{2} *[words] frays *[fights, wears out]
phraseology
phraze frays *[fights, wears out]
phrase^{2} *[words]
phrazle phrasal *[short phrase]$^{+}$
frazzle^{2} *[upset]
phrenetic frenetic
phrenology @phrenologist
physeke physique
physical *[matter and energy] ~ly ~| examination ~| force
fiscal *[money]$^{+}$
physician
physics @physicist
physiognomy
physiology @physiologist
physiotherapist @physiotherapy
physique
phyzicle physical^{+}

> Unable to find your word under **phy**?
> Look under **phi**

pi *[number] pie *[food]$^{+}$
pianeer pioneer^{1}
piaya paella
picalo piccolo
pican pecan
piccher picture^{2+}
piccherresk picturesque^{+}
piccolo
pich pitch^{5} *[throw, substance]$^{+}$
peach^{5+}
pichfork pitchfork
pichuitary pituitary^{+}
pick^{1} *[select, tool] ~ax ~y ~pocket^{1} ~up truck^{1}
peak *[top]$^{+}$
peek^{1} *[look]$^{+}$
pique *[anger]
pickel pickle^{2}
picket^{1} ~| fence ~| line
pickings
pickit picket^{1+}
pickle^{2}
picknick picnic^{+}
picknicked picnicked^{+}
picksee pixie
picksel pixel
picnic ~| basket
picnicked @picnickers
@picnicking
picshure picture^{2+}
pictogram
pictographic
pictorial ~ly
picture^{2} ~| book ~| perfect
picturesque ~ly ~ness
pida pita^{+}
piddle^{2} *[trifle, urinate]
peddle^{2} *[sell]
pedal^{1} *[on a bike, foot lever]
petal *[flower]
pide peed *[urinated]
pidgin *[jargon] pigeon *[bird]$^{+}$
pidiatrics pediatrics
pidius piteous^{+}
pidofile pedophile^{+}
pidy pity^{4+}
pie *[food] ~| chart ~| crust
pi *[number]
piea paella
piebald
piece^{2} *[part] ~meal ~| rate ~work
peace *[calm]$^{+}$
peas *[vegetables]
piedy piety^{4}
pity^{4+}

Key to Suffixes and Compounds

These rules are explained on pages vii to ix.

1 Keep the word the same before adding **ed, er, est, ing**
e.g. cool^{1} → cooled, cooler, coolest, cooling
2 Take off final **e** before adding **ed, er, est, ing**
e.g. fine^{2} → fined, finer, finest, fining
3 Double final consonant before adding **ed, er, est, ing**
e.g. thin^{3} → thinned, thinner, thinnest, thinning
4 Change final **y** to **i** before adding **ed, er, es, est, ly, ness**
e.g. tidy^{4} → tidied, tidier, tidies, tidiest, tidily, tidiness
Keep final **y** before adding **ing** e.g. tidying
5 Add **es** instead of **s** to the end of the word
e.g. bunch^{5} → bunches
6 Change final **f** to **ve** before adding **s**
e.g. calf^{6} → calves

<table>
<tr><td>piel</td><td>pile[2] *[heap]+</td></tr>
<tr><td>pielon</td><td>pylon *[tower]</td></tr>
<tr><td>pien</td><td>pine[2] *[tree, unhappy]+</td></tr>
<tr><td>pieneer</td><td>pioneer[1]</td></tr>
<tr><td>pient</td><td>pint+</td></tr>
<tr><td>piep</td><td>peep[1] *[look]+</td></tr>
<tr><td></td><td>pipe[2] *[tube]+</td></tr>
<tr><td>pier *[structure]</td><td>peer[1] *[look, noble, equal]+</td></tr>
<tr><td></td><td>pyre[2] *[cremation]</td></tr>
<tr><td>pierage</td><td>peerage</td></tr>
<tr><td>pierce[2] *[make a hole]</td><td></td></tr>
<tr><td></td><td>peers *[looks, colleagues]</td></tr>
<tr><td>piety[4]</td><td></td></tr>
<tr><td>pig[3] ~| iron ~let ~skin ~sty ~tail</td><td></td></tr>
<tr><td>pigee</td><td>piggy+</td></tr>
<tr><td>pigeon *[bird] ~hole[2] ~-toed</td><td></td></tr>
<tr><td></td><td>pidgin *[jargon]</td></tr>
<tr><td>piggy ~back ~| bank</td><td></td></tr>
<tr><td>pigheaded ~ness</td><td></td></tr>
<tr><td>pigin</td><td>pidgin *[jargon]</td></tr>
<tr><td></td><td>pigeon *[bird]+</td></tr>
<tr><td>pigment[1] ~ation</td><td></td></tr>
<tr><td>pigsty[4]</td><td></td></tr>
<tr><td>pigy</td><td>piggy+</td></tr>
<tr><td>pijamas</td><td>pajamas</td></tr>
<tr><td>pijin</td><td>pidgin *[jargon]</td></tr>
<tr><td></td><td>pigeon *[bird]+</td></tr>
<tr><td>pik</td><td>peak *[top]+</td></tr>
<tr><td></td><td>peek[1] *[look]+</td></tr>
<tr><td></td><td>Peke *[dog]</td></tr>
<tr><td></td><td>pick[1] *[select]+</td></tr>
<tr><td></td><td>pike[2] *[fish, weapon]</td></tr>
<tr><td></td><td>pique *[anger]</td></tr>
<tr><td>pikant</td><td>piquant+</td></tr>
<tr><td>pike[2] *[fish, weapon]</td><td></td></tr>
<tr><td></td><td>pick[1] *[select]+</td></tr>
<tr><td></td><td>pique *[anger]</td></tr>
<tr><td>pikel</td><td>pickle[2]</td></tr>
<tr><td>piket</td><td>picket[1+]</td></tr>
<tr><td>pikilo</td><td>piccolo</td></tr>
<tr><td>pikings</td><td>pickings</td></tr>
<tr><td>piknik</td><td>picnic+</td></tr>
<tr><td>pikock</td><td>peacock+</td></tr>
<tr><td>piksle</td><td>pixel</td></tr>
<tr><td>piksy</td><td>pixie</td></tr>
<tr><td>piktcheresk</td><td>picturesque+</td></tr>
<tr><td>pikuliarity</td><td>peculiarity[4]</td></tr>
<tr><td>pikulyer</td><td>peculiar+</td></tr>
<tr><td>pilage</td><td>pillage[2]</td></tr>
<tr><td>pilaster *[column]</td><td>plaster[1] *[material]+</td></tr>
<tr><td>pile[2] *[heap] ~up</td><td></td></tr>
<tr><td></td><td>pill *[medicine]+</td></tr>
<tr><td>pilfer[1] ~age</td><td></td></tr>
<tr><td>pilgrim ~age</td><td></td></tr>
<tr><td>pilige</td><td>pillage[2]</td></tr>
<tr><td>pilit</td><td>pilot[1+]</td></tr>
<tr><td>pill *[medicine] ~box</td><td></td></tr>
<tr><td></td><td>pile[2] *[heap]+</td></tr>
<tr><td>pillage[2]</td><td></td></tr>
<tr><td>pillavur</td><td>palaver</td></tr>
<tr><td>pillow ~case</td><td></td></tr>
<tr><td>pilon</td><td>pylon *[tower]</td></tr>
<tr><td>pilot[1] ~| house ~| lamp ~| light ~| scheme</td><td></td></tr>
<tr><td>pilow</td><td>pillow+</td></tr>
<tr><td>pilyon</td><td>pillion</td></tr>
<tr><td>pimiento</td><td></td></tr>
<tr><td>pimple</td><td>@pimply</td></tr>
<tr><td>pin[3] *[point] ~ball ~cushion ~| down ~hole ~point ~prick</td><td></td></tr>
<tr><td></td><td>pine[2] *[tree, unhappy]+</td></tr>
<tr><td>PIN *[Personal Identification Number]</td><td></td></tr>
</table>

> Unable to find your word under **pin**?
> Take off **pin** and look again

<table>
<tr><td>pinacul</td><td>pinnacle</td></tr>
<tr><td>pinash</td><td>panache</td></tr>
<tr><td>pincers</td><td></td></tr>
<tr><td>pinch[5] ~-hit[3]</td><td></td></tr>
<tr><td>pinck</td><td>pink[1+]</td></tr>
<tr><td>pincurs</td><td>pincers</td></tr>
<tr><td>pine[2] *[tree, wish] ~apple ~| cone ~| needle ~| nut ~| tree</td><td></td></tr>
<tr><td></td><td>pin[3] *[point]+</td></tr>
<tr><td>pinickle</td><td>pinnacle</td></tr>
<tr><td>pinion[1]</td><td></td></tr>
<tr><td>pink[1] ~ie ~ish</td><td></td></tr>
<tr><td>pinky[4] *[also spelled pinkie]</td><td></td></tr>
</table>

pinnacle	
pinpoint[1]	
pinsirs	pincers
pinstripe ~d	
pint ~-sized	
pintch	pinch[5+]
pinut	peanut[+]
pinyun	pinion[1]
pioneer[1]	
pious ~ly ~ness	
pip[3] *[seed] ~squeak	
	pipe[2] *[tube][+]
pipaya	papaya
pipe[2] *[tube] ~| dream ~line	
	pip[3] *[seed][+]
pipette [also spelled pipet]	
piquant	@piquancy
pique *[anger]	peak *[top][+]
	peek[1] *[look]
	Peke *[dog]
	pick[1] *[select][+]
pir	per *[rate][+]
	purr[1] *[cat]
pirabola	parabola *[curve][+]
pirade	parade[2]
piralysis	paralysis[+]
piramid	pyramid[+]
piramiter	parameter *[function input]
piranha *[fish]	Purana *[Hindu book]
pirate[2]	@piracy
pirch	perch[5+]
pire	pyre[2] *[cremation]
pireyuh	pariah
pirit	pirate[2+]
pirl	pearl *[gem][+]
	Perl *[computer language]
	purl[1] *[knitting]
piroet	pirouette[2]
pirokial	parochial[+]
piroll	parole[2] *[release]
	payroll *[pay]
piromaniac	pyromaniac
pirotechnics	pyrotechnics
pirouette[2]	
piroxism	paroxysm
pirrfect	perfect[1] *[flawless][+]
Pirric	Pyrrhic[+]
pirut	pirate[2+]
piruwette	pirouette[2]
pis	peace *[harmony]
	peas *[vegetables]
	piss[5] *[urine][+]
Pisces *[Zodiac sign]	
	pisses *[urinates]
piss[5] *[urine, urinate] ~| off	
	peace *[harmony]
	peas *[vegetables]
pissed *[angry, drunk]	
	psst *[attention]
pistachio	
pistal	pistil *[flower]
	pistol *[gun]
pistashio	pistachio
piste *[skiing]	pissed *[angry, drunk]
	psst *[attention]
pisten	piston
pistil *[flower]	pistol *[gun]
pistol *[gun]	pistil *[flower]
piston	
pistramy	pastrami
pit[3] *[hole, fight] ~| bull ~fall	
	peat *[substance][+]
pita ~| bread	
pitasium	potassium
pitch[5] *[throw, substance] ~-black ~dark ~fork	
	peach[5+]
piteous ~ly ~ness	
Pithagoras	Pythagoras
pithie	pithy[4]
pithon	python
pithy[4]	
pitiful ~ly	
pitince	pittance
pitius	piteous[+]
pitsicado	pizzicato
pittance	
pittiful	pitiful[+]
pittins	pittance

Key to Suffixes and Compounds

These rules are explained on pages vii to ix.

1 Keep the word the same before adding **ed, er, est, ing**
e.g. cool[1] → cooled, cooler, coolest, cooling

2 Take off final **e** before adding **ed, er, est, ing**
e.g. fine[2] → fined, finer, finest, fining

3 Double final consonant before adding **ed, er, est, ing**
e.g. thin[3] → thinned, thinner, thinnest, thinning

4 Change final **y** to **i** before adding **ed, er, es, est, ly, ness**
e.g. tidy[4] → tidied, tidier, tidies, tidiest, tidily, tidiness
Keep final **y** before adding **ing** e.g. tidying

5 Add **es** instead of **s** to the end of the word
e.g. bunch[5] → bunches

6 Change final **f** to **ve** before adding **s**
e.g. calf[6] → calves

pitty	pity[4+]
pituitary ~| gland	
pitunia	petunia
pity[4]	@pitiable
pitza	pizza[+]
pitzeria	pizzeria
pitzicato	pizzicato
pius	pious[+]
pivot[1] ~al	
piw	pew *[church seating]
pixel	
pixie	
piyety	piety
pizza	@pizzeria
pizzazz *[excitement]	
	pizzas *[food]
pizzicato	
placard	
placate[2]	
place[2] *[position] ~| mat ~ment ~| value	
	plaice *[fish]
placebo ~| effect	
placenta	
placid ~ity ~ly	
placird	placard
plackate	placate[2]
plackerd	placard
plad	plaid *[cloth pattern]
pladder	platter
plage	plague[2]
plagiarism	
plagiarize[2]	@plagiarist
plague[2]	
plaice *[fish]	place[2] *[position][+]
plaid *[cloth pattern]	
	played *[did play]
plain *[ordinary, flat land] ~ly ~ness ~-clothes ~| sailing ~-spoken	
	plane[2] *[smooth, aircraft]
plaintiff *[legal]	
plaintive *[sad] ~ly	
plait *[hair]	plat[3] *[land survey]
	plate[2] *[flat dish]
plajerise	plagiarize[2+]
plajirism	plagiarism

plak	plaque
plakard	placard
plakate	placate[2]
plan[3] *[design an action]	
	plain *[ordinary, flat land][+]
	plane[2] *[smooth, aircraft]
Planck *[physicist] ~'s constant	
	plank *[wood]
plancton	plankton
plane[2] *[smooth, aircraft]	
	plain *[ordinary, flat land][+]
planet ~arium ~ary	
planetiff	plaintiff *[legal]
	plaintive *[sad][+]
plangton	plankton
planit	planet[+]
plank *[wood]	Planck *[physicist][+]
plankton	
plannet	planet[+]
plant[1] ~ation	
plantain	
plantif	plaintiff *[legal]
plantive	plaintive *[sad][+]
plaque	
plase	place[2] *[position][+]
	plaice *[fish]
	plays *[does play]
plasebo	placebo[+]
plasenta	placenta
plasma	
plassid	placid[+]
plaster[1] ~| board ~| cast	
	pilaster *[column]
plastic *[material, can be shaped] ~| surgeon ~| surgery	
	plastique *[explosive]
plasticity	
plastique *[explosive]	
	plastic *[material, can be shaped][+]
plastir	plaster[1+]
plastisuty	plasticity
platanum	platinum
plate[2] *[flat dish] ~ful ~| glass ~| tectonics	

Key to Spelling Rules

Red words are wrong. **Black** words are correct.

- ~ Add the suffix or word directly to the main word, without a space or hyphen
  e.g. ash ~en ~tray → ashen ashtray
- ~- Add a hyphen to the main word before adding the next word
  e.g. blow ~-dry → blow-dry
- ~| Leave a space between the main word and the next word
  e.g. decimal ~| place → decimal place
- \+ By finding this word in its correct alphabetical order, you can find related words
  e.g. abowt about[+] → about-face
- ★ Draws attention to words that may be confused
- TM Means the word is a trademark
- @ Signifies the word is derived from the main word

plate[2]	plait *[hair]
	plat[3] *[land survey]
	plot[3] *[scheme]
plateau	
platelet	
plater	platter
platform	
platinum	
platipus	platypus[5]
platitude	
platlit	platelet
platoe	plateau
platonic *[just friends] ~ally	
	plutonic *[igneous rock]
platoon	
platow	plateau
platter	
platune	platoon
platunum	platinum
	plutonium
platypus[5]	
plaudits	
plausible	@plausibility

play[1] ~able ~boy ~ground ~| group ~house ~mate ~pen ~room ~thing ~time

> Unable to find your word under **play**?
> Take off **play** and look again

played *[did play]	plaid *[cloth pattern]
playful ~ly ~ness	
playge	plague[2]

playing ~| card ~| field

playjarize	plagiarize[2+]
playn	plain *[ordinary, flat land][+]
	plane[2] *[smooth, aircraft]
playntif	plaintiff *[legal]
playntiv	plaintive *[sad][+]
playrite	playwright
plays *[does play]	place[2] *[position][+]
	plaice *[fish]
playt	plait *[hair]
	plate[2] *[flat dish][+]
playtlet	platelet

playwright	
plazma	plasma
plea *[begging] ~bargain[1]	
	plié *[ballet]
plead[1] ~ingly	
pleas *[appeals]	please[2] *[entreat]
	police[2] *[law and order][+]
pleasant *[enjoyable] ~ly ~ness	
	peasant *[rustic][+]
	pheasant *[bird]
pleasantry[4]	
please[2] *[entreat]	pleas *[appeals]
	police[2] *[law and order][+]
pleasure	@pleasurable
	@pleasurably
pleat ~ed	
pleay	plea *[begging][+]
	plié *[ballet]
plebasite	plebiscite
plebeian	
plebiscite	
plecksus	plexus[+]
plede	plead[1+]
pledge[2]	
plee	plea *[begging][+]
pleeay	plié *[ballet]
pleed	plead[1+]
pleet	pleat[+]
pleeze	please[2] *[entreat]
plej	pledge[2]
plenary[4]	
plenitude	
plentiful ~ly ~ness	
plenty	
plenury	plenary[4]
pleral	pleural *[lungs]
	plural *[several]
plese	pleas *[appeals]
	please[2] *[entreat]
plesenta	placenta
plesint	pleasant[+]
plesintry	pleasantry[4]
plete	pleat[+]
plethora	
pleural *[lungs]	plural *[several]

Key to Suffixes and Compounds

These rules are explained on pages vii to ix.

1 Keep the word the same before adding **ed, er, est, ing**
e.g. cool[1] → cooled, cooler, coolest, cooling
2 Take off final **e** before adding **ed, er, est, ing**
e.g. fine[2] → fined, finer, finest, fining
3 Double final consonant before adding **ed, er, est, ing**
e.g. thin[3] → thinned, thinner, thinnest, thinning
4 Change final **y** to **i** before adding **ed, er, es, est, ly, ness**
e.g. tidy[4] → tidied, tidier, tidies, tidiest, tidily, tidiness
Keep final **y** before adding **ing** e.g. tidying
5 Add **es** instead of **s** to the end of the word
e.g. bunch[5] → bunches
6 Change final **f** to **ve** before adding **s**
e.g. calf[6] → calves

pleurisy
Plexiglas™
pley play[1+]
plea *[begging][+]
pleyable pliable
pleye ply[4+]
pleyful playful[+]
pleying playing[+]
plezant pleasant[+]
plezantry pleasantry[4]
pleze pleas *[appeals]
please[2] *[entreat]
plezher pleasure[+]
pliable
pliant
plié *[ballet] plea *[begging][+]
ply[4] *[layer]
plieant pliant
pliers
pliet plié *[ballet]
plight *[bad situation]
polite[2] *[good][+]
plight *[bad situation]
polite[2] *[good][+]
plite plight *[bad situation]
polite[2] *[good][+]
plod[3]
ploi ploy
ploom plume *[feather][+]
ploorel plural *[several]
pleural *[lungs]
ploorisy pleurisy
plop[3]
plosible plausible[+]
plot[3] *[scheme] plat[3] *[land survey]
plow[1] ~share
ploy
plubean plebeian
pluck[1] @plucky[4]
Pludo Pluto
plug[3] ~hole
pluk pluck[1+]
plum *[fruit] ~| assignment ~| pudding
plume *[feather][+]

plumb[1] *[weight] ~line
plume *[feather][+]
plumber
plume *[feather] @plumage
plum *[fruit][+]
plumb[1] *[weight][+]
plumer plumber
plumit plummet[1]
plummer plumber
plummet[1]
plump[1] ~ness
plunder[1]
plunge[2]
plunk[1] ~| down
pluperfect
plural *[several] pleural *[lungs]
pluralism
plurality
pluralizm pluralism
plurel pleural *[lungs]
plural *[several]
pluricy pleurisy
plurul pleural *[lungs]
plural *[several]
plus ~es and minuses ~| sign
plusebo placebo[+]
plush ~y
pluss plus[+]
Pluto
plutocracy[4]
plutonic *[igneous rock]
platonic *[just friends][+]
plutonium
ply[4] *[layer] ~wood
plyable pliable
plyant pliant
plyers pliers
plyght plight *[bad situation]
polite[2] *[good][+]
p.m. *[time]
pneumatic ~| drill
pneumonia
pneumonic *[lungs] ~| plague
mnemonic *[memory]

Key to Spelling Rules

Red words are wrong. **Black** words are correct.

~ Add the suffix or word directly to the main word, without a space or hyphen
e.g. ash ~en ~tray → ashen ashtray

~- Add a hyphen to the main word before adding the next word
e.g. blow ~-dry → blow-dry

~| Leave a space between the main word and the next word
e.g. decimal ~| place → decimal place

+ By finding this word in its correct alphabetical order, you can find related words
e.g. abowt about[+] → about-face

* Draws attention to words that may be confused

™ Means the word is a trademark

@ Signifies the word is derived from the main word

poach[5] *[cook, trespass] ~ed egg	
	posh[1] *[smart]
poak	poke[2] *[prod, bag]+
poaker	poker *[game, tool]+
poar	paw[1] *[foot]
	poor[1] *[needy]+
	pore[2] *[skin, over]
	pour[1] *[a drink]
poastmodern	postmodern+
poastmortem	post-mortem
poch	poach[5] *[cook, trespass]+
	posh[1] *[smart]
pock *[pustule]	poke[2] *[prod, bag]+
pocker	poker *[game, tool]+
	pucker[1] *[lips]+
pocket[1] ~ful ~book ~| calculator ~| change ~| edition ~| knife ~| money	

> Unable to find your word under **pocket**?
> Take off **pocket** and look again

pockmarked	
pocs	pox
pod *[seed case]	pad[3] *[cushion]
	paid *[given money]
podder	potter[1] *[makes pots]+
	putter[1] *[golf, work at hobby]+
podium	
poeddic	poetic+
poedium	podium
poeit	poet+
poem	
Poep	Pope *[Head of Catholic Church]
	pop[3] *[noise]+
poer	poor[1] *[needy]+
	pore[2] *[skin, over]
	pour[1] *[a drink]
poest	post[1+]
poet ~| Laureate	
poetic ~ally ~| justice ~| license	
poetry[4] *[words]	pottery[4] *[ceramics]
pogrom *[attack on Jewish communities]	program[3] *[schedule, software]+
poignancy	
poignant ~ly	
poinseta	poinsettia
poinsettia	
point[1] ~edly ~-blank ~| duty ~| man ~| person ~| of interest ~| of order ~| of sale ~| of view	

> Unable to find your word under **point**?
> Take off **point** and look again

pointless ~ly ~ness	
pointsetta	poinsettia
poinyinsy	poignancy
poinyint	poignant+
poise[2]	
poison[1] ~ous ~ously ~| pill	
poit	poet+
poitry	poetry[4] *[words]
pok	pock *[pustule]
	poke[2] *[prod, bag]+
poka	polka+
poke[2] *[prod, bag] ~| about ~| around	
poker *[game, tool] ~| dice ~-faced	
poket	pocket[1+]
pokey	poky[4]
pokit	pocket[1+]
pokmarkt	pock-marked
pokre	poker *[game, tool]+
poks	pox
poky[4]	
polar ~| bear ~| cap ~| circle	
polaridy	polarity[4]
Polaris	
polarity[4]	
polarize[2]	@polarization
Polaroid™	
polasy	policy[4+]
polatishin	politician
pole *[post, stick] ~| vault[1]	
	poll[1] *[vote]+

Key to Suffixes and Compounds

These rules are explained on pages vii to ix.

1. Keep the word the same before adding **ed, er, est, ing**
   e.g. cool[1] → cooled, cooler, coolest, cooling
2. Take off final **e** before adding **ed, er, est, ing**
   e.g. fine[2] → fined, finer, finest, fining
3. Double final consonant before adding **ed, er, est, ing**
   e.g. thin[3] → thinned, thinner, thinnest, thinning
4. Change final **y** to **i** before adding **ed, er, es, est, ly, ness**
   e.g. tidy[4] → tidied, tidier, tidies, tidiest, tidily, tidiness
   Keep final **y** before adding **ing** e.g. tidying
5. Add **es** instead of **s** to the end of the word
   e.g. bunch[5] → bunches
6. Change final **f** to **ve** before adding **s**
   e.g. calf[6] → calves

Pole Star *[North Star]	
	pollster *[surveys opinions]
polees	police[2] *[law and order][+]
	pleas *[appeals]
	please[2] *[entreat]
polemic ~al	
polemik	polemic[+]
poler	polar[+]
polerise	polarize[2+]
poleroid	Polaroid™
police[2] *[law and order] ~| dog ~| force ~man ~| officer ~| state ~| station ~woman	
	pleas *[appeals]
	please[2] *[entreat]

> Unable to find your word under **police**?
> Take off **police** and look again

policy[4] ~holder	
polidicle	political[+]
polidisize	politicize[2]
poliester	polyester
polight	polite[2] *[good][+]
	plight *[bad situation]
polinate	pollinate[2+]
polio *[disease] ~myelitis	
	polo *[sport][+]
polip	polyp
polir	polar[+]
polirize	polarize[2+]
polis	police[2] *[law and order][+]
	pleas *[appeals]
	please[2] *[entreat]
polish[5] ~| off ~| up	
polisy	policy[4+]
Politburo	
polite[2] *[good] ~ly ~ness	
	plight *[bad situation]
politic	@politicking
political ~| process ~| risk ~| science	
politically ~| correct	
politician	
politicize[2]	
politicks	politics[+]
politics ~| politicking	
politik	politic[+]
politikal	political[+]
politikly	politically[+]
politishun	politician
politisize	politicize[2]
polka ~dot	
poll[1] *[vote] ~ing booth ~ing place ~| tax	
	pole *[post, stick][+]
	pool[1] *[swimming]
	pull[1] *[tug]
pollar	polar[+]
pollaris	Polaris
polle	pole *[post, stick][+]
	poll[1] *[vote][+]
pollen	
polligon	polygon
pollinate[2]	@pollination
pollio	polio *[disease][+]
pollip	polyp
pollish	polish[5+]
pollite	polite[2] *[good][+]
pollitic	politic[+]
pollster *[surveys opinions]	
	Pole Star *[North Star]
polltergist	poltergeist
pollun	pollen
pollute[2]	@pollution
pollyetheleen	polyethylene
pollyhedron	polyhedron

> Unable to find your word under **poll**?
> Look under **pol**

polo *[sport] ~-neck ~| pony ~| shirt	
	polio *[disease][+]
poloot	pollute[2+]
polow	polo *[sport][+]
polster	Pole Star *[North Star]
	pollster *[surveys opinions]
poltergeist	
poltiss	poultice
poltry	poultry[+]

polup polyp
polyester
polyethylene
polygamy @polygamous
polyglot
polygon
polygumy polygamy[+]
polyhedron
polymer
polyo polio *[disease][+]
polo *[sport][+]
polyp
polysh polish[5+]
polysyllabic
polyte polite[2] *[good][+]
plight *[bad situation]
polytechnic
polytic politic[+]
polytical political[+]
polyticyse politicize[2]
polyunsaturated
pomagranate pomegranate
pome poem
pomegranate
pomigranite pomegranate
pommel *[knob] ~| horse
pummel[1] *[beat]
pommpon pompon
pomp *[ceremony] ~| and circumstance
pump[1] *[fluid][+]
pompis pompous[+]
pom-pom
pompous *[self-important] ~ly
@pomposity
pampas *[plains][+]
poncho
pond *[water] panned *[criticized, camera, gold]
pawned *[sold]
pound[1] *[weight, money][+]
ponder[1] *[think][+] panda *[animal]
pander[1] *[indulge]
ponderous ~ly
ponee pony[4+]
pontiff

pontificate[2]
pontoon
pony[4] ~| express ~tail ~| up
poo[1] *[feces] pooh *[exclamation]
poodle *[dog] puddle[2] *[water]
pooerile puerile
pooh *[exclamation]
poo[1] *[feces]
pool *[swimming] pull[1] *[tug]
pooma puma
poomise pumice[2+]
poop[1] *[stern of ship, information, feces]
poopa pooper[+]
pupa *[of insect][+]
pooper ~-scooper
poor[1] *[needy] ~ly ~| quality ~| service
paw[1] *[foot]
pore[2] *[skin, over]
pour[1] *[a drink]
poosh push[5+]
poot put *[place][+]
pop[3] *[noise] ~| art ~corn ~gun ~| music ~up
Pope *[Head of Catholic Church]
Pope *[Head of Catholic Church]
pop[3] *[noise][+]
poplar *[tree] popular *[well-known][+]
poplarise popularize[2]
popler poplar *[tree]
poppy[4] *[flower] ~| seed
puppy[4] *[dog][+]
populace *[the masses]
populous *[crowded]
popular *[well-known] ~ity ~ly
poplar *[tree]
popularize[2]
populas populous *[crowded]
populase populace *[the masses]
populate[2] @population
populerize popularize[2]
populous *[crowded]
populace *[the masses]
popuri potpourri *[mixture, scent]
popyulate populate[2+]

KEY TO SUFFIXES AND COMPOUNDS

These rules are explained on pages vii to ix.

1 Keep the word the same before adding **ed, er, est, ing**
e.g. cool[1] → cooled, cooler, coolest, cooling
2 Take off final **e** before adding **ed, er, est, ing**
e.g. fine[2] → fined, finer, finest, fining
3 Double final consonant before adding **ed, er, est, ing**
e.g. thin[3] → thinned, thinner, thinnest, thinning
4 Change final **y** to **i** before adding **ed, er, es, est, ly, ness**
e.g. tidy[4] → tidied, tidier, tidies, tidiest, tidily, tidiness
Keep final **y** before adding **ing** e.g. tidying
5 Add **es** instead of **s** to the end of the word
e.g. bunch[5] → bunches
6 Change final **f** to **ve** before adding **s**
e.g. calf[6] → calves

popyuler	popular *[well-known]+
	poplar *[tree]
popyulerize	popularize[2]
popyulis	populous *[crowded]
por	paw[1] *[foot]
	poor[1] *[needy]+
	pore[2] *[skin, over]
	pour[1] *[a drink]
porc	pork+
porcelain	
porch[5]	
porcipine	porcupine
porcity	paucity
porck	pork+
porcupine	
pordabul	portable+
pordico	portico
pore[2] *[skin, over]	
	paw[1] *[foot]
	poor[1] *[needy]+
	pour[1] *[a drink]
poridge	porridge
poris	porous+
pork ~er ~y	
porkypine	porcupine
porn *[sex]	pawn[1] *[deposit, chess]+
pornagrafik	pornographic
pornagrafy	pornography+
pornographic	
pornography	@pornographer
porous	@porosity
porpoise[2] *[animal]	
	purpose[2] *[intent]+
porre	poor[1] *[needy]+
	pour[1] *[a drink]
porridge	
porse	porous+
	pause[2] *[stop]
	paws *[feet]
porshun	portion[1]
porsulin	porcelain
port ~| authority[4] ~folio ~hole	
portable	@portably
portal	
portcullis	
portend[1] *[foretell]	
	pretend[1] *[make believe]
portent *[omen] ~ous	
	important *[valuable]+
portfolio ~| assessment ~| manager	
portible	portable+
portico	
portion[1]	
portkulis	portcullis
portle	portal
portly[4]	
portrait ~ure	
portray[1] ~al	
portul	portal
portunt	portent *[omen]+
	portend[1] *[foretell]
	important *[valuable]+
porus	porous+
posability	possibility[4]
posative	positive+
poscher	posture[2] *[hold oneself]
poschilate	postulate[2]
poschulunt	postulant
poschumus	posthumous+
pose[2] *[position]	posse *[group of citizens]
poseshin	possession
posesive	possessive+
posess	possess[5] *[own]+
posession	possession
posh[1] *[smart]	poach[5] *[cook, trespass]+
poshun	potion
posibility	possibility[4]
posible	possible+
posishun	position
position	
positive ~ly ~ness ~| feedback	
	@positivity
positivism	
positron	
posse *[group of citizens]	
	pose[2] *[hold still]
	posy *[flowers]
possess[5] *[own] ~or	
	poses *[holds still]
possession	

Key to Spelling Rules

Red words are wrong. **Black** words are correct.

~ Add the suffix or word directly to the main word, without a space or hyphen
e.g. ash ~en ~tray → ashen ashtray

~- Add a hyphen to the main word before adding the next word
e.g. blow ~-dry → blow-dry

~| Leave a space between the main word and the next word
e.g. decimal ~| place → decimal place

+ By finding this word in its correct alphabetical order, you can find related words
e.g. abowt about+ → about-face

★ Draws attention to words that may be confused

™ Means the word is a trademark

@ Signifies the word is derived from the main word

possessive ~ly ~ness	
possibility[4]	
possible *[can be done]	
	@possibly
	passable *[can pass, be passed]
	passible *[can suffer]
possim	possum
possterior	posterior
possum	
possy	posse *[group of citizens]
	posy[4] *[flowers]
post[1] ~card ~date[2] ~doctoral ~graduate ~haste ~man ~mark ~| office ~paid	

> Unable to find your word under **post**?
> Take off **post** and look again

postage ~| and handling ~-stamp	
postal ~| service	
poster *[sign]	posture[2] *[hold oneself]
posterior	
posterity	
posthumous ~ly	
postige	postage[+]
postil	postal[+]
postilate	postulate[2]
postir	poster *[sign]
	posture[2] *[hold oneself]
postirior	posterior
postmodern ~ism	
postmortem	
postnatal	
postoperative	
postpartum ~| depression	
postpone[2] ~ment	
postscript	
postul	postal[+]
postulant	
postulate[2]	
postulint	postulant
postur	poster *[sign]
	posture[2] *[hold oneself]
posture[2] *[hold oneself]	
	poster *[sign]
posum	possum
posy[4] *[flowers]	posse *[group of citizens]
posytiv	positive[+]
pot[3] ~| belly ~-bellied ~boiler ~hole ~holing ~| luck	
potado	potato[5+]
potassium	
potato[5] ~| chip	
potency[4]	@potent
potenshil	potential[+]
potensy	potency[4+]
potential ~ly ~| customers ~| market	
poter	potter[1+]
potery	poetry[4] *[words]
	pottery[4] *[ceramics]
potinsy	potency[4+]
potion	
potpourri *[mixture, scent]	
potter[1] *[makes pots] ~y[4]	
	@potter's wheel
	putter[1] *[golf, work at hobby][+]
pottery[4] *[ceramics]	
	poetry[4] *[words]
potty[4] ~-train[1]	
pouch[5]	
pouder	powder[1+]
poultergeist	poltergeist
poultice	
poultry ~| farm	
pounce[2]	
pound[1] *[weight, money] ~| sterling	
pouns	pounce[2]
pour[1] *[a drink]	paw[1] *[foot]
	poor[1] *[needy][+]
	pore[2] *[skin, over]
pournografﬁc	pornographic
pourous	porous[+]
pourt	port[+]
pout[1]	
pou-wou	pow-wow
poverty ~-stricken	
powch	pouch[5+]

KEY TO SUFFIXES AND COMPOUNDS

These rules are explained on pages vii to ix.

1 Keep the word the same before adding **ed, er, est, ing**
e.g. cool[1] → cooled, cooler, coolest, cooling
2 Take off final **e** before adding **ed, er, est, ing**
e.g. fine[2] → fined, finer, finest, fining
3 Double final consonant before adding **ed, er, est, ing**
e.g. thin[3] → thinned, thinner, thinnest, thinning
4 Change final **y** to **i** before adding **ed, er, es, est, ly, ness**
e.g. tidy[4] → tidied, tidier, tidies, tidiest, tidily, tidiness
Keep final **y** before adding **ing** e.g. tidying
5 Add **es** instead of **s** to the end of the word
e.g. bunch[5] → bunches
6 Change final **f** to **ve** before adding **s**
e.g. calf[6] → calves

powder[1] ~y ~| keg ~| puff ~| room
powdium **podium**
power[1] ~less ~boat ~house ~| of attorney ~| pack ~| plant ~| play ~| sharing ~| steering ~| trip

> Unable to find your word under **power**? Take off **power** and look again

powerful ~ly ~ness
powir **power**[1+]
powka **polka**+
powky **poky**[4]
powl **pole** *[post, stick]+
poll[1] *[vote]+
powlio **polio** *[disease]+
pownd **pound**[1] *[weight, money]+
powr **power**[1+]
pow-wow
pox
poynansy **poignancy**
poynant **poignant**+
poynt **point**[1+]
poynyunt **poignant**+
poyze **poise**[2]
poyzin **poison**[1+]
poze **pose**[2] *[position]
posy[4] *[flowers]
pozeshun **possession**
pozeur **poseur** *[pretender]
poser *[puzzle]
pozition **position**
pozitivism **positivism**
pozy **posy**[4] *[flowers]
pose[2] *[position]
PR [public relations]
prablem **problem**+
pracision **precision** *[exactness]+
pracksy **proxy**[4]
practicable @**practicability**
practical ~ity ~ly
practice[2] @**practitioner**
practitioner
practus **practice**[2+]
praddle **prattle**[2]
praduct **product**+
praer **prayer**+
pragmatic @**pragmatism**
pragnosis **prognosis**+
prairie ~| grass
praise[2] *[express admiration] ~worthy
prays *[offers prayers]
preys *[kills for food]
praject **project**[1+]
prakticle **practical**+
pralong **prolong**[1+]
pramere **premiere**
pramise **premise**
promise[2+]
pramordeal **primordial**
pramote **promote**[2]
prampt **prompt**[1+]
pranc **prank**+
prance[2]
prang **prong**
prank ~ster
pranse **prance**[2]
praper **prepare**
proper+
prare **prayer**+
praree **prairie**+
prasise **precise** *[exact]+
précis *[summary]
prattle[2]
praun **prawn**
praverb **proverb**+
pravide **provide**[2]

> Unable to find your word under **pra**? Look under **pro**

prawn
pray[1] *[say prayers]
prey[1] *[kill for food, victim]
prayer ~| beads ~| book
praylude **prelude**[2]
prayr **prayer**+
prays *[offers prayers]
preys *[kills for food]

Key to Spelling Rules

Red words are wrong. **Black** words are correct.

~ Add the suffix or word directly to the main word, without a space or hyphen
e.g. ash ~en ~tray → ashen ashtray

~- Add a hyphen to the main word before adding the next word
e.g. blow ~-dry → blow-dry

~| Leave a space between the main word and the next word
e.g. decimal ~| place → decimal place

\+ By finding this word in its correct alphabetical order, you can find related words
e.g. abowt about+ → about-face

★ Draws attention to words that may be confused

TM Means the word is a trademark

@ Signifies the word is derived from the main word

prays — praise^{2} *[express admiration]$^{+}$
praysee — précis *[summary]
preach^{5}
preamble^{2}
preambul — preamble^{2}
prean — preen^{1}
prearrange^{2}
preast — priest^{+}
precarious ~ly ~ness
precarius — precarious^{+}
precaution ~ary
precawshin — precaution^{+}
precawtion — precaution^{+}
precede^{2} *[go before]
— proceed^{1} *[go on]
precedence *[priority]
— precedents *[happened before]
— presidents *[leaders]
precedent *[example]
— president *[leader]$^{+}$
precept
precession *[wobbling] ~| of the equinoxes
— procession *[march]$^{+}$
— precision *[exactness]$^{+}$
preche — preach^{5+}
precinct
precious ~ly ~ness
precipice
precipitate^{2} — @precipitation
precipitous ~ly ~ness
precipus — precipice
preciputate — precipitate^{2+}
précis *[summary]
precise *[exact] ~ly
precision *[exactness] ~| instrument ~| machining
— precession *[wobbling]$^{+}$
preclude^{2}
precocious ~ly ~ness
preconceive^{2}
preconception
preconseev — preconceive^{2}
preconsepshin — preconception

precorshun — precaution^{+}
precripshun — prescription *[order]$^{+}$
precursor ~y
precus — precious^{+}
predacate — predicate^{2}
predalection — predilection
predasesser — predecessor
predate *[date before]
predator *[kills for food]
predecessor
predestined — @predestination
predetermine^{2}
predicament
predicate^{2}
prediceser — predecessor
predict^{1} ~able ~or
prediction
predikament — predicament
predilection
predispose^{2} — @predisposition
preditor — predator *[kills for food]
predjudiss — prejudice^{2}
predominance
predominant *[foremost] ~ly
predominate^{2} *[prevail]
preech — preach^{5+}
preeclude — preclude^{2}
preejudge — prejudge^{2}
preeliminary — preliminary^{4}
preeminence — @preeminent
preemium — premium^{+}
preempt^{1} ~ion ~ive
preen^{1}
preeocupy — preoccupy^{4+}
preepaid — prepaid
preest — priest^{+}
preevent — prevent^{1+}
preexist^{1} ~ent ~ing condition
prefabricate^{2} — @prefabrication
preface^{2}
prefect *[official] ~ure
— perfect^{1} *[flawless]$^{+}$
prefer^{3} ~able ~ably
preference
preferential ~ly

Key to Suffixes and Compounds

These rules are explained on pages vii to ix.

1 Keep the word the same before adding **ed, er, est, ing** e.g. cool^{1} → cooled, cooler, coolest, cooling
2 Take off final **e** before adding **ed, er, est, ing** e.g. fine^{2} → fined, finer, finest, fining
3 Double final consonant before adding **ed, er, est, ing** e.g. thin^{3} → thinned, thinner, thinnest, thinning
4 Change final **y** to **i** before adding **ed, er, es, est, ly, ness** e.g. tidy^{4} → tidied, tidier, tidies, tidiest, tidily, tidiness
Keep final **y** before adding **ing** e.g. tidying
5 Add **es** instead of **s** to the end of the word e.g. bunch^{5} → bunches
6 Change final **f** to **ve** before adding **s** e.g. calf^{6} → calves

preferment	
preffer	**prefer[3+]**
preficks	**prefix[5]**
prefiss	**preface[2]**
prefix[5]	
prefur	**prefer[3+]**
prefurenshil	**preferential[+]**
prefurins	**preference**
prefurment	**preferment**
prefus	**preface[2]**
	profuse[2+]
pregnancy[4]	
pregnant	
prehensile	
prehistoric ~ally	**@prehistory**
prejidishul	**prejudicial[+]**
prejudge[2]	
prejudice[2]	
prejudicial ~ly	
prejudis	**prejudice[2]**
prejudishul	**prejudicial[+]**
prejuj	**prejudge[2]**
prekirsur	**precursor[+]**
preklude	**preclude[2]**
prekoshus	**precocious[+]**
prekursor	**precursor[+]**
prelate	
preliminary[4]	
prelit	**prelate**
prelood	**prelude[2]**
prelude[2]	
prema	**prima[+]**
premacher	**premature[+]**
premanishun	**premonition**
premarital ~| relations	
premasis	**premises**
premature ~ly	
premeditate[2]	**@premeditation**
premenstrual ~| syndrome *[PMS]	
premeum	**premium[+]**
premiere	
preminition	**premonition**
premise[2]	
premium ~| offer ~| quality	
premmiere	**premiere**

premonition	
premordial	**primordial**
prenatal	
prene	**preen[1]**
preoccupy[4]	**@preoccupation**
preordained	
prepackaged	
prepaid	
prepair	**prepare[2]**
prepakijed	**prepackaged**
preparashin	**preparation[+]**
preparation	**@preparatory**
prepare[2]	
prepay[1] ~ment	
prepayd	**prepaid**
preponderance	**@preponderant**
preposition *[grammar] ~al	
	proposition *[statement, invitation to casual sex]
preposterous ~ly ~ness	
prepozishin	**preposition** *[grammar][+]
pre-rapped	**pre-wrapped**
prere	**prayer[+]**
prerequisite	
prerogative	
prery	**prairie[+]**
pres	**press[5+]**
presadinse	**precedence** *[priority]
	president *[leader][+]
presadunt	**president** *[leader][+]
	precedent *[example]
presapis	**precipice**
Presbyterian ~| Church	
preschool	
prescribe[2] *[write an order]	
	proscribe[2] *[forbid]
prescription *[order] ~| drugs	
	proscription *[ban]
prescriptive ~ly	
presede	**precede[2]** *[go before]
	proceed[1] *[go on]
presedense	**precedence** *[priority][+]
	precedents *[happened before]

KEY TO SPELLING RULES

Red words are wrong. **Black** words are correct.

~ Add the suffix or word directly to the main word, without a space or hyphen
e.g. ash ~en ~tray → ashen ashtray

~- Add a hyphen to the main word before adding the next word
e.g. blow ~-dry → blow-dry

~| Leave a space between the main word and the next word
e.g. decimal ~| place → decimal place

\+ By finding this word in its correct alphabetical order, you can find related words
e.g. abowt about[+] → about-face

* Draws attention to words that may be confused

TM Means the word is a trademark

@ Signifies the word is derived from the main word

presedent	precedent *[example]
	President *[leader][+]
presee	précis *[summary]
preseed	precede[2] *[go before]
presence *[attendance]	
	presents *[gifts, offers]
present[1] *[gift, show] ~ly ~-day	
	presence *[attendance]
presentable	@presentably
presentament	presentiment
presentation	
presentible	presentable[+]
presentiment	
presents *[gifts, offers]	
	presence *[attendance]
presept	precept
preservation ~ist	
preservative	
preserve[2]	
presher	pressure[2+]
presherize	pressurize[2+]
preshus	precious[+]
preside[2]	
presidency[4]	
president *[leader] ~ial	
	precedent *[example]
presied	preside[2]
	precede[2] *[go before]
	proceed[1] *[go on]
presinct	precinct
presinse	presence *[attendance]
	presents *[gifts, offers]
presint	present[1] *[gift, show][+]
presintation	presentation
presipiss	precipice
presipitate	precipitate[2+]
presipitous	precipitous[+]
presippose	presuppose[2]
presise	precise *[exact][+]
	précis *[summary]
preskool	pre-school
preskripshin	prescription *[order][+]
Prespiterian	Presbyterian[+]

presreybe	prescribe[2] *[write an order]
	proscribe[2] *[forbid]
press[5] ~| agency ~| agent ~| box ~| clipping ~| conference ~| corps ~| gallery ~-gang ~| kit ~| release ~| room ~| secretary	

> Unable to find your word under **press**? Take off **press** and look again

pressed *[forced, flattened]	
	priest[+]
pressto	presto
pressure[2] ~| cooker ~| group	
pressurize[2]	@pressurization
preste	priest[+]
	pressed *[forced, flattened]
presteej	prestige[+]
prestige	@prestigious
presto	
presume[2]	@presumably
presumption	@presumptive
presumptuous ~ly ~ness	
presumshin	presumption[+]
presumshis	presumptuous[+]
presuppose[2]	
presurvashun	preservation[+]
presurvative	preservative
presurve	preserve[2]
pretax ~| profit	
pretekst	pretext
pretense	
pretend[1] *[make believe]	
	portend[1] *[foretell]
pretension	
pretentious ~ly ~ness	
preterb	perturb[1]
pretext	
pretsel	pretzel
pretty[4]	
pretzel	
prevail[1]	
prevalence	@prevalant

Key to Suffixes and Compounds

These rules are explained on pages vii to ix.

1 Keep the word the same before adding **ed, er, est, ing**
e.g. cool[1] → cooled, cooler, coolest, cooling

2 Take off final **e** before adding **ed, er, est, ing**
e.g. fine[2] → fined, finer, finest, fining

3 Double final consonant before adding **ed, er, est, ing**
e.g. thin[3] → thinned, thinner, thinnest, thinning

4 Change final **y** to **i** before adding **ed, er, es, est, ly, ness**
e.g. tidy[4] → tidied, tidier, tidies, tidiest, tidily, tidiness
Keep final **y** before adding **ing** e.g. tidying

5 Add **es** instead of **s** to the end of the word
e.g. bunch[5] → bunches

6 Change final **f** to **ve** before adding **s**
e.g. calf[6] → calves

prevalins prevalence+
prevaricate² @prevarication
prevent¹ ~able ~ion
preventive [preventative, alternative spelling]
preveus previous+
preview¹
previlans prevalence+
previous ~ly
prevlans prevalence+
prewar
pre-wrapped
prey¹ *[kill for food, victim]
pray¹ *[say prayers]
pry⁴ *[loosen, nosy]+
preyeminens pre-eminence+
preyempt pre-empt¹+
preyexist preexist¹+
preym prim³ *[very proper]+
prime² *[height of abilities]+
preyor prior+
prayer+
preys *[kills for food]
praise² *[express admiration]+
prays *[offers prayers]
price² *[cost]+
prise² *[lever]
prize² *[award]+
preysing pricing+
prezadint President *[leader]+
precedent *[example]
prezent present¹ *[gift, offer]+
presence *[attendance]
prezentiment presentiment
prezide preside²
prezince presence *[attendance]
presents *[gifts]
prezume presume²+
priambul preamble²
priarange prearrange²
pricarious precarious+
pricaushun precaution+
price² *[cost] ~| control ~| cut ~| differential ~-fixing ~-gouging
price ~| hike ~| index ~| list ~| range ~| reduction ~| tag ~-sensitive ~| war
pries *[curious]
prise² *[lever]
prize² *[award]+

> Unable to find your word under **price**? Take off **price** and look again

priceless ~ly ~ness
pricey *[expensive]
prich preach⁵+
pricing ~| policy⁴
prick¹
prickle² @prickly⁴
priconsepshun preconception

> Unable to find your word under **pri**? Look under **pre**

priddy pretty⁴
pride² *[self-respect]
pried *[curious]
prie pry⁴ *[loosen, nosy]+
pried *[curious] pride² *[self-respect]
priemary primary⁴+
prier prior+
pries *[curious] prize² *[award]+
priest ~ess ~hood ~ly
prifect prefect *[official]+
perfect¹ *[flawless]+
prig³ @priggish
prik prick¹
priliminary preliminary⁴
prim³ *[very proper] ~ly ~ness
prime² *[height of abilities]+
prima ~| donna ~| facie ~| ballerina
primacy
primary⁴ ~| care ~| color ~| school ~| source
primasy primacy
primate
primative primitive+

Key to Spelling Rules

Red words are wrong. **Black** words are correct.

~ Add the suffix or word directly to the main word, without a space or hyphen
e.g. ash ~en ~tray → ashen ashtray

~- Add a hyphen to the main word before adding the next word
e.g. blow ~-dry → blow-dry

~| Leave a space between the main word and the next word
e.g. decimal ~| place → decimal place

\+ By finding this word in its correct alphabetical order, you can find related words
e.g. abowt about+ → about-face

★ Draws attention to words that may be confused

TM Means the word is a trademark

@ Signifies the word is derived from the main word

prime[2] *[height of abilities] ~| factor ~| number ~| rate ~| time ~| Minister
prim[3] *[very proper]+

Unable to find your word under **prime**? Take off **prime** and look again

primeeval primeval
primer
primerdonner prima donna
primeval
priminuns prominence+
primisy primacy
primitive @primitivism
primium premium+
primordial
primusy primacy
prince *[royalty] ~ly @princess
prints *[words or pictures on paper]
principal *[chief] ~ly
principle *[rule, idea]
principle *[rule, idea]
principal *[chief]+
prinnt print[1+]
prinowns pronounce[2] *[announce]+
prins prince *[royalty]+
prints *[words or pictures on paper]
prinsipality principality[4]
prinsuple principal *[chief]+
principle *[rule, idea]
print[1] ~| area ~out ~| run
prioccupy preoccupy[4+]
prior ~| art
prioritize[2]
priority[4]
pripade prepaid
priporshin proportion[1]
prippose propose[2] *[suggest]+
priscribe prescribe[2] *[write an order]
proscribe[2] *[forbid]
priscripshun prescription *[order]+
proscription *[ban]
prise[2] *[lever] pries *[curious]
price[2] *[cost]+
prize[2] *[award]+
priseed precede[2] *[go before]
proceed[1] *[go on]
prisentable presentable+
prising pricing+
prism
prison ~er
prisoom presume[2+]
prisribe prescribe[2] *[write an order]
proscribe[2] *[forbid]
prissy[4] *[fussy]
pristine
prisume presume[2+]
prisy prissy[4] *[fussy]
pricey *[expensive]
pritend pretend[1]
pritty pretty[4]
privacy
privail prevail[1]
privashun privation
private ~ly ~| enterprise ~| ownership
privateys privatize[2+]
privation
privatize[2] @privatization
privent prevent[1+]
privie privy
privilege[2]
privisow proviso
privisy privacy
privit private+
privitize privatize[2+]
privius previous+

Unable to find your word under **pri**? Look under **pre**

privusy privacy
privut private+
privy

KEY TO SUFFIXES AND COMPOUNDS

These rules are explained on pages vii to ix.

1 Keep the word the same before adding **ed, er, est, ing**
e.g. cool[1] → cooled, cooler, coolest, cooling
2 Take off final **e** before adding **ed, er, est, ing**
e.g. fine[2] → fined, finer, finest, fining
3 Double final consonant before adding **ed, er, est, ing**
e.g. thin[3] → thinned, thinner, thinnest, thinning
4 Change final **y** to **i** before adding **ed, er, es, est, ly, ness**
e.g. tidy[4] → tidied, tidier, tidies, tidiest, tidily, tidiness
Keep final **y** before adding **ing** e.g. tidying
5 Add **es** instead of **s** to the end of the word
e.g. bunch[5] → bunches
6 Change final **f** to **ve** before adding **s**
e.g. calf[6] → calves

priyd	pried *[curious]
	pride[2] *[self-respect]
priyz	pries *[curious]
	prise[2] *[lever]
	prize[2] *[award]+
prize[2] *[award] ~-fighter ~-giving ~-winning	
	pries *[curious]
	price[2] *[cost]+
	prise[2] *[lever]
prizm	prism
prizon	prison+
pro ~| forma ~| rata ~| tem	
proab	probe[2]
proan	prone
probability ~| scale	
probable	@probably
probate	
probation ~| officer	
probe[2]	
probibility	probability+
probible	probable+
problem ~| solver ~| solving	
problematic ~al ~ally	
proboscis	
procecute	prosecute[2] *[court]+
procecution	prosecution
procede	proceed[1] *[go on]
	precede[2] *[go before]
procedure	
proceed[1] *[go on]	
	precede[2] *[go before]
procelitize	proselytize[2]
process[5] ~or	
procession *[march] ~al	
	precession *[wobbling]+
procksimate	proximate+
procksimity	proximity
procksy	proxy[4]
proclaim[1]	
proclamation	
proclame	proclaim[1]
proclimashin	proclamation
procrastinate[2]	@procrastination
procreate[2]	@procreation

proctor	
procuration	@procurator
procure[2] ~ment	
prod[3]	
prodigal	
prodigious ~ly ~ness	
prodigy[4]	
prodoos	produce[2]
prodotype	prototype
prodozoa	protozoa+
produce[2]	
product ~| cycle ~| design ~| development ~| engineer ~| launch ~| lifecycle ~| line ~| mix	

> Unable to find your word under **product**?
> Take off **product** and look again

production ~| line ~| standards ~| target	
productive ~ly	
productivity	
produse	produce[2]
proe	pro+
proeduce	produce[2]
proegram	program[3] *[schedule, software]+
proen	prone
proes	prose
profane[2] ~ly ~ness	
profanity[4]	
profer	proffer[1]
	prefer[3]+
profes	profess[5]+
profeseye	prophesy[4] *[predict]
	prophecy[4] *[prediction]
profeshin	profession
profesie	prophesy[4] *[predict]
	prophecy[4] *[prediction]
profess[5] ~or ~orial	
profession	
professional ~ism ~ly	
professionalize[2]	@professionalization
profesy	prophesy[4] *[predict]
profet	prophet *[predictor]+
	profit[1] *[benefit]+

KEY TO SPELLING RULES

Red words are wrong. **Black** words are correct.

~ Add the suffix or word directly to the main word, without a space or hyphen
e.g. ash ~en ~tray → ashen ashtray

~- Add a hyphen to the main word before adding the next word
e.g. blow ~-dry → blow-dry

~| Leave a space between the main word and the next word
e.g. decimal ~| place → decimal place

+ By finding this word in its correct alphabetical order, you can find related words
e.g. abowt about+ → about-face

* Draws attention to words that may be confused

TM Means the word is a trademark

@ Signifies the word is derived from the main word

proffer[1]	
proffesionalise	professionalize[2+]
proffisy	prophesy[4] *[predict]
	prophecy[4] *[prediction]
proffit	profit[1] *[benefit][+]
	prophet *[predictor][+]
proficiency	@proficient
profiel	profile[2]
profilactic	prophylactic
profile[2]	
profishinsy	proficiency[+]
profisie	prophecy[4] *[prediction]
profisiency	proficiency[+]
profit[1] *[benefit] ~| and loss [P & L] ~| center ~| margin ~-oriented ~-sharing ~-taking	
	prophet *[predictor][+]

Unable to find your word under **profit**? Take off **profit** and look again

profitable	@profitability
	@profitably
profiteer[1]	
profligate	
profolus	propolis
profound ~ly	
profownd	profound[+]
profre	proffer[1]
profread	proofread[1]
profundity	
profuse[2] ~ly	
profylactic	prophylactic
profyle	profile[2]
profyoos	profuse[2+]
progect	project[1+]
progenitor	
progeny[4]	
progesterone	
proggress	progress[5+]
proginy	progeny[4]
prognosis	@prognoses
program[3] *[schedule, software] ~mable	
	pogrom *[attack on Jewish communities]

progress[5] ~ion ~| report	
progressive ~ly	
prohibit[1]	@prohibition
prohibitive ~ly	
projecshun	projection
project[1] ~ion ~or ~| management	
projectile	
projenitor	progenitor
projeny	progeny[4]
projesteron	progesterone
proklaim	proclaim[1]
proklamashun	proclamation
prokrastinate	procrastinate[2+]
prokreate	procreate[2+]
proksy	proxy[4]
prokure	procure[2+]
prolang	prolong[1+]
prolapse[2]	
proletarian	@proletariat
proliferate[2]	@proliferation
prolific ~ally	
prolitarian	proletarian[+]
prolog	
prolong[1] ~ation	
promenade[2]	
promenince	prominence[+]
prominaid	promenade[2]
prominence	@prominent
promiscuous	@promiscuity
promise[2]	@promissory note
promoshun	promotion[+]
promote[2]	
promotion ~al	
prompt[1] ~ness ~| payment ~| service	
prone	
prong	
pronoun *[grammar]	
pronounce[2] *[announce] ~ment	
pronounciation	pronunciation
pronunciation	
prood	prude[+]
proodense	prudence[+]
proodenshal	prudential
proodins	prudence[+]

proof[1] *[evidence] ~read[1]
prove[2] *[provide evidence]+
proofread[1]
proon — prune[2]
prooriens — prurience+
proove — prove[2] *[provide evidence]+
proof[1] *[evidence]+
prop[3]
propaganda
propagate[2] — @propagator
propagation
propane ~| gas
propegate — propagate[2+]
propel[3] — @propeller
propellant
propensity[4]
proper ~ly ~| fraction
property[4] *[possession, quality] ~| rights ~| values
propriety[4] *[behavior]
prophane — profane[2+]
propane+
prophecy[4] *[prediction]
prophesy[4] *[predict]
prophet *[predictor] ~ic ~ically
profit[1] *[benefit]+
prophylactic
propigait — propagate[2+]
propishiait — propitiate[2]
propishus — propitious+
propitiate[2]
propitious ~ly ~ness
propolis
proporshun — proportion[1]
proportion[1]
proportional ~ity ~ly
proportionate ~ly
proposal *[suggestion, offer of marriage]
propose[2] *[suggest] ~| a toast
proposition *[statement, invitation to casual sex]
preposition *[grammar]+
propound[1]

propownd — propound[1]
propozal — proposal *[suggestion, offer of marriage]
propoze — propose[2] *[suggest]+
proppel — propel[3+]
proprietary *[ownership]
propriety[4] *[behavior]
proprietor
propriety[4] *[behavior]
proprietary *[ownership]
property[4] *[possession, quality]+
propugashin — propagation
propulsion — @propulsive
proqure — procure[2+]
Prosac — Prozac™
prosaic ~ally
prosciutto
proscribe[2] *[forbid]
prescribe[2] *[write an order]
proscription *[ban]
prescription *[order]+
prose
prosecushun — prosecution
prosecute[2] *[in court]
@prosecutor
persecute[2] *[harass]+
prosecution
prosedure — procedure
proseed — proceed[1] *[go on]
precede[2] *[go before]
proseejer — procedure
prosekute — prosecute[2] *[court]+
persecute[2] *[harass]+
proselytize[2]
prosequte — prosecute[2] *[court]+
persecute[2] *[harass]+
proseshin — procession+
prosess — process[5+]
prosicute — prosecute[2] *[court]+
persecute[2] *[harass]+
prosikution — prosecution

proskribe	proscribe[2] *[forbid]
	prescribe[2] *[write an order]
prospect[1] ~ive ~or	
prospectus[5]	
prosper[1]	@prosperity
prosperous ~ly	
prostate *[gland]	prostrate[2] *[flat]
prosthesis	@prostheses
prosthetic ~ally ~s	
prostitute[2]	@prostitution
prostrate[2] *[flat]	prostate *[gland]
protagonist	
protajay	protégé *[man]
	protégée *[woman]
protan	proton
protect[1] ~ion ~ionist ~or	
protective ~ly ~ness ~| gear ~| tariff	
protectorate	
proteen	protein
protégé *[man]	
protégée *[woman]	
protein	
protekt	protect[1+]
protektiv	protective[+]
protektorate	protectorate
protene	protein
protest[1] ~ation	
Protestant ~ism	
protien	protein
protocol	
proton	
prototype	
protozoa	@protozoan
protract[1] ~or	
protrude[2]	@protrusion
protuberance	
protuge	protégé *[man]
	protégée *[woman]
proud[1] ~ly	
provast	provost
prove[2] *[provide evidence]	
	@proven
	proof[1] *[evidence][+]
proveduns	providence
provenance	
proverb ~ial	
provide[2]	
providence	
provident ~ial ~ially	
provied	provide[2]
provieso	proviso
province	@provincial
provinuns	provenance
provirb	proverb[+]
provision ~al ~ally	
proviso	
provocative	
provoke[2]	@provocation
provost	
provyso	proviso
prow	
prowb	probe[2]
prowd	proud[1+]
prowess	
prowl[1]	
prown	prone
proxie	proxy[4]
proximate ~ly	
proximity	
proxy[4]	
Prozac™	
proze	prose
pruboskus	proboscis
prude	@prudery
	@prudish
prudence	@prudent
prudential	
pruf	proof[1] *[evidence][+]
	prove[2] *[provide evidence][+]
prufread	proofread[1]
prumeer	premiere
prune[2]	
pruportion	proportion[1]
prurience	@prurient
pruve	prove[2] *[provide evidence][+]

pry[4] *[loosen, nosy] ~| into ~| open
prey[1] *[kill for food, victim]
pray[1] *[say prayers]
pryde pride[2] *[self-respect]
pryer prior+
prykul prickle[2+]
prym prim[3] *[very proper]+
prime[2] *[height of abilities]+
prymary primary[4+]
pryvasee privacy
psalm ~ist ~ody
pseudo ~ephedrine ~nym
psoriasis
psst *[attention] pissed *[angry, drunk]
psyche @psyched
psychedelic
psychiatrist @psychiatry
psychic ~ally
psycho
psychoanalyst
psychoanalyze[2] @psychoanalysis
psychodrama
psychological ~ly
psychology @psychologist
psychometric ~| test
psychopath ~ic
psychosis
psychosomatic
psychotherapist @psychotherapy
psychotic ~| illness
psykapath psychopath+
psykiatrist psychiatrist+
psyllium *[seed] cilium *[hairlike]+
ptarmigan
pterodactyl
Ptolemaic ~| system
ptomaine ~| poisoning
pu pew *[church seating]
poo *[feces]
pooh *[exclamation]
pub
pubees pubes *[hair]
puberty
pubes *[hair] pubis *[bone]
pubescence @pubescent
pubesinse pubescence+
pubic ~| hair
pubis *[bone] pubes *[hair]
publasize publicize[2+]
public ~| defender ~| domain ~| enemy ~| finance ~| funds ~| holiday ~| image ~| library ~| nuisance ~| opinion ~| relations ~| sector ~| servant ~| service ~| speaking ~| spending ~| television ~| transportation ~| utility

> Unable to find your word under **public**? Take off **public** and look again

publicity ~| campaign ~| department ~| expense
publicize[2] @publicist
publish[5] ~| or perish
publisity publicity+
puburtie puberty
pubys pubis+
puce *[color]
pucific pacific *[peaceful]
Pacific *[Ocean]+
puck *[hockey] puke[2] *[vomit]
pucka pukka *[genuine]
pucker[1] *[lips] ~| up
poker *[game, tool]+
puddel puddle[2] *[water]
puddie putty[4]
puddle[2] *[water] poodle *[dog]
pue pew *[church seating]
puerile
pueter pewter
puff[1] ~| pastry
puffin
puffy[4]
pug ~| mill ~| nose
pugnacious ~ly @pugnacity
pujorativ pejorative
puk puck *[hockey]
puke[2] *[vomit]
puke[2] *[vomit] puck *[hockey]

Key to Spelling Rules

Red words are wrong. **Black** words are correct.

- ~ Add the suffix or word directly to the main word, without a space or hyphen
  e.g. ash ~en ~tray → ashen ashtray
- ~- Add a hyphen to the main word before adding the next word
  e.g. blow ~-dry → blow-dry
- ~| Leave a space between the main word and the next word
  e.g. decimal ~| place → decimal place
- \+ By finding this word in its correct alphabetical order, you can find related words
  e.g. abowt about+ → about-face
- ★ Draws attention to words that may be confused
- ™ Means the word is a trademark
- @ Signifies the word is derived from the main word

puker	pucker[1] *[lips]*
pulce	pulse[2] *[beat]
pulet	pullet
pull[1] *[tug]	pool *[swimming]
pullet	
pulley	
pullp	pulp[1+]

Unable to find your word under **pull**? Look under **pul**

pulmonary	
pulp[1] ~y	
pulpit	
puls	pulse[2] *[beat]
	pulls *[tugs]
pulsar	
pulsate[2]	@pulsation
pulse[2] *[beat]	pulls *[tugs]
pulute	pollute[2+]
pulverize[2]	
puma	
pumckin	pumpkin
pumel	pummel[1] *[beat]
	pommel *[knob]
pumice[2] ~| stone	
pumkin	pumpkin
pummel[1] *[beat]	pommel *[knob]*
pummis	pumice[2+]
pump[1] *[fluid] ~ing station ~| up	
	pomp *[ceremony]*
pumpernickel ~| bread	
pumpkin	
pumuh	puma
pun[3]	
puncchual	punctual*
punch[5] ~es ~| drunk	
puncher *[one who punches]	
	puncture[2] *[pierce]
punchuate	punctuate[2+]
punctilious ~ly ~ness	
punctual ~ity ~ly ~| delivery	
punctuate[2]	@punctuation
puncture[2] *[pierce]	
	puncher *[one who punches]
pundit	
pungent	
punie	puny[4] *[small]
punish[5] ~able ~ment	
punitive ~ly	
punjent	pungent
punkshual	punctual*
punkshuate	punctuate[2+]
punkshure	puncture[2] *[pierce]
punktilious	punctilious*
punktuate	punctuate[2+]
punkture	puncture[2] *[pierce]
punnish	punish[5+]
punt[1]	
puny[4] *[small]	
punysh	punish[5+]
punytive	punitive*
pupa *[of insect] ~e	
	pooper*
pupe	poop[1] *[stern of ship, information, feces]
pupil	
pupit	puppet*
puppa	pupa *[of insect]*
puppet ~eer ~ry	
puppy[4] *[dog] ~| love	
	poppy[4] *[flower]
pur	per *[rate]*
	pure[2] *[clean]*
	purr[1] *[cat]
purade	parade[2]
purady	purity
purafy	purify[4+]
puralisis	paralysis*
purameter	parameter *[function input]
Purana *[Hindu book]	
	piranha *[fish]
puratin	puritan*
puray	purée *[strained food]
purceive	perceive[2]
purch	perch[5+]

purchase[2] ~| order ~| price
purchasing ~| department ~| manager ~| power
purdah
pure[2] *[clean] ~ly ~st
purée *[strained food]
purest *[most pure]
purist *[person]
purey — purée *[strained food]
pure[2] *[clean]+
pureyah — pariah
purfect — perfect[1] *[flawless]+
purfyoom — perfume[2+]
purgatory
purge[2]
purify[4] — @purification
puritan ~ical
purity
purizhin — Parisian *[person from Paris]
purjer — perjure[2+]
purl[1] *[knitting] — pearl *[gem]+
Perl *[computer language]
purloin[1]
purm — perm[1+]
puroll — parole[2] *[release]
payroll *[pay]
purpiss — purpose[2] *[intent]+
porpoise[2] *[animal]
purple *[color]
Purple Heart *[Medal]
purpleks — perplex[5+]
purport[1]
purpose[2] *[intent] ~ly ~-built
porpoise[2] *[animal]
purposeful ~ly
purr[1] *[cat] — per *[rate]+
pure[2] *[clean]+
purrfikt — perfect[1] *[flawless]+
purse[2]
purseed — precede[2] *[go before]
proceed[1] *[go on]
purson — person *[being]+

Unable to find your word under **pur**?
Look under **per**

pursuant
pursue[2] — @pursuable
pursuit
pursunel — personal *[private]+
personnel *[employees]+
purverce — perverse+
purvey[1] ~or
purytan — puritan+
pus *[infection] — puce *[color]
puss *[cat, face]
push[5] ~chair ~over
@pushy[4]
pusillanimity — @pusillanimous
puss *[cat, face] — puce
pus *[infection]
pussy[4] ~| cat ~foot ~| willow
pustramy — pastrami
put *[place] ~ting ~| off ~| through
putt[1] *[golf]
putella — patella
puternil — paternal+
putite — petite
putrefy[4]
putrid
putrol — patrol[3] *[guard rounds]
putt[1] *[golf] — put *[place]+
putter[1] *[golf, work at hobby] ~| around
potter[1] *[makes pots]+
puttrid — putrid
putty[4]
puzzle[2] ~ment
pwerile — puerile
py — pi *[number]
pie *[food]+
pybald — piebald
pycees — Pisces *[Zodiac sign]
pyckle — pickle[2]
pycnic — picnic+
pyella — paella
pyer — pier *[structure]
pyre[2] *[cremation]
Pygmy[4]

Key to Spelling Rules

Red words are wrong. **Black** words are correct.

~ Add the suffix or word directly to the main word, without a space or hyphen
e.g. ash ~en ~tray → ashen ashtray

~- Add a hyphen to the main word before adding the next word
e.g. blow ~-dry → blow-dry

~| Leave a space between the main word and the next word
e.g. decimal ~| place → decimal place

+ By finding this word in its correct alphabetical order, you can find related words
e.g. abowt about+ → about-face

★ Draws attention to words that may be confused

TM Means the word is a trademark

@ Signifies the word is derived from the main word

pyke	pike[2] *[fish, weapon]
pylon *[tower]	
pynt	pint[+]
pyooberdy	puberty
pyp	pip[3] *[seed][+]
	pipe[2] *[tube][+]
pyque	peak *[top][+]
	peek *[look][+]
	Peke *[dog][+]
	pick[1] *[select, tool][+]
	pike[2] *[fish, weapon]
	pique *[anger]
pyr	pyre[2] *[cremation]

pyramid ~| selling	
pyrate	pirate[2+]
pyre[2] *[cremation]	
	pier *[structure]
Pyrex™	
pyromaniac	
pyrotechnics	
Pyrrhic ~| victory	
pysees	Pisces *[Zodiac sign]
pyt	pit[3] *[hole, fight][+]
Pythagoras	@Pythagorean
python	
pyuce	puce *[color]

Q

Q *[Letter] ~| & A ~-tip	
	queue[2][get in line][+]
	cue *[sign]
qake	quake[2]

> Unable to find your word under **qa**?
> Look under **qua**

quack[1] *[duck's sound] ~ery	
	quake[2] *[tremble]
Quacker	Quaker[+]
quad	
Quad Cities [in Iowa and Illinois]	
quadradic	quadratic[+]
quadrangle	@quadrangular
quadrant	
quadratic ~| equation ~| expression ~| function ~| growth	
quadriceps	
quadrilateral	
quadrille	
quadrint	quadrant
quadriplegic	
quadriseps	quadriceps
quadruple[2]	@quadruplet

quadruplicate[2]	
quaff[1]	
quagmire	
quail[1]	
quaint[1] ~ly ~ness	
quake[2] *[tremble]	quack[1] *[duck's sound][+]
Quaker ~ism	
quale	quail[1]
qualify[4]	@qualification
quality[4] ~| assurance ~| control ~| time	
	@qualitative
qualms	
quams	qualms
quandary[4]	
quansa	Kwanzaa *[African American holidays]
quantam	quantum[+]
quante	quaint[1+]
quantify[4]	
quantitative	
quantity[4] ~| discount	
quantum ~| leap ~| mechanics ~| theory	
quanza	Kwanzaa *[African American holidays]
quarantine[2]	

Key to Suffixes and Compounds

These rules are explained on pages vii to ix.

1 Keep the word the same before adding **ed, er, est, ing**
e.g. cool[1] → cooled, cooler, coolest, cooling

2 Take off final **e** before adding **ed, er, est, ing**
e.g. fine[2] → fined, finer, finest, fining

3 Double final consonant before adding **ed, er, est, ing**
e.g. thin[3] → thinned, thinner, thinnest, thinning

4 Change final **y** to **i** before adding **ed, er, es, est, ly, ness**
e.g. tidy[4] → tidied, tidier, tidies, tidiest, tidily, tidiness
Keep final **y** before adding **ing** e.g. tidying

5 Add **es** instead of **s** to the end of the word
e.g. bunch[5] → bunches

6 Change final **f** to **ve** before adding **s**
e.g. calf[6] → calves

quardo quarto
quark *[particle] quirk *[odd behavior]+
quarms qualms
quarrel[3] ~some
quarrie quarry[4]
quarril quarrel[3+]
quarry[4] *[mine, hunted]
quarter[1] ~ly ~back ~deck ~final ~| hour ~master
quartet
quartir quarter[1+]
quarto
quarts *[measurement]
quartz *[mineral] ~ite
quarum quorum
quary quarry[4] *[mine, hunted]
 query[4] *[question]
quasar
quash[5] *[nullify] squash[5] *[crush]
quasi *[as if]
quasir quasar
quasy quasi *[as if]
 queasy[4] *[feeling sick]
quaternary[4]
quatrain
quaver[1]
quay *[by the sea] ~side
 key *[lock, computer, important]
quayver quaver[1]
que cue *[sign]
 queue[2] *[line up]+
quear queer[1] *[strange]+
queasy[4] *[feeling sick]
queen ~ly ~-size ~-sized
queer[1] *[strange] ~ly ~ness
queerulous querulous+
queery query[4] *[question]
queezy queasy[4] *[feeling sick]
quell[1]
quench[5] ~able
querk quark *[particle]
 quirk *[odd behavior]+
Querty QWERTY+
querulous ~ly ~ness

query[4] *[question]
queschin question[1+]
quest[1]
question[1] ~able ~ably ~| mark
questionnaire
queue[2] *[line] ~up
 Q *[letter]
 cue *[sign]
quibble[2]
quiche *[food] ~| lorraine
quick ~ly ~-change artist ~-freeze ~lime ~sand ~silver ~step ~-tempered ~-witted

> Unable to find your word under **quick**?
> Take off **quick** and look again

quicken[1]
quickie
quid ~| pro quo
quien queen+
quier queer[1] *[strange]+
quiery query[4] *[question]
quiescent @quiescence
quiet[1] *[calm] ~ly
 quit *[leave, stop]+
 quite *[completely]
quik quick+
quiken quicken[1]
quiksotic quixotic+
quiky quickie
quill[1]
quilt[1]
quince
quinine
quintessence @quintessential
quintet
quintuple ~t
quip[3]
quire *[paper] choir *[singers]+
 coir *[coconut fiber]
quirk *[odd behavior] ~y
 quark *[particle]
quirty QWERTY+

quit *[leave, stop] ~ter ~ting
quiet[1] *[calm]+
quite *[completely]
quiet[1] *[calm]+
quit *[leave, stop]+
quits
quiver[1]
quixotic ~ally
quiz[3] ~master ~| show
quizzical ~ly
quod quad+
quoda quota
quodruple quadruple[2] *[four times as much]+
quadrupole[1] *[having four poles]+
quollify qualify[4+]
quollitey quality[4+]
quontity quantity[4+]
quork quark *[particle]
quirk *[odd behavior]+
quorrel quarrel[3+]

Unable to find your word under **quo**? Look under **qua**

quorum *[enough members]
Koran *[holy book]
quoruntine quarantine[2]
quosh quash[5] *[nullify]
quoshunt quotient
quota
quotable
quote[2] @quotable
@quotation
quoted ~| company ~| share price
quotient
Qur'an [also spelled Koran]
quorum *[enough members]
qwack quack[1] *[duck's sound]+
quake[2] *[tremble[]
QWERTY ~| keyboard
qwyer quire *[paper]
choir *[singers]+
coir *[coconut fiber]

R

rabbi *[Jewish minister] ~s ~nic ~nical
rabies *[disease]
rabbit *[animal] rabid *[crazy]+
rabble ~-rouser
rabed rabid *[crazy]+
raped *[forced sex]
rabellious rebellious+
rabeys rabies *[disease]
rabbis *[Jewish ministers]+
rabid *[crazy] ~ly
rabbit *[animal]
rabie rabbi *[Jewish minister]+
rabies *[disease] rabbis *[Jewish minister]+
racall recall[1]
raccoon

race[2] *[contest] ~course
raise[2] *[lift]
rays *[light]
race ~horse ~track ~way
rach rash+
racher rasher
rachit ratchet[1]
racial ~ly ~| discrimination
racie racy[4]
racism @racist
rack[1] *[shelf, pain]
rake[2] *[leaves]
racket[1] *[noise, crime] ~eer ~eering *[criminal]

KEY TO SUFFIXES AND COMPOUNDS

These rules are explained on pages vii to ix.

1 Keep the word the same before adding **ed, er, est, ing**
e.g. cool[1] → cooled, cooler, coolest, cooling
2 Take off final **e** before adding **ed, er, est, ing**
e.g. fine[2] → fined, finer, finest, fining
3 Double final consonant before adding **ed, er, est, ing**
e.g. thin[3] → thinned, thinner, thinnest, thinning
4 Change final **y** to **i** before adding **ed, er, es, est, ly, ness**
e.g. tidy[4] → tidied, tidier, tidies, tidiest, tidily, tidiness
Keep final **y** before adding **ing** e.g. tidying
5 Add **es** instead of **s** to the end of the word
e.g. bunch[5] → bunches
6 Change final **f** to **ve** before adding **s**
e.g. calf[6] → calves

racket[1] racquet[1] *[sports]+
rocket[1] *[missile]+
racquet[1] *[sports] ~ball
racket *[noise, crime]+
rocket[1] *[missile]+
racy[4]
radar
raddesh radish[5]
rade raid[1] *[attack]
rayed *[having rays]
raden radon
radial ~| tire
radiance @radiant
@radiantly
radiashun radiation+
radiate[2] @radiator
radiation ~| sickness
radical *[political] ~ly
radicle *[root]
radicalize[2]
radicchio
radicle *[root] radical *[political]+
radikalize radicalize[2]
radikul radicle *[root]
radical *[political]+
radio[1] ~active ~| astronomy ~| broadcast ~-controlled ~frequency ~isotope ~| telescope ~therapy ~| wave
radiographer *[makes X-ray images]
@radiography
radiologist *[studies X-ray images]
@radiology
radish[5]
radium
radius @radii
radix *[number system base]
@radices
radon
radyal radial+

Unable to find your word under **rady**? Look under **radi**

raffea raffia
raffed raft[1]
raffel raffle[2]
raffesh raffish+
raffia
raffish ~ly
raffle[2]
raft[1]
rag *[cloth] ~| doll ~tag ~time
rage[2] *[anger]
Raj *[British India]+
rag ~| trade ~weed ~wort
ragamuffin
rage[2] *[anger] rag *[cloth]+
Raj *[British India]+
ragged *[torn, dirty]
raged *[anger]
ragout
Rahj Raj *[British India]+
rage[2] *[anger]
raid[1] *[attack] rayed *[having rays]
RAID *[redundant array of inexpensive disks]
raij rage[2] *[anger]
Raj *[British India]+
raik rake[2] *[leaves]
raki *[liquor]
rail[1] *[bar, complain] ~road ~way
rale[2] *[chest sound]
railing *[bar, complaining]
raiment
rain[1] *[water] ~bow ~| check ~coat ~drop ~fall ~| forest ~maker ~proof ~storm ~water
reign[1] *[rule]
rein[1] *[horse]+

Unable to find your word under **rain**? Take off **rain** and look again

raindeer reindeer
rainy[4] ~| day
raip rape[2] *[force sex]+
rap[3] *[music, knock]
raise[2] *[lift] rays *[light]
race[2] *[contest]+

Key to Spelling Rules

Red words are wrong. **Black** words are correct.

~ Add the suffix or word directly to the main word, without a space or hyphen
e.g. ash ~en ~tray → ashen ashtray

~- Add a hyphen to the main word before adding the next word
e.g. blow ~-dry → blow-dry

~| Leave a space between the main word and the next word
e.g. decimal ~| place → decimal place

+ By finding this word in its correct alphabetical order, you can find related words
e.g. abowt about+ → about-face

* Draws attention to words that may be confused

TM Means the word is a trademark

@ Signifies the word is derived from the main word

raisin *[fruit]	resin *[sticky]
raison d'être *[reason]	
rait	rate[2] *[amount][+]
raive	rave[2+]
raiven	raven[+]
raivish	ravish[5]
raize	raze[2] *[demolish]
	raise[2] *[lift]
raizer	razor[+]
Raj *[British India]	
	rage[2] *[anger]
rajah *[prince]	roger[1] *[one has heard]
	Roger *[name]
rake[2] *[leaves]	rack[1] *[shelf, pain]
	raki *[liquor]
rakish ~ly	
rakket	racket[1] *[noise, crime][+]
	racquet[1] *[sports][+]
	rocket[1] *[missile][+]
rakontoor	raconteur
rakoon	raccoon
rale *[chest sound]	
	rail[1] *[bar, complain][+]
ralley	rally[4] *[together][+]
	rallye *[motor sport]
	rely[4] *[trust]
ralling	rallying *[together][+]
	railing *[bar, complaining]
rally[4] *[together] ~| around	
	rallye *[motor sport]
	rely[4] *[trust]
rallye *[motor sport]	
	rally[4] *[together][+]
rallying *[together] ~| cry	
ram[3] *[hit, male sheep] ~rod	
RAM *[random access memory]	
	ROM *[read only memory]
Ramadan *[Islamic fasting month]	
rambal	ramble[2]
ramble[2]	
rambunctious ~ly ~ness	
ramekin	
ramen *[noodles]	
rament	raiment
ramify[4]	@ramification
ramp[1]	
rampage[2]	
rampant ~ly	@rampancy
ramparts	
rampent	rampant[+]
ramshackle	
ran *[moved fast]	rain[1] *[water][+]
	run *[fast][+]
ranch[5] ~| dressing ~ing ~| house	
ranchor	rancor *[resentment]
	rancher *[ranch owner]
	ranker *[serves in ranks, assigns ranks, more foul]
rancid ~ity	
ranck	rank[1+]
rancor *[resentment]	
	ranker *[serves in ranks, assigns ranks, more foul]
random ~ly ~ness ~| number ~| sampling	
random-access memory *[RAM]	
	ROM *[read only memory]
randomize[2]	
rane	rain[1] *[water][+]
	reign[1] *[rule]
	rein[1] *[horse][+]
ranegg	renege[2]
raney	rainy[4+]
rang *[did ring]	
range[2] *[wide area] ~finder	
ranje	range[2+]
rank[1] ~ings ~| and file	
rankel	rankle[2]
ranker *[serves in ranks, assigns ranks, more foul]	
	rancor *[resentment]
rankle[2]	
ransack[1]	
ransid	rancid[+]
ransom[1]	
rant[1] ~| and rave[2]	
rantch	ranch[+]
rap[3] *[music, knock]	
	wrap[3] *[pack]
	rape[2] *[force sex][+]

rapacious ~ly ~ness
rapashus rapacious+
rapcher rapture+
rapcidy rhapsody4+
rapd rapped *[music, knocked]
wrapped *[packed]
rapid *[quickly]+
raped *[forced sex]
rape2 *[force sex] @rapist
raped *[forced sex]
rapped *[music, knocked]
rapell rappel3 *[descend]
repel3 *[push away]
rapeseed ~| oil
rapid *[quickly] ~ity ~ly
raped *[forced sex]
rapid ~-fire ~| transit
rapids
rapier *[sword]
rapore rapport
rappar rapper *[singer]
rapport
rapped *[music, knocked]
raped *[forced sex]
rapt *[absorbed]
rapid *[quickly]+
wrapped *[packed]
rappel3 *[descend]
repeal1 *[law]
repel3 *[push away]
rapper *[singer] wrapper *[packing]
rapport *[communication]
report1 *[description, explosion]
rapsody rhapsody4+
rapt *[absorbed] rapped *[music, knocked]
wrapped *[packed]
raped *[forced sex]
rapture @rapturous
rapyer rapier *[sword]
rarafied rarefied+
rare *[scarce] ~ly ~ness
rear1 *[back, horse]
rarefied ~| air ~| atmosphere
rarity4

rasberry raspberry4
rascal ~ly
rascism racism+
rase race2 *[contest]+
raise2 *[lift]
rays *[light]
rash ~ly ~ness
rashal racial+
rashen ration1
rasheo ratio
rasher
rashio ratio
rashnalize rationalize2+
rashonal rational *[logical]+
rationale *[reason]
rashun ration1
rasisum racism+
raskal rascal+
rasmatass razzmatazz
rasp1
raspberry4
Rastafarian @Rasta
raster *[lines of dots] ~| image
roster *[list]
rasy racy4
raszmatasz razzmatazz
rat3 *[rodent] ~bag ~| fink ~hole ~line ~| race ~ty
rate2 *[amount]+
ratan rattan
ratchet1
rate2 *[amount] ~| of exchange ~| of inflation ~| of interest
rat3 *[rodent]+
rather
ratify4 @ratification
ratio
ration1
rational *[logical] ~ly ~| number
rationale *[reason]
rationalist ~ic @rationalism
rationality
rationalize2 @rationalization
rattan
rattle2 ~bag ~snake ~trap

ratty *[run-down] rate[2] *[amount]+
raucous ~ly ~ness
ravage[2] *[devastate]
ravish[5] *[rape, overcome]
ravanous ravenous+
rave[2] ~| review
raveen ravine
raveeoli ravioli
raven *[bird, black] ~-haired
raving *[mad]
ravenous ~ly ~ness
ravige ravage[2] *[devastate]
ravine
raving *[mad] raven *[bird, black]+
ravioli
ravish[5] *[rape, overcome]
ravage[2] *[devastate]
ravishing *[attractive]
ravive revive[2]
ravyoli ravioli
raw[1] *[not cooked] ~ness ~| data ~| deal ~hide ~| materials
roar[1] *[sound]

Unable to find your word under **raw**?
Take off **raw** and look again

rawbin robin+
rawk rock[1+]
rawkus raucous+
ray[1] *[light, fish] ~| gun ~| tracing
rayed *[having rays]
raid[1] *[attack]
raydar radar
rayl rail[1] *[bar, complain]+
rale[2] *[chest sound]
rayment raiment
rayn rain[1] *[water]+
reign[1] *[rule]
rein[1] *[horse]
rayon
rays *[light] race[2] *[contest]+
raise[2] *[lift]
rayser razor+
rayson raisin *[fruit]
raysondette raison d'être *[meaning]
raze[2] *[demolish] raise[2] *[lift]
razor ~back ~bill ~| blade ~-edged ~-sharp
razp rasp[1]
razzle-dazzle
razzmatazz
reach[5] *[come to a point]
retch[5] *[vomit]
rich[5] *[wealthy]+
wretch *[miserable person]+
react[1] ~ive ~or

Unable to find your word under **re**?
Take off **re** and look again

reaction @reactionary[4]
read *[book] ~able ~ing ~out
red[3] *[color]+
reed *[plant]
readdress[5]
reader ~ship
readjust[1] ~ment
readmission
readmit[3] @readmittance
ready[4] ~-made ~-mix ~-to-wear
reaffirm[1] ~ation
reak
reakchun reaction+
reakt react[1+]
real *[genuine] ~| estate ~| time ~| world
reel[1] *[film, spin]
realism @realist
realistic ~ally
reality[4] *[truth] realty *[real estate]
realize[2] @realizable
@realization
realizm realism+
reallocate[2] @reallocation
really *[actually] rely[4] *[trust]
realm
Realtor™
realty *[real estate]
reality[4] *[truth]

Key to Suffixes and Compounds

These rules are explained on pages vii to ix.

1 Keep the word the same before adding **ed, er, est, ing**
e.g. cool[1] → cooled, cooler, coolest, cooling
2 Take off final **e** before adding **ed, er, est, ing**
e.g. fine[2] → fined, finer, finest, fining
3 Double final consonant before adding **ed, er, est, ing**
e.g. thin[3] → thinned, thinner, thinnest, thinning
4 Change final **y** to **i** before adding **ed, er, es, est, ly, ness**
e.g. tidy[4] → tidied, tidier, tidies, tidiest, tidily, tidiness
Keep final **y** before adding **ing** e.g. tidying
5 Add **es** instead of **s** to the end of the word
e.g. bunch[5] → bunches
6 Change final **f** to **ve** before adding **s**
e.g. calf[6] → calves

ream *[of paper]	REM *[rapid eye movement]
reanimate[2]	@reanimation
reap[1] *[harvest]	rip[3] *[tear]+
reappear[1] ~ance	
reappoint[1] ~ment	
reapportion[1]	
reappraise[2]	@reappraisal
rear[1] *[back, horse, raise] ~| admiral ~| end ~guard	
	rare *[scarce]+
rearm[1] ~ament	
rearrange[2] ~ment	
reashurance	reassurance
reashure	reassure[2]
reason[1] *[explain, explanation]+	
	resin *[sticky]
	rezone[2] *[change zoning]
reassemble[2] *[make again]	
	resemble[2] *[look like]+
reassert[1] ~ion	
reassess[5] ~ment	
reassurance	
reassure[2]	
reassuringly	
reatch	reach[5] *[come to a point]
	retch[5] *[vomit]
reawaken[1]	
rebait	rebate[2]
rebal	rebel[3+]
rebar *[steel]	
rebate[2]	
rebel[3]	@rebellion
rebellious ~ly ~ness	
rebild	rebuild+
rebirth[1]	@reborn
rebound[1]	
rebuff[1]	
rebuild ~ing	@rebuilt
rebuke[2]	
rebul	rebel[3+]
reburth	rebirth[1+]

rebut[3] ~tal	
rebyook	rebuke[2]
recalcitrance	@recalcitrant
recall[1]	
recammend	recommend[1+]
recant[1] *[not true]	
	recent *[just past]+
recap[3]	
recapitulate[2]	@recapitulation
recapture[2]	
recast ~ing	
recede[2] *[farther]	@receding hairline
	reseed *[plant again]
receeve	receive[2+]
receipt[1] *[document]	
	reseat[1] *[seat again]
receivables	
receive[2]	@receivable
receiver ~ship	
recent *[just past] ~ly	
	re-sent *[sent again]
	resent[1] *[grudge]+
receptacle	
reception ~| desk ~ist ~-room	
receptive ~ness	
receptivity	
receptor	
receshun	recession+
recess ~ed	
recession ~ary	
recessive ~ly ~ness	
rech	reach[5] *[come to a point]
	retch[5] *[vomit]
	rich *[wealthy]+
recharge[2] ~able	
recidivism	@recidivist
recievables	receivables
reciever	receiver+
recind	rescind[1]
recipe	
recipient	
reciprocal ~ly ~| agreement	
	@reciprocity
reciprocate[2]	@reciprocation

Key to Spelling Rules

Red words are wrong. **Black** words are correct.

~ Add the suffix or word directly to the main word, without a space or hyphen
e.g. ash ~en ~tray → ashen ashtray

~- Add a hyphen to the main word before adding the next word
e.g. blow ~-dry → blow-dry

~| Leave a space between the main word and the next word
e.g. decimal ~| place → decimal place

\+ By finding this word in its correct alphabetical order, you can find related words
e.g. abowt about+ → about-face

★ Draws attention to words that may be confused

TM Means the word is a trademark

@ Signifies the word is derived from the main word

recite[2] *[speak] @recital
@recitation
resight[1] *[observe agan]
resite[2] *[relocate]
reck
reckin reckon[1]
reckless ~ly ~ness
reckon[1]
reckoncilable reconcilable
reckonoiter reconnoiter[1]
reclaim[1] @reclamation
reclassify[4] @reclassification
recline[2]
recluse
recoarse recourse[+]
recognizable
recognize[2] @recognition
recoil[1]
recollect[1] ~ion
recommence[2]
recommend[1] ~able ~ation
recompense[2]
reconcilable
reconcile[2] @reconciliation
recondition[1]
reconker reconquer[1]
reconnaissance
reconnect[1]
reconnoiter[1]
reconquer[1]
reconsider[1] ~ation
reconsilable reconcilable
reconsile reconcile[2+]
reconstitute[2] @reconstitution
reconstruct[1] ~ion
reconstructive ~| surgery
reconvene[2]
recooperate recuperate[2+]
recooperativ recuperative[+]
record[1] ~-breaking ~| high ~-making
recorded ~| delivery ~| message
recorse recourse[+]
recount[1] *[tell, count again]
recoup[1] ~ment
recourse ~| loan

recover[1] ~able ~| assets
recovery[4] ~| room
recownt recount[1] *[tell, count again]
recreate[2] *[play] @recreation
re-create[2] *[make again]
recrimination
recruit[1] ~ment
rectangle @rectangular
recter rector[+]
rectify[4] @rectifier
@rectifiable
@rectification
rectitude
rector @rectory[4]
rectum @rectal
recuperate[2] @recuperation
recuperative ~| powers
recur[3]
recurrence @recurrent
recuse[2]
recussitate resuscitate[2+]
recycle[2]
red[3] *[color] ~| alert ~-blooded ~-brick ~-carpet ~| cent ~coat ~dish ~-eye ~-faced ~-handed ~| herring ~-hot ~-light district ~line ~neck ~| tape ~wood
read *[book][+]
reed *[water grass]

Unable to find your word under **red**?
Take off **red** and look again

Red Cross *[organization]
redaploy redeploy[1+]
redden[1]
reddy ready[4+]
redeam redeem[1+]
redecorate[2] @redecoration
redeem[1] ~able
redemption @redemptive ~| clause
redeploy[1] ~ment
rederick rhetoric[+]
redevelop[1] ~ment

Key to Suffixes and Compounds

These rules are explained on pages vii to ix.

1 Keep the word the same before adding **ed, er, est, ing**
e.g. cool[1] → cooled, cooler, coolest, cooling
2 Take off final **e** before adding **ed, er, est, ing**
e.g. fine[2] → fined, finer, finest, fining
3 Double final consonant before adding **ed, er, est, ing**
e.g. thin[3] → thinned, thinner, thinnest, thinning
4 Change final **y** to **i** before adding **ed, er, es, est, ly, ness**
e.g. tidy[4] → tidied, tidier, tidies, tidiest, tidily, tidiness
Keep final **y** before adding **ing** e.g. tidying
5 Add **es** instead of **s** to the end of the word
e.g. bunch[5] → bunches
6 Change final **f** to **ve** before adding **s**
e.g. calf[6] → calves

redial^{3}
redid
rediffusion
redile redial^{3}
redirect^{1} ~ion
redistribute^{2} @redistribution
redistrict ~ing
rediyal redial^{3}
redo ~ing
redolence @redolent
redone
redoosed reduced^{+}
redouble^{2}
redress^{5}
reduce^{2} @reduction
reduced ~| rate ~| size
redundancy^{4} @redundant
reech reach^{5} *[come to a point]
retch^{5} *[vomit]
rich^{5} *[wealthy]$^{+}$
reecoo recoup^{1+}
reed *[plant] read *[book]$^{+}$
reeder reader^{+}
reedo redo^{+}
reef^{1} *[underwater, take in sail] ~| knot
reefer *[refrigerated truck, marijuana]
refer^{3} *[pass on]
reek^{1} *[stink] wreak^{1} *[havoc, ruin]
reel^{1} *[film, spin] real *[genuine]$^{+}$
reelay relay^{1+}
reelect^{1} ~ion

> Unable to find your word under **re**?
> Take off **re** and look again

reelter Realtor™
reely really *[actually]
rely^{4} *[trust]
reem ream *[of paper]
re-enact^{1} ~ment
reenal renal
re-engineer^{1}
re-enter^{1}
re-entry^{4}
reep reap^{1} *[harvest]
reer rear^{1} *[back, horse]$^{+}$
reesent recent *[just past]$^{+}$
re-sent *[sent again]
reeson reason^{1} *[explain, explanation]$^{+}$
re-establish^{5} ~ment
refer^{3} *[pass on] reefer *[refrigerated truck, marijuana]
referee *[official] ~d ~ing
reference ~| number
referendum @referenda
referent ~ial
referral
referse reverse^{2+}
refill^{1} *[fill again] ~able
refine^{2} ~ment
refinery^{4}
refit^{3}
reflate^{2}
reflecks reflex^{5} *[automatic response]$^{+}$
reflect^{1} *[bounce light, think] ~ive ~or
reflection ~| symmetry
reflex^{5} *[automatic response] ~ive pronoun
reflux^{5} *[backward flow]$^{+}$
refloat^{1}
reflux^{5} *[backward flow]
reflex^{5} *[automatic response]$^{+}$
reform^{1} *[change] ~ation ~| school
re-form^{1} *[make again]
reformat^{3}
refract^{1} *[bend light] ~ion ~ive
refrain^{1}
refrence reference^{+}
refresh^{5} ~ment
refresher ~| course
refried ~| beans
refrigerate^{2} @refrigerator
refrigeration
refuel^{3}
refuge *[shelter]
refugee *[fugitive]
refulgent *[brilliant]

KEY TO SPELLING RULES

Red words are wrong. **Black** words are correct.

~ Add the suffix or word directly to the main word, without a space or hyphen
e.g. ash ~en ~tray → ashen ashtray

~- Add a hyphen to the main word before adding the next word
e.g. blow ~-dry → blow-dry

~| Leave a space between the main word and the next word
e.g. decimal ~| place → decimal place

\+ By finding this word in its correct alphabetical order, you can find related words
e.g. abowt about^{+} → about-face

★ Draws attention to words that may be confused

™ Means the word is a trademark

@ Signifies the word is derived from the main word

refund[1] ~able deposit
refurbish[5]
refuree — referee *[official][+]
refurendum — referendum[+]
refuse[2] *[garbage, reject] @refusal
refute[2] @refutable @refutal
regain[1]
regal *[king] ~ia ~ly
regale[2] *[entertain]
regalia *[symbolic ornaments]
regard[1] ~less
regatta
regay — reggae
regect — reject[1+]
regency[4] @regent
regenerate[2] @regeneration
regenerative
regergitate — regurgitate[2]
reggae
regicide @regicidal
regime *[government] ~| change
regimen *[treatment plan]
regiment[1] *[military unit] ~al ~ation
region ~al ~alism ~ally
register[1] *[record] ~variable
registered ~| letter ~| nurse
registrar @registry[4]
registration @number
reglate — regulate[2+]
regler — regular[+]
regress[5] ~ion ~ive
regret[3] ~ful ~fully
regrettable @regrettably
regular ~| expression ~ity ~ly ~| size
regularize[2]
regulate[2] @regulator
regulation
regurgitate[2]
rehabilitate[2] @rehabilitation
rehash[5]
rehearse[2] @rehearsal
reheat[1]
rehouse[2]

reicipyent — recipient
reign[1] *[rule] — rain[1] *[water][+] rein[1] *[horse][+]
reimburse[2] ~ment
rein[1] *[horse] ~| in — rain[1] *[water][+] reign[1] *[rule]
reincarnate[2] @reincarnation
reindeer
reinforce[2] ~ment
reinforced ~| concrete
reinstate[2] ~ment
reinvent[1] ~ion ~| the wheel
reinvest[1] ~ment
reippoint — reappoint[1+]
reiterate[2] @reiteration
reject[1] ~ion
rejeem — regime *[government][+]
rejistur — register[1] *[record][+]
rejoice[2] @rejoicingly
rejoin[1] ~der
rejoise — rejoice[2+]
rejuce — reduce[2+]
rejuvenate[2] @rejuvenation
rekall — recall[1]
rekerd — record[1+]
rekindle[2]
rekkanoyta — reconnoiter[1]
reknown — renown *[fame][+]
rekonsider — reconsider[1+]
rekooperate — recuperate[2+]
rekord — record[1+]
rekover — recover[1+]
rekovery — recovery[4+]
rektangle — rectangle[+]
rektify — rectify[4+]

Unable to find your word under **rek**?
Look under **rec**

rekwiem — requiem
rekwisite — requisite[+]
rekwited — requited[+]
relate[2]
relation ~al ~ship

KEY TO SUFFIXES AND COMPOUNDS

These rules are explained on pages vii to ix.

1 Keep the word the same before adding **ed, er, est, ing**
e.g. cool[1] → cooled, cooler, coolest, cooling
2 Take off final **e** before adding **ed, er, est, ing**
e.g. fine[2] → fined, finer, finest, fining
3 Double final consonant before adding **ed, er, est, ing**
e.g. thin[3] → thinned, thinner, thinnest, thinning
4 Change final **y** to **i** before adding **ed, er, es, est, ly, ness**
e.g. tidy[4] → tidied, tidier, tidies, tidiest, tidily, tidiness
Keep final **y** before adding **ing** e.g. tidying
5 Add **es** instead of **s** to the end of the word
e.g. bunch[5] → bunches
6 Change final **f** to **ve** before adding **s**
e.g. calf[6] → calves

relative ~ly ~| frequency ~| strengths
relativism *[philosophy]
  @relativist
relativity *[physics]
  @relativistic
relax[5] ~ation
relay[1] ~| race
release[2] ~| date
relegate[2] @relegation
relent[1] ~less ~lessly
reletive relative+
relevance @relevant
reliable @reliability
  @reliably
reliance @reliant
relic
relidjeous religious+
relief ~| effort
relieve[2] @relievable
religion
religious ~ly ~ness ~| value
relinquish[5] ~ment
relish[5]
relm realm
reload[1]
relocate[2] @relocation
reluctance
reluctant ~ly
rely[4] *[trust] really *[actually]
REM ream *[of paper]
remain[1] ~s
remainder *[left over]
  reminder *[memory]
remake @remaking
  @remade
remand[1]
remaniss reminisce[2+]
remark[1] ~able ~ably
remarry[4]
rematch

> Unable to find your word under **re**?
> Take off **re** and look again

reme ream *[of paper]
  REM *[rapid eye movement]
remedial ~| remediation
remedy[4]
remember[1] @remembrance
remind[1] ~er
reminder *[memory]
  remainder *[left over]
reminisce[2] ~nce ~nt
remiss
remission
remit[3] ~tal ~tance
remix[5]
remoat remote[2+]
remodel[3]
remonstrance
remonstrate[2] @remonstration
remorse ~ful ~fully
remorseless ~ly ~ness
remote[2] ~ly ~ness ~| control ~| location
removal
remove[2] @removable
remunerate[2] @remuneration
renaissance *[rebirth]
Renaissance *[historic period]
renal
rend[1]
render[1]
rendezvous[1]
rendition
renegade
renege[2]
renegotiate[2]
renew[1] ~able ~al
renoun renown *[fame]+
renounce[2] ~ment
renounciation renunciation
renovate[2] @renovation
renown *[fame] ~ed
rent[1] ~-free
rental ~| income ~| property[4]
renunciation
reoccupy[4]

Key to Spelling Rules

Red words are wrong. **Black** words are correct.

~ Add the suffix or word directly to the main word, without a space or hyphen
e.g. ash ~en ~tray → ashen ashtray

~- Add a hyphen to the main word before adding the next word
e.g. blow ~-dry → blow-dry

~| Leave a space between the main word and the next word
e.g. decimal ~| place → decimal place

+ By finding this word in its correct alphabetical order, you can find related words
e.g. abowt about+ → about-face

★ Draws attention to words that may be confused

TM Means the word is a trademark

@ Signifies the word is derived from the main word

reoonion reunion+
reopen[1]
reorganize[2] @reorganization
reorient[1] @re-orientation
repaid
repair[1] ~| man
reparable @reparation
repartee
repatriate[2] @repatriation
repay ~able ~ing ~ment
repatwah repertoire+
repeal[1] *[law] repel[3] *[push away]
repeat[1] ~able ~edly ~| order
repel[3] *[push away]
repeal[1] *[law]
rappel[3] *[descend]
repellent
repent[1] ~ance ~ant
repercussion
repertoire @repertory
repetition @repetitious
repetitive ~ly ~ness
replace[2] ~able ~ment
replay[1]
replenish[5] ~ment
replete
replica
replicate[2] @replication
reply[4]
report[1] *[description, explosion] ~able ~edly
rapport *[communication]
repose[2]
repository[4]
repossess[5]
repreeze reprise[2]+
reprehend[1] @reprehension
reprehensible @reprehensibly
represent[1] ~ation ~ative
repress[5] ~ible ~ion ~ive
reprieve[2]
reprimand[1]
reprint[1]
reprise[2] @reprisal
reproach[5] ~ful ~fully

reprobate[2]
reproduce[2] @reproducible
reproduction @reproductive
reproof *[criticism]
reprove[2] *[criticize]
@reprovingly
reptile @reptilian
republic ~an ~anism *[form of government]
Republican *[U.S. political party]
repudiate[2] @repudiation
repugnance @repugnant
repulse[2] @repulsion
repulsive ~ly ~ness
reputation @reputable
repute ~d ~dly
requer recur[3]
reques recuse[2]
request[1]
requiem
require[2] ~ment
requisite @requisition
requited ~| love
requring recurring+
rere rare+
rear[1] *[back, horse]+
rerifide rarefied+
rerite rewrite+
rerity rarity[4]
rerote rewrote
resadent resident
rescind[1]
rescue[2]
research[5] ~and development [R & D]
reseat[1] *[seat again]
receipt[1] *[document]
reseed *[plant again]
recede[2] *[farther]+
reseet reseat[1] *[seat again]
receipt[1] *[document]
reseeve receive[2]+
resemble[2] *[look like]
@resemblance
reassemble[2] *[make again]

Key to Suffixes and Compounds

These rules are explained on pages vii to ix.

1 Keep the word the same before adding **ed, er, est, ing**
e.g. cool[1] → cooled, cooler, coolest, cooling
2 Take off final **e** before adding **ed, er, est, ing**
e.g. fine[2] → fined, finer, finest, fining
3 Double final consonant before adding **ed, er, est, ing**
e.g. thin[3] → thinned, thinner, thinnest, thinning
4 Change final **y** to **i** before adding **ed, er, es, est, ly, ness**
e.g. tidy[4] → tidied, tidier, tidies, tidiest, tidily, tidiness
Keep final **y** before adding **ing** e.g. tidying
5 Add **es** instead of **s** to the end of the word
e.g. bunch[5] → bunches
6 Change final **f** to **ve** before adding **s**
e.g. calf[6] → calves

resent[1] *[grudge] ~ment
recent *[just past]+
re-sent *[sent again]
resentful ~ly ~ness
resepshun reception+
reseptacle receptacle
reserface resurface[2]
resergence resurgence+
reserrect resurrect[1+]
reservation
reserve[2] ~| bank ~| currency ~| price
reservist
reservoir
resess recess+
resession recession+
reset[3] ~button
resettle[2] ~ment
reshape[2]
reshuffle[2]

Unable to find your word under **re**?
Take off **re** and look again

reside[2]
residence @residency[4] ~| permit
resident
residential
residew residue+
residivism recidivism+
residivisum recidivism+
residue @residual
resight[1] *[observe again]
recite[2] *[speak]+
resite[2] *[relocate]
resign[1] *[leave] resin *[sticky]
risen *[arose]
resignation
resikal recycle[2]
resilience
resilient ~ly
resin *[sticky] raisin *[grape]
resign[1] *[leave]
risen *[arose]
resint recent *[just past]+
resipee recipe
resipient recipient
resiprocal reciprocal+
resiprocate reciprocate[2+]
resipy recipe
resissed resist[1+]
resist[1] ~ant ~ance
resister *[person]
resistible @resistibility
@resistibly
resistor *[electrical]
resite[2] *[relocate] recite[2] *[speak]+
resight[1] *[observe again]

Unable to find your word under **res**?
Look under **rec**

resize[2]
reskue rescue[2]
resolute ~ly ~ness
resolution
resolve[2]
resonance @resonant
resonate[2] @resonator
resondetre raison d'être *[reason]
resonense resonance+
resort[1]
resound[1]
resource ~ful ~fully
respect[1] ~ful ~fully
respectable @respectability
@respectably
respective ~ly
respiration
respire[2] @respirator
respite
resplendence @resplendent
respond[1] ~ent
response
responsibility[4]
responsible @responsibly
responsive ~ly ~ness
ressel wrestle[2]
ressin resin *[sticky]
reason[1] *[explain, explanation]+

Key to Spelling Rules

Red words are wrong. **Black** words are correct.

~ Add the suffix or word directly to the main word, without a space or hyphen
e.g. ash ~en ~tray → ashen ashtray

~- Add a hyphen to the main word before adding the next word
e.g. blow ~-dry → blow-dry

~| Leave a space between the main word and the next word
e.g. decimal ~| place → decimal place

+ By finding this word in its correct alphabetical order, you can find related words
e.g. abowt about+ → about-face

★ Draws attention to words that may be confused

TM Means the word is a trademark

@ Signifies the word is derived from the main word

ressipee recipe
resstront restaurant
rest[1] *[relax, sleep] ~| assured ~| home ~| room
wrest[1] *[pull away]
restate[2]
restaurant
restful ~ly ~ness
restitution
restive ~ly ~ness
restless ~ly ~ness
restorative
restore[2] @restoration
restrain[1] ~ing order
@restraint
restrict[1] ~ion
restrictive ~| practises
restructure[2]
result[1] ~ant
resume[2] *[restart]
résumé *[summary]
resumption
resurface[2]
resurgence @resurgent
resurrect[1] ~ion
resurvor reservoir
resus rhesus⁺
resuscitate[2] @resuscitation
resycle recycle[2]
retacent reticent⁺
retacince reticence
retahd retard[1+]
retired
retail[1] ~| goods ~| outlets ~| price
retain[1]
retake ~n @retaking
retale retail[1+]
retaliate[2] @retaliation
retaliatory
retane retain[1]
retard[1] ~ation @retarded
retired
retayl retail[1+]
retch[5] *[vomit] reach[5] *[come to a point]
rich[5] *[wealthy]⁺

retch[5] *[vomit] wretch *[miserable person]⁺
retena retina
retention @retentive
reterick rhetoric⁺
retern return[1+]
rethink ~ing
retiar retire[2+]
reticence
reticent ~ly
retina
retinue
retire[2] ~ment age
retired retard[1+]
retisense reticence
retisent reticent⁺
retold
retook
retool[1]
retoric rhetoric⁺
retort[1]
retouch[5]
retoul retool[1]
retourt retort[1]
retrace[2]
retract[1] ~able ~ion
retrad retrod *[walked again]⁺
retread[1] *[walk again, tire]
retraise retrace[2]
retrakt retract[1+]
retrawed retrod *[walked again]⁺
retread[1] *[walk again, tire]
retreat[1] *[move back]
retred retread[1] *[walk again, tire]
retreeval retrieval⁺
retreiver retriever
retrench[5] ~ment
retrete retreat[1] *[move back]
retrial
retribution
retrieval ~| system
retrieve[2] @retrievable
retriever

Key to Suffixes and Compounds

These rules are explained on pages vii to ix.

1 Keep the word the same before adding **ed, er, est, ing**
e.g. cool[1] → cooled, cooler, coolest, cooling
2 Take off final **e** before adding **ed, er, est, ing**
e.g. fine[2] → fined, finer, finest, fining
3 Double final consonant before adding **ed, er, est, ing**
e.g. thin[3] → thinned, thinner, thinnest, thinning
4 Change final **y** to **i** before adding **ed, er, es, est, ly, ness**
e.g. tidy[4] → tidied, tidier, tidies, tidiest, tidily, tidiness
Keep final **y** before adding **ing** e.g. tidying
5 Add **es** instead of **s** to the end of the word
e.g. bunch[5] → bunches
6 Change final **f** to **ve** before adding **s**
e.g. calf[6] → calves

retro ~active ~fit ~-rocket
retroactive
retrod *[walked again] ~den
retroevirus — retrovirus
retrograde
retrogress[5] ~ion ~ive
retrospect ~ion ~ive
retrovirus
retrowactive — retroactive
retryal — retrial
retsh — retch[5] *[vomit]
reach[5] *[come to a point]
rich[5] *[wealthy]+
retuch — retouch[5]
retule — retool[1]
return[1] ~able ~| address ~| envelope ~| match ~| on investment [ROI] ~| postage
reubella — rubella
reubrick — rubric
reuhpraise — reappraise[2]+
reumatisum — rheumatism
reumatoid — rheumatoid+
reunion — @reunite[2]
reupholster[1]
reuse[2]
Reuters™
rev[3] ~| up
reval — revel[1] *[fun]+
revallee — reveille
revalue[2] — @revaluation

> Unable to find your word under **re**?
> Take off **re** and look again

revamp[1]
revanue — revenue+
reveal[1] *[show] — revel[1] *[fun]+
reveer — revere[2]
revehl — reveille
reveille *[wake up]
revelry[4] *[fun]+
reveal[1] *[show]
revile[2] *[insult]+

reveiw — review[1] *[survey]
revue *[entertainment]
revel[1] *[fun] ~s
revelry[4] *[fun] — reverie *[daydream]
revelashun — revelation
revelation
revele — reveal[1] *[show]
reveille *[wake up]
revel[1] *[fun]
revenge[2] ~ful ~fully
revenue ~| bond
reverberate[2] — @reverberation
revere[2] *[honor]
reveree — reverie *[daydream]
revelry[4] *[fun]
referee *[official]+
reverence
Reverend *[minister]
reverent *[respectful] ~ly
reverie *[daydream]
revere *[honor]
revelry[4] *[fun]
reveille *[wake up]
reverint — Reverend *[minister]
reverent *[respectful]+
reversal
reverse[2] ~| charge ~| discrimination ~| gear ~| takeover
@reversible
revert[1] — @reversion
revery — reverie *[daydream]
revelry[4] *[fun]
revial — revile[2]
reviir — revere[2]
revil — reveal[1]
revel[1]+
revile[2] *[insult]+
revile[2] *[insult] ~ment
reveille *[wake up]
revise[2]
revision ~ist
revisit[1]
revitalize[2] — @revitalization
revival ~ist
revive[2]

Key to Spelling Rules

Red words are wrong. **Black** words are correct.

~ Add the suffix or word directly to the main word, without a space or hyphen
e.g. ash ~en ~tray → ashen ashtray

~- Add a hyphen to the main word before adding the next word
e.g. blow ~-dry → blow-dry

~| Leave a space between the main word and the next word
e.g. decimal ~| place → decimal place

+ By finding this word in its correct alphabetical order, you can find related words
e.g. abowt about+ → about-face

★ Draws attention to words that may be confused

™ Means the word is a trademark

@ Signifies the word is derived from the main word

revize	revise[2]
revizhun	revision[+]
revizit	revisit[1]
revocation	
revoke[2]	@revocable
revolled	revolt[1]
revolshun	revolution *[overturning][+]
	revulsion *[disgust]
revolt[1]	
revolution *[overturning] ~ize[2]	
revolutionary[4]	
revolutshunary	revolutionary[4]
revolve[2]	
revolver	
revry	reverie *[daydream]
revue *[entertainment]	
	review[1] *[survey]
revulsion *[disgust]	
revurse	reverse[2+]
rew	rue[2] *[regret][+]
reward[1]	
rewarred	reward[1]
rewbella	rubella
rewbric	rubric
rewd	rude[2] *[offensive][+]
	rued *[regretted]
rewind ~ing	
reword[1]	
rework[1]	
rewound	
rewrite	@rewriting
	@rewritten
rewrote	
rewse	ruse[2]
	reuse[2]
rewurd	reword[1]
rewurk	rework[1]
reyaddress	readdress[5]

> Unable to find your word under **rey**?
> Look under **re**

rezervist	reservist
rezidue	residue[+]
rezolution	resolution
rezone[2] *[change zoning]	
	reason[1] *[explain, explanation][+]

> Unable to find your word under **re**?
> Take off **re** and look again

rezurv	reserv[2]
rezuvwah	reservoir

> Unable to find your word under **rez**?
> Look under **res**

Rhamadan	Ramadan *[Islamic fasting month]
rhapsody[4]	@rhapsodise[2]
rhesus ~| monkey	
rhetoric ~al question	
rheumatic ~| fever	
rheumatism	
rheumatoid ~| arthritis	
Rhine *[river]	rind *[skin]
rhinestone	
rhino	@rhinoceros[5]
rho *[Greek letter]	roe *[deer, fish][+]
	row[1] *[boat, line, noise]
rhobe	robe[2] *[clothing]

> Unable to find your word under **rho**?
> Look under **ro**

Rhodes Scholar	
rhodium	
rhododendron	
rhomboid	
rhombus[5]	@rhombi
rhondo	rondo
rhoot	root[1] *[plant][+]
rhubarb	
rhug	rug *[floor covering]
rhum	rum *[liquor]
rhunt	runt

> Unable to find your word under **rhu**?
> Look under **ru**

KEY TO SUFFIXES AND COMPOUNDS

These rules are explained on pages vii to ix.

1 Keep the word the same before adding **ed, er, est, ing**
e.g. cool[1] → cooled, cooler, coolest, cooling

2 Take off final **e** before adding **ed, er, est, ing**
e.g. fine[2] → fined, finer, finest, fining

3 Double final consonant before adding **ed, er, est, ing**
e.g. thin[3] → thinned, thinner, thinnest, thinning

4 Change final **y** to **i** before adding **ed, er, es, est, ly, ness**
e.g. tidy[4] → tidied, tidier, tidies, tidiest, tidily, tidiness
Keep final **y** before adding **ing** e.g. tidying

5 Add **es** instead of **s** to the end of the word
e.g. bunch[5] → bunches

6 Change final **f** to **ve** before adding **s**
e.g. calf[6] → calves

rhyme[2] *[poetry] rime[2] *[frost]
rim[3] *[edge]+
rhythm ~| and blues
rhythmic ~al ~ally
riact react[1+]

> Unable to find your word under **ri**?
> Look under **re**

rial rile[2]
rib[3] ~| steak
ribald ~ry
ribbon
rice *[food] rise *[up]+
rich[5] *[wealthy] ~ly ~ness
richous righteous+
Richter ~| scale
richual ritual+
rickets *[disease]
rickety *[unstable]
rickoshay ricochet[1]
rickshaw
rickter Richter Scale
ricochet[1]
rid[3] @riddance
riddel riddle[2]
ridden
riddle[2]
ride @rider
@riding
ridge ~d
ridicule[2]
ridiculous ~ly ~ness
riep ripe[2] *[ready to eat]+
reap[1] *[harvest]
rip[3] *[tear]+
rife
rifectory refectory[4]
rifel rifle[2] *[gun, plunder]+
rifer reefer *[refrigerated truck, marijuana]
refer[3] *[pass on]
river+
riff *[music] rift *[division]+

riffraff *[disreputable person]
riprap *[rough wall]
rifill refill[1] *[fill again]+
rifle[2] *[gun, plunder]+
rifine refine[2+]
rifinery refinery[4]
riflate reflate[2]
rifle[2] *[gun, plunder] ~man ~| range
riflect reflect[1+]
rift *[division] ~| valley
riff *[music]
rig[3] *[equipment] ~| up
rigged *[equipped]
rigid *[unbending]+
rigger *[one who rigs]
rigor *[stiffness]+
righf rife
right[1] *[correct] ~ly ~| angle ~| hand ~| of way
rite *[ceremony]
write *[text]
righteous ~ly ~ness
rightful ~ly ~| owner
right-hand @right-handed
rights ~| issue
right-wing
rigid *[unbending] ~ity ~ly
rigged *[equipped]
rigmarole
rigor *[stiffness] ~| mortis
rigger *[one who rigs]
Rihch Reich
rijid rigid *[unbending]+
rikant recant[1] *[not true]
Rike Reich
rikkety rickety *[unstable]
rikoko rococo
rikter Richter+
rile[2]
rim[3] *[edge] ~less
rhyme[2] *[poetry]
rime[2] *[frost]
rimain remain[1+]
rime[2] *[frost] rhyme[2] *[poetry]
rim[3] *[edge]+

Key to Spelling Rules

Red words are wrong. **Black** words are correct.

~ Add the suffix or word directly to the main word, without a space or hyphen
e.g. ash ~en ~tray → ashen ashtray

~- Add a hyphen to the main word before adding the next word
e.g. blow ~-dry → blow-dry

~| Leave a space between the main word and the next word
e.g. decimal ~| place → decimal place

\+ By finding this word in its correct alphabetical order, you can find related words
e.g. abowt about+ → about-face

★ Draws attention to words that may be confused

TM Means the word is a trademark

@ Signifies the word is derived from the main word

rince	**rinse**[2]
rind *[skin]	**Rhine** *[river]
rinegg	**renege**[2]
rinestone	**rhinestone**
ring[1] *[bell, circle] ~ing ~| finger ~leader ~master ~side ~worm	
	rink *[event place]
	wring *[squeeze]+
ringer *[one who rings, substitute]	
	wringer *[squeezer]+
ringlet	
rink *[event place]	
	ring[1] *[bell, circle]+
rino	**rhino**+
rinse[2]	
riot[1] ~ous ~ously	
rip[3] *[tear] ~-cord ~-off ~-roaring ~saw	
	ripe[2] *[ready to eat]+
	reap[1] *[harvest]
ripe[2] *[ready to eat] ~ness	
	reap[1] *[harvest]
	rip[3] *[tear]+
ripel	**repel**[3] *[push away]
	repeal[1] *[law]
	rappel[3] *[descend]
	ripple[2] *[wave]+
ripen[1]	
riph-raph	**riffraff** *[disreputable person]
	riprap *[rough wall]
ripple[2] *[wave] ~| effect	
riprap *[rough wall]	
	riffraff *[disreputable person]
risen *[arose]	**resin** *[sticky]
rish	**rich**[5] *[wealthy]+
	reach[5] *[come to a point]
risk[1] *[put in danger]	
risk ~-averse ~-free ~-taking	
risky[4] *[dangerous]	
	risqué *[sexual content]
risollay	**rissole**
risolve	**resolve**[2]
risotto	
risound	**resound**[1]
rispect	**respect**[1+]
rispectabul	**respectable**+
risplendence	**resplendence**+
risponse	**response**
risponsibul	**responsible**+
risqué *[sexual content]	
	risky[4] *[dangerous]
ritch	**rich**[5] *[wealthy]+
	reach[5] *[come to a point]
	retch[5] *[vomit]
rite *[ceremony]	**right**[1] *[correct]+
	write *[text]
rithm	**rhythm**+
rithmic	**rhythmic**+
ritual ~ise ~ism ~istic	
rival[3]	@**rivalry**[4]
river ~front ~side	
riverberate	**reverberate**[2+]

Unable to find your word under **ri**?
Look under **re**

rivet[1]	
Riviera	
rivit	**rivet**[1]
rivulet	
rivyulet	**rivulet**
riyot	**riot**[1+]
rize	**rise** *[up]+
rizome	**rhizome**
ro	**rho** *[Greek letter]
	roe *[deer, fish]+
	row[1] *[boat, line, noise]
roab	**robe**[2] *[clothing]
roach[5]	
roackus	**raucous**+
road *[street] ~block ~hog ~house ~| race ~runner ~show ~side ~| test ~| trip ~work ~worthy	
	rode *[bike]
	rowed *[boat]

Unable to find your word under **road**?
Take off **road** and look again

roadeeo	**rodeo**+

Key to Suffixes and Compounds

These rules are explained on pages vii to ix.

1 Keep the word the same before adding **ed, er, est, ing**
e.g. cool[1] → cooled, cooler, coolest, cooling

2 Take off final **e** before adding **ed, er, est, ing**
e.g. fine[2] → fined, finer, finest, fining

3 Double final consonant before adding **ed, er, est, ing**
e.g. thin[3] → thinned, thinner, thinnest, thinning

4 Change final **y** to **i** before adding **ed, er, es, est, ly, ness**
e.g. tidy[4] → tidied, tidier, tidies, tidiest, tidily, tidiness
Keep final **y** before adding **ing** e.g. tidying

5 Add **es** instead of **s** to the end of the word
e.g. bunch[5] → bunches

6 Change final **f** to **ve** before adding **s**
e.g. calf[6] → calves

Wrong	Correct
Roades scholar	Rhodes Scholar
roadster *[car]	roaster *[cooking]
roag	rogue+
roal	role *[actor]+
	roll[1] *[move]+
roam[1] *[wonder around]	
	Rome *[Italian city]
roaming *[traveling] ~| charges	
	Roman *[from Rome]+
Roaman	Roman *[from Rome]+
roan	
roar[1] *[sound]	raw[1] *[not cooked]+
roast[1]	
roaster *[cooking]	
	roadster *[car]
	rooster *[bird]
	roster *[list]
roat	rote *[repetition]
	rotor *[blade]
roave	rove[2]+
roaws	rose *[flower, up]+
	rows *[boat, lines, noise]
rob[3] *[steal]	robe[2] *[clothing]
robbery[4]	
robe[2] *[clothing]	rob[3] *[steal]
robin ~| redbreast	
	@Robin Hood
robot *[device] ~ics	
	rowboat *[boat]
robust ~ly ~ness	
robyn	robin+
roche	roach[5]
rock[1] ~| and roll ~| bottom ~| climbing ~| garden ~-hard ~| music ~| pool ~-solid ~-steady	

> Unable to find your word under **rock**?
> Take off **rock** and look again

Wrong	Correct
rocked *[moved]	rocket[1] *[missile]+
rocker	
rocket[1] *[missile] ~eer *[fires rockets] ~| science	
	rocked *[moved]
rocket[1]	racket[1] *[noise, crime]+
	racquet[1] *[sports]+
rocketry	
rockfort	Roquefort+
rocking ~| chair ~| horse	
rocky[4] *[stones]	rookie *[beginner]
rococo	
rod *[stick]	road *[street]
	rowed *[boat]
	rode *[bike]
rode *[bike]	road *[street]
	rowed *[boat]
rodent	
rodeo ~| clown	
Rodery	Rotary *[club]+
	rotary[4] *[machine]
rodester	roadster *[car]
rodeyo	rodeo+
rodint	rodent
rodium	rhodium

> Unable to find your word under **ro**?
> Look under **rho**

Wrong	Correct
rodyo	rodeo+
roe *[deer, fish] ~buck	
	row[1] *[boat, line, noise]
	rho *[Greek letter]
roebot	robot *[device]+
	rowboat *[boat]
roebust	robust+
rog	rogue+
roger[1] *[one has heard]	
	rajah *[prince]
Roger *[name]	
rogue	@roguish
roil[1] *[to stir up]	royal *[related to royalty]+
Roiters	Reuters™
rojer	roger[1] *[one has heard]
	Roger *[name]
rok	rock[1]+

> Unable to find your word under **rok**?
> Look under **rock**

Key to Spelling Rules

Red words are wrong. **Black** words are correct.

- **~** Add the suffix or word directly to the main word, without a space or hyphen
  e.g. ash ~en ~tray → ashen ashtray
- **~-** Add a hyphen to the main word before adding the next word
  e.g. blow ~-dry → blow-dry
- **~|** Leave a space between the main word and the next word
  e.g. decimal ~| place → decimal place
- **+** By finding this word in its correct alphabetical order, you can find related words
  e.g. abowt about+ → about-face
- **★** Draws attention to words that may be confused
- **™** Means the word is a trademark
- **@** Signifies the word is derived from the main word

roked	**rocked** *[moved]
	rocket[1] *[missile]+
role *[actor] ~| model[1] ~| play[4]	
roll[1] *[move] ~| call ~out ~over ~-top	
roller ~| coaster ~| derby[4] ~| skate[2]	
Rollerblade™[2]	
rollick[1]	
rolling ~| contract ~| pin ~| plan ~| stock	
ROM *[read only memory]	
	RAM *[random access memory]
	ram[3] *[hit, male sheep]+
Romadon	**Ramadan** *[Islamic fasting month]
Roman *[from Rome] ~| candle ~| Catholic ~| numeral	
romance[2] ~| language	
romantic ~ally	
romanticism *[idealism]	
Romanticism *[artistic movement]	
romboid	**rhomboid**
Rome *[Italian city]	
	roam[1] *[wonder around]
romen	**Roman** *[from Rome]+
	ramen *[noodles]
Romeo ~| and Juliet	
romin	**Roman** *[from Rome]+
	roaming *[traveling]+
	ramen *[noodles]
rommadon	**Ramadan** *[Islamic fasting month]
romp[1] ~er	
rondeau *[poetry]	
rondo *[music]	
rone	**roan**
	run *[fast]+
ronning	**running**+
roo	**rue**[2] *[regret]+
roobarb	**rhubarb**

Unable to find your word under **roo**? Look under **ru**

rood *[cross, area]	
	rude[2] *[offensive]+
	rued *[regretted]
roof[1] *[building] ~less ~| garden ~| rack ~| terrace ~top	
	ruff *[collar, bird]
rooj	**rouge** *[blush]
	rug *[floor covering]
rook[1]	**@rookery**[4]
rookie *[beginner]	
	rocky[4] *[stones]
roolette	**roulette**
room ~ful ~| reservations ~| service	
	@roomy[4]
roomatism	**rheumatism**
roomba	**rumba**
roome	**room**+
roomer *[rents room]	
	rumor *[gossip]+
roomynate	**ruminate**[2]+
roon	**ruin**[1] *[destroy]+
	rune *[letter]
roonous	**ruinous**+
roopee	**rupee**
rooph	**roof**[1] *[building]+
roose	**ruse**[2] *[trick]
roost[1]	
rooster *[bird]	**roster** *[list]
	roaster *[cooking]
root[1] *[plant] ~less ~| directory ~| out ~| vegetable	
	rout[1] *[defeat]
	route *[way]+
rooteen	**routine**+
roothless	**ruthless**+
rope[2] ~| in ~| ladder	
ropy[4]	
Roquefort ~| cheese	
rorcous	**raucous**+
rore	**roar**[1] *[sound]
	raw[1] *[not cooked]+
rosary[4]	
rose *[flower, up] ~bud ~-colored ~water ~| window ~wood	
	rows *[boat, lines, noise]

Key to Suffixes and Compounds

These rules are explained on pages vii to ix.

1 Keep the word the same before adding **ed, er, est, ing**
e.g. cool[1] → cooled, cooler, coolest, cooling

2 Take off final **e** before adding **ed, er, est, ing**
e.g. fine[2] → fined, finer, finest, fining

3 Double final consonant before adding **ed, er, est, ing**
e.g. thin[3] → thinned, thinner, thinnest, thinning

4 Change final **y** to **i** before adding **ed, er, es, est, ly, ness**
e.g. tidy[4] → tidied, tidier, tidies, tidiest, tidily, tidiness
Keep final **y** before adding **ing** e.g. tidying

5 Add **es** instead of **s** to the end of the word
e.g. bunch[5] → bunches

6 Change final **f** to **ve** before adding **s**
e.g. calf[6] → calves

rosemary	
rosery	rosary[4]
rosette	
roste	roost[1]
roster *[list]	raster *[lines of dots]
	roaster
	rooster
rostrum *[speaking platform]	
rostur	roster
rosy[4]	
rot[3] *[decay]	rote *[repetition]
	wrote *[past of write]
rota *[list]	rotor *[blade]
rotachun	rotation+
rotaite	rotate[2+]
rotary[4] *[machine]	
Rotary *[club]	@Rotarian
rotashun	rotation+
rotate[2]	@rotatable
rotation ~| symmetry	
ROTC *[Reserve Officers' Training Corps]	
rote *[repetition]	rot *[decay]
	wrote *[past of write]
rotor *[blade]	Rota *[list]
	rotter *[bad person]
rotten[1] ~ly ~ness	
Rottweiler	
rotund ~a	
rotunned	rotund+
Rotviler	Rottweiler
roubel	ruble *[Russian money]
	rubble *[broken bricks]
roubikund	rubicund
rouck	rook[1+]
roudy	rowdy[4]
rouge *[blush]	rug *[floor covering]
rough[1] *[coarse] ~ly ~ness ~| draft ~| estimate ~-hew ~house ~neck ~shod ~| up	
	ruff *[collar, bird]

Unable to find your word under **rough**? Take off **rough** and look again

roughage	
roughen[1]	
roulette	
roum	room+
	rum *[liquor]
roump	rump+
round[1] ~ly ~ness ~| down ~| up ~| robin ~| table ~| trip	
roundabout	
rouse[2]	
rout[1] *[defeat]	
route *[way] ~| march	
	root[1] *[plant]+
routeen	routine+
routine ~ly ~| work	
rove[2] ~around	
row[1] *[boat, line, noise]	
	roe *[deer, fish]+
	rho *[Greek letter]
rowboat *[boat]	robot *[device]+
rowbust	robust+
rowdy[4]	
rownd	round[1+]
rows *[boat, line, noise]	
	rose *[flower, up]+
	rouse[2]
rowt	rout[1] *[defeat]
	route *[way]+
royal *[related to royalty] ~ly ~ty	
	roil[1] *[to stir up]
Royters	Reuters™
roze	rose *[flower, up]+
	rows *[boat, line, noise]
rozemary	rosemary
rozette	rosette
rozy	rosy[4]
rub[3]	
rubarb	rhubarb
rubbal	ruble *[Russian money]
	rubble *[broken bricks]
rubber ~ize[2] ~| band ~| check ~| dinghy	
rubber-stamp[1]	
rubbesh	rubbish[1] *[garbage]+
rubbish[1] *[garbage] ~y	

rubble *[broken bricks]	
	ruble *[Russian money]
rubella	
rubicund	
rubir	rubber^{+}
ruble *[Russian money]	
	rubble *[broken bricks]
rubric	
rubul	ruble *[Russian money]
	rubble *[broken buildings]
ruby^{4}	
ruch	rush^{5+}
rucksack	
ruckus	
ructions	
rudament	rudiment^{+}
rudder	
ruddy^{4}	
rude^{2} *[offensive] ~ly ~ness	
	rued *[regretted]
	rood *[cross, area]
rudiment ~ary	
rue^{2} *[regret] ~ful ~fully	
rued *[regretted]	rude^{2} *[offensive]$^{+}$
	rood *[cross, area]
ruel	rule^{2+}
rues *[regrets]	ruse *[trick]
ruff *[collar, bird]	roof^{1} *[building]$^{+}$
	rough^{1} *[coarse]$^{+}$
ruffage	roughage
ruffel	ruffle^{2}
ruffen	roughen^{1}
ruffian	
ruffyan	ruffian
rug *[floor covering]	
	rouge *[blush]
rugby	
ruge	rouge *[blush]
	rug *[floor covering]
rugged ~ly ~ness	
rugid	rugged^{+}
ruin^{1} *[destroy] ~ation	
	rune *[letter]
ruinous ~ly	
ruk	rook^{1+}

rukkus	ruckus
rukky	rocky^{4} *[stones]
	rookie *[beginner]
ruksak	rucksack
rule^{2} ~book	
rulette	roulette
rum *[liquor]	room^{+}
rumatic	rheumatic^{+}
rumatisum	rheumatism
rumatoid	rheumatoid^{+}
rumba	
rumble^{2}	
rumenate	ruminate^{2+}
rumer	rumor *[gossip]$^{+}$
	roomer *[rents room]
ruminate^{2}	@rumination
rummage^{2}	
rummer	rumor *[gossip]$^{+}$
	roomer *[rents room]
rummige	rummage^{2}
rummij	rummage^{2}
rummy	
rumor *[gossip] ~ed	
	roomer *[rents room]
rump ~steak	
rumple^{2}	
rumpus^{5}	
rumynate	ruminate^{2+}
run *[fast] ~-on ~| over ~| time	
	rune *[letter]
runaway *[fugitive]	
rune *[letter]	ruin^{1} *[destroy]$^{+}$
	run *[fast]$^{+}$
runegg	renege^{2}
runeway	runaway *[fugitive]
	runway *[airport]
rung *[ladder, bell]	
	wrong^{1} *[not right]$^{+}$
	wrung *[squeezed]
runner ~| bean ~-up	
running ~| battle ~| commentary ~| joke ~| mate ~| total ~| water	

Unable to find your word under **running**? Take off **running** and look again

Key to Suffixes and Compounds

These rules are explained on pages vii to ix.

1 Keep the word the same before adding **ed, er, est, ing**
e.g. cool^{1} → cooled, cooler, coolest, cooling

2 Take off final **e** before adding **ed, er, est, ing**
e.g. fine^{2} → fined, finer, finest, fining

3 Double final consonant before adding **ed, er, est, ing**
e.g. thin^{3} → thinned, thinner, thinnest, thinning

4 Change final **y** to **i** before adding **ed, er, es, est, ly, ness**
e.g. tidy^{4} → tidied, tidier, tidies, tidiest, tidily, tidiness
Keep final **y** before adding **ing** e.g. tidying

5 Add **es** instead of **s** to the end of the word
e.g. bunch^{5} → bunches

6 Change final **f** to **ve** before adding **s**
e.g. calf^{6} → calves

Entry	Correct spelling
runny^{4} ~| nose	
runous	ruinous^{+}
runt	
runway *[airport]	runaway *[fugitive]
rupchure	rupture^{2}
rupee	
ruphian	ruffian
rupture^{2}	
rural ~ness	
rurel	rural^{+}
ruse^{2} *[trick]	rues *[regrets]
ruset	russet^{+}
rush^{5} ~| hour ~| job ~| order	
rusller	rustler
russed	rust^{1+}
russel	rustle^{2+}
russet ~| color	
Russian ~| roulette	
russit	russet^{+}
russul	rustle^{2+}
rust^{1} ~-free ~-proof	
rustic	
rustick	rustic
rustle^{2} ~| up	
rustler	
rusty^{4}	
rut^{3} *[deep hole, mating]	
	root^{1} *[plant]$^{+}$
	route *[way]$^{+}$
ruthless ~ly ~ness	
rutine	routine^{+}
ruze	ruse^{2} *[trick]
ryb	rib^{3+}

Unable to find your word under **ry**? Look under **ri**, **rhi**, and **rhy**

Entry	Correct spelling
rye *[grain] ~| bread ~grass	
	wry *[humor]
ryme	rhyme^{2} *[poetry]
	rim^{3} *[edge]$^{+}$
rythim	rhythm^{+}
ryval	rival^{3+}

S

Entry	Correct spelling
Sabbath	
sabbatical	
sabel	sable
saber ~| rattling	~-toothed
sabetage	sabotage^{2+}
sabith	Sabbath
sable	
sabotage^{2}	@saboteur
saccharin	
sachel	satchel
sachet *[small bag]	
	sashay^{1} *[walk]
sachurate	saturate^{2+}
sack^{1} *[bag, destroy] ~cloth ~ful	
	sake *[benefit of, Japanese drink]
sackarin	saccharin
sackreligious	sacrilegious^{+}
sacrament	
sacred ~ly ~ness	
sacreligious	sacrilegious^{+}
sacrifice^{2}	@sacrificial
sacrilege	
sacrilegious ~ly ~ness	
sacrosanct	
sad ~ly ~ness	
sadden^{1}	
saddle^{2} ~bag ~-sore	
saden	sadden^{1}
sadist ~ic ~ically	
	@sadism
sadomasochist	

safari
safe[2] ~ly ~-conduct ~| deposit ~| haven ~| investment ~keeping ~| sex
safeguard[1]
safety ~| belt ~| catch ~| glass ~| match ~| measure ~| precaution ~| regulation ~| valve
saffire — sapphire
saffron
saftey — safety+
sag[3] *[low] — sage *[wise]+
saga
sagacious ~| sagacity
sage *[wise] ~ly ~ness
— sag[3] *[low]
Sagittarius
said *[did say] — seed *[plant, number]+
saif — safe[2]+
saifety — safety+
saifguard — safeguard[1]
saik — sake *[benefit of, Japanese drink]
sail[1] *[boat] ~or
— sale *[goods]+
sails *[boat] — sales *[business]+
saim — same+
sain — sane+
saint ~ly ~hood ~'s day
saiv — save[2]+
saizmic — seismic+
saje — sage *[wise]+
— sag[3] *[low]
Sajittarius — Sagittarius
sak — sack[1] *[bag, destroy]+
— sake *[benefit of, Japanese drink]
sakarin — saccharin
sake *[benefit of, Japanese drink]
— sack[1] *[bag, destroy]+
sakrament — sacrament
salaam
salad ~| bar ~| dressing
salami
salary[4] *[pay] ~| review
— @salaried
— celery[4] *[vegetable]
sale *[goods] ~ability ~able
— sail[1] *[boat]+
saleen — saline+
salery — salary[4] *[pay]+
— celery[4] *[vegetable]
sales *[business] ~| budget ~| campaign ~| clerk ~| conference ~| curve ~| drive ~| executive ~| figures ~| force ~| forecast ~| ledger ~| literature ~| manager ~| pitch ~| personnel ~| promotion ~| receipt ~| representative ~| revenue ~| tax ~| team ~| volume
— sails *[boat]

> Unable to find your word under **sales**?
> Take off **sales** and look again

saletare — solitaire
saletude — solitude
salient
saline — @salinity
saliva
salivate[2] — @salivation
sallow
salm — psalm+
salmon
salmonella
salon *[hair, beauty]
saloon *[bar]
salow — sallow
salsa
salt[1] ~| marsh ~water
salty[4]
salubrious ~ly ~ness
salune — saloon *[bar]
— salon *[hair, beauty]
salutary
salute[2] — @salutation
salvage[2] *[save] ~able ~| vessel
— selvage[2] *[fabric edge]
— savage[2] *[wild]+

Key to Suffixes and Compounds

These rules are explained on pages vii to ix.

1. Keep the word the same before adding **ed, er, est, ing**
   e.g. cool[1] → cooled, cooler, coolest, cooling
2. Take off final **e** before adding **ed, er, est, ing**
   e.g. fine[2] → fined, finer, finest, fining
3. Double final consonant before adding **ed, er, est, ing**
   e.g. thin[3] → thinned, thinner, thinnest, thinning
4. Change final **y** to **i** before adding **ed, er, es, est, ly, ness**
   e.g. tidy[4] → tidied, tidier, tidies, tidiest, tidily, tidiness
   Keep final **y** before adding **ing** e.g. tidying
5. Add **es** instead of **s** to the end of the word
   e.g. bunch[5] → bunches
6. Change final **f** to **ve** before adding **s**
   e.g. calf[6] → calves

salvation
salve[2]
salvige salvage[2] *[save]+
selvage[2] *[fabric edge]
salvo
salyne saline+
salyvate salivate[2+]
Samaritan
samba *[dance] somber *[gloomy]+
same ~ness ~-sex
samerai samurai
samon salmon
samovar
sample[2]
samurai
samwitch sandwich[5+]
sanatorium @sanatoria
sanchury sanctuary[4]
sancshun sanction[1]
sanctem sanctum
sanctify[4] @sanctification
sanctimonious ~ly ~ness
sanction[1]
sanctity[4]
sanctuary[4]
sanctum
sand[1] ~bag ~bank ~bar ~blast ~box ~| castle ~paper ~stone

> Unable to find your word under **sand**? Take off **sand** and look again

sandal ~wood
sandscript Sanskrit
sandwich[5] ~| board ~| spread
sandy[4]
sane ~ly @sanity
sanguine @sanguinity
sangwitch sandwich[5+]
sanitarium @sanitaria
sanitary[4] ~| certificate ~| napkin
sanitation
sank
sankshun sanction[1]
sans serif

Sanskrit
Santa ~| Fe ~| Claus
sanwich sandwich[5+]
sap[3] ~ling
sapphire
sarcasm
sarcastic ~ally
sarcoma
sarcophagus @sarcophagi
sardine
sardonic ~ally
sari *[garment] sorry[4] *[sad]
sarkasm sarcasm
sarkastik sarcastic+
sarkoma sarcoma
sarm psalm+
sarong
sary sari *[garment]
sorry[4] *[sad]
saryeussis psoriasis
sash[5]
sashabul satiable
sashay[1] *[walk] sachet *[small bag]
sashiate satiate[2+]
sashimi
sat *[past of sit] ~| down
sate[2] *[satisfy]
Satan *[the Devil] ~ic
satin *[glossy material]
satay sauté[1]
satchel
sate[2] *[satisfy] sat *[past of sit]+
satellite ~| dish ~| service
saten satin *[glossy material]
Satan *[the Devil]+
Saterday Saturday
Satern Saturn *[planet]
Satan *[the Devil]+
satiate[2] @satiable
satin *[glossy material]
Satan *[the Devil]+
satire @satirist
satirical ~ly
satirize[2]
satisfactory[4]

satisfy[4]	@satisfaction
saturate[2]	@saturation
Saturday	
Saturn	
satyre	satire[+]
satyrical	satirical[+]
satysfactory	satisfactory[4]
satysfy	satisfy[4+]
sauce *[liquid] ~| boat ~pan	
	source[2] *[origin][+]
saucer	
saucy[4]	
sauder	solder[1] *[join][+]
	soldier[1] *[army][+]
saum	psalm[+]
sauna	
saunter[1]	
sausage ~| meat ~| roll	
sause	sauce *[liquid][+]
	source[2] *[origin][+]
sauser	saucer
sausery	sorcery[4+]
sausy	saucy[4]
sauté[1]	
savage[2] *[wild] ~ly ~ry	
	salvage[2] *[save][+]
	selvage[2] *[fabric edge]
savannah	
savant	
save[2] ~| up	
saver *[one who saves]	
	savor[1] *[enjoy the taste]
savery	savory[4] *[very tasty]
savige	savage[2] *[wild][+]
savings ~| account ~| and loan ~| bank	
savior *[someone who rescues]	
	savor[1] *[enjoy the taste]
	saver *[one who saves]
Savior *[Jesus Christ]	
savoir-faire	
savont	savant
savor[1] *[enjoy the taste]	
	saver *[one who saves]
savory[4] *[very tasty]	
savvy[4] *[knowledgeable]	

savwafair	savoir-faire
saw[1] *[cut, past of see] ~dust ~horse	
	soar[1] *[fly]
	sore[2] *[hurt][+]
sawlt	salt[1+]
sawn	
sawna	sauna
sawnter	saunter[1]
sawsa	saucer
saxofone	saxophone[+]
saxophone	@saxophonist
say *[talk] ~ing	@said
	sea *[water]
sayber	saber[+]
sayder	Seder *[Jewish meal]
sayk	sake *[benefit of, Japanese drink]
saym	same[+]
saynt	saint[+]
sayons	séance
sayvyer	savior *[someone who rescues]
scab[3]	
scabbard	
scabies	
scaffold[1]	
scair	scare[2] *[frighten][+]
scald[1] *[burn]	scold[1] *[tell off][+]
scale[2] ~| down ~| drawing ~| factor ~| up	
scallop *[shell, cook] ~ed	
scalp[1] *[head]	
scalpel	
scaly[4]	
scam[3]	
scamper[1]	
scan[3]	
scandal	@scandalize[2]
scandalous ~ly	
scanner	
scant	@scanty[4]
scapegoat[1]	
scar[3] *[mark] ~-faced	
	scare[2] *[frighten][+]
scarab	

Key to Suffixes and Compounds

These rules are explained on pages vii to ix.

1 Keep the word the same before adding **ed, er, est, ing**
e.g. cool[1] → cooled, cooler, coolest, cooling

2 Take off final **e** before adding **ed, er, est, ing**
e.g. fine[2] → fined, finer, finest, fining

3 Double final consonant before adding **ed, er, est, ing**
e.g. thin[3] → thinned, thinner, thinnest, thinning

4 Change final **y** to **i** before adding **ed, er, es, est, ly, ness**
e.g. tidy[4] → tidied, tidier, tidies, tidiest, tidily, tidiness
Keep final **y** before adding **ing** e.g. tidying

5 Add **es** instead of **s** to the end of the word
e.g. bunch[5] → bunches

6 Change final **f** to **ve** before adding **s**
e.g. calf[6] → calves

scarce^{2} ~ly ~ness
scarcity^{4} ~| value
scare^{2} *[frighten] ~crow
scar^{3} *[mark]+
scarf^{6} ~| pin
scarlet ~| fever
scarse scarce^{2+}
scarsity scarcity^{4+}
scary^{4}
scate skate^{2+}
scathing ~ly
scatter^{1} ~brain ~brained ~| plot
scavenge^{2}
sceleton skeleton+
scematic schematic+
sceme scheme^{2}
scenario
scene *[theater] seen *[eyes]
scenery
scenic ~ally
scent^{1} *[perfume] sent *[away]
cent *[money]
scents *[perfumes]
cents *[money]
sense^{2} *[become aware]
sceptic *[also spelled skeptic]+
septic *[infected]
sceptical ~ly
scerge scourge^{2}
schedule^{2}
schema *[model] ~s
schemer *[plotter]
schematic ~ally
scheme^{2}
schemer *[plotter]
schema *[model]+
schism ~atic
schizo
schizophrenia @schizophrenic
schlep^{3}
schlock^{1}
schmaltz
schmooze^{2}
schmuck
scholar ~ly ~ship
scholastic ~ally
school^{1} ~teacher ~| year
schooner
schwa
sci ski^{1} *[snow sport]+
sciatic ~a ~| nerve
science @scientist ~| fiction
scientific ~ally
scientology
sci-fi *[science fiction]
scintillating
scism schism+
scissor *[cutting instrument] ~s
seizure *[sudden attack]
scit skit *[play]
shit^{3} *[feces]
sclerosis
Scoch Scotch
scoff^{1}
scolar scholar+
scold^{1} *[tell off] ~ing
scald^{1} *[burn]
scone
scooner schooner
scoop^{1}
scoot^{1}
scope^{2} ~| out
scorch^{5}
score^{2} ~board ~card ~sheet
scorn^{1} ~ful ~fully
Scorpio
scorpion
Scotch
scot-free
scoundrel
scour^{1}
scourge^{2}
scout^{1}
scowl^{1}
scowndrel scoundrel
scowt scout^{1}
scrabble^{2} *[scratch]
Scrabble™ *[game]
scrach scratch^{5+}
scraggly^{4}

Key to Spelling Rules

Red words are wrong. **Black** words are correct.

~ Add the suffix or word directly to the main word, without a space or hyphen
e.g. ash ~en ~tray → ashen ashtray

~- Add a hyphen to the main word before adding the next word
e.g. blow ~-dry → blow-dry

~| Leave a space between the main word and the next word
e.g. decimal ~| place → decimal place

+ By finding this word in its correct alphabetical order, you can find related words
e.g. abowt about+ → about-face

* Draws attention to words that may be confused

™ Means the word is a trademark

@ Signifies the word is derived from the main word

scraip scrape^{2} *[remove]
scram^{3}
scramble^{2} @scrambled eggs
scrap^{3} *[get rid of] ~book ~| heap ~| metal ~yard
scrape^{2} *[remove]
scrape^{2} *[remove]
scrap^{3} *[get rid of]$^{+}$
scraper *[scrapes]
scrappy^{4}
scratch^{5} ~card ~| pad ~| paper
scrawl^{1}
scrawny^{4}
scream^{1}
screech^{5} ~| owl
screen^{1} ~play ~writer
screme scream^{1}
screw^{1} ~y ~ball ~driver ~-up
screwpull scruple

> Unable to find your word under **screw**?
> Look under **scru**

scribble^{2}
scribe^{2}
scrimp^{1}
script^{1} ~writer
Scripture
scroll^{1} ~bar
Scrooge
scrotum
scrounge^{2}
scrownge scrounge^{2}
scrub^{3}
scrue screw^{1+}
scruff @scruffy^{4}
scrumptious ~ly ~ness
scrunch^{5} @scrunchy^{4}
scruple
scrupulous ~ly ~ness
scrutinize^{2}
scrutiny^{4} @scrutineer
SCSI *[computer disk]
scuzzy *[dirty]
scuba ~| diver ~| diving ~| gear

scud^{3} *[move like cloud]
scuff^{1}
scuffle^{2}
scule school^{1+}
sculk skulk^{1}
scull^{1} *[boat] skull *[head]$^{+}$
sculptor *[artist]
sculpture^{2} *[what a sculptor produces]
scum ~bag
scuner schooner
scunk skunk
scupe scoop^{1}
scurrilous ~ly
scurry^{4}
scurvy
scute scoot^{1}
scuttle^{2}
scuzzy *[dirty] SCSI *[computer disk]
scythe^{2} *[tool] seethe^{2} *[boil]
sea *[water] ~| anemone ~| freight ~front ~gull ~| level ~| lion ~shore ~sick ~sickness ~side ~| transport
see *[eyes]$^{+}$

> Unable to find your word under **sea**?
> Take off **sea** and look again

sead cede^{2} *[give up]
said *[did say]
seed^{1} *[plant, number]$^{+}$
seady seedy^{4} *[poor condition]
CD *[recording, investment]$^{+}$
seafarer @seafaring
seak seek *[look for]$^{+}$
Sikh *[religion]$^{+}$
seal^{1} *[part of a lid, official, animal] ~skin
sill *[window edge]
sealant
sealed ~| bids ~| envelope
sealing *[shut] ceiling *[roof]
seam *[cloth] ~less
seem^{1} *[appear]$^{+}$
seaman *[sailor] ~ship
semen *[sperm]

Key to Suffixes and Compounds

These rules are explained on pages vii to ix.

1 Keep the word the same before adding **ed, er, est, ing**
e.g. cool^{1} → cooled, cooler, coolest, cooling
2 Take off final **e** before adding **ed, er, est, ing**
e.g. fine^{2} → fined, finer, finest, fining
3 Double final consonant before adding **ed, er, est, ing**
e.g. thin^{3} → thinned, thinner, thinnest, thinning
4 Change final **y** to **i** before adding **ed, er, es, est, ly, ness**
e.g. tidy^{4} → tidied, tidier, tidies, tidiest, tidily, tidiness
Keep final **y** before adding **ing** e.g. tidying
5 Add **es** instead of **s** to the end of the word
e.g. bunch^{5} → bunches
6 Change final **f** to **ve** before adding **s**
e.g. calf^{6} → calves

seament	cement[1+]
seamstress[5]	
seamy[4] *[messy]	semi *[half]+
Sean *[name]	scene *[theater]
	seen *[eyes]
séance	
seap	seep[1+]
sear[1] *[scorch]	seer *[prophet]
	sere *[dried]
search[5] ~| engine ~light ~| warrant	
seasaw	seesaw[1]
sease	cease[2] *[stop]+
	seize[2] *[grab hold]+
seasick ~ness	
season[1] ~able ~ably ~| ticket	
seasonal ~ly ~| adjustments ~| demand ~| variations	
seat[1] *[chair]	set *[put]+
seathe	seethe[2] *[boil]
seaworthy[4]	
sebaceous ~| gland	
secede[2]	@secession
seclude[2]	@seclusion
second[1] ~ly ~| class ~-guess[5] ~hand ~| home ~| quarter ~-rate	
secondary[4] ~| data ~| school ~| source	
secrecy	
secret *[hidden] ~ly ~ive	
	secrete[2] *[produce]+
secretariat ~| secretarial	
secretary[4] ~| general	
secrete[2] *[produce]	
	@secretion
	secret *[hidden]+
secshun	section+
sect ~arian	
section	@sector
sects *[groups]	sex[5] *[gender, intercourse]+
secular ~ize[2] ~ization	
secularism	@secularist
secure[2] ~| funds ~| investment ~| job	
security[4] ~| guard ~| of tenure	

sed	said *[did say]
	cede[2] *[give up]
	seed[1] *[plant, number]+
sedait	sedate+
sedament	sediment+
sedate ~ly ~ness	
sedative	@sedation
sede	cede[2] *[give up]
	said *[did say]
	seed[1] *[plant, number]+
sedentary	
Seder *[Jewish meal]	
	cedar *[tree]
	seeder *[plants seeds]
sedilla	cedilla
sediment ~ary ~ation	
sedition	@seditious
seduce[2]	@seduction
seductive ~ly	
see *[eyes] ~ing ~n	
	sea *[water]+
seed[1] *[plant, number]	
	cede[2] *[give up]
	said *[did say]
seed ~less ~| money	
seeder *[plants seeds]	
	cedar *[tree]
	Seder *[Jewish meal]
seedling	
seedy[4] *[poor condition]	
	CD *[recording, investment]+
seefarer	seafarer+
seek *[look for] ~ing	
	Sikh *[religion]+
seel	seal[1+]
seeling	ceiling *[roof]
	sealing *[shut]
seem[1] *[appear] ~ingly ~ly	
	seam *[cloth]+
seeman	seaman *[sailor]+
	semen *[sperm]
seement	cement[1+]
seemy	seamy[4] *[messy]
seen *[eyes]	scene *[theater]

KEY TO SPELLING RULES

Red words are wrong. **Black** words are correct.

~ Add the suffix or word directly to the main word, without a space or hyphen
e.g. ash ~en ~tray → ashen ashtray

~- Add a hyphen to the main word before adding the next word
e.g. blow ~-dry → blow-dry

~| Leave a space between the main word and the next word
e.g. decimal ~| place → decimal place

+ By finding this word in its correct alphabetical order, you can find related words
e.g. abowt about+ → about-face

* Draws attention to words that may be confused

TM Means the word is a trademark

@ Signifies the word is derived from the main word

seep[1] @seepage
seepia sepia
seer *[prophet] sear[1] *[scorch]
sere *[dried]
seereez series
seeriul cereal *[grain]
serial *[one after another]+
seesar Caesar+
seesaw[1]
seesick seasick+
seeson season[1+]
seesonal seasonal+
seet seat[1]
seethe[2] *[boil] scythe[2] *[tool]
seeworthy seaworthy[4]
segment[1] ~ation
segregate[2] @segregation
seismic @seismograph
seismology @seismologist
seize[2] *[grab hold]
cease[2] *[stop]
size[2] *[measure]
seizure *[sudden attack]
scissor *[for cutting]+
seks sects *[groups]
sex[5] *[gender, intercourse]+
seksual sexual+
seksy sexy[4]
sekure secure[2+]
sekurity security[4+]
sekwel sequel
sekwence sequence+
sekwestrate sequestrate[2+]
sekwin sequin+
seldom
selebrate celebrate[2+]
selebrity celebrity[4]
select[1] ~ion ~or
selective ~ly
selenium
seler cellar *[underground]
seller *[sales person]
selery celery[4] *[vegetable]
salary[4] *[pay]+

selestial celestial+
self[6] ~-centered ~-confessed ~-driven ~-preservation ~-proclaimed ~-promotion ~-confident ~-conscious ~-discipline ~-employed ~-esteem ~-financing ~-government ~-help ~-image ~-important ~-made ~-motivated ~-pity ~-portrait ~-regulating ~-regulation ~-regulatory ~-respect ~-righteous ~-seeking ~-service

> Unable to find your word under **self**?
> Take off **self** and look again

selibate celibate *[unmarried]+
celebrate[2] *[occasion]+
sell *[goods] ~| off ~| out
cell *[prison, unit]+
seller *[sales person] ~'s market
cellar *[space underground]
sellphone cell phone
sellular cellular
Selsius Celsius

> Unable to find your word under **sel**?
> Look under **cel**

semantic ~ally ~s
semaphore
sematary cemetery[4] *[graveyard]
semblance
seme seam *[cloth]+
seem[1] *[appear]+
semen *[sperm] seaman *[sailor]+
sement cement[1+]
semester
semetery cemetery[4] *[graveyard]
symmetry[4] *[similarity]
semi *[half] ~automatic ~circle ~circular ~colon ~conductor ~conscious ~final ~finalist ~precious ~-skilled ~tone
seamy[4] *[messy]

Key to Suffixes and Compounds

These rules are explained on pages vii to ix.

1 Keep the word the same before adding **ed, er, est, ing**
e.g. cool[1] → cooled, cooler, coolest, cooling
2 Take off final **e** before adding **ed, er, est, ing**
e.g. fine[2] → fined, finer, finest, fining
3 Double final consonant before adding **ed, er, est, ing**
e.g. thin[3] → thinned, thinner, thinnest, thinning
4 Change final **y** to **i** before adding **ed, er, es, est, ly, ness**
e.g. tidy[4] → tidied, tidier, tidies, tidiest, tidily, tidiness
Keep final **y** before adding **ing** e.g. tidying
5 Add **es** instead of **s** to the end of the word
e.g. bunch[5] → bunches
6 Change final **f** to **ve** before adding **s**
e.g. calf[6] → calves

Unable to find your word under **semi**?
Take off **semi** and look again

seminal
seminar
seminary[4]
Semite @Semitic
semmi semi+
semolina
semynal seminal
Semyte Semite+
senario scenario
senate @senator
send ~er ~ing @sent
sene scene *[theater]
seen *[eyes]
senic scenic+
senile @senility
senior ~ity ~| manager
senotaph cenotaph
sensational ~ism ~ly
sensationalize[2]
sense[2] *[become aware]
cents *[money]
scents *[perfumes]
senseless ~ly
senses *[sight, hearing, touch]
census *[count of population]
sensibility[4]
sensible @sensibly
sensitive ~ly
sensitivity[4]
sensitize[2]
sensor *[detector]
censer *[incense holder]
censor[1] *[restrict]
censure[2] *[disapprove of]
sensory
sensual *[dominated by senses] ~ist ~ity ~ly
sensuous *[appealing to senses] ~ly ~ness
sensure censer *[incense holder]
censor[1] *[restrict]
censure[2] *[disaprove of]
sensus census *[count of population]
senses *[sight, hearing, touch]
sensytiv sensitive+
sent *[away] cent *[money]
scent[1] *[perfume]
sentence[2]
senter center[2+]
sentigrade centigrade
sentileeter centiliter
sentiment
sentimental ~ism ~ist ~ly
sentimentalize[2]
sentimeter centimeter
sentinel
sentipede centipede
sentral central+
sentralize centralize[2+]
sentry[4] ~| box
sentury century[4]

Unable to find your word under **sen**?
Look under **cen**

separable
separate[2] @separator
separation
separatist @separatism
sepcis sepsis
sepia
sepret separate[2+]
sepsis
September
septic *[infected] @septicemia
skeptic *[doubter]+
septum *[wall]
sepulcher
sequel
sequence @sequential
sequester[1]
sequestrate[2] @sequestration
sequin ~ned
ser sir *[man]
sear[1] *[scorch]

ser	seer *[prophet]
	sere *[dried]
seramic	ceramic
seraph *[angel] ~ic ~im	
	serif *[type]
serch	search[5+]
sercharge	surcharge[2]
sere *[dried]	sear[1] *[scorch]
	seer *[prophet]
sereal	cereal *[grain]
	serial *[one after another][+]
seremony	ceremony[4]
serenade[2]	
serendipity	
serene ~ly	@serenity
serf *[slave] ~dom	
	surf[1] *[sea][+]
	serif *[type]
	seraph *[angel][+]
serface	surface[2+]
serfit	surfeit
sergeant *[army] ~-major	
	surgeon *[doctor]
sergery	surgery[4]
serial *[one after another] ~| comma ~| killer ~| number ~| port	
	cereal *[grain]
serialize[2]	@serialization
seriel	cereal *[grain]
	serial *[one after another][+]
series	
serif *[type]	serf *[slave][+]
	seraph *[angel][+]
serious ~ly ~ness	
serje	surge[2]
serloin	sirloin[+]
serly	surly[4] *[rude]
sermise	surmise[2]
sermon	
sermonize[2]	
sermount	surmount[1]
sername	surname
serocco	sirocco
serong	sarong
serpass	surpass[5]

serpent ~ine	
serpliss	surplice *[robe]
	surplus[5] *[excess]
serprize	surprise[2+]
serrated ~| edge	
serrealism	surrealism
serrealist	surrealist[+]
sertain	certain *[sure][+]
	curtain *[screen][+]
sertax	surtax[5]
sertificate	certificate[+]
sertify	certify[4+]
sertitude	certitude
serum	
servant	
serve[2]	
serveillance	surveillance
servey	survey[1+]
servical	cervical[+]
service[2] ~able ~| charge ~| department ~| industry[4] ~| manual ~| station	
serviette	
servile ~ly	
servility	@servitude
servival	survival[+]
servix	cervix
sesame ~| seed	
sesashun	cessation *[halt]
	session *[period]
sesede	secede[2+]
sessamy	sesame[+]
Sessar	Caesar[+]
Sessarian	Caesarean[+]
sessation	cessation
session *[period] ~al	
	cession *[yielding][+]
sesspit	cesspit[+]
set *[put] ~ting ~| against ~-aside ~back ~| point ~| piece ~| price ~| square ~| target ~up	
	seat[1] *[chair]

Unable to find your word under **set**?
Take off **set** and look again

Key to Suffixes and Compounds

These rules are explained on pages vii to ix.

1 Keep the word the same before adding **ed, er, est, ing**
e.g. cool[1] → cooled, cooler, coolest, cooling

2 Take off final **e** before adding **ed, er, est, ing**
e.g. fine[2] → fined, finer, finest, fining

3 Double final consonant before adding **ed, er, est, ing**
e.g. thin[3] → thinned, thinner, thinnest, thinning

4 Change final **y** to **i** before adding **ed, er, es, est, ly, ness**
e.g. tidy[4] → tidied, tidier, tidies, tidiest, tidily, tidiness
Keep final **y** before adding **ing** e.g. tidying

5 Add **es** instead of **s** to the end of the word
e.g. bunch[5] → bunches

6 Change final **f** to **ve** before adding **s**
e.g. calf[6] → calves

setter
settle[2] ~ment ~| a claim ~| an account
seudo pseudo[+]
seveir severe[+]
seven ~teen ~teenth
seventh ~| heaven ~-Day Adventist
seventy[4] @seventieth
sever[1] ~ance
several ~ly
severe ~ly @severity
sevrel several[+]
sew[1] *[clothes] ~n
sow[1] *[seeds][+]
so *[in this way][+]
sue[2] *[claim]
sewage *[wastewater]
sewed *[did sew] sod *[earth]
sowed *[did sow]
sewer *[drain, sews clothes]
sower *[sows seeds]
sewerage *[drain provisions]
sewn *[clothes] sown *[seeds]
sewur sewer *[drain, sews clothes]
sex[5] *[gender, intercourse] ~less ~y[4] ~| appeal ~| discrimination
sects *[groups]
sexism @sexist
sextant
sextet
sexton
sexual ~ity ~ly ~| abuse ~| harassment ~| intercourse ~| discrimination
sey say *[talk][+]
see *[with eyes]
sfere sphere[2+]
sfincter sphincter[+]
sfinx sphinx[5]
shabang shebang
shabby[4]
shack
shackle[2]
shade[2] @shady[4]
shaded ~| area
shadow[1] ~y
shaft[1]
shaggy[4]
shah
shaid shade[2+]
shaided shaded[+]
shaik shake *[agitate][+]
sheikh *[Arab chief]
shail shale
shaim shame[2] *[guilty][+]
shaip shape[2+]
shair share[2+]
shake *[agitate] ~n ~down ~out ~up
@shaking
sheikh *[Arab chief]
shaky[4]
shalack shellac[+]
shalay chalet
shale *[rock]
shall *[will] ~| not
shallot
shallow[1] ~ness
sham[3] *[not real] shame[2] *[guilty][+]
shaman ~ism
shamble[2]
shame[2] *[guilty] ~-faced
sham[3] *[not real]
shameez chemise *[blouse]
shameful ~ly
shameless ~ly
shamman shaman[+]
shammy chamois *[animal, cloth]
shampain champagne
shampoo[1]
shamrock
Shangri La
shank
shanty[4] ~| town
shape[2] ~less ~ly
shaperon chaperone[2]
sharard charade
shard *[fragment] chard *[beet]
charred *[burned]

Key to Spelling Rules

Red words are wrong. **Black** words are correct.

- ~ Add the suffix or word directly to the main word, without a space or hyphen
  e.g. ash ~en ~tray → ashen ashtray
- ~- Add a hyphen to the main word before adding the next word
  e.g. blow ~-dry → blow-dry
- ~| Leave a space between the main word and the next word
  e.g. decimal ~| place → decimal place
- \+ By finding this word in its correct alphabetical order, you can find related words
  e.g. abowt about[+] → about-face
- ★ Draws attention to words that may be confused
- TM Means the word is a trademark
- @ Signifies the word is derived from the main word

share[2] ~| capital ~| certificate ~cropper ~holder ~holding ~| issue ~| option ~| price ~ware

Unable to find your word under **share**?
Take off **share** and look again

sharia
shark ~-infested
sharlatan charlatan *[fraud]
Charleston *[dance, U.S. city]
sharp[1] ~ly ~ness ~-eared ~-eyed ~shooter ~-tongued ~-witted
sharpen[1]
shassee chassis
shatow chateau+
shatter[1]
shauffer chauffeur[1+]
shaul shawl
shave[2] ~| off
shaving ~| cream ~| gel ~| lotion
shaw shore[2] *[sea, prop up]+
sure[2] *[certain]+
shawl
shawt short[1+]
she *[3rd person feminine] ~-devil ~'d * ~'s *[she is, has]
shy[4] *[horse, timid]+
sheaf[6]
sheap sheep+
shear[1] *[clip] sheer[1] *[thin, steep]
sheat sheet *[bedding]+
sheath *[covering]
sheathe[2] *[put away]
shebang
shed *[building, hair] ~ding
she'd *[she had, would]
shedule schedule[2]
sheef sheaf[6]
sheek chic *[elegant]
cheek *[face, rudeness]
sheikh *[Arab chief]
sheen *[shine] shin[3] *[leg]+
shine[2] *[shoes, sun]+

sheep *[animals] ~dog ~skin ~shank
ship[3] *[boat]+
cheap[1] *[not expensive]+
cheep[1] *[bird]
sheepish ~ly ~ness
sheer[1] *[thin, steep]
shear[1] *[clip]
sheet *[bedding] ~| lightning
shit[3] *[feces]
sheeth sheath *[covering]
sheathe[2] *[put away]
sheikh *[Arab chief]
shake *[agitate]+
chic *[elegant]
sheild shield[1]
Sheite Shiite *[branch of Islam]
shit[3][feces]
shekel
shelf[6] *[piece of wood] ~| life
shelve[2] *[place on]
shell[1] ~fish ~| game ~| out ~| script ~-shocked
shellac ~king
shelter[1]
shelve[2] *[place on]
shelf[6] *[piece of wood]+
shemeez chemise *[blouse]
shepherd[1] ~ess
shepherd's pie
sherbet
sheree sherry[4] *[drink]
sheriff
sherk shirk[1]
sherpa
sherry[4] *[drink] cherry[4] *[fruit]+
shert shirt *[clothing]+
sherty surety[4]
sheur shear[1] *[clip]
sheer[1] *[thin, steep]
sure[2] *[certain]+
shiatsu *[massage]
shih tzu *[dog]
shicanery chicanery

Key to Suffixes and Compounds

These rules are explained on pages vii to ix.

1 Keep the word the same before adding **ed, er, est, ing** e.g. cool[1] → cooled, cooler, coolest, cooling
2 Take off final **e** before adding **ed, er, est, ing** e.g. fine[2] → fined, finer, finest, fining
3 Double final consonant before adding **ed, er, est, ing** e.g. thin[3] → thinned, thinner, thinnest, thinning
4 Change final **y** to **i** before adding **ed, er, es, est, ly, ness** e.g. tidy[4] → tidied, tidier, tidies, tidiest, tidily, tidiness
Keep final **y** before adding **ing** e.g. tidying
5 Add **es** instead of **s** to the end of the word e.g. bunch[5] → bunches
6 Change final **f** to **ve** before adding **s** e.g. calf[6] → calves

shie she[3] *[3rd person feminine]+
shy[4] *[horse, timid]+
shiek sheikh *[Arab chief]
shield[1]
shier *[more shy, one that shies]
sheer[1] *[thin, steep]
shire *[place]+
shiffon chiffon
shift[1] @shifty[4] ~less
shih tzu *[dog] shiatsu *[massage]
Shiite *[branch of Islam]
shit[3] *[feces]
shilling
shimmer[1] ~y
shin[3] *[leg] ~dig
sheen *[shine]
shine[2] *[shoes, sun]
@shining
sheen *[shine]
shingle[2]
shinny[4] *[climb]
shiny[4] *[bright]
ship[3] *[boat] ~builder ~load ~ment ~shape
sheep *[animals]
cheap[1] *[inexpensive]+
cheep[1] *[bird]
chip[3] *[piece]+
shipping ~| agent ~| charges ~| clerk ~| company[4] ~| forecast ~| instructions
shipwreck[1]
shirk[1]
shirt *[clothing] ~-sleeved
shirtee surety[4]
shit[3] *[feces] sheet *[bedding]+
Shiite *[branch of Islam]
shivaree *[wedding pranks]
shivery[4] *[shaky]
shivelry chivalry+
shiver[1] ~y
shivery[4] *[shaky] shivaree *[wedding pranks]
shizum schism+

sho show[1] *[display]+
shore[2] *[sea, prop up]+
sure[2] *[certain]+
shoal ~of fish
shoar shore[2] *[sea, prop up]+
sure[2] *[certain]+
shock[1] ~| absorber ~-proof ~| waves
shod
shoddy[4]
shoe *[foot] ~ing ~box ~horn ~lace[2] ~shine[2] ~string
shoo[1] *[away]+
shofar *[horn] chauffeur[1] *[driver]+
shok shock[1]+
shole shoal+
shone *[lit up, polished]
shown *[displayed]
shoo[1] *[away] ~in
shoe *[foot]+
shood should+
shooger sugar[1]+
shook ~-up
shoot *[weapon, goal] ~er
chute *[slide]
shout *[yell]
shooting ~| star
shop[3] ~| floor ~lift[1] ~keeper ~talk ~| window ~worn
shopping ~| bag ~| cart ~| center ~| mall ~| plaza
shore[2] *[sea, prop up] ~line
chore *[job]
sure[2] *[certain]+
shority surety[4]
shorn
short[1] ~ly ~ness ~bread ~cake ~-change[2] ~-circuit[1] ~coming ~cut ~fall ~| fuse ~hand ~-haul ~| list[1] ~-lived ~-order ~-range ~sighted ~-staffed ~stop ~| story[4] ~-tempered ~-term ~wave

Unable to find your word under **short**? Take off **short** and look again

KEY TO SPELLING RULES

Red words are wrong. **Black** words are correct.

~ Add the suffix or word directly to the main word, without a space or hyphen
e.g. ash ~en ~tray → ashen ashtray

~- Add a hyphen to the main word before adding the next word
e.g. blow ~-dry → blow-dry

~| Leave a space between the main word and the next word
e.g. decimal ~| place → decimal place

+ By finding this word in its correct alphabetical order, you can find related words
e.g. abowt about+ → about-face

* Draws attention to words that may be confused

TM Means the word is a trademark

@ Signifies the word is derived from the main word

shortage
shot *[did shoot] ~gun ~| put
  shoot *[weapon, goal]+
  shout[1] *[yell]
shoud — should+
should ~n't [should not]
shoulder[1] ~-high ~-length
shout[1] *[yell] — shoot *[weapon, goal]+
shove[2]
shovel[3] ~ful
show[1] *[display] ~biz ~boat ~| business ~case[2] ~down ~girl ~man ~off ~piece ~place ~room ~stopper ~-and-tell
  @shown

> Unable to find your word under **show**? Take off **show** and look again

showcase[2]
shower[1] ~proof ~y[4]
showfer — chauffeur[1] *[driver]+
  shofar *[horn]
showlder — shoulder[1+]
shown *[displayed]
  shone *[lit up, polished]
showt — shout[1] *[yell]
  shoot *[weapon, goal]+
showvanist — chauvinist+
showy[4]
shpeel — spiel
shrank
shrapnel
shred[3]
shreik — shriek[1] *[scream]
  shrike *[bird]
shrew ~ish ~ishly
shrewd[1] ~ly ~ness
shriek[1] *[scream] — shrike *[bird]
shrift
shrike *[bird] — shriek *[scream]
shrill[1] ~y ~ness
shrimp ~ing ~| cocktail
shrine
shrink ~ing ~-wrapped
shrinkage
shrivel[3]
shroud[1]
shrub — @shrubbery[4]
shrude — shrewd[1+]
shrue — shrew+
shrug[3] ~| off
shrunk ~en
shryll — shrill[1+]
shryne — shrine
shrynk — shrink+
shud — should+
shudder[1] *[shake]
  shutter *[camera, window]+
shudent — shouldn't [should not]
shuffle[2]
shugar — sugar[1+]
shun[3]
shunt[1]
shurbert — sherbet
shurpa — sherpa
shurt — shirt *[clothing]+
shurtie — surety[4]
shush[5]
shut *[close] ~ting ~-eye ~out *[game] ~| out *[keep out]
  chute *[slide]
  shoot *[weapon, goal]+
shutter *[camera, window] ~ed
  shudder[1] *[shake]
shuttle[2] ~| bus ~cock
shuv — shove[2]
shuvel — shovel[3+]
shyer [also spelled shier]
Siamese ~| cat ~| twin
siatic — sciatic+
sibling ~| rivalry
sic *[thus] — sick *[ill]+
sic[3] *[unleash] — Sikh *[religion]+
sicada — cicada
sicadelic — psychedelic
siccey — sissy[4]
sichuate — situate[2]
siciatrist — psychiatrist+
sicick — psychic+

KEY TO SUFFIXES AND COMPOUNDS

These rules are explained on pages vii to ix.

1 Keep the word the same before adding **ed, er, est, ing**
e.g. cool[1] → cooled, cooler, coolest, cooling
2 Take off final **e** before adding **ed, er, est, ing**
e.g. fine[2] → fined, finer, finest, fining
3 Double final consonant before adding **ed, er, est, ing**
e.g. thin[3] → thinned, thinner, thinnest, thinning
4 Change final **y** to **i** before adding **ed, er, es, est, ly, ness**
e.g. tidy[4] → tidied, tidier, tidies, tidiest, tidily, tidiness
Keep final **y** before adding **ing** e.g. tidying
5 Add **es** instead of **s** to the end of the word
e.g. bunch[5] → bunches
6 Change final **f** to **ve** before adding **s**
e.g. calf[6] → calves

Unable to find your word under **si**?
Look under **psy**

sick *[ill] ~ly ~ness ~bay
sic *[thus]
sic[3] *[unleash]
Sikh *[religion]+
sicken[1]
sickle *[blade] ~-cell anemia
cycle[2] *[turning]
sicks — sics *[unleashes]
six *[number]+
sex[5] *[gender, intercourse]+
sicofant — sycophant+
sicreet — secrete[2] *[produce]+
sics *[unleashes] — six *[number]+
sex[5] *[gender, intercourse]+
sects *[groups]
side[2] *[right, left] ~board ~burns ~car ~| effect ~light ~line[2] ~long ~saddle ~step[3] ~swipe[2] ~track ~ways
sighed *[did sigh]

Unable to find your word under **side**?
Take off **side** and look again

sidel — sidle[2]
sider — cider
sidle[2] ~| up
sie — see *[eyes]+
sea *[water]+
sigh[1] *[let out air]
siedy — seedy[4] *[poor condition]
CD *[recording, investment]+
siege ~| mentality
siense — science+
siesta
sieve[2]
sifalis — syphilis+
sifen — siphon[1] *[tube, take away]
cipher *[code]
sifer — cipher *[code]
siphon[1] *[tube, take away]
sifon — siphon[1] *[tube, take away]
sift[1]
sigar — cigar
sigaret — cigarette+
sigh[1] *[let out air] — sea *[water]+
see *[eyes]+
sighed *[did sigh] — side[2] *[right, left]+
sighkee — psyche+
sight[1] *[seeing] ~read ~reading
site[2] *[place]+
sightseeing — @sightseer
sign[1] *[pointer] ~board ~| language
sin[3] *[wrongdoing]
sine *[trigonometry]
sign ~post
signachure — signature+
signal[3] ~| box
signatory[4]
signature ~| file ~| tune
signet *[ring] — cygnet *[swan]
significance
significant ~ly
signify[4] — @signification
siir — sire[2] *[breed, king]
sir *[man]
sik — sic *[thus]
sick *[ill]+
Sikh *[religion]+
siken — sicken[1]
sikey — psyche+
Sikh *[religion] ~ism
seek *[look for]+
sikle — sickle *[blade]+
sikosis — psychosis+
siks — six *[number]+
sex[5] *[gender, intercourse]+
siksteen — sixteen+
siksth — sixth+
siksty — sixty[4]+
silacone — silicon *[element]
silicone *[compound]
silacosis — silicosis

Key to Spelling Rules

Red words are wrong. **Black** words are correct.

~ Add the suffix or word directly to the main word, without a space or hyphen
e.g. ash ~en ~tray → ashen ashtray

~- Add a hyphen to the main word before adding the next word
e.g. blow ~-dry → blow-dry

~| Leave a space between the main word and the next word
e.g. decimal ~| place → decimal place

+ By finding this word in its correct alphabetical order, you can find related words
e.g. abowt about+ → about-face

* Draws attention to words that may be confused

TM Means the word is a trademark

@ Signifies the word is derived from the main word

silage
silee   silly[4]
silence[2]
silent ~ly
silf   sylph+
silhouette[2]
silica *[mineral]
silicon *[element]
Silicon Valley *[place]
silicone *[compound]
silicosis
silium   cilium *[hairlike]+
   psyllium *[seed]
silk ~-screen ~worm
   @silky[4]
sill *[window edge]
   seal[1] *[part of a lid, official, animal]+
sillabul   syllable+
sillabus   syllabus[5]
sillogisum   syllogism
sillooet   silhouette[2]
silly[4]
silo
silt[1]
silver ~| anniversary[4] ~| birch ~fish ~| lining ~| medal ~| mine ~| plate ~smith ~| spoon ~ware

> Unable to find your word under **silver**?
> Take off **silver** and look again

silvery[4]
simalar   similar+
simalarity   similarity[4]
simaly   simile *[figure of speech]+
simbol   cymbal *[music]
   symbol *[sign]
simbolic   symbolic+
simbolize   symbolize[2+]
simese   Siamese+
simfony   symphony+
similar ~ly
similarity[4]   @similitude
simile *[figure of speech]
   smile[2] *[happy expression]+
simmer[1]
simmetric   symmetric+
simmetry   cemetery[4] *[graveyard]
   symmetry[4] *[similarity]
simmilar   similar+
simpathetic   sympathetic+
simpathize   sympathize[2]
simpathy   sympathy
simper[1]
simphony   symphony+
simple[2] ~| interest ~-minded ~ton
   @simply
simplicity
simplify[4]   @simplification
simplissity   simplicity
simplistic ~ally
simpozeeum   symposium+
simulate[2]   @simulator
simulation
simultaneous ~ly ~| equation
sin[3] *[wrongdoing]
   sign[1] *[pointer]+
   sine *[trigonometry]
sinagog   synagogue
sinammon   cinnamon+
since *[before the present time]
   sins *[religious violations]
sincere[2] ~ly   @sincerity
sinch   cinch[5] *[binding]
   sync *[together]

> Unable to find your word under **si**?
> Look under **sy**

sinchronize   synchronize[2+]
sindicalism   syndicalism
sindicate   syndicate[2+]
sindrome   syndrome
sine *[trigonometry]
   sign[1] *[pointer]+
   sin[3] *[wrongdoing]
sine qua non

Key to Suffixes and Compounds

These rules are explained on pages vii to ix.

1 Keep the word the same before adding **ed, er, est, ing**
e.g. cool[1] → cooled, cooler, coolest, cooling
2 Take off final **e** before adding **ed, er, est, ing**
e.g. fine[2] → fined, finer, finest, fining
3 Double final consonant before adding **ed, er, est, ing**
e.g. thin[3] → thinned, thinner, thinnest, thinning
4 Change final **y** to **i** before adding **ed, er, es, est, ly, ness**
e.g. tidy[4] → tidied, tidier, tidies, tidiest, tidily, tidiness
Keep final **y** before adding **ing** e.g. tidying
5 Add **es** instead of **s** to the end of the word
e.g. bunch[5] → bunches
6 Change final **f** to **ve** before adding **s**
e.g. calf[6] → calves

sinema cinema+
sinematographer cinematographer+
sinew ~y
sinful ~ly ~ness
sing *[song] ~er ~ing ~along ~song
singe[2] *[burn]
single[2] ~| file ~-handed ~-minded
singly
singular ~ity
sinister
sink *[drop, basin] ~ing
sync *[together]
sinnamon cinnamon
sinnee cine *[camera, film]
sign[1] *[mark]+
sine *[trigonometry]
sinner
sinopsis synopsis+
sinse since *[before the present time]
sins *[religious violations]
sintax syntax+
sinthesis synthesis+
sinthetic synthetic+
sintillating scintillating
sinuous ~ly
sinus[5] ~itis
sinuus sinuous+
sip[3]
sipher siphon[1] *[tube, take away]
cipher *[code]
siphilis syphilis+

Unable to find your word under **si**?
Look under **sy**

siphon[1] *[tube, take away]
cipher *[code]
sir *[man] sire[2] *[breed, king]
sircul circle[2]
sircus circus[5]
sire[2] *[breed, king]
sir *[man]
siren

siringe syringe
sirloin ~| steak
sirocco
sirrup syrup+
sirtax surtax[5]
sirum serum
sismic seismic+
sismology seismology+
sissy[4]
sistem system+
sistematic systematic *[planned]+
sistematize systematize[2]
sister ~ly ~hood ~-in-law ~| ship
sistern cistern
sistole systole
sit[3] *[down] seat *[chair]
sight *[seeing]+
sitadel citadel
sitar
sitcom
site[2] *[place] cite[2] *[quote]+
seat *[chair]
sight *[seeing]+
siteseeing sightseeing+
sithe scythe[2] *[tool]
seethe[2] *[boil]
sitizen citizen+
sitrus citrus+
sitting ~| duck ~| room ~| target
situate[2]
situation
sity city[4+]
sityooashun situation
sive sieve[2]
sivic civic+
sivil civil+

Unable to find your word under **si**?
Look under **ci**

six *[number] ~fold ~-pack
sex[5] *[gender, intercourse]+
sics *[unleashes]
sects *[groups]

KEY TO SPELLING RULES

Red words are wrong. **Black** words are correct.

~ Add the suffix or word directly to the main word, without a space or hyphen
e.g. ash ~en ~tray → ashen ashtray

~- Add a hyphen to the main word before adding the next word
e.g. blow ~-dry → blow-dry

~| Leave a space between the main word and the next word
e.g. decimal ~| place → decimal place

+ By finding this word in its correct alphabetical order, you can find related words
e.g. abowt about+ → about-face

★ Draws attention to words that may be confused

™ Means the word is a trademark

@ Signifies the word is derived from the main word

sixteen ~th
sixth ~| sense
sixty[4] @sixtieth
size[2] *[measure] ~able ~ably ~| up
seize[2] *[grab hold]
sizmic seismic+
sizmology seismology+
sizum schism+
sizzle[2]
skab scab[3]
skate[2] ~board ~boarder
skeem scheme[2]
skeema schema *[model]+
skein
skeleton @skeletal
skeptic *[doubter] ~ism
skeptical *[doubting] ~ly
skermish skirmish[1+]
skert skirt[1+]
sketch[5] ~book
sketchy[4]
skew[1]
skewer[1]
ski[1] *[snow sport] ~| jump ~| lift
sky *[space]+
skid[3] *[slip] ~| row
skied *[snow sport]
skidoo
skied *[snow sport]
skid[3] *[slip]+
skiff
skill ~ed labor ~ful ~fully
skim[3] ~| milk
skimp[1]
skimpy[4]
skin[3] ~| care ~-deep ~-dive[2] ~flint ~head ~tight
skinny[4] ~-dipping
skip[3]
skirmish[5] ~er
skirt[1] ~| chaser
skism schism+
skit *[play]
skittish ~ness
skittle[2]
skitzo schizo
skizm schism+
sklerosis sclerosis
skold scald[1] *[burn]
scold[1] *[tell off]+
skulk[1]
skull *[head] ~cap
scull[1] *[boat]
skulpcher sculpture[2] *[what a sculptor produces]
skulpter sculptor *[artist]
skunk
skuttle scuttle[2]

Unable to find your word under **sk**? Look under **sc**

skwall squall[1]
skwod squad
skwolid squalid+
skwot squat[3]

Unable to find your word under **skw**? Look under **squ**

sky *[space] ~-blue ~diving ~-high ~lark ~light ~line ~rocket ~scraper ~wards
ski[1] *[snow sport]+

Unable to find your word under **sky**? Take off **sky** and look again

slack[1] *[lazy, loose] ~ly ~ness
slake[2] *[satisfy thirst]
slacken[1]
slacks *[trousers, stops work]
slakes[1] *[stops thirst]
slaik slake[2] *[satisfy thirst]
slain
slait slate[2] *[rock, list]
sleight *[skill]+
slaiv slave[2+]
slake[2] *[satisfy thirst]
slack[1] *[lazy, loose]+
slam[3] @slammer

Key to Suffixes and Compounds

These rules are explained on pages vii to ix.

1 Keep the word the same before adding **ed, er, est, ing**
e.g. cool[1] → cooled, cooler, coolest, cooling
2 Take off final **e** before adding **ed, er, est, ing**
e.g. fine[2] → fined, finer, finest, fining
3 Double final consonant before adding **ed, er, est, ing**
e.g. thin[3] → thinned, thinner, thinnest, thinning
4 Change final **y** to **i** before adding **ed, er, es, est, ly, ness**
e.g. tidy[4] → tidied, tidier, tidies, tidiest, tidily, tidiness
Keep final **y** before adding **ing** e.g. tidying
5 Add **es** instead of **s** to the end of the word
e.g. bunch[5] → bunches
6 Change final **f** to **ve** before adding **s**
e.g. calf[6] → calves

slander[1] ~ous ~ously
slane slain
slang
slant[1]
slap[3] ~dash ~-happy ~stick
slash[1]
slat *[flat piece]
slate[2] *[rock, list]
slaughter[1] ~house
slave[2] ~| driver ~| labor ~| trade
slavery
slavish ~ly ~ness
slay *[kill] @slain
@slew
sleigh *[snow carriage]
sleap sleep+
sleapless sleepless+
sleat sleet *[ice]
sleave *[skein, in Shakespeare]
sleeve *[tube]+
sleaze
sleazy[4]
sledge ~hammer
sleek[1] ~ly ~ness
sleep ~over ~walk
sleeping ~| bag ~| pill
sleepless ~ly ~ness
sleepy[4] ~head
sleet *[ice] slit *[cut]+
sleeve *[tube] ~d ~less
sleeze sleaze
sleezy sleazy[4]
slege sledge+
sleigh *[snow carriage]
slay *[kill]+
sleight *[skill] ~| of hand
slight[1] *[little]+
slender ~ness
slep sleep+
schlep[3]
slept
sler slur[3]
slerp slurp[1]
sleuth

slew *[killed, turn, many] ~| around ~| rate
slough[1] *[wetland]
sley slay[1] *[kill]+
sleigh *[snow carriage]
slice[2]
slick[1] ~ly ~ness
slid *[moved]
slide *[move, a slope] ~| rule
sliding ~| door ~| scale
slight[1] *[little] ~ly ~ness
sleight[1] *[skill]+
slik slick[1+]
slim[3] *[thin] ~line ~ness
slime *[thick substance]
@slimy[4]
sling[1] ~back ~shot
slink ~ing
slinky[4]
slip[3] ~knot ~shod ~-up ~way
slippage
slipped ~| disk
slipper
slippery[4] @slippy[4]
slipshod
slise slice[2]
slit *[cut] ~ting
sleet *[ice]
slight[1] *[little]+
sleight *[skill]+
slither[1] ~y
sliver
slob[3] ~ber[1]
sloe *[fruit] slow[1] *[not fast]+
slog[3]
slogan
sloo slew *[killed, turn, many]+
slough[1] *[wetland]
sloop *[boat]
sloose sluice[2+]
slooth sleuth
slop[3] *[slosh] ~py[4]
slope[2] *[surface]
slorter slaughter[1+]
slosh[5]
slot[3] ~| machine ~| racing

Key to Spelling Rules

Red words are wrong. **Black** words are correct.

- ~ Add the suffix or word directly to the main word, without a space or hyphen
  e.g. ash ~en ~tray → ashen ashtray
- ~- Add a hyphen to the main word before adding the next word
  e.g. blow ~-dry → blow-dry
- ~| Leave a space between the main word and the next word
  e.g. decimal ~| place → decimal place
- + By finding this word in its correct alphabetical order, you can find related words
  e.g. abowt about+ → about-face
- * Draws attention to words that may be confused
- TM Means the word is a trademark
- @ Signifies the word is derived from the main word

sloth ~ful
slouch[5]
slough[1] *[wetland]
 slew *[killed, turn, many]+
slough[1] *[cast off]
sloup sloop
slovenly[4]
slow[1] *[not fast] ~ly ~down ~| motion ~poke ~-witted ~worm
sludge[2] @sludgy[4]
slue slew *[killed, turn, many]+
 slough[1] *[wetland]
sluff slough[1] *[cast off]
slug[3]
sluggish ~ly ~ness
sluice[2] ~| gate
slum[3] ~lord
slumber[1] ~| party
slump[1]
slung
slunk
slur[3]
slurp[1]
slurry
slush[5] ~| fund @slushy[4]
slut
sluth sleuth
sluvenly slovenly[4]
sly ~ly ~ness
slyme slime *[thick substance]+
slyt slit *[cut]+
 slight[1] *[little]+
 sleight *[skill]+
slyther slither[1]+
slyver sliver
smack[1]
small[1] ~| business ~| change ~| fry ~-minded ~pox ~-scale ~-town
smart[1] ~ly ~ness ~| card
smarten[1] ~| up
smash[5]
smattering
smear[1] ~| campaign ~| tactics ~| test
smell[1] @smelt
 @smelly[4]
smelling ~| salts
smelt[1]
smerk smirk[1]
smidgen
smile[2] *[happy expression] ~y
 simile *[figure of speech]
smirk[1]
smite @smiting
smith @smithy[4]
smithereens
smitten
smock *[dress] ~ed ~ing
 smoke[2] *[fire]+
smog ~gy
smoke[2] *[fire] ~| bomb ~| detector ~-free ~| screen ~| signal ~stack
 smock *[dress]+
smoked ~| glass ~| salmon
smoking ~| area ~| gun
smoky[4]
smolder[1]
smooch[5]
smooth[1] ~ly ~ness
smoothie
smorgasbord
smote
smother[1]
smudge[2]
smug[3] ~ly ~ness
smuggle[2]
smut @smutty[4]
smyle smile[2] *[happy expression]+
snach snatch[5]
snack[1] *[food] ~-bar
 snake[2] *[animal]+
snaffle[2]
snag[3]
snaik snake[2]+
snail ~| mail
snair snare[2]
snake[2] *[animal] ~bite ~| eyes ~skin
 snack[1] *[food]+
snale snail+
snap[3] ~-on ~shot

Key to Suffixes and Compounds

These rules are explained on pages vii to ix.

1 Keep the word the same before adding **ed, er, est, ing**
e.g. cool[1] → cooled, cooler, coolest, cooling
2 Take off final **e** before adding **ed, er, est, ing**
e.g. fine[2] → fined, finer, finest, fining
3 Double final consonant before adding **ed, er, est, ing**
e.g. thin[3] → thinned, thinner, thinnest, thinning
4 Change final **y** to **i** before adding **ed, er, es, est, ly, ness**
e.g. tidy[4] → tidied, tidier, tidies, tidiest, tidily, tidiness
Keep final **y** before adding **ing** e.g. tidying
5 Add **es** instead of **s** to the end of the word
e.g. bunch[5] → bunches
6 Change final **f** to **ve** before adding **s**
e.g. calf[6] → calves

snapper
snappy4
snare2
snarl1 ~-up
snatch5
snazzy4
sneak1 ~ingly ~| preview
sneaky4
sneer1
sneeze2
snich — snitch1
snick1
snicker1
snide ~ly
snier — sneer1
snifel — sniffle2 *[have a cold]
snivel1 *[whine]
sniff1 — @sniffer dog
sniffle2 *[have a cold]
snivel1 *[whine]
snigger1
snikker — snicker1
snip3 *[cut]
snipe2 *[criticize, shoot, bird]
sniper
snippet
snitch5
snivel2 *[have a cold]
sno — snow1+
snob — @snobbery
snobbish ~ly ~ness
snoop1
snooty
snooze2
snorcul — snorkel3
snore2
snorkel3
snort1 *[breathe noisily]
snot3 *[mucus] ~-nosed
snout *[animal's nose]
snow1 ~ball ~boarding ~bound ~-blind ~| blower ~-capped ~| chains ~drift ~drop ~fall ~flake ~man ~plow ~shoe ~storm ~suit ~-white

Unable to find your word under **snow**? Take off **snow** and look again

snowt — snout *[animal's nose]
snot *[mucus]
snowy4
snuck ~| off
snuff1 ~box
snuffle2
snug3
snuggle2 ~| down ~| up
snupe — snoop1
snutey — snooty
snuze — snooze2
snyde — snide+
so *[in this way] ~-and-so ~-called
sew1 *[clothes]+
sow1 *[seeds]+
soak1 *[get wet] — sock1 *[clothing, hit]
soal — sole *[single, shoe]+
soul *[spirit]+
soap1 *[washing] ~box ~suds
sop3 *[blot]
soapy4 *[soap] — soppy4 *[wet]
soar1 *[fly] — saw1 *[cut, past of see]+
sore2 *[hurt]+
sob3 ~| story
sober1
sobriety
soccer
sociable — @sociably
social ~ly ~| climber ~ite ~| security ~| services ~| studies ~| worker
socialism — @socialist
socialize2 — @socialization
society4 — @societal
socio ~-cultural ~-political
socio-economic ~| group
sociology — @sociologist
sock1 *[clothing, hit]
soak1 *[get wet]
socker — soccer
socket
sod *[earth] — sewed *[did sew]
sowed *[did sow]

Key to Spelling Rules

Red words are wrong. **Black** words are correct.

~ Add the suffix or word directly to the main word, without a space or hyphen
e.g. ash ~en ~tray → ashen ashtray

~- Add a hyphen to the main word before adding the next word
e.g. blow ~-dry → blow-dry

~| Leave a space between the main word and the next word
e.g. decimal ~| place → decimal place

+ By finding this word in its correct alphabetical order, you can find related words
e.g. abowt about+ → about-face

* Draws attention to words that may be confused

TM Means the word is a trademark

@ Signifies the word is derived from the main word

soda ~| water

sodden

sodder solder[1] *[join]+

soldier[1] *[army]+

sodium

sodomy

sofa ~| bed

soffamore sophomore

soffen soften[1]+

sofist sophist+

sofmore sophomore

soft[1] ~ly ~ness ~ball ~-boiled ~cover ~| currency ~| drink ~headed ~hearted ~-pedal[3] ~| rock ~| sell ~-spoken

> Unable to find your word under **soft**?
> Take off **soft** and look again

soften[1] ~er

software

softy[4]

soggy[4]

soil[1]

soirée

sojourn[1]

soke soak[1] *[get wet]

sock[1] *[clothing, hit]

soket socket

solace[2]

solar ~| energy ~ium ~| plexus ~| system

solasism solecism *[social error]

solipsism *[belief that only self exists]

sold

solder[1] *[join] ~ing iron

soldier[1] *[army]+

soldier[1] *[army] ~| of fortune

solder[1] *[join]+

sole *[single, shoe] ~ly

soul *[spirit]+

solecism *[social error]

solipsism *[belief that only self exists]

solejur solder[1] *[join]

soldier[1] *[army]+

solem solemn+

solemn ~ity[4] ~ly[4] ~ify[4]

solenoid

solepcism solipsism *[belief that only self exists]

soler solar+

solesism solecism *[social error]

solipsism *[belief that only self exists]

solichude solitude

solicit[1] ~ation ~or

solicitous ~ly @solicitude

solid ~ity ~ly

solidarity

solidify[4]

soliloquy[4]

solipsism *[belief that only self exists]

solecism *[social error]

solis solace[2]

solissit solicit[1]+

solitaire

solitary[4]

solitude

sollace solace[2]

solo ~ist

solstice

solt salt[1]+

solty salty[4]

soluble @solubility

solute @solution

solve[2]

solvency

solvent ~| abuse

som psalm+

somber *[gloomy] ~ly ~ness

samba *[dance]

sombrero

some *[a quantity] ~body ~how ~one ~thing ~time ~times ~what ~where

sum[3] *[total]

> Unable to find your word under **some**?
> Take off **some** and look again

Key to Suffixes and Compounds

These rules are explained on pages vii to ix.

1 Keep the word the same before adding **ed, er, est, ing**
e.g. cool[1] → cooled, cooler, coolest, cooling

2 Take off final **e** before adding **ed, er, est, ing**
e.g. fine[2] → fined, finer, finest, fining

3 Double final consonant before adding **ed, er, est, ing**
e.g. thin[3] → thinned, thinner, thinnest, thinning

4 Change final **y** to **i** before adding **ed, er, es, est, ly, ness**
e.g. tidy[4] → tidied, tidier, tidies, tidiest, tidily, tidiness
Keep final **y** before adding **ing** e.g. tidying

5 Add **es** instead of **s** to the end of the word
e.g. bunch[5] → bunches

6 Change final **f** to **ve** before adding **s**
e.g. calf[6] → calves

somersault[1]
son *[male child] ~| et lumière ~-in-law
sun[3] *[shine]+
sonar
sonata
soner sonar
sonet sonnet
song ~bird ~book ~ster ~writer
sonic ~| boom
sonnet
sonorous
sonter saunter[1]
sooave suave[2+]
soocher suture[2] *[sew up]
sooder suitor *[for marriage]
soodoe pseudo+
sooflay soufflé
soon[1]
soony Sunni *[branch of Islam]
soop soup[1] *[food]+
sop[3] *[blot]
sooper

> Unable to find your word under **sooper**?
> Look under **super**

soot *[black dust] ~y
suit[1] *[clothes, lawsuit]+
soothe[2]
soothsayer @soothsaying
soovineer souvenir+
sop[3] *[blot] soap[1] *[washing]+
soup[1] *[food]+
sopey soapy[4]
sophist ~ry
sophisticated @sophistication
sophomore
soporific
soppy[4] *[wet] soapy[4] *[soap]
soprano
sor saw[1] *[cut, past of see]+
soar[1] *[fly]
sore[2] *[hurt]+
sorce sauce *[liquid]+
source[2] *[origin]+

sorcer saucer
sorcery[4] @sorcerer
sorcy saucy[4]
sord sword+
sordid ~ly ~ness
sore[2] *[hurt] ~ly
saw[1] *[cut, past of see]+
soar[1] *[fly]
sorel sorrel
soriasis psoriasis
sorn sawn+
sorna sauna
sornter saunter[1]
sorow sorrow+
sorrel
sorrow ~ful ~fully ~fulness
sorry[4] *[sad] sari *[garment]
sorsery sorcery[4+]
sort[1] *[kind] ~| algorithm
sought *[looked for]
sory sorry[4] *[sad]
sari *[garment]
soshall social+
sossige sausage+
sotay sauté[1]

> Unable to find your word under **so**?
> Look under **sau**

sotto voce
soufflé
sought *[looked for]
sort[1] *[kind]+
soul *[spirit] ~ful ~fully ~less ~-destroying ~| food ~mate ~| music ~-searching
sole *[single, shoe]+

> Unable to find your word under **soul**?
> Take off **soul** and look again

sound[1] ~ly ~ness ~| barrier ~| effects ~track
soundless ~ly
soundproof[1]

KEY TO SPELLING RULES

Red words are wrong. **Black** words are correct.

~ Add the suffix or word directly to the main word, without a space or hyphen
e.g. ash ~en ~tray → ashen ashtray

~- Add a hyphen to the main word before adding the next word
e.g. blow ~-dry → blow-dry

~| Leave a space between the main word and the next word
e.g. decimal ~| place → decimal place

+ By finding this word in its correct alphabetical order, you can find related words
e.g. abowt about+ → about-face

* Draws attention to words that may be confused

TM Means the word is a trademark

@ Signifies the word is derived from the main word

soup[1] *[food] ~y ~| spoon
sop[3] *[blot]
sour[1] ~ness ~dough ~puss
source[2] *[origin] ~| code
sauce *[liquid]+
souse[2]
south ~bound ~east ~easterly ~erner ~erly ~-seeking ~paw ~| pole ~wards ~west ~westerly

Unable to find your word under **south**?
Take off **south** and look again

southern @Southern Baptist
southmore sophomore
souvenir ~| hunter
sovereign ~ty
Soviet
sovren sovereign+
sow[1] *[seeds] ~n
sew[1] *[clothes]+
so *[in this way]+
sow[1] *[pig]
sowed *[did sow] sewed *[did sew]
sod *[earth]
sower *[sows seeds]
sewer *[sews clothes]
sown *[seeds] sewn *[clothes]
sownd sound[1+]
sowndprufe soundproof[1]
sowr sour[1+]
sowse souse[2]
sowth south+
soy ~| bean ~| sauce
spa *[mineral springs]
spar[3] *[fight, mast]
space[2] ~| age ~craft ~| flight ~| probe ~ship ~| shuttle ~suit ~| travel ~walk

Unable to find your word under **space**?
Take off **space** and look again

spachula spatula
spacial spatial
spacious ~ly ~ness
spade *[tool, card] ~work
spayed *[sterilized]
spaghetti
spair spare[2] *[left over, save]+
spairing sparing *[using little]+
spait spate *[large number]
span[3]
spaner spanner
spangle ~d
spaniel
spank[1]
spanner
spanyel spaniel
spar[3] *[fight, mast] ~ring partner
spare[2] *[left over, save]+
spa *[mineral springs]
sparce sparse+
spare[2] *[left over, save] ~| part ~| time ~| tire
spar[3] *[fight, mast]+
sparing *[using little] ~ly
sparring *[fighting]+
spark[1] ~| plug
sparkle[2]
sparring *[fighting] ~| partner
sparing *[using little]+
sparrow ~hawk
sparse ~ly ~ness ~r
sparsity
spartan
spase space[2+]
spashul special+
spashus spacious+
spasm
spasmodic *[proceeding by spasms] ~ally
spastic *[afflicted with spasms] ~ally
spat *[argument, past of spit]
spate *[large number]
spatial
spatter[1]
spatula
spaun spawn[1]
spaw spoor *[smell, track]
spore *[seed, germ]
spa *[mineral springs]

Key to Suffixes and Compounds

These rules are explained on pages vii to ix.

1 Keep the word the same before adding **ed, er, est, ing** e.g. cool[1] → cooled, cooler, coolest, cooling
2 Take off final **e** before adding **ed, er, est, ing** e.g. fine[2] → fined, finer, finest, fining
3 Double final consonant before adding **ed, er, est, ing** e.g. thin[3] → thinned, thinner, thinnest, thinning
4 Change final **y** to **i** before adding **ed, er, es, est, ly, ness** e.g. tidy[4] → tidied, tidier, tidies, tidiest, tidily, tidiness
Keep final **y** before adding **ing** e.g. tidying
5 Add **es** instead of **s** to the end of the word e.g. bunch[5] → bunches
6 Change final **f** to **ve** before adding **s** e.g. calf[6] → calves

spawn[1]
spay[1]
spayr spare[2] *[left over, save]+
spazum spasm
speach speech+
spead speed[1] *[move fast]+
speady speedy[4]
speak *[talk] ~er ~ing ~-easy ~erphone
spec *[speculation, specification]+
speck[1] *[spot]
spear[1] ~head ~mint
spare[2] *[left over, save]+
spec *[speculation, specification] ~| sheet
speak *[talk]+
speck[1] *[spot]
speces species
special ~| delivery ~| education ~ist ~ly ~| offer

> Unable to find your word under **special**?
> Take off **special** and look again

specialize[2] @specialization
specialty[4]
species
specific ~ally ~s
specify[4] @specification
specimen
specious ~ly ~ness
speck[1] *[spot] speak *[talk]+
spec *[speculation, specification]+
speckle[2]
spectacle @spectacles
@spectacled
spectacular ~ly
spectator ~| sport
specter
spectrum
speculate[2] @speculation
speculative
speculator
sped *[past of speed]
speech ~less ~| therapy ~writer
speed[1] *[move fast] ~y[4] ~boat ~| bump ~| limit ~way
sped *[past of speed]
spied *[looked]
speedometer
speek speak *[talk]+
spec *[on spec, specification]+
speck[1] *[spot]
speer spear[1]+
speesheez species
speeshus specious+
spek speak *[talk]+
spec *[speculation, specification]+
speck[1] *[spot]
spektakel spectacle+
spell[1] ~checker
spellbinding @spellbound
spend ~er ~ing ~thrift
@spent
sper spur[3]+
spare[2] *[left over, save]+
sperm ~atozoa ~| bank ~| count ~icide ~| whale
spern spurn[1]
spert spurt[1]
speshul special+
speshus specious+
spesial special+
spesies species
spessimen specimen
spew[1]
spewed *[sprayed]
spud *[potato]
sphere[2] @spherical
sphincter ~| muscle
sphinx[5]
spice[2] @spicy[4]
spider ~'s web @spidery
spied *[looked] speed[1] *[move fast]+
spiel
spight spite[2] *[resentment]
spigot

Key to Spelling Rules

Red words are wrong. **Black** words are correct.

~ Add the suffix or word directly to the main word, without a space or hyphen
e.g. ash ~en ~tray → ashen ashtray

~- Add a hyphen to the main word before adding the next word
e.g. blow ~-dry → blow-dry

~| Leave a space between the main word and the next word
e.g. decimal ~| place → decimal place

+ By finding this word in its correct alphabetical order, you can find related words
e.g. abowt about+ → about-face

* Draws attention to words that may be confused

™ Means the word is a trademark

@ Signifies the word is derived from the main word

spike[2]	@spiky[4]
spill[1] ~age	@spilt
spin[3] *[turn fast] ~cast ~| doctor ~-dryer	
	@spun
	spine *[backbone]+
spinach	
spinal ~| column ~| cord ~| tap	
spindle	@spindly
spine *[backbone] ~less ~-chilling ~-tingling	
	spin *[turn fast]+
spineker	spinnaker
spinet	
spinich	spinach
spinnaker •	
spinster ~hood	
spiral[3] ~-bound ~| staircase	
spire	
spirichual	spiritual+
spirit[1] ~| lamp ~| level	
spiritual ~ly ~ism ~ist ~ity ~| advisor ~| counseling	
spise	spice[2+]
spit[3] *[saliva] ~ball ~fire	
spite[2] *[resentment]	
spiteful ~ly ~ness	
spittle	
splaie	splay[1+]
splash[5] ~y ~back ~down	
splatter[2]	
splay[1] ~| out	
spleen	
splendid ~ly	
splendor	
splerge	splurge[2]
splice[2]	
splint *[limb support]	
splinter[1] *[sharp piece]	
splise	splice[2]
split ~ting ~-level ~-screen ~| up	
splurge[2]	
splutter[1]	
splyt	split+
spoak	spoke+

spoar	spore *[seed, germ]
	spoor *[smell, track]
spoil[1]	@spoilage ~sport
spoke ~n	
spokesman	@spokeswoman
sponge[2] ~| bath ~| cake	
spongy[4]	
sponsor[1] ~ship	
spontaneity	
spontaneous ~ly ~ness ~| combustion	
spontenaity	spontaneity
spoof[1]	
spook[1]	@spooky[4]
spool[1]	
spoon[1] *[utensil] ~-fed ~feed ~feeding ~ful	
	spun *[past of spin]
spoor *[smell, track]	
	spore *[seed, germ]
sporadic ~ally	
spore *[seed, germ]	
	spoor *[smell, track]
sporran	
sport[1] *[game] ~y[4] ~| coat ~| utility	
	spot[3] *[mark]+
	spurt[1] [liquid]
sporting ~| chance	
sports ~| car ~wear	
sportsman ~like ~ship	
spot[3] *[mark] ~less ~| check[1]	
	sport[1] *[game]+
spotless ~ly ~ness	
spotlight[1]	
spoure	spore *[seed, germ]
	spoor *[smell, track]
spourt	sport[1] *[game]+
	spurt[1] *[liquid]
spourts	sports+
spourtsman	sportsman+
spouse	@spousal
spout[1]	
spoylige	spoilage
spraie	spray[1+]
sprain[1]	
sprang	

KEY TO SUFFIXES AND COMPOUNDS

These rules are explained on pages vii to ix.

1 Keep the word the same before adding **ed, er, est, ing**
e.g. cool[1] → cooled, cooler, coolest, cooling

2 Take off final **e** before adding **ed, er, est, ing**
e.g. fine[2] → fined, finer, finest, fining

3 Double final consonant before adding **ed, er, est, ing**
e.g. thin[3] → thinned, thinner, thinnest, thinning

4 Change final **y** to **i** before adding **ed, er, es, est, ly, ness**
e.g. tidy[4] → tidied, tidier, tidies, tidiest, tidily, tidiness
Keep final **y** before adding **ing** e.g. tidying

5 Add **es** instead of **s** to the end of the word
e.g. bunch[5] → bunches

6 Change final **f** to **ve** before adding **s**
e.g. calf[6] → calves

sprawl[1]
spray[1] ~| gun ~| paint
spread ~er ~ing ~-eagle[2] ~sheet
spree *[binge]
sprig
sprightly[4]
spring ~ing ~y[4] ~board ~bok
~| chicken ~-clean ~-loaded ~time

> Unable to find your word under **spring**?
> Take off **spring** and look again

sprinkle[2]
sprint[1]
sprite ~ly
spritely sprightly[4]
sprocket
sprout[1]
spruce[2] ~ly ~-up
sprung
spruse spruce[2+]
spry *[energetic] ~ly
spree *[binge]
spryng spring+
spryngy springy[4]
sprynt sprint[1]
spryte sprite+
sprytely sprightly[4]
spud *[potato] spewed *[sprayed]
spue spew[1]
spufe spoof[1]
spuk spook[1+]
spule spool[1]
spume[2]
spun *[past of spin]
spoon[1] *[utensil]+
spunk
spunky[4]
spur[3] ~-of-the-moment
spurious ~ly ~ness
spurm sperm+
spurn[1]
spurt[1] *[liquid] sport[1] *[game]+
spuryius spurious+
sputter[1]

sputum
spy[4] ~-glass ~-hole
spyed spied *[looked]
speed[1] *[move fast]+
spyne spine *[backbone]+
spin *[turn fast]+
spyrit spirit[1+]
squabble[2]
squad
squadron
squalid ~ly
squall[1]
squalor
squander[1]
square[2] ~ly ~| dance[2] ~off ~| root
squash[5] *[crush] quash[5] *[nullify]
squat[3]
squawk[1]
squeak[1] @squeaky[4]
squeal[1]
squeamish ~ly ~ness
squeek squeak[1+]
squeel squeal[1]
squeemish squeamish+
squeeze[2]
squelch[5]
squerl squirrel
squerm squirm[1]
squert squirt[1]
squid
squiggle[2]
squint[1]
squirm[1]
squirrel
squirt[1]
squish[5] @squishy[4]
squobble squabble[2]
squok squawk[1]
stab[3]
stabel stable[2+]
stability
stabilize[2]
stable[2] *[steady, horses] ~| currency[4]
~| economy[4] ~| exchange rate
~hand ~mate ~| prices

Key to Spelling Rules

Red words are wrong. **Black** words are correct.

~ Add the suffix or word directly to the main word, without a space or hyphen
e.g. ash ~en ~tray → ashen ashtray

~- Add a hyphen to the main word before adding the next word
e.g. blow ~-dry → blow-dry

~| Leave a space between the main word and the next word
e.g. decimal ~| place → decimal place

+ By finding this word in its correct alphabetical order, you can find related words
e.g. abowt about+ → about-face

* Draws attention to words that may be confused

TM Means the word is a trademark

@ Signifies the word is derived from the main word

staccato
stacher — stature
stachue — statue+
stachute — statute+
stack[1]
stadium ~s — @stadia
staek — stake[2] *[post, share]+
steak *[beef]+
staer — stair *[step]+
stare[2] *[gaze]
staff[1] ~| nurse
stag *[deer] — stage[2] *[time, theater]+
stagar — stagger[1]
stage[2] *[time, theater] ~coach ~craft ~hand ~-manage[2] ~struck
stag *[deer]
stagger[1]
stagnant
stagnate[2] — @stagnation
staid *[prim] — stayed *[remained]
staik — stake[2] *[post, share]+
stail — stale[2+]
stain[1] ~ed glass ~less steel
stair *[step] ~case ~way ~well
stare[2] *[gaze]
stait — state[2+]
staites — states+
staiv — stave[2]
stak — stack[1]
stakato — staccato
stake[2] *[post, share] ~holder ~-out
steak *[beef]+
stalactite *[rock, down]
stalagmite *[rock, up]
stale[2] ~mate
staletto — stiletto+
stalk[1] *[stem, follow]
stock[1] *[keep, have]+
stork *[bird]
stalking *[following]
stocking *[legwear]
stall[1]
stallion
stalwart
stamen *[part of flower]
stamina *[endurance]
stammer[1]
stamp[1]
stampede[2]
stance
stand ~ing ~-alone ~| down ~-in ~off ~offish ~point ~still
standard ~-bearer ~-issue ~| of living ~| time
standardize[2] — @standardization
standby ~| arrangement ~| credit ~| ticket
standing ~| order
stane — stain[1+]
stank
stanse — stance
stanza
staple[2] ~| industry[4] ~| product
@stapler
star[3] *[in sky, actor] ~less ~ry ~board ~burst ~dom ~dust ~fish ~gaze ~gazer ~light ~ship ~struck ~-studded
stare[2] *[gaze]
stair *[step]+

> Unable to find your word under **star**?
> Take off **star** and look again

starch[5]
stare[2] *[gaze] — stair *[step]+
star[3] *[in sky, actor]+
stark *[empty, utter] ~ly
stalk[1] *[stem, follow]
stock[1] *[keep, have]+
stork *[bird]
starlight *[brightness]
starlit *[bright]
start[1] ~-up
starting ~| date ~| point ~| salary[4]
startle[2]
start-up ~| costs
starve[2] — @starvation
stash[5]

KEY TO SUFFIXES AND COMPOUNDS

These rules are explained on pages vii to ix.

1 Keep the word the same before adding **ed, er, est, ing**
e.g. cool[1] → cooled, cooler, coolest, cooling
2 Take off final **e** before adding **ed, er, est, ing**
e.g. fine[2] → fined, finer, finest, fining
3 Double final consonant before adding **ed, er, est, ing**
e.g. thin[3] → thinned, thinner, thinnest, thinning
4 Change final **y** to **i** before adding **ed, er, es, est, ly, ness**
e.g. tidy[4] → tidied, tidier, tidies, tidiest, tidily, tidiness
Keep final **y** before adding **ing** e.g. tidying
5 Add **es** instead of **s** to the end of the word
e.g. bunch[5] → bunches
6 Change final **f** to **ve** before adding **s**
e.g. calf[6] → calves

stashun station¹
stashuner stationer
state² ~less ~ly ~ment ~hood ~-of-the-art
states ~man ~woman
static ~ally
station¹
stationary *[not moving] — stationery *[paper]
stationer
stationery *[paper] — stationary *[not moving]
statistic ~ian ~s
statistical ~ly ~| analysis ~| analyst
statuary
statue ~sque ~tte
stature
status ~| quo ~| symbol
statute ~| law ~| of limitations
staunch⁵
stave²
staw store²⁺
stay¹ ~-at-home ~| of execution
stayed *[remained] — staid *[prim]
stayje stage² *[time, theater]⁺
staymin stamen *[flower]
steadfast ~ly ~ness
steady⁴
steak *[beef] ~| house ~| tartare — stake² *[post, share]⁺
steal *[take] ~ing — steel¹ *[iron]⁺
stealth @stealthy⁴
steam¹ *[hot air] ~er ~boat ~| engine ~roller ~ship — stem³ *[grow]⁺
stedfast steadfast⁺
stedy steady⁴
steed
steel¹ *[iron] ~| band ~| wool ~y⁴ — steal *[take]⁺
steep¹ ~ly ~ness
steeple ~chase
steer¹ *[drive, ox] ~age
stellar
stelth stealth⁺
stem³ *[grow] ~| cell — steam¹ *[hot air]⁺
stench⁵
stencil³
stenography @stenographer
stensil stencil³
step³ *[pace] ~ing stone ~ladder ~brother ~sister ~son ~father ~mother ~parent — steppe *[land]

Unable to find your word under **step**? Take off **step** and look again

stepchild ~ren
steppe *[land] — step³ *[pace]⁺
ster stir³ *[move]⁺; steer¹ *[drive, ox]⁺; star³ *[in sky, actor]⁺
sterdy sturdy⁴
stere stare² *[gaze]; stair *[step]⁺; steer¹ *[drive, ox]⁺
stereo ~phonic ~scopic
stereotype² @stereotypical
stergeon sturgeon *[fish]
sterile @sterility
sterilize² @sterilization
sterio stereo⁺
steriotype stereotype²⁺
sterling ~| silver
stern¹ ~ly ~ness
sternum
steroid
steryle sterile⁺
sterylize sterilize²⁺
stethoscope
stew¹ ~pot
steward ~ess ~ship
stewdent student⁺
sticelback stickleback
stich stitch⁵⁺
stick ~er ~y⁴ ~-up

stickleback
stickler
stie — sty[4] *[pigpen]
— stye[1] *[eyelid infection]
stiep — steep[1+]
stieple — steeple[+]
stier — steer[1] *[drive, ox][+]
— stir[3] *[move][+]
stifel — stifle[2]
stiff[1] ~ly ~ness
stiffen[1]
stifle[2]
stigma — @stigmata
stigmatize[2]
stik — stick[+]
stile *[steps] — style[2] *[appearance][+]
stiletto ~| heel
stilist — stylist[+]
stilize — stylize[2]
still ~birth ~born ~| image ~| life ~ness
stilt ~ed
stilus — stylus[5]
stimie — stymie[+]
stimulant
stimulate[2] — @stimulation
stimulus — @stimuli
sting ~er ~ing ~-ray ~y[4]
stink ~er ~ing — @stinky[4]
stint[1]
stipend
stipple[2]
stipulate[2] — @stipulation
stir[3] *[move] ~-crazy ~-fry
stirrup
stitch[5] ~| up
sto — stow[1+]
stoal — stole[+]
stoan — stone[2+]
stoav — stove[2]
stock[1] *[keep, have] ~y[4] ~broker ~| car ~| exchange ~| level ~| market ~| option ~room ~| size ~| still ~| turnover ~| up ~| valuation
— stalk[1] *[stem, follow]
stock[1] — stoke[2] *[a fire]
— stork *[bird]

> Unable to find your word under **stock**?
> Take off **stock** and look again

stocking *[legwear]
— stalking *[following]
— stoking *[making a fire]
stockpile[2]
stodgy[4] *[dull]
stogie *[cigar] — stooge[2] *[subordinate]
stoic ~al ~ally ~ism
stoke[2] *[a fire] — stock[1] *[keep, have][+]
— stork *[bird]
stoking *[making a fire]
— stalking *[following]
— stocking *[legwear]
stokpile — stockpile[2]
stoky — stocky[4]
stole ~n
stolid ~ly
stolwort — stalwart
stomach[1] ~ache ~| pump
stomp[1] ~ing ground
stone[2] ~-cold ~mason ~wall
Stone Age *[a period of time]

> Unable to find your word under **stone**?
> Take off **stone** and look again

stony[4] ~-faced
stood
stooge[2] *[subordinate]
— stogie *[cigar]
— stodgy[4] *[dull]
stool ~ie ~| pigeon ~| specimen
stoop[1] *[bend down]
— stoup *[container]
stop[3] *[quit] ~page ~gap ~light ~watch
stopper
storage ~| capacity[4] ~| facility[4] ~| unit
store[2] ~house ~keeper
storeybord — storyboard[1]
stork *[bird] — stalk[1] *[stem, follow]
— stock[1] *[keep, have][+]

KEY TO SUFFIXES AND COMPOUNDS

These rules are explained on pages vii to ix.

1 Keep the word the same before adding **ed, er, est, ing**
e.g. cool[1] → cooled, cooler, coolest, cooling
2 Take off final **e** before adding **ed, er, est, ing**
e.g. fine[2] → fined, finer, finest, fining
3 Double final consonant before adding **ed, er, est, ing**
e.g. thin[3] → thinned, thinner, thinnest, thinning
4 Change final **y** to **i** before adding **ed, er, es, est, ly, ness**
e.g. tidy[4] → tidied, tidier, tidies, tidiest, tidily, tidiness
Keep final **y** before adding **ing** e.g. tidying
5 Add **es** instead of **s** to the end of the word
e.g. bunch[5] → bunches
6 Change final **f** to **ve** before adding **s**
e.g. calf[6] → calves

storm^{1} ~y^{4} ~| cloud ~| damage ~| trooper
stornch — **staunch**^{5}
story^{4} *[tale, building] ~book ~line ~teller ~telling
storyboard^{1}
stoup *[container] — **stoop**^{1} *[bend down]
stourk — **stork** *[bird]
stourm — **storm**$^{1+}$
stout^{1} ~ly ~ness
stove^{2}
stow^{1} ~away — @**stowage**
stowick — **stoic**$^{+}$
stowt — **stout**$^{1+}$
straddle^{2}
straey — **stray**^{1}
strafe^{2}
straggle^{2}
straight *[not bent] ~| away ~-faced ~forward ~| line ~| man
— **strait** *[narrow passage]

> Unable to find your word under **straight**?
> Take off **straight** and look again

straighten^{1}
strain^{1}
strait *[narrow passage] ~jacket ~laced
— **straight** *[not bent]$^{+}$
straiten — **straighten**^{1}
strand^{1}
strane — **strain**^{1}
strange^{2} ~ly ~ness
stranger *[unknown person]
— **strangler** *[killer]
strangle^{2} ~hold
strangler *[killer] — **stranger** *[unknown person]
strangulated — @**strangulation**
strap^{3} ~less
stratagem
strategic ~ally ~| planning
— @**strategist**
strategy^{4}
stratify^{4}
stratosphere — @**stratospheric**
stratum — @**strata**
straw ~| boss ~| hat ~| man ~| poll
strawberry^{4}
stray^{1}
strayt — **straight** *[not bent]$^{+}$
— **strait** *[narrow passage]
streak^{1} — @**streaky**^{4}
stream^{1} ~line^{2}
strech — **stretch**$^{1+}$
streek — **streak**$^{1+}$
streem — **stream**$^{1+}$
street ~light ~| smarts ~| value ~wise
strength ~en^{1}
strenuous ~ly ~ness
streptococcus — @**streptococci**
stress^{5} ~ful ~fully ~| fracture
stretch^{5} ~| limo ~| mark ~| pants
stretcher ~-bearer
strew^{1} ~n
strickcher — **stricture**
stricken
stricknine — **strychnine**
strict^{1} ~ly ~ness ~ure
stricture
stride — @**striding**
strident ~ly
strife
strike^{2} ~breaker ~| down
— @**struck**
— @**stricken**
strike ~| force ~out ~| price
striken — **stricken**
strikt — **strict**$^{1+}$
string ~er ~ing
stringent — @**stringency**
strip^{3} *[naked] ~-search ~tease
stripe^{2} *[pattern] — @**stripy**^{4}
strive^{2} — @**strove**
stroad — **strode**
stroak — **stroke**^{2}
strobe ~| light
strode
stroke^{2}
stroll^{1}

strong[1] ~ly ~-arm[1] ~box ~| currency[4] ~| growth ~hold ~-minded ~room
strore straw[+]
strove
struck
structural ~ism ~ly ~| adjustment
structure[2]
strudel
strue strew[1+]
struggle[2]
strum[3]
strung
strut[3]
strychnine
strydent strident[+]
stub[3]
stubble @stubbly[4]
stubborn ~ly ~ness
stucco[5]
stuck ~-up
stucko stucco[1+]
stud[3]
studded *[decorated]
studied *[worked]
student ~| body ~| council ~| teaching
studie study[4]
studied *[worked] studded *[decorated]
studio
studious ~ly ~ness
study[4]
studyo studio
stue stew[1+]
stueard steward[+]
stuff[1] ~y[4]
stuge stooge[2] *[subordinate]
stuk stuck[+]
stule stool[+]
stultify[4]
stumble[2] @stumbling block
stummick stomach[1+]
stump[1]
stun[3] ~| grenade ~| gun
stung
stunk
stunt[1] ~| double
stupe stoop[1] *[bend down]
stupefy[4]
stupendous ~ly ~ness
stuper stupor
stupid[1] ~ly
stupidity[4]
stupify stupefy[4]
stupor
stupyd stupid[1+]
stur stir[3] *[move][+]
sturdy[4]
sturgeon *[fish] surgeon *[doctor]
sturling sterling[+]
sturn stern[1+]
sturnum sternum
stutter[1]
sty[4] *[pigpen]
stye[1] *[eyelid infection]
stygma stigma[+]
style[2] *[appearance]
@styling
stile *[steps]
stylish ~ly ~ness
stylist ~ic ~ically ~ics
stylize[2]
stylus[5]
stymie ~d
stymulant stimulant

Unable to find your word under **sty**?
Look under **sti**

su sue[2]
suave[2] ~ly ~ness
sub[3] ~| judice
subcommittee
subconscious ~ly ~ness
subcontinent
subcontract[1] ~or
subculture
subdew subdue[2]
subdivide[2] @subdivision
subdue[2]

Key to Suffixes and Compounds

These rules are explained on pages vii to ix.

1 Keep the word the same before adding **ed, er, est, ing**
e.g. cool[1] → cooled, cooler, coolest, cooling
2 Take off final **e** before adding **ed, er, est, ing**
e.g. fine[2] → fined, finer, finest, fining
3 Double final consonant before adding **ed, er, est, ing**
e.g. thin[3] → thinned, thinner, thinnest, thinning
4 Change final **y** to **i** before adding **ed, er, es, est, ly, ness**
e.g. tidy[4] → tidied, tidier, tidies, tidiest, tidily, tidiness
Keep final **y** before adding **ing** e.g. tidying
5 Add **es** instead of **s** to the end of the word
e.g. bunch[5] → bunches
6 Change final **f** to **ve** before adding **s**
e.g. calf[6] → calves

suberb	suburb+
	superb+
subheading	
subject[1] ~| matter	
subjective	@subjectivity
subjugate[2]	@subjugation
subjunctive	
sublet[3]	
sublimate[2]	
sublime	@subliminal
submachine gun	
submarine	
submerge[2]	
submersion	@submersible
submission	
submissive ~ly	
submit[3]	
submurge	submerge[2]
submurshun	submersion+
subordinate[2]	@subordination
subplot	
subpoena[1]	
subscribe[2]	@subscription
subsequent ~ly	
subservience	@subservient
subset	
subside[2]	@subsidence
subsidiary[4]	
subsidize[2]	
subsidy[4]	
subsist[1] ~ence	
subskribe	subscribe[2]+
subsoil	
subsonic	
substance	
substandard	
substantial ~ly ~| losses	
substantiate[2]	@substantiation
substantive ~ly	
substence	substance
substitute[2]	@substitution
substratum	@substrata
subsume[2]	
subsurvience	subservience+
subsyde	subside[2]+
subsydiary	subsidiary[4]
subterfuge	
subterranean	
subtitle[2]	
subtle[2]	@subtly
subtlety[4]	
subtotal	
subtract[1] ~ion	
subtropical	
subturranean	subterranean
suburb ~an ~ia	
subversion	@subversive
subvert[1]	
subvurtion	subversion+
subway ~| station	
subzero	

Unable to find your word under **sub**?
Take off **sub** and look again

succeed[1]	
succer	succor[1] *[help]
	sucker *[victim, plant]
success ~ion ~ive ~or	
successful ~ly ~| bidder	
succinct ~ly	
succor[1] *[help]	sucker *[victim, plant]
succulent	@succulence
succumb[1]	
sucessful	successful+
such ~like	
suck[1]	@suction
sucker *[victim, plant]	
	succor[1] *[help]
suckle[2]	
sucrose	
sucseed	succeed[1]
sucshun	suction
suction	
sudden ~ly ~ness	
sudo	pseudo+
suds	
sue[2] *[claim]	sew[1] *[sew clothes]+
sued *[claimed]	
suede *[leather]	Swede *[from Sweden]

Key to Spelling Rules

Red words are wrong. **Black** words are correct.

~ Add the suffix or word directly to the main word, without a space or hyphen
e.g. ash ~en ~tray → ashen ashtray

~- Add a hyphen to the main word before adding the next word
e.g. blow ~-dry → blow-dry

~| Leave a space between the main word and the next word
e.g. decimal ~| place → decimal place

+ By finding this word in its correct alphabetical order, you can find related words
e.g. abowt about+ → about-face

★ Draws attention to words that may be confused

TM Means the word is a trademark

@ Signifies the word is derived from the main word

suedo	pseudo[+]
sueur	sewer *[drain][+]
	sure[2] *[certain][+]
suffer[1] ~ance ~er ~| damage	
suffice[2]	
sufficiency	
sufficient ~ly	
sufficks	suffix[5+]
suffix[5]	
sufflay	soufflé
suffocate[2]	@suffocation
suffrage	@suffragette
suffuse[2]	
sugar[1] ~less ~y	
suggest[1] ~ion ~ive	
suicide	@suicidal
suit[1] *[clothes, lawsuit] ~case ~or	
	suite *[rooms]
	soot *[black dust][+]
suitable	@suitably
	@suitability
suite *[rooms]	suit[1] *[clothes, lawsuit][+]
	sweet *[sugar taste][+]
suitor *[for marriage]	
	suture[2] *[sew up]
suitten	sweeten[1+]
sukculent	succulent[+]
sukcumb	succumb[1]
suker	succor[1] *[help]
	sucker *[victim, plant]
sukrose	sucrose
sukul	suckle[2]
sulen	sullen
sulfate	sulfate
sulfer	sulfur[+]
sulfide	sulfide
sulfur ~ous	
sulfuric ~| acid	
sulk[1]	@sulky[4]
sullen	
sully[4]	
sultan ~a	
sultry[4]	
suly	sully[4]
sum[3] *[total]	some *[a quantity][+]

sumchuous	sumptuous[+]
Sumer *[ancient nation] ~ian	
	summer *[season][+]
sumerily	summarily
sumerize	summarize[2]
sumery	summary *[quick]
	summery *[warm]
sumit	summit
summarily	
summarize[2]	
summary *[quick]	
	summery *[warm]
summen	summon[1] *[call forth]
summens	summons[5] *[before court]
summer *[season] ~house ~time	
	Sumer *[ancient nation][+]
summersault	somersault[1]
summery *[warm]	
	summary *[quick]
summit	
summon[1] *[call forth]	
summons[5] *[before court]	
sump ~| pump	
sumptuous ~ly ~ness	
sun[3] *[shine] ~bathe ~bathing ~beam ~burn ~dial ~down ~dress ~-dried ~fish ~flower ~glasses ~| hat ~lamp ~| porch ~rise ~screen ~set ~shade ~spot ~stroke ~| tan ~| worshipper	
	son *[male child][+]

> Unable to find your word under **sun**?
> Take off **sun** and look again

Sunbelt	
sundae *[ice cream]	
Sunday *[day of week] ~| best ~| school	
sundry[4] *[various]	
sune	soon[1]
sung	
sunie	sunny[4] *[brightly lit]
	Sunni *[branch of Islam]
sunk ~en	

Key to Suffixes and Compounds

These rules are explained on pages vii to ix.

1 Keep the word the same before adding **ed, er, est, ing**
e.g. cool[1] → cooled, cooler, coolest, cooling

2 Take off final **e** before adding **ed, er, est, ing**
e.g. fine[2] → fined, finer, finest, fining

3 Double final consonant before adding **ed, er, est, ing**
e.g. thin[3] → thinned, thinner, thinnest, thinning

4 Change final **y** to **i** before adding **ed, er, es, est, ly, ness**
e.g. tidy[4] → tidied, tidier, tidies, tidiest, tidily, tidiness
Keep final **y** before adding **ing** e.g. tidying

5 Add **es** instead of **s** to the end of the word
e.g. bunch[5] → bunches

6 Change final **f** to **ve** before adding **s**
e.g. calf[6] → calves

sunlight *[brightness]
sunlit *[bright]
Sunni *[branch of Islam]
sunny[4] *[brightly lit]
super *[great] supper *[meal]+
Super ~| Bowl ~man
superabundance
superannuated @superannuation
superb ~ly
supercilious ~ly ~ness
supercomputer
superconductor @superconductivity
superficial ~ly ~ity
superfluous ~ly ~ness
superhero[5]
superhuman
superimpose[2]
superintendent
superior ~ity ~| court
superlative ~ly
supermarket
supernatural ~ly
supernova
supersede[2]
supersillius supercilious+
supersonic
superstar
superstition
superstitious ~ly ~ness
supervise[2] @supervisor
supervision @supervisory

> Unable to find your word under **super**?
> Take off **super** and look again

supine
suplant supplant[1]
suply supply[4+]
suport support[1+]
supose suppose[2+]

> Unable to find your word under **sup**?
> Look under **supp**

supper *[meal] ~| time
super *[great]
suppervise supervise[2+]
supplant[1]
supple ~ness
supplement[1] ~ary
supply[4] ~| and demand ~-side economics
support[1] ~ive ~| price
suppose[2] ~dly @supposition
suppository
suppress[5] ~ant ~or
supremacy @supremacist
supreme ~ly @supremo
supress suppress[1+]
supurfluous superfluous+
surcharge[2]
sure[2] *[certain] ~ly ~fire ~-footed
shore[2] *[sea, prop up]+
surealist surrealist+
surely *[certainly] surly[4] *[rude]
surender surrender[1]
surene serene+
sureptishus surreptitious+
surety[4]
surf[1] *[sea] ~board ~-side
serf *[slave]+
surface[2] ~| area ~| mail ~| tension ~| transport
surfeit
surge[2]
surgeon *[doctor] sergeant *[army]+
sturgeon *[fish]
surgery[4]
surgical ~ly ~| spirit
suriesis psoriasis
surje surge[2]
surjen sergeant *[army]+
surgeon *[doctor]
surly[4] *[rude] surely *[certainly]
surmise[2]
surmon sermon
surmonize sermonize[2]
surmount[1]
surname
surogate surrogate+
suround surround[1+]

Key to Spelling Rules

Red words are wrong. **Black** words are correct.

~ Add the suffix or word directly to the main word, without a space or hyphen
e.g. ash ~en ~tray → ashen ashtray

~- Add a hyphen to the main word before adding the next word
e.g. blow ~-dry → blow-dry

~| Leave a space between the main word and the next word
e.g. decimal ~| place → decimal place

+ By finding this word in its correct alphabetical order, you can find related words
e.g. abowt about+ → about-face

* Draws attention to words that may be confused

TM Means the word is a trademark

@ Signifies the word is derived from the main word

surpass[5]
surpent serpent+
surplice *[robe]
surplus[5] *[excess]
surprise[2] @surprisingly
surrated serrated+
surrealism
surrealist ~ic
surrender[1]
surreptitious ~ly ~ness
surrogate ~| mother ~| father
surround[1] ~ings
surtax[5]
survalence surveillance
surve serve[2]
surveillance
survey[1] ~or
survice service[2+]

Unable to find your word under **sur**? Look under **ser**

survival ~| kit ~| mode
survive[2] @survivor
suryasiss psoriasis
susceptible @susceptibility
suseptible susceptible+
suspect[1]
suspend[1] ~ers
suspense ~ful
suspension ~| bridge
suspicion
suspicious ~ly ~ness
sussinct succinct+
sustain[1] ~able ~ability
sustenance
sutch such+
sute soot *[black dust]+
suit[1] *[clothes, lawsuit]+
suite *[rooms]
suter suitor *[for marriage]
suthe soothe[2]
suthern southern
suttel subtle[2+]
suttlety subtlety[4]

suture[2] *[sew up] suitor *[for marriage]
suvenear souvenir+
swab[3]
swach swatch *[sample]
Swatch™ *[watch]
swaddle[2] @swaddling clothes
swade suede *[leather]
swagger[1]
swaie sway[1]
swallow[1]
swam *[past of swim]
swarm[1] *[of insects]
swamp[1] @swampy[4]
swan[3] ~song
swank[1] @swanky[4]
swap[3]
swarm[1] *[of insects]
swam *[past of swim]
swarthy[4]
swarve suave[2+]
swastika
swat[3]
swatch *[sample]
Swatch™ *[watch]
swath *[path of damage]
swathe[2] *[wrap]
swaw swore+
sway[1]
swayd suede *[leather]
swear ~ing ~| word
sweat[1] *[hot] ~band ~pants ~shirt ~shop
sweet *[sugar taste]+
suite *[rooms]
sweaten sweeten[1+]
sweater *[clothing]
sweeter *[sugary]
sweaty[4]
Swede *[from Sweden]
suede *[leather]
sweet *[sugar taste] ~er ~ing ~ly ~ness ~bread ~heart ~meat ~pea ~| pepper ~| potato ~| talk ~-talk[1] ~-tempered ~| tooth

---

KEY TO SUFFIXES AND COMPOUNDS

These rules are explained on pages vii to ix.

1 Keep the word the same before adding **ed, er, est, ing**
e.g. cool[1] → cooled, cooler, coolest, cooling
2 Take off final **e** before adding **ed, er, est, ing**
e.g. fine[2] → fined, finer, finest, fining
3 Double final consonant before adding **ed, er, est, ing**
e.g. thin[3] → thinned, thinner, thinnest, thinning
4 Change final **y** to **i** before adding **ed, er, es, est, ly, ness**
e.g. tidy[4] → tidied, tidier, tidies, tidiest, tidily, tidiness
Keep final **y** before adding **ing** e.g. tidying
5 Add **es** instead of **s** to the end of the word
e.g. bunch[5] → bunches
6 Change final **f** to **ve** before adding **s**
e.g. calf[6] → calves

sweet	sweat[1] *[hot]+
	suite *[rooms]

> Unable to find your word under **sweet**?
> Take off **sweet** and look again

sweeten[1] ~er	
sweeter *[sugary]	
	sweater *[clothing]
swell[1]	
swelter[1]	
swept ~-back	
swerl	swirl[1]
swerve[2]	
swet	sweat[1] *[hot]+
	sweet *[sugar taste]+
swetter	sweater *[clothing]
	sweeter *[sugary]
swhere	swear+
swich	switch[5+]
swift[1] ~ly ~ness	
swig[3]	
swill[1]	
swim ~mer ~suit ~wear	
swimming ~| pool	
swindle[2]	
swine	
swing ~ing	
swipe[2]	
swirl[1]	
swish[5]	
switch[5] ~back ~blade ~board	
swivel[3] ~| chair ~| round	
swizzle[2] ~| stick	
swob	swab[3]
swollen	
swollow	swallow[1]
swoon[1]	
swoop[1]	
swoosh[5]	
swopp	swap[3]
sword ~fish ~sman	
swore	@sworn
swotch	swatch *[sample]
	Swatch™ *[watch]
swoth	swath *[path of damage]

> Unable to find your word under **swo**?
> Look under **swa**

swoup	swoop[1]
swum	
swune	swoon[1]
swung	
swurve	swerve[2]
syanide	cyanide
syche	psyche+
syclamate	cyclamate
sycle	cycle[2] *[turning]
	sickle *[blade]+

> Unable to find your word under **sy**?
> Look under **cy**, **psy**, or **si**

sycophant ~ic	
syfer	cipher *[code]
	siphon[1] *[tube, take away]
syfilis	syphilis+
syft	sift[1]
sygn	sign[1] *[pointer]+
sykee	psyche+
sylent	silent+
sylinder	cylinder
sylk	silk+
syllable	@syllabic
syllabus[5]	
syllogism	
sylph ~like	
symbiosis	@symbiotic
symbol *[sign]	cymbal *[music]
symbolic ~al ~ally	
symbolize[2]	@symbolism
symfony	symphony+
symmetric ~al ~ally	
symmetry[4] *[similarity]	
	cemetery[4] *[graveyard]
sympathetic ~ally	
sympathize[2]	
sympathy	
symphony	@symphonic
symposium	@symposia
symptom ~atic	
synagogue	

Key to Spelling Rules

Red words are wrong. **Black** words are correct.

~ Add the suffix or word directly to the main word, without a space or hyphen
e.g. ash ~en ~tray → ashen ashtray

~- Add a hyphen to the main word before adding the next word
e.g. blow ~-dry → blow-dry

~| Leave a space between the main word and the next word
e.g. decimal ~| place → decimal place

\+ By finding this word in its correct alphabetical order, you can find related words
e.g. abowt about+ → about-face

* Draws attention to words that may be confused

™ Means the word is a trademark

@ Signifies the word is derived from the main word

synaptic *[of nerve junction]
@synapse
synoptic *[general view]+
sync *[together] sink *[drop, basin]+
syncere sincere[2+]
synchronize[2] @synchronization
syncopate[2] @syncopation
syncronize synchronize[2+]
syndicalism
syndicate[2] @syndication
syndrome
syng sing *[song]+
synge singe[2] *[burn]
synic cynic+
synk sink *[drop, basin]+
sync *[together]
synod
synonym ~ous ~ously
synopsis @synopses
synoptic *[general view]
@Synoptic Gospels
synaptic *[of nerve junction]
synovial
syntax @syntactic
synthesis @syntheses
synthesize[2]
synthetic ~ally
synus sinus[5+]

syoodoe pseudo+
sypher cipher *[code]
siphon[1] *[tube, take away]
syphilis @syphilitic
syphon siphon[1] *[tube, take away]
cipher *[code]
sypress cypress+
syre sir *[man]
sire[2] *[breed, king]
syren siren
Syrillic Cyrillic
syringe
syrup @syrupy
sysop *[System Operator]
syst cyst+
system ~| operator ~s analysis
systematic *[planned] ~ally
systematize[2]
systemic *[affecting all] ~ally
systole
sytar sitar
syte cite[2] *[quote]+
sight *[seeing]+
site[2] *[place]
sythe scythe[2] *[tool]
seethe[2] *[boil]
syze size[2] *[measure]+
seize[2] *[grab hold]+

Key to Suffixes and Compounds

These rules are explained on pages vii to ix.

1 Keep the word the same before adding **ed, er, est, ing**
e.g. cool[1] → cooled, cooler, coolest, cooling
2 Take off final **e** before adding **ed, er, est, ing**
e.g. fine[2] → fined, finer, finest, fining
3 Double final consonant before adding **ed, er, est, ing**
e.g. thin[3] → thinned, thinner, thinnest, thinning
4 Change final **y** to **i** before adding **ed, er, es, est, ly, ness**
e.g. tidy[4] → tidied, tidier, tidies, tidiest, tidily, tidiness
Keep final **y** before adding **ing** e.g. tidying
5 Add **es** instead of **s** to the end of the word
e.g. bunch[5] → bunches
6 Change final **f** to **ve** before adding **s**
e.g. calf[6] → calves

T

T *[letter] ~| bill ~-bone ~-square ~-shirt
tea *[drink]+
tee *[golf]+
tab[3] ~-delimited text ~| stop
tabby ~| cat
tabacco — tobacco+
tabbernackel — tabernacle
tabel — table[2+]
tabelspune — tablespoon+
tabernacle
table[2] ~cloth ~| manners ~| mat ~| tennis ~ware
tablespoon ~ful
tablet
tabloid ~| journalism
taboggan — toboggan[1]
taboo
tabu — taboo
tabul — table[2+]
tabular
tabulate[2] — @tabulation
tabulspoon — tablespoon+
taburnakul — tabernacle
tachometer
tacit ~ly ~ness ~| agreement ~| approval
taciturn
tack[1] *[approach, nail, sailing]
take *[obtain]+
tackee — tacky[4]
tackle[2]
tackometer — tachometer
tacks *[nails] — tax[5] *[money]+
tacksidermy — taxidermy+
tacksonomy — taxonomy[4]
tackt — tact+
tacktile — tactile
tackul — tackle[2]
tacky[4]
taco
tact ~ful ~fully ~less ~lessly
tactic ~al ~ally @tactician
tactile
tad *[little bit, child]
taday — today
tadpole
taffeta
taffy *[stretchy candy] ~| apple ~| pull
toffee *[brittle candy]
tag[3] ~| along ~| sale
t'ai chi
tail[1] *[follow, body part] ~back ~coat ~gate[2] ~light ~piece ~pipe ~spin ~wind
tale *[story]

Unable to find your word under **tail**? Take off **tail** and look again

tailor[1] ~-made
taim — tame[2+]
taing — tang+
taint[1] *[spoil]
taip — tape[2] *[adhesive, for recording]+
taiper — taper[1] *[narrow, candle]+
tapir *[animal]
tair — tear *[cry, rip]+
tare[2] *[empty weight]
taist — taste[2+]
take *[obtain] ~n ~| after ~| apart ~| away ~| down ~-home pay ~| in ~| legal action ~| legal advice

KEY TO SPELLING RULES

Red words are wrong. **Black** words are correct.

~ Add the suffix or word directly to the main word, without a space or hyphen
e.g. ash ~en ~tray → ashen ashtray

~- Add a hyphen to the main word before adding the next word
e.g. blow ~-dry → blow-dry

~| Leave a space between the main word and the next word
e.g. decimal ~| place → decimal place

\+ By finding this word in its correct alphabetical order, you can find related words
e.g. abowt about+ → about-face

★ Draws attention to words that may be confused

TM Means the word is a trademark

@ Signifies the word is derived from the main word

take ~| out *[get rid of] ~out *[fast food] ~| up ~off ~over *[of a company] ~| over ~| to *[get control]
@taking
tack[1] *[approach, nail, sailing]

Unable to find your word under **take**? Take off **take** and look again

takeela tequila
takes *[removes] tacks *[nails]
tax[5] *[money]+
takle tackle[2]
tako taco
taks tacks *[nails]
takes *[removes]
tax[5] *[money]+
taksi taxi+
takt tact+
talc *[substance] ~um powder
talk[1] *[speak]+
tale *[story] tail[1] *[follow, body part]+
tall *[high]+
tally[4] *[count]+
talen talon
talent ~ed ~| scout
talisman
talk[1] *[speak] ~ative ~| back ~| over ~| radio ~| show
talc *[substance]+
tall *[high] ~ness ~| order
tale *[story]
tail[1] *[follow, body part]+
tallent talent+
tallie tally[4] *[count]+
tale *[story]
tallisman talisman
tallow
tally[4] *[count] ~up
tale *[story]
Talmud
talon
talysman talisman
tamarin *[monkey]
tamarind *[fruit]
tamarisk *[bush]
tamber timbre *[sound]
tambourine
tame[2] ~able ~ly ~ness
tamirisk tamarisk *[bush]
tamper[1]
tampon
tan[3]
tandem
tang @tangy
tangel tangle[2]
tangent ~ial
tangerine
tangible @tangibly
tangle[2]
tango[1]
tanjable tangible+
tanjent tangent+
tanjerine tangerine
tanjunt tangent+
tank[1] *[container] ~ard ~ful
thank[1] *[acknowledge]+
tanks *[liquid, military]
thanks *[acknowledgment]
tannery[4]
tantalize[2] @tantalizingly
tantamount
tante taint[1] *[spoil]
taunt[1] *[jeer]
tantra @tantric
tantrum
Tao ~ism
tap[3] *[hit lightly] ~root ~| water
tape[2] *[adhesive, for recording]+
tapas
tap-dance[2]
tape[2] *[adhesive, for recording] ~| deck ~| measure
tap[3] *[hit lightly]+
taper[1] *[narrow, candle] ~| off
tapir *[animal]
tape-record[1]

Key to Suffixes and Compounds

These rules are explained on pages vii to ix.

1 Keep the word the same before adding **ed, er, est, ing**
e.g. cool[1] → cooled, cooler, coolest, cooling
2 Take off final **e** before adding **ed, er, est, ing**
e.g. fine[2] → fined, finer, finest, fining
3 Double final consonant before adding **ed, er, est, ing**
e.g. thin[3] → thinned, thinner, thinnest, thinning
4 Change final **y** to **i** before adding **ed, er, es, est, ly, ness**
e.g. tidy[4] → tidied, tidier, tidies, tidiest, tidily, tidiness
Keep final **y** before adding **ing** e.g. tidying
5 Add **es** instead of **s** to the end of the word
e.g. bunch[5] → bunches
6 Change final **f** to **ve** before adding **s**
e.g. calf[6] → calves

tapestry^{4}	
tapeworm	
tapioca	
tapir *[animal]	taper^{1} *[narrow, candle]+
tapistry	tapestry^{4}
tappas	tapas
tappet	
tapyoca	tapioca
taquila	tequila
tar^{3} *[black liquid]	tear *[cry, rip]+
	tare^{2} *[empty weight]
taraggon	tarragon
tarantella *[dance]	
tarantula *[spider]	
tardy^{4}	
tare^{2} *[empty weight]	
	tear *[cry, rip]+
	tar^{3} *[black liquid]
target^{1} ~| area ~| market	
tariff	
tarmac	
tarmigan	ptarmigan
tarmik	tarmac
tarn	
tarnish^{5}	
taro *[plant]	
tarot *[cards]	
tarp ~aulin	
tarragon	
tarrific	terrific+
tarrot	taro *[plant]
	tarot *[cards]
tarry^{4} *[delay]	terry *[cloth]
tarsus	@tarsi
	@tarsal
tart ~ly ~ness	
tartan	
tartar *[teeth] ~| sauce	
	tarter *[more tart]
tartare *[raw]	
tarten	tartan
tarter *[more tart]	tartar *[teeth]+
	tartare *[raw]
tartrate	

tasit	tacit+
tasiturn	taciturn
task ~| force ~master	
tassel ~led	
tassit	tacit+
taste^{2} ~buds ~less	
tasteful ~ly ~ness	
tasty^{4}	
tattered	@tatters
tattoo^{1} ~ist	
taudry	tawdry^{4}
taught *[did teach]	
	taut *[tight]+
taunt^{1} *[jeer]	
taupe *[color]	top *[highest, lid]+
	tope *[drink alcohol]
Taurus *[stars]	torus *[ring]
taut *[tight] ~ly ~ness	
	taught *[did teach]
	tort *[law]
tautology	@tautological
tavern ~a	
tawang	twang^{1}
tawdry^{4}	
tawfee	toffee+
tawhnee	tawny^{4} *[color]
tawn	torn+
tawnt	taunt^{1} *[jeer]
tawny^{4} *[color]	
tawso	torso
tawtology	tautology+
tax^{5} *[money] ~able ~ation ~adjustment ~| assessment ~| avoidance ~| break ~| code ~| collection ~| collector ~| consultant ~-deductible ~| deduction ~-exempt ~-exemption ~-free ~| inspector ~payer ~| refund ~| return ~| shelter	
	tacks *[nails]
	takes *[removes]

Unable to find your word under **tax**?
Take off **tax** and look again

Key to Spelling Rules

Red words are wrong. **Black** words are correct.

~ Add the suffix or word directly to the main word, without a space or hyphen
e.g. ash ~en ~tray → ashen ashtray

~- Add a hyphen to the main word before adding the next word
e.g. blow ~-dry → blow-dry

~| Leave a space between the main word and the next word
e.g. decimal ~| place → decimal place

+ By finding this word in its correct alphabetical order, you can find related words
e.g. abowt about+ → about-face

* Draws attention to words that may be confused

TM Means the word is a trademark

@ Signifies the word is derived from the main word

taxi ~cab ~| stand
taxidermy @taxidermist
taxonomy[4]
taylor tailor[1]+
taynt taint[1] *[spoil]
TB *[tuberculosis] TV *[television]
tea *[drink] ~| bag ~| cake ~cup ~pot ~spoon ~room ~| time
T *[letter]
tee[2] *[golf]+
teach ~able ~ing
teacher ~'s pet
teak *[wood] tic *[twitch]
tick[1] *[clock, mark, insect]+
teal
team[1] *[group] ~mate ~| player ~| spirit
teem[1] *[swarm]
teamster
teanage teenage+
teanie teeny+
tear *[cry, rip] ~ing ~away ~drop ~| gas ~-jerker ~| off
tier *[layer]
tire[2] *[sleep, wheel]+
tearful ~ly ~ness
teas *[plural of tea]
tease[2] *[annoy]+
teashert T-shirt
teaspoon ~ful
teasquare T-square
teat
teater teeter[1]
teather tether[1]
teatotal teetotal+
techer teacher+
techie
technalogy technology[4]
technical ~ly ~| support
technicality[4]
technician
technique
technocrat ~ic
technological ~ly

technology[4]
technophobe
tectonic ~| plates
teddy[4] ~| bear
tedious ~ly ~ness
tedium
tedy teddy[4]+
tedyum tedium
tee[2] *[golf] ~d ~ing ~| off
T *[letter]
tea *[drink]+
teeara tiara
teecher teacher+
tee-entie TNT *[explosive]
teek teak *[wood]
tic *[twitch]
tick[1] *[clock, mark, insect]+
teel teal
teem[1] *[swarm] team[1] *[group]+
teen *[teenager] ten *[number]+
tin *[metal]+
teenage ~d ~r
teeny ~bopper ~-weeny
teepee tepee
teese teas *[tea]
tease[2] *[annoy]+
tee-shirt [also spelled T-shirt]
teespoon teaspoon+
teesquare T-square
teet teat
teeter[1]
teeth *[plural of tooth]
teethe[2] *[develop teeth]
teetotal ~ism ~er
teevee TV *[television]
TB *[tuberculosis]
Teflon™
tegether together+
tekie techie
tekilla tequila
teknical technical+

Unable to find your word under **tek**? Look under **tech**

Key to Suffixes and Compounds

These rules are explained on pages vii to ix.

1 Keep the word the same before adding **ed, er, est, ing** e.g. cool[1] → cooled, cooler, coolest, cooling
2 Take off final **e** before adding **ed, er, est, ing** e.g. fine[2] → fined, finer, finest, fining
3 Double final consonant before adding **ed, er, est, ing** e.g. thin[3] → thinned, thinner, thinnest, thinning
4 Change final **y** to **i** before adding **ed, er, es, est, ly, ness** e.g. tidy[4] → tidied, tidier, tidies, tidiest, tidily, tidiness
Keep final **y** before adding **ing** e.g. tidying
5 Add **es** instead of **s** to the end of the word e.g. bunch[5] → bunches
6 Change final **f** to **ve** before adding **s** e.g. calf[6] → calves

tekst text[1+]
telakinesis telekinesis+
tele ~communications ~gram ~graph[1] ~marketing ~port[1]
telecommute[2]
telefone telephone[2+]
telefoto telephoto+
telekinesis @telekinetic
teleks telex[5]
telepathy @telepathic
telephone[2] ~| book ~| call ~| directory ~| line ~| number ~| subscriber

> Unable to find your word under **telephone**? Take off **telephone** and look again

telephoto ~| lens
telesales
telescope[2] @telescopic
teletext
telethon
televise[2]
television ~| program
telex[5]
telivise televise[2]
tell ~er ~ing ~| off ~tale
telnet
temerity
temp[1] *[temporary work] ~| agency[4]
tempt[1] *[seduce]+
tempel temple
temper[1] ~| tantrum
tempera *[paint] tempura *[food]
temperament ~al ~ally
temperance
temperary temporary[4]
temperate
temperature
tempermint temperament+
tempertcher temperature
tempest ~uous ~uously
template
temple
tempo
tempoora tempura *[food]

temporary[4]
tempra tempera *[paint]
tempura *[food]
tempracher temperature
tempritcher temperature
tempt[1] *[seduce] ~ation
temp[1] *[temporary work]+
tempul temple
tempur temper[1+]
tempura *[food] tempera *[paint]
ten *[number] ~fold ~th ~pin
teen *[teenager]
tin *[metal]+
tenable
tenacious ~ly
tenacity
tenament tenement+
tenancy[4] *[being a tenant]
tendency[4] *[habit]
tenant *[renter] ~| farmer
tenet *[principle]
tenashus tenacious+
tenasity tenacity
tend[1]
tendency[4] *[habit]
tenancy[4] *[being a tenant]
tender ~ly ~ness ~foot ~-hearted ~loin ~| offer
tenderhooks tenterhooks
tenderize[2]
tendinitis
tendon *[sinew]
tendril
tendur tender+
tendurize tenderize[2]
tenement ~| house
tenency tenancy[4] *[being a tenant]
tendency[4] *[habit]
tenent tenant *[renter]+
tenet *[principle]
tenet *[principle] tenant *[renter]+
tennis ~| court ~| elbow ~| shoe
tenor *[voice] tenure *[job]+
tenpin ~| bowling
tens *[number] teens *[teenagers]

tense^{2} *[stressed] ~ly	
tenshun	tension
tensile ~| strength	
tension	
tent	
tentacle	
tentative ~ly	
tentecle	tentacle
tenterhooks	
tentitive	tentative+
tenuous ~ly ~ness	
tenure *[job] ~d	
	tenor *[voice]
tepee	
tephlon	Teflon™
tepid	
tequila	
terban	turban *[head covering]+
terbine	turbine *[engine]
	turban *[head covering]+
terbo	turbo *[engine]+
terbulence	turbulence+
terer	terror+
terf	turf^{1+}
terific	terrific+
terify	terrify^{4}
teritory	territory^{4}
terkey	turkey *[bird]
	Turkey *[country]
term^{1} ~| loan ~| insurance	
terminal ~ly	
terminate^{2}	@termination clause
terminology^{4}	
terminus	
termite	
termoil	turmoil
tern *[bird]	turn^{1} *[go around]+
ternary	
terodactyl	pterodactyl
teror	terror+
terrace^{2}	
terra-cotta *[clay]	
terra firma *[solid ground]	
terrain	
terra incognita *[unknown territory]	
terratory	territory^{4}
terrestrial	
terret	turret
terrible	@terribly
terrice	terrace^{2}
terrier	
terrific ~ally	
terrify^{4}	
territorial ~ly	
territory^{4}	
terror ~ism ~ist	
terrorize^{2}	
terry *[cloth]	tarry^{4} *[delay]
terse ~ly ~ness	
tertiary	
tertle	turtle+

> Unable to find your word under **ter**?
> Look under **tur**

teshtule	textual
tessellate^{2}	@tessellation
test^{1} ~| ban ~| case ~-drive ~-drove ~| match ~| pilot ~| tube	
testafy	testify^{4}
testament	
testamony	testimony+
testicle	@testicular
testie	testy^{4}
testify^{4}	
testimony	@testimonial
testis	@testes
testosterone	
testy^{4}	
tetanus	
tete	teat
tête-à-tête	
tether^{1}	
tetnus	tetanus
tetrahedron	
Teutonic	
tewlip	tulip
tewn	tune^{2} *[song]+
tewnic	tunic
Tewsday	Tuesday

Key to Suffixes and Compounds

These rules are explained on pages vii to ix.

1 Keep the word the same before adding **ed, er, est, ing**
e.g. cool^{1} → cooled, cooler, coolest, cooling

2 Take off final **e** before adding **ed, er, est, ing**
e.g. fine^{2} → fined, finer, finest, fining

3 Double final consonant before adding **ed, er, est, ing**
e.g. thin^{3} → thinned, thinner, thinnest, thinning

4 Change final **y** to **i** before adding **ed, er, es, est, ly, ness**
e.g. tidy^{4} → tidied, tidier, tidies, tidiest, tidily, tidiness
Keep final **y** before adding **ing** e.g. tidying

5 Add **es** instead of **s** to the end of the word
e.g. bunch^{5} → bunches

6 Change final **f** to **ve** before adding **s**
e.g. calf^{6} → calves

Wrong	Correct
tewter	tutor[1] *[teacher]+
Tex-Mex	
text[1] ~book	
textile	
textual	
texture[2]	
thaaw	thaw[1]
thach	thatch[5]
thaht	thought+
Thai *[from Thailand]	
	tie *[bind, equal score]+
thai chi	t'ai chi
thallium	
than *[comparison]	
	then *[time]
thank[1] *[acknowledge] ~ful ~fully ~less ~-you *[noun] ~-you *[adjective]	
	tank[1] *[container]+

> Unable to find your word under **thank**?
> Take off **thank** and look again

Wrong	Correct
thanks *[acknowledgment]	
	tanks *[liquid, military]
thanksgiving *[giving thanks]	
Thanksgiving *[celebration] ~| Day	
tharill	thrill[1] *[excitement]+
tharive	thrive[2]
that	
thatch[5]	
thaw[1]	
thawng	thong
thawtful	thoughtful+
thay	they+
the *[article]	thee *[old form of "you"]
thealagy	theology[4+]
theam	theme *[main idea]+
thearam	theorem
thearst	thirst[1+]
theater	@theatrical
	@theatrics
thee *[old form of "you"]	
	the *[article]
theef	thief[6]
theery	theory[4+]
theese	these *[nearby things]
theeter	theater+
theezm	theism
theft	
their *[possession]	
	there *[place]+
theirs *[belonging]	
	there's *[there is]
theism	
them *[they] ~selves	
	theme *[main idea]+
thematic ~ally	
theme *[main idea] ~| park ~| song	
	them *[they]+
then *[time]	than *[comparison]
thence ~forth	
theology[4]	@theologian
theorem	
theoretical ~ly ~| probability	
theorize[2]	
theory[4]	@theorist
therapeutic ~ally	
therapy[4]	@therapist
there *[place] ~| abouts	
	their *[possession]
there ~after ~by ~fore	
thereputic	therapeutic+
there's *[there is]	theirs *[belonging]
therfour	therefore+
therift	thrift+
thermal	
thermodynamics	
thermoelectric ~ity	
thermometer	
thermonuclear	
Thermos™ ~| bottle	
thermostat	
therough	thorough *[complete]+
thers	there's *[there is]
	theirs *[belonging]
Thersday	Thursday
therteen	thirteen+
therty	thirty[4+]
thesaurus	

Key to Spelling Rules

Red words are wrong. **Black** words are correct.

~ Add the suffix or word directly to the main word, without a space or hyphen
e.g. ash ~en ~tray → ashen ashtray

~- Add a hyphen to the main word before adding the next word
e.g. blow ~-dry → blow-dry

~| Leave a space between the main word and the next word
e.g. decimal ~| place → decimal place

+ By finding this word in its correct alphabetical order, you can find related words
e.g. abowt about+ → about-face

★ Draws attention to words that may be confused

™ Means the word is a trademark

@ Signifies the word is derived from the main word

these *[nearby things]
this *[referring to]
thesis @theses
they ~'d ~'ll ~'ve [have]
they're *[they are]
there *[place]+
their *[possession]
thick[1] ~ly ~ness ~-skinned
thicken[1]
thie thigh *[part of leg]
thy *[your]
thief[6]
thier their *[possession]
there *[place]+
thigh *[part of leg]
thy *[your]
thik thick[1+]
thimble ~ful
thin[3] *[slender] ~ly ~| client ~-layer ~-skinned
thine *[yours]
thine *[yours] thin[3] *[slender]+
thing ~amabob ~amajig
@thingy[4]
think ~er ~ing ~| tank
third ~ly ~| base ~| class ~| degree ~| party[4] ~| quarter
Third World
thirmal thermal
thiroyd thyroid+
thirst[1] @thirsty[4]
thirteen ~th
thirty[4] @thirtieth
this *[referring to] these *[nearby things]
thissel thistle+
thistle ~down
thither
thiye thigh *[part of leg]
Thomas *[name] @Thomist
thong
thorax @thoracic
thore thaw[1]
thorn @thorny[4]
thorough *[complete] ~ly ~ness ~bred ~fare

those
thou *[you]
though *[but]
thoughs those
thought ~-provoking
thoughtful ~ly ~ness
thousand ~fold ~th
thow thou *[you]
though *[but]
thowrn thorn+
thowsand thousand+
thrab throb[3]
thrach thrash[5]
thrahng throng[1]
thrall *[bondage] through all *[continuing]
thrambosis thrombosis
thrash[5]
thrattle throttle[2+]
thrawl thrall *[bondage]
trawl[1] *[fish with net]+
thread[1] ~bare
threash thresh[5]
threat *[danger] treat[1] *[give]+
threaten[1]
thred thread[1+]
three ~-dimensional ~fold ~-legged ~-quarters ~-piece ~-point ~| R's ~some ~-wheeler

Unable to find your word under **three**? Take off **three** and look again

thresh[5]
thret threat *[danger]
threten threaten[1]
threw *[did throw] through *[transit]+
thrice
thrift ~shop @thrifty[4]
thrill[1] *[excitement] ~er ~| ride
trill *[music]
thrive[2]
thrize thrice
throat ~y
throb[3]

Key to Suffixes and Compounds

These rules are explained on pages vii to ix.

1 Keep the word the same before adding **ed, er, est, ing**
e.g. cool[1] → cooled, cooler, coolest, cooling
2 Take off final **e** before adding **ed, er, est, ing**
e.g. fine[2] → fined, finer, finest, fining
3 Double final consonant before adding **ed, er, est, ing**
e.g. thin[3] → thinned, thinner, thinnest, thinning
4 Change final **y** to **i** before adding **ed, er, es, est, ly, ness**
e.g. tidy[4] → tidied, tidier, tidies, tidiest, tidily, tidiness
Keep final **y** before adding **ing** e.g. tidying
5 Add **es** instead of **s** to the end of the word
e.g. bunch[5] → bunches
6 Change final **f** to **ve** before adding **s**
e.g. calf[6] → calves

throes *[middle of]
throws *[ball]
thrombosis
throne *[chair] thrown *[ball]
throng[1]
throte throat+
throttle[2] ~| back
through *[transit] ~out ~put ~way
threw *[did throw]
throw *[a ball]+
true[2] *[correct]+
throw *[a ball] ~ing ~back ~| up ~| away *[get rid of] ~away *[not important]
through *[transit]+

> Unable to find your word under **throw**? Take off **throw** and look again

thrown *[ball] throne *[chair]
throws *[ball] throes *[middle of]
thrush[5]
thrust ~ing
thryve thrive[2]
thud[3]
thug ~gery ~gish
thumb[1] ~nail ~screw ~tack
thumbs ~| down ~| up
thump[1]
thunder[1] ~bolt ~clap ~cloud ~storm ~struck
thunderous ~ly
thurmal thermal
thurow thorough *[complete]+
Thursday
thus
thwack[1]
thwart[1]
thy *[your] thigh *[part of leg]
thyme *[herb] time[2] *[clock]+
thyn thin[3] *[slender]+
thine *[yours]
thyng thing+
thynk think+
thyroid ~| gland
thystle thistle+
thyther thither
tiara
tibia
tic *[twitch] tick[1] *[clock, mark, insect]+
teak *[wood]
tyke *[small child]
tichie t'ai chi
tichular titular
tick[1] *[clock, mark, insect] ~-tock
tic *[twitch]
tyke *[small child]
ticket[1] ~| agency
tickle[2] @ticklish
ticoon tycoon
tic-tac-toe
tidal *[tide] ~| pool
title *[name]+
tidbit
tiddlywinks
tide *[sea] ~line ~mark
tied *[rope, score]
tidel tidal *[tide]+
title *[name]+
tidings
tidy[4] ~| up
tie *[bind, equal score] ~d ~breaker ~-dye ~| pin ~| up
@tying
Thai *[from Thailand]
tie chee t'ai chi
tied *[rope, score] tide *[sea]+
tiem time[2] *[clock]+
teem[1] *[swarm]
tier *[layer] tear *[cry, rip]+
tire[2] *[sleep, wheel]+
tiersome tiresome+
tieter teeter[1]
tighter *[more tight]
titer *[concentration]
tiff *[quarrel]
TIFF *[file format]
tiffus typhus+

Key to Spelling Rules

Red words are wrong. **Black** words are correct.

~ Add the suffix or word directly to the main word, without a space or hyphen
e.g. ash ~en ~tray → ashen ashtray

~- Add a hyphen to the main word before adding the next word
e.g. blow ~-dry → blow-dry

~| Leave a space between the main word and the next word
e.g. decimal ~| place → decimal place

\+ By finding this word in its correct alphabetical order, you can find related words
e.g. abowt about+ → about-face

★ Draws attention to words that may be confused

™ Means the word is a trademark

@ Signifies the word is derived from the main word

Unable to find your word under **ti**?
Look under **ty**

tifune **typhoon**
tiger ~| lily[4] ~| moth
@tigress
tight[1] *[pulled firmly] ~-fisted ~-knit ~-lipped ~rope
tit *[bird, breast]+
tighten[1] *[firm up]
titan *[important person]+
tighter *[more tight]
titer *[concentration]
tighth **tithe**[2] *[give income]+
tights *[stockings]
tighty **tidy**[4+]
tik **teak** *[wood]
tic *[twitch]
tick[1] *[clock, mark, insect]+
tikkel **tickle**[2+]
tikket **ticket**[1+]
tikul **tickle**[2+]
tilde
tile[2] *[floor covering]
till[1] *[soil, cash register, until]
tilt[1] *[slope] **tilled** *[the land]
timber *[wood] ~land ~line
timbre *[sound]
time[2] *[clock] ~less ~| bomb ~| capsule ~| card ~-consuming ~| frame ~-honored ~-lapse ~keeping ~keeper ~| limit ~-out ~piece ~-saving ~| scale ~table ~| warp ~-worn ~| zone
thyme *[herb]

Unable to find your word under **time**?
Take off **time** and look again

timid ~ity
timorous ~ly ~ness
tin *[metal] ~foil ~| opener
teen *[teenager]
ten *[number]+
tinchure **tincture**
tinckle **tinkle**[2]
tincture
tinder ~| box
tingal **tingle**[2]
tinge[2]
tingle[2]
tinitis **tinnitus**
tinj **tinge**[2]
tinker[1]
tinkle[2]
tinnitus
tinsel ~| town
tint[1]
tiny[4] *[very small]
tinny[4] *[metallic sound]
tip[3] *[end, advice] ~ster ~| off *[warn] ~-off *[told a secret]
type[2] *[kind, printing]+
tipee **tepee**
tiph **tiff** *[quarrel]
TIFF *[file format]
tiphoon **typhoon**
tipi [also spelled tepee]
tipical **typical**+
tipography **typography**[4] *[printing]+
topography[4] *[land shape]+
tipsy[4]
tiptoe[2]
tiptop
tirade
tiranny **tyranny**[4]
tirant **tyrant**
tire[2] *[sleep, wheel] ~less ~lessly
tier *[layer]
tiresome ~ly ~ness
tirn **tern** *[bird]
turn[1] *[go around]+
tissue ~| paper
tit *[bird, breast] **tight**[1] *[pulled firmly]+
titainium **titanium**
tital **title** *[name]+
tidal *[tide]+
titan *[important person] ~ic
tighten[1] *[firm up]
titanic

Key to Suffixes and Compounds

These rules are explained on pages vii to ix.

1 Keep the word the same before adding **ed, er, est, ing** e.g. cool[1] → cooled, cooler, coolest, cooling
2 Take off final **e** before adding **ed, er, est, ing** e.g. fine[2] → fined, finer, finest, fining
3 Double final consonant before adding **ed, er, est, ing** e.g. thin[3] → thinned, thinner, thinnest, thinning
4 Change final **y** to **i** before adding **ed, er, es, est, ly, ness** e.g. tidy[4] → tidied, tidier, tidies, tidiest, tidily, tidiness
Keep final **y** before adding **ing** e.g. tidying
5 Add **es** instead of **s** to the end of the word e.g. bunch[5] → bunches
6 Change final **f** to **ve** before adding **s** e.g. calf[6] → calves

titanium	
tite	tit *[bird, breast][+]
	tight[1+]
titelate	titillate[2+]
titen	titan *[important person][+]
	tighten[1] *[firm up]
titer *[concentration]	
	tighter *[more tight]
	titter[1] *[laugh]
titevate	titivate[2+]
tithe[2] *[give income] ~| barn	
	tight[1+]
titie	tidy[4+]
titillate[2]	@titillation
titivate[2]	@titivation
title *[name] ~d ~| deed ~-holder ~| page	
	tidal *[tide][+]
titraight	titrate[+]
titrate	@titration
titter[1] *[laugh]	titer *[concentration]
tittle-tattle	
tittur	titter[1]
titular	
tizzy[4]	
TNT *[explosive]	
to *[for, toward] ~| and fro ~-do	
	too *[also, very]
	two *[number][+]
toad *[animal] ~stool	
	towed *[pulled]
toaken	token[+]
toan	tone[2] *[sound][+]
toast[1] ~master ~| rack	
tobacco ~| leaf ~nist	
toberculosis	tuberculosis
toboggan[1]	
tocksin	toxin *[poison]
	tocsin *[bell]
tocksisity	toxic[+]
tocsin *[bell]	toxin *[poison]
today	
toddle[2] ~r	
toddy[4]	

tode	toad *[animal][+]
	towed *[pulled]
todel	toddle[2]
toe *[on foot] ~hold ~nail	
	to *[for, toward][+]
	tow[1] *[pull][+]
	two *[number][+]
toem	tome *[large book]
toffee *[brittle candy]	
	taffy *[stretchy candy][+]
tofu	
toga	
together ~ness	
toggle[2] ~| switch	
toi	toy[1+]
toil[1]	
toilet *[bathroom] ~| paper ~-trained	
	toilette *[cosmetic chores]
toiletry[4]	
toilette *[cosmetic chores]	
	toilet *[bathroom][+]
token ~ism	
toksic	toxic[+]
Tolemaic	Ptolemaic[+]
tolerable	@tolerably
tolerance	@tolerant
tolerate[2]	@toleration
toll *[money] ~booth ~| call ~-free ~| gate	
	tool[1] *[utensil][+]
tom ~boy ~cat ~foolery ~-tom	
tomahawk	
tomain	ptomaine[+]
tomato[5]	
tomb *[burial] ~stone	
tome *[large book]	
tommult	tumult[+]
tomorrow	
ton *[2000 lb] ~nage	
	tone[2] *[sound][+]
	tonne *[1000 kg]
	tun *[large cask]
tonal ~ity	

KEY TO SPELLING RULES

Red words are wrong. **Black** words are correct.

~ Add the suffix or word directly to the main word, without a space or hyphen
e.g. ash ~en ~tray → ashen ashtray

~- Add a hyphen to the main word before adding the next word
e.g. blow ~-dry → blow-dry

~| Leave a space between the main word and the next word
e.g. decimal ~| place → decimal place

\+ By finding this word in its correct alphabetical order, you can find related words
e.g. abowt about[+] → about-face

★ Draws attention to words that may be confused

TM Means the word is a trademark

@ Signifies the word is derived from the main word

tone[2] *[sound] ~-deaf ~| down ~less
ton *[2000 lb]+
tonne *[1000 kg]
toner
tongs
tongue[2] *[body, language] ~-in-cheek ~-lashing ~-tied ~-twister
tung *[tree]+
tonguesten — tungsten+
tonic ~| water
tonight
tonne *[1000 kg] — ton *[2000 lb]+
tun *[large cask]
tonsil ~litis
too *[also, very] — to *[to work]+
two *[number]+
toob — tube[2] *[pipe, of paste]+
tooba — tuba *[music]
tooberculosis — tuberculosis
took
tool[1] *[utensil] ~bar ~box ~kit
toll *[money]+
toolip — tulip
toom — tomb *[burial]+
toomer — tumor
toon — tune[2] *[song]+
toona — tuna+
toopay — toupée
toosday — Tuesday
tooshay — touché *[admiration]
toot[1] *[noise] — tout[1] *[praise]
tootelaj — tutelage
tooter *[one who toots]
tutor[1] *[teacher]+
tooth ~less ~y ~ache ~brush ~comb ~paste ~pick
tootle[2]
too-too *[excessive]
tutu *[ballet skirt]

> Unable to find your word under **too**?
> Look under **tu**

top[3] *[highest, lid] ~less ~| brass ~coat ~-down ~| dog ~-flight ~| hat ~heavy ~knot ~-level ~-notch ~| off ~-rated ~sail ~| secret ~-selling ~soil ~spin ~-up
taupe *[color]
tope *[drink alcohol]

> Unable to find your word under **top**?
> Take off **top** and look again

topaz
tope *[drink alcohol]
taupe *[color]
top *[highest, lid]+
topic ~al ~ally
topography[4] *[land shape]
@topographer
typography[4] *[printing]+
topology[4] *[mathematics]
@topological
typology[4] *[study of examples]+
topple[2]
topsy-turvy
Torah *[Jewish law]
tor
torch[5] ~light
torcher — torture[2]
tordry — tawdry[4]
tore *[pulled apart]
tour[1] *[journey]+
toreador
torid — torrid
torism — tourism
torment[1] ~or
torn ~| off ~| up
tornado[5]
tornament — tournament
torney — tawny[4] *[color]
tourney[1] *[competition]
torniquet — tourniquet
tornt — taunt[1] *[jeer]
torpedo[5] ~es
torpid
torpor
torque

Key to Suffixes and Compounds

These rules are explained on pages vii to ix.

1 Keep the word the same before adding **ed, er, est, ing**
e.g. cool[1] → cooled, cooler, coolest, cooling
2 Take off final **e** before adding **ed, er, est, ing**
e.g. fine[2] → fined, finer, finest, fining
3 Double final consonant before adding **ed, er, est, ing**
e.g. thin[3] → thinned, thinner, thinnest, thinning
4 Change final **y** to **i** before adding **ed, er, es, est, ly, ness**
e.g. tidy[4] → tidied, tidier, tidies, tidiest, tidily, tidiness
Keep final **y** before adding **ing** e.g. tidying
5 Add **es** instead of **s** to the end of the word
e.g. bunch[5] → bunches
6 Change final **f** to **ve** before adding **s**
e.g. calf[6] → calves

torrent ~ial
torrid
Torrus — Taurus *[stars]
torus *[ring]
torso
tort *[law] — taught *[did teach]
taut *[tight]+
tortilla ~| chips
tortoise ~shell
tortology — tautology+
tortoys — tortoise+
tortuous ~ly ~ness
torture[2]
tortuss — tortoise+
tortylla — tortilla+
torus *[ring] — Taurus *[stars]
toss[5] ~-up
toste — toast[1]+
tot[1] *[small child] ~| up
tote *[bag, carry]
total[3] ~ity ~ly ~| amount ~| assets ~| cost ~| eclipse ~| expenditure ~| income ~| output ~| revenue ~| quality management [TQM]

> Unable to find your word under **total**?
> Take off **total** and look again

totalitarian ~ism
tote *[bag, carry] — toad *[animal]+
tot[1] *[small child]+
totem ~| pole
totter[1]
touch[5] ~-and-go ~down ~| off ~| panel ~| screen ~stone ~-tone ~| up ~y
touché *[admiration]
touched *[emotionally affected]
touchy[4] *[irritable]
tough[1] ~-minded ~ness
toughen[1]
toughft — tuft[1]
tought — taught *[did teach]
toupée

tour[1] *[journey] ~| operator
tore *[pulled apart]
tower[1] *[tall building]+
tourism
tourist ~y ~| attraction
tournament
tourney[1] *[competition]
tourniquet
tousle[2]
tout[1] *[praise] — toot[1] *[noise]
toutonic — Teutonic
tow[1] *[pull] ~| bar ~line ~path ~| truck
toe *[on foot]+
two *[number]+
toward ~s
to-way — two-way
towed *[pulled] — toad *[animal]+
towel[1] ~| bar ~| rack
tower[1] *[tall building] ~| block
tour[1] *[journey]+
tow-fu — tofu
towga — toga
towle — towel[1]+
town ~| hall ~house ~| planning ~ship
towns ~folk ~people
towt — tout[1]
toxic ~ity ~ology ~ologist
toxin *[poison] — tocsin *[bell]
toy[1] ~shop
toyl — toil[1]
toylet — toilet *[bathroom]+
toilette *[cosmetic chores]
toyletry — toiletry[4]
trace[2] ~able — @tracing paper
trachea — @tracheotomy
track[1] ~| and field ~| down ~| event ~| meet ~| record ~suit
tracked *[followed]
tract *[land, article]+
tracking ~| station
tract *[land, article] ~able
tracked *[followed]
traction
tractor ~-trailor

Key to Spelling Rules

Red words are wrong. **Black** words are correct.

~ Add the suffix or word directly to the main word, without a space or hyphen
e.g. ash ~en ~tray → ashen ashtray

~- Add a hyphen to the main word before adding the next word
e.g. blow ~-dry → blow-dry

~| Leave a space between the main word and the next word
e.g. decimal ~| place → decimal place

+ By finding this word in its correct alphabetical order, you can find related words
e.g. abowt about+ → about-face

★ Draws attention to words that may be confused

TM Means the word is a trademark

@ Signifies the word is derived from the main word

trade[2] ~| deficit ~| discount ~-in ~| journal ~mark ~name ~-off ~| route ~| secret ~| school

> Unable to find your word under **trade**?
> Take off **trade** and look again

trades ~man ~person
tradishun — tradition+
tradition ~al ~alist ~ally
trae — tray
traffic ~ked ~king ~| circle ~| jam ~| light
trafic — traffic+
tragectory — trajectory[4]
tragedy[4]
tragic ~ally
tragicomedy
traid — trade[2+]
trail[1] *[track] ~blazer ~blazing
  trial *[legal]+
train[1] ~ee ~| line ~| of thought ~spotting ~track
traipse[2]
trais — trace[2+]
trait
traitor ~ous
trajacomedy — tragicomedy
trajectory[4]
trajedy — tragedy[4]
trak — track[1+]
trakea — trachea+
trakia — trachea+
trakshun — traction
trakt — tracked *[followed]
  tract *[land, article]+
trale — trail[1] *[track]+
  trial *[legal]+
trall — trawl[1] *[fish with net]+
  thrall *[bondage]
  troll[1] *[monster, fish with line]
tram ~car ~line
tramendous — tremendous+
tramma — trauma+
tramp[1]
trample[2]
trampoline — @trampolining
trance
trancept — transept
trane — train[1+]
trankwil — tranquil+
trankwilize — tranquilize[2]
tranquil ~ity ~ly
tranquilize[2]
transact[1] — @transaction
transatlantic
transceiver
transcend[1] ~ence ~ent
transcendental ~ism
transcontinental
transcribe[2]
transcript ~ion
transducer
transe — trance
transect ~ion
transeever — transceiver
transekshual — transsexual
transend — transcend[1+]
transept
transet — transit+
transfer[3] ~able ~al ~ence
transfigure[2] — @transfiguration
transfix[5]
transform[1] ~ation
transfuse[2] — @transfusion
transgender
transgress[5] ~ion ~or
transient
transishun — transition+
transistor
transit ~ory
transition ~al
transitive ~| verb
transjender — transgender
transjucer — transducer
transkribe — transcribe[2]
transkript — transcript+
translatable
translate[2] — @translation

KEY TO SUFFIXES AND COMPOUNDS

These rules are explained on pages vii to ix.

1 Keep the word the same before adding **ed, er, est, ing**
e.g. cool[1] → cooled, cooler, coolest, cooling
2 Take off final **e** before adding **ed, er, est, ing**
e.g. fine[2] → fined, finer, finest, fining
3 Double final consonant before adding **ed, er, est, ing**
e.g. thin[3] → thinned, thinner, thinnest, thinning
4 Change final **y** to **i** before adding **ed, er, es, est, ly, ness**
e.g. tidy[4] → tidied, tidier, tidies, tidiest, tidily, tidiness
Keep final **y** before adding **ing** e.g. tidying
5 Add **es** instead of **s** to the end of the word
e.g. bunch[5] → bunches
6 Change final **f** to **ve** before adding **s**
e.g. calf[6] → calves

translucence	@translucent
transmishun	transmission
transmission	
transmit[3]	
transparent ~ly	@transparency[4]
transpire[2]	
transplant[1] ~ation	
transport[1] ~ation	
transpose[2]	
transpyre	transpire[2]
transseiver	transceiver
transseksual	transsexual
transsend	transcend[1+]
transsexual	

> Unable to find your word under **trans**? Take off **trans** and look again

transubstantiation	
transverse ~ly	
transvestite	
transyent	transient
tranzact	transact[1+]
trap[3] ~door	@trappings
trapeze	
trapezium	
trascript	transcript+
trase	trace[2+]
trash[5] ~y[4] ~| bin ~| compactor	
trate	trait
trater	traitor+
trattoria	
traught	trot[3] *[fast walk]
traul	trawl[1] *[fish with net]+
trauma ~tic	
travail *[suffering]	
travel[3] *[visit other places] ~| agency ~| agent	
traveler ~'s check	
traverse[2]	
travesty[4]	
travler	traveler+
travurse	traverse[2]
trawl[1] *[fish with net] ~er	
	troll[1] *[monster, fish with line]
trawl[1]	thrall *[bondage]
tray	
trayl	trail[1] *[track]+
	trial *[legal]+
traypse	traipse[2]
trayt	trait
traytor	traitor+
trea	tree+
treacherous ~ly	
treachery[4]	
treacle	
tread ~ing ~mill	
treason ~able	
treasure[2] ~| hunt ~| trove	
treasury[4] ~| bond	
	@treasurer
Treasury ~| bill ~| note	
treat[1] *[give]+ ~able ~ment	
	threat *[danger]
treatise *[long statement]	
	treaties *[agreements]
treaty[4]	
treble[2] ~| clef	
trecherus	treacherous+
trechery	treachery[4]
tred	tread+
tree ~line ~-lined ~tops ~| trunk	
treeaj	triage
treet	treat[1] *[give]+
treety	treaty[4]
trefoil	
trehspass	trespass[5+]
trek[3]	
trellis ~work	
tremble[2]	
tremendous ~ly	
tremor	
tremulous ~ly	
trench ~es ~| coat	
trenchant	
trend[1] ~setter ~-setting	
trendy[4]	
trenned	trend[1+]
trentch	trench+

Key to Spelling Rules

Red words are wrong. **Black** words are correct.

- **~** Add the suffix or word directly to the main word, without a space or hyphen
  e.g. ash ~en ~tray → ashen ashtray
- **~-** Add a hyphen to the main word before adding the next word
  e.g. blow ~-dry → blow-dry
- **~|** Leave a space between the main word and the next word
  e.g. decimal ~| place → decimal place
- **+** By finding this word in its correct alphabetical order, you can find related words
  e.g. abowt about+ → about-face
- ***** Draws attention to words that may be confused
- **TM** Means the word is a trademark
- **@** Signifies the word is derived from the main word

trepidation
treshere treasure[2+]
treshery treasury[4+]
trespass[5] ~es
tressur treasure[2+]
trestle ~| table
treverse traverse[2]
trew true *[correct]+
triab tribe+
triad *[group of three]
tried *[made an effort]+
triage
trial *[legal] ~| and error ~| balance ~| lawyer ~| period ~| run ~| sample
trail[1] *[track]+

Unable to find your word under **trial**?
Take off **trial** and look again

triangle @triangulate
triangular ~| number ~| prism
triathlon
tribe ~sman @tribal @tribalism
tribulation
tribunal
tribune
tributary[4]
tribute
tribyoot tribute
tribyunal tribunal
triceps
trick[1] *[stunt, deceive] ~ery ~ster
trike *[tricycle]
trick-or-treat ~ing
trickle[2]
tricky[4]
tricuspid ~| valve
tricycle
trident
trie try[4+]
trieb tribe+
tried *[made an effort] ~| and true
triad *[group of three]
trite *[not important]+

triel trial[3] *[legal]+
triep tripe *[food]
triffel trifle[2]
trifle[2]
trigger[1] ~-happy
trigger treet trick-or-treat+
trigonometry
trike *[tricycle] trick[1] *[stunt, deceive]+
trikkel trickle[2]
triky tricky[4]
trilateral @Trilateral Commission
trile trial *[legal]+
trill[1] *[music] trial *[legal]+
thrill[1] *[excitement]+
trillion
trilobite
trilogy[4]
trilyun trillion
trim[3]
trimester
trinity
trinket
trio
trip[3] *[fall] ~wire
tripe *[food]
tripartite
tripe *[food] trip[3] *[fall]+
triple[2] ~| jump @triplet
triplicate
tripod
triptych
trisect[1]
triseps triceps
trist tryst
trite *[not important] ~ly ~ness
tried *[made an effort]+
triumf triumph[1+]
triumph[1] ~al ~ant ~antly
triveal trivial+
trivia
trivial @trivialize[2]
triviality[4]
triyal trial[3] *[legal]+
trod ~den
trofee trophy[4]

KEY TO SUFFIXES AND COMPOUNDS

These rules are explained on pages vii to ix.

1 Keep the word the same before adding **ed, er, est, ing**
e.g. cool[1] → cooled, cooler, coolest, cooling
2 Take off final **e** before adding **ed, er, est, ing**
e.g. fine[2] → fined, finer, finest, fining
3 Double final consonant before adding **ed, er, est, ing**
e.g. thin[3] → thinned, thinner, thinnest, thinning
4 Change final **y** to **i** before adding **ed, er, es, est, ly, ness**
e.g. tidy[4] → tidied, tidier, tidies, tidiest, tidily, tidiness
Keep final **y** before adding **ing** e.g. tidying
5 Add **es** instead of **s** to the end of the word
e.g. bunch[5] → bunches
6 Change final **f** to **ve** before adding **s**
e.g. calf[6] → calves

troff trough *[low point, container]
trofy trophy[4]
troika
troll[1] *[monster, fish with line]
trolley ~| car
troma trauma+
trombone @trombonist
troo true *[correct]+
trooancy truancy+
troobadoor troubadour
trooism truism
troop[1] *[soldiers] troupe *[actors]
trooso trousseau
trophy[4]
tropic ~al ~ally
tropism
troposphere
trot[3] *[fast walk] trout *[fish]
troubadour
trouble[2] ~maker ~some ~shooter
trough *[low point, container]
through *[transit]+
trounce[2]
troupe *[actors] troop[1] *[soldiers]
trouser ~s
trousseau
trout *[fish] trot[3] *[fast walk]
trowel
trowle trowel
trownce trounce[2]
troyka troika
truancy @truant
trubadoor troubadour
trubbel trouble[2+]
truce
truck[1] ~load ~| stop
truculence
truculent ~ly
trudge[2]
trudj trudge[2]
true[2] *[correct] ~| blue ~| colors
through *[transit]
threw *[did throw]
truely truly *[correctly]

truff trough *[low point, container]
truffle
truge trudge[2]
truhmp trump[1+]
truhs truss[5+]
truism
truj trudge[2]
trukulence truculence
truly *[correctly]
trump[1] ~| card ~ed-up
trumpet[1]
truncate[2] @truncation
truncheon
trunck trunk+
trundle[2] ~| bed
trunk ~| line
trunkate truncate[2+]
trunshun truncheon
trup troop[1] *[soldiers]
troupe *[actors]
trupeez trapeze
truse truce
truss[5] ~es
trusseau trousseau
trust[1] ~ful ~buster ~| company[4] ~| fund
trustee *[overseer] ~ship
trusty *[trustworthy]+
trustworthy[4]
trusty *[trustworthy] ~| sword
trustee *[overseer]+
truth *[correct] ~ful ~fully ~fulness ~| serum ~| table
try[4] ~| out *[compete for entry]
try ~out *[competition for entry]
tryaj triage
tryangel triangle
tryll thrill[1] *[excitement]+
trill *[music]
tryst
tryumf triumph[1+]

Unable to find your word under **try**? Look under **tri**

Key to Spelling Rules

Red words are wrong. **Black** words are correct.

- ~ Add the suffix or word directly to the main word, without a space or hyphen
  e.g. ash ~en ~tray → ashen ashtray
- ~- Add a hyphen to the main word before adding the next word
  e.g. blow ~-dry → blow-dry
- ~| Leave a space between the main word and the next word
  e.g. decimal ~| place → decimal place
- + By finding this word in its correct alphabetical order, you can find related words
  e.g. abowt about+ → about-face
- ★ Draws attention to words that may be confused
- ™ Means the word is a trademark
- @ Signifies the word is derived from the main word

tsar ~ina @czar ~ina
tsetse fly
tsunami
tub[3] *[bath] @tubby[4]
tube[2] *[pipe, of paste]+
tuba *[music] tuber *[root]
tube[2] *[pipe, of paste]
@tubular
tub[3] *[bath]+
tube[2] @tubular
tuber *[root] tuba *[music]
tuberculosis
tuch touch[5+]
tuched touched *[emotionally affected]
touché *[admiration]
tucks *[makes a fold]
tux *[clothing]+
Tuesday
tuffen toughen[1]
tuft[1]
tug[3] ~boat ~-of-war
tuishun tuition
tuition
tuk took
tuks tucks *[makes a fold]
tux *[clothing]+
tule tool[1+]
tulip
tumble[2] ~down
tume tomb *[burial]+
tumor
tumult ~uous ~uously
tun *[large cask] ton *[2000 lbs]+
tonne *[1000 kg]
tune[2] *[song]+
tuna ~| fish ~| salad
tundra
tune[2] *[song] ~| in ~| out ~| up *[adjust] ~-up *[adjustment]
tun *[large cask]
tuna+
tuneful ~ly ~ness

tung *[tree] ~| oil
tongue[2] *[body, language]+
tungsten ~| lighting
tunic
tuning ~| fork
tunnel[3] ~| vision
Tuparwear Tupperware™
tupay toupée
Tupperware™
turban *[head covering] ~ed
turbine *[engine]
turbo *[engine] ~charge ~jet ~prop
turbot *[fish]
turbot *[fish] turbo *[engine]+
turbulence @turbulent
turd
tureen
turf[1] ~| out
turgid
turkey *[bird] turnkey *[guard, ready to run]+
Turkey *[country]
Turkish ~| bath ~| delight
turkwoise turquoise
turm term[1+]
turminology terminology[4]
turmoil
turn[1] *[go around] ~about ~| around *[change direction] ~around *[improvement] ~| down ~-off ~-on ~out ~over ~table
tern *[bird]

> Unable to find your word under **turn**?
> Take off **turn** and look again

turning ~| point
turnip
turnkey *[guard, ready to run] ~| operation ~| operator
turkey *[bird]
Turkey *[country]
turpentine

KEY TO SUFFIXES AND COMPOUNDS

These rules are explained on pages vii to ix.

1 Keep the word the same before adding **ed, er, est, ing**
e.g. cool[1] → cooled, cooler, coolest, cooling
2 Take off final **e** before adding **ed, er, est, ing**
e.g. fine[2] → fined, finer, finest, fining
3 Double final consonant before adding **ed, er, est, ing**
e.g. thin[3] → thinned, thinner, thinnest, thinning
4 Change final **y** to **i** before adding **ed, er, es, est, ly, ness**
e.g. tidy[4] → tidied, tidier, tidies, tidiest, tidily, tidiness
Keep final **y** before adding **ing** e.g. tidying
5 Add **es** instead of **s** to the end of the word
e.g. bunch[5] → bunches
6 Change final **f** to **ve** before adding **s**
e.g. calf[6] → calves

turpitude
turquoise
turrain terrain
turrestrial terrestrial
turret
turse terse+
turshiary tertiary
turtle ~dove ~neck
tussle[2]
tutelage
tuter tutor[1] *[teacher]+
tooter *[one who toots]
tuth tooth+
Tutonic Teutonic
tutor[1] *[teacher] ~ial
tooter *[one who toots]
tutti-frutti
tut-tut[3]
tutu *[ballet skirt] too-too *[excessive]
tuward toward+
tux *[clothing] ~edo
tucks *[makes a fold]
TV *[television] TB *[tuberculosis]
twaddle
twain
twang[1]
twead tweed+
tweak[1]
tweazers tweezers
tweed ~y
tweek tweak[1]
tweet[1]
tweezers
twelve @twelfth
twentieth
twenty[4] ~-first ~-twenty
twerl twirl[1]+
twice ~| as much
twich twitch[5]+
twiddle[2] ~| one's thumbs
@twiddly
twig[1]
twilight ~| world ~| zone
twill[1]

twin[3] *[two] ~| beds ~-engined ~| pack
twine *[string]
twine *[string] twin[3] *[two]+
twinge[2]
twinj twinge[2]
twinkle[2]
twirl[1] ~| around
twis twice+
twist[1] ~y
twit[3]
twitch[5] ~es ~y
twitter[1] ~y
twittle twiddle[2]+
two *[number] ~-dimensional ~-faced ~fold ~-man ~-piece ~-ply ~some ~-time ~-way
to *[for, toward]+
too *[also, very]

> Unable to find your word under **two**?
> Take off **two** and look again

twylight twilight+
twyn twin[3] *[two]+
twyne twine *[string]
twyst twist[1]+
ty tie *[bind, equal score]+
Thai *[from Thailand]
tycket ticket[1]+
tycoon
tyde tide *[sea]+
tied *[rope, score]
tydings tidings
tydul tidal *[tide]+
title *[name]+
tyer tear *[cry, rip]+
tier *[layer]
tire[2] *[sleep, wheel]+
tyfoon typhoon
tyght tight[1] *[stretched firmly]+
tit *[bird]+
tyll till[1] *[soil, cash register, until]
tymber timber *[wood]+
timbre *[sound]

Key to Spelling Rules

Red words are wrong. **Black** words are correct.

~ Add the suffix or word directly to the main word, without a space or hyphen
e.g. ash ~en ~tray → ashen ashtray

~- Add a hyphen to the main word before adding the next word
e.g. blow ~-dry → blow-dry

~| Leave a space between the main word and the next word
e.g. decimal ~| place → decimal place

+ By finding this word in its correct alphabetical order, you can find related words
e.g. abowt about+ → about-face

★ Draws attention to words that may be confused

™ Means the word is a trademark

@ Signifies the word is derived from the main word

tyme time[2] *[clock]⁺
thyme *[herb]
type[2] *[kind, printing] ~cast ~face ~writer
tip[3] *[end, advice]⁺
typhoon
typhus @typhoid
typical ~ly
typify[4]
typist
typo
typography[4] *[printing]
@typographer
topography[4] *[land shape]⁺
typology[4] *[study of examples]
@typological
topology[4] *[mathematics]⁺

tyrade tirade
tyrannical ~ly
tyrannize[2]
Tyrannosaurus ~| rex
tyranny[4]
tyrant
tyt tit *[bird, breast]⁺
tight[1] [stretched firmly]⁺
tytan titan *[important person]⁺
tighten[1] *[firm up]
tytanic titanic
tytle title *[name]⁺
tidal *[tide]⁺

Unable to find your word under **ty**?
Look under **ti**

U

U *[letter] ~-boat ~-turn
you *[person]⁺
U.S. *[United States] ~| U.S.A.
us *[group of two or more]
ubiquitous ~ly
ucalayli ukulele
ucalyptus eucalyptus

Unable to find your word under **u**?
Look under **eu**

udder *[cows] utter[1] *[express]⁺
ufemism euphemism
uffishant efficient *[gets things done]⁺
officiant *[officiates]
UFO [unidentified flying object]
uforia euphoria⁺
ugenics eugenics
ugh
ugly[4] ~| duckling

uh ~-huh ~oh ~uh
ujeniks eugenics
ukeliptis eucalyptus
ukerist Eucharist
uclid Euclid
ukulele
ulcer *[wound] ~ated ~ous
Ulster *[Northern Ireland]
ule Yule *[Christmas]⁺
you'll *[you will]
uliteration alliteration
ulna ~e
ulogise eulogize[2]⁺
ulogy eulogy[4] *[funeral oration]
elegy[4] *[poem]⁺
Ulster *[Northern Ireland]
ulcer *[wound]⁺
ulterior ~| motive
ultimate ~ly
ultimatum
ultireor ulterior⁺

Key to Suffixes and Compounds

These rules are explained on pages vii to ix.

1 Keep the word the same before adding **ed, er, est, ing**
e.g. cool[1] → cooled, cooler, coolest, cooling
2 Take off final **e** before adding **ed, er, est, ing**
e.g. fine[2] → fined, finer, finest, fining
3 Double final consonant before adding **ed, er, est, ing**
e.g. thin[3] → thinned, thinner, thinnest, thinning
4 Change final **y** to **i** before adding **ed, er, es, est, ly, ness**
e.g. tidy[4] → tidied, tidier, tidies, tidiest, tidily, tidiness
Keep final **y** before adding **ing** e.g. tidying
5 Add **es** instead of **s** to the end of the word
e.g. bunch[5] → bunches
6 Change final **f** to **ve** before adding **s**
e.g. calf[6] → calves

ultra ~conservative ~liberal ~microscopic ~modern
ultrasonic ~ally
ultrasound
ultraviolet
ululate @ululation
umbilical ~| cord
umbrage
umbrella ~| policy[4]
umpire[2] *[game] empire *[lands]
umpteen
umpyre umpire[2] *[game] empire *[lands]
UN [United Nations]
unabashed
unabated
unable *[not able] enable[2] *[to make able]+
unabridged
unacceptable
unacclaimed
unaccommodating
unaccompanied
unaccountable
unaccounted *[not explained] ~| for uncounted *[not counted]
unaccredited
unaccustomed
unacknowledged
unacquainted
unadapted
unaded unaided
unadulterated
unaffected
unaffiliated
unaform uniform+
unafraid ~| of
unaided
unaknoleged unacknowledged
unalienable
unalterable @unalterably
unambiguous ~ly
unambitious
un-American
unamortized ~| investment ~| premium

unanimous @unanimity
unannounced
unanticipated
unapatizing unappetizing
unapologetic ~ally
unappetizing
unappologetic unapologetic+
unarmed
unarmored
unasecks unisex
unashamed ~ly
unasimalated unassimilated
unasin unison
unasined unassigned
unasked
unassailable
unassertive
unassigned
unassimilated
unassuming
unatarian Unitarian+
unatary unitary+
unattached
unattended
unattractive
unaudited ~| accounts
unauthorized ~| entry ~| expenditure ~| use
unavailabe
unavoidable
unaware *[not knowing] ~ness underwear *[clothing]
unawthorised unauthorized+
unaybul unable *[not able] enable[2] *[to make able]+
unbalance[2]
unbeatable
unbeaten
unbeknownst
unblinking
unblock[1]
unborn
unbounded
unbowed
unbreakable

Key to Spelling Rules

Red words are wrong. **Black** words are correct.

~ Add the suffix or word directly to the main word, without a space or hyphen
e.g. ash ~en ~tray → ashen ashtray

~- Add a hyphen to the main word before adding the next word
e.g. blow ~-dry → blow-dry

~| Leave a space between the main word and the next word
e.g. decimal ~| place → decimal place

+ By finding this word in its correct alphabetical order, you can find related words
e.g. abowt about+ → about-face

* Draws attention to words that may be confused

TM Means the word is a trademark

@ Signifies the word is derived from the main word

unbridled
unbroken
unbuckle[2]
unburden[1]
unbutton[1]
uncanny
unceremonious ~ly
uncertain ~ly ~ty
unchanged
uncharitable @uncharitably
unchecked ~| figures
uncivilized
unclaimed ~| baggage
uncle
unclear
uncollectible ~| account
uncomfortable
uncomprehending ~ly
unconditional ~ly
unconfirmed
unconnected
unconscionable *[cannot be accepted in conscience] ~| contract @unconscionably
unconscious ~ly
uncontrolled
unconvincing
uncoordinated
uncorrected
uncorroborated
uncorrupted
uncounted *[not counted] unaccounted *[not explained]+
uncouth ~ness
uncover[1]
uncultured
uncumfterble uncomfortable
uncustomary
uncuver uncover[1]
undafeeted undefeated
undafined undefined
undaklared undeclared
undamaged
undasided undecided
undated
undaware underwear *[clothing] unaware *[not knowing]+
undavided undivided+
undawkyoomented undocumented+
undecided
undecyrabul undesirable+
undeclared
undefeated
undefined
undeniable @undeniably
under ~| class ~| construction ~| contract ~| control ~| new management ~achieve[2] ~-age ~-aged ~| budget ~capitalized ~cover ~employed ~graduate ~ground ~growth ~hand ~insured ~neath ~populated ~powered ~priced ~water ~wear ~weight ~went ~world ~write ~writing ~written

> Unable to find your word starting with **under**? Take off **under** and look again

undercided undecided
undercut ~ting
underdeveloped
undereport underreport[1]
underequipped
underestimate[2]
underfeated undefeated
underfoot
undergo ~ing
undergone
underkut undercut[3]
underlay *[to place under] ~ment @underlaid
underlie *[to be under]
underline[2]
underlying ~| debt[1] ~| mortgage[2] ~| security[4]
undermine[2]
undernyble undeniable+

Key to Suffixes and Compounds

These rules are explained on pages vii to ix.

1 Keep the word the same before adding **ed, er, est, ing** e.g. cool[1] → cooled, cooler, coolest, cooling
2 Take off final **e** before adding **ed, er, est, ing** e.g. fine[2] → fined, finer, finest, fining
3 Double final consonant before adding **ed, er, est, ing** e.g. thin[3] → thinned, thinner, thinnest, thinning
4 Change final **y** to **i** before adding **ed, er, es, est, ly, ness** e.g. tidy[4] → tidied, tidier, tidies, tidiest, tidily, tidiness
Keep final **y** before adding **ing** e.g. tidying
5 Add **es** instead of **s** to the end of the word e.g. bunch[5] → bunches
6 Change final **f** to **ve** before adding **s** e.g. calf[6] → calves

underpaid
underpass
underplay[1]
underprivileged
underreport[1]
underright underwrite+
underscore[2]
undersell ~ing @undersold
undersided undecided
undersign[1]
undersirable undesirable+
underspend ~ing @underspent
understand ~able ~ably ~ing
understood
undersyne undersign[1]
undertake ~n ~r @undertaking
undertone *[low sound, suggestion]
undertook
undertow *[water current]
undervalued
underwear *[clothing]
unaware *[not knowing]+
underwrite[2]
undesided undecided
undesirable @undesirably
undevided undivided+
undew undo *[reverse]+ undue *[excessive]
undignified
undiniabel undeniable+
undisciplined
undisclosed ~| amount
undisguised
undisided undecided
undisiplined undisciplined
undisirable undesirable+
undiskized undisguised
undisklozed undisclosed+
undivided ~| attention ~| interest
undo *[reverse] ~ing
undue *[excessive]
undocumented ~| alien
undone

undoubtedly
undreamed ~| of @undreamt of
undrinkable
undue *[excessive]
undo *[reverse]+
undun undone
unduniabel undeniable+
undur under+
undurgo undergo+
unearned ~| discount ~| income ~| interest ~| premium
unearth[1]
uneasy[4]
uneatable @uneaten
unebasht unabashed
unecessary unnecessary[4]
unecksiting unexciting
uneconomic ~al
unedifying
uneducated
uneek unique *[one and only]+
uneetable uneatable+
uneeven uneven+
uneezy uneasy[4]
unekonomik uneconomic+
uneksiting unexciting
unekspected unexpected+
unekspIaned unexplained
unekwal unequal+
unemotional
unemployed @unemployable
unemployment ~| compensation ~| insurance
unenthusiastic ~ally
unenviable
unequal ~led ~ly

> Unable to find your word under **un**?
> Take off **un** and look again

unerned unearned+
unerth unearth[1]
unesasary unnecessary[4]
unesey uneasy[4]
unetabel uneatable+

KEY TO SPELLING RULES

Red words are wrong. **Black** words are correct.

~ Add the suffix or word directly to the main word, without a space or hyphen
e.g. ash ~en ~tray → ashen ashtray

~- Add a hyphen to the main word before adding the next word
e.g. blow ~-dry → blow-dry

~| Leave a space between the main word and the next word
e.g. decimal ~| place → decimal place

+ By finding this word in its correct alphabetical order, you can find related words
e.g. abowt about+ → about-face

* Draws attention to words that may be confused

TM Means the word is a trademark

@ Signifies the word is derived from the main word

unethical
uneven ~ly ~ness
unexaggerated
unexciting
unexpected ~ly
unexplained
unfair ~ly ~| competition ~| dismissal
unfaithful
unfamiliar
unfare unfair+
unfashionable @unfashionably
unfavorable ~| exchange rate
unfaythful unfaithful
unferl unfurl[1]
unfernished unfurnished
unfertilized ~| egg
unfettered
unfinished
unfirl unfurl[1]
unfirnished unfurnished
unflagging
unflattering
unflinching ~ly
unfocused
unfold[1]
unforchenit unfortunate+
unforeseeable ~| future
unforgettable @unforgettably
unforgivable @unforgivably
unfortunate ~ly
unfounded *[without basis] ~| allegation
unfunded *[without money]+
unfourgettabul unforgettable+
unfourgivabul unforgivable+
unfourseeabul unforeseeable+
unfourtunate unfortunate+
unfownded unfounded
unfriendly
unfulfilled ~| order
unfunded *[without money] ~| mandate
unfounded *[without basis]+
unfurl[1]
unfurnished

ungainly
ungarded unguarded
unglewd unglued
unglued
ungodly
ungovernable
ungracious ~ly ~ness
ungraitful ungrateful+
ungrammatical
ungrashous ungracious+
ungrateful ~ly ~ness
unguarded
unguvernable ungovernable
unhampered
unhappy[4]
unheard ~| of
unhelpful
unherd unheard+
unhesitatingly
unhurd unheard+
unianise unionize[2]
unien union+
uniform ~| resource locator [URL]
unike unique *[one and only]+
unimaginable @unimaginably
unincorporated
uninsured ~| motorist
union *[uniting] ~| contract ~| rate ~| shop
onion *[vegetable]
Union ~| Jack
Unionist
unionize[2]
unionized *[not in a labor union]
un-ionized *[not turned into ions]
unique *[one and only] ~ly ~ness
unisex
unison
unit *[single thing] ~| cost ~| price ~| trust
unite[2] *[put together]
Unitarian ~ism
unitary ~| tax
unite[2] *[put together]
unit *[single thing]+

Key to Suffixes and Compounds

These rules are explained on pages vii to ix.

1 Keep the word the same before adding **ed, er, est, ing** e.g. cool[1] → cooled, cooler, coolest, cooling
2 Take off final **e** before adding **ed, er, est, ing** e.g. fine[2] → fined, finer, finest, fining
3 Double final consonant before adding **ed, er, est, ing** e.g. thin[3] → thinned, thinner, thinnest, thinning
4 Change final **y** to **i** before adding **ed, er, es, est, ly, ness** e.g. tidy[4] → tidied, tidier, tidies, tidiest, tidily, tidiness
Keep final **y** before adding **ing** e.g. tidying
5 Add **es** instead of **s** to the end of the word e.g. bunch[5] → bunches
6 Change final **f** to **ve** before adding **s** e.g. calf[6] → calves

unite[2] — unity[4] *[togetherness]
untie *[take apart]+
United States ~| of America
unity[4] *[togetherness]
untie *[take apart]+
universal ~ity ~ly
universe
university[4]
UNIX *[operating system]
eunuchs *[castrated males]
unizy — uneasy[4]
unjust ~ified ~ly
unkanny — uncanny
unkempt *[not groomed]
unkept *[not kept]
unkind ~ly ~ness
unkle — uncle
unklear — unclear
unknowing ~ly
unknown
unkomfortable — uncomfortable
unkonshous — unconscious+
unkontrolled — uncontrolled
unkover — uncover[1]
unkulchered — uncultured
unkumfterble — uncomfortable
unkwenchable — unquenchable
unkynd — unkind+

> Unable to find your word under **unk**?
> Look under **unc**

unleaded
unlicensed
unlimited ~| liability[4]
unlisted ~| number

> Unable to find your word under **un**?
> Take off **un** and look again

unload[1]
unlovable
unloved
unmached — unmatched
unmanned
unmapped
unmarked
unmatched
unmentionable
unmerciful ~ly
unmitigated ~| disaster
unmoved
unmursafully — unmerciful+
unnabated — unabated
unnabriged — unabridged
unnanounced — unannounced
unnaware — unaware *[not knowing]+
underwear *[clothing]
unnecessary[4]
unnowing — unknowing+
unnown — unknown
unobtrusive ~ly
unopened
unotherized — unauthorized+
unowing — unknowing+
unpaid ~| dividend ~| invoice
unpalatable
unpardonable
unpaved ~| road
unpayd — unpaid+
unplug[3]
unpopular ~ity
unprafesional — unprofessional+
unpredictable — @unpredictably
unprejudiced
unprepared
unpretentious ~ly ~ness
unprincipled
unprintable
unpripared — unprepared
unprofessional ~ly
unprompted
unpronounceable
unprotected
unproven
unprovoked
unprufeshional — unprofessional+
unpruven — unproven
unpunished
unquenchable

Key to Spelling Rules

Red words are wrong. **Black** words are correct.

~ Add the suffix or word directly to the main word, without a space or hyphen
e.g. ash ~en ~tray → ashen ashtray

~- Add a hyphen to the main word before adding the next word
e.g. blow ~-dry → blow-dry

~| Leave a space between the main word and the next word
e.g. decimal ~| place → decimal place

\+ By finding this word in its correct alphabetical order, you can find related words
e.g. abowt about+ → about-face

★ Draws attention to words that may be confused

TM Means the word is a trademark

@ Signifies the word is derived from the main word

unquestionable @unquestionably
unquestioning ~ly
unralenting unrelenting
unrap unwrap[3]
unreal *[imaginary, fantastic]
unreel[1] *[unwind]
unrealized ~| appreciation ~| depreciation
unreckwitted unrequited+
unrecorded ~| profit
unrecovered ~| cost
unreel[1] *[unwind] unreal *[imaginary, fantastic]
unreelized unrealized+
unregistered ~| stock
unrekovered unrecovered+
unrekwighted unrequited+
unrelenting
unreliable
unremitting
unrepentant
unreported ~| income
unrequited ~| love
unresponsive
unritten unwritten
unsafe
unsaid
unsanitary *[dirty]
unsaported unsupported
unsatisfactory
unsayf unsafe
unscene unseen
unscientific ~ally
unscramble[2]
unscrew[1]
unscrupulous ~ly ~ness
unsealed
unsecured ~| debt ~| creditor
unsed unsaid
unseeled unsealed
unseen
unsekured unsecured+
unselfconscious ~ly ~ness
unselfish ~ly ~ness
unseramonius unceremonious+
unsertain uncertain+
unshakable
unsher unsure
unsien unseen
unsientific unscientific+
unsightly
unsine unseen
unsivilised uncivilized
unskilled
unskramble unscramble[2]
unskrew unscrew[1]
unskrupulous unscrupulous+
unskylled unskilled
unsociable
unsofisticated unsophisticated
unsolved
unsoopervized unsupervised
unsooted unsuited
unsophisticated
unsoshable unsociable
unspeakable
unspecified
unspoiled
unspoken
unsporting
unspoyled unspoiled
unstated
unsteady
unstructured
unsubstantiated
unsuffisticated unsophisticated
unsuited
unsung ~| hero
unsupervised
unsupported
unsure
unsurten uncertain+
untacksed untaxed
untactful
untainted
untaktfull untactful
untangle[2]
untanted untainted
untarnished ~| reputation
untaught

KEY TO SUFFIXES AND COMPOUNDS

These rules are explained on pages vii to ix.

1 Keep the word the same before adding **ed, er, est, ing**
e.g. cool[1] → cooled, cooler, coolest, cooling
2 Take off final **e** before adding **ed, er, est, ing**
e.g. fine[2] → fined, finer, finest, fining
3 Double final consonant before adding **ed, er, est, ing**
e.g. thin[3] → thinned, thinner, thinnest, thinning
4 Change final **y** to **i** before adding **ed, er, es, est, ly, ness**
e.g. tidy[4] → tidied, tidier, tidies, tidiest, tidily, tidiness
Keep final **y** before adding **ing** e.g. tidying
5 Add **es** instead of **s** to the end of the word
e.g. bunch[5] → bunches
6 Change final **f** to **ve** before adding **s**
e.g. calf[6] → calves

untaxed	
untaynted	untainted
unteachable	
unterned	unturned
untested	
unthankful	
unthinkable	
unthinking ~ly	
untidy[4]	
untie *[take apart] ~d	@untying
	unite[2] *[put together]
until	
untimely ~| death	
untold	
untot	untaught
untraceable	
untranslatable	
untraveled	
untrooth	untruth+
untroubled	
untrustworthy[4]	
untruth ~ful	
unturned	
untwist[1]	
untye	unite[2] *[put together]
	unity[4] *[togetherness]
	untie *[take apart]+
untydy	untidy[4]
untymley	untimely+
unuch	eunuch
unurth	unearth[1]
unusable	
unwelcome	@unwelcoming
unworthy[4]	
unwrap[3]	
unwritten	
unyen	onion *[vegetable]
	union *[uniting]
unyen jack	Union Jack
unyenize	unionize[2]
unyform	uniform+
Unyionist	Unionist
unyon	onion *[vegetable]
	union *[uniting]
unyoozable	unusable
unyque	unique+
unyson	unison
unyte	unite[2] *[put together]
unyty	unity[4]
unyun	onion *[vegetable]
	union *[uniting]
unyverse	universe

Unable to find your word under **uny**?
Look under **uni**

unzip[3]

Unable to find your word under **un**?
Take off **un** and look again

up[3] ~-and-coming ~chuck[1] ~end[1] ~-front ~| market ~right ~river ~| state ~s and downs ~-to-date ~-to-the-minute

Unable to find your word under **up**?
Take off **up** and look again

upawn	upon
upbeat	
upbringing	
update[2]	
uper	upper+
upgrade[2]	
upheaval	@upheave[2]
upheld	
uphemism	euphemism
uphemistic	euphemistic+
upheval	upheaval+
uphill	
uphold ~ing	
upholster[1] ~y	
uphoria	euphoria+
uphyll	uphill
upkeep	
upland	
uplift[1]	
upload[1]	
upolster	upholster[1]+

Key to Spelling Rules

Red words are wrong. **Black** words are correct.

~ Add the suffix or word directly to the main word, without a space or hyphen
e.g. ash ~en ~tray → ashen ashtray

~- Add a hyphen to the main word before adding the next word
e.g. blow ~-dry → blow-dry

~| Leave a space between the main word and the next word
e.g. decimal ~| place → decimal place

+ By finding this word in its correct alphabetical order, you can find related words
e.g. abowt about+ → about-face

* Draws attention to words that may be confused

TM Means the word is a trademark

@ Signifies the word is derived from the main word

upon
upper ~case ~| class ~| crust
uprise @uprising
uprite upright
uprize uprise+
uproar ~ious ~iously
uproot[1]
uprore uproar+
upryse uprise+
upryt upright
upset ~ting ~| price
upshot
upside ~-down ~| potential
upskale upscale
upstage[2]
upstairs
upstanding
upstart
upstarze upstairs
upstream
upswing
upsyde-down upside-down
uptern upturn[1]
uptight
uptime
uptirn upturn[1]
uptite uptight
uptrend
upturn[1]
upward ~ly ~s ~| mobility ~| trend
uranate urinate[2]
uranium
Uranus
urase erase[2+]
urban *[city] ~| renewal ~| sprawl
urbane *[worldly]
urbanize[2] @urbanization
urchin
urea
uren urine *[waste]+
ureter *[from kidney to bladder]
urethra *[from bladder to outside]
urge[2]
urgency
urgent ~ly

urhythmee eurythmy+
uria urea
urinate[2]
urine *[waste] @urinal
@urinary
uriter ureter *[from kidney to bladder]
urithmy eurythmy+
urithra urethra *[from bladder to outside]
urje urge[2]
urjensy urgency
urjent urgent+
url earl *[noble]+
URL *[uniform resource locator]
urly early[4+]
urmine ermine
urn *[vase] earn[1] *[receive payment]
urnest earnest+
uro euro
urode erode[2+]
urology @urologist
Uropean European+
urotic erotic+
urr err[1+]
urratic erratic+
urth earth+
urupt erupt[1+]

Unable to find your word under **ur**?
Look under **ear** and **er**

uryne urine *[waste]+
us *[group of two or more]
U.S. *[United States]+
use[2] *[put into service]
@usable
@usage
yews *[evergreen trees]
useful ~ly ~ness
useless ~ly ~ness
user ~| fee ~-friendly ~| ID
userp usurp[1]
usery usury

Key to Suffixes and Compounds

These rules are explained on pages vii to ix.

1 Keep the word the same before adding **ed, er, est, ing**
e.g. cool[1] → cooled, cooler, coolest, cooling
2 Take off final **e** before adding **ed, er, est, ing**
e.g. fine[2] → fined, finer, finest, fining
3 Double final consonant before adding **ed, er, est, ing**
e.g. thin[3] → thinned, thinner, thinnest, thinning
4 Change final **y** to **i** before adding **ed, er, es, est, ly, ness**
e.g. tidy[4] → tidied, tidier, tidies, tidiest, tidily, tidiness
Keep final **y** before adding **ing** e.g. tidying
5 Add **es** instead of **s** to the end of the word
e.g. bunch[5] → bunches
6 Change final **f** to **ve** before adding **s**
e.g. calf[6] → calves

usful	useful+
usher[1] ~| in	
usirp	usurp[1]
usless	useless+
usual ~ly	
usurp[1]	
usury	
utalize	utilize[2+]
utensil	
uter	utter[1] *[express]+
	udder *[cows]
uterly	utterly
uterus	
uthanasia	euthanasia
uther	other
utilitarian ~ism	
utility[4] ~| easement	
utilize[2]	@utilization
utmost	
utopia ~n	
utter[1] *[express] ~ance ~ly	
	udder *[cows]
uturus	uterus
utylitarian	utilitarian+
utylity	utility[4+]
utylize	utilize[2+]
uven	oven
uvre	oeuvre+
uze	ooze[2]
uzer	user+
uzery	usury
uzual	usual+

V

V ~-neck ~-necked ~-shaped ~| sign	
vacancy[4] ~| rate	
vacant ~ly	
vacate[2]	
vacation *[holiday] ~| home ~| pay	
	vocation *[occupation]
vaccinate[2]	@vaccination
vaccine	
vace	vase *[for flowers]
vacency	vacancy[4+]
vacillate[2]	@vacillation
vackyoom	vacuum[1+]
vackyuous	vacuous+
vacsinate	vaccinate[2+]
vacum	vacuum[1+]
vacuous ~ly ~ness	
vacuum[1] ~| bottle ~| cleaner ~| flask ~-packed ~| tube	
vael	vale *[valley]
	veil[1] *[cloth]
	veal *[meat]
vagabond	
vagary[4]	
vage	vague+
vagina ~l	
vagrant	@vagrancy
vague ~ly ~ness	
vaguery	vagary[4]
vahz	vase *[for flowers]
	vas *[in body]+
vain *[proud] ~ly	
	vane *[weather]
	vein *[blood]+
vaiporize	vaporize[2]
vajina	vagina+
vakant	vacant+
vakation	vacation *[holiday]+
	vocation *[occupation]
vakensy	vacancy[4+]
vaksinate	vaccinate[2+]

Unable to find your word under **vak**?
Look under **vac**

KEY TO SPELLING RULES

Red words are wrong. **Black** words are correct.

~ Add the suffix or word directly to the main word, without a space or hyphen
e.g. ash ~en ~tray → ashen ashtray

~- Add a hyphen to the main word before adding the next word
e.g. blow ~-dry → blow-dry

~| Leave a space between the main word and the next word
e.g. decimal ~| place → decimal place

\+ By finding this word in its correct alphabetical order, you can find related words
e.g. abowt about+ → about-face

★ Draws attention to words that may be confused

TM Means the word is a trademark

@ Signifies the word is derived from the main word

valance *[drapery]	
	valence *[chemistry]+
valantine	valentine
valauble	valuable *[worth money]+
valay	valet *[servant]
	valley *[lowland]
	volley[1] *[projectiles]+
vale *[valley]	valet *[servant]
valed	valid+
valedait	validate[2+]
valedictorian	
valence *[chemistry] ~| band ~| electron	
	valance *[drapery]
valentine	
valer	valor *[bravery]
valet *[servant]	valley *[lowland]
	volley *[projectiles]+
valew	value[2+]
vali	valley *[lowland]
	valet *[servant]
	volley[1] *[projectiles]+
valiant ~ly	
valid ~ity	
validate[2]	@validation
valley *[lowland]	volley[1] *[projectiles]+
	valet *[servant]
valor *[bravery]	valet *[servant]
valuable *[worth money] ~| consideration	
	voluble *[talkative]+
value[2] ~-added ~less ~| date	
~| judgment	@valuation
valuntine	valentine
valve	
valyd	valid+
valydate	validate[2+]
valyent	valiant+
valyu	value[2+]
valyuble	valuable *[worth money]+
	voluble *[talkative]+
vamoose	
vamp[1]	
vampire	
van *[truck] ~guard	
	vane *[weather]
vandal ~ize[2] ~ism	
vane *[weather]	van *[truck]+
	vain *[proud]+
	vein *[blood]+
vanilla	
vanish[5] *[disappear]	
	varnish[5] *[polish]
vanity ~| case ~| unit ~| table	
vanquish[5]	
vantage ~| point	
vanysh	vanish[5]
vaper	vapor+
vapid	
vapor ~ware	
vaporize[2]	
varekose	varicose+
variable ~| annuity[4] ~| cost ~| interest ~-rate mortgage	
	@variability
variant	@variance
variation	
variaty	variety[4]
varicose ~| veins	
varied	
varient	variant+
variety[4]	
varikoze	varicose+
various ~ly	
varnish[5] *[polish]	vanish[5] *[disappear]
varse	vase
varsity	
vary[4] *[change]	very *[much]
varyabel	variable+
varyation	variation
varyent	variable+
vascular	
vase	
vasectomy[4]	
vasillate	vacillate[2+]
vaskyooler	vascular
vassal *[under lord]	
	vessel *[ship, container]
vast ~ly ~ness	
Vatican ~| City ~| Council	
vault[1] *[jump, safe place]	
	volt *[electric]+

Key to Suffixes and Compounds

These rules are explained on pages vii to ix.

1. Keep the word the same before adding **ed, er, est, ing**
   e.g. cool[1] → cooled, cooler, coolest, cooling
2. Take off final **e** before adding **ed, er, est, ing**
   e.g. fine[2] → fined, finer, finest, fining
3. Double final consonant before adding **ed, er, est, ing**
   e.g. thin[3] → thinned, thinner, thinnest, thinning
4. Change final **y** to **i** before adding **ed, er, es, est, ly, ness**
   e.g. tidy[4] → tidied, tidier, tidies, tidiest, tidily, tidiness
   Keep final **y** before adding **ing** e.g. tidying
5. Add **es** instead of **s** to the end of the word
   e.g. bunch[5] → bunches
6. Change final **f** to **ve** before adding **s**
   e.g. calf[6] → calves

vaunt[1]	
vauze	vase
vaygrent	vagrant[+]
vayn	vain *[proud][+]
	vane *[weather]
	vein *[blood][+]
VCR [video cassette recorder]	
VD [venereal disease]	
veal *[meat]	veil[1] *[cloth]
veamence	vehemence
vecks	vex[5+]
vector ~| graphic ~| image ~| calculus	
vedderan	veteran *[served in war][+]
veddernarian	veterinarian *[treats animals][+]
vee eye pee	VIP[+]
veea	via *[through]
	vie *[compete][+]
veegen	vegan
veeickle	vehicle[+]
veel	veal *[meat]
veenal	venal *[corrupt]
	venial *[less grave][+]
veenus	Venus *[planet][+]
	venous *[veins]
veer[1]	
veermuns	vehemence
veeto	veto[1+]
ve eye pee	VIP[+]
veezavee	vis-à-vis
vegan	
vegetable	
vegetarian ~ism	
vegetate[2]	@vegetation
vegtable	vegetable
vehemence	
vehement ~ly	
vehicle	@vehicular
veikel	vehicle[+]
veil[1] *[cloth]	vale *[valley]
	valley *[lowland]
	veal *[meat]
vein *[blood] ~ed	
	vain *[proud][+]
	vane *[weather]
veiw	view[1+]
vejetable	vegetable
veks	vex[5+]
vektor	vector[+]
veladrome	velodrome
Velcro™	
vellum	
velociraptor	
velocity	
velodrome	
velosarapter	velociraptor
velosity	velocity
velour	
velur	velour
velvet ~een ~y	
ven diagram	Venn diagram
vena cava	
venal *[corrupt]	venial *[less grave][+]
venarability	venerability *[wisdom]
	vulnerability[4] *[weakness]
venarable	venerable *[wise]
	vulnerable *[weak]
venarait	venerate[2+]
venasin	venison
vencher	venture[2+]
vend ~ing machine ~or	
vendetta	
veneer[1]	
veneerial	venereal[+]
veneeshun	Venetian *[from Venice][+]
venerability *[wisdom]	
	vulnerability[4] *[weakness]
venerable *[wise]	
	vulnerable *[weak]
venerate[2]	@veneration
venereal ~| disease [VD]	
Venetian *[from Venice] ~| blinds	
venew	venue
vengeance	
vengeful	
venial *[less grave] ~| sin	
	venal *[corrupt]

Key to Spelling Rules

Red words are wrong. **Black** words are correct.

~ Add the suffix or word directly to the main word, without a space or hyphen
e.g. ash ~en ~tray → ashen ashtray

~- Add a hyphen to the main word before adding the next word
e.g. blow ~-dry → blow-dry

~| Leave a space between the main word and the next word
e.g. decimal ~| place → decimal place

\+ By finding this word in its correct alphabetical order, you can find related words
e.g. abowt about[+] → about-face

* Draws attention to words that may be confused

™ Means the word is a trademark

@ Signifies the word is derived from the main word

Venice *[city] | Venus *[planet]+
| venous *[veins]
venim | venom+
venir | veneer[1]
venirial | venereal+
venis | venous *[veins]
| Venus *[planet]+
| Venice *[city]
venison
venjful | vengeful
venjuns | vengeance
Venn diagram
vennis | Venice *[city]
| venous *[veins]
| Venus *[planet]+
vennison | venison
venom ~ous
venous *[veins] | Venus *[planet]+
venrable | venerable *[wise]
venrate | venerate[2+]
vent[1]
ventilate[2] | @ventilation
| @ventilator
ventricle
ventriloquist | @ventriloquism
venture[2] ~| capital ~| team
ventylate | ventilate[2+]
venue
venum | venom+
venurate | venerate[2+]
Venus *[planet] ~| flytrap
| venous *[veins]
| Venice *[city]
venyoo | venue
venyson | venison
veracity *[truth] | voracity *[greed]
verafy | verify[4+]
veranda
verasity | veracity *[truth]
| voracity *[greed]
verb
verbal ~ize[2] ~ly ~| agreement
verbatim
verbiage
verbose ~ly | @verbosity

vercabulary | vocabulary[4]
verchoo | virtue+
verdant
verdge | verge[2]
verdict
verdure
verge[2]
vergin | virgin+
veri | very *[much]
| vary[4] *[change]
veriashun | variation
veriety | variety[4]
verify[4] | @verifiable
| @verification
verisimilitude
veritable | @veritably
| @verity
verius | various+
vermen | vermin
vermicelli
vermilion
vermin
vermiselly | vermicelli
vermitchelly | vermicelli
vermouth
vernacular
vernal ~| equinox
verology | virology+
verruca
versatile | @versatility
verse ~d
verses *[poetry] | versus *[against]
versimilitude | verisimilitude
version
versus *[against] | verses *[poetry]
vertacle | vertical+
vertago | vertigo+
vertebra ~e ~te
vertex | @vertices
vertical ~ly ~| analysis ~| discount ~| marketing ~| merger ~| integration ~| organization ~| promotion ~| specialization ~| union

KEY TO SUFFIXES AND COMPOUNDS

These rules are explained on pages vii to ix.

1 Keep the word the same before adding **ed, er, est, ing**
e.g. cool[1] → cooled, cooler, coolest, cooling
2 Take off final **e** before adding **ed, er, est, ing**
e.g. fine[2] → fined, finer, finest, fining
3 Double final consonant before adding **ed, er, est, ing**
e.g. thin[3] → thinned, thinner, thinnest, thinning
4 Change final **y** to **i** before adding **ed, er, es, est, ly, ness**
e.g. tidy[4] → tidied, tidier, tidies, tidiest, tidily, tidiness
Keep final **y** before adding **ing** e.g. tidying
5 Add **es** instead of **s** to the end of the word
e.g. bunch[5] → bunches
6 Change final **f** to **ve** before adding **s**
e.g. calf[6] → calves

Unable to find your word under **vertical**? Take off **vertical** and look again

vertigo @vertiginous
vertu virtue+
vertual virtual *[not quite real]+
vertuos virtuous *[morals]+
vertuoso virtuoso *[art]+
veruka verruca
verve
very *[much] vary[4] *[change]
verzhen version
vesal vessel *[ship, container]
vassal *[under lord]
vespers
vessel *[ship, container]
vassal *[under lord]
vest[1] ~ment ~ure
vestage vestige+
vestal ~| virgin
vessel *[ship, container]
vassal *[under lord]
vested ~| interest
vestige @vestigial
vestle vestal+
vessel *[ship, container]
vestry[4]
vet[3] *[inspect, veteran, veterinarian]
veteran *[served in war] ~s' benefits
veterinarian *[treats animals]
@veterinary
veto[5] ~es
vex[5] ~es ~ation ~atious
via *[through] vie *[compete]+
viable @viability
viaduct
Viagra™
vial *[glass] vile *[awful]
viol *[old instrument]
vibe
vibrant
vibrate[2] @vibration
@vibrator
vicar ~age
vicarious ~ly ~| liability

vice *[bad habit] ~| squad ~| versa
vise *[clamp]
Vice ~-Chancellor ~-President
viceral visceral+
vicinity[4]
vicious *[wicked] ~ly ~ness ~| circle
viscose *[fabric]
viscous *[sticky]+
vicissitude
vickchooals victuals
vicker vicar+
vicksen vixen
vickter victory[4]
victim
victimize[2] @victimization
victor ~ious ~iously
Victorian ~a
victory[4]
victuals
video ~| cassette recorder [VCR] ~disk ~| game ~phone ~tape ~text ~-conference[2] ~-conferencing

Unable to find your word under **video**? Take off **video** and look again

vidgel vigil+
vidgelante vigilant *[careful]+
vigilante *[civilian law enforcer]
vidio video+
vie *[compete] ~d ~s
@vying
via *[through]
vieble viable+
vieduct viaduct
viel veil[1] *[cloth]
vile *[awful]
veal *[meat]
vielence violence+
vielet violet
viemense vehemence
vien vain *[proud]+
vane *[weather]
vein *[blood]+

Key to Spelling Rules

Red words are wrong. **Black** words are correct.

~ Add the suffix or word directly to the main word, without a space or hyphen
e.g. ash ~en ~tray → ashen ashtray

~- Add a hyphen to the main word before adding the next word
e.g. blow ~-dry → blow-dry

~| Leave a space between the main word and the next word
e.g. decimal ~| place → decimal place

+ By finding this word in its correct alphabetical order, you can find related words
e.g. abowt about+ → about-face

* Draws attention to words that may be confused

™ Means the word is a trademark

@ Signifies the word is derived from the main word

vier	veer[1]
view[1] ~finder ~point	
vigger	vigor
vigil ~| light	
vigilant *[careful] ~ly	
	@vigilance
vigilante *[civilian law enforcer]	
vignette	
vigor	
vigorous ~ly	
vijil	vigil+
vijilantee	vigilante *[civilian law enforcer]
vikarious	vicarious+
Viking	
viksen	vixen
vikter	victory[4]
viktim	victim
viktimize	victimize[2+]
vila	villa
vilafy	vilify[4+]
vilage	village
vilas	villas *[houses]
	villus *[intestine]+
vile *[awful]	vial *[glass]
	viol *[old instrument]
vilen	villain+
	violin+
vilence	violence+
	violins
vilidge	village
vilify[4]	@vilification
vilis	villus *[intestine]+
	villas *[houses]
villa	
villas *[houses]	villus *[intestine]+
village	
villain ~ous ~y	
villus *[intestine]	@villi
	villas *[houses]
vim ~| and vigor	
vinacava	vena cava
vinager	vinegar+
vinaigrette	

vinal	vinyl *[plastic]
	venal *[corrupt]
	venial *[less grave]+
vindicate[2]	@vindication
vindictive ~ly ~ness	
vine ~yard	
vinegar ~y	
vinegrette	vinaigrette
vinil	vinyl *[plastic]
	venal *[corrupt]
	venial *[less grave]+
vintage	
vinyerd	vineyard
vinyet	vignette
vinyl *[plastic]	venal *[corrupt]
	venial *[less grave]+
viol *[old instrument]	
	vial *[glass]
	vile *[awful]
viola *[instrument]	
	voilà *[here is]
violate[2]	@violation
violence *[destruction]	
	@violent
	@violently
	violins *[music]
violet	
violin ~ist	
violins *[music]	violence *[destruction]
VIP [very important person] ~| lounge	
viper	
viralense	virulence+
virb	verb
virchoo	virtue+
virchuus	virtuous *[morals]+
vires	virus[5]
virgin ~al ~ity	
Virgo	
virile	@virility
viris	virus[5]
virjin	virgin+
virnackular	vernacular
virology	@virologist
virse	verse+
virtual *[not quite real] ~ly ~| reality	

Key to Suffixes and Compounds

These rules are explained on pages vii to ix.

1 Keep the word the same before adding **ed, er, est, ing**
e.g. cool[1] → cooled, cooler, coolest, cooling

2 Take off final **e** before adding **ed, er, est, ing**
e.g. fine[2] → fined, finer, finest, fining

3 Double final consonant before adding **ed, er, est, ing**
e.g. thin[3] → thinned, thinner, thinnest, thinning

4 Change final **y** to **i** before adding **ed, er, es, est, ly, ness**
e.g. tidy[4] → tidied, tidier, tidies, tidiest, tidily, tidiness
Keep final **y** before adding **ing** e.g. tidying

5 Add **es** instead of **s** to the end of the word
e.g. bunch[5] → bunches

6 Change final **f** to **ve** before adding **s**
e.g. calf[6] → calves

Word	Correct / related
virtue	
virtuoso *[art]	@virtuosity
virtuous *[morals]	~ly ~ness
virulence	@virulent
virus^{5}	
virve	verve

> Unable to find your word under **vir**?
> Look under **ver**

Word	Correct / related
visa *[permit]	vise *[clamp]
	vice *[bad habit]$^{+}$
visage	
visaje	visage
vis-à-vis	
visceral	@viscera
viscose *[fabric]	
viscous *[sticky]	@viscosity
	vicious *[wicked]$^{+}$
vise *[clamp]	visa *[permit]
	vice *[bad habit]$^{+}$
viseral	visceral^{+}
vishous	vicious *[wicked]$^{+}$
	viscose *[fabric]
	viscous *[sticky]$^{+}$
visible ~| means of support ~| trade	
	@visibility
	@visibly
visidge	visage
visinity	vicinity^{4}
vision ~ary	
visissitude	vicissitude
visit^{1} ~ation	
visitor	
viskose	viscose *[fabric]
viskus	viscous *[sticky]$^{+}$
viss	vice *[bad habit]$^{+}$
	vise *[clamp]
visseral	visceral^{+}
vista	
visual ~ly ~| aid	
visualize^{2}	@visualization
vital ~ity ~ly ~| statistics	
vitamin	
vitle	vital^{+}

Word	Correct / related
vito	veto^{5+}
vitreous ~| humor	
vitriol ~ic	
vittles [also spelled victuals]	
viue	view^{1+}
viva	
vivacious	@vivacity
vivarium	
vivasect	vivisect^{1+}
vivasious	vivacious^{+}
vivid ~ly ~ness	
vivisect^{1}	@vivisection
vixen	
viyul	vial *[glass]
	vile *[awful]
	viol *[old instrument]
vizable	visible^{+}
vizavee	vis-à-vis
vizhen	vision^{+}
vizidge	visage
vizit	visit^{1+}
vizual	visual^{+}
vizualize	visualize^{2+}
voag	vogue
	voyage^{2}
voat	vote^{2+}
vocabulary^{4}	
vocal ~ist ~ly	
vocalize^{2}	@vocalization
vocation *[occupation]	
	vacation *[holiday]$^{+}$
vocational ~| guidance ~| rehabilitiation	
vociferous ~ly ~ness	
vodka	
voel	vole
	vowel
vogue	
voiage	voyage^{2}
voice^{2} ~-activated ~mail ~-over	
void^{1} ~able	
voier	voyeur
voilà *[here is]	viola *[instrument]
voise	voice^{2+}
vokabulary	vocabulary^{4}
vokal	vocal^{+}

Key to Spelling Rules

Red words are wrong. **Black** words are correct.

~ Add the suffix or word directly to the main word, without a space or hyphen
e.g. ash ~en ~tray → ashen ashtray

~- Add a hyphen to the main word before adding the next word
e.g. blow ~-dry → blow-dry

~| Leave a space between the main word and the next word
e.g. decimal ~| place → decimal place

\+ By finding this word in its correct alphabetical order, you can find related words
e.g. abowt about^{+} → about-face

★ Draws attention to words that may be confused

TM Means the word is a trademark

@ Signifies the word is derived from the main word

vokation	vocation *[occupation]
volatile	@volatility
volcanic ~| ash	
volcano[5]	@volcanic
vole	
volenteer	volunteer[1]
volentery	voluntary⁺
voletile	volatile⁺
voley	volley[1] *[projectiles]⁺
volition	
volkanic	volcanic⁺
volley[1] *[projectiles] ~ball	
	valley *[lowland]
vollume	volume⁺
volt *[electric] ~age ~meter	
	vault[1] *[jump, safe place]
voluble *[talkative]	
	@volubility
	@volubly
	valuable *[worth money]⁺
volume ~| discount	
	@voluminous
voluntary ~| accumulation ~| bankruptcy ~| conveyance ~| lien ~| liquidation ~| redundancy[4]	
	@voluntarily

> Unable to find your word under **voluntary**? Take off **voluntary** and look again

volunteer[1]	
voluptuous	
volyuble	voluble *[talkative]⁺
	valuable *[worth money]⁺
volyum	volume⁺
vomit[1]	
vont	vaunt[1]
voodoo ~ism	
voracious ~ly ~ness	
voracity *[greed]	veracity *[truth]
vorasious	voracious⁺
vorasity	veracity *[truth]
	voracity *[greed]
vorlt	vault[1] *[jump, place]
vornt	vaunt[1]
vortex	@vortices
vosiferous	vociferous⁺
vote[2] ~| of thanks	
voting ~| right ~| stock	
votive ~| candle	
vouch[5] ~| for	
voucher	
voul	vowel
vow[1]	
vowch	vouch[5]⁺
vowel	
voyage[2]	
voyce	voice[2]⁺
voyd	void[1]⁺
voyeur	
voys	voice[2]⁺
vudu	voodoo⁺
vue	view[1]⁺
vulcher	vulture
vulgar ~ity	
vulgarize[2]	@vulgarization
vulnerability[4] *[weakness]	
	venerability *[wisdom]
vulnerable *[weak]	
	venerable *[wise]
vulture	
vulva	
vunrabel	vulnerable *[weak]
vurb	verb
vurge	verge[2]
vurse	verse⁺

> Unable to find your word under **vur**? Look under **ver**

vurtue	virtue⁺
vwalla	voilà *[here is]
vya	via *[through]
	vie *[compete]⁺
vyagra	Viagra™
vybe	vibe
vydeo	video⁺
vye	vie *[compete]⁺
	via *[through]
vykarious	vicarious⁺

Key to Suffixes and Compounds

These rules are explained on pages vii to ix.

1 Keep the word the same before adding **ed, er, est, ing**
e.g. cool[1] → cooled, cooler, coolest, cooling
2 Take off final **e** before adding **ed, er, est, ing**
e.g. fine[2] → fined, finer, finest, fining
3 Double final consonant before adding **ed, er, est, ing**
e.g. thin[3] → thinned, thinner, thinnest, thinning
4 Change final **y** to **i** before adding **ed, er, es, est, ly, ness**
e.g. tidy[4] → tidied, tidier, tidies, tidiest, tidily, tidiness
Keep final **y** before adding **ing** e.g. tidying
5 Add **es** instead of **s** to the end of the word
e.g. bunch[5] → bunches
6 Change final **f** to **ve** before adding **s**
e.g. calf[6] → calves

vylalin violin+
villain+
vyle vile *[awful]
vial *[glass]
viol *[old instrument]
vylense violence+
violins
vynil vinyl *[plastic]
venal *[corrupt]
venial *[less grave]+

vyola viola *[instrument]
voilà *[here is]
vyolate violate[2+]
vyshus vicious *[wicked]+
viscose *[fabric]
viscous *[sticky]+

Unable to find your word under **vy**? Look under **vi**

wacen waken[1+]
wack whack[1]
wacko
wacks whacks *[hits]
wax[5] *[candle]+
wacky[4]
wad[3] *[tight lump] ~ding
wade[2] *[water]+
waddle[2]
wade[2] *[water] ~| in ~| through
weighed *[how heavy]
wad[3] *[tight lump]+
wader *[one who wades]
waiter *[meal server]+
water[1+]
wading ~| pool
wafe waif+
wafer ~-thin
waffle[2] ~| iron
waft[1]
wafull waffle[2+]
wag[3] *[tail]
wage[2] *[earned money] ~| bracket ~| ceiling ~| claim ~| control ~| earner ~| freeze ~| level ~| incentive ~| negotiations ~| rate ~| scale

Unable to find your word under **wage**? Take off **wage** and look again

wager[1]
waggen wagon+
waggle[2]
wagon ~| train
waid wade *[water]
weighed *[how heavy]
waie way *[direction]+
weigh[1] *[how heavy]+
waif ~| and stray
waifer wafer+
waik wake+
waiken waken[1+]
wail[1] *[cry] whale *[mammal]+
wair ware *[product]
wear *[clothes]+
where *[in what place]+
weir *[dam]
wairhouse warehouse+
wairily warily
wairs wares *[goods]
wears *[clothes]
waist *[body] ~band ~coat ~line
waste[2] *[garbage, not use well]+
wait[1] *[delay] weight *[heaviness]+

Key to Spelling Rules

Red words are wrong. **Black** words are correct.

~ Add the suffix or word directly to the main word, without a space or hyphen
e.g. ash ~en ~tray → ashen ashtray

~- Add a hyphen to the main word before adding the next word
e.g. blow ~-dry → blow-dry

~| Leave a space between the main word and the next word
e.g. decimal ~| place → decimal place

+ By finding this word in its correct alphabetical order, you can find related words
e.g. abowt about+ → about-face

* Draws attention to words that may be confused

TM Means the word is a trademark

@ Signifies the word is derived from the main word

waiter *[meal server]
@waitress
wader *[one who wades]
waiting ~| game ~| list ~| room
waive[2] *[give up] wave[2] *[sea, hand]+
waiver *[permit] waver[1] *[unsteady]
waj wage[2] *[earned money]+
wajer wager[1]
wake *[not asleep, funeral] ~-up ~ful ~fullness
walk[1] *[move forward]+
waken[1] @waking
waks walks *[moves forward]
wax[5] *[candle]+
wale wail[1] *[cry]
whale *[mammal]+
walk[1] *[move forward] ~| away ~about ~-in ~| off ~out *[strike] ~| out *[leave] ~over ~| up *[approach] ~-up *[building with no elevator]
wake *[not asleep, funeral]+
wok *[frying bowl]

Unable to find your word under **walk**? Take off **walk** and look again

walkie-talkie
walking ~| frame ~| papers ~| stick
Walkman™
wall[1] *[barrier] ~board ~flower ~paper ~-to-wall
wail[1] *[cry]+
whale *[mammal]+
Wall Street [place]
wallaby[4]
wallet
wallop[1]
walnut
walrus[5]
waltz[5]
wan *[pale] ~ly
wane[2] *[decrease]
won *[victory]
one *[single]

wand
wander[1] *[roam] ~lust
wonder[1] *[think, marvel]+
wane[2] *[decrease]
wan *[pale]+
won *[victory]
wangle[2] *[get through trickery]
wrangle[2] *[quarrel bitterly]
wannabe
want[1] *[desire] ~| ad
wont *[habit]
won't *[will not]
wanting *[lacking, desiring]
wanton *[thoughtless] ~ly ~ness
wonton *[food]+
wants *[needs, desires]
once *[one time]+
WAP [Wireless Application Protocol] ~| phone
war[3] *[battle] ~| chest ~| crime ~| cry ~fare ~| games ~head ~horse ~like ~lord ~| paint ~path ~plane ~ship ~time ~-torn ~| zone
wear *[clothes]+
were *[past of be]
where *[in what place]+
wore *[clothes]

Unable to find your word under **war**? Take off **war** and look again

warble[2]
ward[1] ~en ~| off
wardrobe
ware *[product] wear *[clothes]+
where *[in what place]+
weir *[dam]
warehouse ~| club
@warehousing
wares *[goods] wears *[clothes]
warily
warm[1] ~ly ~th ~-blooded ~-hearted ~-up *[exercise] ~| up *[heat]
warmonger[1]

Key to Suffixes and Compounds

These rules are explained on pages vii to ix.

1 Keep the word the same before adding **ed, er, est, ing**
e.g. cool[1] → cooled, cooler, coolest, cooling
2 Take off final **e** before adding **ed, er, est, ing**
e.g. fine[2] → fined, finer, finest, fining
3 Double final consonant before adding **ed, er, est, ing**
e.g. thin[3] → thinned, thinner, thinnest, thinning
4 Change final **y** to **i** before adding **ed, er, es, est, ly, ness**
e.g. tidy[4] → tidied, tidier, tidies, tidiest, tidily, tidiness
Keep final **y** before adding **ing** e.g. tidying
5 Add **es** instead of **s** to the end of the word
e.g. bunch[5] → bunches
6 Change final **f** to **ve** before adding **s**
e.g. calf[6] → calves

warn[1] *[alert] worn *[used]+
warning ~| sign
warp[1] ~| speed
warrant[1]
warranty ~| deed
warren
warrior *[one who fights]
worrier *[one who worries]
wart *[on skin] ~hog
wort *[in brewing]
wary[4] *[cautious] weary[4] *[tired]+
was ~n't [was not]
wash[5] ~able ~basin ~board ~| down ~| off ~room ~stand ~| up ~| out *[cause failure] ~out *[failure]

> Unable to find your word under **wash**?
> Take off **wash** and look again

washed ~-out ~-up
wasn't *[was not]
wasp ~ish ~like
wastage
waste[2] *[garbage, not use well] ~| away ~basket ~| disposal ~land ~| paper
@wastage
waist *[body]+

> Unable to find your word under **waste**?
> Take off **waste** and look again

watch[5] ~es ~ful ~dog ~man ~word
wate wait[1] *[delay]
what *[question]+
weight *[heaviness]+
water[1] ~y ~bed ~-borne ~color ~cress ~| cycle ~fall ~fowl ~front[1] ~logged ~main ~mark[1] ~-repellent ~shed ~side ~melon ~| polo ~-ski[1] ~tight ~way ~works
wader *[one who wades]
waiter *[meal server]+

> Unable to find your word under **water**?
> Take off **water** and look again

waterproof[1]
watt *[power] ~age
what *[question]+
wait[1] *[delay]
wave[2] *[sea, hand] ~length
waive[2] *[give up]
waver[1] *[unsteady]
waiver *[permit]
wavy
wax[5] *[candle] ~en ~y ~| paper ~work
whacks *[hits]
way *[direction] ~bill ~side ~ward
weigh[1] *[how heavy]+
wayder wader *[one who wades]
waiter *[meal server]+
waylay ~ing @waylaid
wayst waist *[body]+
waste[2] *[garbage, not use well]+
wayt wait[1] *[delay]
weight *[heaviness]+
wayting waiting+
wayv wave[2] *[sea, hand]+
waive[2] *[give up]

> Unable to find your word under **way**?
> Look under **wa** or **wai**

we *[us] wee *[very small]+
whee *[happy sound]
weak *[feeble] ~ly *[feebly] ~-kneed ~ling ~ness ~| link
week *[seven days]+
weaken[1]
weakly *[feebly] weekly *[every week]
weal *[mark] we'll *[we will]
wheel[1] *[tire]+
wealth @wealthy[4]
wean[1] *[off milk, stop]
when *[at what time]+
wen *[growth on skin]
weapon ~ry
wear *[clothes] ~| and tear
war[3] *[battle]+
ware *[product]

KEY TO SPELLING RULES

Red words are wrong. **Black** words are correct.

~ Add the suffix or word directly to the main word, without a space or hyphen
e.g. ash ~en ~tray → ashen ashtray

~- Add a hyphen to the main word before adding the next word
e.g. blow ~-dry → blow-dry

~| Leave a space between the main word and the next word
e.g. decimal ~| place → decimal place

+ By finding this word in its correct alphabetical order, you can find related words
e.g. abowt about+ → about-face

* Draws attention to words that may be confused

TM Means the word is a trademark

@ Signifies the word is derived from the main word

wear *[clothes] were *[past of be]
where *[in what place]+
weir *[dam]
wearhouse warehouse+
wears *[clothes] wares *[goods]
weary[4] *[tired] @wearisome
wiry[4] *[body type]
wary[4] *[cautious]
weasel[3]
weather[1] *[sun, rain] ~-beaten ~| forecast ~| vane
whether *[if]
wether *[castrated sheep]
weave[2] *[fabric] we've *[we have]
web[3] ~| address ~| browser ~cam ~cast ~-footed ~log ~master ~| page ~| server ~site ~-toed

Unable to find your word under **web**? Take off **web** and look again

wed[3] *[marriage] ~lock
we'd *[we had, we would]
we'd *[we had, we would]
weed[1] *[plant]+
wedding ~| party
Wedensday Wednesday
wedge[2]
Wednesday
wee *[very small] we *[us]
whee *[happy sound]
weed[1] *[plant] ~killer ~| out
we'd *[we had, we would]
weedle wheedle[2]
weedy[4]
week *[seven days] ~end
weak *[feeble]+
weeken weaken[1]
weekly *[every week]
weakly *[feebly]
weel we'll *[we will]
weal *[mark]
wheel[1] *[tire]+
weeld wield[1] *[use weapon]
wheeled *[having wheels]
ween wean[1]
weep *[cry] ~ing ~y
wipe[2] *[clean]+
weer weir *[dam]
weerd weird+
weerwolf werewolf[6]
weery weary[4] *[tired]+
weet wheat+
weev weave[2] *[fabric]
weeze wheeze[2+]
weezle weasel[3]
weigh[1] *[how heavy] ~| in ~| on
way *[direction]+
weight *[heaviness] ~less ~lessness ~lifter ~lifting ~| training
wait[1] *[delay]
weighted *[weight-related] ~| average ~| index
waited *[delayed action]
weighty[4]
weild wield[1]
weir *[dam] wear *[clothes]+
where *[in what place]+
ware *[product]
weird *[strange] ~ly ~ness
wired *[tense, set up with wire]
wej wedge[2]
we'll *[we will] well *[health, water]
weal *[mark]
wheel[1] *[tire]+
welch welsh[5] *[cheat]
Welsh *[from Wales]
welcome[2]
weld[1]
welfare ~| state
welk whelk
welkum welcome[2]
well[1] *[health, water] ~-advised ~-balanced ~-behaved ~being ~-bred ~-built ~-done ~-founded ~-groomed ~-heeled ~-informed

Key to Suffixes and Compounds

These rules are explained on pages vii to ix.

1 Keep the word the same before adding **ed, er, est, ing**
e.g. cool[1] → cooled, cooler, coolest, cooling
2 Take off final **e** before adding **ed, er, est, ing**
e.g. fine[2] → fined, finer, finest, fining
3 Double final consonant before adding **ed, er, est, ing**
e.g. thin[3] → thinned, thinner, thinnest, thinning
4 Change final **y** to **i** before adding **ed, er, es, est, ly, ness**
e.g. tidy[4] → tidied, tidier, tidies, tidiest, tidily, tidiness
Keep final **y** before adding **ing** e.g. tidying
5 Add **es** instead of **s** to the end of the word
e.g. bunch[5] → bunches
6 Change final **f** to **ve** before adding **s**
e.g. calf[6] → calves

well[1] ~-kept ~-known ~-liked ~-mannered ~-meaning ~-meant ~-nigh ~-paid ~-off ~-read ~-rounded ~-spoken ~-thought-of ~-to-do ~-versed ~-wisher
weal *[mark]
we'll *[we will]
wheel[1] *[tire]+

Unable to find your word under **well**?
Take off **well** and look again

welp — whelp[1]
Welsh *[from Wales]
welsh[5] *[cheat]
welt ~er
welth — wealth+
wen *[growth on skin]
wean[1] *[off milk, stop]
when *[at what time]+
wench[5] *[girl] — wrench[5] *[force, tool]
winch[5] *[machine]
wensday — Wednesday
went
weppen — weapon+
wept
werd — weird+
word[1]+
were *[past of be]
whir[1] *[sound]
we're *[we are] — weir *[dam]
where *[in what place]+
weren't *[were not]
werewolf[6]
werk — work[1]+
werl — whirl[1] *[spin]+
whorl *[pattern]
werld — world+
whirled *[spun]+
werr — were *[past of be]
whir[1] *[sound]
wery — wary[4] *[cautious]
weary[4] *[tired]+
west ~| coast ~bound ~erly ~ern ~ward

westernize[2] — @westernization
wet[3] *[soak] ~land ~ness ~suit
wheat *[grain]
whet[3] *[sharpen]
wether *[castrated sheep]
weather[1] *[sun, rain]+
whether *[if]
we've *[we have] — weave[2] *[fabric]
whack[1]
whacks *[hits] — wax[5] *[candle]+
whacky — wacky[4]
whale *[mammal] — @whaling
wail[1] *[cry]
wharf[6]
what *[question] ~ever ~soever
watt *[power]+
wheat *[grain] ~| bread
wet[3] *[soak]+
whee *[happy sound]
we *[us]
wee *[very tiny]+
wheedle[2] — wheat *[grain]
wet[3] *[soak]+
wheel[1] *[tire] ~barrow ~chair ~wright
weal *[mark]
wheeled *[having wheels]
wield[1] *[use weapon]
wheeze[2] — @wheezy[4]
whelk
whelp[1] — wean
when *[at what time] ~ever ~soever
wean[1] *[off milk, stop]
wen *[growth on skin]
whence *[from what place]
where *[in what place] ~abouts ~as ~by ~upon ~withal ~ver
wear *[clothes]+
were *[past of be]
ware *[product]
weir *[dam]

Unable to find your word under **where**?
Take off **where** and look again

wherefore *[why]

Key to Spelling Rules

Red words are wrong. **Black** words are correct.

~ Add the suffix or word directly to the main word, without a space or hyphen
e.g. ash ~en ~tray → ashen ashtray

~- Add a hyphen to the main word before adding the next word
e.g. blow ~-dry → blow-dry

~| Leave a space between the main word and the next word
e.g. decimal ~| place → decimal place

+ By finding this word in its correct alphabetical order, you can find related words
e.g. abowt about+ → about-face

* Draws attention to words that may be confused

TM Means the word is a trademark

@ Signifies the word is derived from the main word

whet[3] *[sharpen] wheat *[grain]
wet[3] *[soak]+
whether *[if] weather[1] *[sun, rain]+
wether *[castrated sheep]
whew
whey *[milk] way *[direction]+
whi why *[question]
whee *[sound]
which *[which one] ~ever
witch[5] *[hag]+
whiff[1] *[smell] wife *[married woman]+
whicker *[horse sound]
wicker *[woven twigs]+
while *[when]
whilst *[meantime]
whim ~sical @whimsy[4]
whimper[1]
whine[2] *[complain]
wine *[drink]+
whined *[complained]
wind[1] *[turn, air]+
whinge[2] *[complain] ~r
whinny[4] *[horse sound]
whiny *[moaning] winey *[like wine]
whip[3] *[beat] ~cord ~lash
wipe[2] *[clean]+
whippersnapper
whippet
whip-poor-will *[bird]
whir[1] *[sound] were *[past of be]
we're *[we are]
where *[in what place]+
whirl[1] *[spin] ~pool ~wind
whorl *[pattern]
whirled *[spun] world+
whisk[1]
whisker ~y
whiskey *[Irish, bourbon]
whisky[4] *[Scotch]
whisper[1]
whist ~| drive
whistful wistful+
whistle[2] ~blower

whit *[least bit] wit *[flair, humor]
wheat *[grain]
white[2] *[color] ~caps ~-collar ~| dwarf ~| elephant ~| goods ~-out ~| knight ~| lie ~| paper ~water
wit *[flair, humor]
wheat *[grain]
White ~| House ~| Pages

Unable to find your word under **white**?
Take off **white** and look again

whiten[1]
whitewash[5]
whither *[toward what place]
wither[1] *[dry up]
whittle[2]
whiz[3] *[move fast, brilliant] ~| kid
wise[2] *[knowledgeable]+
who *[question] ~'d [who would] ~ever
hew[1] *[cut]+
whoa *[stop] woe *[misery]+
wow *[exclamation]
whole *[full] ~hearted ~heartedly ~some ~someness
hole[2] *[cavity]+
wholesale ~r ~| price index ~| discount
wholistic holistic
wholly *[fully] holy[4] *[sacred]+
holly *[shrub]
woolly *[not clear, wool texture]+
wholocost holocaust *[blood sacrifice]
whom ~ever
whoop[1] *[shout] ~ing cough
hoop[1] *[circle]
whopper @whopping
whore[2] *[prostitute] ~house
hoar *[frost]
who're *[who are]
whorer horror+
whorl *[pattern] whirl[1] *[spin]+
whorse hoarse *[voice]+
horse *[animal]+
who's *[who is, who has]

Key to Suffixes and Compounds

These rules are explained on pages vii to ix.

1 Keep the word the same before adding **ed, er, est, ing**
e.g. cool[1] → cooled, cooler, coolest, cooling
2 Take off final **e** before adding **ed, er, est, ing**
e.g. fine[2] → fined, finer, finest, fining
3 Double final consonant before adding **ed, er, est, ing**
e.g. thin[3] → thinned, thinner, thinnest, thinning
4 Change final **y** to **i** before adding **ed, er, es, est, ly, ness**
e.g. tidy[4] → tidied, tidier, tidies, tidiest, tidily, tidiness
Keep final **y** before adding **ing** e.g. tidying
5 Add **es** instead of **s** to the end of the word
e.g. bunch[5] → bunches
6 Change final **f** to **ve** before adding **s**
e.g. calf[6] → calves

whose *[possessive]
who've *[who have]
why *[question] we *[us]
whee *[sound]
wye *[Y-shaped pipe fitting]
Y *[letter]
whydah *[bird] widow *[husband dead]+
wi we *[us]
wee *[very small]
whee *[sound]
wye *[Y-shaped pipe fitting]
Y *[letter]
Wiccipedia Wikipedia
wich witch[5] *[hag]+
which *[which one]+
wick *[on candle]
wicked[1] ~ly ~ness
wicker *[woven twigs] ~work
whicker *[horse sound]
wide[2] ~ly ~-angle ~-area network ~-eyed ~| open ~spread
widen[1]
widget
widow *[husband dead] ~ed ~er *[wife dead]
whydah *[bird]
width *[distance across]
with *[in the company of]+
wied weed[1] *[plant]+
wide[2]+
wiegh weigh[1] *[how heavy]+
wiek weak *[feeble]+
week *[seven days]+
wiekly weakly *[feebly]
weekly *[every week]
wield[1] *[use weapon]
wheeled *[having wheels]
wiell we'll *[we shall, we will]
wheel[1] *[tire]+
wiep weep+

wier weir *[dam]
we're *[we are]
wier[2] *[metal thread]
wierd weird *[strange]+
wired *[tense, set up with wire]
wiery weary[4] *[tired]+
wiry[4] *[body type]
wiesal weasel[3]
wieve weave[2] *[fabric]
we've *[we have]
wife *[married woman]
@wives
whiff[1] *[smell]
wig
wiget widget
wiggle[2] @wiggly
wigwam
wijit widget
wik wick *[on candle]
week *[feeble]+
week *[seven days]+
Wikipedia
wikker wicker *[woven twigs]+
whicker *[horse sound]
wikkid wicked[1]+
wild ~ly ~ness ~cat ~fire ~flower ~life
wilderness
wiles *[tricks] @wily[4]
while *[when]
will[1] *[do, power] ~-o'-the-wisp ~| power
while *[when]
willful ~ly ~ness
willing ~ly ~ness
willow ~y ~| tree
wilt[1]
wim whim+
wimen women *[more than one woman]+
wimper whimper[1]
wimsy whimsy[4]
win *[be first] ~ner ~ning ~some ~-win
wine *[drink]+
wince[2]

KEY TO SPELLING RULES

Red words are wrong. **Black** words are correct.

~ Add the suffix or word directly to the main word, without a space or hyphen
e.g. ash ~en ~tray → ashen ashtray

~- Add a hyphen to the main word before adding the next word
e.g. blow ~-dry → blow-dry

~| Leave a space between the main word and the next word
e.g. decimal ~| place → decimal place

\+ By finding this word in its correct alphabetical order, you can find related words
e.g. abowt about+ → about-face

* Draws attention to words that may be confused

™ Means the word is a trademark

@ Signifies the word is derived from the main word

winch^{5} *[machine]	
	wench^{5} *[girl]
winck	wink^{1}
wind^{1} *[turn, air] ~bag ~| chill ~| fall ~mill ~shield ~surfing ~swept ~| turbine ~| up ~ward	
	whined *[complained]

> Unable to find your word under **wind**?
> Take off **wind** and look again

window ~| display ~| dressing ~pane ~| shade ~| shop ~| shopping	
windy^{4}	
wine *[drink] ~| cellar ~| cooler ~| glass	
	whine^{2} *[complain]
winey *[like wine]	whiny *[moaning]
wing^{1} *[of a bird] ~span	
winge	whinge^{2} *[complain]$^{+}$
wink^{1}	
winnow^{1}	
winny	whinny^{4} *[horse sound]
winse	wince^{2}
winsome	
wintch	winch^{5} *[machine]
winter^{1} ~time	
wintry	
wip	weep *[cry]$^{+}$
	whip^{3} *[beat]$^{+}$
wipe^{2} *[clean] ~| out *[obliterate]	
wipeout *[disaster]	
wipper-snapper	whippersnapper
wipperwill	whip-poor-will *[bird]
wippet	whippet
wire^{2} *[metal thread] ~less ~tap	
	weir *[dam]
	we're *[we are]
wired	weird *[strange]$^{+}$
wiry^{4} *[body type]	weary^{4} *[tired]$^{+}$
wisdom ~| teeth ~| tooth	
wise^{2} *[knowledgeable] ~acre ~crack^{1} ~| guy	
	whiz^{3} *[move fast, brilliant]$^{+}$
wish^{5} ~bone ~ful ~fully	
wishy-washy	
wisk	whisk^{1}
wisker	whisker^{+}
wiskey	whiskey *[Irish, bourbon]
	whisky^{4} *[Scotch]
wisp ~y	
wisper	whisper^{1}
wissel	whistle^{2+}
wist	whist^{+}
wisteria *[vine]	listeria *[germ]
wistful ~ly ~ness	
wit *[flair, humor]	whit *[least bit]
	white^{2} *[color]$^{+}$
witasizm	witticism
witch^{5} *[hag] ~craft ~| doctor ~| hunt	
	which *[which one]$^{+}$
wite	white^{2} *[color]$^{+}$
	whit *[least bit]
	wheat *[grain]
with *[in the company of] ~in ~out	
	width *[distance across]
withdraw ~al ~ing ~n	
	@withdrew
wither^{1} *[dry up]	whither *[toward what place]
withers *[of a horse]	
withhold ~ing	@withheld
withstand	@withstood
witness^{5} ~es ~| stand	
witticism	
wittle	whittle^{2}
witty^{4}	
wiz	wise *[knowledgeable]
	whiz^{3} *[move fast, brilliant]$^{+}$

> Unable to find your word under **wi**?
> Look under **whi**

wizard	
wize	wise^{2+}
wizened *[old]	
wizzywig	WYSIWYG
wobble^{2}	@wobbly^{4}

KEY TO SUFFIXES AND COMPOUNDS

These rules are explained on pages vii to ix.

1 Keep the word the same before adding **ed, er, est, ing** e.g. cool^{1} → cooled, cooler, coolest, cooling
2 Take off final **e** before adding **ed, er, est, ing** e.g. fine^{2} → fined, finer, finest, fining
3 Double final consonant before adding **ed, er, est, ing** e.g. thin^{3} → thinned, thinner, thinnest, thinning
4 Change final **y** to **i** before adding **ed, er, es, est, ly, ness** e.g. tidy^{4} → tidied, tidier, tidies, tidiest, tidily, tidiness
Keep final **y** before adding **ing** e.g. tidying
5 Add **es** instead of **s** to the end of the word e.g. bunch^{5} → bunches
6 Change final **f** to **ve** before adding **s** e.g. calf^{6} → calves

wod wad[3] *[tight lump]+
word[1]+
would *[past of will]
wood *[trees]+
woddle waddle[2]
woe *[misery] ~ful ~fully
whoa *[stop]
wow *[exclamation]
woffel waffle[2]+
woft waft[1]
wok *[frying bowl] walk[1] *[move forward]+
woke *[awakened] ~n
wokky-tokky walkie-talkie
wokman Walkman™
wolf[6] ~ish ~ishly
woll wall[1]+
wool *[sheep hair]
wollet wallet
wolnut walnut

Unable to find your word under **wol**?
Look under **wal**

woman ~ly ~ize[2] ~kind
womb
women *[more than one woman] ~folk
won *[victory] one *[number]+
wan *[pale]
wond wand
wonder[1] *[think, marvel] ~ful ~fully
wander[1] *[roam]+
wondrous ~ly
wonk
wonnabe wannabe
wons once
wont *[habit] want[1] *[desire]+
won't *[will not]
wonton *[food] ~| soup
wanton *[thoughtless]+
wanting *[lacking, desiring]
woo[1]
wood *[trees] ~chuck ~cut ~land ~pecker ~shed ~| stove ~wind ~work
wood *[trees] would *[past of will]
wooed *[did woo]

Unable to find your word under **wood**?
Take off **wood** and look again

wooden ~ly ~ness
wooed *[did woo] wood *[trees]+
would *[past of will]
woof
wool *[sheep hair] ~len ~ly
woolly *[not clear, wool texture] ~| mammoth
wholly *[fully]
woom womb
woop whoop[1] *[shout]+
woozy
wopper whopper+
wor war[3] *[battle]+
wore *[clothes]
worantee warrantee *[person]
woranty warranty+
word[1] ~y
word-process[5] ~or
wore *[clothes] war[3] *[battle]+
whore[2] *[prostitute]+
worenty warranty+
worf wharf[6]
work[1] ~able ~aholic ~bench ~book ~day ~| ethic ~force ~horse ~| release ~| week ~| station ~| stoppage ~load ~| order ~-out ~| permit

Unable to find your word under **work**?
Take off **work** and look again

worker's ~| compensation ~| rights
working ~| capital ~| class ~| day ~| papers
workman ~like ~ship
world *[planet] ~-class ~wide
whirled *[spun]
World ~| Series ~| War I ~| War II ~| Wide Web @worldly[4]
worm
wormunger warmonger[1]

Key to Spelling Rules

Red words are wrong. **Black** words are correct.

~ Add the suffix or word directly to the main word, without a space or hyphen
e.g. ash ~en ~tray → ashen ashtray

~- Add a hyphen to the main word before adding the next word
e.g. blow ~-dry → blow-dry

~| Leave a space between the main word and the next word
e.g. decimal ~| place → decimal place

\+ By finding this word in its correct alphabetical order, you can find related words
e.g. abowt about+ → about-face

★ Draws attention to words that may be confused

™ Means the word is a trademark

@ Signifies the word is derived from the main word

worn *[used] ~-out
warn[1] *[alert]
worning warning+
worrier *[one who worries]
warrior *[one who fights]
worry[4]
worse
worsen[1]
worship[3]
worst ~case
wort *[in brewing] wart *[on skin]+
worter water[1]+

> Unable to find your word under **wor**?
> Look under **war**

worth ~less ~while ~y[4]
wos was+
wot watt *[power]+
what *[question]+
would *[past of will]
wood *[trees]+
wound[1]
wove ~n
wow[1] *[exclamation]
whoa *[stop]
woe *[misery]+
wrangle[2] *[quarrel bitterly]
wangle[2] *[get through trickery]
wrap[3] *[pack] ~around ~| up
rap[3] *[music, knock]
wrapping ~| paper
wrath ~ful
wreak[1] *[inflict] ~| havoc ~| ruin
wreck[1] *[smash]+
reek[1] *[stink]
wreath[5]
wrech wretch+
wreck[1] *[smash] ~age
wreak[1] *[inflict]+
reek[1] *[stink]
wreckless reckless+
wreeth wreath[5]

wren
wrench[5] *[force, tool]
wench[5] *[girl]
wrest[1] *[pull away]
wrestle[2]
wretch *[miserable person] ~ed
retch[5] *[vomit]
wrinckle wrinkle[2+]
wring *[squeeze] ~ing
ring[1] *[circle, bell]+
wringer *[squeezer] ~| washer
ringer *[one who rings, substitute]
wrinkle[2] @wrinkly[4]
wrist ~watch
writ *[legal order] rite *[ceremony]
write *[with a pen] ~r ~-down ~-off ~-protect[1] ~-up
right *[correct]+
rite *[ceremony]
writing ~| out ~| paper ~| desk
written ~| down ~| off
wrong[1] *[not right] ~-footed ~doer ~doing ~headed
wrung *[squeezed]
rung *[ladder, bell]
wrongful ~ly ~| dismissal ~| termination
wrote *[past of write]
rote *[repetition]
wrought ~| iron
wrung *[squeezed]
wrong[1] *[not right]+
rung *[ladder, bell]
wry *[slightly amusing] ~ly
rye *[grain]+
wryte write *[with a pen]
right *[correct]+
wu woo[1]
wud wood *[trees]+
would *[past of will]
wooed *[did woo]
wulf wolf[6+]
wull wool *[sheep hair]+
wuman woman+
wume womb

Key to Suffixes and Compounds

These rules are explained on pages vii to ix.

1 Keep the word the same before adding **ed, er, est, ing**
e.g. cool[1] → cooled, cooler, coolest, cooling
2 Take off final **e** before adding **ed, er, est, ing**
e.g. fine[2] → fined, finer, finest, fining
3 Double final consonant before adding **ed, er, est, ing**
e.g. thin[3] → thinned, thinner, thinnest, thinning
4 Change final **y** to **i** before adding **ed, er, es, est, ly, ness**
e.g. tidy[4] → tidied, tidier, tidies, tidiest, tidily, tidiness
Keep final **y** before adding **ing** e.g. tidying
5 Add **es** instead of **s** to the end of the word
e.g. bunch[5] → bunches
6 Change final **f** to **ve** before adding **s**
e.g. calf[6] → calves

wunder wander[1] *[roam]+
wonder[1] *[think, marvel]+
wurd word[1+]
wuren't weren't *[were not]
wurk work[1+]
wurld world *[planet]+
whirled *[spun]
wurr were *[past of be]
where *[in what place]+
whir[1] *[quiet sound]
wuz was+
wyde wide[2+]
wydow widow[1] *[husband dead]+
whydah *[bird]
wydth width *[distance across]
with *[in the company of]+
wye *[Y-shaped pipe fitting]
why *[question]
wyfe wife *[married woman]+
whiff[1] *[smell]
wylderness wilderness
wyle while *[when]
wiles *[tricks]+
wylful willful+
WYSIWYG
wyth width *[distance across]
with *[in the company of]+
wyzard wizard

Unable to find your word your word under **wy**?
Look under **wi**

X

X *[letter] ~-rated ~-ray[1]
~| chromosome
xaggerate exaggerate[2+]
xenofobe xenophobe+
xenofobia xenophobia
xenophobe @xenophobic
xenophobia
Xerox™
Xmas
xylem
xylophone

Unable to find your word under **x**?
Look under **ex**

Key to Spelling Rules

Red words are wrong. **Black** words are correct.

~ Add the suffix or word directly to the main word, without a space or hyphen
e.g. ash ~en ~tray → ashen ashtray

~- Add a hyphen to the main word before adding the next word
e.g. blow ~-dry → blow-dry

~| Leave a space between the main word and the next word
e.g. decimal ~| place → decimal place

+ By finding this word in its correct alphabetical order, you can find related words
e.g. abowt about+ → about-face

★ Draws attention to words that may be confused

™ Means the word is a trademark

@ Signifies the word is derived from the main word

Y

Y *[letter] ~-axis ~| chromosome[2]
~-coordinate
why *[question]⁺
wye *[Y-shaped pipe fitting]
yaa — yeah *[yes, slang]⁺
yacht ~ing ~sman ~swoman
yack — yak
yahoo *[exclamation]
Yahoo™ *[search engine]
yaht — yacht⁺
yahu — yahoo *[exclamation]
yak
y'all *[you all] — yawl *[boat]
yam ~| yammer[1]
yamuka — yarmulke
yanck — yank[1]
yander — yonder
yang
yank[1]
Yankee
yap[3]
yard ~age ~| sale ~stick
yarmulke
yarn
yashmak
yat — yacht⁺
yaun — yawn[1]
yaw *[swerve]
yawl *[boat] — y'all *[you all]
yawn[1] *[open wide]
yon *[over there, poetic]
yaws *[disease]
yeah *[yes, slang] — yeh *[yes, slang]
yes *[agreed]

year *[365 days] ~ly ~book ~-end
~ling ~long ~-round
your *[belonging]
you're *[you are]
yearn[1] *[desire]
yeast ~y ~| extract
yeeld — yield[1+]
yeer — year *[365 days]⁺
yeest — yeast⁺
yeild — yield[1+]
yell[1]
yellow *[color] ~ish ~| fever ~| jacket
Yellow Pages™ *[book]
yelp[1]
yen *[wish, Japanese currency]
yer — year *[365 days]⁺
your *[belonging]
you're *[you are]
yern — yearn[1] *[desire]
urine *[waste]⁺
yers — yours⁺
yerself — yourself[6]
yert — yurt
yes *[agreed]
yeshiva
yest — yeast⁺
yesterday — @yesteryear
yet *[already]
yeti *[monster]
yew *[tree] — ewe *[sheep]
you *[person]
yews *[evergreen trees]
use[2] *[put into service]
us *[group of two or more]
ewes *[sheep]
Yiddish

Key to Suffixes and Compounds

These rules are explained on pages vii to ix.

1 Keep the word the same before adding **ed, er, est, ing**
e.g. cool[1] → cooled, cooler, coolest, cooling
2 Take off final **e** before adding **ed, er, est, ing**
e.g. fine[2] → fined, finer, finest, fining
3 Double final consonant before adding **ed, er, est, ing**
e.g. thin[3] → thinned, thinner, thinnest, thinning
4 Change final **y** to **i** before adding **ed, er, es, est, ly, ness**
e.g. tidy[4] → tidied, tidier, tidies, tidiest, tidily, tidiness
Keep final **y** before adding **ing** e.g. tidying
5 Add **es** instead of **s** to the end of the word
e.g. bunch[5] → bunches
6 Change final **f** to **ve** before adding **s**
e.g. calf[6] → calves

yield[1] ~| curve ~| equivalence ~| spread
yier — **year** *[365 days]+ **your** *[belonging] **you're** *[you are]
yiest — **yeast**+
yin ~| and yang
yip[3] *[make a cry]
yipe *[exclamation of pain]
yippee *[exclamation of delight]
yirn — **yearn**[1]
yirt — **yurt**
yo ~-yo
yoak — **yoke** *[on neck] **yolk** *[egg]
yodel[3]
yoega — **yoga**
yoegi — **yogi**
yoeman — **yeoman**+
yoer — **your** *[belonging] **you're** *[you are] **yore** *[years ago]
yoers — **yours**+
yoerself — **yourself**[6]
yoga
yogurt
yoke *[on neck] — **yolk** *[egg]
yokel
yolk *[egg] — **yoke** *[on neck]
Yom Kippur
yon *[over there, poetic] — **yawn**[1] *[open wide]
yonder
yoo — **yew** *[tree] **you** *[person]+
yood — **you'd** [you had]
yool — **you'll** *[you will] **Yule** *[Christmas]+
yooth — **youth**+
yoov — **you've** [you have]

> Unable to find your word under **yoo**? Look under **you**

yore *[years ago] — **your** *[belonging] **you're** *[you are]
yors — **yours**+
yorself — **yourself**[6]
yot — **yacht**+
you *[person] ~| all — **ewe** *[sheep] **yew** *[tree]
you'd [you had, you would]
you'll *[you will] — **Yule** *[Christmas]+
young ~| adult ~ish ~ster ~| gun
your *[belonging] — **yore** *[years ago] **you're** *[you are]
yours ~| sincerely ~| truly
yourself[6]
youth ~ful ~| hostel
you've [you have]
yo-yo
ytterbium *[element 70]
yttrium *[element 39]
yu — **yew** *[tree] **you** *[person]+
Yuan *[Chinese currency]
yucca ~| plant
yuck ~y
yud — **you'd** [you had, you would]
yue — **ewe** *[female sheep] **yew** *[tree] **you** *[person]
yuk — **yuck**+
yuka — **yucca**+
yul — **you'll** *[you will] **Yule** *[Christmas]+
Yule *[Christmas] ~| log ~tide — **you'll** *[you will]
yummy — @yum-yum
yung — **young**+
yup *[yes, slang] — **yes** *[agreed]
yuppie
yurn — **yearn**[1] **urine**+
yurt
yus — **yews** *[evergreen trees] **ewes** *[sheep]

Key to Spelling Rules

Red words are wrong. **Black** words are correct.

~ Add the suffix or word directly to the main word, without a space or hyphen
e.g. ash ~en ~tray → ashen ashtray

~- Add a hyphen to the main word before adding the next word
e.g. blow ~-dry → blow-dry

~| Leave a space between the main word and the next word
e.g. decimal ~| place → decimal place

+ By finding this word in its correct alphabetical order, you can find related words
e.g. abowt about+ → about-face

★ Draws attention to words that may be confused

TM Means the word is a trademark

@ Signifies the word is derived from the main word

yus	use[2] *[put into service]
	us *[group of two or more]
yushiva	yeshiva
yuterus	uterus
yuth	youth+
yuthanasia	euthanasia
yutility	utility4+
yutilize	utilize2+

Unable to find your word under **yu**?
Look under **u** or **eu**

yuv	you've *[you have]
yyn	yin+

Z

Z *[letter] ~| particle

Unable to find your word under **z**?
Look under **s** or **th**

zany[4]	
zap[3] ~py	
zapper	
zat	that
zeal ~ot	
zealous ~ously ~ousness	
zebra	
zeel	zeal+
zeen	zine *[small magazine]
zeenith	zenith
zeero	zero1+
zeerox	Xerox™1
zeffer	zephyr
zeitgeist	
zelis	zealous+
zel	zeal+
Zen *[philosophy] ~| Buddhism	
	zine *[small magazine]
zener ~| diode	
zenith	
zenofobe	xenophobe+
zepelin	zeppelin
zephyr	
zeplin	zeppelin
zeppelin	
zerkonium	zirconium *[metal]
zero[1] ~-base budgeting ~| in on ~| tolerance	
zerox	Xerox™1
zest ~ful ~y	
zewm	zoom1+
zibra	zebra
ziel	zeal+
ziero	zero1+
zigoat	zygote
zigzag[3]	
zilafone	xylophone
zilch	
zillion	
zilophone	xylophone
zinc	
zine *[small magazine]	
	Zen *[philosophy]+
zineth	zenith
zinfandel	
zing[1]	
zink	zinc
Zion ~ism ~ist	
zip[3] ~| up	
ZIP ~| code	
zircon *[zirconium silicate, natural]	
zirconia *[zirconium oxide, synthetic]	
zirconium *[metal]	
ziro	zero1+
zis	this+
zit	
zitegist	zeitgeist

KEY TO SUFFIXES AND COMPOUNDS

These rules are explained on pages vii to ix.

1 Keep the word the same before adding **ed, er, est, ing**
e.g. cool[1] → cooled, cooler, coolest, cooling
2 Take off final **e** before adding **ed, er, est, ing**
e.g. fine[2] → fined, finer, finest, fining
3 Double final consonant before adding **ed, er, est, ing**
e.g. thin[3] → thinned, thinner, thinnest, thinning
4 Change final **y** to **i** before adding **ed, er, es, est, ly, ness**
e.g. tidy[4] → tidied, tidier, tidies, tidiest, tidily, tidiness
Keep final **y** before adding **ing** e.g. tidying
5 Add **es** instead of **s** to the end of the word
e.g. bunch[5] → bunches
6 Change final **f** to **ve** before adding **s**
e.g. calf[6] → calves

zither	
ziyon	Zion+
ziytgiyst	zeitgeist
zoalogy	zoology+
zoan	zone2
zodiac	
zohn	zone2
zombie	
zone2	
zonked ~| out	
zoo ~-keeper ~logist	
zookini	zucchini
zoology	@zoological
Zoolu	Zulu+
zoom1 ~| in ~lens ~| out	
zoot ~| suit	
Zoroastrian ~ism	
zowdiac	zodiac
zoze	those
zu	zoo+
zucchini	
zukini	zucchini
Zulu ~| warrior	
zum	zoom1+
zurconium	zirconium *[metal]
zygospore	
zygote	
zygzag	zigzag3
zylafone	xylophone
zylch	zilch
zylem	xylem
zylofone	xylophone
zylum	xylem
zyne	zine *[small magazine]
zyng	zing1
zyp	zip3+
zyt	zit
zyther	zither

Unable to find your word under **zy**?
Look under **zi**

Key to Spelling Rules

Red words are wrong. **Black** words are correct.

- ~ Add the suffix or word directly to the main word, without a space or hyphen
  e.g. ash ~en ~tray → ashen ashtray
- ~- Add a hyphen to the main word before adding the next word
  e.g. blow ~-dry → blow-dry
- ~| Leave a space between the main word and the next word
  e.g. decimal ~| place → decimal place
- + By finding this word in its correct alphabetical order, you can find related words
  e.g. abowt about+ → about-face
- ★ Draws attention to words that may be confused
- TM Means the word is a trademark
- @ Signifies the word is derived from the main word

Commonly Misspelled Words

Words with a * and a descriptor are often confused with another word in this list.

absence
abundance
acceptable
accessible
accidentally
acclaim
accommodate
accomplish
accordion
accumulate
accuracy
achievement
acknowledgement
acquaint
acquaintance
acquire
acquitted
across
actually
adapt
addition *[add]
address
adequately
admission
adolescent
advertise
advertisement
advice
advise
affect *[influence]
afterwards
against
aggravate
all right
alleged
although
always
amateur
amendment
American
among
amount
analysis
analyze
annual
annually
answer
anticipated
apartment
apparatus
apparent
appearance
appropriate
arctic
argument
around
article
ascend
assassination
atheist
athletic
attacked
attendance
attendance
audience
author
auxiliary
awkward
balloon
barbecue
bargain
basically
battery
beautiful
beggar
beginning
belief
believe
beneficial
beneficiary
benefit
biscuit
bought
boundaries
breathe
brilliant
broadcast
bureaucracy
bureaucrat
business
calendar
camera
camouflage
candidate
capital *[asset, city]
capitol *[building]
career
carefully
Caribbean
catalog
category
caught
cemetery
certain
challenge
changeable
changing
character
characteristic
chief
choose
chose
cigarette
climbed
cloth
clothes
clothing
collectible
college
colonel
column
coming
commission
commitment
committed
committee
communication
comparative
compare
competent
competition
complement
completely
completely
compliment
concede
conceivable
conceive
condemn
condemned
condescend
conscience
conscientious
conscious
consistent
continuous
controlled
controversial
controversy
convenient
copyright
correlate
correspondence
couldn't
council *[assembly]
counsel *[advise]
counselor
country
courteous
courtesy
cried
criticism
criticize
criticized
curiosity
death
deceive
decide
defeat
defendant
deferred
definite
definitely
definition
dependent
descend
describe
description
desirable
despair
desperate
develop
diagnosis
diagonal
dictionary
difference
different
dilemma
dining
disappear
disappearance
disappoint
disapprove
disassociate
disastrous
discipline
discussion
disease
dispensable
dissatisfied
dividend
division
doesn't
dominant
don't
drunkenness
during
easily
ecstasy
edition
effect *[result]
efficiency
efficient
eighth
either
eligible

eliminate
embarrass
embarrassed
emit *[light]
emperor
encouragement
encouraging
enemy
entirely
envelope
environment
epitome
equipment
equipped
equivalent
escape
escape
especially
etc.
etcetera
exaggerate
exceed
excel
excellence
excellent
except
excite
exercise
exhaust
existence
existent
expense
experience
experiment
experiment
explanation
extremely
exuberance
facsimile
fallacious
fallacy
familiar
fascinate
fascinating
fascist
favorite
feasible
February
fictitious
fiery
fight
finally
financially
fluorescent
forcibly
foreign
foresee
forfeit
formerly
forty
fourth
fueling
fulfill
fundamentally
gauge
genealogy
generally
genius
government
governor
grammar
grateful
grievous
guarantee
guaranteed
guardian
guerilla
guidance
handkerchief
happened
happily
harass
height
heinous
hemorrhage
hero
heroes
hesitancy
hindrance
hoarse
hole *[cavity]
hoping
horizontal
humorous
hygiene
hypocrisy
hypocrite
ideally
idiosyncrasy
ignorance
illogical
imaginary
immediate
immediately
implement
incidentally
incredible
independence
independent
indict
indicted
indispensable
individual
inevitable
influence
influential
information
input
insurance
intelligence
intelligent
interest
interference
interrupt
interruption
introduce
invariable
irregardless
irrelevant
irresistible
irresistible
Islam
island
January
jealously
jewelry
judgment
judicial
know *[knowledge]
knowledge
knowledgeable
label
laboratory
laid
later *[afterwards]
latter *[last]
legitimate
leisure
length
liaison
library
license
lieutenant
lightning
likelihood
likely
literature
lonely
loose *[not tight]
lose *[not win]
losing
lovely
luxury
luxury
magazine
magnificent
maintain
maintenance
manageable
maneuver
manufacture
marriage
mathematics
meant
meat *[flesh]
medicine
meet *[encounter]
millennium
millionaire
miniature
minuscule
minutes
miscellaneous
mischievous
misspelled
missile
mortgage
mosquito
mosquitoes
mountain
murmur
muscle
Muslim
mysterious
mystery
narrative
naturally
necessary
necessity
negotiate
neighbor
neutron
nickel
ninety
ninth
notary public
noticeable
now *[this minute]
nuclear
nuisance
obedience
obstacle
occasion
occasionally
occur
occurrence
occurring
official
omission
omit *[leave out]
omitted
opinion
opponent
opportunity
oppressed
oppression
optimism
optimistic
orchestra
ordinarily
orientated
origin
outrageous
overrun
paid
pamphlets

parallel
parameter
paroled
particle
particular
particularly
pastime
pavilion
peace *[calm]
peculiar
penetrate
perceive
performance
performance
perimeter
permanent
permissible
permissible
permitted
perseverance
persistence
personal
personnel
perspiration
physical
physician
piece *[part]
pilgrimage
pitiful
planning
pleasant
poison
politician
pollute
portray
possess
possession
possessive
possibility
possible
potato
potatoes
practically
prairie
precede
precedence
precedent
preceding
preceding
preference
preferred
prejudice
preparation
prescription
prevalent
primitive
principal *[chief]
principle *[rule, idea]
privilege
probably
procedure
procedure
proceed
profession
professor
prominent
pronounce
pronunciation
propaganda
psychiatry
psychology
publicly
pursue
quantity
quarantine
questionnaire
quiet *[silent]
quite *[to some degree]
quizzes
realistically
realize
really
realtor
recede
receipt
receive
received
recognize
recommend
reference
referring
rehearsal
relevant
relieving
religious
remember
remembrance
reminiscence
repetition
representative
resemblance
reservoir
resistance
responsibility
responsible
restaurant
reversible
rheumatism
rhythm
rhythmical
ridiculous
right *[correct]
roommate
sacrifice
sacrilegious
safety
said
salary
sandwich
satellite
Saturday
sausage
scarcity
scary
scene *[theater]
scenery
schedule
sea *[waves]
secede
secretary
see *[eyes]
seen *[past of see]
seize
sense
sentence
separate
separation
September
sergeant
several
severely
sexual
shepherd
shining
siege
sight *[seeing]
signature
significance
significant
similar
simile
simply
simultaneous
sincerely
site *[place]
skiing
society
soluble
someone
sophomore
sound
souvenir
specifically
specimen
speech
sponsor
spontaneous
stationary *[not moving]
stationery *[paper]
statistics
stopped
straight
strategy
strength
strenuous
strictly
stubbornness
studied
studies
studying
subordinate
subtle
suburban
succeed
success
succession
sufficient
summarized
superintendent
supersede
supposedly
suppress
surprise
surround
susceptible
suspicious
swimming
syllable
symmetrical
synonymous
technical
technicality
technique
temperamental
temperature
tendency
tendency
tension
their *[possession]
themselves
theories
there *[place]
therefore
they're *[short for they are]
thorough *[complete]
though *[but]
thought *[thinking]
thousandth
threw *[ball]
through *[go through]
Thursday
together
tomorrow
too *[also, very]
tournament
towards
tragedy
transferred
transferring
traveled
tries
truly
Tuesday

twelfth
two *[number]
tyranny
unanimous
worthwhile
write *[text]
writing
written
undoubtedly
unforgettable
unfortunate
unique
unnecessary
until
usable
usage
used
useful
usually
utilization
vacuum
valuable
vengeance
vertical
vigilant
village
villain
violence
virtue
visibility
visible
vision
vitamin
volume
warrant
warrior
weather *[sun, rain]
Wednesday
weird
were *[past of are]
where *[place]
wherever
whether
which
whole *[complete]
wholly
withdrawal
woman *[singular]
women *[plural]
yacht
y'all
yield
young

Country, Capital, Citizen, and Language(s)

Country	Capital	Citizen	Language(s)
Afghanistan	Kabul	Afghan	Dari (Farsi), Pashto
Albania	Tirana	Albanian	Albanian, Greek
Algeria	Algiers	Algerian	Arabic, French, Amazigh
Angola	Luanda	Angolan	Portuguese
Antigua & Barbuda	St. John's City	Citizen of ...	English
Argentina	Buenos Aires	Argentine	Spanish
Armenia	Yerevan	Armenian	Armenian, Russian
Australia	Canberra	Australian	English
Austria	Vienna	Austrian	German
Azerbaijan	Baku	Azerbaijani	Azeri, Russian, Armenian
Bahamas	Nassau	Bahamian	English, Creole
Bahrain	Manama	Bahraini	Arabic, English
Bangladesh	Dhaka	Bangladeshi	Bengali (Bangla), English
Barbados	Bridgetown	Barbadian	English
Belarus	Minsk	Belarusian	Belarusian, Russian
Belgium	Brussels	Belgian	Flemish (Dutch), French, German
Belize	Belmopan	Citizen of ...	English, Spanish, Creole
Benin	Porto-Novo	Beninese	French, Fon, Yoruba
Bhutan	Thimphu	Bhutanese	Dzongkha, Tibetan
Bolivia	La Paz	Bolivian	Spanish, Quechua, Aymara
Bosnia & Herzegovina	Sarajevo	Citizen of ...	Bosnian, Croatian, Serbian
Botswana	Gaborone	Citizen of ...	English, Setswana
Brazil	Brasília	Brazilian	Portuguese
Brunei	Bandar Seri Begawan	Citizen of ...	Malay, English, Chinese
Bulgaria	Sofia	Bulgarian	Bulgarian
Burkina Faso	Ouagadougou	Burkinan	French, Sudanic African
Burma (Myanmar)	Rangoon	Burmese	Burmese
Burundi	Bujumbura	Citizen of ...	Kirundi, French, Swahili
Cambodia	Phnom Penh	Cambodian	Khmer/Cambodian
Cameroon	Yaounde	Cameroonian	French, English, Fulfulde, Ewondo
Canada	Ottawa	Canadian	English, French
Central African Republic	Bangui	Citizen of ...	French, Sangho
Chad	N'Djamena	Chadian	French, Arabic
Chile	Santiago de Chile	Chilean	Spanish, English, Mapuche, Aymara, Quecha
China	Beijing	Chinese	Mandarin (Putonghua),
Colombia	Bogotá	Colombian	Spanish
Comoros	Moroni	Comoran	French, Arabic, Comoran
Congo (Democratic Republic of)	Kinshasa	Citizen of ...	French, Lingala, Kingwana, Kikongo, Tshiluba
Congo (Republic of)	Brazzaville	Congolese	French, Lingala, Munukutuba, Kikongo

Country	Capital	Citizen	Language(s)
Costa Rica	San José	Costa Rican	Spanish
Croatia	Zagreb	Croat	Croatian, Serbian, Italian, Slovene, Slovac, German
Cuba	Havana	Cuban	Spanish
Cyprus	Nicosia	Cypriot	Greek, Turkish, English
Czech Republic	Prague	Czech	Czech
Denmark	Copenhagen	Dane	Danish, English, German
Djibouti	Djibouti	Djiboutian	French, Arabic, Somali, Afar
Dominican Republic	Santo Domingo	Citizen of ...	Spanish
East Timor	Dila	East Timorese	Tetum, Portugese
Ecuador	Quito	Ecuadorean	Spanish
Egypt	Cairo	Egyptian	Arabic, English, French
El Salvador	San Salvador	Salvadorean	Spanish
Equatorial Guinea	Malabo	Equatorian Guinean	Spanish, French, Fang, Bubi, Ibo
Eritrea	Asmara	Eritrean	Tigrinya, Tigre Arabic, English
Estonia	Tallinn	Estonian	Estonian, Russian
Ethiopia	Addis Ababa	Ethiopian	Amharic, Tigrinya, Oromigna, Somali, Arabic, English, Guaragigna
Fiji	Suva	Fijian	English, Fijian, Hindu
Finland	Helsinki	Finn	Finnish, Swedish, Lapp, Russian
France	Paris	Frenchman / woman	French
Gabon	Libreville	Gabonese	French, Fang, Myene, Bateke, Bapoumon
Gambia	Banjul	Gambian	English, Mandinka, Wolof, Fula
Georgia	Tbilisi	Georgian	Georgian, Russian, Armenian, Abkhaz, Azeri
Germany	Berlin	German	German
Ghana	Accra	Ghanaian	English, Akan, Moshi-Dagomba, Ewe, Ga
Greece	Athens	Greek	Greek
Grenada	St. George's	Grenadian	English
Guatemala	Guatemala City	Guatemalan	Spanish
Guinea	Conakry	Guinean	French
Guinea – Bissau	Bissau	Citizen of ...	Portuguese, Crioulo
Guyana	Georgetown	Guyanese	English, Ameridian Dialects, Creole, Hindi, Urdu
Haiti	Port au Prince	Haitian	French, Creole
Honduras	Tegucigalpa	Honduran	Spanish
Hungary	Budapest	Hungarian	Hungarian
Iceland	Reykjavik	Icelander	Icelandic, English, Danish
India	New Delhi	Indian	Hindi, English, Bengali, Kannada, Kashmiri, Marathi, Oriya, Punjabi, Sindhi, Sanskrit, Tamil, Telugu, Urdu & many others

Country	Capital	Citizen	Language(s)
Indonesia	Jakarta	Indonesian	Bahasa Indonesian, English & many others
Iran	Tehran	Iranian	Persian (Farsi), Azeri, Kurdish Arabic
Iraq	Baghdad	Iraqi	Arabic, Kurdish, Assyrian, Armenian, Turkoman
Ireland	Dublin	Irish Citizen	Irish, English
Israel	Tel Aviv	Israeli	Hebrew, Arabic, Yiddish
Italy	Rome	Italian	Italian
Ivory Coast	Yamoussoukro	Citizen of ...	French, Dioula
Jamaica	Kingston	Jamaican	Patois English
Japan	Tokyo	Japanese	Japanese
Jordan	Amman	Jordanian	Arabic, English
Kazakhstan	Astana	Kazakh	Kazakh, Russian
Kenya	Nairobi	Kenyan	English, Kiswahili
Korea, North	Pyongyang	Citizen of the DPRK	Korean
Korea, South	Seoul	South Korean	Korean
Kuwait	Kuwait	Kuwaiti	Arabic, English
Kyrgyzstan	Bishkek	Kyrgyz / Russian	Kyrgyz, Russian
Laos	Vientiane	Lao	Lao
Latvia	Riga	Latvian	Latvian, Russian
Lebanon	Beirut	Lebanese	Arabic, French, English, Armenian
Lesotho	Maseru	Citizen of ...	English, Sesotho
Liberia	Monrovia	Liberian	English
Libya	Tripoli	Libyan	Arabic, Italian, English
Liechtenstein	Vaduz	Citizen of ...	German
Lithuania	Vilnius	Lithuanian	Lithuanian
Luxembourg	Luxembourg	Luxembourger	Luxembourgish, German, French
Macedonia	Skopje	Macedonian	Macedonian, Albanian, Turkish, Serbian
Madagascar	Antananarivo	Citizen of ...	Malagasy, French
Malawi	Lilongwe	Malawian	English, Chichewa
Malaysia	Kuala Lumpur	Citizen of ...	Bahasa Malaysian, English, Chinese, Tamil
Maldives	Malé	Maldivian	Dhivehi, English
Mali	Bamako	Malian	French, Bambara
Malta	Valletta	Maltese	Maltese, English
Mauritania	Nouakchott	Mauritanian	Hassaniya Arabic, French
Mauritius	Port Louis	Mauritian	English, French, Creole
Mexico	Mexico City	Mexican	Spanish
Micronesia	Palikir	Micronesian	English
Moldova	Chisinau	Moldovan	Moldovan, Russian, Gagauz, Ukranian
Monaco	Monaco	Monegasque	French, English, Italian, Monegasque
Mongolia	Ulaanbaatar	Mongolian	Khalk, Mongol, Kazakh
Morocco	Rabat	Moroccan	Arabic, Berber
Mozambique	Maputo	Mozambican	Portuguese, Makhuwa, Tsonga, Lomwe, Sena
Namibia	Windhoek	Namibian	English, Afrikaans
Nepal	Kathmandu	Nepalese	Nepali and many others

Country	Capital	Citizen	Language(s)
Netherlands	The Hague	Dutchman / woman	Dutch
New Zealand	Wellington	New Zealander	English, Maori
Nicaragua	Managua	Nicaraguan	Spanish
Niger	Niamey	Citizen of ...	French, Arabic
Nigeria	Abuja	Nigerian	English, Hausa, Yoruba, Igbo (Ibo), Fulani
Norway	Oslo	Norwegian	Bokma°l, Nynorsk, Sami
Oman	Muscat	Omani	Arabic, English, Fasi, Baluchi, Urdu
Pakistan	Islamabad	Pakistani	Punjabi, Sindhi, Pashtun, Urdu, English,
Panama	Panama City	Panamanian	Spanish, English
Papua New Guinea	Port Moresby	Papua New Guinean	Pidgin, Hiri, Motu, English & many others
Paraguay	Asuncion	Paraguayan	Spanish, Guarani
Peru	Lima	Peruvian	Spanish, Quechua, Aymara
Philippines	Metro Manila	Filipino / Filipina	Filipino, English, Tagalog & many others
Poland	Warsaw	Pole	Polish
Portugal	Lisbon	Portuguese	Portuguese
Puerto Rico	San Juan	Puerto Rican	Spanish, English
Qatar	Doha	Qatari	Arabic, English, Urdu
Romania	Bucharest	Romanian	Romanian, English, French, German
Russia	Moscow	Russian	Russian & many others
Rwanda	Kigali	Rwandese	Kinyarwanda, French, English, Kiswahili
Samoa	Apia	Samoan	Samoan, English
Saudi Arabia	Riyadh	Saudi Arabian	Arabic, English
Senegal	Dakar	Senegalese	French, Wolof, Mandinka
Serbia and Montenegro	Belgrade	Citizen of ...	Serbian, Albanian, Hungarian
Seychelles	Victoria	Citizen of ...	English, French, Creole
Sierra Leone	Freetown	Sierra Leonean	English, Mende, Temnel
Singapore	Singapore	Singaporean	Chinese, Malay, Tamil, English
Slovakia	Bratislava	Slovak	Slovak, Hungarian
Slovenia	Ljubljana	Slovene	Slovene, Italian, Hungarian, English
Solomon Islands	Honoria	Solomon Islander	English, Pidgin & many others
Somalia	Mogadishu	Somali	Somali, Arabic
South Africa	Pretoria	South African	Afrikaans, English, Xhosa, Sotho, Swazi, Tsonga, Zulu & many others
Spain	Madrid	Spaniard	Spanish, Catalan, Galician, Basque
Sri Lanka	Colombo	Citizen of ...	Sinhalese, Tamil, English
St. Kitts & Nevis	Basseterre	Citizen of ...	English
St. Lucia	Castries	St. Lucian	English, Patois

Country	Capital	Citizen	Language(s)
St. Vincent	Kingstown	Vincentian	English
Sudan	Khartoum	Sudanese	Arabic, Nubian, Ta Bedawie & many others
Surinam	Paramaribo	Surinamer	Dutch, English, Creole
Swaziland	Mbabane	Swazi	English, siSwati
Sweden	Stockholm	Swede	Swedish, English
Switzerland	Berne	Swiss	Swiss German, French, Italian, Romansch
Syria	Damascus	Syrian	Arabic, Kurdish, Armenian
Tajikistan	Dushanbe	Tajik	Russian
Taiwan	Taipei	Chinese / Taiwanese	Chinese, Taiwanese, Minnanyu, Hakka
Tanzania	Dar es Salaam	Tanzanian	Kiswahili, English, Arabic
Thailand	Bangkok	Thai	Thai, English & others
Togo	Lome	Togolese	French, Kabiye & others
Tonga	Nuku'alofa	Tongan	Tongan, English
Trinidad and Tobago	Port of Spain	Citizen of ...	English, Spanish
Turkmenistan	Ashgabat	Turkmen	Russian, Turkmen
Tunisia	Tunis	Tunisian	Arabic, French
Turkey	Ankara	Turk	Turkish, Kurdish, Armenian, Greek
Tuvalu	Funafuti	Citizen of ...	Tuvaluan, English
Uganda	Kampala	Ugandan	English, Luganda & others
Ukraine	Kiev	Ukrainian	Ukrainian, Russian, Polish, Romanian, Hungarian
United Arab Emirates	Abu Dhabi	Citizen of ...	Arabic, English
United States of America	Washington D.C.	American	English, Spanish
Uruguay	Montevideo	Uruguayan	Spanish, Portunol, Brazilero
Uzbekistan	Tashkent	Uzbeki	Uzbek, Russian, Tajik
Vanuatu	Port Villa	Citizen of ...	Bislama, English, French & many others
Vatican City (Holy See)	Vatican City	Citizen of ...	Italian, Latin, French
Venezuela	Caracas	Venezuelan	Spanish
Vietnam	Hanoi	Vietnamese	Vietnamese, French
Yemen	Sanaá	Yemeni	Arabic
Zambia	Lusaka	Zambian	English, Bemba, Kaonda, Lozi, Lunda & many others
Zimbabwe	Greater Harare	Zimbabwean	English, Shona, Ndebele

About the Author

Christine Maxwell began her career as a teacher's aide in a HeadStart program in California in the early 1970s and went on to teach middle school in Oxford, England. As a teacher she came up with the idea of writing a dictionary that students could use even if they did not know how to spell. After writing the first edition of this spelling dictionary for the use of her own students, Ms. Maxwell published it in 1977.

Over the years—during which, among many other accomplishments, Ms. Maxwell ran a market research company in Berkeley, California; wrote one of the very first Internet guides, published by Macmillan in 1994; and created the MAGELLAN online directory featured on Netscape's homepage in the mid-1990s—she has received countless requests from parents, teachers, and others for a new edition of her spelling dictionary. Berlitz proved to be, she says, the perfect publishing partner for the American English edition. Today she divides her time between California and Aix-en-Provence, France.